STUDENT SOLUTIONS MANUAL

MARK McCOMBS

COLLEGE ALGEBRA

GRAPHING, DATA, AND ANALYSIS

THIRD EDITION

MICHAEL SULLIVAN • MICHAEL SULLIVAN, III

PEARSON
Prentice
Hall

Pearson Education, Inc.
Upper Saddle River, NJ 07458

Editor-in-Chief: Sally Yagan
Senior Acquisitions Editor: Eric Frank
Supplement Editor: Aja Shevelew
Assistant Managing Editor: John Matthews
Production Editor: Allyson Kloss
Supplement Cover Manager: Paul Gourhan
Supplement Cover Designer: Joanne Alexandris
Manufacturing Buyer: Ilene Kahn

© 2004 Pearson Education, Inc.
Pearson Prentice Hall
Pearson Education, Inc.
Upper Saddle River, NJ 07458

Pearson Prentice Hall® is a trademark of Pearson Education, Inc.

Printed in the United States of America

10 9 8 7 6 5 4 3 2 1

ISBN 0-13-182792-8

Pearson Education Ltd., *London*
Pearson Education Australia Pty. Ltd., *Sydney*
Pearson Education Singapore, Pte. Ltd.
Pearson Education North Asia Ltd., *Hong Kong*
Pearson Education Canada, Inc., *Toronto*
Pearson Educación de Mexico, S.A. de C.V.
Pearson Education—Japan, *Tokyo*
Pearson Education Malaysia, Pte. Ltd.
Pearson Education, *Upper Saddle River, New Jersey*

Contents

Chapter 4　Additional Functions and Models

Chapter 5　Polynomial and Rational Functions

Chapter 6　Exponential and Logarithmic Functions

Chapter 7　Analytic Geometry

Chapter 8   Systems of Equations and Inequalities

Chapter 9   Sequences; Induction; The Binomial Theorem

Chapter 10   Counting and Probability

Preface

The <u>Student</u> <u>Solutions</u> <u>Manual</u> to accompany <u>College Algebra: Graphing, Data and Analysis</u>, <u>3rd</u> <u>Edition</u> by Michael Sullivan and Michael Sullivan, III contains detailed solutions to all of the odd-numbered problems in the textbook. TI-83 graphing calculator screens have been included to demonstrate the use of the graphics calculator in solving and in checking solutions to the problems where requested. Every attempt has been made to make this manual as error free as possible. If you have suggestions, error corrections, or comments please feel free to write to me about them.

A number of people need to be recognized for their contributions in the preparation of this manual. Thanks go to Sally Yagan, Aja Shevelew and Dawn Murrin at Prentice Hall. Special thanks also to Halle Amick for her timely and meticulous error-checking of the solutions. (Go Bengals!)

I especially wish to thank my mother, Sarah, and my brothers, Kirk and Doug, for their unwavering support and encouragement.

Finally, I am also greatly indebted to John Lydon and Otis Spann for helping me endure the long hours of editing the manuscript.

Mark A. McCombs
Department of Mathematics
Campus Box 3250
University of North Carolina at Chapel Hill
Chapel Hill, NC 27599
mccombs@math.unc.edu

Review

R.1 Classification of Numbers

1. (a) $\{2, 5\}$
   (b) $\{-6, 2, 5\}$
   (c) $\left\{-6, \dfrac{1}{2}, -1.333\ldots, 2, 5\right\}$
   (d) $\{\pi\}$
   (e) $\left\{-6, \dfrac{1}{2}, -1.333\ldots, \pi, 2, 5\right\}$

3. (a) $\{1\}$
   (b) $\{0, 1\}$
   (c) $\left\{0, 1, \dfrac{1}{2}, \dfrac{1}{3}, \dfrac{1}{4}\right\}$
   (d) None
   (e) $\left\{0, 1, \dfrac{1}{2}, \dfrac{1}{3}, \dfrac{1}{4}\right\}$

5. (a) None
   (b) None
   (c) None
   (d) $\left\{\sqrt{2}, \pi, \sqrt{2}+1, \pi+\dfrac{1}{2}\right\}$
   (e) $\left\{\sqrt{2}, \pi, \sqrt{2}+1, \pi+\dfrac{1}{2}\right\}$

7. (a) 18.953
   (b) 18.952

9. (a) 28.653
   (b) 28.653

11. (a) 0.063
    (b) 0.062

13. (a) 9.999
    (b) 9.998

15. (a) 0.429
    (b) 0.428

17. (a) 34.733
    (b) 34.733

19. $3 + 2 = 5$

21. $x + 2 = 3 \cdot 4$

23. $3y = 1 + 2$

25. $x - 2 = 6$

27. $\dfrac{x}{2} = 6$

29. $9 - 4 + 2 = 5 + 2 = 7$

31. $-6 + 4 \cdot 3 = -6 + 12 = 6$

33. $4 + 5 - 8 = 9 - 8 = 1$

35. $4 + \dfrac{1}{3} = \dfrac{12+1}{3} = \dfrac{13}{3}$

37. $6 - \left[3 \cdot 5 + 2 \cdot (3 - 2)\right]$
    $= 6 - \left[15 + 2 \cdot (1)\right]$
    $= 6 - 17 = -11$

39. $2 \cdot (3 - 5) + 8 \cdot 2 - 1$
    $= 2 \cdot (-2) + 16 - 1$
    $= -4 + 16 - 1$
    $= 12 - 1 = 11$

41. $10 - \left[6 - 2 \cdot 2 + (8 - 3)\right] \cdot 2$
    $= 10 - \left[6 - 4 + 5\right] \cdot 2$
    $= 10 - \left[2 + 5\right] \cdot 2$
    $= 10 - \left[7\right] \cdot 2 = 10 - 14$
    $= -4$

43. $(5 - 3)\dfrac{1}{2} = (2)\dfrac{1}{2} = 1$

45. $\dfrac{4+8}{5-3} = \dfrac{12}{2} = 6$

47. $\dfrac{3}{5} \cdot \dfrac{10}{21} = \dfrac{2}{7}$

49. $\dfrac{6}{25} \cdot \dfrac{10}{27} = \dfrac{4}{45}$

51. $\dfrac{3}{4} + \dfrac{2}{5} = \dfrac{15+8}{20} = \dfrac{23}{20}$

53. $\dfrac{5}{6} + \dfrac{9}{5} = \dfrac{25+54}{30} = \dfrac{79}{30}$

55. $\dfrac{5}{18} + \dfrac{1}{12} = \dfrac{10+3}{36} = \dfrac{13}{36}$

57. $\dfrac{1}{30} - \dfrac{7}{18} = \dfrac{3-35}{90}$

$= -\dfrac{32}{90} = -\dfrac{16}{45}$

59. $\dfrac{3}{20} - \dfrac{2}{15} = \dfrac{9-8}{60}$

$= \dfrac{1}{60}$

61. $\dfrac{\left(\dfrac{5}{18}\right)}{\left(\dfrac{11}{27}\right)} = \dfrac{5}{18} \cdot \dfrac{27}{11} = \dfrac{15}{22}$

63. $6(x+4) = 6x + 24$

65. $x(x-4) = x^2 - 4x$

67. $(x+2)(x+4)$
$= x^2 + 4x + 2x + 8$
$= x^2 + 6x + 8$

69. $(x-2)(x+1)$
$= x^2 + x - 2x - 2$
$= x^2 - x - 2$

71. $(x-8)(x-2)$
$= x^2 - 2x - 8x + 16$
$= x^2 - 10x + 16$

73. $(x+2)(x-2)$
$= x^2 - 2x + 2x - 4$
$= x^2 - 4$

75. $2x + 3x$
$= x(2+3)$
$= x(5) = 5x$

77.   Natural Numbers, Rational Numbers, Integers

79.   If $a \cdot b = 0$, then $a = 0$, or $b = 0$, or both $a = 0$ and $b = 0$.

81.   The sum of an irrational number and a rational number must be irrational. Otherwise, the irrational number would then be the difference of two rational numbers, and therefore would have to be rational.

Review

R.2 Algebra Review

1.

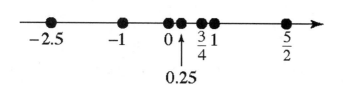

3. $\dfrac{1}{2} > 0$ 5. $-1 > -2$ 7. $\pi > 3.14$

9. $\dfrac{1}{2} = 0.5$ 11. $\dfrac{2}{3} < 0.67$ 13. $x > 0$

15. $x < 2$ 17. $x \le 1$

19. Graph on the number line: $x \ge -2$

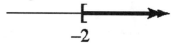

21. Graph on the number line: $x > -1$

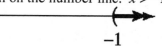

23. $d(C,D) = d(0,1) = |1-0| = |1| = 1$ 25. $d(D,E) = d(1,3) = |3-1| = |2| = 2$

27. $d(A,E) = d(-3,3) = |3-(-3)| = |6| = 6$ 29. $x + 2y = -2 + 2 \cdot 3 = -2 + 6 = 4$

31. $5xy + 2 = 5(-2)(3) + 2 = -30 + 2 = -28$ 33. $\dfrac{2x}{x-y} = \dfrac{2(-2)}{-2-3} = \dfrac{-4}{-5} = \dfrac{4}{5}$

35. $\dfrac{3x + 2y}{2 + y} = \dfrac{3(-2) + 2(3)}{2 + 3} = \dfrac{-6 + 6}{5} = \dfrac{0}{5} = 0$ 37. $|x + y| = |3 + (-2)| = |1| = 1$

39. $|x| + |y| = |3| + |-2| = 3 + 2 = 5$ 41. $\dfrac{|x|}{x} = \dfrac{|3|}{3} = \dfrac{3}{3} = 1$

43. $|4x - 5y| = |4(3) - 5(-2)| = |12 + 10| = |22| = 22$

45. $\big||4x| - |5y|\big| = \big||4(3)| - |5(-2)|\big| = \big||12| - |-10|\big| = |12 - 10| = |2| = 2$

47. $\dfrac{x^2-1}{x}$ Part (c) must be excluded.

The value $x = 0$ must be excluded from the domain because it causes division by 0.

49. $\dfrac{x}{x^2-9} = \dfrac{x}{(x-3)(x+3)}$ Part (a) must be excluded.

The values $x = -3$ and $x = 3$ must be excluded from the domain because they cause division by 0.

51. $\dfrac{x^2}{x^2+1}$ None of the given values are excluded. The domain is all real numbers.

53. $\dfrac{x^2+5x-10}{x^3-x} = \dfrac{x^2+5x-10}{x(x-1)(x+1)}$ Parts (b), (c), and (d) must be excluded.

The values $x = 0$, $x = 1$, and $x = -1$ must be excluded from the domain because they cause division by 0.

55. $\dfrac{4}{x-5}$ Domain $= \{x \mid x \neq 5\}$

57. $\dfrac{x}{x+4}$ Domain $= \{x \mid x \neq -4\}$

59. $C = \dfrac{5}{9}(F-32) = \dfrac{5}{9}(32-32) = \dfrac{5}{9}(0) = 0°C$

61. $C = \dfrac{5}{9}(F-32) = \dfrac{5}{9}(77-32) = \dfrac{5}{9}(45) = 25°C$

63. $(-4)^2 = (-4)(-4) = 16$

65. $4^{-2} = \dfrac{1}{4^2} = \dfrac{1}{16}$

67. $3^{-6} \cdot 3^4 = 3^{-6+4} = 3^{-2} = \dfrac{1}{3^2} = \dfrac{1}{9}$

69. $\left(3^{-2}\right)^{-1} = 3^{(-2)(-1)} = 3^2 = 9$

71. $\sqrt{25} = \sqrt{5^2} = |5| = 5$

73. $\sqrt{(-4)^2} = |-4| = 4$

75. $\left(8x^3\right)^2 = \left(8x^3\right)^2 = 8^2 \cdot x^6 = 64x^6$

77. $\left(x^2 y^{-1}\right)^2 = \left(\dfrac{x^2}{y}\right)^2 = \dfrac{x^{2\cdot2}}{y^{1\cdot2}} = \dfrac{x^4}{y^2}$

79. $\dfrac{x^2 y^3}{xy^4} = \dfrac{x^2}{x} \cdot \dfrac{y^3}{y^4} = x^{2-1}y^{3-4} = x^1 y^{-1} = \dfrac{x}{1} \cdot \dfrac{1}{y} = \dfrac{x}{y}$

81. $\dfrac{(-2)^3 x^4 (yz)^2}{3^2 xy^3 z} = \dfrac{-8x^4 y^2 z^2}{9xy^3 z} = \dfrac{-8}{9}x^{4-1}y^{2-3}z^{2-1} = \dfrac{-8}{9}x^3 y^{-1}z^1 = \dfrac{-8}{9}x^3 \cdot \dfrac{1}{y} \cdot z = -\dfrac{8x^3 z}{9y}$

83. $\left(\dfrac{3x^{-1}}{4y^{-1}}\right)^{-2} = \left(\dfrac{3y^1}{4x^1}\right)^{-2} = \dfrac{1}{\left(\dfrac{3y^1}{4x^1}\right)^2} = \dfrac{1}{\left(\dfrac{3^2 y^{1\cdot2}}{4^2 x^{1\cdot2}}\right)} = \dfrac{1}{\left(\dfrac{9y^2}{16x^2}\right)} = \dfrac{16x^2}{9y^2}$

85. Given the expression $2x^3 - 3x^2 + 5x - 4$:

$$x = 2 \Rightarrow 2(2)^3 - 3(2)^2 + 5(2) - 4 = 2 \cdot 8 - 3 \cdot 4 + 10 - 4 = 16 - 12 + 10 - 4 = 10$$
$$x = 1 \Rightarrow 2(1)^3 - 3(1)^2 + 5(1) - 4 = 2 - 3 + 5 - 4 = 0$$

87. $\dfrac{(666)^4}{(222)^4} = \left(\dfrac{666}{222}\right)^4 = (3)^4 = 81$

89. $(8.2)^6 \approx 304006.671$

91. $(6.1)^{-3} \approx 0.004$

93. $(-2.8)^6 \approx 481.890$

95. $(-8.11)^{-4} \approx 0.000$

97. $454.2 = 4.542 \times 10^2$

99. $0.013 = 1.3 \times 10^{-2}$

101. $32{,}155 = 3.2155 \times 10^4$

103. $0.000423 = 4.23 \times 10^{-4}$

105. $6.15 \times 10^4 = 61{,}500$

107. $1.214 \times 10^{-3} = 0.001214$

109. $1.1 \times 10^8 = 110{,}000{,}000$

111. $8.1 \times 10^{-2} = 0.081$

113.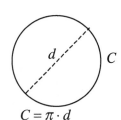

$A = l \cdot w$

All variables are positive real numbers.

115.

$C = \pi \cdot d$

All variables are positive real numbers.

117.

$A = \dfrac{\sqrt{3}}{4} \cdot x^2$

All variables are positive real numbers.

119.

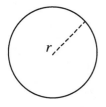

$$V = \frac{4}{3} \cdot \pi \cdot r^3$$

All variables are positive real numbers.

121.

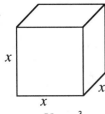

$$V = x^3$$

All variables are positive real numbers.

123. (a)   If $x = 1000$, $C = 4000 + 2x = 4000 + 2(1000) = 4000 + 2000 = \$6000$
       (b)   If $x = 2000$, $C = 4000 + 2x = 4000 + 2(2000) = 4000 + 4000 = \$8000$

125. $|x - 115| \le 5$
       (a) $|x - 115| = |113 - 115| = |-2| = 2 \le 5$ 113 volts is acceptable.
       (b) $|x - 115| = |109 - 115| = |-6| = 6 > 5$ 109 volts is not acceptable.

127. $|x - 3| \le 0.01$
       (a) $|x - 3| = |2.999 - 3| = |-0.001| = 0.001 \le 0.01$
              A radius of 2.999 centimeters is acceptable.
       (b) $|x - 3| = |2.89 - 3| = |-0.11| = 0.11 > 0.01$
              A radius of 2.89 centimeters is _not_ acceptable.

129. $4 \times 10^8 = 400,000,000$ meters   131. $5 \times 10^{-7} = 0.0000005$ meters

133. $0.0005 = 5 \times 10^{-4}$ inches

135. $186,000 \cdot 60 \cdot 60 \cdot 24 \cdot 365 = \left(1.86 \times 10^5\right)\left(6 \times 10^1\right)\left(6 \times 10^1\right)\left(2.4 \times 10^1\right)\left(3.65 \times 10^2\right)$
              $= 586.5696 \times 10^{10} = 5.865696 \times 10^{12}$ miles

137. $\frac{1}{3} = 0.333333\ldots > 0.333 \implies \frac{1}{3}$ is larger by approximately $0.0003333\ldots$

139. No.

141.   Answers will vary.

Review

R.3   Geometry Review

1. $a = 5, \ b = 12, \ c^2 = a^2 + b^2 = 5^2 + 12^2 = 25 + 144 = 169 \ \Rightarrow \ c = 13$

3. $a = 10, \ b = 24, \ c^2 = a^2 + b^2 = 10^2 + 24^2 = 100 + 576 = 676 \ \Rightarrow \ c = 26$

5. $a = 7, \ b = 24, \ c^2 = a^2 + b^2 = 7^2 + 24^2 = 49 + 576 = 625 \ \Rightarrow \ c = 25$

7. $5^2 = 3^2 + 4^2 \ \Rightarrow \ 25 = 9 + 16 \ \Rightarrow \ 25 = 25$
   The given triangle is a right triangle. The hypotenuse is 5.

9. $6^2 = 4^2 + 5^2 \ \Rightarrow \ 36 = 16 + 25 \ \Rightarrow \ 36 \neq 41$
   The given triangle is not a right triangle.

11. $25^2 = 7^2 + 24^2 \ \Rightarrow \ 625 = 49 + 576 \ \Rightarrow \ 625 = 625$
    The given triangle is a right triangle. The hypotenuse is 25.

13. $6^2 = 3^2 + 4^2 \ \Rightarrow \ 36 = 9 + 16 \ \Rightarrow \ 36 \neq 25$
    The given triangle is not a right triangle.

15. $A = l \cdot w = 4 \cdot 2 = 8 \text{ in}^2$ 17. $A = \dfrac{1}{2} b \cdot h = \dfrac{1}{2}(2)(4) = 4 \text{ in}^2$

19. $A = \pi r^2 = \pi(5)^2 = 25\pi \text{ m}^2$ $C = 2\pi r = 2\pi(5) = 10\pi \text{ m}$

21. $V = l\,w\,h = 8 \cdot 4 \cdot 7 = 224 \text{ ft}^3$

23. $V = \dfrac{4}{3}\pi r^3 = \dfrac{4}{3}\pi \cdot 4^3 = \dfrac{256}{3}\pi \text{ cm}^3$ $S = 4\pi r^2 = 4\pi \cdot 4^2 = 64\pi \text{ cm}^2$

25. $V = \pi r^2 h = \pi(9)^2(8) = 648\pi \text{ in}^3$

27. The diameter of the circle is 2, so its radius is 1. $A = \pi r^2 = \pi(1)^2 = \pi$ square units

29. The diameter of the circle is the length of the diagonal of the square.
    $$d^2 = 2^2 + 2^2 = 4 + 4 = 8 \ \Rightarrow \ d = \sqrt{8} = 2\sqrt{2} \qquad r = \sqrt{2}$$
    The area of the circle is: $A = \pi r^2 = \pi\left(\sqrt{2}\right)^2 = 2\pi$ square units

Review

31. The total distance traveled is 4 times the circumference of the wheel.

$$\text{Total distance} = 4C = 4(\pi d) = 4\pi \cdot 16 = 64\pi = \frac{16\pi}{3} \approx 16.8 \text{ feet}.$$

33. Area of the border = area of EFGH − area of ABCD = $10^2 - 6^2 = 100 - 36 = 64 \text{ ft}^2$

35. Area of the window = area of the rectangle + area of the semicircle.

$$A = (6)(4) + \frac{1}{2} \cdot \pi \cdot 2^2 = 24 + 2\pi \approx 30.28 \text{ ft}^2$$

Perimeter of the window = 2 heights + width + one-half the circumference.

$$P = 2(6) + 4 + \frac{1}{2} \cdot \pi(4) = 12 + 4 + 2\pi = 16 + 2\pi \approx 22.28 \text{ feet}$$

37. Convert 20 feet to miles, and solve the Pythagorean theorem to find the distance:

$$20 \text{ feet} = 20 \text{ feet} \cdot \frac{1 \text{ mile}}{5280 \text{ feet}} \approx 0.003788 \text{ miles}$$

$$d^2 = (3960 + 0.003788)^2 - 3960^2 = 30$$

$$d \approx 5.477 \text{ miles}$$

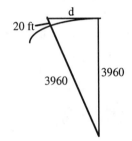

39. Convert 100 feet to miles, and solve the Pythagorean theorem to find the distance:

$$100 \text{ feet} = 100 \text{ feet} \cdot \frac{1 \text{ mile}}{5280 \text{ feet}} = 0.018939 \text{ miles}$$

$$d^2 = (3960 + 0.018939)^2 - 3960^2 = 150 \Rightarrow d \approx 12.247 \text{ miles}$$

Convert 150 feet to miles, and solve the Pythagorean theorem to find the distance:

$$150 \text{ feet} = 150 \text{ feet} \cdot \frac{1 \text{ mile}}{5280 \text{ feet}} \approx 0.028409 \text{ miles}$$

$$d^2 = (3960 + 0.028409)^2 - 3960^2 = 225 \Rightarrow d \approx 15.000 \text{ miles}$$

41. Given a rectangle with perimeter = 1000 feet, the largest area will be enclosed by a square with dimensions 250 by 250 feet. That is, the area = $250^2 = 62500$ square feet.

A circular pool with circumference = 1000 feet yields the equation : $2\pi r = 1000 \Rightarrow r = \dfrac{500}{\pi}$

The area enclosed by the circular pool is: $A = \pi r^2 = \pi \left(\dfrac{500}{\pi}\right)^2 = \dfrac{500^2}{\pi} \approx 79577.47$ square feet

Therefore, a circular pool will enclose the most area.

Review

R.4 Polynomials

1. $2x^3$ Monomial; Variable: x; Coefficient: 2; Degree: 3

3. $\dfrac{8}{x}$ Not a monomial.

5. $-2xy^2$ Monomial; Variable: x, y; Coefficient: –2; Degree: 3

7. $\dfrac{8x}{y}$ Not a monomial   9. $x^2 + y^2$ Not a monomial.

11. $3x^2 - 5$ Polynomial; Degree: 2   13.   5   Polynomial; Degree: 0

15. $3x^2 - \dfrac{5}{x}$ Not a polynomial.   17. $2y^3 - \sqrt{2}$ Polynomial; Degree: 3

19. $\dfrac{x^2 + 5}{x^3 - 1}$ Not a polynomial.

21. $(x^2 + 4x + 5) + (3x - 3) = x^2 + (4x + 3x) + (5 - 3) = x^2 + 7x + 2$

23. $(x^3 - 2x^2 + 5x + 10) - (2x^2 - 4x + 3) = x^3 - 2x^2 + 5x + 10 - 2x^2 + 4x - 3$
$$= x^3 + (-2x^2 - 2x^2) + (5x + 4x) + (10 - 3)$$
$$= x^3 - 4x^2 + 9x + 7$$

25. $\left(6x^5 + x^3 + x\right) + \left(5x^4 - x^3 + 3x^2\right) = 6x^5 + 5x^4 + 3x^2 + x$

27. $(x^2 - 3x + 1) + 2(3x^2 + x - 4) = x^2 - 3x + 1 + 6x^2 + 2x - 8 = 7x^2 - x - 7$

29. $6(x^3 + x^2 - 3) - 4(2x^3 - 3x^2) = 6x^3 + 6x^2 - 18 - 8x^3 + 12x^2 = -2x^3 + 18x^2 - 18$

31. $\left(x^2 - x + 2\right) + \left(2x^2 - 3x + 5\right) - \left(x^2 + 1\right) = x^2 - x + 2 + 2x^2 - 3x + 5 - x^2 - 1$
$$= 2x^2 - 4x + 6$$

33. $9\left(y^2 - 3y + 4\right) - 6\left(1 - y^2\right) = 9y^2 - 27y + 36 - 6 + 6y^2 = 15y^2 - 27y + 30$

35. $x(x^2 + x - 4) = x^3 + x^2 - 4x$ 37. $-2x^2(4x^3 + 5) = -8x^5 - 10x^2$

39. $(x+1)(x^2+2x-4) = x(x^2+2x-4)+1(x^2+2x-4)$
$$= x^3+2x^2-4x+x^2+2x-4 = x^3+3x^2-2x-4$$

41. $(x+2)(x+4) = x^2+4x+2x+8 = x^2+6x+8$

43. $(2x+5)(x+2) = 2x^2+4x+5x+10 = 2x^2+9x+10$

45. $(x-4)(x+2) = x^2+2x-4x-8 = x^2-2x-8$

47. $(x-3)(x-2) = x^2-2x-3x+6 = x^2-5x+6$

49. $(2x+3)(x-2) = 2x^2-4x+3x-6 = 2x^2-x-6$

51. $(-2x+3)(x-4) = -2x^2+8x+3x-12 = -2x^2+11x-12$

53. $(-x-2)(-2x-4) = 2x^2+4x+4x+8 = 2x^2+8x+8$

55. $(x-2y)(x+y) = x^2+xy-2xy-2y^2 = x^2-xy-2y^2$

57. $(-2x-3y)(3x+2y) = -6x^2-4xy-9xy-6y^2 = -6x^2-13xy-6y^2$

59. $(x-7)(x+7) = x^2-7^2 = x^2-49$

61. $(2x+3)(2x-3) = (2x)^2-3^2 = 4x^2-9$

63. $(x+4)^2 = x^2+2\cdot x\cdot4+4^2 = x^2+8x+16$

65. $(x-4)^2 = x^2-2\cdot x\cdot4+4^2 = x^2-8x+16$

67. $(3x+4)(3x-4) = (3x)^2-4^2 = 9x^2-16$

69. $(2x-3)^2 = (2x)^2-2(2x)(3)+3^2 = 4x^2-12x+9$

71. $(x+y)(x-y) = (x)^2-(y)^2 = x^2-y^2$

73. $(3x+y)(3x-y) = (3x)^2-(y)^2 = 9x^2-y^2$

75. $(x+y)^2 = x^2+2xy+y^2$

77. $(x-2y)^2 = x^2+2(x\cdot(-2y))+(2y)^2 = x^2-4xy+4y^2$

79. $(x-2)^3 = x^3-3\cdot x^2\cdot2+3\cdot x\cdot2^2-2^3 = x^3-6x^2+12x-8$

81. $(2x+1)^3 = (2x)^3+3(2x)^2(1)+3(2x)\cdot1^2+1^3 = 8x^3+12x^2+6x+1$

83. $-3x^2 + 4\sqrt{x}$ is not a polynomial since $4\sqrt{x} = 4x^{1/2}$.

85.   When we add two polynomials $p_1(x)$ and $p_2(x)$, where the degree of $p_1(x) \neq$ the degree of $p_2(x)$, each term of $p_1(x)$ will be added to each term of $p_2(x)$. Since only the terms with equal degrees will combine via addition, the degree of the sum polynomial will be the degree of the highest powered term overall, that is, the degree of the polynomial that had the higher degree.

87.   Answers will vary.

Review

R.5   Polynomial Division; Synthetic Division

1.   Divide:

$$
\begin{array}{r}
4x^2 - 11x + 23 \\
x+2\overline{\smash{\big)}\,4x^3 - 3x^2 + x + 1} \\
\underline{4x^3 + 8x^2} \\
-11x^2 + x + 1 \\
\underline{-11x^2 - 22x} \\
23x + 1 \\
\underline{23x + 46} \\
-45
\end{array}
$$

Check:

$(x+2)(4x^2 - 11x + 23) + (-45)$

$= 4x^3 - 11x^2 + 23x + 8x^2 - 22x + 46 - 45$

$= 4x^3 - 3x^2 + x + 1$

The quotient is $4x^2 - 11x + 23$; the remainder is –45.

3.   Divide:

$$
\begin{array}{r}
4x^2 + 13x + 53 \\
x-4\overline{\smash{\big)}\,4x^3 - 3x^2 + x + 1} \\
\underline{4x^3 - 16x^2} \\
13x^2 + x \\
\underline{13x^2 - 52x} \\
53x + 1 \\
\underline{53x - 212} \\
213
\end{array}
$$

Check:

$(x-4)(4x^2 + 13x + 53) + 213$

$= 4x^3 + 13x^2 + 53x - 16x^2 - 52x - 212 + 213$

$= 4x^3 - 3x^2 + x + 1$

The quotient is $4x^2 + 13x + 53$; the remainder is 213.

5.   Divide:

$$
\begin{array}{r}
4x - 3 \\
x^2+2\overline{\smash{\big)}\,4x^3 - 3x^2 + x + 1} \\
\underline{4x^3 \qquad + 8x} \\
-3x^2 - 7x \\
\underline{-3x^2 \qquad -6} \\
-7x + 7
\end{array}
$$

Check:

$(x^2 + 2)(4x - 3) + (-7x + 7)$

$= 4x^3 - 3x^2 + 8x - 6 - 7x + 7$

$= 4x^3 - 3x^2 + x + 1$

The quotient is $4x - 3$; the remainder is $-7x + 7$.

7.   Divide:

$$\begin{array}{r} 2 \\ 2x^3-1\overline{\smash{\big)}\ 4x^3-3x^2+x+1} \\ \underline{4x^3\qquad\qquad -2} \\ -3x^2+x+3 \end{array}$$

Check:

$(2x^3-1)(2)+(-3x^2+x+3)$

$=4x^3-2-3x^2+x+3=4x^3-3x^2+x+1$

The quotient is 2; the remainder is $-3x^2+x+3$.

9.   Divide:

$$\begin{array}{r} 2x-\dfrac{5}{2} \\ 2x^2+x+1\overline{\smash{\big)}\ 4x^3-3x^2+\ x+1} \\ \underline{4x^3+2x^2+2x} \\ -5x^2-\ x \\ \underline{-5x^2-\dfrac{5}{3}x-\dfrac{5}{2}} \\ \dfrac{3}{2}x+\dfrac{7}{2} \end{array}$$

Check:

$\left(2x^2+x+12\right)\left(x-\dfrac{5}{2}\right)+\left(\dfrac{3}{2}x+\dfrac{7}{2}\right)$

$=4x^3-5x^2+2x^2-\dfrac{5}{2}x+2x-\dfrac{5}{2}+\dfrac{3}{2}x+\dfrac{7}{2}=4x^3-3x^2+x+1$

The quotient is $2x-\dfrac{5}{2}$; the remainder is $\dfrac{3}{2}x+\dfrac{7}{2}$.

11.   Divide:

$$\begin{array}{r} x-\dfrac{3}{4} \\ 4x^2+1\overline{\smash{\big)}\ 4x^3-\ 3x^2+x+\ 1} \\ \underline{4x^3\qquad\quad +x} \\ -3x^2\qquad +1 \\ \underline{-3x^2\qquad -\dfrac{3}{4}} \\ \dfrac{7}{4} \end{array}$$

Check:

$(4x^2+1)\left(x-\dfrac{3}{4}\right)+\dfrac{7}{4}$

$=4x^3-3x^2+x-\dfrac{3}{4}+\dfrac{7}{4}$

$=4x^3-3x^2+x+1$

The quotient is $x-\dfrac{3}{4}$; the remainder is $\dfrac{7}{4}$.

13.   Divide:

$$\begin{array}{r} x^3+x^2+x+1 \\ x-1\overline{\smash{\big)}\ x^4+0x^3+0x^2+0x-1} \\ \underline{x^4-\ x^3} \\ x^3 \\ \underline{x^3-\ x^2} \\ x^2 \\ \underline{x^2-\ x} \\ x-1 \\ \underline{x-1} \\ 0 \end{array}$$

Check:

$(x-1)(x^3+x^2+x+1)+0$

$=x^4+x^3+x^2+x-x^3-x^2-x-1$

$=x^4-1$

The quotient is x^3+x^2+x+1; the remainder is 0.

15. Divide:

$$\begin{array}{r} x^2 + 1 \\ x^2 - 1 \overline{)\smash{x^4 + 0x^3 + 0x^2 + 0x - 1}} \\ \underline{x^4 \quad\quad - x^2} \\ x^2 \\ \underline{x^2 \quad - 1} \\ 0 \end{array}$$

Check:

$(x^2 - 1)(x^2 + 1) + 0$

$= x^4 + x^2 - x^2 - 1$

$= x^4 - 1$

The quotient is $x^2 + 1$; the remainder is 0.

17. Divide:

$$\begin{array}{r} -4x^2 - 3x - 3 \\ x - 1 \overline{)\smash{-4x^3 + \;\; x^2 + 0x - 4}} \\ \underline{-4x^3 + 4x^2} \\ -3x^2 \\ \underline{-3x^2 + 3x} \\ -3x - 4 \\ \underline{-3x + 3} \\ -7 \end{array}$$

Check:

$(x - 1)(-4x^2 - 3x - 3) + (-7)$

$= -4x^3 - 3x^2 - 3x + 4x^2 + 3x + 3 - 7$

$= -4x^3 + x^2 - 4$

The quotient is $-4x^2 - 3x - 3$; the remainder is –7.

19. Divide:

$$\begin{array}{r} x^2 - x - 1 \\ x^2 + x + 1 \overline{)\smash{x^4 + 0x^3 - \;\; x^2 + 0x + 1}} \\ \underline{x^4 + \;\; x^3 + \;\; x^2} \\ -x^3 - 2x^2 \\ \underline{-x^3 - \;\; x^2 - x} \\ -x^2 + x + 1 \\ \underline{-x^2 - x - 1} \\ 2x + 2 \end{array}$$

Check:

$(x^2 + x + 1)(x^2 - x - 1) + 2x + 2$

$= x^4 + x^3 + x^2 - x^3 - x^2 - x - x^2 - x - 1 + 2x + 2$

$= x^4 - x^2 + 1$

The quotient is $x^2 - x - 1$; the remainder is $2x + 2$.

21. Divide:

$$\begin{array}{r} -x^2 \\ -x^2 + 1 \overline{)\smash{x^4 + 0x^3 - x^2 + 0x + 1}} \\ \underline{x^4 \quad\quad - x^2} \\ 1 \end{array}$$

Check:

$-x^2(-x^2 + 1) + 1$

$= x^4 - x^2 + 1$

The quotient is $-x^2$; the remainder is 1.

23. Divide:

$$x - a \overline{\smash{\big)}\ x^3 + 0x^2 + 0x - a^3}$$
$$\underline{x^3 - ax^2}$$
$$ax^2$$
$$\underline{ax^2 - a^2x}$$
$$a^2x - a^3$$
$$\underline{a^2x - a^3}$$
$$0$$

with quotient $x^2 + ax + a^2$

Check:

$(x - a)(x^2 + ax + a^2) + 0$
$= x^3 + ax^2 + a^2x - ax^2 - a^2x - a^3$
$= x^3 - a^3$

The quotient is $x^2 + ax + a^2$; the remainder is 0.

25. Divide:

$$x - a \overline{\smash{\big)}\ x^4 + 0x^3 + 0x^2 + 0x - a^4}$$
$$\underline{x^4 - ax^3}$$
$$ax^3$$
$$\underline{ax^3 - a^2x^2}$$
$$a^2x^2$$
$$\underline{a^2x^2 - a^3x}$$
$$a^3x - a^4$$
$$\underline{a^3x - a^4}$$
$$0$$

with quotient $x^3 + ax^2 + a^2x + a^3$

Check:

$(x - a)(x^3 + ax^2 + a^2x + a^3) + 0$
$= x^4 + ax^3 + a^2x^2 + a^3x - ax^3 - a^2x^2 - a^3x - a^4$
$= x^4 - a^4$

The quotient is $x^3 + ax^2 + a^2x + a^3$; the remainder is 0.

27. Use synthetic division:

$$
\begin{array}{r|rrrr}
2 & 1 & -1 & 2 & 4 \\
  &   & 2 & 2 & 8 \\
\hline
  & 1 & 1 & 4 & 12
\end{array}
$$

Quotient: $x^2 + x + 4$ Remainder: 12

29. Use synthetic division:

$$
\begin{array}{r|rrrr}
3 & 3 & 2 & -1 & 3 \\
  &   & 9 & 33 & 96 \\
\hline
  & 3 & 11 & 32 & 99
\end{array}
$$

Quotient: $3x^2 + 11x + 32$ Remainder: 99

31. Use synthetic division:

$$
\begin{array}{r|rrrrrr}
-3 & 1 & 0 & -4 & 0 & 1 & 0 \\
   &   & -3 & 9 & -15 & 45 & -138 \\
\hline
   & 1 & -3 & 5 & -15 & 46 & -138
\end{array}
$$

Quotient: $x^4 - 3x^3 + 5x^2 - 15x + 46$ Remainder: -138

33. Use synthetic division:

$$1 \overline{)\,4 \quad 0 \quad -3 \quad 0 \quad 1 \quad 0 \quad 5}$$
$$\phantom{1 \overline{)\,}} 4 \quad 4 \quad 1 \quad 1 \quad 2 \quad 2$$
$$\overline{ 4 \quad 4 \quad 1 \quad 1 \quad 2 \quad 2 \quad 7}$$

Quotient: $4x^5 + 4x^4 + x^3 + x^2 + 2x + 2$ Remainder: 7

35. Use synthetic division:

$$-1.1 \overline{)\,0.1 \quad 0 \quad 0.2 \quad 0}$$
$$\phantom{-1.1 \overline{)\,}} -0.11 \quad 0.121 \quad -0.3531$$
$$\overline{ 0.1 \quad -0.11 \quad 0.321 \quad -0.3531}$$

Quotient: $0.1x^2 - 0.11x + 0.321$ Remainder: –0.3531

37. Use synthetic division:

$$1 \overline{)\,1 \quad 0 \quad 0 \quad 0 \quad 0 \quad -1}$$
$$\phantom{1 \overline{)\,}} 1 \quad 1 \quad 1 \quad 1 \quad 1$$
$$\overline{ 1 \quad 1 \quad 1 \quad 1 \quad 1 \quad 0}$$

Quotient: $x^4 + x^3 + x^2 + x + 1$ Remainder: 0

39. Use synthetic division:

$$2 \overline{)\,4 \quad -3 \quad -8 \quad 4}$$
$$\phantom{2 \overline{)\,}} 8 \quad 10 \quad 4$$
$$\overline{ 4 \quad 5 \quad 2 \quad 8}$$

Remainder = $8 \neq 0$; therefore $x - 2$ is not a factor of $f(x)$.

41. Use synthetic division:

$$2 \overline{)\,3 \quad -6 \quad 0 \quad -5 \quad 10}$$
$$\phantom{2 \overline{)\,}} 6 \quad 0 \quad 0 \quad -10$$
$$\overline{ 3 \quad 0 \quad 0 \quad -5 \quad 0}$$

Remainder = 0; therefore $x - 2$ is a factor of $f(x)$.

43. Use synthetic division:

$$-3 \overline{)\,3 \quad 0 \quad 0 \quad 82 \quad 0 \quad 0 \quad 27}$$
$$\phantom{-3 \overline{)\,}} -9 \quad 27 \quad -81 \quad -3 \quad 9 \quad -27$$
$$\overline{ 3 \quad -9 \quad 27 \quad 1 \quad -3 \quad 9 \quad 0}$$

Remainder = 0; therefore $x + 3$ is a factor of $f(x)$.

45. Use synthetic division:

$$-4 \overline{)\,4 \quad 0 \quad -64 \quad 0 \quad 1 \quad 0 \quad -15}$$
$$\phantom{-4 \overline{)\,}} -16 \quad 64 \quad 0 \quad 0 \quad -4 \quad 16$$
$$\overline{ 4 \quad -16 \quad 0 \quad 0 \quad 1 \quad -4 \quad 1}$$

Remainder = $1 \neq 0$; therefore $x + 3$ is not a factor of $f(x)$.

47. Use synthetic division:

$$\frac{1}{2} \overline{)\, 2 \;\; -1 \;\; 0 \;\; 2 \;\; -1}$$

$$\underline{\qquad\;\; 1 \;\; 0 \;\; 0 \;\;\;\; 1}$$

$$\;\;\;\; 2 \;\;\; 0 \;\; 0 \;\; 2 \;\;\;\; 0$$

Remainder $= 0$; therefore $x - \dfrac{1}{2}$ is a factor of $f(x)$.

49. Answers will vary.

Review

R.6 Factoring Polynomials

1. $3x + 6 = 3(x + 2)$

3. $ax^2 + a = a(x^2 + 1)$

5. $x^3 + x^2 + x = x(x^2 + x + 1)$

7. $2x^2 - 2x = 2x(x - 1)$

9. $3x^2y - 6xy^2 + 12xy = 3xy(x - 2y + 4)$

11. $x^2 - 1 = x^2 - 1^2 = (x - 1)(x + 1)$

13. $4x^2 - 1 = (2x)^2 - 1^2 = (2x - 1)(2x + 1)$

15. $x^2 - 16 = x^2 - 4^2 = (x - 4)(x + 4)$

17. $25x^2 - 4 = (5x - 2)(5x + 2)$

19. $x^2 + 2x + 1 = (x + 1)^2$

21. $x^2 + 4x + 4 = (x + 2)^2$

23. $x^2 - 10x + 25 = (x - 5)^2$

25. $4x^2 + 4x + 1 = (2x + 1)^2$

27. $16x^2 + 8x + 1 = (4x + 1)^2$

29. $x^3 - 27 = x^3 - 3^3 = (x - 3)(x^2 + 3x + 9)$

31. $x^3 + 27 = x^3 + 3^3 = (x + 3)(x^2 - 3x + 9)$

33. $8x^3 + 27 = (2x)^3 + 3^3 = (2x + 3)(4x^2 - 6x + 9)$

35. $x^2 + 5x + 6 = (x + 2)(x + 3)$

37. $x^2 + 7x + 6 = (x + 6)(x + 1)$

39. $x^2 + 7x + 10 = (x + 2)(x + 5)$

41. $x^2 - 10x + 16 = (x - 2)(x - 8)$

43. $x^2 - 7x - 8 = (x + 1)(x - 8)$

45. $x^2 + 7x - 8 = (x + 8)(x - 1)$

47. $2x^2 + 4x + 3x + 6 = 2x(x + 2) + 3(x + 2) = (x + 2)(2x + 3)$

49. $2x^2 - 4x + x - 2 = 2x(x - 2) + 1(x - 2) = (x - 2)(2x + 1)$

51. $6x^2 + 9x + 4x + 6 = 3x(2x + 3) + 2(2x + 3) = (2x + 3)(3x + 2)$

53. $3x^2 + 4x + 1 = (3x + 1)(x + 1)$

55. $2z^2 + 5z + 3 = (2z + 3)(z + 1)$

57. $3x^2 + 2x - 8 = (3x - 4)(x + 2)$

59. $3x^2 - 2x - 8 = (3x + 4)(x - 2)$

61. $3x^2 + 14x + 8 = (3x + 2)(x + 4)$

63. $3x^2 + 10x - 8 = (3x - 2)(x + 4)$

65. $x^2 - 36 = (x - 6)(x + 6)$ 67. $2 - 8x^2 = 2(1 - 4x^2) = 2(1 - 2x)(1 + 2x)$

69. $x^2 + 7x + 10 = (x + 2)(x + 5)$ 71. $x^2 - 10x + 21 = (x - 7)(x - 3)$

73. $4x^2 - 8x + 32 = 4(x^2 - 2x + 8)$

75. $x^2 + 4x + 16$ is prime because there are no factors of 16 whose sum is 4.

77. $15 + 2x - x^2 = -(x^2 - 2x - 15) = -(x - 5)(x + 3)$

79. $3x^2 - 12x - 36 = 3(x^2 - 4x - 12) = 3(x - 6)(x + 2)$

81. $y^4 + 11y^3 + 30y^2 = y^2(y^2 + 11y + 30) = y^2(y + 5)(y + 6)$

83. $4x^2 + 12x + 9 = (2x + 3)^2$

85. $6x^2 + 8x + 2 = 2(3x^2 + 4x + 1) = 2(3x + 1)(x + 1)$

87. $x^4 - 81 = (x^2 - 9)(x^2 + 9) = (x - 3)(x + 3)(x^2 + 9)$

89. $x^6 - 2x^3 + 1 = (x^3 - 1)^2 = \left[(x - 1)(x^2 + x + 1)\right]^2 = (x - 1)^2(x^2 + x + 1)^2$

91. $x^7 - x^5 = x^5(x^2 - 1) = x^5(x - 1)(x + 1)$

93. $16x^2 + 24x + 9 = (4x + 3)^2$

95. $5 + 16x - 16x^2 = -(16x^2 - 16x - 5) = -(4x - 5)(4x + 1)$

97. $4y^2 - 16y + 15 = (2y - 5)(2y - 3)$

99. $1 - 8x^2 - 9x^4 = -(9x^4 + 8x^2 - 1) = -(9x^2 - 1)(x^2 + 1) = -(3x - 1)(3x + 1)(x^2 + 1)$

101. $x(x + 3) - 6(x + 3) = (x + 3)(x - 6)$

103. $(x + 2)^2 - 5(x + 2) = (x + 2)[(x + 2) - 5] = (x + 2)(x - 3)$

105. $(3x - 2)^3 - 27 = [(3x - 2) - 3][(3x - 2)^2 + 3(3x - 2) + 9]$
$= (3x - 5)(9x^2 - 12x + 4 + 9x - 6 + 9) = (3x - 5)(9x^2 - 3x + 7)$

107. $3(x^2 + 10x + 25) - 4(x + 5) = 3(x + 5)^2 - 4(x + 5)$
$= (x + 5)[3(x + 5) - 4] = (x + 5)(3x + 15 - 4) = (x + 5)(3x + 11)$

109. $x^3 + 2x^2 - x - 2 = x^2(x + 2) - (x + 2) = (x + 2)(x^2 - 1) = (x + 2)(x - 1)(x + 1)$

111. $x^4 - x^3 + x - 1 = x^3(x-1) + (x-1) = (x-1)(x^3+1) = (x-1)(x+1)(x^2-x+1)$

113. $2(3x+4)^2 + (2x+3) \cdot 2(3x+4) \cdot 3 = 2 \cdot (3x+4)[(3x+4)+(2x+3) \cdot 3]$
$$= 2 \cdot (3x+4)[3x+4+6x+9] = 2 \cdot (3x+4)(9x+13)$$

115. $2x(2x+5) + x^2 \cdot 2 = 2x(2x+5+x) = 2x(3x+5)$

117. $2(x+3)(x-2)^3 + (x+3)^2 \cdot 3(x-2)^2 = (x+3)(x-2)^2[2(x-2)+3 \cdot (x+3)]$
$$= (x+3)(x-2)^2[2x-4+3x+9] = (x+3)(x-2)^2(5x+5) = 5(x+3)(x-2)^2(x+1)$$

119. $(4x-3)^2 + x \cdot 2(4x-3) \cdot 4 = (4x-3)[4x-3+x \cdot 2 \cdot 4] = (4x-3)(4x-3+8x)$
$$= (4x-3)(12x-3) = 3(4x-3)(4x-1)$$

121. $2(3x-5) \cdot 3(2x+1)^3 + (3x-5)^2 \cdot 3(2x+1)^2 \cdot 2 = 6(3x-5)(2x+1)^2[2x+1+3x-5]$
$$= 6(3x-5)(2x+1)^2(5x-4)$$

123. Factors of 4   1, 4   2, 2   −1, −4   −2, −2
Sum   5   4   −5   −4
None of the sums of the factors is 0, so x^2+4 is prime.

125. Answers will vary.

Review

R.7   Rational Expressions

1. $\dfrac{3x+9}{x^2-9} = \dfrac{3(x+3)}{(x-3)(x+3)} = \dfrac{3}{x-3}$

3. $\dfrac{x^2-2x}{3x-6} = \dfrac{x(x-2)}{3(x-2)} = \dfrac{x}{3}$

5. $\dfrac{24x^2}{12x^2-6x} = \dfrac{24x^2}{6x(2x-1)} = \dfrac{4x}{2x-1}$

7. $\dfrac{y^2-25}{2y^2-8y-10} = \dfrac{(y+5)(y-5)}{2(y^2-4y-5)} = \dfrac{(y+5)(y-5)}{2(y-5)(y+1)} = \dfrac{y+5}{2(y+1)}$

9. $\dfrac{x^2+4x-5}{x^2-2x+1} = \dfrac{(x+5)(x-1)}{(x-1)(x-1)} = \dfrac{x+5}{x-1}$

11. $\dfrac{x^2+5x-14}{2-x} = \dfrac{(x+7)(x-2)}{2-x} = \dfrac{(x+7)(x-2)}{(-1)(-2+x)} = \dfrac{(x+7)(x-2)}{(-1)(x-2)} = -(x+7)$

13. $\dfrac{3x+6}{5x^2} \cdot \dfrac{x}{x^2-4} = \dfrac{3(x+2)}{5x^2} \cdot \dfrac{x}{(x-2)(x+2)} = \dfrac{3}{5x(x-2)}$

15. $\dfrac{4x^2}{x^2-16} \cdot \dfrac{x-4}{2x} = \dfrac{4x^2}{(x-4)(x+4)} \cdot \dfrac{x-4}{2x} = \dfrac{2x}{x+4}$

17. $\dfrac{4x-8}{-3x} \cdot \dfrac{12}{12-6x} = \dfrac{4(x-2)}{-3x} \cdot \dfrac{12}{6(2-x)} = \dfrac{4(x-2)}{-3x} \cdot \dfrac{2}{(-1)(x-2)} = \dfrac{8}{3x}$

19. $\dfrac{x^2-3x-10}{x^2+2x-35} \cdot \dfrac{x^2+4x-21}{x^2+9x+14} = \dfrac{(x-5)(x+2)}{(x+7)(x-5)} \cdot \dfrac{(x+7)(x-3)}{(x+7)(x+2)} = \dfrac{x-3}{x+7}$

21. $\dfrac{\left(\dfrac{6x}{x^2-4}\right)}{\left(\dfrac{3x-9}{2x+4}\right)} = \dfrac{6x}{x^2-4} \cdot \dfrac{2x+4}{3x-9} = \dfrac{6x}{(x-2)(x+2)} \cdot \dfrac{2(x+2)}{3(x-3)} = \dfrac{4x}{(x-2)(x-3)}$

23. $\dfrac{\left(\dfrac{8x}{x^2-1}\right)}{\left(\dfrac{10x}{x+1}\right)} = \dfrac{8x}{x^2-1} \cdot \dfrac{x+1}{10x} = \dfrac{8x}{(x-1)(x+1)} \cdot \dfrac{x+1}{10x} = \dfrac{4}{5(x-1)}$

25. $\dfrac{\left(\dfrac{4-x}{4+x}\right)}{\left(\dfrac{4x}{x^2-16}\right)} = \dfrac{4-x}{4+x} \cdot \dfrac{x^2-16}{4x} = \dfrac{4-x}{4+x} \cdot \dfrac{(x+4)(x-4)}{4x} = \dfrac{(4-x)(x-4)}{4x} = -\dfrac{(x-4)^2}{4x}$

27. $\dfrac{\left(\dfrac{x^2+7x+12}{x^2-7x+12}\right)}{\left(\dfrac{x^2+x-12}{x^2-x-12}\right)} = \dfrac{x^2+7x+12}{x^2-7x+12} \cdot \dfrac{x^2-x-12}{x^2+x-12} = \dfrac{(x+3)(x+4)}{(x-3)(x-4)} \cdot \dfrac{(x-4)(x+3)}{(x+4)(x-3)} = \dfrac{(x+3)^2}{(x-3)^2}$

29. $\dfrac{\left(\dfrac{2x^2-x-28}{3x^2-x-2}\right)}{\left(\dfrac{4x^2+16x+7}{3x^2+11x+6}\right)} = \dfrac{2x^2-x-28}{3x^2-x-2} \cdot \dfrac{3x^2+11x+6}{4x^2+16x+7} = \dfrac{(2x+7)(x-4)}{(3x+2)(x-1)} \cdot \dfrac{(3x+2)(x+3)}{(2x+7)(2x+1)}$

$= \dfrac{(x-4)(x+3)}{(x-1)(2x+1)}$

31. $\dfrac{x}{2} + \dfrac{5}{2} = \dfrac{x+5}{2}$

33. $\dfrac{x^2}{2x-3} - \dfrac{4}{2x-3} = \dfrac{x^2-4}{2x-3} = \dfrac{(x+2)(x-2)}{2x-3}$

35. $\dfrac{x+1}{x-3} + \dfrac{2x-3}{x-3} = \dfrac{x+1+2x-3}{x-3} = \dfrac{3x-2}{x-3}$

37. $\dfrac{3x+5}{2x-1} - \dfrac{2x-4}{2x-1} = \dfrac{(3x+5)-(2x-4)}{2x-1} = \dfrac{3x+5-2x+4}{2x-1} = \dfrac{x+9}{2x-1}$

39. $\dfrac{4}{x-2} + \dfrac{x}{2-x} = \dfrac{4}{x-2} - \dfrac{x}{x-2} = \dfrac{4-x}{x-2}$

41. $\dfrac{4}{x-1} - \dfrac{2}{x+2} = \dfrac{4(x+2)}{(x-1)(x+2)} - \dfrac{2(x-1)}{(x+2)(x-1)} = \dfrac{4x+8-2x+2}{(x+2)(x-1)} = \dfrac{2x+10}{(x+2)(x-1)}$

$= \dfrac{2(x+5)}{(x+2)(x-1)}$

43. $\dfrac{x}{x+1} + \dfrac{2x-3}{x-1} = \dfrac{x(x-1)}{(x+1)(x-1)} + \dfrac{(2x-3)(x+1)}{(x-1)(x+1)} = \dfrac{x^2-x+2x^2-x-3}{(x-1)(x+1)}$

$= \dfrac{3x^2-2x-3}{(x-1)(x+1)}$

45. $\dfrac{x-3}{x+2} - \dfrac{x+4}{x-2} = \dfrac{(x-3)(x-2)}{(x+2)(x-2)} - \dfrac{(x+4)(x+2)}{(x-2)(x+2)} = \dfrac{x^2-5x+6-(x^2+6x+8)}{(x+2)(x-2)}$

$= \dfrac{x^2-5x+6-x^2-6x-8}{(x+2)(x-2)} = \dfrac{-11x-2}{(x+2)(x-2)}$

47. $\dfrac{x}{x^2-4}+\dfrac{1}{x}=\dfrac{x^2+x^2-4}{(x)(x^2-4)}=\dfrac{2x^2-4}{(x)(x^2-4)}=\dfrac{2(x^2-2)}{(x)(x-2)(x+2)}$

49. $x^2-4=(x+2)(x-2)$
$x^2-x-2=(x+1)(x-2)$
$\therefore \text{LCM is } (x+2)(x-2)(x+1)$

51. $x^3-x=x(x^2-1)=x(x+1)(x-1)$
$x^2-x=x(x-1)$
$\therefore \text{LCM is } x(x+1)(x-1)$

53. $4x^3-4x^2+x=x(4x^2-4x+1)=x(2x-1)(2x-1)$
$2x^3-x^2=x^2(2x-1)$
x^3
$\therefore \text{LCM is } x^3(2x-1)^2$

55. $x^3-x=x(x^2-1)=x(x+1)(x-1)$
$x^3-2x^2+x=x(x^2-2x+1)=x(x-1)^2$
$x^3-1=(x-1)(x^2+x+1)$
$\therefore \text{LCM is } x(x+1)(x-1)^2(x^2+x+1)$

57. $\dfrac{x}{x^2-7x+6}-\dfrac{x}{x^2-2x-24}=\dfrac{x}{(x-6)(x-1)}-\dfrac{x}{(x-6)(x+4)}$
$=\dfrac{x(x+4)}{(x-6)(x-1)(x+4)}-\dfrac{x(x-1)}{(x-6)(x+4)(x-1)}$
$=\dfrac{x^2+4x-x^2+x}{(x-6)(x+4)(x-1)}=\dfrac{5x}{(x-6)(x+4)(x-1)}$

59. $\dfrac{4x}{x^2-4}-\dfrac{2}{x^2+x-6}=\dfrac{4x}{(x-2)(x+2)}-\dfrac{2}{(x+3)(x-2)}$
$=\dfrac{4x(x+3)}{(x-2)(x+2)(x+3)}-\dfrac{2(x+2)}{(x+3)(x-2)(x+2)}$
$=\dfrac{4x^2+12x-2x-4}{(x-2)(x+2)(x+3)}=\dfrac{4x^2+10x-4}{(x-2)(x+2)(x+3)}$
$=\dfrac{2(2x^2+5x-2)}{(x-2)(x+2)(x+3)}$

61. $\dfrac{3}{(x-1)^2(x+1)}+\dfrac{2}{(x-1)(x+1)^2}=\dfrac{3(x+1)+2(x-1)}{(x-1)^2(x+1)^2}=\dfrac{3x+3+2x-2}{(x-1)^2(x+1)^2}$
$=\dfrac{5x+1}{(x-1)^2(x+1)^2}$

63. $\dfrac{x+4}{x^2-x-2}-\dfrac{2x+3}{x^2+2x-8}=\dfrac{x+4}{(x-2)(x+1)}-\dfrac{2x+3}{(x+4)(x-2)}$

$$=\dfrac{(x+4)(x+4)}{(x-2)(x+1)(x+4)}-\dfrac{(2x+3)(x+1)}{(x+4)(x-2)(x+1)}$$

$$=\dfrac{x^2+8x+16-(2x^2+5x+3)}{(x-2)(x+1)(x+4)}=\dfrac{-x^2+3x+13}{(x-2)(x+1)(x+4)}$$

65. $\dfrac{1}{x}-\dfrac{2}{x^2+x}+\dfrac{3}{x^3-x^2}=\dfrac{1}{x}-\dfrac{2}{x(x+1)}+\dfrac{3}{x^2(x-1)}=\dfrac{x(x+1)(x-1)-2x(x-1)+3(x+1)}{x^2(x+1)(x-1)}$

$$=\dfrac{x(x^2-1)-2x^2+2x+3x+3}{x^2(x+1)(x-1)}=\dfrac{x^3-x-2x^2+5x+3}{x^2(x+1)(x-1)}=\dfrac{x^3-2x^2+4x+3}{x^2(x+1)(x-1)}$$

67. $\dfrac{1}{h}\left(\dfrac{1}{x+h}-\dfrac{1}{x}\right)=\dfrac{1}{h}\left(\dfrac{1\cdot x}{(x+h)x}-\dfrac{1(x+h)}{x(x+h)}\right)=\dfrac{1}{h}\left(\dfrac{x-x-h}{x(x+h)}\right)=\dfrac{-h}{hx(x+h)}=\dfrac{-1}{x(x+h)}$

69. $\dfrac{1+\dfrac{1}{x}}{1-\dfrac{1}{x}}=\dfrac{\left(\dfrac{x}{x}+\dfrac{1}{x}\right)}{\left(\dfrac{x}{x}-\dfrac{1}{x}\right)}=\dfrac{\left(\dfrac{x+1}{x}\right)}{\left(\dfrac{x-1}{x}\right)}=\dfrac{x+1}{x}\cdot\dfrac{x}{x-1}=\dfrac{x+1}{x-1}$

71. $\dfrac{x-\dfrac{1}{x}}{x+\dfrac{1}{x}}=\dfrac{\left(\dfrac{x^2}{x}-\dfrac{1}{x}\right)}{\left(\dfrac{x^2}{x}+\dfrac{1}{x}\right)}=\dfrac{\left(\dfrac{x^2-1}{x}\right)}{\left(\dfrac{x^2+1}{x}\right)}=\dfrac{x^2-1}{x}\cdot\dfrac{x}{x^2+1}=\dfrac{(x-1)(x+1)}{x^2+1}$

73. $\dfrac{\left(\dfrac{x+4}{x-2}-\dfrac{x-3}{x+1}\right)}{x+1}=\dfrac{\left(\dfrac{(x+4)(x+1)}{(x-2)(x+1)}-\dfrac{(x-3)(x-2)}{(x+1)(x-2)}\right)}{x+1}=\dfrac{\left(\dfrac{x^2+5x+4-(x^2-5x+6)}{(x-2)(x+1)}\right)}{x+1}$

$$=\dfrac{10x-2}{(x-2)(x+1)}\cdot\dfrac{1}{x+1}=\dfrac{2(5x-1)}{(x-2)(x+1)^2}$$

75. $\dfrac{\left(\dfrac{x-2}{x+2}+\dfrac{x-1}{x+1}\right)}{\left(\dfrac{x}{x+1}-\dfrac{2x-3}{x}\right)}=\dfrac{\left(\dfrac{(x-2)(x+1)}{(x+2)(x+1)}+\dfrac{(x-1)(x+2)}{(x+1)(x+2)}\right)}{\left(\dfrac{x^2}{(x+1)(x)}-\dfrac{(2x-3)(x+1)}{x(x+1)}\right)}=\dfrac{\left(\dfrac{x^2-x-2+x^2+x-2}{(x+2)(x+1)}\right)}{\left(\dfrac{x^2-(2x^2-x-3)}{x(x+1)}\right)}$

$$=\dfrac{\left(\dfrac{2x^2-4}{(x+2)(x+1)}\right)}{\left(\dfrac{-x^2+x+3}{x(x+1)}\right)}=\dfrac{2(x^2-2)}{(x+2)(x+1)}\cdot\dfrac{x(x+1)}{-(x^2-x-3)}=\dfrac{2x(x^2-2)}{-(x+2)(x^2-x-3)}=\dfrac{-2x(x^2-2)}{(x+2)(x^2-x-3)}$$

77. $1 - \dfrac{1}{\left(1 - \dfrac{1}{x}\right)} = 1 - \dfrac{1}{\left(\dfrac{x-1}{x}\right)} = 1 - 1 \cdot \dfrac{x}{x-1} = \dfrac{x-1-x}{x-1} = \dfrac{-1}{x-1}$

79. $\dfrac{(2x+3) \cdot 3 - (3x-5) \cdot 2}{(3x-5)^2} = \dfrac{6x+9-6x+10}{(3x-5)^2} = \dfrac{19}{(3x-5)^2}$

81. $\dfrac{x \cdot 2x - (x^2+1) \cdot 1}{(x^2+1)^2} = \dfrac{2x^2 - x^2 - 1}{(x^2+1)^2} = \dfrac{x^2-1}{(x^2+1)^2} = \dfrac{(x+1)(x-1)}{(x^2+1)^2}$

83. $\dfrac{(3x+1) \cdot 2x - x^2 \cdot 3}{(3x+1)^2} = \dfrac{6x^2 + 2x - 3x^2}{(3x+1)^2} = \dfrac{3x^2+2x}{(3x+1)^2} = \dfrac{x(3x+2)}{(3x+1)^2}$

85. $\dfrac{(x^2+1) \cdot 3 - (3x+4) \cdot 2x}{(x^2+1)^2} = \dfrac{3x^2+3-6x^2-8x}{(x^2+1)^2} = \dfrac{-3x^2-8x+3}{(x^2+1)^2} = \dfrac{(-3x+1)(x+3)}{(x^2+1)^2}$

87. $\dfrac{1}{f} = (n-1)\left(\dfrac{1}{R_1} + \dfrac{1}{R_2}\right)$

$\dfrac{R_1 \cdot R_2}{f} = (n-1)\left(\dfrac{1}{R_1} + \dfrac{1}{R_2}\right) R_1 \cdot R_2 \Rightarrow \dfrac{R_1 \cdot R_2}{f} = (n-1)(R_2 + R_1)$

$\dfrac{f}{R_1 \cdot R_2} = \dfrac{1}{(n-1)(R_2 + R_1)} \Rightarrow f = \dfrac{R_1 \cdot R_2}{(n-1)(R_2 + R_1)}$

$f = \dfrac{0.1(0.2)}{(1.5-1)(0.2+0.1)} = \dfrac{0.02}{0.5(0.3)} = \dfrac{0.02}{0.15} = \dfrac{2}{15}$ meters

89. $1 + \dfrac{1}{x} = \dfrac{x+1}{x} \Rightarrow a = 1, b = 1, c = 0$

$1 + \dfrac{1}{1 + \dfrac{1}{x}} = 1 + \dfrac{1}{\left(\dfrac{x+1}{x}\right)} = 1 + \dfrac{x}{x+1} = \dfrac{x+1+x}{x+1} = \dfrac{2x+1}{x+1} \Rightarrow a = 2, b = 1, c = 1$

$1 + \dfrac{1}{1 + \dfrac{1}{1 + \dfrac{1}{x}}} = 1 + \dfrac{1}{\left(\dfrac{2x+1}{x+1}\right)} = 1 + \dfrac{x+1}{2x+1} = \dfrac{2x+1+x+1}{2x+1} = \dfrac{3x+2}{2x+1} \Rightarrow a = 3, b = 2, c = 1$

$1 + \dfrac{1}{1 + \dfrac{1}{1 + \dfrac{1}{1 + \dfrac{1}{x}}}} = 1 + \dfrac{1}{\left(\dfrac{3x+2}{2x+1}\right)} = 1 + \dfrac{2x+1}{3x+2} = \dfrac{3x+2+2x+1}{3x+2} = \dfrac{5x+3}{3x+2} \Rightarrow a = 5, b = 3, c = 2$

If we continue this process, the values of a, b and c produce the following sequences:

$a : 1, 2, 3, 5, 8, 13, 21, \ldots$

$b : 1, 1, 2, 3, 5, 8, 13, 21, \ldots$

$c : 0, 1, 1, 2, 3, 5, 8, 13, 21, \ldots$

In each case we have the *Fibonacci Sequence*, where the next value in the list is obtained from the sum of the previous 2 values in the list.

91.   Answers will vary.

Review

R.8   *n*th Roots; Rational Exponents

1. $\sqrt[3]{27} = 3$

3. $\sqrt[3]{-8} = -2$

5. $\sqrt{8} = \sqrt{4 \cdot 2} = 2\sqrt{2}$

7. $\sqrt[3]{-8x^4} = \sqrt[3]{-8 \cdot x^3 \cdot x} = -2x\sqrt[3]{x}$

9. $\sqrt[4]{x^{12}y^8} = \sqrt[4]{\left(x^3\right)^4\left(y^2\right)^4} = x^3 y^2$

11. $\sqrt[4]{\dfrac{x^9 y^7}{x\,y^3}} = \sqrt[4]{x^8 y^4} = x^2 y$

13. $\sqrt{36x} = 6\sqrt{x}$

15. $\sqrt{3x^2}\sqrt{12x} = \sqrt{36x^2 \cdot x} = 6x\sqrt{x}$

17. $\left(\sqrt{5} \ \sqrt[3]{9}\right)^2 = 5\left(\sqrt[3]{81}\right) = 5\left(\sqrt[3]{27 \cdot 3}\right) = 5 \cdot 3\left(\sqrt[3]{3}\right) = 15\sqrt[3]{3}$

19. $\left(3\sqrt{6}\right)\left(2\sqrt{2}\right) = 6\sqrt{12} = 6\sqrt{4 \cdot 3} = 12\sqrt{3}$

21. $\left(\sqrt{3} + 3\right)\left(\sqrt{3} - 1\right) = \left(\sqrt{3}\right)^2 - \sqrt{3} + 3\sqrt{3} - 3 = 3 + 2\sqrt{3} - 3 = 2\sqrt{3}$

23. $\left(\sqrt{x} - 1\right)^2 = \left(\sqrt{x}\right)^2 - 2\sqrt{x} + 1 = x - 2\sqrt{x} + 1$

25. $3\sqrt{2} - 4\sqrt{8} = 3\sqrt{2} - 4\sqrt{4 \cdot 2} = 3\sqrt{2} - 8\sqrt{2} = -5\sqrt{2}$

27. $\sqrt[3]{16x^4} - \sqrt[3]{2x} = \sqrt[3]{8 \cdot 2 \cdot x^3 \cdot x} - \sqrt[3]{2x} = 2x\sqrt[3]{2x} - \sqrt[3]{2x} = (2x - 1)\sqrt[3]{2x}$

29. $\dfrac{1}{\sqrt{2}} \cdot \dfrac{\sqrt{2}}{\sqrt{2}} = \dfrac{\sqrt{2}}{2}$

31. $\dfrac{-\sqrt{3}}{\sqrt{5}} \cdot \dfrac{\sqrt{5}}{\sqrt{5}} = \dfrac{-\sqrt{15}}{5} = -\dfrac{\sqrt{15}}{5}$

33. $\dfrac{\sqrt{3}}{5 - \sqrt{2}} \cdot \dfrac{5 + \sqrt{2}}{5 + \sqrt{2}} = \dfrac{\sqrt{3}\left(5 + \sqrt{2}\right)}{25 - 2} = \dfrac{\sqrt{3}\left(5 + \sqrt{2}\right)}{23}$

35. $\dfrac{2 - \sqrt{5}}{2 + 3\sqrt{5}} \cdot \dfrac{2 - 3\sqrt{5}}{2 - 3\sqrt{5}} = \dfrac{4 - 6\sqrt{5} - 2\sqrt{5} + 3\left(\sqrt{5}\right)^2}{4 - 9\left(\sqrt{5}\right)^2} = \dfrac{4 - 8\sqrt{5} + 3 \cdot 5}{4 - 9 \cdot 5}$

$$= \dfrac{4 - 8\sqrt{5} + 15}{4 - 45} = \dfrac{19 - 8\sqrt{5}}{-41} = \dfrac{-19 + 8\sqrt{5}}{41}$$

37. $\dfrac{5}{\sqrt[3]{2}}\cdot\dfrac{\left(\sqrt[3]{2}\right)^2}{\left(\sqrt[3]{2}\right)^2}=\dfrac{5\left(\sqrt[3]{2}\right)^2}{\left(\sqrt[3]{2}\right)^3}=\dfrac{4\left(\sqrt[3]{2^2}\right)}{2}=\dfrac{5\sqrt[3]{4}}{2}$

39. $\dfrac{\sqrt{x+h}-\sqrt{x}}{\sqrt{x+h}+\sqrt{x}}\cdot\dfrac{\sqrt{x+h}-\sqrt{x}}{\sqrt{x+h}-\sqrt{x}}=\dfrac{\left(\sqrt{x+h}\right)^2-2\sqrt{x}\cdot\sqrt{x+h}+\left(\sqrt{x}\right)^2}{\left(\sqrt{x+h}\right)^2-\left(\sqrt{x}\right)^2}$

$=\dfrac{x+h-2\sqrt{x(x+h)}+x}{x+h-x}=\dfrac{2x+h-2\sqrt{x(x+h)}}{h}$

41. $8^{2/3}=\left(2^3\right)^{2/3}=2^2=4$ **43.** $(-27)^{1/3}=\left((-3)^3\right)^{1/3}=-3$

45. $16^{3/2}=\left(2^4\right)^{3/2}=2^6=64$ **47.** $9^{-3/2}=\left(3^2\right)^{-3/2}=3^{-3}=\dfrac{1}{3^3}=\dfrac{1}{27}$

49. $\left(\dfrac{9}{8}\right)^{3/2}=\left(\dfrac{3^2}{2^3}\right)^{3/2}=\dfrac{3^{6/2}}{2^{9/2}}=\dfrac{3^3}{2^{8/2}\cdot2^{1/2}}=\dfrac{27}{2^4\cdot2^{1/2}}=\dfrac{27}{16\cdot\sqrt{2}}\cdot\dfrac{\sqrt{2}}{\sqrt{2}}=\dfrac{27\sqrt{2}}{16\cdot2}=\dfrac{27\sqrt{2}}{32}$

51. $\left(\dfrac{8}{9}\right)^{-3/2}=\left(\dfrac{2^3}{3^2}\right)^{-3/2}=\dfrac{2^{-9/2}}{3^{-6/2}}=\dfrac{2^{-8/2}\cdot2^{-1/2}}{3^{-3}}=\dfrac{2^{-4}\cdot2^{-1/2}}{3^{-3}}=\dfrac{27}{16\cdot\sqrt{2}}\cdot\dfrac{\sqrt{2}}{\sqrt{2}}=\dfrac{27\sqrt{2}}{16\cdot2}=\dfrac{27\sqrt{2}}{32}$

53. $x^{3/4}\cdot x^{1/3}\cdot x^{-1/2}=x^{3/4+1/3-1/2}=x^{(9+4-6)/12}=x^{7/12}$

55. $\left(x^3y^6\right)^{1/3}=\left(x^3\right)^{1/3}\left(y^6\right)^{1/3}=x\,y^2$

57. $\left(x^2y\right)^{1/3}\left(x\,y^2\right)^{2/3}=x^{2/3}y^{1/3}x^{2/3}y^{4/3}=x^{4/3}y^{5/3}$

59. $\left(16x^2y^{-1/3}\right)^{3/4}=\left(2^4x^2y^{-1/3}\right)^{3/4}=2^3x^{3/2}y^{-1/4}=\dfrac{8x^{3/2}}{y^{1/4}}$

61. $\dfrac{x}{(1+x)^{1/2}}+2(1+x)^{1/2}=\dfrac{x+2(1+x)^{1/2}(1+x)^{1/2}}{(1+x)^{1/2}}=\dfrac{x+2(1+x)}{(1+x)^{1/2}}=\dfrac{x+2+2x}{(1+x)^{1/2}}=\dfrac{3x+2}{(1+x)^{1/2}}$

63. $\dfrac{\left(\sqrt{1+x}-x\cdot\dfrac{1}{2\sqrt{1+x}}\right)}{1+x}=\dfrac{\left(\sqrt{1+x}-\dfrac{x}{2\sqrt{1+x}}\right)}{1+x}=\dfrac{\left(\dfrac{2\sqrt{1+x}\sqrt{1+x}-x}{2\sqrt{1+x}}\right)}{1+x}$

$=\dfrac{2(1+x)-x}{2(1+x)^{1/2}}\cdot\dfrac{1}{1+x}=\dfrac{2+x}{2(1+x)^{3/2}}$

65. $\dfrac{(x+4)^{1/2}-2x(x+4)^{-1/2}}{x+4}=\dfrac{\left((x+4)^{1/2}-\dfrac{2x}{(x+4)^{1/2}}\right)}{x+4}=\dfrac{\left((x+4)^{1/2}\cdot\dfrac{(x+4)^{1/2}}{(x+4)^{1/2}}-\dfrac{2x}{(x+4)^{1/2}}\right)}{x+4}$

$=\dfrac{\left(\dfrac{x+4-2x}{(x+4)^{1/2}}\right)}{x+4}=\dfrac{-x+4}{(x+4)^{1/2}}\cdot\dfrac{1}{x+4}=\dfrac{4-x}{(x+4)^{3/2}}$

67. $(x+1)^{3/2}+x\cdot\dfrac{3}{2}(x+1)^{1/2}=(x+1)^{1/2}\left(x+1+\dfrac{3}{2}x\right)=(x+1)^{1/2}\left(\dfrac{5}{2}x+1\right)=\dfrac{1}{2}(x+1)^{1/2}(5x+2)$

69. $6x^{1/2}\left(x^2+x\right)-8x^{3/2}-8x^{1/2}=2x^{1/2}\left(3(x^2+x)-4x-4\right)=2x^{1/2}\left(3x^2-x-4\right)$

$=2x^{1/2}(3x-4)(x+1)$

71. $x\left(\dfrac{1}{2}\right)\left(8-x^2\right)^{-1/2}(-2x)+\left(8-x^2\right)^{1/2}=-x^2\left(8-x^2\right)^{-1/2}+\left(8-x^2\right)^{1/2}=\left(8-x^2\right)^{-1/2}\left[-x^2+\left(8-x^2\right)\right]$

$=\left(8-x^2\right)^{-1/2}\left[-x^2+8-x^2\right]=\left(8-x^2\right)^{-1/2}\left[8-2x^2\right]$

$=\dfrac{8-2x^2}{\left(8-x^2\right)^{1/2}}=\dfrac{2\left(4-x^2\right)}{\left(8-x^2\right)^{1/2}}=\dfrac{2(2-x)(2+x)}{\left(8-x^2\right)^{1/2}}$

Equations, Inequalities and Functions

1.1 Solving Equations and Inequalities in One Variable Algebraically

1.
$$x + 2 = 10$$
$$x + 2 - 2 = 10 - 2$$
$$x = 8$$
Solution set is $\{8\}$.

3.
$$2t - 6 = 4$$
$$2t - 6 + 6 = 4 + 6$$
$$2t = 10$$
$$\frac{2t}{2} = \frac{10}{2}$$
$$t = 5$$
Solution set is $\{5\}$.

5.
$$3 + 2n = 5n + 7$$
$$3 + 2n - 2n = 5n + 7 - 2n$$
$$3 = 3n + 7$$
$$3 - 7 = 3n + 7 - 7$$
$$-4 = 3n$$
$$\frac{-4}{3} = \frac{3n}{3}$$
$$-\frac{4}{3} = n$$
Solution set is $\left\{-\frac{4}{3}\right\}$.

7.
$$x^2 - 7x + 12 = 0$$
$$(x - 4)(x - 3) = 0$$
$$x - 4 = 0 \Rightarrow x = 4$$
$$x - 3 = 0 \Rightarrow x = 3$$
Solution set $\{3, 4\}$.

9.
$$2x^2 + 5x - 3 = 0$$
$$(2x - 1)(x + 3) = 0$$
$$2x - 1 = 0 \Rightarrow x = \frac{1}{2}$$
$$x + 3 = 0 \Rightarrow x = -3$$
Solution set $\left\{-3, \frac{1}{2}\right\}$.

11.
$$x^2 - 9 = 0$$
$$(x - 3)(x + 3) = 0$$
$$x - 3 = 0 \Rightarrow x = 3$$
$$x + 3 = 0 \Rightarrow x = -3$$
Solution set $\{-3, 3\}$.

13. $x^3 + x^2 - 20x = 0$
$x(x^2 + x - 20) = 0 \Rightarrow x(x + 5)(x - 4) = 0$
$$x = 0$$
$$x + 5 = 0 \Rightarrow x = -5$$
$$x - 4 = 0 \Rightarrow x = 4$$
Solution set $\{-5, 0, 4\}$.

15. $4x^2 = x$
$4x^2 - x = 0 \Rightarrow x(4x - 1) = 0$
$$x = 0$$
$$4x - 1 = 0 \Rightarrow x = \frac{1}{4}$$
Solution set $\left\{0, \frac{1}{4}\right\}$.

17. $x^3 = 9x$
$x^3 - 9x = 0 \Rightarrow x(x^2 - 9) = 0$
$$x(x - 3)(x + 3) = 0$$
$$x = 0$$
$$x - 3 = 0 \Rightarrow x = 3$$
$$x + 3 = 0 \Rightarrow x = -3$$
Solution set $\{-3, 0, 3\}$.

19. $x^4 = x^2$
$x^4 - x^2 = 0 \Rightarrow x^2(x^2 - 1) = 0$
$$x(x - 1)(x + 1) = 0$$
$$x = 0$$
$$x - 1 = 0 \Rightarrow x = 1$$
$$x + 1 = 0 \Rightarrow x = -1$$
Solution set $\{-1, 0, 1\}$.

21. $x^3 + x^2 + x + 1 = 0$
$x^2(x + 1) + x + 1 = 0 \Rightarrow (x + 1)(x^2 + 1) = 0$
$$x + 1 = 0 \Rightarrow x = -1$$
$$x^2 + 1 = 0 \text{ has no real solution}$$
Solution set $\{-1\}$.

23. $x^3 - 2x^2 - 4x + 8 = 0$
$x^2(x - 2) - 4(x - 2) = 0 \Rightarrow (x - 2)(x^2 - 4) = 0$
$$(x - 2)(x - 2)(x + 2) = 0$$
$$x - 2 = 0 \Rightarrow x = 2$$
$$x + 2 = 0 \Rightarrow x = -2$$
Solution set $\{-2, 2\}$.

25. $x^2 = 25 \Rightarrow x = \pm\sqrt{25} \Rightarrow x = \pm 5$
The solution set is $\{-5, 5\}$.

27. $(x - 1)^2 = 4$
$$x - 1 = \pm\sqrt{4} \Rightarrow x - 1 = \pm 2$$
$$x - 1 = 2 \text{ or } x - 1 = -2$$
$$\Rightarrow x = 3 \text{ or } x = -1$$
The solution set is $\{-1, 3\}$.

29. $(2x + 3)^2 = 9$
$$2x + 3 = \pm\sqrt{9} \Rightarrow 2x + 3 = \pm 3$$
$$2x + 3 = 3 \text{ or } 2x + 3 = -3$$
$$\Rightarrow x = 0 \text{ or } x = -3$$
The solution set is $\{-3, 0\}$.

31. $[0, 2]$ $0 \le x \le 2$

33. $(-1, 2)$ $-1 < x < 2$

35. $[0, 3)$ $0 \le x < 3$

37. (a) $6 < 8$
    (b) $-2 < 0$
    (c) $9 < 15$
    (d) $-6 > -10$

39. (a) $7 > 0$
    (b) $-1 > -8$
    (c) $12 > -9$
    (d) $-8 < 6$

41. (a) $2x + 4 < 5$
    (b) $2x - 4 < -3$
    (c) $6x + 3 < 6$
    (d) $-4x - 2 > -4$

43. $[0, 4]$
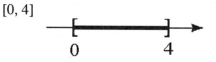

45. $[4, 6)$

47. $[4, \infty)$

49. $(-\infty, -4)$

51. $2 \leq x \leq 5$
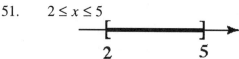

53. $-3 < x < -2$
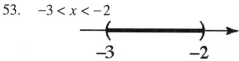

55. $x \geq 4$

57. $x < -3$

59. If $x < 5$, then $x - 5 < 0$.

61. If $x > -4$, then $x + 4 > 0$.

63. If $x \geq -4$, then $3x \geq -12$.

65. If $x > 6$, then $-2x < -12$.

67. If $x \geq 5$, then $-4x \leq -20$.

69. If $2x < 6$, then $x < 3$.

71. If $-\dfrac{1}{2}x \leq 3$, then $x \geq -6$.

73. $x - 4 < 0 \Rightarrow x < 4$
    $\{x \mid x < 4\}$ or $(-\infty, 4)$

75. $1 - 2x \leq 3$
    $-2x \leq 2 \Rightarrow x \geq -1$
    $\{x \mid x \geq -1\}$ or $[-1, +\infty)$

77. $3x - 7 > 2$
    $3x > 9 \Rightarrow x > 3$
    $\{x \mid x > 3\}$ or $(3, +\infty)$

79. $3x - 1 \geq 3 + x$

$2x \geq 4 \Rightarrow x \geq 2$
$\{x \mid x \geq 2\}$ or $[2, +\infty)$

81. $-2(x + 3) < 8$

$-2x - 6 < 8 \Rightarrow -2x < 14 \Rightarrow x > -7$
$\{x \mid x > -7\}$ or $(-7, +\infty)$

83. $4 - 3(1 - x) \leq 3$
$4 - 3 + 3x \leq 3$

$3x + 1 \leq 3 \Rightarrow 3x \leq 2 \Rightarrow x \leq \dfrac{2}{3}$

$\left\{x \mid x \leq \dfrac{2}{3}\right\}$ or $\left(-\infty, \dfrac{2}{3}\right]$

85. $\dfrac{1}{2}(x - 4) > x + 8$

$\dfrac{1}{2}x - 2 > x + 8 \Rightarrow -\dfrac{1}{2}x > 10 \Rightarrow x < -20$

$\{x \mid x < -20\}$ or $(-\infty, -20)$

87. $\dfrac{x}{2} \geq 1 - \dfrac{x}{4}$

$2x \geq 4 - x \Rightarrow 3x \geq 4 \Rightarrow x \geq \dfrac{4}{3}$

$\left\{x \mid x \geq \dfrac{4}{3}\right\}$ or $\left[\dfrac{4}{3}, +\infty\right)$

89. $0 \leq 2x - 6 \leq 4$

$6 \leq 2x \leq 10 \Rightarrow 3 \leq x \leq 5$
$\{x \mid 3 \leq x \leq 5\}$ or $[3, 5]$

91. $-5 \leq 4 - 3x \leq 2$

$-9 \leq -3x \leq -2 \Rightarrow 3 \geq x \geq \dfrac{2}{3}$

$\left\{x \mid \dfrac{2}{3} \leq x \leq 3\right\}$ or $\left[\dfrac{2}{3}, 3\right]$

93. $-3 < \dfrac{2x - 1}{4} < 0$

$-12 < 2x - 1 < 0$

$-11 < 2x < 1 \Rightarrow -\dfrac{11}{2} < x < \dfrac{1}{2}$

$\left\{x \mid -\dfrac{11}{2} < x < \dfrac{1}{2}\right\}$ or $\left(-\dfrac{11}{2}, \dfrac{1}{2}\right)$

95. $1 < 1 - \dfrac{1}{2}x < 4$

$0 < -\dfrac{1}{2}x < 3 \Rightarrow 0 > x > -6 \Rightarrow -6 < x < 0$
$\{x \mid -6 < x < 0\}$ or $(-6, 0)$

97. $(x + 2)(x - 3) > (x - 1)(x + 1)$
$x^2 - x - 6 > x^2 - 1$

$-x - 6 > -1 \Rightarrow -x > 5 \Rightarrow x < -5$
$\{x \mid x < -5\}$ or $(-\infty, -5)$

99. $x(4x+3) \le (2x+1)^2$
$4x^2 + 3x \le 4x^2 + 4x + 1$

$3x \le 4x + 1 \Rightarrow -x \le 1 \Rightarrow x \ge -1$
$\{x \mid x \ge -1\}$ or $[-1, +\infty)$

101. $\dfrac{1}{2} \le \dfrac{x+1}{3} < \dfrac{3}{4}$
$6 \le 4x + 4 < 9$

$2 \le 4x < 5 \Rightarrow \dfrac{1}{2} \le x < \dfrac{5}{4}$

$\left\{ x \mid \dfrac{1}{2} \le x < \dfrac{5}{4} \right\}$ or $\left[\dfrac{1}{2}, \dfrac{5}{4} \right)$

103. $21 <$ young adult's age < 30

105. A temperature x that differs from 98.6°F by at most 1.5°:
$-1.5° \le x - 98.6° \le 1.5°$

$97.1° \le x \le 100.1°$
The temperatures that are considered healthy are those that are greater than or equal to 97.1°F but less than or equal to 100.1°F.

107. (a) An average 25-year-old male can expect to live at least 50.6 more years.
$25 + 50.6 = 75.6$. Therefore, the average age of a 25-year-old male will be ≥ 75.6.
(b) An average 25-year-old female can expect to live at least 55.4 more years.
$25 + 55.4 = 80.4$. Therefore, the average age of a 25-year-old female will be ≥ 80.4.
(c) By the given information, a female can expect to live 4.8 years longer.

109. Let P represent the selling price in dollars and C represent the commission in dollars.
Calculating the commission:
$C = 45,000 + 0.25(P - 900,000) = 45,000 + 0.25P - 225,000 = 0.25P - 180,000$
Solving for P: $C = 0.25P - 180,000$
$$C + 180,000 = 0.25P \Rightarrow \frac{C + 180,000}{0.25} = P$$
Calculate the commission range, given the price range:
$$900,000 \le P \le 1,100,000 \Rightarrow 900,000 \le \frac{C + 180,000}{0.25} \le 1,100,000$$
$$0.25(900,000) \le C + 180,000 \le 0.25(1,100,000) \Rightarrow 225,000 \le C + 180,000 \le 275,000$$
$$225,000 - 180,000 \le C \le 275,000 - 180,000$$
$$45,000 \le C \le 95,000$$
The agent's commission ranges from \$45,000 to \$95,000, inclusive.
$$\frac{45,000}{900,000} = 0.05 = 5\% \text{ to } \frac{95,000}{1,100,000} = 0.086 = 8.6\%, \text{ inclusive.}$$
As a percent of selling price, the commission ranges from 5% to 8.6%.

111. Let W represent the weekly wage in dollars and T represent the withholding tax in dollars.
Calculating the tax:
$T = 75.15 + 0.27(W - 552) = 75.15 + 0.27W - 149.04 = 0.27W - 73.89$

Solving for W: $T = 0.27W - 73.89$

$$T + 73.89 = 0.27W \Rightarrow \frac{T + 73.89}{0.27} = W$$

Calculating the withholding tax range, given the range of weekly wages:

$$575 \le W \le 650 \Rightarrow 575 \le \frac{T + 73.89}{0.27} \le 650$$

$$0.27(575) \le T + 73.89 \le 0.27(650) \Rightarrow 155.25 \le T + 73.89 \le 175.50$$

$$155.25 - 73.89 \le T \le 175.50 - 73.89$$

$$81.36 \le T \le 101.61$$

The amount of withholding tax ranges from \$81.36 to \$101.61, inclusive.

113. Let K represent the monthly usage in kilowatt-hours.
   Let C represent the monthly customer bill in dollars.
   Calculating the bill: $C = 0.10494K + 9.36$
   Calculating the range of kilowatt-hours, given the range of bills:

   $$80.24 \le \quad C \quad \le 271.80$$
   $$80.24 \le 0.10494K + 9.36 \le 271.80$$
   $$70.88 \le \quad 0.10494K \quad \le 262.44$$
   $$675.43 \le \quad K \quad \le 2500.86$$

   The range of usage in kilowatt-hours varied from 675.43 to 2500.86, inclusive.

115. Let C represent the dealer's cost in dollars and M represent the markup over dealer's cost.
   If the price is \$8800, then $8800 = C + MC = C(1 + M)$

   Solving for C: $C = \dfrac{8800}{1 + M}$

   Calculating the range of dealer costs, given the range of markups:

   $$0.12 \le \quad M \quad \le 0.18 \Rightarrow 1.12 \le 1 + M \le 1.18$$

   $$\frac{1}{1.12} \ge \frac{1}{1 + M} \ge \frac{1}{1.18} \Rightarrow \frac{8800}{1.12} \ge \frac{8800}{1 + M} \ge \frac{8800}{1.18}$$

   $$7857.14 \ge \quad C \quad \ge 7457.63$$

   The dealer's cost ranged from \$7457.63 to \$7857.14, inclusive.

117. Let T represent the score on the last test and G represent the course grade.
   Calculating the course grade and solving for the last test:

   $$G = \frac{68 + 82 + 87 + 89 + T}{5} = \frac{326 + T}{5} \Rightarrow T = 5G - 326$$

   Calculating the range of scores on the last test, given the grade range:

   $$80 \le \quad G \quad < 90 \Rightarrow 400 \le \quad 5G \quad < 450$$

   $$74 \le 5G - 326 < 124 \Rightarrow 74 \le \quad T \quad < 124$$

   The fifth test must be greater than or equal to 74.

119. Let g represent the number of gallons of gasoline in the gas tank.
   Since the car averages 25 miles per gallon, a trip of at least 300 miles will require
   at least $\dfrac{300}{25} = 12$ gallons of gas. Therefore the range of the amount of
   gasoline is $12 \le g \le 20$.

121. Since $a < b$

$$\frac{a}{2} < \frac{b}{2}$$

$$\frac{a}{2} + \frac{a}{2} < \frac{a}{2} + \frac{b}{2}$$

$$a < \frac{a+b}{2}$$

$$\frac{a}{2} < \frac{b}{2}$$

$$\frac{a}{2} + \frac{b}{2} < \frac{b}{2} + \frac{b}{2}$$

$$\frac{a+b}{2} < b$$

Thus, $a < \dfrac{a+b}{2} < b$

123. If $0 < a < b$, then $0 < a^2 < ab$ and $0 < ab < b^2$

$$ab - a^2 > 0$$

$$ab > a^2 > 0$$

$$\left(\sqrt{ab}\right)^2 > a^2$$

$$\sqrt{ab} > a$$

$$b^2 - ab > 0$$

$$b^2 > ab > 0$$

$$b^2 > \left(\sqrt{ab}\right)^2$$

$$b > \sqrt{ab}$$

Thus, $a < \sqrt{ab} < b$.

125. For $0 < a < b$, $\dfrac{1}{h} = \dfrac{1}{2}\left(\dfrac{1}{a} + \dfrac{1}{b}\right)$

$$h \cdot \frac{1}{h} = \frac{1}{2}\left(\frac{b+a}{ab}\right) \cdot h \;\Rightarrow\; 1 = \frac{1}{2}\left(\frac{b+a}{ab}\right) \cdot h \;\Rightarrow\; \frac{2ab}{a+b} = h$$

$$h - a = \frac{2ab}{a+b} - a$$

$$= \frac{2ab - a(a+b)}{a+b}$$

$$= \frac{2ab - a^2 - ab}{a+b} = \frac{ab - a^2}{a+b}$$

$$= \frac{a(b-a)}{a+b} > 0$$

Therefore, $h > a$.

$$b - h = b - \frac{2ab}{a+b}$$

$$= \frac{b(a+b) - 2ab}{a+b}$$

$$= \frac{ab + b^2 - 2ab}{a+b} = \frac{b^2 - ab}{a+b}$$

$$= \frac{b(b-a)}{a+b} > 0$$

Therefore, $h < b$.   Thus, $a < h < b$.

127. $x^2 + 1 < -5$ has no solution because $x^2 \geq 0$ for every number x. Therefore, adding 1 cannot yield a negative number.

129. Answers will vary.

Equations, Inequalities and Functions

1.2   Rectangular Coordinates; Graphing Utilities

1. (a)   Quadrant II
    (b)   Positive x-axis
    (c)   Quadrant III
    (d)   Quadrant I
    (e)   Negative y-axis
    (f)   Quadrant IV

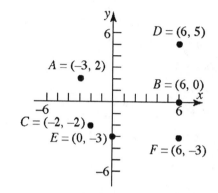

3.   The points will be on a vertical line that is two units to the right of the y-axis.

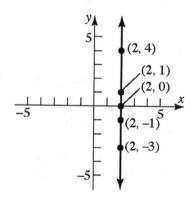

5. (−1, 4); Quadrant II

7. (3, 1); Quadrant I

9.

$X \min = -11$

$X \max = 5$

$X \operatorname{scl} = 1$

$Y \min = -3$

$Y \max = 6$

$Y \operatorname{scl} = 1$

11.

$X \min = -30$

$X \max = 50$

$X \operatorname{scl} = 10$

$Y \min = -90$

$Y \max = 50$

$Y \operatorname{scl} = 10$

13.

$X \min = -10$

$X \max = 110$

$X \operatorname{scl} = 10$

$Y \min = -10$

$Y \max = 160$

$Y \operatorname{scl} = 10$

15.

$X \min = -6$

$X \max = 6$

$X \operatorname{scl} = 2$

$Y \min = -4$

$Y \max = 4$

$Y \operatorname{scl} = 2$

17.

$X \min = -6$

$X \max = 6$

$X \operatorname{scl} = 2$

$Y \min = -1$

$Y \max = 3$

$Y \operatorname{scl} = 1$

19.

$X \min = 3$

$X \max = 9$

$X \operatorname{scl} = 1$

$Y \min = 2$

$Y \max = 10$

$Y \operatorname{scl} = 2$

21. $d(P_1, P_2) = \sqrt{(2-0)^2 + (1-0)^2} = \sqrt{4+1} = \sqrt{5}$

23. $d(P_1, P_2) = \sqrt{(-2-1)^2 + (2-1)^2} = \sqrt{9+1} = \sqrt{10}$

25. $d(P_1, P_2) = \sqrt{(5-3)^2 + (4-8)^2} = \sqrt{2^2 + (-4)^2} = \sqrt{4+16} = \sqrt{20} = 2\sqrt{5}$

27. $d(P_1, P_2) = \sqrt{(6-(-3))^2 + (0-2)^2} = \sqrt{9^2 + (-2)^2} = \sqrt{81+4} = \sqrt{85}$

29. $d(P_1, P_2) = \sqrt{(6-4)^2 + (4-(-3))^2} = \sqrt{2^2 + 7^2} = \sqrt{4+49} = \sqrt{53}$

31. $d(P_1, P_2) = \sqrt{(2.3-(-0.2))^2 + (1.1-0.3)^2} = \sqrt{(2.5)^2 + (0.8)^2}$
$$= \sqrt{6.25+0.64} = \sqrt{6.89} \approx 2.62$$

33. $d(P_1, P_2) = \sqrt{(0-a)^2 + (0-b)^2} = \sqrt{a^2 + b^2}$

35. $P_1 = (1,3); P_2 = (5,15)$
$$d(P_1, P_2) = \sqrt{(5-1)^2 + (15-3)^2}$$
$$= \sqrt{(4)^2 + (12)^2}$$
$$= \sqrt{16+144}$$
$$= \sqrt{160} = 4\sqrt{10}$$

37. $P_1 = (-4,6); P_2 = (4,-8)$
$$d(P_1, P_2) = \sqrt{(4-(-4))^2 + (-8-6)^2}$$
$$= \sqrt{(8)^2 + (-14)^2}$$
$$= \sqrt{64+196}$$
$$= \sqrt{260} = 2\sqrt{65}$$

39. $A = (-2,5)$, $B = (1,3)$, $C = (-1,0)$

$$d(A,B) = \sqrt{(1-(-2))^2 + (3-5)^2} = \sqrt{3^2 + (-2)^2}$$
$$= \sqrt{9+4} = \sqrt{13}$$
$$d(B,C) = \sqrt{(-1-1)^2 + (0-3)^2} = \sqrt{(-2)^2 + (-3)^2}$$
$$= \sqrt{4+9} = \sqrt{13}$$
$$d(A,C) = \sqrt{(-1-(-2))^2 + (0-5)^2} = \sqrt{1^2 + (-5)^2}$$
$$= \sqrt{1+25} = \sqrt{26}$$

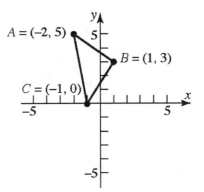

Verifying that $\triangle$ ABC is a right triangle by the Pythagorean Theorem:
$$[d(A,B)]^2 + [d(B,C)]^2 = [d(A,C)]^2$$
$$\left(\sqrt{13}\right)^2 + \left(\sqrt{13}\right)^2 = \left(\sqrt{26}\right)^2$$
$$13 + 13 = 26$$
$$26 = 26$$

The area of a triangle is $A = \dfrac{1}{2} \cdot bh$. In this problem,

$$A = \frac{1}{2} \cdot [d(A,B)] \cdot [d(B,C)] = \frac{1}{2} \cdot \sqrt{13} \cdot \sqrt{13} = \frac{1}{2} \cdot 13 = \frac{13}{2} \text{ square units}$$

41. $A = (-5,3)$, $B = (6,0)$, $C = (5,5)$

$$d(A,B) = \sqrt{(6-(-5))^2 + (0-3)^2} = \sqrt{11^2 + (-3)^2}$$
$$= \sqrt{121+9} = \sqrt{130}$$
$$d(B,C) = \sqrt{(5-6)^2 + (5-0)^2} = \sqrt{(-1)^2 + 5^2}$$
$$= \sqrt{1+25} = \sqrt{26}$$
$$d(A,C) = \sqrt{(5-(-5))^2 + (5-3)^2} = \sqrt{10^2 + 2^2}$$
$$= \sqrt{100+4} = \sqrt{104} = 2\sqrt{26}$$

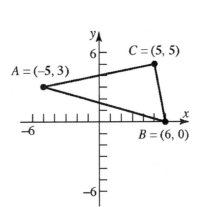

Verifying that $\triangle$ ABC is a right triangle by the Pythagorean Theorem:
$$[d(A,C)]^2 + [d(B,C)]^2 = [d(A,B)]^2$$
$$\left(\sqrt{104}\right)^2 + \left(\sqrt{26}\right)^2 = \left(\sqrt{130}\right)^2$$
$$104 + 26 = 130$$
$$130 = 130$$

The area of a triangle is $A = \dfrac{1}{2} \cdot bh$. In this problem,

$$A = \frac{1}{2} \cdot [d(A,C)] \cdot [d(B,C)] = \frac{1}{2} \cdot \sqrt{104} \cdot \sqrt{26} = \frac{1}{2} \cdot \sqrt{2704} = \frac{1}{2} \cdot 52 = 26 \text{ square units}$$

43. $A = (4,-3)$, $B = (0,-3)$, $C = (4,2)$

$$d(A,B) = \sqrt{(0-4)^2 + (-3-(-3))^2} = \sqrt{(-4)^2 + 0^2}$$
$$= \sqrt{16+0} = \sqrt{16} = 4$$
$$d(B,C) = \sqrt{(4-0)^2 + (2-(-3))^2} = \sqrt{4^2 + 5^2}$$
$$= \sqrt{16+25} = \sqrt{41}$$
$$d(A,C) = \sqrt{(4-4)^2 + (2-(-3))^2} = \sqrt{0^2 + 5^2}$$
$$= \sqrt{0+25} = \sqrt{25} = 5$$

Verifying that $\triangle$ ABC is a right triangle by the Pythagorean Theorem:
$$[d(A,B)]^2 + [d(A,C)]^2 = [d(B,C)]^2$$
$$4^2 + 5^2 = \left(\sqrt{41}\right)^2 \Rightarrow 16 + 25 = 41 \Rightarrow 41 = 41$$

The area of a triangle is $A = \dfrac{1}{2} \cdot bh.$ In this problem,

$$A = \frac{1}{2} \cdot [d(A,B)] \cdot [d(A,C)] = \frac{1}{2} \cdot 4 \cdot 5 = 10 \text{ square units}$$

45.   All points having an x-coordinate of 2 are of the form (2, y). Those which are 5 units from
       (–2, –1) are:
$$\sqrt{(2-(-2))^2 + (y-(-1))^2} = 5 \Rightarrow \sqrt{4^2 + (y+1)^2} = 5$$
       Squaring both sides: $4^2 + (y+1)^2 = 25$
$$16 + y^2 + 2y + 1 = 25$$
$$y^2 + 2y - 8 = 0$$
$$(y+4)(y-2) = 0$$
$$y = -4 \text{ or } y = 2$$
Therefore, the points are (2, –4) or (2, 2).

47.   All points on the x-axis are of the form $(x, 0)$. Those which are 5 units from $(4, -3)$ are:
$$\sqrt{(x-4)^2 + (0-(-3))^2} = 5 \Rightarrow \sqrt{(x-4)^2 + 3^2} = 5$$
       Squaring both sides: $(x-4)^2 + 9 = 25$
$$x^2 - 8x + 16 + 9 = 25 \Rightarrow x^2 - 8x = 0$$
$$x(x-8) = 0 \Rightarrow x = 0 \text{ or } x = 8$$
Therefore, the points are (0, 0) or (8, 0).

49.   The coordinates of the midpoint are:
$$(x,y) = \left(\frac{x_1 + x_2}{2}, \frac{y_1 + y_2}{2}\right) = \left(\frac{5+3}{2}, \frac{4+2}{2}\right) = \left(\frac{8}{2}, \frac{6}{2}\right) = (4,3)$$

51. The coordinates of the midpoint are:

$$(x,y) = \left(\frac{x_1 + x_2}{2}, \frac{y_1 + y_2}{2}\right) = \left(\frac{-3+6}{2}, \frac{2+0}{2}\right) = \left(\frac{3}{2}, \frac{2}{2}\right) = \left(\frac{3}{2}, 1\right)$$

53. The coordinates of the midpoint are:

$$(x,y) = \left(\frac{x_1 + x_2}{2}, \frac{y_1 + y_2}{2}\right) = \left(\frac{4+6}{2}, \frac{-3+1}{2}\right) = \left(\frac{10}{2}, \frac{-2}{2}\right) = (5,-1)$$

55. The coordinates of the midpoint are:

$$(x,y) = \left(\frac{x_1 + x_2}{2}, \frac{y_1 + y_2}{2}\right) = \left(\frac{-0.2+2.3}{2}, \frac{0.3+1.1}{2}\right) = \left(\frac{2.1}{2}, \frac{1.4}{2}\right) = (1.05, 0.7)$$

57. The coordinates of the midpoint are:

$$(x,y) = \left(\frac{x_1 + x_2}{2}, \frac{y_1 + y_2}{2}\right) = \left(\frac{a+0}{2}, \frac{b+0}{2}\right) = \left(\frac{a}{2}, \frac{b}{2}\right)$$

59. The midpoint of AB is: $D = \left(\frac{0+6}{2}, \frac{0+0}{2}\right) = (3,0)$

The midpoint of AC is: $E = \left(\frac{0+4}{2}, \frac{0+4}{2}\right) = (2,2)$

The midpoint of BC is: $F = \left(\frac{6+4}{2}, \frac{0+4}{2}\right) = (5,2)$

$$d(C,D) = \sqrt{(0-4)^2 + (3-4)^2} = \sqrt{(-4)^2 + (-1)^2} = \sqrt{16+1} = \sqrt{17}$$

$$d(B,E) = \sqrt{(2-6)^2 + (2-0)^2} = \sqrt{(-4)^2 + 2^2} = \sqrt{16+4} = \sqrt{20} = 2\sqrt{5}$$

$$d(A,F) = \sqrt{(2-0)^2 + (5-0)^2} = \sqrt{2^2 + 5^2} = \sqrt{4+25} = \sqrt{29}$$

61. $d(P_1,P_2) = \sqrt{(-4-2)^2 + (1-1)^2} = \sqrt{(-6)^2 + 0^2} = \sqrt{36} = 6$

$d(P_2,P_3) = \sqrt{(-4-(-4))^2 + (-3-1)^2} = \sqrt{0^2 + (-4)^2} = \sqrt{16} = 4$

$d(P_1,P_3) = \sqrt{(-4-2)^2 + (-3-1)^2} = \sqrt{(-6)^2 + (-4)^2} = \sqrt{36+16} = \sqrt{52} = 2\sqrt{13}$

Since $[d(P_1,P_2)]^2 + [d(P_2,P_3)]^2 = [d(P_1,P_3)]^2$, the triangle is a right triangle.

63. $d(P_1,P_2) = \sqrt{(0-(-2))^2 + (7-(-1))^2} = \sqrt{2^2 + 8^2} = \sqrt{4+64} = \sqrt{68} = 2\sqrt{17}$

$d(P_2,P_3) = \sqrt{(3-0)^2 + (2-7)^2} = \sqrt{3^2 + (-5)^2} = \sqrt{9+25} = \sqrt{34}$

$d(P_1,P_3) = \sqrt{(3-(-2))^2 + (2-(-1))^2} = \sqrt{5^2 + 3^2} = \sqrt{25+9} = \sqrt{34}$

Since $d(P_2,P_3) = d(P_1,P_3)$, the triangle is isosceles.

Since $[d(P_1,P_3)]^2 + [d(P_2,P_3)]^2 = [d(P_1,P_2)]^2$, the triangle is also a right triangle.

Therefore, the triangle is an isosceles right triangle.

65.   Using the Pythagorean Theorem:

$$90^2 + 90^2 = d^2$$
$$8100 + 8100 = d^2$$
$$16200 = d^2$$
$$d = \sqrt{16200} = 90\sqrt{2} \approx 127.28 \text{ feet}$$

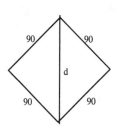

67.   (a)   First: (90, 0), Second: (90, 90)
       Third: (0, 90)

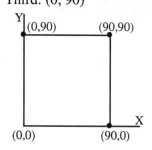

(b)   Using the distance formula:
$$d = \sqrt{(310-90)^2 + (15-90)^2}$$
$$= \sqrt{220^2 + (-75)^2}$$
$$= \sqrt{54025} \approx 232.43 \text{ feet}$$

(c)   Using the distance formula:
$$d = \sqrt{(300-0)^2 + (300-90)^2}$$
$$= \sqrt{300^2 + 210^2}$$
$$= \sqrt{134100} \approx 366.20 \text{ feet}$$

69.   The Intrepid heading east moves a distance $30t$ after t hours. The truck heading south moves a distance $40t$ after t hours. Their distance apart after t hours is:

$$d = \sqrt{(30t)^2 + (40t)^2}$$
$$= \sqrt{900t^2 + 1600t^2}$$
$$= \sqrt{2500t^2}$$
$$= 50t$$

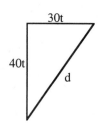

71.   Answers will vary.

Equations, Inequalities and Functions

1.3 Introduction to Graphing Equations

1. $y = x^4 - \sqrt{x}$

    $0 = 0^4 - \sqrt{0}$ $1 = 1^4 - \sqrt{1}$ $0 = (-1)^4 - \sqrt{-1}$

    $0 = 0$ $1 \neq 0$ $0 \neq 1 - \sqrt{-1}$

    $(0, 0)$ is on the graph of the equation.

3. $y^2 = x^2 + 9$

    $3^2 = 0^2 + 9$ $0^2 = 3^2 + 9$ $0^2 = (-3)^2 + 9$

    $9 = 9$ $0 \neq 18$ $0 \neq 18$

    $(0, 3)$ is on the graph of the equation.

5. $x^2 + y^2 = 4$

    $0^2 + 2^2 = 4$ $(-2)^2 + 2^2 = 4$ $\sqrt{2}^2 + \sqrt{2}^2 = 4$

    $4 = 4$ $8 \neq 4$ $4 = 4$

    $(0, 2)$ and $\left(\sqrt{2}, \sqrt{2}\right)$ are on the graph of the equation.

7. $(-1, 0), (1, 0)$

9. $\left(-\dfrac{\pi}{2}, 0\right), \left(\dfrac{\pi}{2}, 0\right), (0, 1)$

11. $(0, 0)$

13. $(-4, 0), (-1, 0), (4, 0), (0, -3)$

15. $y = 5x + 4$

    $2 = 5a + 4$

    $-2 = 5a \Rightarrow a = -\dfrac{2}{5}$

17. $2x + 3y = 6$

    $2a + 3b = 6$

19. $y = x + 2$

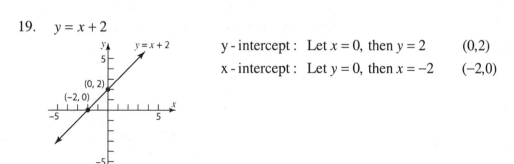

    $y\text{-intercept}:$ Let $x = 0$, then $y = 2$ $(0, 2)$

    $x\text{-intercept}:$ Let $y = 0$, then $x = -2$ $(-2, 0)$

21. $y = 2x + 8$

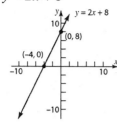

y - intercept : Let $x = 0$, then $y = 8$ $(0,8)$

x - intercept : Let $y = 0$, then $x = -4$ $(-4,0)$

23. $y = x^2 - 1$

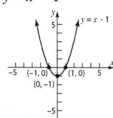

y - intercept : Let $x = 0$, then $y = -1$ $(0,-1)$

x - intercept : Let $y = 0$, then $x = \pm 1$ $(-1,0);(1,0)$

25. $y = -x^2 + 4$

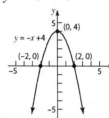

y - intercept : Let $x = 0$, then $y = 4$ $(0,4)$

x - intercept : Let $y = 0$, then $x = \pm 2$ $(-2,0);(2,0)$

27. $2x + 3y = 6$

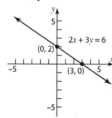

y - intercept : Let $x = 0$, then $y = 2$ $(0,2)$

x - intercept : Let $y = 0$, then $x = 3$ $(3,0)$

29. $9x^2 + 4y = 36$

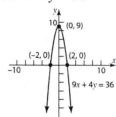

y - intercept : Let $x = 0$, then $y = 9$ $(0,9)$

x - intercept : Let $y = 0$, then $x = \pm 2$ $(-2,0);(2,0)$

31. $y = 2x - 13$

Use VALUE and ZERO (or ROOT) on the graph of $y_1 = 2x - 13$.

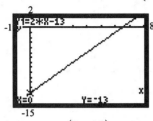 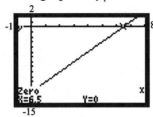

y-intercept: $(0, -13)$ x-intercept: $(6.5, 0)$

33. $y = 2x^2 - 15$

Use VALUE and ZERO (or ROOT) on the graph of $y_1 = 2x^2 - 15$.

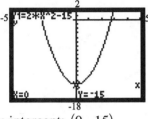 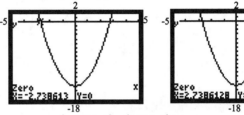

y-intercept: $(0, -15)$ x-intercepts: $(-2.74, 0)$, $(2.74, 0)$

35. $3x - 2y = 43$

Use VALUE and ZERO (or ROOT) on the graph of $y_1 = 1.5x - 43/2$.

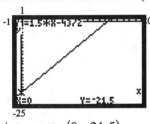 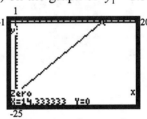

y-intercept: $(0, -21.5)$ x-intercept: $(14.33, 0)$

37. $5x^2 + 3y = 37$

Use VALUE and ZERO (or ROOT) on the graph of $y_1 = (-5/3)x^2 + 37/3$.

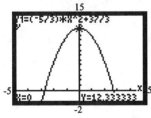 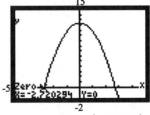 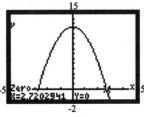

y-intercept: $(0, 12.33)$ x-intercepts: $(-2.72, 0)$, $(2.72, 0)$

39. (a)

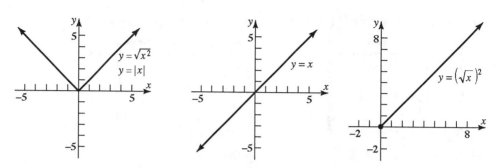

(b)   Since $\sqrt{x^2} = |x|$, then for all x, the graphs of $y = \sqrt{x^2}$ and $y = |x|$ are the same.

(c)   For $y = \left(\sqrt{x}\right)^2$, the domain of the variable x is $x \geq 0$; for $y = x$, the domain of the variable x is all real numbers. Thus, $\left(\sqrt{x}\right)^2 = x$ only for $x \geq 0$.

(d)   For $y = \sqrt{x^2}$, the range of the variable y is $y \geq 0$; for $y = x$, the range of the variable y is all real numbers. Also, $\sqrt{x^2} = x$ only if $x \geq 0$.

41.   The standard viewing window is given by

$X \min = -10$

$X \max = 10$

$X \operatorname{scl} = 1$

$Y \min = -10$

$Y \max = 10$

$Y \operatorname{scl} = 1$

43.   Answers will vary

Equations, Inequalities and Functions

1.4   Symmetry; Graphing Key Equations; Circles

1.

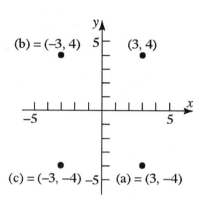

3.

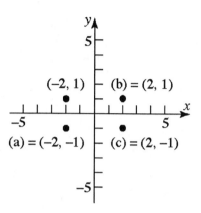

5.

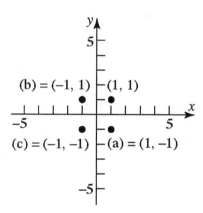

7.

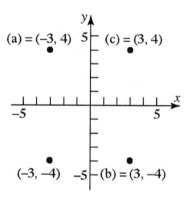

9.

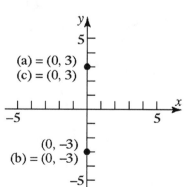

11.   symmetric to the x-axis, y-axis and origin

13.   symmetric to the y-axis

15.   symmetric to the x-axis

17.   not symmetric to x-axis, y-axis, or origin

19.

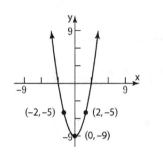

21.

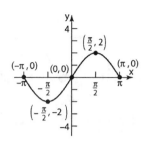

23. $x^2 = y + 5$

    y-intercept : Let $x = 0$, then $y = -5$ $(0,-5)$

    x-intercept : Let $y = 0$, then $x = \pm\sqrt{5}$ $\left(-\sqrt{5},0\right),\left(\sqrt{5},0\right)$

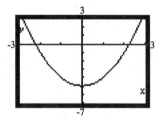

    Test for symmetry:

        x-axis : Replace y by $-y$ so $x^2 = -y + 5$, which is not equivalent to $x^2 = y + 5$.

        y-axis : Replace x by $-x$ so $(-x)^2 = y$ or $x^2 = y + 5$, which is equivalent to $x^2 = y + 5$.

        Origin : Replace x by $-x$ and y by $-y$ so $(-x)^2 = -y + 5$ or $x^2 = -y + 5$,

                which is not equivalent to $x^2 = y + 5$.

    Therefore, the graph is symmetric with respect to the y-axis.

25. $y = 3x$

    y-intercept: Let $x = 0$, then $y = 0$ $(0,0)$

    x-intercept: Let $y = 0$, then $x = 0$ $(0,0)$

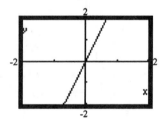

    Test for symmetry:

        x-axis : Replace y by $-y$ so $-y = 3x$, which is not equivalent to $y = 3x$.

        y-axis : Replace x by $-x$ so $y = 3(-x)$ or $y = -3x$, which is not equivalent to $y = 3x$.

        Origin : Replace x by $-x$ and y by $-y$ so $-y = 3(-x) \Rightarrow y = 3x$,

                which is equivalent to $y = 3x$.

    Therefore, the graph is symmetric with respect to the origin.

27. $x^2 + y - 9 = 0$

    y-intercept : Let $x = 0$, then $y = 9$ $(0,9)$

    x-intercept : Let $y = 0$, then $x = \pm 3$ $(-3,0),(3,0)$

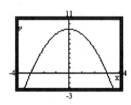

    Test for symmetry:

        x-axis : Replace y by $-y$ so $x^2 + (-y) - 9 = 0 \Rightarrow x^2 - y - 9 = 0$,

                which is not equivalent to $x^2 + y - 9 = 0$.

y-axis: Replace x by $-x$ so $(-x)^2 + y - 9 = 0 \Rightarrow x^2 + y - 9 = 0$,

which is equivalent to $x^2 + y - 9 = 0$.

Origin: Replace x by $-x$ and y by $-y$ so $(-x)^2 + (-y) - 9 = 0 \Rightarrow x^2 - y - 9 = 0$,

which is not equivalent to $x^2 + y - 9 = 0$.

Therefore, the graph is symmetric with respect to the y-axis.

29. $y = x^3 - 27$

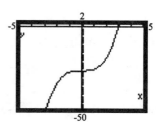

   y-intercept: Let $x = 0$, then $y = 0^3 - 27$

$y = -27$ $(0, -27)$

   x-intercept: Let $y = 0$, then $0 = x^3 - 27$

$x^3 = 27 \Rightarrow x = 3$ $(3, 0)$

Test for symmetry:

   x-axis: Replace y by $-y$ so $-y = x^3 - 27$, which is not equivalent to $y = x^3 - 27$.

   y-axis: Replace x by $-x$ so $y = (-x)^3 - 27 \Rightarrow y = -x^3 - 27$,

which is not equivalent to $y = x^3 - 27$.

   Origin: Replace x by $-x$ and y by $-y$ so $-y = (-x)^3 - 27$

$\Rightarrow y = x^3 + 27$, which is not equivalent to $y = x^3 - 27$.

Therefore, the graph is not symmetric to the x-axis, the y-axis, or the origin.

31. $y = x^2 - 3x - 4$

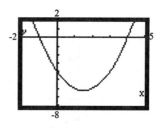

   y-intercept: Let $x = 0$, then $y = 0^2 - 3(0) - 4$

$y = -4$ $(0, -4)$

   x-intercept: Let $y = 0$, then $0 = x^2 - 3x - 4$

$(x - 4)(x + 1) = 0$

$x = 4$ $x = -1$ $(4, 0), (-1, 0)$

Test for symmetry:

   x-axis: Replace y by $-y$ so $-y = x^2 - 3x - 4$, which is not equivalent to $y = x^2 - 3x - 4$.

   y-axis: Replace x by $-x$ so $y = (-x)^2 - 3(-x) - 4 \Rightarrow y = x^2 + 3x - 4$,

which is not equivalent to $y = x^2 - 3x - 4$.

   Origin: Replace x by $-x$ and y by $-y$ so $-y = (-x)^2 - 3(-x) - 4$

$\Rightarrow y = -x^2 - 3x + 4$, which is not equivalent to $y = x^2 - 3x - 4$.

Therefore, the graph is not symmetric to the x-axis, the y-axis, or the origin.

33. $y = \dfrac{x}{x^2 + 9}$

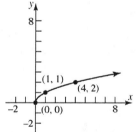

y-intercept: Let $x = 0$, then $y = \dfrac{0}{0 + 9}$

$$y = 0 \qquad (0, 0)$$

x-intercept: Let $y = 0$, then $0 = \dfrac{x}{x^2 + 9}$

$$x = 0 \Rightarrow x = 0 \quad (0, 0)$$

Test for symmetry:

x-axis: Replace y by $-y$ so $-y = \dfrac{x}{x^2 + 9}$, which is not equivalent to $y = \dfrac{x}{x^2 + 9}$.

y-axis: Replace x by $-x$ so $y = \dfrac{(-x)}{(-x)^2 + 9} \Rightarrow y = \dfrac{-x}{x^2 + 9}$,

which is not equivalent to $y = \dfrac{3x}{x^2 + 9}$.

Origin: Replace x by $-x$ and y by $-y$ so $-y = \dfrac{-x}{(-x)^2 + 9}$

$$\Rightarrow y = \dfrac{x}{x^2 + 9}, \text{ which is equivalent to } y = \dfrac{x}{x^2 + 9}.$$

Therefore, the graph is symmetric with respect to the origin.

35. $y = x^3$

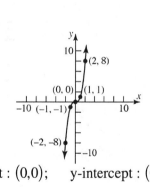

x-intercept : $(0,0)$;   y-intercept : $(0,0)$

37. $y = \sqrt{x}$

x-intercept : $(0,0)$;   y-intercept : $(0,0)$

39. $\left(\dfrac{8}{2}\right)^2 = (4)^2 = 16$

41. $\left(\dfrac{-\dfrac{1}{2}}{2}\right)^2 = \left(-\dfrac{1}{4}\right)^2 = \dfrac{1}{16}$

43. Center = (2, 1)
Radius = distance from (0,1) to (2,1)
$$= \sqrt{(2-0)^2 + (1-1)^2} = \sqrt{4} = 2$$
$$(x-2)^2 + (y-1)^2 = 4$$

45. Center = midpoint of (1,2) and (4,2)
$$= \left(\frac{1+4}{2}, \frac{2+2}{2} \right) = \left(\frac{5}{2}, 2 \right)$$
Radius = distance from $\left(\frac{5}{2}, 2 \right)$ to (4,2)
$$= \sqrt{\left(4 - \frac{5}{2} \right)^2 + (2-2)^2} = \sqrt{\frac{9}{4}} = \frac{3}{2}$$
$$\left(x - \frac{5}{2} \right)^2 + (y-2)^2 = \frac{9}{4}$$

47. $(x-h)^2 + (y-k)^2 = r^2$
$(x-0)^2 + (y-0)^2 = 2^2$
$$x^2 + y^2 = 4$$
General form:
$x^2 + y^2 - 4 = 0$

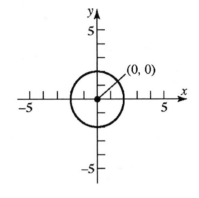

49. $(x-h)^2 + (y-k)^2 = r^2$
$(x-0)^2 + (y-2)^2 = 2^2$
$$x^2 + (y-2)^2 = 4$$
General form:
$x^2 + y^2 - 4y + 4 = 4$
$x^2 + y^2 - 4y = 0$

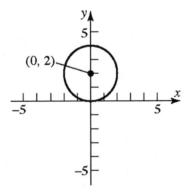

51. $(x-h)^2 + (y-k)^2 = r^2$
$(x-4)^2 + (y-(-3))^2 = 5^2$
$(x-4)^2 + (y+3)^2 = 25$
General form:
$x^2 - 8x + 16 + y^2 + 6y + 9 = 25$
$x^2 + y^2 - 8x + 6y = 0$

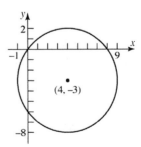

53. $(x-h)^2+(y-k)^2=r^2$

$(x-(-2))^2+(y-1)^2=4^2$

$(x+2)^2+(y-1)^2=16$

General form:

$x^2+4x+4+y^2-2y+1=16$

$x^2+y^2+4x-2y-11=0$

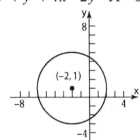

55. $(x-h)^2+(y-k)^2=r^2$

$\left(x-\dfrac{1}{2}\right)^2+(y-0)^2=\left(\dfrac{1}{2}\right)^2$

$\left(x-\dfrac{1}{2}\right)^2+y^2=\dfrac{1}{4}$

General form:

$x^2-x+\dfrac{1}{4}+y^2=\dfrac{1}{4}$

$x^2+y^2-x=0$

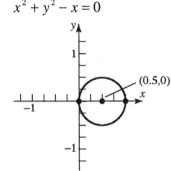

57. $x^2+y^2=25$

$x^2+y^2=5^2$

Center : (0,0)

Radius = 5

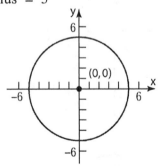

59. $(x-2)^2+y^2=4$

$(x-2)^2+y^2=2^2$

Center: (2,0)

Radius = 2

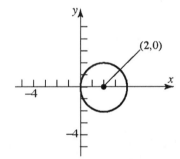

61. $x^2 + y^2 + 4x - 4y - 1 = 0$

$$x^2 + 4x + y^2 - 4y = 1$$

$$(x^2 + 4x + 4) + (y^2 - 4y + 4) = 1 + 4 + 4$$

$$(x + 2)^2 + (y - 2)^2 = 3^2$$

Center: $(-2, 2)$

Radius = 3

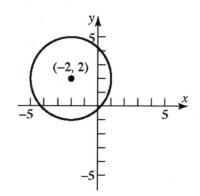

63. $x^2 + y^2 - x + 2y + 1 = 0$

$$x^2 - x + y^2 + 2y = -1$$

$$\left(x^2 - x + \frac{1}{4}\right) + (y^2 + 2y + 1) = -1 + \frac{1}{4} + 1$$

$$\left(x - \frac{1}{2}\right)^2 + (y + 1)^2 = \left(\frac{1}{2}\right)^2$$

Center: $\left(\frac{1}{2}, -1\right)$

Radius = $\dfrac{1}{2}$

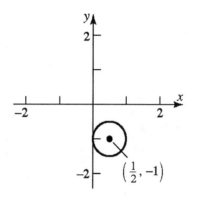

65. $2x^2 + 2y^2 - 12x + 8y - 24 = 0$

$$x^2 + y^2 - 6x + 4y = 12$$

$$x^2 - 6x + y^2 + 4y = 12$$

$$(x^2 - 6x + 9) + (y^2 + 4y + 4) = 12 + 9 + 4$$

$$(x - 3)^2 + (y + 2)^2 = 5^2$$

Center: $(3, -2)$

Radius = 5

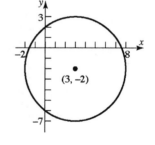

67. Center at $(0,0)$; containing point $(-2, 3)$.

$$r = \sqrt{(-2-0)^2 + (3-0)^2} = \sqrt{4+9} = \sqrt{13}$$

Equation: $(x - 0)^2 + (y - 0)^2 = \left(\sqrt{13}\right)^2$

$$x^2 + y^2 = 13 \Rightarrow x^2 + y^2 - 13 = 0$$

69. Center at $(2,3)$; tangent to the x-axis.

$$r = 3$$

Equation: $(x - 2)^2 + (y - 3)^2 = 3^2$

$$x^2 - 4x + 4 + y^2 - 6y + 9 = 9 \Rightarrow x^2 + y^2 - 4x - 6y + 4 = 0$$

71. Endpoints of a diameter are $(1,4)$ and $(-3,2)$.
The center is at the midpoint of that diameter:

Center: $\left(\dfrac{1+(-3)}{2}, \dfrac{4+2}{2}\right) = (-1, 3)$

$$\text{Radius: } r = \sqrt{(1-(-1))^2 + (4-3)^2} = \sqrt{4+1} = \sqrt{5}$$

$$\text{Equation: } \qquad (x-(-1))^2 + (y-3)^2 = \left(\sqrt{5}\right)^2$$

$$x^2 + 2x + 1 + y^2 - 6y + 9 = 5 \Rightarrow x^2 + y^2 + 2x - 6y + 5 = 0$$

73. (c)   75.   (b)

77. $(x+3)^2 + (y-1)^2 = 16$ 79. $(x-2)^2 + (y-2)^2 = 9$

81. $x^2 + y^2 + 2x + 4y - 4091 = 0$

$$x^2 + 2x + 1 + y^2 + 4y + 4 = 4091 + 5 \Rightarrow (x+1)^2 + (y+2)^2 = 4096$$

The circle representing Earth has center $(-1,-2)$ and radius $= \sqrt{4096} = 64$
So the radius of the satellite's orbit is $64 + 0.6 = 64.6$ units.
The equation of the orbit is $(x+1)^2 + (y+2)^2 = (64.6)^2$

$$x^2 + y^2 + 2x + 4y - 4168.6 = 0$$

83.   If the equation has x-axis and y-axis symmetry, then we have the following:
$x-$ axis symmetry means $(x,y) \leftrightarrow (x,-y)$; $y-$ axis symmetry means $(x,y) \leftrightarrow (-x,y)$

$\therefore (x,-y) \leftrightarrow (-x,y)$ which is equivalent to origin symmetry.

If the equation has x-axis and origin symmetry, then we have the following:
$x-$ axis symmetry means $(x,y) \leftrightarrow (x,-y)$

origin symmetry means $(x,y) \leftrightarrow (-x,-y)$

$\therefore (x,-y) \leftrightarrow (-x,-y)$, which is equivalent to y - axis symmetry.

If the equation has y-axis and origin symmetry, then we have the following:
$y-$ axis symmetry means $(x,y) \leftrightarrow (-x,y)$

origin symmetry means $(x,y) \leftrightarrow (-x,-y)$

$\therefore (-x,y) \leftrightarrow (-x,-y)$, which is equivalent to x - axis symmetry

85. (b), (c), (e) and (g)

Equations, Inequalities and Functions

1.5 Solving Equations and Inequalities in One Variable Using a Graphing Utility

1. $x^3 - 4x + 2 = 0$; Use ZERO (or ROOT) on the graph of $y_1 = x^3 - 4x + 2$.

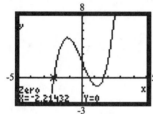 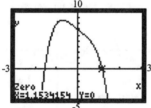 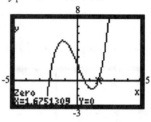

The solution set is $\{-2.21, 0.54, 1.68\}$.

3. $-2x^4 + 5 = 3x - 2$; Use ZERO (or ROOT) on the graph of $y_1 = -2x^4 - 3x + 7$.

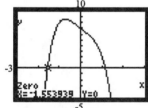 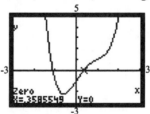

The solution set is $\{-1.55, 1.15\}$.

5. $x^4 - 2x^3 + 3x - 1 = 0$; Use ZERO (or ROOT) on the graph of $y_1 = x^4 - 2x^3 + 3x - 1$.

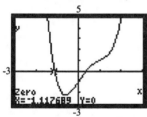 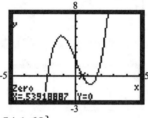

The solution set is $\{-1.12, 0.36\}$.

7. $-x^3 - \dfrac{5}{3}x^2 + \dfrac{7}{2}x + 2 = 0$;

Use ZERO (or ROOT) on the graph of $y_1 = -x^3 - (5/3)x^2 + (7/2)x + 2$.

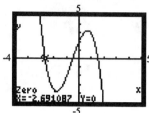 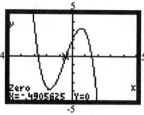 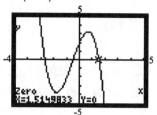

The solution set is $\{-2.69, -0.49, 1.51\}$.

9. $-\dfrac{2}{3}x^4 - 2x^3 + \dfrac{5}{2}x = -\dfrac{2}{3}x^2 + \dfrac{1}{2}$

Use ZERO (or ROOT) on the graph of $y_1 = -(2/3)x^4 - 2x^3 + (2/3)x^2 + (5/2)x - 1/2$.

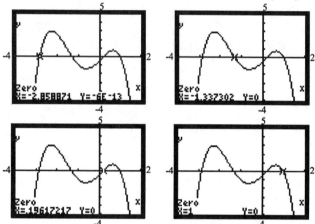

The solution set is $\{-2.86, -1.34, 0.20, 1.00\}$.

11. $x^4 - 5x^2 + 2x + 11 = 0$; Use ZERO (or ROOT) on the graph of $y_1 = x^4 - 5x^2 + 2x + 11$.

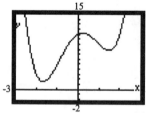   There are no real solutions.

13.
$$3x - 4 = 0$$
$$3x - 4 + 4 = 0 + 4$$
$$3x = 4$$
$$\dfrac{3x}{3} = \dfrac{4}{3} \Rightarrow x = \dfrac{4}{3}$$
The solution set is $\left\{\dfrac{4}{3}\right\}$.

15.
$$6 - x = 2x + 12$$
$$6 - x - 6 = 2x + 12 - 6$$
$$-x = 2x + 6$$
$$-x - 2x = 2x + 6 - 2x$$
$$-3x = 6 \Rightarrow \dfrac{-3x}{-3} = \dfrac{6}{-3} \Rightarrow x = -2$$
The solution set is $\{-2\}$.

17. $2(3+2x) = 3(x-4)$
$$6+4x = 3x-12$$
$$6+4x-6 = 3x-12-6$$
$$4x = 3x-18$$
$$4x-3x = 3x-18-3x$$
$$x = -18$$
The solution set is $\{-18\}$.

19. $8x-(2x+1) = 3x-13$
$$8x-2x-1 = 3x-13$$
$$6x-1 = 3x-13$$
$$6x-1+1 = 3x-13+1$$
$$6x = 3x-12$$
$$6x-3x = 3x-12-3x$$
$$3x = -12$$
$$\frac{3x}{3} = \frac{-12}{3} \Rightarrow x = -4$$
The solution set is $\{-4\}$.

21. $\frac{2}{3}p = \frac{1}{2}p + \frac{1}{3}$
$$6\left(\frac{2}{3}p\right) = 6\left(\frac{1}{2}p + \frac{1}{3}\right)$$
$$4p = 3p+2$$
$$4p-3p = 3p+2-3p$$
$$p = 2$$
The solution set is $\{2\}$.

23. $0.9t = 0.4 + 0.1t$
$$0.9t - 0.1t = 0.4 + 0.1t - 0.1t$$
$$0.8t = 0.4$$
$$\frac{0.8t}{0.8} = \frac{0.4}{0.8}$$
$$t = 0.5$$
The solution set is $\{0.5\}$.

25. $\frac{x+1}{3} + \frac{x+2}{7} = 5$
$$(21)\left(\frac{x+1}{3} + \frac{x+2}{7}\right) = (5)(21)$$
$$(21)\left(\frac{x+1}{3}\right) + (21)\left(\frac{x+2}{7}\right) = 105$$
$$7(x+1) + (3)(x+2) = 105$$
$$7x+7+3x+6 = 105$$
$$10x+13 = 105$$
$$10x+13-13 = 105-13$$
$$10x = 92$$
$$\frac{10x}{10} = \frac{92}{10}$$
$$x = \frac{46}{5}$$
The solution set is $\left\{\frac{46}{5}\right\}$.

27. $\frac{5}{y} + \frac{4}{y} = 3$
$$y\left(\frac{5}{y} + \frac{4}{y}\right) = y(3)$$
$$5+4 = 3y$$
$$9 = 3y \Rightarrow \frac{9}{3} = \frac{3y}{3} \Rightarrow y = 3$$
and since y = 3 does not cause a denominator to equal zero, the solution set is $\{3\}$.

29.
$$(x+7)(x-1)=(x+1)^2$$
$$x^2-x+7x-7=x^2+2x+1$$
$$x^2+6x-7=x^2+2x+1$$
$$x^2+6x-7-x^2=x^2+2x+1-x^2$$
$$6x-7=2x+1$$
$$6x-7-2x=2x+1-2x$$
$$4x-7=1$$
$$4x-7+7=1+7$$
$$4x=8$$
$$\frac{4x}{4}=\frac{8}{4}\Rightarrow x=2$$

The solution set is $\{2\}$.

31. $x-4<0$
Graph $y_1=x-4$ and $y_2=0$.

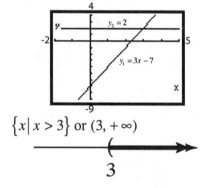

$\{x\,|\,x<4\}$ or $(-\infty,4)$

4

33. $1-2x\le 3$
Graph $y_1=1-2x$ and $y_2=3$.

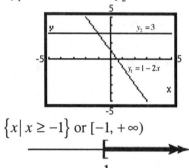

$\{x\,|\,x\ge -1\}$ or $[-1,+\infty)$

-1

35. $3x-7>2$
Graph $y_1=3x-7$ and $y_2=2$.

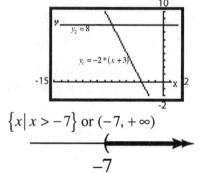

$\{x\,|\,x>3\}$ or $(3,+\infty)$

3

37. $3x-1\ge 3+x$
Graph $y_1=3x-1$ and $y_2=3+x$.

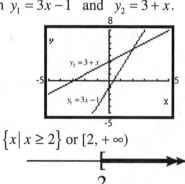

$\{x\,|\,x\ge 2\}$ or $[2,+\infty)$

2

39. $-2(x+3)<8$
Graph $y_1=-2*(x+3)$ and $y_2=8$.

$\{x\,|\,x>-7\}$ or $(-7,+\infty)$

-7

41. $4 - 3(1 - x) \le 3$

Graph $y_1 = 4 - 3*(1 - x)$ and $y_2 = 3$.

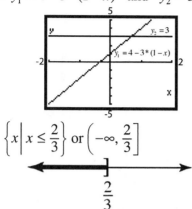

$$\left\{ x \mid x \le \frac{2}{3} \right\} \text{ or } \left(-\infty, \frac{2}{3} \right]$$

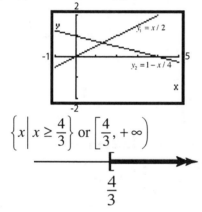

$$\frac{2}{3}$$

43. $\frac{1}{2}(x - 4) > x + 8$

Graph $y_1 = (x - 4)/2$ and $y_2 = x + 8$.

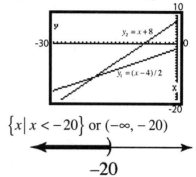

$$\left\{ x \mid x < -20 \right\} \text{ or } (-\infty, -20)$$

$$-20$$

45. $\frac{x}{2} \ge 1 - \frac{x}{4}$

Graph $y_1 = x/2$ and $y_2 = 1 - x/4$.

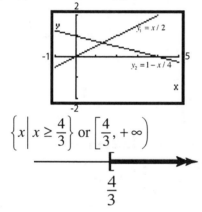

$$\left\{ x \mid x \ge \frac{4}{3} \right\} \text{ or } \left[\frac{4}{3}, +\infty \right)$$

$$\frac{4}{3}$$

47. $0 \le 2x - 6 \le 4$

Graph $y_1 = 0$; $y_2 = 2x - 6$ and $y_3 = 4$.

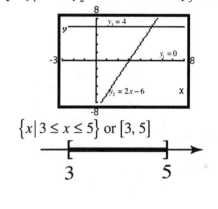

$$\left\{ x \mid 3 \le x \le 5 \right\} \text{ or } [3, 5]$$

$$3 \qquad 5$$

49. $-5 \le 4 - 3x \le 2$

Graph $y_1 = -5$; $y_2 = 4 - 3x$ and $y_3 = 2$.

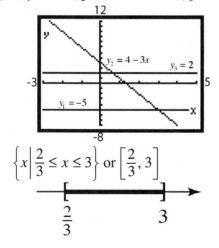

$$\left\{ x \mid \frac{2}{3} \le x \le 3 \right\} \text{ or } \left[\frac{2}{3}, 3 \right]$$

$$\frac{2}{3} \qquad 3$$

51. $-3 < \frac{2x - 1}{4} < 0$

Graph $y_1 = -3$; $y_2 = (2x - 1)/4$ and $y_3 = 0$.

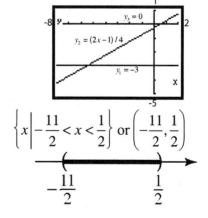

$$\left\{ x \mid -\frac{11}{2} < x < \frac{1}{2} \right\} \text{ or } \left(-\frac{11}{2}, \frac{1}{2} \right)$$

$$-\frac{11}{2} \qquad \frac{1}{2}$$

53. $1 < 1 - \dfrac{1}{2}x < 4$

Graph $y_1 = 1$; $y_2 = 1 - x/2$ and $y_3 = 4$.

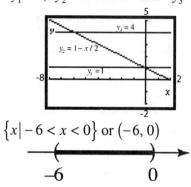

$\{x \mid -6 < x < 0\}$ or $(-6, 0)$

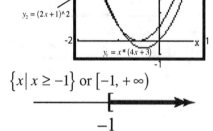

55. $(x + 2)(x - 3) > (x - 1)(x + 1)$
Graph
$y_1 = (x + 2)*(x - 3)$ and $y_2 = (x - 1)*(x + 1)$

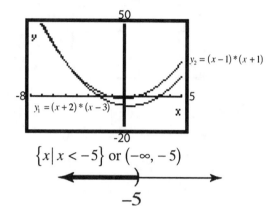

$\{x \mid x < -5\}$ or $(-\infty, -5)$

57. $x(4x + 3) \le (2x + 1)^2$
Graph
$y_1 = x*(4x + 3)$ and $y_2 = (2x + 1)^{\wedge}2$.

$\{x \mid x \ge -1\}$ or $[-1, +\infty)$

59. $\dfrac{1}{2} \le \dfrac{x + 1}{3} < \dfrac{3}{4}$

Graph
$y_1 = 1/2$; $y_2 = (x + 1)/3$ and $y_3 = 3/4$.

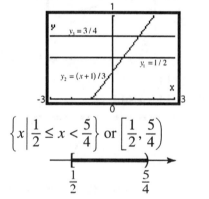

$\left\{x \mid \dfrac{1}{2} \le x < \dfrac{5}{4}\right\}$ or $\left[\dfrac{1}{2}, \dfrac{5}{4}\right)$

Equations, Inequalities and Functions

1.6   Introduction to Functions

1. Function
   Domain: {Dad, Colleen, Kaleigh,
                 Marissa}
   Range: {Jan. 8, Mar. 15, Sept. 17}

3. Not a function

5. Not a function.

7. Function
   Domain: {1, 2, 3, 4}
   Range: {3}

9. Not a function

11. Function
    Domain: {−2, −1, 0, 1}
    Range: {0, 1, 4}

13. $f(x) = 2x + 5$
    (a) $f(0) = 2(0) + 5 = 5$
    (b) $f(1) = 2(1) + 5 = 7$
    (c) $f(-1) = 2(-1) + 5 = 3$
    (d) $f(-x) = 2(-x) + 5 = -2x + 5$
    (e) $-f(x) = -(2x + 5) = -2x - 5$
    (f) $f(x + 1) = 2(x + 1) + 5 = 2x + 2 + 5 = 2x + 7$
    (g) $f(2x) = 2(2x) + 5 = 4x + 5$
    (h) $f(x + h) = 2(x + h) + 5 = 2x + 2h + 5$

15. $f(x) = 3x^2 + 2x - 4$
    (a) $f(0) = 3(0)^2 + 2(0) - 4 = -4$
    (b) $f(1) = 3(1)^2 + 2(1) - 4 = 3 + 2 - 4 = 1$
    (c) $f(-1) = 3(-1)^2 + 2(-1) - 4 = 3 - 2 - 4 = -3$
    (d) $f(-x) = 3(-x)^2 + 2(-x) - 4 = 3x^2 - 2x - 4$
    (e) $-f(x) = -(3x^2 + 2x - 4) = -3x^2 - 2x + 4$
    (f) $f(x + 1) = 3(x + 1)^2 + 2(x + 1) - 4 = 3(x^2 + 2x + 1) + 2x + 2 - 4$
        $= 3x^2 + 6x + 3 + 2x + 2 - 4 = 3x^2 + 8x + 1$
    (g) $f(2x) = 3(2x)^2 + 2(2x) - 4 = 12x^2 + 4x - 4$
    (h) $f(x + h) = 3(x + h)^2 + 2(x + h) - 4 = 3(x^2 + 2xh + h^2) + 2x + 2h - 4$
        $= 3x^2 + 6xh + 3h^2 + 2x + 2h - 4$

17. $f(x) = \dfrac{x}{x^2+1}$

(a) $f(0) = \dfrac{0}{0^2+1} = \dfrac{0}{1} = 0$

(b) $f(1) = \dfrac{1}{1^2+1} = \dfrac{1}{2}$

(c) $f(-1) = \dfrac{-1}{(-1)^2+1} = \dfrac{-1}{1+1} = -\dfrac{1}{2}$

(d) $f(-x) = \dfrac{-x}{(-x)^2+1} = \dfrac{-x}{x^2+1}$

(e) $-f(x) = -\dfrac{x}{x^2+1} = \dfrac{-x}{x^2+1}$

(f) $f(x+1) = \dfrac{x+1}{(x+1)^2+1} = \dfrac{x+1}{x^2+2x+1+1} = \dfrac{x+1}{x^2+2x+2}$

(g) $f(2x) = \dfrac{2x}{(2x)^2+1} = \dfrac{2x}{4x^2+1}$

(h) $f(x+h) = \dfrac{x+h}{(x+h)^2+1} = \dfrac{x+h}{x^2+2xh+h^2+1}$

19. $f(x) = |x| + 4$

(a) $f(0) = |0| + 4 = 0 + 4 = 4$

(b) $f(1) = |1| + 4 = 1 + 4 = 5$

(c) $f(-1) = |-1| + 4 = 1 + 4 = 5$

(d) $f(-x) = |-x| + 4 = |x| + 4$

(e) $-f(x) = -(|x| + 4) = -|x| - 4$

(f) $f(x+1) = |x+1| + 4$

(g) $f(2x) = |2x| + 4 = 2|x| + 4$

(h) $f(x+h) = |x+h| + 4$

21. Graph $y = x^2$. The graph passes the vertical line test. Thus, the equation represents a function.

23. Graph $y = \dfrac{1}{x}$. The graph passes the vertical line test. Thus, the equation represents a function.

25. $y^2 = 4 - x^2$

Solve for y: $y = \pm\sqrt{4 - x^2}$

For $x = 0$, $y = \pm 2$. Thus, (0,2) and (0,–2) are on the graph. This is not a function, since a distinct x corresponds to two different y's.

27. $x = y^2$

Solve for y: $y = \pm\sqrt{x}$

For $x = 1$, $y = \pm 1$. Thus, (1,1) and (1,–1) are on the graph. This is not a function, since a distinct x corresponds to two different y's.

29. Graph $y = 2x^2 - 3x + 4$. The graph passes the vertical line test. Thus, the equation represents a function.

31. $2x^2 + 3y^2 = 1$

Solve for y: $2x^2 + 3y^2 = 1 \Rightarrow 3y^2 = 1 - 2x^2 \Rightarrow y^2 = \dfrac{1 - 2x^2}{3} \Rightarrow y = \pm\sqrt{\dfrac{1 - 2x^2}{3}}$

For $x = 0, y = \pm\sqrt{\dfrac{1}{3}}$. Thus, $\left(0, \sqrt{\dfrac{1}{3}}\right)$ and $\left(0, -\sqrt{\dfrac{1}{3}}\right)$ are on the graph. This is not a function, since a distinct x corresponds to two different y's.

33. $f(x) = -5x + 4$

Domain: {Real Numbers}

35. $f(x) = \dfrac{x}{x^2 + 1}$

Domain: {Real Numbers}

37. $g(x) = \dfrac{x}{x^2 - 16}$

$x^2 - 16 \neq 0$

$x^2 \neq 16 \Rightarrow x \neq \pm 4$

Domain: $\{x \mid x \neq -4, \ x \neq 4\}$

39. $F(x) = \dfrac{x - 2}{x^3 + x}$

$x^3 + x \neq 0$

$x(x^2 + 1) \neq 0$

$x \neq 0, \quad x^2 \neq -1$

Domain: $\{x \mid x \neq 0\}$

41. $h(x) = \sqrt{3x - 12}$

$3x - 12 \geq 0$

$3x \geq 12$

$x \geq 4$

Domain: $\{x \mid x \geq 4\}$

43. $f(x) = \dfrac{4}{\sqrt{x - 9}}$

$x - 9 > 0$

$x > 9$

Domain: $\{x \mid x > 9\}$

45. $p(x) = \sqrt{\dfrac{2}{x - 1}}$

$\dfrac{2}{x - 1} \geq 0 \Rightarrow x - 1 > 0 \Rightarrow x > 1$

Domain: $\{x \mid x > 1\}$

47. $f(x) = 3x + 4 \qquad g(x) = 2x - 3$

(a) $(f + g)(x) = 3x + 4 + 2x - 3 = 5x + 1$ The domain is all real numbers.

(b) $(f - g)(x) = (3x + 4) - (2x - 3) = 3x + 4 - 2x + 3 = x + 7$

The domain is all real numbers.

(c) $(f \cdot g)(x) = (3x + 4)(2x - 3) = 6x^2 - 9x + 8x - 12 = 6x^2 - x - 12$

The domain is all real numbers.

(d) $\left(\dfrac{f}{g}\right)(x) = \dfrac{3x + 4}{2x - 3}$ The domain is all real numbers except $\dfrac{3}{2}$.

49. $f(x) = x - 1$ $g(x) = 2x^2$

  (a) $(f + g)(x) = x - 1 + 2x^2 = 2x^2 + x - 1$ The domain is all real numbers.

  (b) $(f - g)(x) = (x - 1) - (2x^2) = x - 1 - 2x^2 = -2x^2 + x - 1$ The domain is all real numbers.

  (c) $(f \cdot g)(x) = (x - 1)(2x^2) = 2x^3 - 2x^2$ The domain is all real numbers.

  (d) $\left(\dfrac{f}{g}\right)(x) = \dfrac{x - 1}{2x^2}$ The domain is all real numbers except 0.

51. $f(x) = \sqrt{x}$ $g(x) = 3x - 5$

  (a) $(f + g)(x) = \sqrt{x} + 3x - 5$ The domain is $\{x \mid x \geq 0\}$.

  (b) $(f - g)(x) = \sqrt{x} - (3x - 5) = \sqrt{x} - 3x + 5$ The domain is $\{x \mid x \geq 0\}$.

  (c) $(f \cdot g)(x) = \sqrt{x}(3x - 5) = 3x\sqrt{x} - 5\sqrt{x}$ The domain is $\{x \mid x \geq 0\}$.

  (d) $\left(\dfrac{f}{g}\right)(x) = \dfrac{\sqrt{x}}{3x - 5}$ The domain is $\left\{x \mid x \geq 0 \text{ and } x \neq \dfrac{5}{3}\right\}$.

53. $f(x) = 1 + \dfrac{1}{x}$ $g(x) = \dfrac{1}{x}$

  (a) $(f + g)(x) = 1 + \dfrac{1}{x} + \dfrac{1}{x} = 1 + \dfrac{2}{x}$ The domain is $\{x \mid x \neq 0\}$.

  (b) $(f - g)(x) = 1 + \dfrac{1}{x} - \dfrac{1}{x} = 1$ The domain is $\{x \mid x \neq 0\}$.

  (c) $(f \cdot g)(x) = \left(1 + \dfrac{1}{x}\right)\dfrac{1}{x} = \dfrac{1}{x} + \dfrac{1}{x^2}$ The domain is $\{x \mid x \neq 0\}$.

  (d) $\left(\dfrac{f}{g}\right)(x) = \dfrac{\left(1 + \dfrac{1}{x}\right)}{(1/x)} = \dfrac{\left(\dfrac{x+1}{x}\right)}{(1/x)} = \dfrac{x+1}{x} \cdot \dfrac{x}{1} = x + 1$ The domain is $\{x \mid x \neq 0\}$.

55. $f(x) = \dfrac{2x + 3}{3x - 2}$ $g(x) = \dfrac{4x}{3x - 2}$

  (a) $(f + g)(x) = \dfrac{2x + 3}{3x - 2} + \dfrac{4x}{3x - 2} = \dfrac{2x + 3 + 4x}{3x - 2} = \dfrac{6x + 3}{3x - 2}$

   The domain is $\left\{x \mid x \neq \dfrac{2}{3}\right\}$.

  (b) $(f - g)(x) = \dfrac{2x + 3}{3x - 2} - \dfrac{4x}{3x - 2} = \dfrac{2x + 3 - 4x}{3x - 2} = \dfrac{-2x + 3}{3x - 2}$

   The domain is $\left\{x \mid x \neq \dfrac{2}{3}\right\}$.

  (c) $(f \cdot g)(x) = \left(\dfrac{2x + 3}{3x - 2}\right)\left(\dfrac{4x}{3x - 2}\right) = \dfrac{8x^2 + 12x}{(3x - 2)^2}$ The domain is $\left\{x \mid x \neq \dfrac{2}{3}\right\}$.

  (d) $\left(\dfrac{f}{g}\right)(x) = \dfrac{\left(\dfrac{2x + 3}{3x - 2}\right)}{\left(\dfrac{4x}{3x - 2}\right)} = \dfrac{2x + 3}{3x - 2} \cdot \dfrac{3x - 2}{4x} = \dfrac{2x + 3}{4x}$ The domain is $\left\{x \mid x \neq \dfrac{2}{3} \text{ and } x \neq 0\right\}$.

57. $f(x) = 3x + 1$ $(f + g)(x) = 6 - \dfrac{1}{2}x$

$6 - \dfrac{1}{2}x = 3x + 1 + g(x) \Rightarrow 5 - \dfrac{7}{2}x = g(x) \Rightarrow g(x) = 5 - \dfrac{7}{2}x$

59. $f(x) = 4x + 3$

$\dfrac{f(x + h) - f(x)}{h} = \dfrac{4(x + h) + 3 - 4x - 3}{h} = \dfrac{4x + 4h + 3 - 4x - 3}{h} = \dfrac{4h}{h} = 4$

61. $f(x) = x^2 - x + 4$

$\dfrac{f(x + h) - f(x)}{h} = \dfrac{(x + h)^2 - (x + h) + 4 - (x^2 - x + 4)}{h}$

$= \dfrac{x^2 + 2xh + h^2 - x - h + 4 - x^2 + x - 4}{h} == \dfrac{2xh + h^2 - h}{h} = 2x + h - 1$

63. $f(x) = x^3 - 2$

$\dfrac{f(x + h) - f(x)}{h} = \dfrac{(x + h)^3 - 2 - (x^3 - 2)}{h}$

$= \dfrac{x^3 + 3x^2h + 3xh^2 + h^3 - 2 - x^3 + 2}{h} = \dfrac{3x^2h + 3xh^2 + h^3}{h} = 3x^2 + 3xh + h^2$

65. Solving for C:

$f(x) = 2x^3 - 4x^2 + 4x + C$ and $f(2) = 5$

$f(2) = 2(2)^3 - 4(2)^2 + 4(2) + C$

$\quad 5 = 16 - 16 + 8 + C$

$\quad -3 = C$

67. Solving for A:

$f(x) = \dfrac{3x + 8}{2x - A}$ and $f(0) = 2$

$f(0) = \dfrac{3(0) + 8}{2(0) - A}$

$2 = \dfrac{8}{-A} \Rightarrow -2A = 8 \Rightarrow A = -4$

69. Solving for A:

$f(x) = \dfrac{2x - A}{x - 3}$ and $f(4) = 0$

$f(4) = \dfrac{2(4) - A}{4 - 3}$

$0 = \dfrac{8 - A}{1}$

$0 = 8 - A$

$A = 8$

f is undefined when $x = 3$.

71. Let x represent the length of the rectangle.

Then $\dfrac{x}{2}$ represents the width of the rectangle, since the length is twice the width.

The function for the area is: $A(x) = x \cdot \dfrac{x}{2} = \dfrac{x^2}{2} = \dfrac{1}{2}x^2$

73. Let x represent the number of hours worked.

The function for the gross salary is: $G(x) = 10x$

75. $R(x) = \left(\dfrac{L}{P}\right)(x) = \dfrac{L(x)}{P(x)}$

77. $H(x) = (P \cdot I)(x) = P(x) \cdot I(x)$

79. (a) $h(x) = 2x$

$h(a+b) = 2(a+b) = 2a + 2b = h(a) + h(b); \quad h(x) = 2x$ has the property.

(b) $g(x) = x^2$

$g(a+b) = (a+b)^2 = a^2 + 2ab + b^2 \neq a^2 + b^2 = h(a) + h(b)$

$g(x) = x^2$ does not have the property.

(c) $F(x) = 5x - 2$

$F(a+b) = 5(a+b) - 2 = 5a + 5b - 2 \neq 5a - 2 + 5b - 2 = h(a) + h(b)$

$F(x) = 5x - 2$ does not have the property.

(d) $G(x) = \dfrac{1}{x}$

$G(a+b) = \dfrac{1}{a+b} \neq \dfrac{1}{a} + \dfrac{1}{b} = h(a) + h(b)$

$G(x) = \dfrac{1}{x}$ does not have the property.

81.   Answers will vary.

Chapter 1

Equations, Inequalities and Functions

1.7 The Graph of a Function

1. (a) $f(0) = 3$ since $(0,3)$ is on the graph.

   $f(-6) = -3$ since $(-6,-3)$ is on the graph.

   (b) $f(6) = 0$ since $(6, 0)$ is on the graph.

   $f(11) = 1$ since $(11, 1)$ is on the graph.

   (c) $f(3)$ is positive since $f(3) \approx 3.7$.

   (d) $f(-4)$ is negative since $f(-4) = -1$.

   (e) $f(x) = 0$ when $x = -3$, $x = 6$, and $x = 10$.

   (f) $f(x) > 0$ when $-3 < x < 6$, and $10 < x \leq 11$.

   (g) The domain of f is $\{x | -6 \leq x \leq 11\}$ or $[-6, 11]$

   (h) The range of f is $\{y | -3 \leq y \leq 4\}$ or $[-3, 4]$

   (i) The x-intercepts are –3, 6 and 10.

   (j) The y-intercept is 3.

   (k) The line $y = \dfrac{1}{2}$ intersect the graph 3 times.

   (l) The line $x = 5$ intersects the graph 1 time

   (m) $f(x) = 3$ when $x = 0$ and $x = 4$.

   (n) $f(x) = -2$ when $x = -5$ and $x = 8$.

3. Not a function since vertical lines will intersect the graph in more than one point.

5. Function   (a) Domain: $\{x | -\pi \leq x \leq \pi\}$;   Range: $\{y | -1 \leq y \leq 1\}$

   (b) $\left(-\dfrac{\pi}{2}, 0\right)$, $\left(\dfrac{\pi}{2}, 0\right)$,   (0,1)

7. Not a function since vertical lines will intersect the graph in more than one point.

9. Function   (a) Domain: $\{x | x > 0\}$;   Range: $\{y | y \in \text{Real Numbers}\}$

   (b) $(1, 0)$

11. Function   (a) Domain: $\{x | x \in \text{Real Numbers}\}$;   Range: $\{y | y \leq 2\}$

   (b) $(-3,0)$, $(3,0)$, $(0,2)$

13. Function   (a)   Domain: $\{x\,|\,x \in \text{Real Numbers}\}$;   Range: $\{y\,|\,y \geq -3\}$
                   (b) $(1,0), (3,0), (0,9)$

15. $f(x) = 2x^2 - x - 1$
     (a) $f(-1) = 2(-1)^2 - (-1) - 1 = 2$ $(-1,2)$ is on the graph of f.
     (b) $f(-2) = 2(-2)^2 - (-2) - 1 = 9$ $(-2,9)$ is on the graph of f.
     (c)   Solve for x:
$$-1 = 2x^2 - x - 1 \Rightarrow 0 = 2x^2 - x$$
$$0 = x(2x - 1) \Rightarrow x = 0, x = \frac{1}{2}$$
          $(0, -1)$ and $\left(\frac{1}{2}, -1\right)$ are points on the graph of f.
     (d)   The domain of f is: $\{x\,|\,x \text{ is any real number}\}$.
     (e)   x-intercepts:
$$f(x) = 0 \Rightarrow 2x^2 - x - 1 = 0$$
$$(2x + 1)(x - 1) = 0 \Rightarrow x = -\frac{1}{2}, x = 1$$
          $\left(-\frac{1}{2}, 0\right)$ and $(1,0)$
     (f)   y-intercept: $f(0) = 2(0)^2 - 0 - 1 = -1 \Rightarrow (0, -1)$

17. $f(x) = \dfrac{x+2}{x-6}$
     (a) $f(3) = \dfrac{3+2}{3-6} = -\dfrac{5}{3} \neq 14$ $(3,14)$ is not on the graph of f.
     (b) $f(4) = \dfrac{4+2}{4-6} = \dfrac{6}{-2} = -3$ $(4,-3)$ is the point on the graph of f.
     (c)   Solve for x:
$$2 = \frac{x+2}{x-6}$$
$$2x - 12 = x + 2 \qquad\qquad (14, 2) \text{ is a point on the graph of } f.$$
$$x = 14$$
     (d)   The domain of f is: $\{x\,|\,x \neq 6\}$.
     (e)   x-intercepts:
$$f(x) = 0 \Rightarrow \frac{x+2}{x-6} = 0$$
$$x + 2 = 0 \Rightarrow x = -2$$
$$(-2, 0)$$
     (f)   y-intercept: $f(0) = \dfrac{0+2}{0-6} = -\dfrac{1}{3} \Rightarrow \left(0, -\dfrac{1}{3}\right)$

68

19. $f(x) = \dfrac{2x^2}{x^4 + 1}$

  (a) $f(-1) = \dfrac{2(-1)^2}{(-1)^4 + 1} = \dfrac{2}{2} = 1$ $(-1, 1)$ is a point on the graph of f.

  (b) $f(2) = \dfrac{2(2)^2}{(2)^4 + 1} = \dfrac{8}{17}$ $\left(2, \dfrac{8}{17}\right)$ is a point on the graph of f.

  (c)   Solve for x:

  $$1 = \dfrac{2x^2}{x^4 + 1}$$

  $$x^4 + 1 = 2x^2$$

  $$x^4 - 2x^2 + 1 = 0 \qquad (1, 1) \text{ and } (-1, 1) \text{ are points on the graph of } f.$$

  $$(x^2 - 1)^2 = 0$$

  $$x^2 - 1 = 0 \Rightarrow x = \pm 1$$

  (d)   The domain of f is: $\{\text{Real Numbers}\}$.

  (e)   x-intercepts:

  $$f(x) = 0 \Rightarrow \dfrac{2x^2}{x^4 + 1} = 0$$

  $$2x^2 = 0 \Rightarrow x = 0 \qquad (0, 0)$$

  (f)   y-intercept: $f(0) = \dfrac{2x^2}{x^4 + 1} = \dfrac{0}{0 + 1} = 0 \Rightarrow (0, 0)$

21. (a)   Graphing: $H(x) = 20 - 4.9x^2$

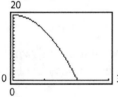

  (b) $H(1) = 20 - 4.9(1)^2 = 20 - 4.9 = 15.1$ meters

  $H(1.1) = 20 - 4.9(1.1)^2 = 20 - 4.9(1.21) = 20 - 5.929 = 14.07$ meters

  $H(1.2) = 20 - 4.9(1.2)^2 = 20 - 4.9(1.44) = 20 - 7.056 = 12.94$ meters

  $H(1.3) = 20 - 4.9(1.3)^2 = 20 - 4.9(1.69) = 20 - 8.281 = 11.72$ meters

  (c) $H(x) = 15$ $\qquad\qquad\qquad$ $H(x) = 10$ $\qquad\qquad\qquad$ $H(x) = 5$

  $\quad 15 = 20 - 4.9x^2$ $\qquad\qquad$ $10 = 20 - 4.9x^2$ $\qquad\qquad$ $5 = 20 - 4.9x^2$

  $\quad -5 = -4.9x^2$ $\qquad\qquad\quad$ $-10 = -4.9x^2$ $\qquad\qquad\quad$ $-15 = -4.9x^2$

  $\quad x^2 \approx 1.0204$ $\qquad\qquad\quad$ $x^2 \approx 2.0408$ $\qquad\qquad\quad$ $x^2 \approx 3.0612$

  $\quad x \approx 1.01$ seconds $\qquad\quad$ $x \approx 1.43$ seconds $\qquad\quad$ $x \approx 1.75$ seconds

  (d) $H(x) = 0$

  $\quad 0 = 20 - 4.9x^2$

  $\quad -20 = -4.9x^2$

  $\quad x^2 \approx 4.0816$

  $\quad x \approx 2.02$ seconds

23. $h(x) = \dfrac{-32x^2}{130^2} + x$

  (a) $h(100) = \dfrac{-32(100)^2}{130^2} + 100 = \dfrac{-320000}{16900} + 100 \approx -18.93 + 100 = 81.07$ feet

  (b) $h(300) = \dfrac{-32(300)^2}{130^2} + 300 = \dfrac{-2880000}{16900} + 300 \approx -170.41 + 300 = 129.59$ feet

  (c) $h(500) = \dfrac{-32(500)^2}{130^2} + 500 = \dfrac{-8000000}{16900} + 500 \approx -473.37 + 500 = 26.63$ feet

  (d) Graphing $h(x) = \dfrac{-32x^2}{130^2} + x$

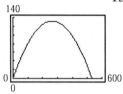

  (e) Solve $h(x) = \dfrac{-32x^2}{130^2} + x = 90$

$$\left(-\dfrac{32}{130^2}\right)x^2 + x - 90 = 0$$

$$x = \dfrac{-1 \pm \sqrt{1^2 - 4\left(-\dfrac{32}{130^2}\right)(-90)}}{2\left(-\dfrac{32}{130^2}\right)} \approx \dfrac{-1 \pm \sqrt{1 - 0.68166}}{-0.00379} \approx \dfrac{-1 \pm 0.5642}{-0.00379}$$

$$x = \dfrac{-1 + 0.5642}{-0.00379} \approx 115.07 \text{ feet} \qquad \text{or} \qquad x = \dfrac{-1 - 0.5642}{-0.00379} \approx 413.05 \text{ feet}$$

  Therefore, the ball reaches a height of 90 feet twice. The first time is when the ball has traveled 115.07 feet, and the second time is when the ball has traveled 413.05 feet.

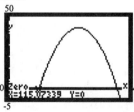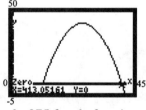

  (f) The ball travels approximately 275 feet before it reaches its maximum height of approximately 131.8 feet.

X	Y1
0	0
25	23.817
50	45.266
75	64.349
100	81.065
125	95.414
150	107.4

X=0

X	Y1
200	124.26
225	129.14
250	131.66
275	131.8
300	129.59
325	125
350	118.05

X=350

(g)   The ball travels approximately 264 feet before it reaches its maximum height of approximately 132.03 feet.

X	Y1	
263.5	132.03	
264	132.03	
264.5	132.03	
265	132.03	
265.5	132.03	
266	132.02	
266.5	132.02	

X=265.5

(h)   Solving $h(x) = \dfrac{-32x^2}{130^2} + x = 0$

$$\dfrac{-32x^2}{130^2} + x = 0 \Rightarrow x\left(\dfrac{-32x}{130^2} + 1\right) = 0 \Rightarrow x = 0 \ \text{ or } \ \dfrac{-32x}{130^2} + 1 = 0$$

$$\dfrac{-32x}{130^2} + 1 = 0 \Rightarrow 1 = \dfrac{32x}{130^2} \Rightarrow 130^2 = 32x \Rightarrow x = \dfrac{130^2}{32} \approx 528.125 \text{ feet}$$

Therefore, the domain of h is $\{x \mid 0 \le x \le 528.125\}$.

25. $C(x) = 100 + \dfrac{x}{10} + \dfrac{36000}{x}$

(a) $C(500) = 100 + \dfrac{500}{10} + \dfrac{36000}{500} = 100 + 50 + 72 = \$222$

(b) $C(450) = 100 + \dfrac{450}{10} + \dfrac{36000}{450} = 100 + 45 + 80 = \$225$

(c) $C(600) = 100 + \dfrac{600}{10} + \dfrac{36000}{600} = 100 + 60 + 60 = \$220$

(d) $C(400) = 100 + \dfrac{400}{10} + \dfrac{36000}{400} = 100 + 40 + 90 = \$230$

(e)   Graphing:

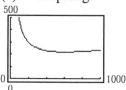

(f)   As x varies from 400 to 600 mph, the cost decreases from $230 to $220.

27.   Answers will vary.

29.   The graph of a function may have at most one y-intercept, otherwise the graph would fail the Vertical Line Test for the line $x = 0$.

31.   (a)   III   (b)   IV   (c)   I   (d)   V   (e)   II

33.

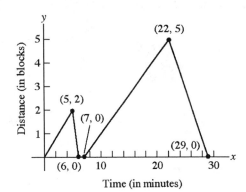

35.   (a)   2 hours elapsed; $0 \leq d \leq 3$ miles.
       (b)   0.5 hours elapsed; $d = 3$ miles.
       (c)   0.3 hours elapsed; $0 \leq d \leq 3$ miles.
       (d)   0.2 hours elapsed; $d = 0$ miles.
       (e)   0.9 hours elapsed; $0 \leq d \leq 2.8$ miles.
       (f)   0.3 hours elapsed; $d = 2.8$ miles.
       (g)   1.1 hours elapsed; $0 \leq d \leq 2.8$ miles.
       (h)   The furthest distance Kevin is from home is 3 miles.
       (i)   2 times.

37.   No points of the form $(5, y)$ or of the form $(x, 0)$ can be on the graph of the function.

Equations, Inequalities and Functions

1.8 Properties of Functions

1. Yes

3. No It only increases on (5, 10).

5. f is increasing on the intervals: (–8, –2), (0, 2), (5, 10).

7. Yes. The local maximum at $x = 2$ is 10.

9. f has local maxima at $x = -2$ and $x = 2$. The local maxima are 6 and 10, respectively.

11. (a) Intercepts: (–2,0), (2,0), and (0,3).
    (b) Domain: $\{x \mid -4 \le x \le 4\}$; Range: $\{y \mid 0 \le y \le 3\}$.
    (c) Interval notation: Increasing: (–2, 0) and (2, 4); Decreasing: (–4, –2) and (0, 2).
    Inequality notation: Increasing: $-2 < x < 0$ and $2 < x < 4$
    Decreasing: $-4 < x < -2$ and $0 < x < 2$
    (d) Since the graph is symmetric to the y-axis, the function is <u>even</u>.

13. (a) Intercepts: (0,1).
    (b) Domain: { Real Numbers }; Range: $\{y \mid y > 0\}$.
    (c) Interval notation: Increasing: $(-\infty, +\infty)$; Decreasing: never.
    Inequality notation: Increasing: $-\infty < x < +\infty$
    Decreasing: never
    (d) Since the graph is not symmetric to the y-axis or the origin, the function is <u>neither</u> even nor odd.

15. (a) Intercepts: $(-\pi, 0)$, (0,0), and $(\pi, 0)$.
    (b) Domain: $\{x \mid -\pi \le x \le \pi\}$; Range: $\{y \mid -1 \le y \le 1\}$.
    (c) Interval notation: Increasing: $\left(-\dfrac{\pi}{2}, \dfrac{\pi}{2}\right)$; Decreasing: $\left(-\pi, -\dfrac{\pi}{2}\right)$ and $\left(\dfrac{\pi}{2}, \pi\right)$.

    Inequality notation: Increasing: $-\dfrac{\pi}{2} < x < \dfrac{\pi}{2}$

    Decreasing: $-\pi < x < -\dfrac{\pi}{2}$ and $\dfrac{\pi}{2} < x < \pi$
    (d) Since the graph is symmetric to the origin, the function is <u>odd</u>.

33. $g(x) = \dfrac{1}{x^2}$

$$g(-x) = \dfrac{1}{(-x)^2} = \dfrac{1}{x^2}$$

g is even.

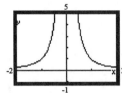

35. $h(x) = \dfrac{-x^3}{3x^2 - 9}$

$$h(-x) = \dfrac{-(-x)^3}{3(-x)^2 - 9} = \dfrac{x^3}{3x^2 - 9}$$

h is odd.

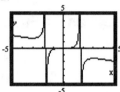

37. $f(x) = x^3 - 3x + 2$ on the interval $(-2,2)$

Use MAXIMUM and MINIMUM on the graph of $y_1 = x^3 - 3x + 2$.

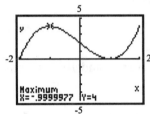
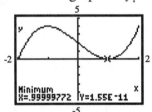

local maximum at: $(-1,4)$;   local minimum at: $(1,0)$

f is increasing on: $(-2,-1) \cup (1,2)$; f is decreasing on: $(-1,1)$

39. $f(x) = x^5 - x^3$ on the interval $(-2,2)$

Use MAXIMUM and MINIMUM on the graph of $y_1 = x^5 - x^3$.

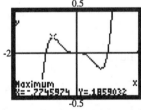

local maximum at: $(-0.77, 0.19)$;   local minimum at: $(0.77, -0.19)$

f is increasing on: $(-2, -0.77) \cup (0.77, 2)$; f is decreasing on: $(-0.77, 0.77)$

41. $f(x) = -0.2x^3 - 0.6x^2 + 4x - 6$ on the interval $(-6,4)$

Use MAXIMUM and MINIMUM on the graph of $y_1 = -0.2x^3 - 0.6x^2 + 4x - 6$.

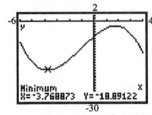
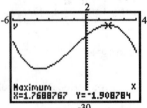

local maximum at: $(1.77, -1.91)$;   local minimum at: $(-3.77, -18.89)$

f is increasing on: $(-3.77, 1.77)$; f is decreasing on: $(-6, -3.77) \cup (1.77, 4)$

43. $f(x) = 0.25x^4 + 0.3x^3 - 0.9x^2 + 3$ on the interval $(-3, 2)$

Use MAXIMUM and MINIMUM on the graph of $y_1 = 0.25x^4 + 0.3x^3 - 0.9x^2 + 3$.

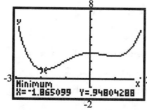 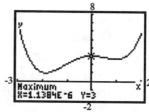 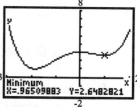

local maximum at: $(0, 3)$;   local minimum at: $(-1.87, 0.95)$, $(0.97, 2.65)$

f is increasing on: $(-1.87, 0) \cup (0.97, 2)$; f is decreasing on: $(-3, -1.87) \cup (0, 0.97)$

45. $f(x) = 5x$

The average rate of change of f from c to x is given by:

$$\frac{f(x) - f(c)}{x - c} = \frac{5x - 5c}{x - c} = \frac{5(x - c)}{x - c} = 5$$

   (a)   From $c = 0$ to $x = 2$; average rate of change = 5
   (b)   From $c = 0$ to $x = 4$; average rate of change = 5
   (c)   From $c = 1$ to $x = x$; average rate of change = 5

47. $f(x) = 1 - 3x$

The average rate of change of f from c to x is given by:

$$\frac{f(x) - f(c)}{x - c} = \frac{1 - 3x - (1 - 3c)}{x - c} = \frac{1 - 3x - 1 + 3c}{x - c} = \frac{-3x + 3c}{x - c} = \frac{-3(x - c)}{x - c} = -3$$

   (a)   From $c = 0$ to $x = 2$; average rate of change = –3
   (b)   From $c = 0$ to $x = 4$; average rate of change = –3
   (c)   From $c = 1$ to $x = x$; average rate of change = –3

49. $f(x) = x^2 - 2x$

The average rate of change of f from c to x is given by:

$$\frac{f(x) - f(c)}{x - c} = \frac{x^2 - 2x - (c^2 - 2c)}{x - c} = \frac{x^2 - 2x - c^2 + 2c}{x - c} = \frac{x^2 - c^2 - 2x + 2c}{x - c}$$

$$= \frac{(x + c)(x - c) - 2(x - c)}{x - c} = \frac{(x - c)(x + c - 2)}{x - c} = x + c - 2$$

   (a)   From $c = 0$ to $x = 2$; average rate of change = $2 + 0 - 2 = 0$
   (b)   From $c = 0$ to $x = 4$; average rate of change = $4 + 0 - 2 = 2$
   (c)   From $c = 1$ to $x = x$; average rate of change = $x + 1 - 2 = x - 1$

17. (a)   Intercepts: $\left(0, \dfrac{1}{2}\right), \left(\dfrac{1}{2}, 0\right),$ and $\left(\dfrac{5}{2}, 0\right).$

(b)   Domain: $\{x \mid -3 \le x \le 3\}$; Range: $\{y \mid -1 \le y \le 2\}.$

(c)   Interval notation: Increasing: $(2, 3)$; Decreasing: $(-1, 1)$;
$\qquad\qquad\qquad\qquad$ Constant: $(-3, -1)$ and $(1, 2)$.
$\quad$ Inequality notation: Increasing: $2 < x < 3$; Decreasing: $-1 < x < 1$;
$\qquad\qquad\qquad\qquad$ Constant: $-3 < x < -1$ and $1 < x < 2$.

(d)   Since the graph is not symmetric to the y-axis or the origin, the function is <u>neither</u> even nor odd.

19. (a)   Intercepts: $(0, 2), (-2, 0),$ and $(2, 0).$

(b)   Domain: $\{x \mid -4 \le x \le 4\}$; Range: $\{y \mid 0 \le y \le 2\}.$

(c)   Interval notation: Increasing: $(-2, 0)$ and $(2, 4)$;
$\qquad\qquad\qquad\qquad$ Decreasing: $(-4, -2)$ and $(0, 2)$.
$\quad$ Inequality notation: Increasing: $-2 < x < 0$ and $2 < x < 4$;
$\qquad\qquad\qquad\qquad$ Decreasing: $-4 < x < -2$ and $0 < x < 2$.

(d)   Since the graph is symmetric to the y-axis, the function is <u>even</u>.

21. (a) f has a local maximum of 3 at $x = 0.$

(b) f has a local minimum of 0 at both $x = -2$ and $x = 2.$

23. (a) f has a local maximum of 1 at $x = \dfrac{\pi}{2}.$

(b) f has a local minimum of -1 at $x = -\dfrac{\pi}{2}.$

25. $f(x) = 4x^3$
$\qquad f(-x) = 4(-x)^3 = -4x^3$
$\quad f$ is odd.

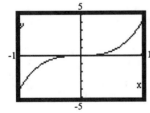

27. $g(x) = -3x^2 - 5$
$\qquad g(-x) = -3(-x)^2 - 5 = -3x^2 - 5$
$\quad g$ is even.

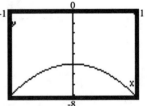

29. $F(x) = \sqrt[3]{x}$
$\qquad F(-x) = \sqrt[3]{-x} = -\sqrt[3]{x}$
$\quad F$ is odd.

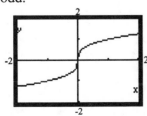

31. $f(x) = x + |x|$
$\qquad f(-x) = -x + |-x| = -x + |x|$
$\quad f$ is neither even nor odd.

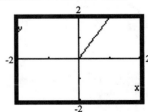

51. $f(x) = x^3 - x$
The average rate of change of f from c to x is given by:

$$\frac{f(x) - f(c)}{x - c} = \frac{x^3 - x - \left(c^3 - c\right)}{x - c} = \frac{x^3 - x - c^3 + c}{x - c} = \frac{x^3 - c^3 - x + c}{x - c}$$

$$= \frac{(x-c)\left(x^2 + xc + c^2\right) - (x-c)}{x - c} = \frac{(x-c)\left(x^2 + xc + c^2 - 1\right)}{x - c}$$

$$= x^2 + xc + c^2 - 1$$

(a)   From $c = 0$ to $x = 2$; average rate of change $= 2^2 + 2 \cdot 0 + 0^2 - 1 = 3$
(b)   From $c = 0$ to $x = 4$; average rate of change $= 4^2 + 4 \cdot 0 + 0^2 - 1 = 15$
(c)   From $c = 1$ to $x = x$; average rate of change $= x^2 + x \cdot 1 + 1^2 - 1 = x^2 + x$

53.   Graphing: $V(x) = x\left(24 - 2x^2\right)$

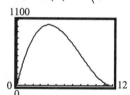

Use MAXIMUM.
The volume is largest when $x = 4$ inches.

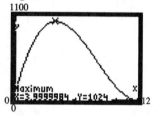

55. $s(t) = -16t^2 + 80t + 6$
(a)   Graphing:

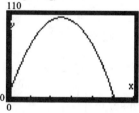

(b) Use MAXIMUM. The maximum value for s occurs at t = 2.5 seconds.
(c) The maximum height is $s(2.5) = -16(2.5)^2 + (80)(2.5) + 6 = -100 + 200 + 6 = 106$ feet.

57.   One at most because if f is increasing it could only cross the x-axis at most one time.
It could not "turn" and cross it again or it would start to decrease.

59.   The only function that is both even and odd is the function $f(x) = 0$.

Equations, Inequalities and Functions

1.R   Chapter Review

1. $6 + \dfrac{x}{3} = 0$

$18 + x = 0 \Rightarrow x = -18$

The solution set is $\{-18\}$.

3. $-2(5 - 3x) + 8 = 4 + 5x$

$-10 + 6x + 8 = 4 + 5x$

$6x - 2 = 4 + 5x$

$x = 6$

The solution set is $\{6\}$.

5. $\dfrac{3x}{4} - \dfrac{x}{3} = \dfrac{1}{12}$

$9x - 4x = 1 \Rightarrow 5x = 1 \Rightarrow x = \dfrac{1}{5}$

The solution set is $\left\{\dfrac{1}{5}\right\}$.

7. $\dfrac{x}{x-1} = \dfrac{6}{5}$

$5x = 6x - 6$

$6 = x$

and since $x = 6$ does not cause a denominator to equal zero, the solution set is $\{6\}$.

9. $x(1 - x) = 6$

$x - x^2 = 6$

$0 = x^2 - x + 6$

$b^2 - 4ac = (-1)^2 - 4(1)(6) = 1 - 24 = -23 < 0$

No real solution.

11. $\dfrac{1}{2}\left(x - \dfrac{1}{3}\right) = \dfrac{3}{4} - \dfrac{x}{6}$

$\dfrac{x}{2} - \dfrac{1}{6} = \dfrac{3}{4} - \dfrac{x}{6}$

$6x - 2 = 9 - 2x$

$8x = 11 \Rightarrow x = \dfrac{11}{8}$

The solution set is $\left\{\dfrac{11}{8}\right\}$.

13. $x^3 = 16x$

$x^3 - 16x = 0$

$x(x^2 - 16) = 0$

$x(x - 4)(x + 4) = 0$

$x = 0$ or $x = 4$ or $x = -4$

The solution set is $\{-4, 0, 4\}$.

15. $x^3 + x^2 - 9x - 9 = 0$

$x^2(x + 1) - 9(x + 1) = 0$

$(x + 1)(x^2 - 9) = 0$

$(x + 1)(x - 3)(x + 3) = 0$

$x = -1$ or $x = 3$ or $x = -3$

The solution set is $\{-3, -1, 3\}$.

17. $x^2 = 16$
$x = \pm 4$
The solution set is $\{-4, 4\}$.

19. $(2x+1)^2 = 4$
$2x+1 = \pm 2$

$$2x+1 = 2 \Rightarrow 2x = 1 \Rightarrow x = \frac{1}{2}$$

$$2x+1 = -2 \Rightarrow 2x = -3 \Rightarrow x = -\frac{3}{2}$$

The solution set is $\left\{-\frac{3}{2}, \frac{1}{2}\right\}$.

21. $[3, \infty)$

23. $2 < x < 5$

25.   If $x \le -2$, then $x+2 \le 0$.

27. $\dfrac{2x-3}{5} + 2 \le \dfrac{x}{2}$
$2(2x-3) + 10(2) \le 5x$
$4x - 6 + 20 \le 5x$
$14 \le x \Rightarrow x \ge 14$

$\{x \mid x \ge 14\}$ or $[14, +\infty)$

29. $-9 \le \dfrac{2x+3}{-4} \le 7$
$36 \ge 2x + 3 \ge -28$
$33 \ge 2x \ge -31$
$\dfrac{33}{2} \ge x \ge -\dfrac{31}{2}$
$-\dfrac{31}{2} \le x \le \dfrac{33}{2}$

$\left\{x \mid -\dfrac{31}{2} \le x \le \dfrac{32}{2}\right\}$ or $\left[-\dfrac{31}{2}, \dfrac{32}{2}\right]$

31. $6 > \dfrac{3-3x}{12} > 2$
$72 > 3 - 3x > 24$
$69 > -3x > 21$
$-23 < x < -7$

$\{x \mid -23 < x < -7\}$ or $(-23, -7)$

33.   Given the points $(0,1)$ and $(-2,3)$.

(a) Distance: $d = \sqrt{(0-(-2))^2 + (1-3)^2}$
$= \sqrt{4+4} = \sqrt{8} = 2\sqrt{2}$

(b) Midpoint: $\left(\dfrac{0+(-2)}{2}, \dfrac{1+3}{2}\right) = (-1, 2)$

35.   Given the points $(-1,2)$ and $(5,-2)$.
(a) Distance:
$$d = \sqrt{(-1-5)^2 + (2-(-2))^2}$$
$$= \sqrt{36+16} = \sqrt{52} = 2\sqrt{13}$$

(b) Midpoint: $\left(\dfrac{-1+5}{2}, \dfrac{2+(-2)}{2}\right) = (2, 0)$

37. $2x - 3y = 6 \Rightarrow y = \dfrac{2}{3}x - 2$

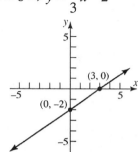

39. $y = x^2 - 9$

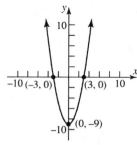

41. $x^2 + 2y = 16 \Rightarrow y = -\dfrac{1}{2}x^2 + 8$

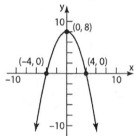

43. Test for symmetry: $2x = 3y^2$

   x-axis: Replace y by $-y$ so $2x = 3(-y)^2 \Rightarrow 2x = 3y^2$, which is
   equivalent to $2x = 3y^2$.

   y-axis: Replace x by $-x$ so $2(-x) = 3y^2 \Rightarrow -2x = 3y^2$,
   which is not equivalent to $2x = 3y^2$.

   Origin: Replace x by $-x$ and y by $-y$ so $2(-x) = 3(-y)^2$
   $\Rightarrow -2x = 3y^2$, which is not equivalent to $2x = 3y^2$.

   Therefore, the graph is symmetric with respect to the x-axis.

45. Test for symmetry: $x^2 + 4y^2 = 16$

   x-axis: Replace y by $-y$ so $x^2 + 4(-y)^2 = 16 \Rightarrow x^2 + 4y^2 = 16$,
   which is equivalent to $x^2 + 4y^2 = 16$.

   y-axis: Replace x by $-x$ so $(-x)^2 + 4y^2 = 16 \Rightarrow x^2 + 4y^2 = 16$,
   which is equivalent to $x^2 + 4y^2 = 16$.

   Origin: Replace x by $-x$ and y by $-y$ so $(-x)^2 + 4(-y)^2 = 16 \Rightarrow x^2 + 4y^2 = 16$,
   which is equivalent to $x^2 + 4y^2 = 16$.

   Therefore, the graph is symmetric with respect to the x-axis, the y-axis and the origin.

47. Test for symmetry: $y = x^4 + 2x^2 + 1$

    x - axis :   Replace y by $-y$ so $-y = x^4 + 2x^2 + 1,$

              which is not equivalent to $y = x^4 + 2x^2 + 1.$

    y - axis :   Replace x by $-x$ so $y = (-x)^4 + 2(-x)^2 + 1 \Rightarrow y = x^4 + 2x^2 + 1,$

              which is equivalent to $y = x^4 + 2x^2 + 1.$

    Origin :   Replace x by $-x$ and y by $-y$ so $-y = (-x)^4 + 2(-x)^2 + 1 \Rightarrow -y = x^4 + 2x^2 + 1,$

              which is not equivalent to $y = x^4 + 2x^2 + 1.$

    Therefore, the graph is symmetric with respect to the y-axis.

49. Test for symmetry: $x^2 + x + y^2 + 2y = 0$

    x - axis :   Replace y by $-y$ so $x^2 + x + (-y)^2 + 2(-y) = 0 \Rightarrow x^2 + x + y^2 - 2y = 0,$

              which is not equivalent to $x^2 + x + y^2 + 2y = 0.$

    y - axis :   Replace x by $-x$ so $(-x)^2 + (-x) + y^2 + 2y = 0 \Rightarrow x^2 - x + y^2 + 2y = 0,$

              which is not equivalent to $x^2 + x + y^2 + 2y = 0.$

    Origin :   Replace x by $-x$ and y by $-y$ so $(-x)^2 + (-x) + (-y)^2 + 2(-y) = 0$

          $\Rightarrow x^2 - x + y^2 - 2y = 0,$ which is not equivalent to $x^2 + x + y^2 + 2y = 0.$

    Therefore, the graph is not symmetric to the x-axis, the y-axis, or the origin.

51. $y = x^3$

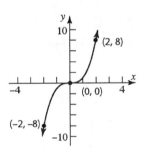

53.   Center $= (-1, 2)$

Radius $= 1$

$$\left(x - (-1)\right)^2 + (y - 2)^2 = 1^2$$

$$(x + 1)^2 + (y - 2)^2 = 1$$

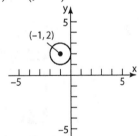

55.   Center $= (1, -1)$

Radius $= 2$

$$(x - 1)^2 + \left(y - (-1)\right)^2 = 2^2$$

$$(x - 1)^2 + (y + 1)^2 = 4$$

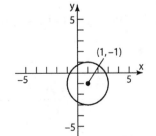

57. $x^2 + y^2 - 2x + 4y - 4 = 0$

$$x^2 - 2x + y^2 + 4y = 4$$

$$(x^2 - 2x + 1) + (y^2 + 4y + 4) = 4 + 1 + 4$$

$$(x-1)^2 + (y+2)^2 = 9$$

$$(x-1)^2 + (y+2)^2 = 3^2$$

Center: $(1,-2)$ Radius $= 3$

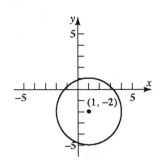

59. $3x^2 + 3y^2 - 6x + 12y = 0$

$$x^2 + y^2 - 2x + 4y = 0$$

$$x^2 - 2x + y^2 + 4y = 0$$

$$(x^2 - 2x + 1) + (y^2 + 4y + 4) = 1 + 4$$

$$(x-1)^2 + (y+2)^2 = 5$$

$$(x-1)^2 + (y+2)^2 = \left(\sqrt{5}\right)^2$$

Center: $(1,-2)$ Radius $= \sqrt{5}$

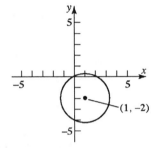

61. $x^3 - 5x + 3 = 0$; Use ZERO (or ROOT) on the graph of $y_1 = x^3 - 5x + 3$.

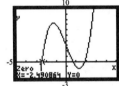 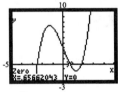 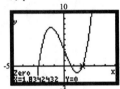

The solution set is $\{-2.49, 0.66, 1.83\}$.

63. $x^4 - 3 = 2x + 1$; Use ZERO (or ROOT) on the graph of $y_1 = x^4 - 2x - 4$.

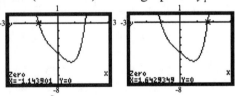

The solution set is $\{-1.14, 1.64\}$.

65.   Function, Domain $= \{-1, 2, 4\}$; Range $= \{0, 3\}$.

67. $f(x) = \dfrac{3x}{x^2 - 1}$

(a) $f(2) = \dfrac{3(2)}{(2)^2 - 1} = \dfrac{6}{4-1} = \dfrac{6}{3} = 2$

(b) $f(-2) = \dfrac{3(-2)}{(-2)^2 - 1} = \dfrac{-6}{4-1} = \dfrac{-6}{3} = -2$

(c) $f(-x) = \dfrac{3(-x)}{(-x)^2 - 1} = \dfrac{-3x}{x^2 - 1}$

(d) $-f(x) = -\left(\dfrac{3x}{x^2 - 1}\right) = \dfrac{-3x}{x^2 - 1}$

69. $f(x) = \sqrt{x^2 - 4}$

   (a) $f(2) = \sqrt{(2)^2 - 4} = \sqrt{4 - 4} = \sqrt{0} = 0$

   (b) $f(x - 2) = \sqrt{(-2)^2 - 4} = \sqrt{4 - 4} = \sqrt{0} = 0$

   (c) $f(-x) = \sqrt{(-x)^2 - 4} = \sqrt{x^2 - 4}$

   (d) $-f(x) = -\sqrt{x^2 - 4}$

71. $f(x) = \dfrac{x^2 - 4}{x^2}$

   (a) $f(2) = \dfrac{(2)^2 - 4}{(2)^2} = \dfrac{4 - 4}{4} = \dfrac{0}{4} = 0$

   (b) $f(-2) = \dfrac{(-2)^2 - 4}{(-2)^2} = \dfrac{4 - 4}{4} = \dfrac{0}{4} = 0$

   (c) $f(-x) = \dfrac{(-x)^2 - 4}{(-x)^2} = \dfrac{x^2 - 4}{x^2}$

   (d) $-f(x) = -\left(\dfrac{x^2 - 4}{x^2}\right) = -\dfrac{x^2 - 4}{x^2}$

73. $f(x) = \dfrac{x}{x^2 - 9}$

   The denominator cannot be zero:
   $$x^2 - 9 \neq 0$$
   $$(x + 3)(x - 3) \neq 0$$
   $$x \neq -3 \text{ or } 3$$
   Domain: $\{x \mid x \neq -3,\ x \neq 3\}$

75. $f(x) = \sqrt{2 - x}$

   The radicand must be positive:
   $$2 - x \geq 0$$
   $$x \leq 2$$
   Domain: $\{x \mid x \leq 2\}$ or $(-\infty, 2]$

77. $f(x) = \dfrac{\sqrt{x}}{|x|}$

   The radicand must be positive and the
   denominator cannot be zero: $x > 0$
   Domain: $\{x \mid x > 0\}$ or $(0, +\infty)$

79. $f(x) = \dfrac{x}{x^2 + 2x - 3}$

   The denominator cannot be zero:
   $$x^2 + 2x - 3 \neq 0$$
   $$(x + 3)(x - 1) \neq 0$$
   $$x \neq -3 \text{ or } 1$$
   Domain : $\{x \mid x \neq -3, x \neq 1\}$

81. $f(x) = 2 - x \quad g(x) = 3x + 1$

   (a) $(f + g)(x) = f(x) + g(x) = 2 - x + 3x + 1 = 2x + 3$, Domain: {Real Numbers}

   (b) $(f - g)(x) = f(x) - g(x) = 2 - x - (3x + 1) = 2 - x - 3x - 1 = -4x + 1$
        Domain: {Real Numbers}

   (c) $(f \cdot g)(x) = f(x) \cdot g(x) = (2 - x)(3x + 1) = 6x + 2 - 3x^2 - x = -3x^2 + 5x + 2$
        Domain: {Real Numbers}

   (d) $\left(\dfrac{f}{g}\right)(x) = \dfrac{f(x)}{g(x)} = \dfrac{2 - x}{3x + 1}$, Domain : $\left\{x \mid x \neq -\dfrac{1}{3}\right\}$

83. $f(x) = 3x^2 + x + 1$ $g(x) = 3x$

(a) $(f + g)(x) = f(x) + g(x) = 3x^2 + x + 1 + 3x = 3x^2 + 4x + 1$, Domain: {Real Numbers}

(b) $(f - g)(x) = f(x) - g(x) = 3x^2 + x + 1 - 3x = 3x^2 - 2x + 1$, Domain: {Real Numbers}

(c) $(f \cdot g)(x) = f(x) \cdot g(x) = (3x^2 + x + 1)(3x) = 9x^3 + 3x^2 + 3x$, Domain: {Real Numbers}

(d) $\left(\dfrac{f}{g}\right)(x) = \dfrac{f(x)}{g(x)} = \dfrac{3x^2 + x + 1}{3x}$, Domain: $\left\{x \mid x \neq 0\right\}$

85. $f(x) = \dfrac{x+1}{x-1}$ $g(x) = \dfrac{1}{x}$

(a) $(f + g)(x) = f(x) + g(x) = \dfrac{x+1}{x-1} + \dfrac{1}{x} = \dfrac{x(x+1) + 1(x-1)}{x(x-1)} = \dfrac{x^2 + x + x - 1}{x(x-1)}$

$$= \dfrac{x^2 + 2x - 1}{x(x-1)}$$

Domain: $\left\{x \mid x \neq 0, x \neq 1\right\}$

(b) $(f - g)(x) = f(x) - g(x) = \dfrac{x+1}{x-1} - \dfrac{1}{x} = \dfrac{x(x+1) - 1(x-1)}{x(x-1)} = \dfrac{x^2 + x - x + 1}{x(x-1)}$

$$= \dfrac{x^2 + 1}{x(x-1)}$$

Domain: $\left\{x \mid x \neq 0, x \neq 1\right\}$

(c) $(f \cdot g)(x) = f(x) \cdot g(x) = \left(\dfrac{x+1}{x-1}\right)\left(\dfrac{1}{x}\right) = \dfrac{x+1}{x(x-1)}$

Domain: $\left\{x \mid x \neq 0, x \neq 1\right\}$

(d) $\left(\dfrac{f}{g}\right)(x) = \dfrac{f(x)}{g(x)} = \dfrac{\left(\dfrac{x+1}{x-1}\right)}{\left(\dfrac{1}{x}\right)} = \left(\dfrac{x+1}{x-1}\right)\left(\dfrac{x}{1}\right) = \dfrac{x^2 + x}{x-1}$

Domain: $\left\{x \mid x \neq 0, x \neq 1\right\}$

87. $f(x) = \dfrac{Ax + 5}{6x - 2}$ and $f(1) = 4$

Solving:

$$\dfrac{A(1) + 5}{6(1) - 2} = 4$$

$$\dfrac{A + 5}{4} = 4$$

$$A + 5 = 16$$

$$A = 11$$

89.   (b), (c), and (d) pass the vertical line test and therefore are functions.

91.   (a)   Domain: $\left\{x \mid -4 \leq x \leq 4\right\}$ Range: $\left\{y \mid -3 \leq y \leq 1\right\}$

(b)   Increasing on: $(-4, -1)$ and $(3, 4)$;   Decreasing: $(-1, 3)$;   Constant: $(-5, -1)$

(c)   Local minimum $(3, -3)$; Local maximum $(-1, 1)$

(d) The graph is not symmetric to the x-axis, the y-axis or the origin.

(e) The function is neither even nor odd.

(f) x-intercepts: $-2, 0, 4$;   y-intercept: 0

93. $f(x) = x^3 - 4x$

$$f(-x) = (-x)^3 - 4(-x) = -x^3 + 4x = -\left(x^3 - 4x\right) = -f(x) \qquad f \text{ is odd.}$$

95. $h(x) = \dfrac{1}{x^4} + \dfrac{1}{x^2} + 1$

$$h(-x) = \frac{1}{(-x)^4} + \frac{1}{(-x)^2} + 1 = \frac{1}{x^4} + \frac{1}{x^2} + 1 = h(x) \qquad h \text{ is even.}$$

97. $G(x) = 1 - x + x^3$

$$G(-x) = 1 - (-x) + (-x)^3 = 1 + x - x^3 \neq -G(x) \neq G(x)$$

G is neither even nor odd.

99. $f(x) = \dfrac{x}{1 + x^2}$

$$f(-x) = \frac{-x}{1 + (-x)^2} = \frac{-x}{1 + x^2} = -f(x) \qquad f \text{ is odd.}$$

101. $f(x) = 2x^3 - 5x + 1$ on the interval $(-3, 3)$

Use MAXIMUM and MINIMUM on the graph of $y_1 = 2x^3 - 5x + 1$.

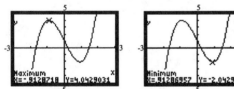

local maximum at: $(-0.91, 4.04)$;   local minimum at: $(0.91, -2.04)$

f is increasing on: $(-3, -0.91) \cup (0.91, 3)$; f is decreasing on: $(-0.91, 0.91)$

103. $f(x) = 2x^4 - 5x^3 + 2x + 1$ on the interval $(-2, 3)$

Use MAXIMUM and MINIMUM on the graph of $y_1 = 2x^4 - 5x^3 + 2x + 1$.

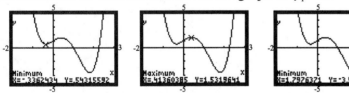

local maximum at: $(0.41, 1.53)$; local minimum at: $(-0.34, 0.54)$, $(1.80, -3.56)$

f is increasing on: $(-0.34, 0.41) \cup (1.80, 3)$; f is decreasing on: $(-2, -0.34) \cup (0.41, 1.80)$

105. $f(x) = 2 - 5x$

$$\frac{f(x) - f(2)}{x - 2} = \frac{2 - 5x - (-8)}{x - 2} = \frac{-5x + 10}{x - 2} = \frac{-5(x - 2)}{x - 2} = -5$$

107. $f(x) = 3x - 4x^2$

$$\frac{f(x) - f(2)}{x - 2} = \frac{3x - 4x^2 - (-10)}{x - 2} = \frac{-4x^2 + 3x + 10}{x - 2}$$

$$= \frac{-(4x^2 - 3x - 10)}{x - 2} = \frac{-(4x + 5)(x - 2)}{x - 2} = -4x - 5$$

Linear Functions and Models

2.1 Properties of Linear Functions

1.

x	$y = f(x) = 2x - 5$	(x, y)
-2	$y = f(-2) = 2(-2) - 5 = -9$	$(-2, -9)$
-1	$y = f(-1) = 2(-1) - 5 = -7$	$(-1, -7)$
0	$y = f(0) = 2(0) - 5 = -5$	$(0, -5)$
1	$y = f(1) = 2(1) - 5 = -3$	$(1, -3)$
2	$y = f(2) = 2(2) - 5 = -1$	$(2, -1)$
3	$y = f(3) = 2(3) - 5 = 1$	$(3, 1)$

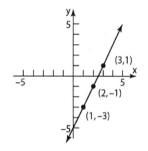

3.

x	$y = g(x) = -4x + 9$	(x, y)
-2	$y = g(-2) = -4(-2) + 9 = 17$	$(-2, 17)$
-1	$y = g(-1) = -4(-1) + 9 = 13$	$(-1, 13)$
0	$y = g(0) = -4(0) + 9 = 9$	$(0, 9)$
1	$y = g(1) = -4(1) + 9 = 5$	$(1, 5)$
2	$y = g(2) = -4(2) + 9 = 1$	$(2, 1)$
3	$y = g(3) = -4(3) + 9 = -3$	$(3, -3)$

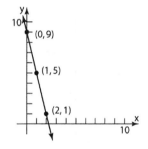

5.

x	$y = G(x) = \dfrac{1}{3}x - 3$	(x, y)
-2	$y = G(-2) = \dfrac{1}{3}(-2) - 3 = -\dfrac{11}{3}$	$\left(-2, -\dfrac{11}{3}\right)$
-1	$y = G(-1) = \dfrac{1}{3}(-1) - 3 = -\dfrac{10}{3}$	$\left(-1, -\dfrac{10}{3}\right)$
0	$y = G(0) = \dfrac{1}{3}(0) - 3 = -3$	$(0, -3)$
1	$y = G(1) = \dfrac{1}{3}(1) - 3 = -\dfrac{8}{3}$	$\left(1, -\dfrac{8}{3}\right)$
2	$y = G(2) = \dfrac{1}{3}(2) - 3 = -\dfrac{7}{3}$	$\left(2, -\dfrac{7}{3}\right)$
3	$y = G(3) = \dfrac{1}{3}(3) - 3 = -2$	$(3, -2)$

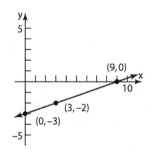

7. $f(x) = 2x + 3$
    Slope = 2; y-intercept = 3
    Increasing function

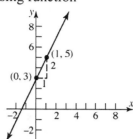

9. $h(x) = -3x + 4$
    Slope = -3; y-intercept = 4
    Decreasing function

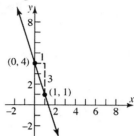

11. $f(x) = \dfrac{1}{4}x - 3$

    Slope $= \dfrac{1}{4}$; y-intercept = -3

    Increasing function

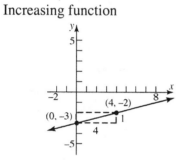

13. $F(x) = 4$
    Slope = 0; y-intercept = 4
    Constant function

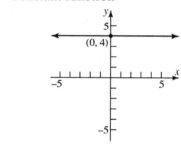

15. $g(x) = 2x - 8$
    (a) $g(x) = 2x - 8 = 0$
    $\quad\quad 2x = 8$
    $\quad\quad\quad x = 4$
    (b) y-intercept = -8

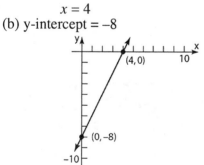

17. $f(x) = -5x + 10$
    (a) $f(x) = -5x + 10 = 0$
    $\quad\quad -5x = -10$
    $\quad\quad\quad x = 2$
    (b) y-intercept = 10

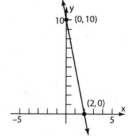

19. $H(x) = -\dfrac{1}{2}x + 4$

(a) $H(x) = -\dfrac{1}{2}x + 4 = 0$

$-\dfrac{1}{2}x = -4$

$x = 8$

(b) y-intercept = 4

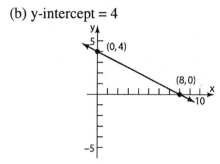

21.

x	$y = f(x)$	Avg. rate of change $= \dfrac{\Delta y}{\Delta x}$
−2	4	
−1	1	$\dfrac{1-4}{-1-(-2)} = \dfrac{-3}{1} = -3$
0	−2	$\dfrac{-2-1}{0-(-1)} = \dfrac{-3}{1} = -3$
1	−5	$\dfrac{-5-(-2)}{1-0} = \dfrac{-3}{1} = -3$
2	−8	$\dfrac{-8-(-5)}{2-1} = \dfrac{-3}{1} = -3$

This is a linear function with slope = −3, since the average rate of change is constant at −3.

23.

x	$y = f(x)$	Avg. rate of change $= \dfrac{\Delta y}{\Delta x}$
−2	−8	
−1	−3	$\dfrac{-3-(-8)}{-1-(-2)} = \dfrac{5}{1} = 5$
0	0	$\dfrac{0-(-3)}{0-(-1)} = \dfrac{3}{1} = 3$
1	1	
2	0	

This is not a linear function, since the average rate of change is not constant.

25.

x	$y = f(x)$	Avg. rate of change $= \dfrac{\Delta y}{\Delta x}$
−2	−26	
−1	−4	$\dfrac{-4-(-26)}{-1-(-2)} = \dfrac{22}{1} = 22$
0	2	$\dfrac{2-(-4)}{0-(-1)} = \dfrac{6}{1} = 6$
1	−2	
2	−10	

This is not a linear function, since the average rate of change is not constant.

27.

x	$y = f(x)$	Avg. rate of change $= \dfrac{\Delta y}{\Delta x}$
-2	8	
-1	8	$\dfrac{8-8}{-1-(-2)} = \dfrac{0}{1} = 0$
0	8	$\dfrac{8-8}{0-(-1)} = \dfrac{0}{1} = 0$
1	8	$\dfrac{8-8}{1-0} = \dfrac{0}{1} = 0$
2	8	$\dfrac{8-8}{2-1} = \dfrac{0}{1} = 0$

This is a linear function with slope $= 0$, since the average rate of change is constant at 0.

29. $f(x) = 4x - 1;\quad g(x) = -2x + 5$

(a) $f(x) = 4x - 1 = 0 \Rightarrow x = \dfrac{1}{4}$

(b) $f(x) = 4x - 1 > 0 \Rightarrow x > \dfrac{1}{4}$

(c) $f(x) = g(x) \Rightarrow 4x - 1 = -2x + 5$
$$4x - 1 = -2x + 5$$
$$6x = 6$$
$$x = 1$$

(d) $f(x) \le g(x) \Rightarrow 4x - 1 \le -2x + 5$
$$4x - 1 \le -2x + 5$$
$$6x \le 6$$
$$x \le 1$$

(e)

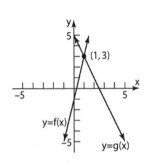

31. In each case, we must identify the x-coordinate of the point whose y-coordinate is given.

(a) $f(x) = 50 \Rightarrow y = 50 \Rightarrow x = 40$

(b) $f(x) = 80 \Rightarrow y = 80 \Rightarrow x = 88$

(c) $f(x) = 0 \Rightarrow y = 0 \Rightarrow x = -40$

(d) $f(x) > 50 \Rightarrow y > 50 \Rightarrow x > 40$

(e) $f(x) \le 80 \Rightarrow y \le 80 \Rightarrow x \le 88$

(f) $0 < f(x) < 80 \Rightarrow 0 < y < 80 \Rightarrow -40 < x < 88$

33. (a) $f(x) = g(x)$ when their graphs intersect, that is, when $x = -4$.

(b) $f(x) > g(x)$ when the graph of f is above the graph of g, that is, when $x < -4$.

35. (a) $f(x) = g(x)$ when their graphs intersect, that is, when $x = -6$.

(b) $g(x) \le f(x) < h(x)$ when the graph of f is above or intersects the graph of g and below the graph of h, that is, when $-6 \le x < 5$.

37. $C(x) = 0.25x + 35$

(a) $C(40) = 0.25(40) + 35 = 45$ dollars.

(b) Solve $C(x) = 0.25x + 35 = 80$

$$0.25x + 35 = 80 \Rightarrow 0.25x = 45 \Rightarrow x = \frac{45}{0.25} = 180 \text{ miles}$$

(c) Solve $C(x) = 0.25x + 35 < 100$

$$0.25x + 35 < 100$$

$$0.25x < 65 \Rightarrow x < \frac{65}{0.25} = 260 \text{ miles}$$

39. $B(t) = 19.25t + 585.72$

(a) $B(10) = 19.25(10) + 585.72 = 778.22$ dollars.

(b) Solve $B(t) = 19.25t + 585.72 = 893.72$

$$19.25t + 585.72 = 893.72$$

$$19.25t = 308$$

$$t = \frac{308}{19.25} = 16 \text{ years}$$

Therefore, the average monthly benefit will be $893.72 in the year 2006.

(c) Solve $B(t) = 19.25t + 585.72 > 1000$

$$19.25t + 585.72 > 1000$$

$$19.25t > 414.28$$

$$t > \frac{414.28}{19.25} \approx 21.52 \text{ years}$$

Therefore, the average monthly benefit will exceed $1000 in the year 2012.

41. $S(p) = -200 + 50p; \quad D(p) = 1000 - 25p$

(a) Solve $S(p) = D(p) \Rightarrow -200 + 50p = 1000 - 25p$

$$-200 + 50p = 1000 - 25p$$

$$75p = 1200$$

$$p = \frac{1200}{75} = 16$$

The equilibrium price is $16.

The equilibrium quantity is $S(16) = -200 + 50(16) = 600$ T-shirts.

(b) Solve $D(p) > S(p) \Rightarrow 1000 - 25p > -200 + 50p$

$$1000 - 25p > -200 + 50p$$

$$1200 > 75p$$

$$\frac{1200}{75} > p$$

$$16 > p$$

The demand will exceed supply when the price is less than $16.

(c) The price will eventually be increased.

43. $R(x) = 8x; \ C(x) = 4.5x + 17500$
   (a) Solve $R(x) = C(x) \Rightarrow 8x = 4.5x + 17500$

$$8x = 4.5x + 17500 \Rightarrow 3.5x = 17500 \Rightarrow x = \frac{17500}{3.5} = 5000$$

   The break-even point occurs when the company sells 5000 units.
   (b) Solve $R(x) > C(x) \Rightarrow 8x > 4.5x + 17500$

$$8x > 4.5x + 17500 \Rightarrow 3.5x > 17500 \Rightarrow x > \frac{17500}{3.5} = 5000$$

   The company makes a profit if it sells more than 5000 units.

45. (a) Consider the data points (x, y), where $x =$ the age in years of the computer and
   $y =$ the value in dollars of the computer. So we have the points $(0, 3000)$ and $(3, 0)$.
   The slope formula yields:

   $$\text{slope} = \frac{\Delta y}{\Delta x} = \frac{0 - 3000}{3 - 0} = \frac{-3000}{3} = -1000 = m$$

   $(0, 3000)$ is the y-intercept, so $b = 3000$
   Therefore, the linear function is $f(x) = mx + b = -1000x + 3000$.

   (b) The graph of $f(x) = -1000x + 3000$

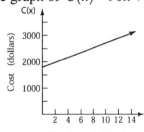

Book Value (dollars) — V(x) — Age

   (c) The computer's value after 2 years is
      given by
      $$f(2) = -1000(2) + 3000$$
      $$= -2000 + 3000 = \$1000$$

   (d) Solve $f(x) = -1000x + 3000 = 2000$
      $$-1000x + 3000 = 2000$$
      $$-1000x = -1000$$
      $$x = 1$$
   The computer will be worth $2000 after 1 year.

47.(a) Let $x =$ the number of bicycles manufactured. We can use the cost function
      $C(x) = mx + b$, with $m = 90$ and $b = 1800$.
   Therefore $C(x) = 90x + 1800$

   (b) The graph of $C(x) = 90x + 1800$

C(x) — Cost (dollars) — 3000, 2000, 1000 — 2 4 6 8 10 12 14 — Number of Bicycles

   (c) The cost of manufacturing 14 bicycles is given by $C(14) = 90(14) + 1800 = \$3060$.
   (d) Solve $C(x) = 90x + 1800 = 3780$
      $$90x + 1800 = 3780$$
      $$90x = 1980 \Rightarrow x = 22$$
   So 22 bicycles could be manufactured for $3780.

49. (a) Let x = number of miles driven, and let C = cost in dollars.
Total cost = (cost per mile)(number of miles) + fixed cost
$$C(x) = 0.07x + 29$$
(b) $C(110) = (0.07)(110) + 29 = \$36.70.$
$C(230) = (0.07)(230) + 29 = \$45.10.$

51. (d) and (e)

53. A linear function $f(x) = mx + b$ will be odd provided $f(-x) = -f(x)$.
That is, provided $m(-x) + b = -(mx + b)$.
$$-mx + b = -mx - b$$
$$b = -b \Rightarrow 2b = 0 \Rightarrow b = 0$$
So a linear function $f(x) = mx + b$ will be odd provided $b = 0$.
A linear function $f(x) = mx + b$ will be even provided $f(-x) = f(x)$.
That is, provided $m(-x) + b = mx + b$.
$$-mx + b = mx + b$$
$$-mxb = mx \Rightarrow 0 = 2mx \Rightarrow m = 0$$
So a linear function $f(x) = mx + b$ will be even provided $m = 0$.

55. Answers will vary.

Linear Functions and Models

2.2 Equations of Lines; Building Linear Functions

1. (a) Slope $= \dfrac{1-0}{2-0} = \dfrac{1}{2}$

   (b) If x increases by 2 units, y will increase by 1 unit.

3. (a) Slope $= \dfrac{1-2}{1-(-2)} = -\dfrac{1}{3}$

   (b) If x increases by 3 units, y will decrease by 1 unit.

5. (2,3) and (4,0) are points on the line.

   (a) Slope $= \dfrac{0-3}{4-2} = \dfrac{-3}{2} = -\dfrac{3}{2}$

   (b) point-slope form of line with (4,0):
   $$y - y_1 = m(x - x_1)$$
   $$y - 0 = -\dfrac{3}{2}(x - 4)$$

7. (−2,3) and (2,1) are points on the line.

   (a) Slope $= \dfrac{1-3}{2-(-2)} = \dfrac{-2}{4} = -\dfrac{1}{2}$

   (b) point-slope form of line with (2,1):
   $$y - y_1 = m(x - x_1)$$
   $$y - 1 = -\dfrac{1}{2}(x - 2)$$

9. (−3,−1) and (2,−1) are points on the line.

   (a) Slope $= \dfrac{-1-(-1)}{2-(-3)} = \dfrac{0}{5} = 0$

   (b) point-slope form of line with (2,−1):
   $$y - y_1 = m(x - x_1)$$
   $$y - (-1) = 0 \cdot (x - 2)$$

11. (−1,2) and (−1,−2) are points on the line.

   (a) Slope $= \dfrac{-2-2}{-1-(--1)} = \dfrac{-4}{0}$

   $\Rightarrow$ slope is undefined

   (b) no point-slope form of line.

   Equation is $x = -1$.

13. (0,0) and (2,1) are points on the line.

   Slope $= \dfrac{1-0}{2-0} = \dfrac{1}{2}$

   y-intercept is 0; using $y = mx + b$:
   $$y = \dfrac{1}{2}x + 0$$
   $$2y = x$$
   $$0 = x - 2y$$
   $$x - 2y = 0 \quad \text{or} \quad y = \dfrac{1}{2}x$$

15. (−1,3) and (1,1) are points on the line.

   Slope $= \dfrac{1-3}{1-(-1)} = \dfrac{-2}{2} = -1$

   Using $y - y_1 = m(x - x_1)$
   $$y - 1 = -1(x - 1)$$
   $$y - 1 = -x + 1$$
   $$y = -x + 2$$
   $$x + y = 2 \quad \text{or} \quad y = -x + 2$$

17. $y - y_1 = m(x - x_1),\ \ m = 2$
$$y - 3 = 2(x - 3)$$
$$y - 3 = 2x - 6$$
$$y = 2x - 3$$
$$2x - y = 3\ \ \text{or}\ \ y = 2x - 3$$

19. $y - y_1 = m(x - x_1),\ \ m = -\dfrac{1}{2}$
$$y - 2 = -\frac{1}{2}(x - 1)$$
$$y - 2 = -\frac{1}{2}x + \frac{1}{2}$$
$$y = -\frac{1}{2}x + \frac{5}{2}$$
$$x + 2y = 5\ \ \text{or}\ \ y = -\frac{1}{2}x + \frac{5}{2}$$

21. Slope = 3; containing (–2,3)
$$y - y_1 = m(x - x_1)$$
$$y - 3 = 3(x - (-2))$$
$$y - 3 = 3x + 6$$
$$y = 3x + 9$$
$$3x - y = -9\ \ \text{or}\ \ y = 3x + 9$$

23. Slope $= -\dfrac{2}{3}$; containing (1,–1)
$$y - y_1 = m(x - x_1)$$
$$y - (-1) = -\frac{2}{3}(x - 1)$$
$$y + 1 = -\frac{2}{3}x + \frac{2}{3}$$
$$y = -\frac{2}{3}x - \frac{1}{3}$$
$$2x + 3y = -1\ \ \text{or}\ \ y = -\frac{2}{3}x - \frac{1}{3}$$

25. Containing (1,3) and (–1,2)
$$m = \frac{2 - 3}{-1 - 1} = \frac{-1}{-2} = \frac{1}{2}$$
$$y - y_1 = m(x - x_1)$$
$$y - 3 = \frac{1}{2}(x - 1)$$
$$y - 3 = \frac{1}{2}x - \frac{1}{2}$$
$$y = \frac{1}{2}x + \frac{5}{2}$$
$$x - 2y = -5\ \ \text{or}\ \ y = \frac{1}{2}x + \frac{5}{2}$$

27. Slope = –3; y-intercept = 3
$$y = mx + b$$
$$y = -3x + 3$$
$$3x + y = 3\ \ \text{or}\ \ y = -3x + 3$$

29. x-intercept = 2; y-intercept = –1
Points are (2,0) and (0,–1)
$$m = \frac{-1 - 0}{0 - 2} = \frac{-1}{-2} = \frac{1}{2}$$
$$y = mx + b$$
$$y = \frac{1}{2}x - 1$$
$$x - 2y = 2\ \ \text{or}\ \ y = \frac{1}{2}x - 1$$

31. Slope undefined; passing through (2,4)
This is a vertical line.
$$x = 2$$
No slope intercept form.

33. Parallel to $y = 2x$; Slope = 2
     Containing $(-1,2)$
     $$y - y_1 = m(x - x_1)$$
     $$y - 2 = 2(x - (-1))$$
     $$y - 2 = 2x + 2 \Rightarrow y = 2x + 4$$
     $$2x - y = -4 \text{ or } y = 2x + 4$$

35. Parallel to $2x - y = -2$;
     $$2x - y = -2$$
     $$-y = -2x - 2 \Rightarrow y = 2x + 2$$
     Slope = 2
     Containing the point $(0,0)$
     $$y - y_1 = m(x - x_1)$$
     $$y - 0 = 2(x - 0)$$
     $$y = 2x$$
     $$2x - y = 0 \text{ or } y = 2x$$

37. Parallel to $x = 5$;
     Containing $(4,2)$
     This is a vertical line.
     $x = 4$
          No slope intercept form.

39. Perpendicular to $y = \dfrac{1}{2}x + 4$;
     Slope of perpendicular = -2
     Containing $(1,-2)$
     $$y - y_1 = m(x - x_1)$$
     $$y - (-2) = -2(x - 1)$$
     $$y + 2 = -2x + 2 \Rightarrow y = -2x$$
     $$2x + y = 0 \text{ or } y = -2x$$

41. Perpendicular to $2x + y = 2$;
     $2x + y = 2 \Rightarrow y = -2x + 2$
     Containing $(-3,0)$
     Slope of perpendicular $= \dfrac{1}{2}$
     $$y - y_1 = m(x - x_1)$$
     $$y - 0 = \dfrac{1}{2}(x - (-3)) \Rightarrow y = \dfrac{1}{2}x + \dfrac{3}{2}$$
     $$x - 2y = -3 \text{ or } y = \dfrac{1}{2}x + \dfrac{3}{2}$$

43. Perpendicular to $x = 8$;
     Slope of perpendicular = 0
     Containing $(3,4)$
     $$y - y_1 = m(x - x_1)$$
     $$y - 4 = 0(x - 3) \Rightarrow y - 4 = 0 \Rightarrow y = 4$$
     $$y = 4 \text{ or } y = 0x + 4$$

45. $y = 2x + 3$
     Slope = 2
     y-intercept = 3

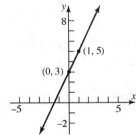

47. $\dfrac{1}{2}y = x - 1$
     $y = 2x - 2$; Slope = 2
     y-intercept = -2

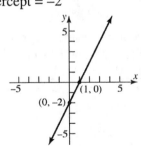

49. $y = \dfrac{1}{2}x + 2$

Slope $= \dfrac{1}{2}$

y-intercept $= 2$

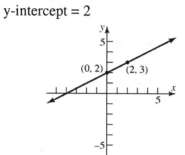

51. $x + 2y = 4$

$2y = -x + 4 \Rightarrow y = -\dfrac{1}{2}x + 2$

Slope $= -\dfrac{1}{2}$

y-intercept $= 2$

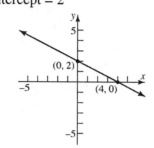

53. $2x - 3y = 6$

$-3y = -2x + 6 \Rightarrow y = \dfrac{2}{3}x - 2$

Slope $= \dfrac{2}{3}$

y-intercept $= -2$

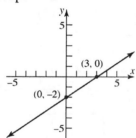

55. $x + y = 1$

$y = -x + 1$

Slope $= -1$

y-intercept $= 1$

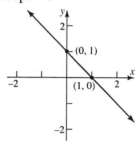

57. $x = -4$

Slope is undefined

y-intercept - none

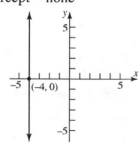

59. $y = 5$

Slope $= 0$

y-intercept $= 5$

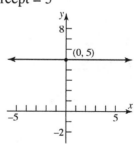

61. $y - x = 0$
     $y = x$
     Slope = 1
     y-intercept = 0

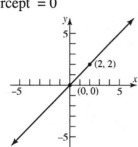

63. $2y - 3x = 0$

     $2y = 3x \Rightarrow y = \dfrac{3}{2}x$

     Slope = $\dfrac{3}{2}$; y-intercept = 0

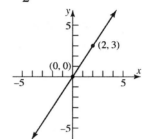

65. The equation of the x-axis is $y = 0$. (The slope is 0 and the y-intercept is 0.)

67. $f(x) = 5x$
(a) $\dfrac{f(x) - f(1)}{x - 1} = \dfrac{5x - 5}{x - 1} = \dfrac{5(x - 1)}{x - 1} = 5$

(b) $\dfrac{f(2) - f(1)}{2 - 1} = \dfrac{10 - 5}{2 - 1} = \dfrac{5}{1} = 5$

(c) Slope = 5; Containing $(1, 5)$:
     $y - 5 = 5(x - 1)$

     $y - 5 = 5x - 5 \Rightarrow y = 5x$

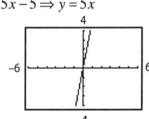

69. $f(x) = 1 - 3x$
(a) $\dfrac{f(x) - f(1)}{x - 1} = \dfrac{1 - 3x - (-2)}{x - 1}$

     $= \dfrac{-3x + 3}{x - 1} = \dfrac{-3(x - 1)}{x - 1} = -3$

(b) $\dfrac{f(2) - f(1)}{2 - 1} = \dfrac{1 - 3(2) - (-2)}{2 - 1} = \dfrac{-3}{1} = -3$

(c) Slope = -3; Containing $(1, -2)$:
     $y - (-2) = -3(x - 1)$

     $y + 2 = -3x + 3 \Rightarrow y = -3x + 1$

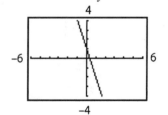

71. $f(x) = x^2 - 2x$
(a) $\dfrac{f(x) - f(1)}{x - 1} = \dfrac{x^2 - 2x - (-1)}{x - 1}$

     $= \dfrac{x^2 - 2x + 1}{x - 1} = \dfrac{(x - 1)^2}{x - 1} = x - 1$

(b) $\dfrac{f(2) - f(1)}{2 - 1} = \dfrac{2^2 - 2(2) - (-1)}{2 - 1} = \dfrac{1}{1} = 1$

(c) Slope = 1; Containing $(1, -1)$:
     $y - (-1) = 1(x - 1)$

     $y + 1 = 1x - 1 \Rightarrow y = x - 2$

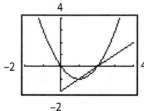

73. $f(x) = x^3 - x$

(a) $\dfrac{f(x) - f(1)}{x - 1} = \dfrac{x^3 - x - 0}{x - 1} = \dfrac{x^3 - x}{x - 1}$

$= \dfrac{x(x-1)(x+1)}{x-1} = x^2 + x = x(x+1)$

(b) $\dfrac{f(2) - f(1)}{2 - 1} = \dfrac{2^3 - 2 - 0}{2 - 1} = \dfrac{6}{1} = 6$

(c) Slope = 6; Containing (1, 0):

$y - 0 = 6(x - 1) \Rightarrow y = 6x - 6$

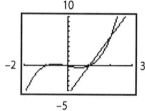

75. $f(x) = \dfrac{2}{x+1}$

(a)

$\dfrac{f(x) - f(1)}{x - 1} = \dfrac{\left(\dfrac{2}{x+1} - 1\right)}{x - 1} = \dfrac{\left(\dfrac{2 - x - 1}{x+1}\right)}{x - 1}$

$= \dfrac{1 - x}{(x-1)(x+1)} = \dfrac{-1}{x+1}$

(b)

$\dfrac{f(2) - f(1)}{2 - 1} = \dfrac{\left(\dfrac{2}{2+1} - 1\right)}{2 - 1} = \dfrac{\left(-\dfrac{1}{3}\right)}{1} = -\dfrac{1}{3}$

(c) Slope $= -\dfrac{1}{3}$; Containing (1, 1):

$y - 1 = -\dfrac{1}{3}(x - 1)$

$y - 1 = -\dfrac{1}{3}x + \dfrac{1}{3} \Rightarrow y = -\dfrac{1}{3}x + \dfrac{4}{3}$

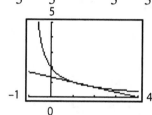

77. $f(x) = \sqrt{x}$

(a) $\dfrac{f(x) - f(1)}{x - 1} = \dfrac{\sqrt{x} - 1}{x - 1}$

(b) $\dfrac{f(2) - f(1)}{2 - 1} = \dfrac{\sqrt{2} - 1}{1} = \sqrt{2} - 1$

(c) Slope $= \sqrt{2} - 1$; Containing (1, 1):

$y - 1 = \left(\sqrt{2} - 1\right)(x - 1)$

$y - 1 = \left(\sqrt{2} - 1\right)x - \left(\sqrt{2} - 1\right)$

$y = \left(\sqrt{2} - 1\right)x - \sqrt{2} + 2$

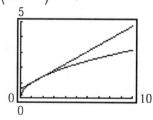

79. $f(x) = 2x + 5$

    (a) $m_{sec} = \dfrac{f(x+h) - f(x)}{h} = \dfrac{2(x+h) + 5 - 2x - 5}{h} = \dfrac{2h}{h} = 2$

    (b)   When $x = 1$,

        $h = 0.5 \Rightarrow m_{sec} = 2$

        $h = 0.1 \Rightarrow m_{sec} = 2$

        $h = 0.01 \Rightarrow m_{sec} = 2$

        as $h \to 0$, $m_{sec} \to 2$

    (c)   Using point $(1, f(1)) = (1, 7)$ and slope $= 2$, we get the secant line:

        $y - 7 = 2(x - 1) \Rightarrow y - 7 = 2x - 2 \Rightarrow y = 2x + 5$

    (d)   Graphing:

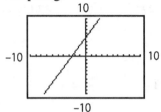

81. $f(x) = x^2 + 2x$

    (a) $m_{sec} = \dfrac{f(x+h) - f(x)}{h} = \dfrac{(x+h)^2 + 2(x+h) - (x^2 + 2x)}{h}$

        $= \dfrac{x^2 + 2xh + h^2 + 2x + 2h - x^2 - 2x}{h} = \dfrac{2xh + h^2 + 2h}{h} = 2x + h + 2$

    (b)   When $x = 1$,

        $h = 0.5 \Rightarrow m_{sec} = 2 \cdot 1 + 0.5 + 2 = 4.5$

        $h = 0.1 \Rightarrow m_{sec} = 2 \cdot 1 + 0.1 + 2 = 4.1$

        $h = 0.01 \Rightarrow m_{sec} = 2 \cdot 1 + 0.01 + 2 = 4.01$

        as $h \to 0$, $m_{sec} \to 2 \cdot 1 + 0 + 2 = 4$

    (c)   Using point $(1, f(1)) = (1, 3)$ and slope $= 4.01$, we get the secant line:

        $y - 3 = 4.01(x - 1) \Rightarrow y - 3 = 4.01x - 4.01 \Rightarrow y = 4.01x - 1.01$

    (d)   Graphing:

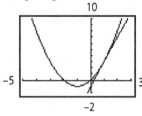

83. $f(x) = 2x^2 - 3x + 1$

(a)
$$m_{sec} = \frac{f(x+h) - f(x)}{h} = \frac{2(x+h)^2 - 3(x+h) + 1 - (2x^2 - 3x + 1)}{h}$$

$$= \frac{2(x^2 + 2xh + h^2) - 3x - 3h + 1 - 2x^2 + 3x - 1}{h}$$

$$= \frac{2x^2 + 4xh + 2h^2 - 3x - 3h + 1 - 2x^2 + 3x - 1}{h}$$

$$= \frac{4xh + 2h^2 - 3h}{h} = 4x + 2h - 3$$

(b) When $x = 1$,
$h = 0.5 \Rightarrow m_{sec} = 4 \cdot 1 + 2(0.5) - 3 = 2$
$h = 0.1 \Rightarrow m_{sec} = 4 \cdot 1 + 2(0.1) - 3 = 1.2$
$h = 0.01 \Rightarrow m_{sec} = 4 \cdot 1 + 2(0.01) - 3 = 1.02$
as $h \to 0$, $m_{sec} \to 4 \cdot 1 + 2(0) - 3 = 1$

(c) Using point $(1, f(1)) = (1, 0)$ and slope = 1.02, we get the secant line:
$y - 0 = 1.02(x - 1) \Rightarrow y = 1.02x - 1.02$

(d) Graphing:

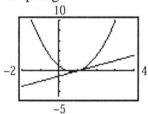

85. $f(x) = \dfrac{1}{x}$

(a)
$$m_{sec} = \frac{f(x+h) - f(x)}{h} = \frac{\left(\dfrac{1}{x+h} - \dfrac{1}{x}\right)}{h}$$

$$= \frac{\left(\dfrac{x - (x+h)}{(x+h)x}\right)}{h} = \left(\frac{x - x - h}{(x+h)x}\right)\left(\frac{1}{h}\right) = \left(\frac{-h}{(x+h)x}\right)\left(\frac{1}{h}\right) = -\frac{1}{(x+h)x}$$

(b) When $x = 1$,
$$h = 0.5 \Rightarrow m_{sec} = -\frac{1}{(1+0.5)(1)} = -\frac{1}{1.5} = -\frac{2}{3}$$

$$h = 0.1 \Rightarrow m_{sec} = -\frac{1}{(1+0.1)(1)} = -\frac{1}{1.1} = -\frac{10}{11}$$

$$h = 0.01 \Rightarrow m_{sec} = -\frac{1}{(1+0.01)(1)} = -\frac{1}{1.01} = -\frac{100}{101}$$

as $h \to 0$, $m_{sec} \to -\dfrac{1}{(1+0)(1)} = -\dfrac{1}{1} = -1$

(c) Using point $\left(1, f(1)\right) = (1,1)$ and slope $= -\dfrac{100}{101}$, we get the secant line:

$$y - 1 = -\frac{100}{101}(x - 1) \Rightarrow y - 1 = -\frac{100}{101}x + \frac{100}{101} \Rightarrow y = -\frac{100}{101}x + \frac{201}{101}$$

(d) Graphing:

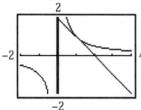

87. (b)

89. (d)

91. Slope = 1; y-intercept = 2
$y = x + 2$ or $x - y = -2$

93. Slope $= -\dfrac{1}{3}$; y-intercept = 1

$y = -\dfrac{1}{3}x + 1$ or $x + 3y = 3$

95. $(^\circ C, ^\circ F) = (0, 32);$ $(^\circ C, ^\circ F) = (100, 212)$

$$\text{slope} \;=\; \frac{212 - 32}{100 - 0} = \frac{180}{100} = \frac{9}{5}$$

$$^\circ F - 32 = \frac{9}{5}(^\circ C - 0)$$

$$^\circ F - 32 = \frac{9}{5}(^\circ C)$$

$$^\circ C = \frac{5}{9}(^\circ F - 32)$$

If $^\circ F = 70$, then

$$^\circ C = \frac{5}{9}(70 - 32) = \frac{5}{9}(38)$$

$$^\circ C \approx 21.11^\circ$$

97. (a) Since there is only a profit of $0.50 per copy and the expense of $100 must be deducted, the profit is:
$$P = 0.50x - 100$$
(b) $P = 0.50(1000) - 100$
$$= 500 - 100 = \$400$$
(c) $P = 0.50(5000) - 100$
$$= 2500 - 100 = \$2400$$

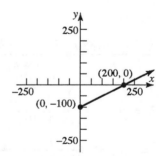

99. $C = 0.06543x + 5.65$
For 300 kWh,
$$C = 0.06543(300) + 5.65 = \$25.28$$
For 750 kWh,
$$C = 0.06543(750) + 5.65 = \$54.72$$

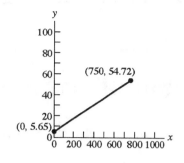

101. $2x - y = C$
Graph the lines:
$$2x - y = -4$$
$$2x - y = 0$$
$$2x - y = 2$$
All the lines have the same slope, 2.
The lines are parallel.

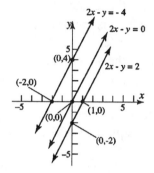

103. (c)

105. No, the equation of a vertical line cannot be written in slope-intercept form since the slope is undefined.

107. If two lines have equal slopes and equal y-intercepts, then their equations must be equivalent.

109. If two lines have the same slope, but different x-intercepts, then the lines cannot have the same y-intercept.
Proof:
Case 1: The two lines are vertical with different x-intercepts.
Suppose Line 1 has equation $x = a_1$ and Line 2 has equation $x = a_2$, with $a_1 \neq a_2$.
The only possible y-intercept is if either $a_1 = 0$ or $a_2 = 0$. And since we are assuming that $a_1 \neq a_2$, the lines cannot have the same y-intercept.
Case 2: The two lines are horizontal with different x-intercepts.
Suppose Line 1 has equation $y = b_1$ and Line 2 has equation $y = b_2$, with $b_1 \neq b_2$.
The only possible x-intercept is if either $b_1 = 0$ or $b_2 = 0$. And since we are assuming that $b_1 \neq b_2$, the lines cannot have the same y-intercept
Case 3: The two lines are non-vertical and non-horizontal with different x-intercepts.
Suppose Line 1 has equation $y = mx + b_1$ and Line 2 has equation $y = mx + b_1$, with $b \neq 0$. That is, suppose Line 1 and Line 2 have the same non-zero slope and the same y-intercept.
To find the x-intercept of each line, we solve $0 = mx + b_1$ for x.
$$0 = mx + b_1 \Rightarrow -b_1 = mx \Rightarrow x = \frac{-b_1}{m}$$
Therefore, Line 1 and Line 2 would have the same x-intercept, which contradicts the original assumption. Therefore, the lines cannot have the same y-intercept.

Linear Functions and Models

2.3   Setting up Linear Equations; Applications

1. Let A represent the area of the circle and r the radius.
    The area of a circle is the product of π times the square of the radius. $A = \pi r^2$

3. Let A represent the area of the square and s the length of a side.
    The area of the square is the square of the length of a side. $A = s^2$

5. Let F represent the force, m the mass, and a the acceleration.
    Force equals the product of the mass times the acceleration. $F = ma$

7. Let W represent the work, F the force, and d the distance.
    Work equals force times distance. $W = Fd$

9. C = total variable cost in dollars, x = number of dishwashers manufactured.
    $C = 150x$

11.

Amount in Bonds	Amount in CD's	Total
x	$x - 3000$	20,000

$x + x - 3000 = 20000$

$2x - 3000 = 20000 \Rightarrow 2x = 23000 \Rightarrow x = 11500$

$11,500 will be invested in bonds. $8,500 will be invested in CD's

13.

Scott	Alice	Tricia	Total
x	$\dfrac{3}{4}x$	$\dfrac{1}{2}x$	900,000

$$x + \frac{3}{4}x + \frac{1}{2}x = 900,000 \Rightarrow \frac{9}{4}x = 900,000$$

$$x = \frac{4}{9}(900,000) \Rightarrow x = 400,000$$

Scott receives $400,000. Alice receives $\dfrac{3}{4}(400000) = \$300,000$.

Tricia receives $\dfrac{1}{2}(400000) = \$200,000$.

15.

	Dollars per hour	Number of hours worked	Money earned
Regular wage	x	40	$40x$
Overtime wage	$1.5x$	8	$(1.5x)(8)$

$40x + (1.5x)(8) = 442$

$40x + 12x = 442$

$52x = 442$

$x = \dfrac{442}{52} = 8.50$

Sandra's regular hourly wage is $8.50.

17.   Let x represent the score on the final exam and construct the table

	Test1	Test2	Test3	Test4	Test5	Final Exam
score	80	83	71	61	95	x
weight	1/7	1/7	1/7	1/7	1/7	2/7

Compute the final average and set equal to 80.

$(1/7)(80 + 83 + 71 + 61 + 95) + (2/7)x = 80$

Now solve for x:

$(1/7)(390) + (2/7)x = 80$

$390 + 2x = 560$

$2x = 170 \Rightarrow x = 85$

Brooke needs to score an 85 on the final exam to get an average of 80 in the course.

19.   Let x represent the original price of the house.

Then $0.15x$ represents the reduction in the price of the house.

original price – reduction = new price

$x - 0.15x = 125,000$

$0.85x = 125,000$

$x = 147,058.82$

The original price of the house was $147,058.82.

The amount of the savings is $0.15($147,058.82) = $22,058.82$.

21.   Let x represent the price the bookstore pays for the book (publisher price).

Then $0.35x$ represents the mark up on the book.

The selling price of the book is $56.00.

publisher price + mark up = selling price

$x + 0.35x = 56.00$

$1.35x = 56.00$

$x = \dfrac{56.00}{1.35} \approx 41.48$

The bookstore pays $41.48 for the book.

23.

	Number of tickets sold	Price per ticket	Money earned
adults	x	4.75	$4.75x$
children	$5200 - x$	2.5	$(5200 - x)(2.5)$

money from adult tickets + money from children tickets = total receipts
$$4.75x + (5200 - x)(2.5) = 20,335 \Rightarrow 4.75x + 13,000 - 2.5x = 20,335$$

$$2.25x = 7335 \Rightarrow x = \frac{7335}{2.25} = 3260$$

There were 3260 adult patrons.

25. l = length, w = width
$$2l + 2w = 60 \qquad \text{Perimeter } = 2l + 2w$$

$$l = w + 8 \qquad \text{The length is 8 more than the width.}$$

$$2(w + 8) + 2w = 60$$

$$2w + 16 + 2w = 60 \Rightarrow 4w + 16 = 60$$

$$4w = 44 \Rightarrow w = 11 \text{ feet, } l = 19 \text{ feet}$$

27. Let x represent the amount of money invested in bonds.
Then $50,000 - x$ represents the amount of money invested in CD's.

	Principle	Rate	Time (yrs)	Interest
Bonds	x	0.15	1	$0.15x$
CD's	$50,000 - x$	0.07	1	$0.07(50,000 - x)$

Since the total interest is to be $6,000, we have:
$$0.15x + 0.07(50,000 - x) = 6,000$$

$$(100)(0.15x + 0.07(50,000 - x)) = (6,000)(100)$$

$$15x + 7(50,000 - x) = 600,000$$

$$15x + 350,000 - 7x = 600,000$$

$$8x + 350,000 = 600,000 \Rightarrow 8x = 250,000 \Rightarrow x = 31,250$$

$31,250 should be invested in bonds at 15% and $18,750 should be invested in CD's at 7%.

29. Let x represent the amount of money loaned at 8%.
Then $12,000 - x$ represents the amount of money loaned at 18%.

	Principle	Rate	Time (yrs)	Interest
Loan at 8%	x	0.08	1	$0.08x$
Loan at 18%	$12,000 - x$	0.18	1	$0.18(12,000 - x)$

Since the total interest is to be $1,000, we have:
$$0.08x + 0.18(12,000 - x) = 1,000$$

$$(100)(0.08x + 0.18(12,000 - x)) = (1,000)(100)$$

$$8x + 18(12,000 - x) = 100,000$$

$$8x + 216,000 - 18x = 100,000$$

$$-10x + 216,000 = 100,000 \Rightarrow -10x = -116,000 \Rightarrow x = 11,600$$

$11,600 is loaned at 8% and $400 is loaned at 18%.

31.   Let x represent the number of pounds of Earl Gray tea.
       Then $100 - x$ represents the number of pounds of Orange Pekoe tea.

	No. of pounds	Price per pound	Total Value
Earl Gray	x	\$5.00	$5x$
Orange Pekoe	$100 - x$	\$3.00	$3(100 - x)$
Blend	100	\$4.50	$4.50(100)$

$$5x + 3(100 - x) = 4.50(100) \Rightarrow 5x + 300 - 3x = 450$$

$$2x + 300 = 450 \Rightarrow 2x = 150 \Rightarrow x = 75$$

75 pounds of Earl Gray tea must be blended with 25 pounds of Orange Pekoe.

33.   Let x represent the number of pounds of cashews.
       Then $x + 60$ represents the number of pounds in the mixture.

	No. of pounds	Price per pound	Total Value
cashews	x	\$4.00	$4x$
peanuts	60	\$1.50	$1.50(60)$
mixture	$x + 60$	\$2.50	$2.50(x + 60)$

$$4x + 1.50(60) = 2.50(x + 60) \Rightarrow 4x + 90 = 2.50x + 150$$

$$1.5x = 60 \Rightarrow x = 40$$

40 pounds of cashews must be added to the 60 pounds of peanuts.

35.   Let r represent the speed of the current.

	Rate	Time	Distance
Upstream	$16 - r$	$\dfrac{20}{60} = \dfrac{1}{3}$	$\dfrac{16 - r}{3}$
Downstream	$16 + r$	$\dfrac{15}{60} = \dfrac{1}{4}$	$\dfrac{16 + r}{4}$

Since the distance is the same in each direction:

$$\frac{16 - r}{3} = \frac{16 + r}{4}$$

$$4(16 - r) = 3(16 + r)$$

$$64 - 4r = 48 + 3r \Rightarrow 16 = 7r \Rightarrow r = \frac{16}{7} \approx 2.286$$

The speed of the current is approximately 2.286 miles per hour.

37.   Let r represent the rate of the Metra commuter train.
       Then $r + 50$ represents the rate of the Amtrak train.

	Rate	Time	Distance
Metra train	r	3	$3r$
Amtrak train	$r + 50$	1	$r + 50$

Amtrak distance = Metra distance $- 10$

$$r + 50 = 3r - 10$$

$$60 = 2r \Rightarrow r = 30$$

The Metra commuter train travels at a rate of 30 miles per hour.
The Amtrak train travels at a rate of 80 miles per hour.

39. Let t represent the time it takes to do the job together.

	Time to do job	Part of job done in one minute
Trent	30	1/30
Lois	20	1/20
Together	t	$1/t$

$$\frac{1}{30} + \frac{1}{20} = \frac{1}{t} \Rightarrow 2t + 3t = 60 \Rightarrow 5t = 60 \Rightarrow t = 12$$

Working together, the job can be done in 12 minutes.

41. l = length of the garden
w = width of the garden
(a) The length of the garden is to be twice its width. Thus, $l = 2w$.
The dimensions of the fence are $l + 4$ and $w + 4$.
The perimeter is 46 feet, so:
$$2(l+4) + 2(w+4) = 46$$
$$2(2w+4) + 2(w+4) = 46$$
$$4w + 8 + 2w + 8 = 46$$
$$6w + 16 = 46$$
$$6w = 30$$
$$w = 5$$
The dimensions of the garden are 10 feet by 5 feet.
(b) Area $= l \cdot w = 5 \cdot 10 = 50$ square feet
(c) If the dimensions of the garden are the same, then the length and width of the fence are also the same $(l + 4)$. The perimeter is 46 feet, so:
$$2(l+4) + 2(l+4) = 46$$
$$2l + 8 + 2l + 8 = 46$$
$$4l + 16 = 46$$
$$4l = 30$$
$$l = 7.5$$
The dimensions of the garden are 7.5 feet by 7.5 feet.
(d) Area $= l \cdot w = 7.5(7.5) = 56.25$ square feet.

43. Let t represent the time it takes for the defensive back to catch the tight end.

	Time to run 100 yards	Time	Rate	Distance
Tight End	12 sec	t	$100/12 = 25/3$	$25t/3$
Defensive Back	10 sec	t	$100/10 = 10$	$10t$

Since the defensive back has to run 5 yards farther, we have:
$$\frac{25}{3}t + 5 = 10t \Rightarrow 25t + 15 = 30t$$
$$15 = 5t \Rightarrow t = 3 \qquad \Rightarrow \qquad 10t = 30$$
The defensive back will catch the tight end at the 45 yard line.

45. Let x represent the number of ounces of pure water.
     Then $x + 1$ represents the number of gallons in the 60% solution.

	No. of gallons	Conc. of Antifreeze	Pure Antifreeze
water	x	0	0
100% antifreeze	1	1.00	1(1)
60% antifreeze	$x + 1$	0.60	$0.60(x + 1)$

$$0 + 1(1) = 0.60(x + 1)$$

$$1 = 0.6x + 0.6 \Rightarrow 0.4 = 0.6x \Rightarrow x = \frac{4}{6} = \frac{2}{3}$$

$\frac{2}{3}$ gallon of pure water should be added.

47. Let x represent the number of ounces of water to be evaporated.

	No. of ounces	Conc. of Salt	Pure Salt
Water	x	0.00	0
4% Salt	32	0.04	0.04(32)
6% Salt	$32 - x$	0.06	$0.06(32 - x)$

$$0 + 0.04(32) = 0.06(32 - x)$$

$$1.28 = 1.92 - 0.06x \Rightarrow 0.06x = 0.64 \Rightarrow x = \frac{0.64}{0.06} = \frac{32}{3} \approx 10.67$$

10.67 ounces of water need to be evaporated.

49. Let x represent the number of grams of pure gold.
     Then $60 - x$ represents the number of grams of 12 karat gold to be used.

	No. of grams	Conc. of gold	Pure gold
Pure gold	x	1.00	x
12 karat gold	$60 - x$	1/2	$\frac{1}{2}(60 - x)$
16 karat gold	60	2/3	$\frac{2}{3}(60) = 20$

$$x + \frac{1}{2}(60 - x) = 20 \Rightarrow x + 30 - 0.5x = 40 \Rightarrow 0.5x = 10 \Rightarrow x = 20$$

20 grams of pure gold should be mixed with 40 grams of 12 karat gold.

51. Let t represent the time it takes for Mike to catch up with Dan.

	Time to run mile	Time	Part of mile run in one minute	Distance
Mike	6	t	1/6	$t/6$
Dan	9	$t + 1$	1/9	$(t + 1)/9$

Since the distances are the same, we have:

$$\frac{1}{6}t = \frac{1}{9}(t + 1) \Rightarrow 3t = 2t + 2 \Rightarrow t = 2$$

Mike will pass Dan after 2 minutes, which is a distance of 1/3 mile.

53.   Let t represent the time the auxiliary pump needs to run.

	Time to do job alone	Part of job done in one hour	Time on Job	Part of total job done by each pump
Main Pump	4	1/4	3	3/4
Auxiliary Pump	9	1/9	t	$t/9$

Since the two pumps are emptying one tanker, we have:

$$\frac{3}{4} + \frac{1}{9}t = 1 \Rightarrow 27 + 4t = 36 \Rightarrow 4t = 9 \Rightarrow t = \frac{9}{4} = 2.25$$

The auxiliary pump must run for 2.25 hours. It must be started at 9:45 a.m.

55.   Let t represent the time for the tub to fill with the faucets on and the stopper removed.

	Time to do job alone	Part of job done in one minute	Time on Job	Part of total job done by each
Faucets open	15	1/15	t	$t/15$
Stopper removed	20	−1/20	t	$-t/20$

Since one tub is being filled, we have:

$$\frac{t}{15} + \left(-\frac{t}{20}\right) = 1$$

$$4t - 3t = 60 \qquad \therefore \ \ 60 \text{ minutes is required to fill the tub.}$$

$$t = 60$$

57.   Let $p =$ the monthly payment and $B =$ the amount borrowed.

Consider the ordered pair (B,p).

We can use the points $(0,0)$ and $(1000,6.49)$.

Now compute the slope:

$$\text{slope} = \frac{\Delta y}{\Delta x} = \frac{6.49 - 0}{1000 - 0} = \frac{6.49}{1000} = 0.00649$$

Therefore we have the linear function $p(B) = 0.00649B + 0 = 0.00649B$.

If $B = 145000$, then $p = (0.00649)(145000) = \$941.05$.

59.   Let $R =$ the revenue and $g =$ the number of gallons of gasoline sold.

Consider the ordered pair (g,R).

We can use the points $(0,0)$ and $(12,15.84)$.

Now compute the slope:

$$\text{slope} = \frac{\Delta y}{\Delta x} = \frac{15.84 - 0}{12 - 0} = \frac{15.84}{12} = 1.32$$

Therefore we have the linear function $R(g) = 1.32g + 0 = 1.32g$.

If $g = 10.5$, then $R = (1.32)(10.5) \approx \$13.86$.

61. $v = kt$

    $64 = k(2) \Rightarrow k = 32$

    in 3 seconds

    $v = (32)(3) = 96$ feet per second

63. To say that a student's average in the class is directly proportional to the amount of time that the student studies implies that the more a student studies, the higher the student's average will be.

65. Answers will vary.

Linear Functions and Models

2.4   Building Linear Functions from Data

1.   Linear, $m > 0$ 3.   Linear, $m < 0$ 5.   Nonlinear

7.   (a)

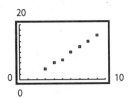

(b)   Answers will vary. We select (3,4) and (9,16). The slope of the line containing these points is:
$$m = \frac{16-4}{9-3} = \frac{12}{6} = 2$$
The equation of the line is:
$$y - y_1 = m(x - x_1)$$
$$y - 4 = 2(x - 3)$$
$$y - 4 = 2x - 6$$
$$y = 2x - 2$$

(c)

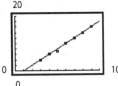

(d)   Using the LINear REGresssion program, the line of best fit is:
$$y = 2.0357x - 2.3571$$

(e)

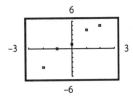

9.   (a)

(b)   Answers will vary. We select (−2,−4) and (2,5). The slope of the line containing these points is:
$$m = \frac{5-(-4)}{2-(-2)} = \frac{9}{4}$$
The equation of the line is:
$$y - y_1 = m(x - x_1)$$
$$y - (-4) = \frac{9}{4}(x - (-2))$$
$$y + 4 = \frac{9}{4}x + \frac{9}{2} \Rightarrow y = \frac{9}{4}x + \frac{1}{2}$$

(c)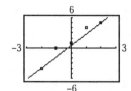

(d) Using the LINear REGresssion program, the line of best fit is:
$$y = 2.2x + 1.2$$

(e)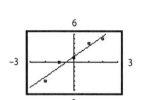

11. (a)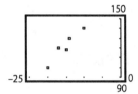

(b) Answers will vary. We select $(-20, 100)$ and $(-10, 140)$. The slope of the line containing these points is:
$$m = \frac{140 - 100}{-10 - (-20)} = \frac{40}{10} = 4$$
The equation of the line is:
$$y - y_1 = m(x - x_1)$$
$$y - 100 = 4(x - (-20))$$
$$y - 100 = 4x + 80$$
$$y = 4x + 180$$

(c)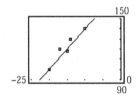

(d) Using the LINear REGresssion program, the line of best fit is:
$$y = 3.8613x + 180.292$$

(e)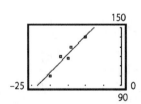

13. (a)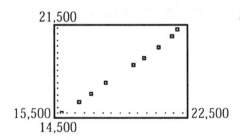

(b) Using the LINear REGression program, the line of best fit is:
$$C = 1.03748I - 1897.5071$$

(c) For each $1 increase in disposable income, the per capita consumption increases by $1.04

(d) $C = 1.03748(21500) - 1897.5071$
$\approx \$20,408$

(e) $17200 = 1.03748I - 1897.5071$
$17200 = 1.03748I$

$19097.5071 = 1.03748I$

$\dfrac{19097.5071}{1.03748} = I \Rightarrow I \approx \$18,408$

15. (a)

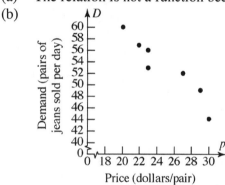

(b) Using the LINear REGression program, the line of best fit is:
$L = 0.0261G + 7.8738$

(c) For each 1 day increase in Gestation period, the life expectancy increases by 0.0261 years.

(d) $L = 0.0261(89) + 7.8738$
≈ 10.2 years

17. (a) The relation is not a function because 23 is paired with both 56 and 53.

(b)

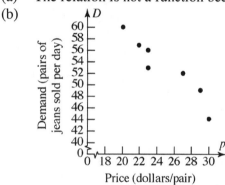

(c) Using the LINear REGression program, the line of best fit is:
$D = -1.3355p + 86.1974$

(d) As the price of the jeans increases by $1, the demand for the jeans decreases by approximately 1.34.

(e) $D(p) = -1.3355p + 86.1974$

(f) Domain: $\{p \mid p > 0\}$

(g) $D(28) = -1.3355(28) + 86.1974$

≈ 48.8034
Demand is about 49 pairs.

19.

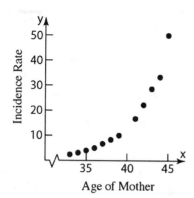

Age of Mother

This scatter diagram does not yield a linear relationship between between the data. Thus, the line of best fit does not make sense.

21. Given the ordered pair (1,5) and (3,8), the line of best fit is determined as follows.

$$\text{slope} = \frac{\Delta y}{\Delta x} = \frac{8-5}{3-1} = \frac{3}{2}$$

using the point-slope formula:

$$y - y_1 = m(x - x_1) \Rightarrow y - 5 = \frac{3}{2}(x - 1)$$

$$y = \frac{3}{2}x - \frac{3}{2} + 5$$

$$y = \frac{3}{2}x + \frac{7}{2} = 1.5x + 3.5$$

The correlation for this data equals 1 since the points are collinear.

Linear Functions and Models

2.R   Chapter Review

1. $f(x) = 2x - 5$
    Slope = 2; y-intercept = –5
    Increasing function

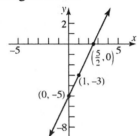

3. $h(x) = \frac{4}{5}x - 6$

    Slope = $\frac{4}{5}$; y-intercept = –6

    Increasing function

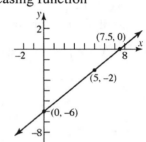

5. $G(x) = 4$
    Slope = 0; y-intercept = 4
    Constant function

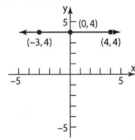

7. $f(x) = 2x + 14$
    (a) $f(x) = 2x + 14 = 0$
    $$2x = -14 \Rightarrow x = -7$$
    (b) y-intercept = 14

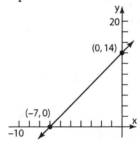

9. Slope = –2; containing $(3, -1)$
    $$y - y_1 = m(x - x_1)$$
    $$y - (-1) = -2(x - 3)$$
    $$y + 1 = -2x + 6 \Rightarrow y = -2x + 5$$
    $$2x + y = 5 \ \text{ or } \ y = -2x + 5$$

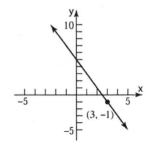

11. Slope undefined; containing $(-3,4)$
This is a vertical line.
$x = -3$

    No slope intercept form.

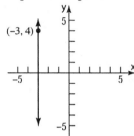

13. y-intercept = -2; containing $(5,-3)$
Points are $(5,-3)$ and $(0,-2)$
$$m = \frac{-2-(-3)}{0-5} = \frac{1}{-5} = -\frac{1}{5}$$
$$y = mx + b$$
$$y = -\frac{1}{5}x - 2$$
$$x + 5y = -10 \ \text{ or } \ y = -\frac{1}{5}x - 2$$

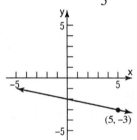

15. Parallel to $2x - 3y = -4$;
$2x - 3y = -4$
$$-3y = -2x - 4 \Rightarrow y = \frac{2}{3}x + \frac{4}{3}$$
Slope $= \frac{2}{3}$; containing $(-5,3)$
$$y - y_1 = m(x - x_1)$$
$$y - 3 = \frac{2}{3}(x - (-5)) \Rightarrow y - 3 = \frac{2}{3}x + \frac{10}{3}$$
$$y = \frac{2}{3}x + \frac{19}{3}$$
$$2x - 3y = -19 \ \text{ or } \ y = \frac{2}{3}x + \frac{19}{3}$$

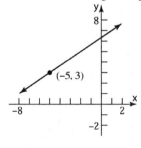

17. Perpendicular to $x + y = 2$;
$x + y = 2 \Rightarrow y = -x + 2$
Containing $(4,-3)$
Slope of perpendicular = 1
$$y - y_1 = m(x - x_1)$$
$$y - (-3) = 1(x - 4)$$
$$y + 3 = x - 4$$
$$y = x - 7$$
$$-x + y = -7 \ \text{ or } \ y = x - 7$$

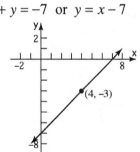

117

19. $3x - 2y = 12$
    $-2y = -3x + 12$

    $y = \dfrac{3}{2}x - 6$

    slope $= \dfrac{3}{2}$; y-intercept $= -6$

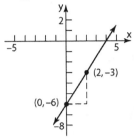

21.(a) Let x = the total number of minutes on the phone. We can construct the following cost functions for each company.
    Company A: $A(x) = (\text{cost per minute})(\#\,\text{of minutes}) + \text{monthly fee}$
    $$A(x) = (0.05)(x) + 7.00 = 0.05x + 7.00$$
    Company B: $B(x) = (\text{cost per minute})(\#\,\text{of minutes}) + \text{monthly fee}$
    $$B(x) = (0.08)(x) + 0 = 0.08x$$
   (b) The bills will be equal when $A(x) = B(x)$.
    $$0.05x + 7 = 0.08x \Rightarrow 7 = 0.03x \Rightarrow \dfrac{7}{0.03} = x \Rightarrow x \approx 233.3 \text{ minutes}$$
   (c) The bill from Company B will be less than the bill from Company A when $B(x) < A(x)$.
    $$0.08x < 0.05x + 7 \Rightarrow 0.03x < 7 \Rightarrow x < \dfrac{7}{0.03} \Rightarrow x < 233.33 \text{ minutes}$$

23.   Let P represent the perimeter of a rectangle, l represent the length and w represent the width of the rectangle.
    The perimeter of a rectangle is the sum of two times the length and two times the width.
    $$P = 2l + 2w$$

25.   Using the simple interest formula: $I = P \cdot r \cdot t$, we have
    $$I = (9000) \cdot (0.07) \cdot (1) = \$630$$

27.

% acid	amount	amount of acid
40%	60	$(0.40)(60)$
15%	x	$(0.15)(x)$
25%	$60 + x$	$(0.25)(60 + x)$

    $$(0.40)(60) + (0.15)(x) = (0.25)(60 + x)$$

    $$24 + .15x = 15 + .25x \Rightarrow 9 = 0.1x \Rightarrow x = 90$$
    90 cubic centimeters of the 15% solution must be added, producing 150 cubic centimeters of the 25% solution.

29.

% salt	amount	amount of salt
10%	64	$(0.10)(64)$
0%	x	$(0.00)(x)$
2%	$64 + x$	$(0.02)(64 + x)$

$(0.10)(64) + (0.00)(x) = (0.02)(64 + x)$

$6.4 = 1.28 + .02x$

$5.12 = 0.2x$

$x = 256$

256 ounces of water must be added.

31. Let s represent the distance the plane can travel.

	Rate	Time	Distance
With wind	250+30=280	$\dfrac{(s/2)}{280}$	$\dfrac{s}{2}$
Against wind	250–30=220	$\dfrac{(s/2)}{220}$	$\dfrac{s}{2}$

Since the total time is at most 5 hours, we have:

$$\frac{(s/2)}{280} + \frac{(s/2)}{220} \le 5 \Rightarrow \frac{s}{560} + \frac{s}{440} \le 5$$

$$11s + 14s \le 5(6160) \Rightarrow 25s \le 30800 \Rightarrow s \le 1232$$

The plane can travel at most 1232 miles or 616 miles one way and return 616 miles.

33. Let t represent the time it takes the helicopter to reach the raft.

	Rate	Time	Distance
Raft	5	t	$5t$
Helicopter	90	t	$90t$

Since the total distance is 150 miles, we have:

$$5t + 90t = 150 \Rightarrow 95t = 150 \Rightarrow t = 1.58 \text{ hours } = 1 \text{ hour and 35 minutes}$$

The helicopter will reach the raft in 1 hour and 35 minutes.

35. Let t represent the time it takes Clarissa to complete the job by herself.

	Time to do job alone (hours)	Part of job done in one day	Time on Job (hours)	Part of total job done by each person
Clarissa	t	$\dfrac{1}{t}$	6	$\dfrac{6}{t}$
Shawna	$t + 5$	$\dfrac{1}{t+5}$	6	$\dfrac{6}{t+5}$

Since the two people paint one house, we have:

$$\frac{6}{t} + \frac{6}{t+5} = 1 \Rightarrow 6(t+5) + 6t = t(t+5) \Rightarrow 6t + 30 + 6t = t^2 + 5t$$

$$t^2 - 7t - 30 = 0 \Rightarrow (t-10)(t+3) = 0 \Rightarrow t = 10 \text{ or } t = -3$$

It takes Clarissa 10 days to paint the house when working by herself.

37. Let t represent the time it takes the smaller pump to fill the tank.

	Time to do job alone (hours)	Part of job done in one hour	Time on Job (hours)	Part of total job done by each pump
3hp Pump	12	$\dfrac{1}{12}$	$t+4$	$\dfrac{t+4}{12}$
8hp Pump	8	$\dfrac{1}{8}$	4	$\dfrac{4}{8}$

Since the two pumps fill one tank, we have:
$$\frac{t+4}{12}+\frac{4}{8}=1 \Rightarrow \frac{t+4}{12}=\frac{1}{2}$$
$$2t+8=12 \Rightarrow 2t=4 \Rightarrow t=2$$
It takes the small pump a total of 2 more hours to fill the tank.

39. Let p = the monthly payment in dollars, and B = the amount borrowed in dollars.
Consider the ordered pair (B,p).
We can use the points $(0,0)$ and $(130000,854)$.
Now compute the slope:
$$\text{slope}=\frac{\Delta y}{\Delta x}=\frac{854-0}{130000-0}=\frac{854}{130000}\approx 0.0065692$$
Therefore we have the linear function $p(B)=0.0065692B+0=0.0065692B$.
If $B=165000$, then $p=(0.006569)(165000)\approx \$1083.92$.

41.

x	$y=f(x)$	Avg. rate of change $=\dfrac{\Delta y}{\Delta x}$
-1	-2	
0	3	$\dfrac{3-(-2)}{0-(-1)}=\dfrac{5}{1}=5$
1	8	$\dfrac{8-3}{1-0}=\dfrac{5}{1}=5$
2	13	$\dfrac{13-8}{2-1}=\dfrac{5}{1}=5$
3	18	$\dfrac{18-13}{3-2}=\dfrac{5}{1}=5$

This is a linear function with slope = 5, since the average rate of change is constant at 5.

43. (a)

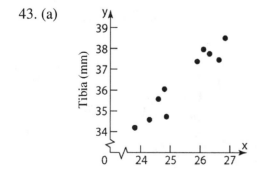

(b)   The relation appears to be linear.

(c)   Using the LINear REGression program, the line of best fit is:
$$y = 1.3902x + 1.114$$

(d)   When $x = 26.5$, $y = 1.3902(26.5) + 1.114 \approx 38.0$ mm.

45. (a)   The relation is a function. Each HS GPA value is paired with exactly one College GPA value.

(b)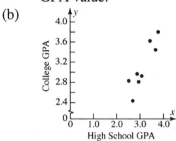

(c)   Using the LINear REGression program, the line of best fit is:
$$G = 0.9639x + 0.0724$$

(d)   As the high school GPA increases by 1 point, the college GPA increases by approximately 0.964 point.

(e) $G(x) = 0.964x + 0.072$

(f)   Domain: $\{x \mid 0 \le x \le 4\}$

(g) $G(3.23) = (0.964)(3.23) + 0.072 \approx 3.186$
       The college GPA is approximately 3.19.

47. $f(x) = 2x^2 + 7$

(a) $\dfrac{f(x) - f(2)}{x - 2} = \dfrac{2x^2 + 7 - 15}{x - 2}$

       $= \dfrac{2x^2 - 8}{x - 2} = \dfrac{2(x^2 - 4)}{x - 2} = \dfrac{2(x + 2)(x - 2)}{x - 2}$

       $= 2(x + 2)$

(b)   Using $x = 3$ and part (a):
       $\dfrac{f(3) - f(2)}{3 - 2} = 2(3 + 2) = 10$

(c)   Slope = 10; Containing (2, 15):
       $y - 15 = 10(x - 2)$
       $y - 15 = 10x - 20 \Rightarrow y = 10x + 35$

(d)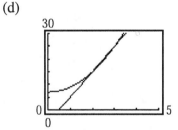

49. $f(x) = x^2 - 3x + 2$

(a) $\dfrac{f(x) - f(2)}{x - 2} = \dfrac{x^2 - 3x + 2 - 0}{x - 2}$

       $= \dfrac{x^2 - 3x + 2}{x - 2} = \dfrac{(x - 2)(x - 1)}{x - 2}$

       $= x - 1$

(b) Using $x = 3$ and part (a):
       $\dfrac{f(3) - f(2)}{3 - 2} = 3 - 1 = 2$

(c)   Slope = 2; Containing (2, 0):

$$y - 0 = 2(x - 2)$$
$$y = 2x - 4$$

(d)

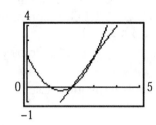

Linear Functions and Models

2.CR Cumulative Review

1. $P = (-1,3); Q = (4,-2)$
   Distance between P and Q:
   $$d(P,Q) = \sqrt{(4-(-1))^2 + (-2-3)^2}$$
   $$= \sqrt{(5)^2 + (5)^2}$$
   $$= \sqrt{25 + 25}$$
   $$= \sqrt{50} = 5\sqrt{2}$$

   Midpoint between P and Q:
   $$\left(\frac{-1+4}{2}, \frac{3-2}{2}\right) = \left(\frac{3}{2}, \frac{1}{2}\right)$$

3. $y_1 = x^4 - 3x^3 + 4x - 1$

   Using ROOT or ZERO on the graph yields the solution set $\{-1.10, 0.26, 1.48, 2.36\}$.

5. $(-1,4)$ and $(2,-2)$ are points on the line.
   $$\text{Slope} = \frac{-2-4}{2-(-1)} = \frac{-6}{3} = -2$$
   $$y - y_1 = m(x - x_1)$$
   $$y - 4 = -2(x - (-1))$$
   $$y - 4 = -2(x + 1)$$
   $$y - 4 = -2x - 2 \Rightarrow y = -2x + 2$$

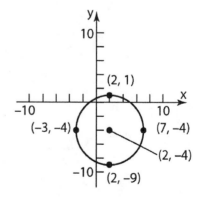

7. $x^2 + y^2 - 4x + 8y - 5 = 0$
   $$x^2 - 4x + y^2 + 8y = 5$$
   $$(x^2 - 4x + 4) + (y^2 + 8y + 16) = 5 + 4 + 16$$
   $$(x - 2)^2 + (y + 4)^2 = 25$$
   $$(x - 2)^2 + (y + 4)^2 = 5^2$$
   Center: $(2,-4)$ Radius $= 5$

9. $f(x) = x^2 - 4x + 1$

(a) $f(2) = 2^2 - 4(2) + 1 = 4 - 8 + 1 = -3$

(b) $f(x) + f(2) = x^2 - 4x + 1 + (-3) = x^2 - 4x - 2$

(c) $f(-x) = (-x)^2 - 4(-x) + 1 = x^2 + 4x + 1$

(d) $-f(x) = -(x^2 - 4x + 1) = -x^2 + 4x - 1$

(e) $f(x + 2) = (x + 2)^2 - 4(x + 2) + 1 = x^2 + 4x + 4 - 4x - 8 + 1 = x^2 - 3$

(f) $\dfrac{f(x+h) - f(x)}{h} = \dfrac{(x+h)^2 - 4(x+h) + 1 - (x^2 - 4x + 1)}{h}$

$$= \frac{x^2 + 2xh + h^2 - 4x - 4h + 1 - x^2 + 4x - 1}{h} = \frac{2xh + h^2 - 4h}{h}$$

$$= \frac{h(2x + h - 4)}{h} = 2x + h - 4$$

11. Yes, the graphs passes the Vertical Line Test.

13. $f(x) = \dfrac{x^2}{2x + 1}$

$$f(-x) = \frac{(-x)^2}{2(-x) + 1} = \frac{x^2}{-2x + 1} \neq f(x) \text{ or } -f(x)$$

Therefore, f is neither even nor odd.

15. $f(x) = 3x + 5; \quad g(x) = 2x + 1$

(a) $f(x) = g(x) \Rightarrow 3x + 5 = 2x + 1$

$3x + 5 = 2x + 1$

$x = -4$

(b) $f(x) > g(x) \Rightarrow 3x + 5 > 2x + 1$

$3x + 5 > 2x + 1$

$x > -4$

Solution set: $\{x | x > -4\}$ or $(-4, \infty)$.

Quadratic Functions and Models

3.1 Quadratic Equations

1. $x^2 - 9x = 0$
   $x(x-9) = 0$
   $x = 0$
   or $x - 9 = 0 \Rightarrow x = 9$
   The solution set is $\{0, 9\}$.

3. $x^2 - 25 = 0$
   $(x-5)(x+5) = 0$
   $x - 5 = 0 \Rightarrow x = 5$
   or $x + 5 = 0 \Rightarrow x = -5$
   The solution set is $\{-5, 5\}$.

5. $z^2 + z - 6 = 0$
   $(z+3)(z-2) = 0$
   $z + 3 = 0 \Rightarrow z = -3$
   or $z - 2 = 0 \Rightarrow z = 2$
   The solution set is $\{-3, 2\}$.

7. $2x^2 - 5x - 3 = 0$
   $(2x+1)(x-3) = 0$
   $2x + 1 = 0 \Rightarrow x = -\dfrac{1}{2}$
   or $x - 3 = 0 \Rightarrow x = 3$
   The solution set is $\left\{-\dfrac{1}{2}, 3\right\}$

9. $3t^2 - 48 = 0$
   $3(t^2 - 16) = 0$
   $3(t+4)(t-4) = 0$
   $t + 4 = 0 \Rightarrow t = -4$
   or $t - 4 = 0 \Rightarrow t = 4$
   The solution set is $\{-4, 4\}$.

11. $x(x+8) + 12 = 0$
    $x^2 + 8x + 12 = 0$
    $(x+6)(x+2) = 0 \Rightarrow x = -6, x = -2$
    The solution set is $\{-6, -2\}$.

13. $4x^2 + 9 = 12x$
    $4x^2 - 12x + 9 = 0$
    $(2x-3)^2 = 0 \Rightarrow x = \dfrac{3}{2}$
    The solution set is $\left\{\dfrac{3}{2}\right\}$.

15. $2x^2 - x = 15$
    $2x^2 - x - 15 = 0$
    $(2x+5)(x-3) = 0$
    $2x + 5 = 0 \Rightarrow x = -\dfrac{5}{2}$
    or $x - 3 = 0 \Rightarrow x = 3$
    The solution set is $\left\{-\dfrac{5}{2}, 3\right\}$.

17. $x^3 + x^2 - 20x = 0$
$x(x^2 + x - 20) = 0$
$x(x+5)(x-4) = 0$
$x = 0$
$x + 5 = 0 \Rightarrow x = -5$
or $x - 4 = 0 \Rightarrow x = 4$
The solution set is $\{-5, 0, 4\}$.

19. $x^2 + 4x = 21$
$x^2 + 4x + 4 = 21 + 4 \Rightarrow (x+2)^2 = 25$
$x + 2 = \pm\sqrt{25} \Rightarrow x + 2 = \pm 5$
$x = -2 \pm 5 \Rightarrow x = 3$ or $x = -7$
The solution set is $\{-7, 3\}$.

21. $x^2 - \dfrac{1}{2}x - \dfrac{3}{16} = 0$
$x^2 - \dfrac{1}{2}x = \dfrac{3}{16}$
$x^2 - \dfrac{1}{2}x + \dfrac{1}{16} = \dfrac{3}{16} + \dfrac{1}{16}$
$\left(x - \dfrac{1}{4}\right)^2 = \dfrac{1}{4}$
$x - \dfrac{1}{4} = \pm\sqrt{\dfrac{1}{4}}$
$x - \dfrac{1}{4} = \pm\dfrac{1}{2}$
$x = \dfrac{1}{4} \pm \dfrac{1}{2} \Rightarrow x = \dfrac{3}{4}$
or $x = -\dfrac{1}{4}$
The solution set is $\left\{-\dfrac{1}{4}, \dfrac{3}{4}\right\}$.

23. $3x^2 + x - \dfrac{1}{2} = 0$
$x^2 + \dfrac{1}{3}x - \dfrac{1}{6} = 0$
$x^2 + \dfrac{1}{3}x = \dfrac{1}{6}$
$x^2 + \dfrac{1}{3}x + \dfrac{1}{36} = \dfrac{1}{6} + \dfrac{1}{36}$
$\left(x + \dfrac{1}{6}\right)^2 = \dfrac{7}{36}$
$x + \dfrac{1}{6} = \pm\sqrt{\dfrac{7}{36}}$
$x + \dfrac{1}{6} = \pm\dfrac{\sqrt{7}}{6}$
$x = -\dfrac{1}{6} \pm \dfrac{\sqrt{7}}{6}$
The solution set is $\left\{\dfrac{-1-\sqrt{7}}{6}, \dfrac{-1+\sqrt{7}}{6}\right\}$.

25. $x^2 - 4x + 2 = 0$
$a = 1, \quad b = -4, \quad c = 2$
$x = \dfrac{-(-4) \pm \sqrt{(-4)^2 - 4(1)(2)}}{2(1)}$
$= \dfrac{4 \pm \sqrt{16 - 8}}{2} = \dfrac{4 \pm \sqrt{8}}{2}$
$= \dfrac{4 \pm 2\sqrt{2}}{2} = 2 \pm \sqrt{2}$
The solution set is $\{2 - \sqrt{2}, 2 + \sqrt{2}\}$.

27. $x^2 - 4x - 1 = 0$
$a = 1, \quad b = -4, \quad c = -1$
$x = \dfrac{-(-4) \pm \sqrt{(-4)^2 - 4(1)(-1)}}{2(1)}$
$= \dfrac{4 \pm \sqrt{16 + 4}}{2} = \dfrac{4 \pm \sqrt{20}}{2}$
$= \dfrac{4 \pm 2\sqrt{5}}{2} = 2 \pm \sqrt{5}$
The solution set is $\{2 - \sqrt{5}, 2 + \sqrt{5}\}$.

29. $2x^2 - 5x + 3 = 0$
$a = 2, \quad b = -5, \quad c = 3$

$$x = \frac{-(-5) \pm \sqrt{(-5)^2 - 4(2)(3)}}{2(2)}$$

$$= \frac{5 \pm \sqrt{25 - 24}}{4} = \frac{5 \pm 1}{4}$$

The solution set is $\left\{ 1, \ \dfrac{3}{2} \right\}$.

31. $4y^2 - y + 2 = 0$
$a = 4, \quad b = -1, \quad c = 2$

$$y = \frac{-(-1) \pm \sqrt{(-1)^2 - 4(4)(2)}}{2(4)}$$

$$= \frac{1 \pm \sqrt{1 - 32}}{8} = \frac{1 \pm \sqrt{-31}}{8}$$

No real solution.

33. $4x^2 = 1 - 2x$
$4x^2 + 2x - 1 = 0$
$a = 4, \quad b = 2, \quad c = -1$

$$x = \frac{-2 \pm \sqrt{2^2 - 4(4)(-1)}}{2(4)}$$

$$= \frac{-2 \pm \sqrt{4 + 16}}{8} = \frac{-2 \pm \sqrt{20}}{8}$$

$$= \frac{-2 \pm 2\sqrt{5}}{8} = \frac{-1 \pm \sqrt{5}}{4}$$

The solution set is $\left\{ \dfrac{-1 - \sqrt{5}}{4}, \dfrac{-1 + \sqrt{5}}{4} \right\}$.

35. $4x^2 = 9x + 2$
$4x^2 - 9x - 2 = 0$
$a = 4, \quad b = -9, \quad c = -2$

$$x = \frac{-(-9) \pm \sqrt{(-9)^2 - 4(4)(-2)}}{2(4)}$$

$$= \frac{9 \pm \sqrt{81 + 32}}{8} = \frac{9 \pm \sqrt{113}}{8}$$

The solution set is $\left\{ \dfrac{9 - \sqrt{113}}{8}, \dfrac{9 + \sqrt{113}}{8} \right\}$.

37. $9t^2 - 6t + 1 = 0$
$a = 9, \quad b = -6, \quad c = 1$

$$x = \frac{-(-6) \pm \sqrt{(-6)^2 - 4(9)(1)}}{2(9)} = \frac{6 \pm \sqrt{36 - 36}}{18} = \frac{6 \pm \sqrt{0}}{18} = \frac{1}{3}$$

The solution set is $\left\{ \dfrac{1}{3} \right\}$.

39. $\dfrac{3}{4}x^2 - \dfrac{1}{4}x - \dfrac{1}{2} = 0 \Rightarrow 4\left(\dfrac{3}{4}x^2 - \dfrac{1}{4}x - \dfrac{1}{2} \right) = (0)(4) \Rightarrow 3x^2 - x - 2 = 0$
$a = 3, \quad b = -1, \quad c = -2$

$$x = \frac{-(-1) \pm \sqrt{(-1)^2 - 4(3)(-2)}}{2(3)} = \frac{1 \pm \sqrt{1 + 24}}{6} = \frac{1 \pm \sqrt{25}}{6} = \frac{1 \pm 5}{6}$$

$$\Rightarrow x = \frac{1 + 5}{6} \ \text{ or } \ x = \frac{1 - 5}{6} \Rightarrow x = \frac{6}{6} = 1 \ \text{ or } \ x = \frac{-4}{6} = -\frac{2}{3}$$

The solution set is $\left\{ -\dfrac{2}{3}, 1 \right\}$.

41. $4 - \dfrac{1}{x} - \dfrac{2}{x^2} = 0$

$$\left(x^2\right)\left(4 - \dfrac{1}{x} - \dfrac{2}{x^2}\right) = (0)\left(x^2\right)$$

$$4x^2 - x - 2 = 0$$

$$a = 4, \quad b = -1, \quad c = -2$$

$$x = \dfrac{-(-1) \pm \sqrt{(-1)^2 - 4(4)(-2)}}{2(4)}$$

$$= \dfrac{1 \pm \sqrt{1 + 32}}{8} = \dfrac{1 \pm \sqrt{33}}{8}$$

Since neither of these values causes a denominator to equal zero, the solution set is

$$\left\{\dfrac{1 - \sqrt{33}}{8}, \dfrac{1 + \sqrt{33}}{8}\right\}.$$

43. $x^2 - 5 = 0$

$\quad x^2 = 5 \Rightarrow x = \pm\sqrt{5}$

The solution set is $\left\{-\sqrt{5}, \sqrt{5}\right\}$.

45. $16x^2 - 8x + 1 = 0$

$\quad (4x - 1)(4x - 1) = 0$

$$4x - 1 = 0 \Rightarrow x = \dfrac{1}{4}$$

The solution set is $\left\{\dfrac{1}{4}\right\}$.

47. $10x^2 - 19x - 15 = 0$

$\quad (5x + 3)(2x - 5) = 0$

$5x + 3 = 0 \quad$ or $\quad 2x - 5 = 0$

$$\Rightarrow x = -\dfrac{3}{5} \quad \text{or} \quad x = \dfrac{5}{2}$$

The solution set is $\left\{-\dfrac{3}{5}, \dfrac{5}{2}\right\}$.

49. $2 + z = 6z^2$

$\quad 0 = 6z^2 - z - 2$

$\quad 0 = (3z - 2)(2z + 1)$

$3z - 2 = 0 \quad$ or $\quad 2z + 1 = 0$

$$\Rightarrow z = \dfrac{2}{3} \quad \text{or} \quad z = -\dfrac{1}{2}$$

The solution set is $\left\{-\dfrac{1}{2}, \dfrac{2}{3}\right\}$.

51. $x^2 + \sqrt{2}x = \dfrac{1}{2}$

$$x^2 + \sqrt{2}x - \dfrac{1}{2} = 0$$

$$2\left(x^2 + \sqrt{2}x - \dfrac{1}{2}\right) = (0)(2)$$

$$2x^2 + 2\sqrt{2}x - 1 = 0$$

$$a = 2, \quad b = 2\sqrt{2}, \quad c = -1$$

$$x = \dfrac{-(2\sqrt{2}) \pm \sqrt{(2\sqrt{2})^2 - 4(2)(-1)}}{2(2)}$$

$$= \dfrac{-2\sqrt{2} \pm \sqrt{8 + 8}}{4} = \dfrac{-2\sqrt{2} \pm \sqrt{16}}{4}$$

$$= \dfrac{-2\sqrt{2} \pm 4}{4} = \dfrac{-\sqrt{2} \pm 2}{2}$$

The solution set is $\left\{\dfrac{-\sqrt{2} + 2}{2}, \dfrac{-\sqrt{2} - 2}{2}\right\}.$

53.
$$x^2 + x = 4$$
$$x^2 + x - 4 = 0$$

$$a = 1, \quad b = 1, \quad c = -4$$

$$x = \frac{-(1) \pm \sqrt{(1)^2 - 4(1)(-4)}}{2(1)}$$

$$= \frac{-1 \pm \sqrt{1 + 16}}{2} = \frac{-1 \pm \sqrt{17}}{2}$$

The solution set is $\left\{ \dfrac{-1 - \sqrt{17}}{2}, \dfrac{-1 + \sqrt{17}}{2} \right\}$.

55.
$$2x^2 - 6x + 7 = 0$$
$$a = 2, \quad b = -6, \quad c = 7$$

$$b^2 - 4ac = (-6)^2 - 4(2)(7)$$

$$= 36 - 56 = -20$$
since the discriminant < 0, we have no real solutions.

57.
$$9x^2 - 30x + 25 = 0$$
$$a = 9, \quad b = -30, \quad c = 25$$

$$b^2 - 4ac = (-30)^2 - 4(9)(25)$$

$$= 900 - 900 = 0$$
since the discriminant $= 0$, we have one repeated real solution.

59.
$$3x^2 + 5x - 8 = 0$$
$$a = 3, \quad b = 5, \quad c = -8$$

$$b^2 - 4ac = (5)^2 - 4(3)(-8)$$

$$= 25 + 96 = 121$$
since the discriminant > 0, we have two unequal real solutions.

61.
$$t^4 - 16 = 0$$
$$(t^2 - 4)(t^2 + 4) = 0$$

$$t^2 - 4 = 0 \ \text{ or } \ t^2 + 4 = 0$$

$t = \pm 2$ or $t^2 = -4$, which is impossible
The solution set is $\{-2, 2\}$.

63.
$$x^4 - 5x^2 + 4 = 0$$
$$(x^2 - 4)(x^2 - 1) = 0$$

$$x^2 - 4 = 0 \ \text{ or } \ x^2 - 1 = 0$$

$$x = \pm 2 \ \text{ or } \ x = \pm 1$$
The solution set is $\{-2, -1, 1, 2\}$.

65.
$$3x^4 - 2x^2 - 1 = 0$$
$$(3x^2 + 1)(x^2 - 1) = 0$$

$$3x^2 + 1 = 0 \ \text{ or } \ x^2 - 1 = 0$$

$$3x^2 = -1 \ \text{, which is impossible}$$

or $x = \pm 1$
The solution set is $\{-1, 1\}$.

67.
$$x^6 + 7x^3 - 8 = 0$$
$$(x^3 + 8)(x^3 - 1) = 0$$

$$x^3 + 8 = 0 \ \text{ or } \ x^3 - 1 = 0$$

$$x^3 = -8 \Rightarrow x = -2$$

or $x^3 = 1 \Rightarrow x = 1$
The solution set is $\{-2, 1\}$.

69. $(x + 2)^2 + 7(x + 2) + 12 = 0$

let $p = x + 2 \Rightarrow p^2 = (x + 2)^2$

$$p^2 + 7p + 12 = 0$$

$$(p + 3)(p + 4) = 0$$

$p + 3 = 0 \ \text{ or } \ p + 4 = 0$

$p = -3 \Rightarrow x + 2 = -3 \Rightarrow x = -5$

or $p = -4 \Rightarrow x + 2 = -4 \Rightarrow x = -6$
The solution set is $\{-6, -5\}$.

71. $(3x+4)^2 - 6(3x+4) + 9 = 0$

let $p = 3x + 4 \Rightarrow p^2 = (3x+4)^2$

$p^2 - 6p + 9 = 0$

$(p-3)(p-3) = 0$

$p - 3 = 0$

$p = 3 \Rightarrow 3x + 4 = 3 \Rightarrow x = -\dfrac{1}{3}$

The solution set is $\left\{-\dfrac{1}{3}\right\}$.

73. Let w represent the width of window.
Then $l = w + 2$ represents the length of the window.
Since the area is 143 square feet, we have: $w(w+2) = 143$

$\qquad w^2 + 2w - 143 = 0 \Rightarrow (w+13)(w-11) = 0 \Rightarrow w = -13$ which is not practical

$\qquad$ or $w = 11$
The width of the rectangular window is 11 feet and the length is 13 feet.

75. Let l represent the length of the rectangle.
Let w represent the width of the rectangle.
The perimeter is 26 meters and the area is 40 square meters.

$\qquad 2l + 2w = 26 \quad \Rightarrow \quad l + w = 13 \quad \Rightarrow \quad w = 13 - l$

$\qquad l\,w = 40$

$\qquad l(13 - l) = 40 \Rightarrow 13l - l^2 = 40 \Rightarrow l^2 - 13l + 40 = 0 \Rightarrow (l-8)(l-5) = 0$

$\qquad l = 8 \ \text{ or } \ l = 5$

$\qquad w = 5 \qquad w = 8$

The dimensions are 5 meters by 8 meters.

77. Let x represent the length of the side of the sheet metal.

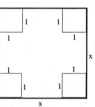

$\qquad (x-2)(x-2)(1) = 4$

$\qquad\qquad x^2 - 4x + 4 = 4$

$\qquad\qquad\quad x^2 - 4x = 0$

$\qquad\quad x(x-4) = 0 \Rightarrow x = 0 \ \text{ or } \ x = 4$

Since the side cannot be 0 feet long, the length of a side of the sheet metal is 4 feet.
Hence, the dimensions of the sheet metal before the cut are 4 feet by 4 feet.

79. (a) $s = 96 + 80t - 16t^2$. The ball strikes the ground when the height = 0.
So we solve $0 = 96 + 80t - 16t^2$.

$\qquad\qquad 0 = -16t^2 + 80t + 96 \Rightarrow \dfrac{0}{-16} = \dfrac{-16t^2 + 80t + 96}{-16}$

$\qquad 0 = t^2 - 5t - 6 \Rightarrow 0 = (t-6)(t+1) \Rightarrow t = 6 \ \text{ or } \ t = -1$, we discard the negative value

since t represents elapsed time. Therefore, the ball hits the ground after 6 seconds.

(b) $s = 96 + 80t - 16t^2$. The ball passes the top of the building when the
height = 96.
So we solve $96 = 96 + 80t - 16t^2$.

$96 = 96 + 80t - 16t^2 \Rightarrow 0 = 80t - 16t^2 \Rightarrow 0 = 16t(5-t) \Rightarrow t = 0$ or $t = 5$

We know that the ball starts ($t = 0$) at a height of 96 feet. Therefore, the ball passes the top of the building on the way down after 5 seconds.

81.   Let x = number of boxes in excess of 150.
The total number of boxes ordered = $150 + x$
The price per box = $200 - x$
The customer's total bill = (# boxes ordered)(price per box)
$$= (150 + x)(200 - x)$$
So we need to solve the equation $(150 + x)(200 - x) = 30{,}525$.
$$30{,}000 + 50x - x^2 = 30{,}525$$

$0 = x^2 - 50x + 525 \Rightarrow 0 = (x - 15)(x - 35) \Rightarrow x = 15$ or $x = 35$

So the customer ordered a total of $150 + 15 = 165$ boxes or $150 + 35 = 185$ boxes.

83.   Let x represent the width of the border measured in feet.
The total area is $A_T = (6 + 2x)(10 + 2x)$.
The area of the garden is $A_G = 6 \cdot 10 = 60$.
The area of the border is $A_B = A_T - A_G = (6 + 2x)(10 + 2x) - 60$.
Since the concrete is 3 inches or 0.25 feet thick, the volume of the concrete in the border is
$$0.25 A_B = 0.25\big((6 + 2x)(10 + 2x) - 60\big)$$
Solving the volume equation:
$$0.25\big((6 + 2x)(10 + 2x) - 60\big) = 27$$

$$60 + 32x + 4x^2 - 60 = 108$$

$$4x^2 + 32x - 108 = 0 \Rightarrow x^2 + 8x - 27 = 0$$

$$x = \frac{-8 \pm \sqrt{8^2 - 4(1)(-27)}}{2(1)} = \frac{-8 \pm \sqrt{172}}{2}$$

$$\approx \frac{-8 \pm 13.11}{2} \approx 2.56 \text{ or } -10.56 \text{ which is not practical}.$$

The width of the border is approximately 2.56 feet.

85.   Let x represent the number of centimeters the length and width should be reduced.
$12 - x$ = the new length, $7 - x$ = the new width.
The new volume is 90% of the old volume.
$$(12 - x)(7 - x)(3) = 0.9(12)(7)(3)$$

$$3x^2 - 57x + 252 = 226.8 \Rightarrow 3x^2 - 57x + 25.2 = 0 \Rightarrow x^2 - 19x + 8.4 = 0$$

$$x = \frac{-(-19) \pm \sqrt{(-19)^2 - 4(1)(8.4)}}{2(1)} = \frac{19 \pm \sqrt{327.4}}{2} \approx \frac{19 \pm 18.09}{2} = 0.45 \text{ or } 18.55$$

Since 18.55 exceeds the dimensions, it is discarded.
The dimensions of the new chocolate bar are: 11.55 cm by 6.55 cm by 3 cm.

87.   Let x represent the width of the border measured in feet.
The radius of the pool is 5 feet.
Then $x + 5$ represents the radius of the circle, including both the pool and the border.
The total area of the pool and border is $A_T = \pi(x+5)^2$.
The area of the pool is $A_P = \pi(5)^2 = 25\pi$.
The area of the border is $A_B = A_T - A_P = \pi(x+5)^2 - 25\pi$.
Since the concrete is 3 inches or 0.25 feet thick, the volume of the concrete in the border is
$$0.25A_B = 0.25\left(\pi(x+5)^2 - 25\pi\right)$$
Solving the volume equation:
$$0.25\left(\pi(x+5)^2 - 25\pi\right) = 27 \Rightarrow \pi\left(x^2 + 10x + 25 - 25\right) = 108 \Rightarrow \pi x^2 + 10\pi x - 108 = 0$$
$$x = \frac{-10\pi \pm \sqrt{(10\pi)^2 - 4(\pi)(-108)}}{2(\pi)} \approx \frac{-31.42 \pm \sqrt{2344.1285}}{6.28} \approx \frac{-31.42 \pm 48.42}{6.28} = 2.71 \text{ or } -12.71$$
The width of the border is approximately 2.71 feet.

89.   Given a quadratic equation $ax^2 + bx + c = 0$,
the solutions are given by $x = \dfrac{-b + \sqrt{b^2 - 4ac}}{2a}$ and $x = \dfrac{-b - \sqrt{b^2 - 4ac}}{2a}$.
Adding these two values we get
$$\frac{-b + \sqrt{b^2 - 4ac}}{2a} + \frac{-b - \sqrt{b^2 - 4ac}}{2a} = \frac{-b + \sqrt{b^2 - 4ac} - b - \sqrt{b^2 - 4ac}}{2a} = \frac{-2b}{2a} = -\frac{b}{a}.$$

91.   The quadratic equation $kx^2 + x + k = 0$ will have a repeated solution provided the
discriminant $= 0$. That is, we need $b^2 - 4ac = 0$ in the given quadratic equation.
$b^2 - 4ac = (1)^2 - 4(k)(k) = 1 - 4k^2$
So we solve $1 - 4k^2 = 0 \Rightarrow 1 = 4k^2 \Rightarrow \dfrac{1}{4} = k^2 \Rightarrow \pm\sqrt{\dfrac{1}{4}} = k \Rightarrow \pm\dfrac{1}{2} = k$

93.   The quadratic equation $ax^2 + bx + c = 0$ has solutions given by
$$x_1 = \frac{-b + \sqrt{b^2 - 4ac}}{2a} \text{ and } x_2 = \frac{-b - \sqrt{b^2 - 4ac}}{2a}.$$
The quadratic equation $ax^2 - bx + c = 0$ has solutions given by
$$x_3 = \frac{-(-b) + \sqrt{(-b)^2 - 4ac}}{2a} = \frac{b + \sqrt{b^2 - 4ac}}{2a} = -x_2$$
and
$$x_4 = \frac{-(-b) - \sqrt{(-b)^2 - 4ac}}{2a} = \frac{b - \sqrt{b^2 - 4ac}}{2a} = -x_1$$
So we have the negatives of the first pair of solutions.

95.   We need to solve the equation $\frac{1}{2}n(n+1) = 666$

$$2\left(\frac{1}{2}\right)n(n+1) = (666)(2) \Rightarrow n(n+1) = 1332$$

$$n^2 + n = 1332 \Rightarrow n^2 + n - 1332 = 0 \Rightarrow (n+37)(n-36) = 0 \Rightarrow n = -37 \text{ or } n = 36$$

Since n must be a positive integer (it represents how many numbers we add together), we discard the negative value. Therefore, we conclude that $1 + 2 + 3 + \ldots\ldots + 36 = 666$.

97.   Let t_1 and t_2 represent the times for the two segments of the trip.

	Rate	Time	Distance
Chicago to Atlanta	45	t_1	$45t_1$
Atlanta to Miami	55	t_2	$55t_2$

Since Atlanta is halfway between Chicago and Miami, the distances are equal.

$$45t_1 = 55t_2 \quad \Rightarrow \quad t_1 = \frac{55}{45}t_2 = \frac{11}{9}t_2$$

Computing the average speed:

$$\text{Avg Speed} = \frac{\text{Distance}}{\text{Time}} = \frac{45t_1 + 55t_2}{t_1 + t_2} = \frac{45(11t_2/9) + 55t_2}{(11t_2/9 + t_2)}$$

$$= \frac{55t_2 + 55t_2}{((11t_2 + 9t_2)/9)} = \frac{110t_2}{(20t_2/9)} = \frac{990t_2}{20t_2} = \frac{99}{2} = 49.5 \text{ miles per hour}$$

The average speed for the trip from Chicago to Miami is 49.5 miles per hour.

99 – 101. Answers will vary.

Quadratic Functions and Models

3.2 The Graph of a Quadratic Function

1. C   3. F   5. G   7. H   9. B   11. D

13. $f(x) = x^2 + 2x$
     $a = 1, b = 2, c = 0.$ Since $a = 1 > 0$, the graph opens up.

     The x-coordinate of the vertex is $x = \dfrac{-b}{2a} = \dfrac{-(2)}{2(1)} = \dfrac{-2}{2} = -1.$

     The y-coordinate of the vertex is $f\left(\dfrac{-b}{2a}\right) = f(-1) = (-1)^2 + 2(-1) = 1 - 2 = -1.$

     Thus, the vertex is $(-1, -1)$.
     The axis of symmetry is the line $x = -1$.
     The discriminant is:
     $$b^2 - 4ac = (2)^2 - 4(1)(0) = 4 > 0,$$
     so the graph has two x-intercepts.
     The x-intercepts are found by solving:
     $$x^2 + 6x = 0$$
     $$x(x + 2) = 0$$
     $$x = 0 \ \text{ or } \ x = -2$$
     The x-intercepts are –2 and 0.
     The y-intercept is $f(0) = 0$.
     Domain: $(-\infty, \infty)$.
     Range: $[-1, \infty)$.
     f is increasing on $(-1, \infty)$
     f is decreasing on $(-\infty, -1)$

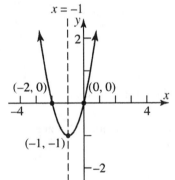

15. $f(x) = -x^2 - 6x$
     $a = -1, b = -6, c = 0.$ Since $a = -1 < 0$, the graph opens down.

     The x-coordinate of the vertex is $x = \dfrac{-b}{2a} = \dfrac{-(-6)}{2(-1)} = \dfrac{6}{-2} = -3.$

     The y-coordinate of the vertex is $f\left(\dfrac{-b}{2a}\right) = f(-3) = -(-3)^2 - 6(-3) = -9 + 18 = 9.$

     Thus, the vertex is $(-3, 9)$.
     The axis of symmetry is the line $x = -3$.
     The discriminant is:
     $$b^2 - 4ac = (-6)^2 - 4(-1)(0) = 36 > 0, \text{ so the graph has two x-intercepts.}$$

The x-intercepts are found by solving:
$$-x^2 - 6x = 0$$
$$-x(x + 6) = 0$$
$$x = 0 \text{ or } x = -6$$
The x-intercepts are –6 and 0.
The y-intercept is $f(0) = 0$.
Domain: $(-\infty, \infty)$.
Range: $(-\infty, 9]$.
f is increasing on $(-\infty, -3)$
f is decreasing on $(-3, \infty)$

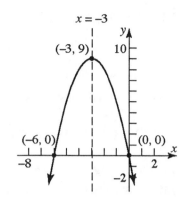

17. $f(x) = 2x^2 - 8x$
   $a = 2, b = -8, c = 0$. Since $a = 2 > 0$, the graph opens up.

   The x-coordinate of the vertex is $x = \dfrac{-b}{2a} = \dfrac{-(-8)}{2(2)} = \dfrac{8}{4} = 2$.

   The y-coordinate of the vertex is $f\left(\dfrac{-b}{2a}\right) = f(2) = 2(2)^2 - 8(2) = 8 - 16 = -8$.

   Thus, the vertex is (2, –8).
   The axis of symmetry is the line $x = 2$.
   The discriminant is: $b^2 - 4ac = (-8)^2 - 4(2)(0) = 64 > 0$,
   so the graph has two x-intercepts.
   The x-intercepts are found by solving:
   $$2x^2 - 8x = 0$$
   $$2x(x - 4) = 0$$
   $$x = 0 \text{ or } x = 4$$
   The x-intercepts are 0 and 4.
   The y-intercept is $f(0) = 0$.
   Domain: $(-\infty, \infty)$.
   Range: $[-8, \infty)$.
   f is increasing on $(2, \infty)$
   f is decreasing on $(-\infty, 2)$

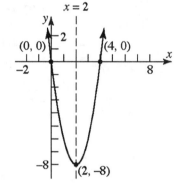

19. $f(x) = x^2 + 2x - 8$
   $a = 1, b = 2, c = -8$. Since $a = 1 > 0$, the graph opens up.

   The x-coordinate of the vertex is $x = \dfrac{-b}{2a} = \dfrac{-2}{2(1)} = \dfrac{-2}{2} = -1$.

   The y-coordinate of the vertex is $f\left(\dfrac{-b}{2a}\right) = f(-1) = (-1)^2 + 2(-1) - 8 = 1 - 2 - 8 = -9$.

   Thus, the vertex is (–1, –9).
   The axis of symmetry is the line $x = -1$.
   The discriminant is:
   $$b^2 - 4ac = 2^2 - 4(1)(-8) = 4 + 32 = 36 > 0, \text{ so the graph has two x-intercepts.}$$

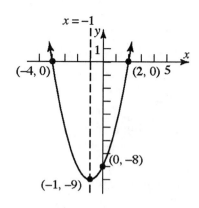

The x-intercepts are found by solving:
$$x^2 + 2x - 8 = 0$$
$$(x + 4)(x - 2) = 0$$
$$x = -4 \text{ or } x = 2$$
The x-intercepts are –4 and 2.
The y-intercept is $f(0) = -8$.
Domain: $(-\infty, \infty)$.
Range: $[-9, \infty)$.
f is increasing on $(-1, \infty)$
f is decreasing on $(-\infty, -1)$

21. $f(x) = x^2 + 2x + 1$
$a = 1, b = 2, c = 1$. Since $a = 1 > 0$, the graph opens up.

The x-coordinate of the vertex is $x = \dfrac{-b}{2a} = \dfrac{-2}{2(1)} = \dfrac{-2}{2} = -1$.

The y-coordinate of the vertex is $f\left(\dfrac{-b}{2a}\right) = f(-1) = (-1)^2 + 2(-1) + 1 = 1 - 2 + 1 = 0$.

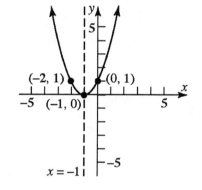

Thus, the vertex is $(-1, 0)$.
The axis of symmetry is the line $x = -1$.
The discriminant is:
$$b^2 - 4ac = 2^2 - 4(1)(1) = 4 - 4 = 0,$$
so the graph has one x-intercept.
The x-intercept is found by solving:
$$x^2 + 2x + 1 = 0$$
$$(x + 1)^2 = 0$$
$$x = -1$$
The x-intercept is –1.
The y-intercept is $f(0) = 1$.
Domain: $(-\infty, \infty)$.
Range: $[0, \infty)$.
f is increasing on $(-1, \infty)$
f is decreasing on $(-\infty, -1)$

23. $f(x) = 2x^2 - x + 2$
$a = 2, b = -1, c = 2$. Since $a = 2 > 0$, the graph opens up.

The x-coordinate of the vertex is $x = \dfrac{-b}{2a} = \dfrac{-(-1)}{2(2)} = \dfrac{1}{4}$.

The y-coordinate of the vertex is $f\left(\dfrac{-b}{2a}\right) = f\left(\dfrac{1}{4}\right) = 2\left(\dfrac{1}{4}\right)^2 - \dfrac{1}{4} + 2 = \dfrac{1}{8} - \dfrac{1}{4} + 2 = \dfrac{15}{8}$.

Thus, the vertex is $\left(\dfrac{1}{4}, \dfrac{15}{8}\right)$.

The axis of symmetry is the line $x = \dfrac{1}{4}$.

The discriminant is: $b^2 - 4ac = (-1)^2 - 4(2)(2) = 1 - 16 = -15$, so the graph has no x-intercepts.

The y-intercept is $f(0) = 2$.

Domain: $(-\infty,\infty)$.

Range: $\left[\dfrac{15}{8},\infty\right)$.

f is increasing on $\left(\dfrac{1}{4},\infty\right)$

f is decreasing on $\left(-\infty,\dfrac{1}{4}\right)$

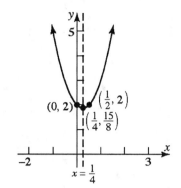

25. $f(x) = -2x^2 + 2x - 3$

$a = -2$, $b = 2$, $c = -3$. Since $a = -2 < 0$, the graph opens down.

The x-coordinate of the vertex is $x = \dfrac{-b}{2a} = \dfrac{-(2)}{2(-2)} = \dfrac{-2}{-4} = \dfrac{1}{2}$.

The y-coordinate of the vertex is $f\left(\dfrac{-b}{2a}\right) = f\left(\dfrac{1}{2}\right) = -2\left(\dfrac{1}{2}\right)^2 + 2\left(\dfrac{1}{2}\right) - 3 = -\dfrac{1}{2} + 1 - 3 = -\dfrac{5}{2}$.

Thus, the vertex is $\left(\dfrac{1}{2}, -\dfrac{5}{2}\right)$.

The axis of symmetry is the line $x = \dfrac{1}{2}$.

The discriminant is:

$b^2 - 4ac = 2^2 - 4(-2)(-3) = 4 - 24 = -20$,

so the graph has no x-intercepts.

The y-intercept is $f(0) = -3$.

Domain: $(-\infty,\infty)$.

Range: $\left(-\infty,-\dfrac{5}{2}\right]$.

f is increasing on $\left(-\infty,\dfrac{1}{2}\right)$

f is decreasing on $\left(\dfrac{1}{2},\infty\right)$

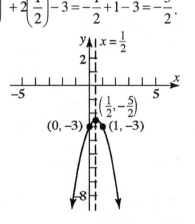

27. $f(x) = 3x^2 + 6x + 2$

$a = 3$, $b = 6$, $c = 2$. Since $a = 3 > 0$, the graph opens up.

The x-coordinate of the vertex is $x = \dfrac{-b}{2a} = \dfrac{-6}{2(3)} = \dfrac{-6}{6} = -1$.

The y-coordinate of the vertex is $f\left(\dfrac{-b}{2a}\right) = f(-1) = 3(-1)^2 + 6(-1) + 2 = 3 - 6 + 2 = -1$.

Thus, the vertex is $(-1, -1)$.

The axis of symmetry is the line $x = -1$.

The discriminant is:

$b^2 - 4ac = 6^2 - 4(3)(2) = 36 - 24 = 12$, so the graph has two x-intercepts.

The x-intercepts are found by solving:

$$x = \frac{-b \pm \sqrt{b^2 - 4ac}}{2a} = \frac{-6 \pm \sqrt{12}}{2(3)}$$

$$= \frac{-6 \pm 2\sqrt{3}}{6} = \frac{-3 \pm \sqrt{3}}{3} \approx \frac{-3 \pm 1.732}{3}$$

The x-intercepts are approximately –0.42 and –1.58.
The y-intercept is $f(0) = 2$.
Domain: $(-\infty, \infty)$.
Range: $[-1, \infty)$.
f is increasing on $(-1, \infty)$
f is decreasing on $(-\infty, -1)$

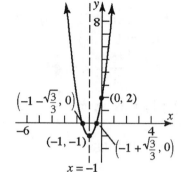

29. $f(x) = -4x^2 - 6x + 2$
$a = -4, b = -6, c = 2$. Since $a = -4 < 0$, the graph opens down.

The x-coordinate of the vertex is $x = \frac{-b}{2a} = \frac{-(-6)}{2(-4)} = \frac{6}{-8} = -\frac{3}{4}$.

The y-coordinate of the vertex is

$$f\left(\frac{-b}{2a}\right) = f\left(-\frac{3}{4}\right) = -4\left(-\frac{3}{4}\right)^2 - 6\left(-\frac{3}{4}\right) + 2 = -\frac{9}{4} + \frac{9}{2} + 2 = \frac{17}{4}.$$

Thus, the vertex is $\left(-\frac{3}{4}, \frac{17}{4}\right)$.

The axis of symmetry is the line $x = -\frac{3}{4}$.

The discriminant is: $b^2 - 4ac = (-6)^2 - 4(-4)(2) = 36 + 32 = 68$, so the graph has two x-intercepts.

The x-intercepts are found by solving:

$$x = \frac{-b \pm \sqrt{b^2 - 4ac}}{2a} = \frac{-(-6) \pm \sqrt{68}}{2(-4)} = \frac{6 \pm 2\sqrt{17}}{-8} = \frac{-3 \pm \sqrt{17}}{4} \approx \frac{-3 \pm 4.123}{4}$$

The x-intercepts are approximately –1.78 and 0.28.
The y-intercept is $f(0) = 2$.
Domain: $(-\infty, \infty)$.

Range: $\left(-\infty, \frac{17}{4}\right]$.

f is increasing on $\left(-\infty, -\frac{3}{4}\right)$

f is decreasing on $\left(-\frac{3}{4}, \infty\right)$

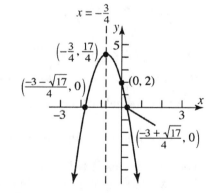

31.   Given that the graph of $f(x) = ax^2 + bx + c$ has vertex $(-1, -2)$ and passes through the point $(0, -1)$, we can conclude

$$\frac{-b}{2a} = -1, \qquad f(-1) = -2, \quad \text{and} \qquad f(0) = -1$$

Notice that $f(0) = -1 \Rightarrow a(0)^2 + b(0) + c = -1 \Rightarrow c = -1$

Therefore $f(x) = ax^2 + bx + c = ax^2 + bx - 1$.

Furthermore, $\dfrac{-b}{2a} = -1 \Rightarrow b = 2a$

and $f(-1) = -2 \Rightarrow a(-1)^2 + b(-1) - 1 = -2 \Rightarrow a - b - 1 = -2$

$$\Rightarrow a - b = -1$$

Replacing b with $2a$ in this equation yields

$a - 2a = -1 \Rightarrow -a = -1 \Rightarrow a = 1$.

So $b = 2a = 2(1) = 2$.

Therefore, we have the function $f(x) = x^2 + 2x - 1$.

33. Given that the graph of $f(x) = ax^2 + bx + c$ has vertex $(-3,5)$ and passes through the point $(0,-4)$, we can conclude

$$\dfrac{-b}{2a} = -3, \qquad f(-3) = 5, \qquad \text{and} \qquad f(0) = -4$$

Notice that $f(0) = -4 \Rightarrow a(0)^2 + b(0) + c = -4 \Rightarrow c = -4$

Therefore $f(x) = ax^2 + bx + c = ax^2 + bx - 4$.

Furthermore, $\dfrac{-b}{2a} = -3 \Rightarrow b = 6a$

and $f(-3) = 5 \Rightarrow a(-3)^2 + b(-3) - 4 = 5 \Rightarrow 9a - 3b - 4 = 5 \Rightarrow 9a - 3b = 9$

$$\Rightarrow 3a - b = 3$$

Replacing b with $6a$ in this equation yields

$3a - 6a = 3 \Rightarrow -3a = 3 \Rightarrow a = -1$.

So $b = 6a = 6(-1) = -6$.

Therefore, we have the function $f(x) = -x^2 - 6x - 4$.

35. Given that the graph of $f(x) = ax^2 + bx + c$ has vertex $(1,-3)$ and passes through the point $(3,5)$, we can conclude

$$\dfrac{-b}{2a} = 1, \qquad f(1) = -3, \qquad \text{and} \qquad f(3) = 5$$

Notice that $f(3) = 5 \Rightarrow a(3)^2 + b(3) + c = 5 \Rightarrow 9a + 3b + c = 5$

Furthermore, $\dfrac{-b}{2a} = 1 \Rightarrow b = -2a$

and $f(1) = -3 \Rightarrow a(1)^2 + b(1) + c = -3 \Rightarrow a + b + c = -3$

Replacing b with $-2a$ in each of these equations yields

$9a + 3b + c = 5 \Rightarrow 9a + 3(-2a) + c = 5 \Rightarrow 9a - 6a + c = 5$

$$\Rightarrow 3a + c = 5 \Rightarrow c = 5 - 3a$$

$a + (-2a) + c = -3 \rightarrow a - 2a + c = -3 \Rightarrow -a + c = -3 \Rightarrow c = -3 + a$

Finally, since $c = 5 - 3a$ and $c = -3 + a$, setting these two expressions equal and solving for a yields

$5 - 3a = -3 + a \Rightarrow 8 = 4a \Rightarrow 2 = a$

So $c = 5 - 3a = 5 - 3 \cdot 2 = 5 - 6 = -1$.

And $b = -2a = (-2)(2) = -4$.

Therefore, we have the function $f(x) = 2x^2 - 4x - 1$.

37. (a) $f(x) = 1(x-(-3))(x-1) = 1(x+3)(x-1) = 1(x^2+2x-3) = x^2+2x-3$

$f(x) = 2(x-(-3))(x-1) = 2(x+3)(x-1) = 2(x^2+2x-3) = 2x^2+4x-6$

$f(x) = -2(x-(-3))(x-1) = -2(x+3)(x-1) = -2(x^2+2x-3) = -2x^2-4x+6$

$f(x) = 5(x-(-3))(x-1) = 5(x+3)(x-1) = 5(x^2+2x-3) = 5x^2+10x-15$

(b)   The value of a multiplies the value of the y-intercept by the value of a. The values
of the x-intercepts are not changed.

(c)   The axis of symmetry is unaffected by the value of a.

(d)   The y-coordinate of the vertex is multiplied by the value of a.

(e)   The x-coordinate of the vertex is the midpoint of the x-intercepts.

39.   Given that the graph of $f(x) = ax^2+bx+c$ has vertex $(0,2)$ and passes through
the point $(1,8)$, we can conclude

$$\frac{-b}{2a} = 0, \qquad\qquad f(0) = 2, \qquad \text{and} \qquad\qquad f(1) = 8$$

Notice that $\dfrac{-b}{2a} = 0 \Rightarrow b = 0$ and $f(0) = 2 \Rightarrow a(0)^2 + b(0) + c = 2 \Rightarrow c = 2$

Therefore $f(x) = ax^2+bx+c = ax^2+2$.

And since $f(1) = 8$, we have $f(1) = a(1)^2 + 2 = 8 \Rightarrow a+2 = 8 \rightarrow a = 6$

So we have the function $f(x) = 6x^2+2$.

41. $f(x) = x^2+2$, $a = 1, b = 0, c = 2$. Since $a = 1 > 0$, the graph opens up, so

the vertex is a minimum point. The minimum occurs at $x = \dfrac{-b}{2a} = \dfrac{-(0)}{2(1)} = \dfrac{0}{2} = 0$.

The minimum value is $f\left(\dfrac{-b}{2a}\right) = f(0) = (0)^2 + 2 = 0+2 = 2$.

X	Y1
-3	11
-2	6
-1	3
0	2
1	3
2	6
3	11

X=0

43. $f(x) = -x^2-4x$, $a = -1, b = -4, c = 0$. Since $a = -1 < 0$, the graph opens down, so

the vertex is a maximum point. The maximum occurs at $x = \dfrac{-b}{2a} = \dfrac{-(-4)}{2(-1)} = \dfrac{4}{-2} = -2$.

The maximum value is $f\left(\dfrac{-b}{2a}\right) = f(-2) = -(-2)^2 - 4(-2) = -4+8 = 4$.

X	Y1
-5	-5
-4	0
-3	3
-2	4
-1	3
0	0
1	-5

X=-2

45. $f(x) = 2x^2 + 12x$, $a = 2$, $b = 12$, $c = 0$. Since $a = 2 > 0$, the graph opens up, so
the vertex is a minimum point. The minimum occurs at $x = \dfrac{-b}{2a} = \dfrac{-12}{2(2)} = \dfrac{-12}{4} = -3$.

The minimum value is $f\left(\dfrac{-b}{2a}\right) = f(-3) = 2(-3)^2 + 12(-3) = 18 - 36 = -18$.

X	Y1
-5	-10
-4	-16
-3	-18
-2	-16
-1	-10
0	0
1	14

X=-3

47. $f(x) = 2x^2 + 12x - 3$, $a = 2$, $b = 12$, $c = -3$. Since $a = 2 > 0$, the graph opens up,
so the vertex is a minimum point. The minimum occurs at $x = \dfrac{-b}{2a} = \dfrac{-12}{2(2)} = \dfrac{-12}{4} = -3$.

The minimum value is $f\left(\dfrac{-b}{2a}\right) = f(-3) = 2(-3)^2 + 12(-3) - 3 = 18 - 36 - 3 = -21$.

X	Y1
-6	-3
-5	-13
-4	-19
-3	-21
-2	-19
-1	-13
0	-3

X=-3

49. $f(x) = -x^2 + 10x - 4$
$a = -1$, $b = 10$, $c = -4$. Since $a = -1 < 0$, the graph opens down, so the vertex is a
maximum point. The maximum occurs at $x = \dfrac{-b}{2a} = \dfrac{-10}{2(-1)} = \dfrac{-10}{-2} = 5$.

The maximum value is $f\left(\dfrac{-b}{2a}\right) = f(5) = -(5)^2 + 10(5) - 4 = -25 + 50 - 4 = 21$.

X	Y1
3	17
4	20
5	21
6	20
7	17
8	12
9	5

X=5

51. $f(x) = -3x^2 + 12x + 1$
$a = -3$, $b = 12$, $c = 1$. Since $a = -3 < 0$, the graph opens down, so the vertex is a
maximum point. The maximum occurs at $x = \dfrac{-b}{2a} = \dfrac{-12}{2(-3)} = \dfrac{-12}{-6} = 2$.

The maximum value is $f\left(\dfrac{-b}{2a}\right) = f(2) = -3(2)^2 + 12(2) + 1 = -12 + 24 + 1 = 13$.

X	Y1
-1	-14
0	1
1	10
2	13
3	10
4	1
5	-14

X=2

53. $R(p) = -4p^2 + 4000p$, $a = -4$, $b = 4000$, $c = 0$. Since $a = -4 < 0$, the graph is a parabola that opens down, so the vertex is a maximum point. The maximum occurs at

$$p = \frac{-b}{2a} = \frac{-4000}{2(-4)} = 500 .$$

Thus, the unit price should be \$500 for maximum revenue.

The maximum revenue is

$$R(500) = -4(500)^2 + 4000(500) = -1000000 + 2000000 = \$1,000,000$$

55. $C(x) = x^2 - 80x + 2000$, $a = 1, b = -80, c = 2000$. Since $a = 1 > 0$, the graph opens up, so the vertex is a minimum point.

The minimum marginal cost occurs at $x = \dfrac{-b}{2a} = \dfrac{-(-80)}{2(1)} = \dfrac{80}{2} = 40$ televisions produced.

The minimum marginal cost is

$$f\left(\frac{-b}{2a}\right) = f(40) = (40)^2 - 80(40) + 2000 = 1600 - 3200 + 2000 = \$400 .$$

57. (a) $a = -\dfrac{32}{2500}, b = 1, c = 200$. The maximum height occurs when

$$x = \frac{-b}{2a} = \frac{-1}{2(-32/2500)} = \frac{2500}{64} \approx 39 \text{ feet from base of the cliff.}$$

(b) The maximum height is $h(39.0625) = \dfrac{-32(39.0625)^2}{2500} + 39.0625 + 200 \approx 219.5$ feet.

(c) Solving when $h(x) = 0$:

$$-\frac{32}{2500}x^2 + x + 200 = 0$$

$$x = \frac{-1 \pm \sqrt{1^2 - 4(-32/2500)(200)}}{2(-32/2500)} \approx \frac{-1 \pm \sqrt{11.24}}{-0.0256} \Rightarrow x \approx -91.90 \text{ or } x \approx 170$$

Since the distance cannot be negative, the projectile strikes the water approximately 170 feet from the base of the cliff.

(d) Graphing:

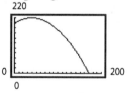

(e) Using the MAXIMUM function

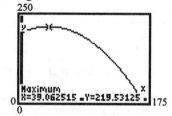

Using the ZERO function

(f)   Solving when $h(x) = 100$:

$$-\frac{32}{2500}x^2 + x + 200 = 100 \Rightarrow -\frac{32}{2500}x^2 + x + 100 = 0$$

$$x = \frac{-1 \pm \sqrt{1^2 - 4(-32/2500)(100)}}{2(-32/2500)} \approx \frac{-1 \pm \sqrt{6.12}}{-0.0256}; \quad x \approx -57.57 \text{ or } x \approx 135.70$$

Since the distance cannot be negative, the projectile is 100 feet above the water when it is approximately 135.7 feet from the base of the cliff.

59.   (a) $a = -1.01, b = 114.3, c = 451.0$ The maximum number of hunters occurs when the income level is

$$x = \frac{-b}{2a} = \frac{-114.3}{2(-1.01)} = \frac{-114.3}{-2.02} \approx 56.584158 \text{ thousand dollars } \approx \$56,600$$

The number of hunters earning this amount is:

$$H(56.584158) = -1.01(56.584158)^2 + 114.3(56.584158) + 451.0 \approx 3685 \text{ hunters.}$$

(b)   Graphing:

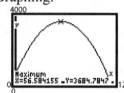

The function H is increasing on $(0, 56)$, therefore the number of hunters is increasing for individuals earning between 20 thousand and 40 thousand dollars.

61.   (a) $M(23) = 0.76(23)^2 - 107.00(23) + 3854.18 \approx 1795$ victims.

(b)   Solve for x: $M(x) = 0.76x^2 - 107.00x + 3854.18 = 1456$

$$0.76x^2 - 107.00x + 3854.18 = 1456$$

$$0.76x^2 - 107.00x + 2398.18 = 0$$

$$a = 0.76, b = -107.00, c = 2398.18$$

$$x = \frac{-b \pm \sqrt{b^2 - 4ac}}{2a} = \frac{-(-107) \pm \sqrt{(-107)^2 - 4(0.76)(2398.18)}}{2(0.76)}$$

$$= \frac{107 \pm \sqrt{4158.5328}}{1.52} \approx \frac{107 \pm 64.49}{1.52} \approx 112.82 \text{ or } 27.98$$

Since the model is valid on the interval $20 \le x < 90$, the only solution is $x \approx 28$ years old

(c)   Graphing:

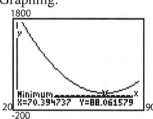

(d)   As age increases between the ages of 20 and 70.39, the number of murder victims decreases. After age 70.39, the number of murder victims increases as age increases.

63. (a) $R(x) = 75x - 0.2x^2$

$a = -0.2, b = 75, c = 0$ The maximum revenue occurs when

$$x = \frac{-b}{2a} = \frac{-75}{2(-0.2)} = \frac{-75}{-0.4} = 187.5 \approx 188 \text{ wrist watches}$$

The maximum revenue is: $R(188) = 75(188) - 0.2(188)^2 = \$7031.20$

(b) $P(x) = R(x) - C(x) = 75x - 0.2x^2 - (32x + 1750) = -0.2x^2 + 43x - 1750$

(c) $P(x) = -0.2x^2 + 43x - 1750$

$a = -0.2, b = 43, c = -1750$ The maximum profit occurs when

$$x = \frac{-b}{2a} = \frac{-43}{2(-0.2)} = \frac{-43}{-0.4} = 107.5 \approx 108 \text{ wrist watches}$$

The maximum profit is: $P(108) = -0.2(108)^2 + 43(108) - 1750 = \$561.20$

65. Answers will vary.

67. $y = x^2 - 4x + 1; \quad y = x^2 + 1; \quad y = x^2 + 4x + 1$

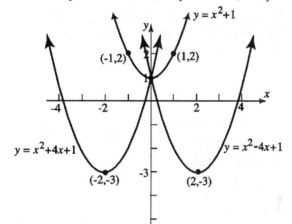

Each member of this family will be a parabola with the following characteristics:

(i) opens upwards since a > 0
(ii) y-intercept occurs at (0, 1)

69.   By completing the square on the quadratic function $f(x) = ax^2 + bx + c$ we obtain the

equation $y = a\left(x + \dfrac{b}{2a}\right)^2 + c - \dfrac{b^2}{4a}$. We can then draw the graph by applying

transformations to the graph of the basic parabola $y = x^2$, which opens up. When $a > 0$, the basic parabola will either be stretched or compressed vertically. When $a < 0$, the basic parabola will either be stretched or compressed vertically as well as reflected across the x-axis. Therefore, when $a > 0$, the graph of $f(x) = ax^2 + bx + c$ will open up, and when $a < 0$, the graph of $f(x) = ax^2 + bx + c$ will open down.

Chapter 3

Quadratic Functions and Models

3.3 Inequalities Involving Quadratic Functions

1. (a) $f(x) > 0$ when the graph of f is above the x-axis.
   That is, for $\{x | x < -2 \text{ or } x > 2\}$.

   (b) $f(x) \leq 0$ when the graph of f is below or intersects the x-axis. That is when That is, for $\{x | -2 \leq x \leq 2\}$.

3. (a) $g(x) \geq f(x)$ when the graph of g is above or intersects the graph of f.
   That is, for $\{x | -2 \leq x \leq 1\}$.

   (b) $f(x) > g(x)$ when the graph of f is above the graph of g.
   That is, for $\{x | x < -2 \text{ or } x > 1\}$.

5. $x^2 - 3x - 10 < 0$
   $(x - 5)(x + 2) < 0$
   $x = 5, x = -2$ are the zeros. $f(x) = (x - 5)(x + 2)$

Interval	Test Number	$f(x)$	Positive/Negative
$-\infty < x < -2$	-3	8	Positive
$-2 < x < 5$	0	-10	Negative
$5 < x < \infty$	6	8	Positive

   The solution set is $\left\{ x | -2 < x < 5 \right\}$.

7. $x^2 - 4x > 0$
   $x(x - 4) > 0$
   $x = 0, x = 4$ are the zeros. $f(x) = x^2 - 4x$

Interval	Test Number	$f(x)$	Positive/Negative
$-\infty < x < 0$	-1	5	Positive
$0 < x < 4$	1	-3	Negative
$4 < x < \infty$	5	5	Positive

   The solution set is $\left\{ x | x < 0 \text{ or } x > 4 \right\}$.

9. $x^2 - 9 < 0$
   $(x + 3)(x - 3) < 0$
   $x = -3, x = 3$ are the zeros $f(x) = x^2 - 9$

Interval	Test Number	$f(x)$	Positive/Negative
$-\infty < x < -3$	-4	7	Positive
$-3 < x < 3$	0	-9	Negative
$3 < x < \infty$	4	7	Positive

   The solution set is $\left\{ x | -3 < x < 3 \right\}$.

11. $x^2 + x > 12$

$$x^2 + x - 12 > 0 \Rightarrow (x+4)(x-3) > 0$$

$x = -4$, $x = 3$ are the zeros. $f(x) = x^2 + x - 12$

Interval	Test Number	$f(x)$	Positive/Negative
$-\infty < x < -4$	-5	8	Positive
$-4 < x < 3$	0	-12	Negative
$3 < x < \infty$	4	8	Positive

The solution set is $\left\{ x \mid x < -4 \ \text{ or } \ x > 3 \right\}$.

13. $2x^2 < 5x + 3$

$$2x^2 - 5x - 3 < 0$$

$$(2x+1)(x-3) < 0$$

$x = -\dfrac{1}{2}$, $x = 3$ are the zeros. $f(x) = 2x^2 - 5x - 3$

Interval	Test Number	$f(x)$	Positive/Negative
$-\infty < x < -1/2$	-1	4	Positive
$-1/2 < x < 3$	0	-3	Negative
$3 < x < \infty$	4	9	Positive

The solution set is $\left\{ x \mid -\dfrac{1}{2} < x < 3 \right\}$.

15. $x(x-7) > 8$

$$x^2 - 7x > 8$$

$$x^2 - 7x - 8 > 0$$

$$(x+1)(x-8) > 0$$

$x = -1$, $x = 8$ are the zeros. $f(x) = x^2 - 7x - 8$

Interval	Test Number	$f(x)$	Positive/Negative
$-\infty < x < -1$	-2	10	Positive
$-1 < x < 8$	0	-8	Negative
$8 < x < \infty$	9	10	Positive

The solution set is $\left\{ x \mid x < -1 \ \text{ or } \ x > 8 \right\}$.

17. $4x^2 + 9 < 6x$

$$4x^2 - 6x + 9 < 0$$

$f(x) = 4x^2 - 6x + 9$

$$b^2 - 4ac = (-6)^2 - 4(4)(9) = 36 - 144 = -108$$

Since the discriminant is negative, there are no real zeros.
There is only one interval, the entire number line; choose any value and test.
For $x = 0$, $4x^2 - 6x + 9 = 9 > 0$. Thus, there is no solution.

19. $6(x^2 - 1) > 5x$

$$6x^2 - 6 > 5x$$

$$6x^2 - 5x - 6 > 0$$

$$(3x+2)(2x-3) > 0$$

$x = -\dfrac{2}{3}, x = \dfrac{3}{2}$ are the zeros. $f(x) = 6x^2 - 5x - 6$

Interval	Test Number	$f(x)$	Positive/Negative
$-\infty < x < -2/3$	-1	5	Positive
$-2/3 < x < 3/2$	0	-6	Negative
$3/2 < x < \infty$	2	8	Positive

The solution set is $\left\{ x \,\middle|\, x < -\dfrac{2}{3} \text{ or } x > \dfrac{3}{2} \right\}$.

21. The domain of the expression $f(x) = \sqrt{x^2 - 16}$ includes all values for which
$x^2 - 16 \geq 0 \Rightarrow (x + 4)(x - 4) \geq 0$
The zeros are $x = -4$ and $x = 4$. $p(x) = x^2 - 16$

Interval	Test Number	$p(x)$	Positive/Negative
$-\infty < x < -4$	-5	9	Positive
$-4 < x < 4$	0	-16	Negative
$4 < x < \infty$	5	9	Positive

The solution or domain is $\left\{ x \,\middle|\, x \leq -4 \text{ or } x \geq 4 \right\}$.

23. $f(x) = x^2 - 1;\quad g(x) = 3x + 3$

(a) $f(x) = 0$
$x^2 - 1 = 0$

$(x - 1)(x + 1) = 0$

$x = 1; x = -1$
Solution set: $\{-1, 1\}$.

(b) $g(x) = 0$
$3x + 3 = 0$

$3x = -3$

$x = -1$
Solution set: $\{-1\}$.

(c) $f(x) = g(x)$
$x^2 - 1 = 3x + 3$

$x^2 - 3x - 4 = 0$

$(x - 4)(x + 1) = 0$

$x = 4; x = -1$
Solution set: $\{-1, 4\}$.

(d) $f(x) > 0$
$x^2 - 1 > 0$

$(x - 1)(x + 1) > 0$
The zeros are $x = -1$ and $x = 1$.

Interval	Test Number	$f(x)$	Positive/Negative
$-\infty < x < -1$	-2	3	Positive
$-1 < x < 1$	0	-1	Negative
$1 < x < \infty$	2	3	Positive

The solution set is $\left\{ x \,\middle|\, x < -1 \text{ or } x > 1 \right\}$.

(e) $g(x) \leq 0$

$\quad 3x + 3 \leq 0$

$\quad 3x \leq -3$

$\quad x \leq -1$

$\quad$ The solution set is $\{ x | x \leq -1 \}$.

(f) $f(x) > g(x)$

$\quad x^2 - 1 > 3x + 3$

$\quad x^2 - 3x - 4 > 0$

$\quad (x - 4)(x + 1) > 0$

$\quad$ The zeros are $x = -1$ and $x = 4$.　　　$p(x) = x^2 - 3x - 4$

Interval	Test Number	$p(x)$	Positive/Negative
$-\infty < x < -1$	-2	6	Positive
$-1 < x < 4$	0	-4	Negative
$4 < x < \infty$	5	6	Positive

$\quad$ The solution set is $\{ x | x < -1 \text{ or } x > 4 \}$.

(g) $f(x) \geq 1$

$\quad x^2 - 1 > 1$

$\quad x^2 - 2 > 0$

$\quad \left(x - \sqrt{2} \right)\left(x + \sqrt{2} \right) > 0$

$\quad$ The zeros are $x = -\sqrt{2}$ and $x = \sqrt{2}$.　　　$p(x) = x^2 - 2$

Interval	Test Number	$p(x)$	Positive/Negative
$-\infty < x < -\sqrt{2}$	-2	2	Positive
$-\sqrt{2} < x < \sqrt{2}$	0	-2	Negative
$\sqrt{2} < x < \infty$	2	2	Positive

$\quad$ The solution set is $\left\{ x | x < -\sqrt{2} \text{ or } x > \sqrt{2} \right\}$.

25. $f(x) = -x^2 + 1; \quad g(x) = 4x + 1$

(a) $f(x) = 0$

$\quad -x^2 + 1 = 0 \Rightarrow 1 - x^2 = 0$

$\quad (1 - x)(1 + x) = 0$

$\quad x = 1; x = -1$

$\quad$ Solution set: $\{ -1, 1 \}$.

(b) $g(x) = 0$

$\quad 4x + 1 = 0$

$\quad 4x = -1$

$\quad x = -\dfrac{1}{4}$

$\quad$ Solution set: $\left\{ -\dfrac{1}{4} \right\}$.

(c) $f(x) = g(x)$

$\quad -x^2 + 1 = 4x + 1$

$\quad 0 = x^2 + 4x \Rightarrow 0 = x(x + 4)$

$\quad x = -4; x = 0$

$\quad$ Solution set: $\{ -4, 0 \}$.

(d) $f(x) > 0$

$-x^2 + 1 > 0 \Rightarrow 1 - x^2 > 0$

$(1-x)(1+x) > 0$

$x = 1; x = -1$

The zeros are $x = -1$ and $x = 1$.

Interval	Test Number	$f(x)$	Positive/Negative
$-\infty < x < -1$	-2	-3	Negative
$-1 < x < 1$	0	1	Positive
$1 < x < \infty$	2	-3	Negative

The solution set is $\left\{ x \mid -1 < x < 1 \right\}$.

(e) $g(x) \le 0$

$4x + 1 \le 0$

$4x \le -1$

$x \le -\dfrac{1}{4}$

The solution set is $\left\{ x \mid x \le -\dfrac{1}{4} \right\}$.

(f) $f(x) > g(x)$

$-x^2 + 1 > 4x + 1$

$0 > x^2 + 4x$

$0 > x(x+4)$

The zeros are $x = -4$ and $x = 0$. $p(x) = x(x+4)$

Interval	Test Number	$p(x)$	Positive/Negative
$-\infty < x < -4$	-5	5	Positive
$-4 < x < 0$	-1	-3	Negative
$0 < x < \infty$	1	5	Positive

The solution set is $\left\{ x \mid -4 < x < 0 \right\}$.

(g) $f(x) \ge 1$

$-x^2 + 1 \ge 1 \Rightarrow -x^2 \ge 0 \Rightarrow x^2 \le 0$

The zero is $x = 0$. $p(x) = x^2$

Interval	Test Number	$p(x)$	Positive/Negative
$-\infty < x < 0$	-1	1	Positive
$0 < x < \infty$	1	1	Positive

The solution set is $\{0\}$.

27. $f(x) = x^2 - 4; \quad g(x) = -x^2 + 4$

(a) $f(x) = 0$

$x^2 - 4 = 0$

$(x-2)(x+2) = 0$

$x = 2; x = -2$

Solution set: $\{-2, 2\}$.

(b) $g(x) = 0$

$-x^2 + 4 = 0 \Rightarrow 4 - x^2 = 0$

$(2-x)(2+x) = 0$

$x = 2; x = -2$

Solution set: $\{-2, 2\}$.

(c) $f(x) = g(x)$

$x^2 - 4 = -x^2 + 4$

$2x^2 - 8 = 0$

$2(x^2 - 4) = 0$

$2(x - 2)(x + 2) = 0$

$x = 2; x = -2$

Solution set: $\{-2, 2\}$.

(d) $f(x) > 0$

$x^2 - 4 > 0$

$(x - 2)(x + 2) > 0$

The zeros are $x = -2$ and $x = 2$.

Interval	Test Number	$f(x)$	Positive/Negative
$-\infty < x < -2$	-3	5	Positive
$-2 < x < 2$	0	-4	Negative
$2 < x < \infty$	3	5	Positive

The solution set is $\{x \mid x < -2 \text{ or } x > 2\}$.

(e) $g(x) \le 0$

$-x^2 + 4 \le 0 \Rightarrow 4 - x^2 \le 0$

$(2 - x)(2 + x) \le 0$

The zeros are $x = -2$ and $x = 2$.

Interval	Test Number	$g(x)$	Positive/Negative
$-\infty < x < -2$	-3	-5	Negative
$-2 < x < 2$	0	4	Positive
$2 < x < \infty$	3	-5	Negative

The solution set is $\{x \mid x \le -2 \text{ or } x \ge 2\}$.

(f) $f(x) > g(x)$

$x^2 - 4 > -x^2 + 4$

$2x^2 - 8 > 0$

$2(x^2 - 4) > 0$

$2(x - 2)(x + 2) > 0$

The zeros are $x = -2$ and $x = 2$. $p(x) = 2(x - 2)(x + 2)$

Interval	Test Number	$p(x)$	Positive/Negative
$-\infty < x < -2$	-3	10	Positive
$-2 < x < 2$	0	-8	Negative
$2 < x < \infty$	3	10	Positive

The solution set is $\{x \mid x < -2 \text{ or } x > 2\}$.

(g) $f(x) \geq 1$

$x^2 - 4 \geq 1$

$x^2 - 5 \geq 0$

$\left(x - \sqrt{5}\right)\left(x + \sqrt{5}\right) \geq 0$

The zeros are $x = -\sqrt{5}$ and $x = \sqrt{5}$. $p(x) = \left(x - \sqrt{5}\right)\left(x + \sqrt{5}\right)$

Interval	Test Number	$p(x)$	Positive/Negative
$-\infty < x < -\sqrt{5}$	-3	4	Positive
$-\sqrt{5} < x < \sqrt{5}$	0	-5	Negative
$\sqrt{5} < x < \infty$	3	4	Positive

The solution set is $\left\{ x \mid x \leq -\sqrt{5} \text{ or } x \geq \sqrt{5} \right\}$.

29. $f(x) = x^2 - x - 2; \quad g(x) = x^2 + x - 2$

(a) $f(x) = 0$

$x^2 - x - 2 = 0$

$(x - 2)(x + 1) = 0$

$x = 2, x = -1$

Solution set: $\{-1, 2\}$.

(b) $g(x) = 0$

$x^2 + x - 2 = 0$

$(x + 2)(x - 1) = 0$

$x = -2; x = 1$

Solution set: $\{-2, 1\}$.

(c) $f(x) = g(x)$

$x^2 - x - 2 = x^2 + x - 2$

$-2x = 0$

$x = 0$

Solution set: $\{0\}$.

(d) $f(x) > 0$

$x^2 - x - 2 > 0 \Rightarrow (x - 2)(x + 1) > 0$

The zeros are $x = -1$ and $x = 2$.

Interval	Test Number	$f(x)$	Positive/Negative
$-\infty < x < -1$	-2	4	Positive
$-1 < x < 2$	0	-2	Negative
$2 < x < \infty$	3	4	Positive

The solution set is $\left\{ x \mid x < -1 \text{ or } x > 2 \right\}$.

(e) $g(x) \leq 0$

$x^2 + x - 2 \leq 0 \Rightarrow (x + 2)(x - 1) \leq 0$

The zeros are $x = -2$ and $x = 1$.

Interval	Test Number	$g(x)$	Positive/Negative
$-\infty < x < -2$	-3	4	Positive
$-2 < x < 1$	0	-2	Negative
$1 < x < \infty$	2	4	Positive

The solution set is $\left\{ x \mid -2 \leq x \leq 1 \right\}$

(f) $f(x) > g(x)$

$x^2 - x - 2 > x^2 + x - 2 \Rightarrow -2x > 0 \Rightarrow x < 0$

The solution set is $\{x \mid x < 0\}$.

(g) $f(x) \geq 1$

$x^2 - x - 2 \geq 1 \Rightarrow x^2 - x - 3 \geq 0$

$x = \dfrac{-(-1) \pm \sqrt{(-1)^2 - 4(1)(-3)}}{2(1)} = \dfrac{1 \pm \sqrt{1+12}}{2} = \dfrac{1 \pm \sqrt{13}}{2}$

The zeros are $x = \dfrac{1 - \sqrt{13}}{2} \approx -1.30$ and $x = \dfrac{1 + \sqrt{13}}{2} \approx 2.30$.

$$p(x) = x^2 - x - 3$$

Interval	Test Number	$p(x)$	Positive/Negative
$-\infty < x < \dfrac{1-\sqrt{13}}{2}$	-2	3	Positive
$\dfrac{1-\sqrt{13}}{2} < x < \dfrac{1+\sqrt{13}}{2}$	0	-3	Negative
$\dfrac{1+\sqrt{13}}{2} < x < \infty$	3	3	Positive

The solution set is $\left\{ x \mid x \leq \dfrac{1-\sqrt{13}}{2} \text{ or } x \geq \dfrac{1+\sqrt{13}}{2} \right\}$.

31. (a) $s(t) = 80t - 16t^2 \Rightarrow a = -16, b = 80$

The maximum height occurs when $t = -\dfrac{b}{2a} = -\dfrac{80}{2(-16)} = 2.5$ seconds.

(b) The maximum height is when $s\left(-\dfrac{b}{2a}\right) = 80(2.5) - 16(2.5)^2 = 100$ feet.

(c) The ball strikes the ground when $s(t) = 80t - 16t^2 = 0$.

$80t - 16t^2 = 0 \Rightarrow 16t(5 - t) = 0 \Rightarrow t = 0, t = 5$

The ball strikes the ground after 5 seconds.

(d) Find the values of t for which

$80t - 16t^2 > 96 \Rightarrow -16t^2 + 80t - 96 > 0$

$16t^2 - 80t + 96 < 0 \Rightarrow 16(t^2 - 5t + 6) < 0 \Rightarrow 16(t - 2)(t - 3) < 0$

The zeros are $t = 2$ and $t = 3$. $s(t) = 16t^2 - 80t + 96$

Interval	Test Number	$s(t)$	Positive/Negative
$-\infty < t < 2$	1	32	Positive
$2 < t < 3$	2.5	-4	Negative
$3 < t < \infty$	4	32	Positive

The solution set is $\{t \mid 2 < t < 3\}$. The ball is more than 96 feet above the ground for times between 2 and 3 seconds.

33. $R(p) = -4p^2 + 4000p$, $a = -4$, $b = 4000$, $c = 0$. Since $a = -4 < 0$, the graph is a parabola that opens down, so the vertex is a maximum point.

(a)   The maximum occurs at
$$p = \frac{-b}{2a} = \frac{-4000}{2(-4)} = 500.$$
Thus, the unit price should be \$500 for maximum revenue.

(b)   The maximum revenue is
$$R(500) = -4(500)^2 + 4000(500) = -1000000 + 2000000 = \$1,000,000$$

(c) $R(p) = -4p^2 + 4000p = 0$
$$-4p(p - 1000) = 0 \Rightarrow p = 0, p = 1000$$
Thus, the revenue equals zero when $p = \$0$ and when $p = \$1000$.

(d)   Find the values of P for which $R(p) = -4p^2 + 4000p > 800000$
$$-4p^2 + 4000p > 800000 \Rightarrow -4p^2 + 4000p - 800000 > 0$$
$$4p^2 - 4000p + 800000 < 0 \Rightarrow 4\left(p^2 - 1000p + 200000\right) < 0$$
$$p^2 - 1000p + 200000 = 0$$
when $p = \dfrac{-(-1000) \pm \sqrt{(-1000)^2 - 4(1)(200000)}}{2(1)} = \dfrac{1000 \pm \sqrt{200000}}{2}$

$$= \frac{1000 \pm 200\sqrt{5}}{2} = 500 \pm 100\sqrt{5}$$

The zeros are $p \approx 276.39$ and $p \approx 723.61$. $s(p) = -4p^2 + 4000p - 800000$

Interval	Test Number	$s(t)$	Positive/Negative
$-\infty < p < 276.39$	276	-704	Negative
$276.39 < p < 723.61$	277	1084	Positive
$723.61 < p < \infty$	724	-704	Negative

The solution set is $\{p \,|\, 276.39 < p < 723.61\}$. The revenue is more than \$800,000 for prices between \$276.39 and \$723.61.

35.   Solving $(x - 4)^2 \le 0$

The only zero is $x = 4$. $f(x) = (x - 4)^2$

Interval	Test Number	$f(x)$	Positive/Negative
$-\infty < x < 4$	-5	81	Positive
$4 < x < \infty$	5	1	Positive

The solution is $\{x \,|\, x = 4\}$. Therefore, the given inequality has exactly one real solution.

37.   Solving $x^2 + x + 1 > 0$

The discriminant $b^2 - 4ac = 1^2 - 4(1)(1) = -3 < 0 \Rightarrow$ there are no real zeros.

So $f(x) = x^2 + x + 1$ is either always positive or always negative.

Interval	Test Number	$f(x)$	Positive/Negative
$-\infty < x < \infty$	0	1	Positive

The solution is $\{x \,|-\infty < x < \infty\}$. Therefore, the given inequality has all real numbers as the solution set.

Quadratic Functions and Models

3.4 Quadratic Models: Building Quadratic Functions

1. (a) $R(x) = x\left(-\dfrac{1}{6}x + 100\right) = -\dfrac{1}{6}x^2 + 100x$

   (b) $R(200) = -\dfrac{1}{6}(200)^2 + 100(200) = \dfrac{-20000}{3} + 20000 = \dfrac{40000}{3} \approx \$13{,}333$

   (c) $x = \dfrac{-b}{2a} = \dfrac{-100}{2(-1/6)} = \dfrac{-100}{(-1/3)} = \dfrac{300}{1} = 300$ maximizes revenue

   $R(300) = -\dfrac{1}{6}(300)^2 + 100(300) = -15000 + 30000 = \$15{,}000 = $ maximum revenue

   (d) $p = -\dfrac{1}{6}(300) + 100 = -50 + 100 = \$50$ maximizes revenue

3. (a) If $x = -5p + 100$, then $p = \dfrac{100 - x}{5}$. $R(x) = x\left(\dfrac{100 - x}{5}\right) = -\dfrac{1}{5}x^2 + 20x$

   (b) $R(15) = -\dfrac{1}{5}(15)^2 + 20(15) = -45 + 300 = \$255$

   (c) $x = \dfrac{-b}{2a} = \dfrac{-20}{2(-1/5)} = \dfrac{-20}{(-2/5)} = \dfrac{100}{2} = 50$ maximizes revenue

   $R(50) = -\dfrac{1}{5}(50)^2 + 20(50) = -500 + 1000 = \$500 = $ maximum revenue

   (d) $p = \dfrac{100 - 50}{5} = \dfrac{50}{5} = \$10$ maximizes revenue

5. (a) Let $x = $ width and $y = $ length of the rectangular area.

   $P = 2x + 2y = 400 \Rightarrow y = \dfrac{400 - 2x}{2} = 200 - x$

   Then $A(x) = (200 - x)x = 200x - x^2 = -x^2 + 200x$

   (b) $x = \dfrac{-b}{2a} = \dfrac{-200}{2(-1)} = \dfrac{-200}{-2} = 100$ yards maximizes area

   (c) $A(100) = -100^2 + 200(100) = -10000 + 20000 = 10{,}000$ sq. yds. $= $ maximum area

7. Let $x = $ width and $y = $ length of the rectangular area.

   $2x + y = 4000 \quad \Rightarrow \quad y = 4000 - 2x$

   Then $A(x) = (4000 - 2x)x = 4000x - 2x^2 = -2x^2 + 4000x$

   $x = \dfrac{-b}{2a} = \dfrac{-4000}{2(-2)} = \dfrac{-4000}{-4} = 1000$ maximizes area

   $A(1000) = -2(1000)^2 + 4000(1000) = -2000000 + 4000000 = 2{,}000{,}000$

   The largest area that can be enclosed is 2,000,000 square meters.

9. Locate the origin at the point where the cable touches the road. Then the equation of the parabola is of the form: $y = ax^2$, where $a > 0$. Since the point (200, 75) is on the parabola, we can find the constant a:

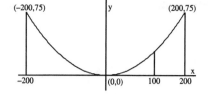

$$75 = a(200)^2 \quad \Rightarrow \quad a = \frac{75}{200^2} = 0.001875$$

When $x = 100$, we have:
$$y = 0.001875(100)^2 = 18.75 \text{ meters}.$$

11. Let $x =$ the depth of the gutter and $y =$ the width of the gutter.
    Then $A = xy$ is the cross-sectional area of the gutter.
    Since the aluminum sheets for the gutter are 12 inches wide, we have
    $$2x + y = 12 \quad \Rightarrow \quad y = 12 - 2x.$$
    The area is to be maximized, so: $A = xy = x(12 - 2x) = -2x^2 + 12x$.
    This equation is a parabola opening down; thus, it has a maximum when
    $$x = \frac{-b}{2a} = \frac{-12}{2(-2)} = \frac{-12}{-4} = 3.$$
    Thus, a depth of 3 inches produces a maximum cross-sectional area.

13. Let $x =$ the width of the rectangle or the diameter of the semicircle.
    Let $y =$ the length of the rectangle.

    The perimeter of each semicircle is $\dfrac{\pi x}{2}$.

    The perimeter of the track is given by: $\dfrac{\pi x}{2} + \dfrac{\pi x}{2} + y + y = 400$.

    Solving for x:

    $$\frac{\pi x}{2} + \frac{\pi x}{2} + y + y = 1500 \Rightarrow \pi x + 2y = 400 \Rightarrow \pi x = 400 - 2y \Rightarrow x = \frac{400 - 2y}{\pi}$$

    The area of the rectangle is: $A = xy = \left(\dfrac{400 - 2y}{\pi}\right)y = \dfrac{-2}{\pi}y^2 + \dfrac{400}{\pi}y$

    This equation is a parabola opening down; thus, it has a maximum when

    $$y = \frac{-b}{2a} = \frac{(-400/\pi)}{2(-2/\pi)} = \frac{-400}{-4} = 100. \quad \text{Thus, } x = \frac{400 - 2(100)}{\pi} = \frac{200}{\pi} \approx 63.7$$

    The dimensions for the rectangle with maximum area are $\dfrac{200}{\pi} \approx 63.7$ meters by 100 meters.

Problems 15 – 17. The equations for the curves that are graphed on the screens use many more decimal places in order to get the desired accuracy.

15. (a) Graphing: The data appear to be quadratic with $a < 0$.

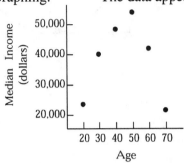

(b) Using the QUADratic REGression program, the quadratic function of best fit is:
$$I(x) = -47.71x^2 + 4262.66x - 42777.73$$

(c) $$x = \frac{-b}{2a} = \frac{-4262.66}{2(-47.71)} \approx 44.673$$

An individual will earn the most income at an age of approximately 45 years.

(d) The maximum income will be:
$$I(44.7) = -47.71(44.7)^2 + 4262.66(44.7) - 42777.73 \approx \$52,434$$

(e) Graphing the quadratic function of best fit:

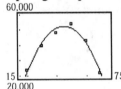

17. (a) Graphing: The data appears to be quadratic with $a < 0$.

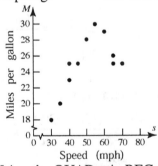

(b) Using the QUADratic REGression program, the quadratic function of best fit is:
$$M(s) = -0.0175s^2 + 1.93s - 25.34$$

(c) $$s = \frac{-b}{2a} = \frac{-1.93}{2(-0.0175)} \approx 55.1$$ The speed that maximizes miles per gallon is about 55.1

miles per hour.

(d) The predicted miles per gallon when the speed is 63 miles per hour is:
$$M(63) = -0.0175(63)^2 + 1.93(63) - 25.34 \approx 26.8 \text{ miles per gallon.}$$

(e)   Graphing the quadratic function of best fit:

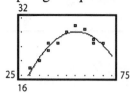

19.   We are given: $V(x) = kx(a - x) = -kx^2 + akx$

The reaction rate is a maximum when: $x = \dfrac{-b}{2a} = \dfrac{-ak}{2(-k)} = \dfrac{ak}{2k} = \dfrac{a}{2}$

21. $f(x) = -5x^2 + 8$ $h = 1$:

$\text{Area} = \dfrac{h}{3}\left(2ah^2 + 6c\right) = \dfrac{1}{3}\left(2(-5)(1)^2 + 6(8)\right) = \dfrac{1}{3}(-10 + 48) = \dfrac{38}{3} \approx 12.67$ sq. units

23. $f(x) = x^2 + 3x + 5$, $h = 4$

$\text{Area} = \dfrac{h}{3}\left(2ah^2 + 6c\right) = \dfrac{4}{3}\left(2(1)(4)^2 + 6(5)\right) = \dfrac{4}{3}(32 + 30) = \dfrac{248}{3} \approx 82.67$ sq. units.

Chapter 3

Quadratic Functions and Models

3.5 Complex Numbers; Quadratic Equations with a Negative Discriminant

1. $(2-3i)+(6+8i)=(2+6)+(-3+8)i=8+5i$

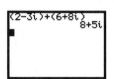

3. $(-3+2i)-(4-4i)=(-3-4)+(2-(-4))i=-7+6i$

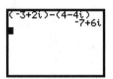

5. $(2-5i)-(8+6i)=(2-8)+(-5-6)i=-6-11i$

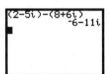

7. $3(2-6i)=6-18i$

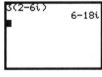

9. $2i(2-3i)=4i-6i^2=4i-6(-1)=6+4i$

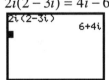

11. $(3-4i)(2+i)=6+3i-8i-4i^2$
$=6-5i-4(-1)=10-5i$

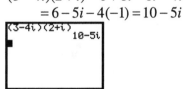

13. $(-6+i)(-6-i)=36+6i-6i-i^2$
$=36-(-1)=37$

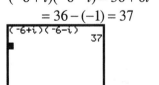

15. $\dfrac{10}{3-4i}=\dfrac{10}{3-4i}\cdot\dfrac{3+4i}{3+4i}=\dfrac{30+40i}{9+12i-12i-16i^2}$
$=\dfrac{30+40i}{9-16(-1)}=\dfrac{30+40i}{25}$
$=\dfrac{30}{25}+\dfrac{40}{25}i=\dfrac{6}{5}+\dfrac{8}{5}i$

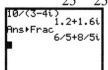

158

17. $\dfrac{2+i}{i} = \dfrac{2+i}{i} \cdot \dfrac{-i}{-i} = \dfrac{-2i-i^2}{-i^2}$

$= \dfrac{-2i-(-1)}{-(-1)} = \dfrac{1-2i}{1} = 1-2i$

```
(2+i)/i
            1-2i
■
```

19. $\dfrac{6-i}{1+i} = \dfrac{6-i}{1+i} \cdot \dfrac{1-i}{1-i} = \dfrac{6-6i-i+i^2}{1-i+i-i^2}$

$= \dfrac{6-7i+(-1)}{1-(-1)} = \dfrac{5-7i}{2} = \dfrac{5}{2} - \dfrac{7}{2}i$

```
(6-i)/(1+i)
         2.5-3.5i
Ans▶Frac
         5/2-7/2i
■
```

21. $\left(\dfrac{1}{2} + \dfrac{\sqrt{3}}{2}i\right)^2 = \dfrac{1}{4} + 2\left(\dfrac{1}{2}\right)\left(\dfrac{\sqrt{3}}{2}i\right) + \dfrac{3}{4}i^2$

$= \dfrac{1}{4} + \dfrac{\sqrt{3}}{2}i + \dfrac{3}{4}(-1) = -\dfrac{1}{2} + \dfrac{\sqrt{3}}{2}i$

```
(1/2+√(3)i/2)^2
-.5+.8660254038i
Ans▶Frac
-1/2+.866025403…
■
```

23. $(1+i)^2 = 1 + 2i + i^2 = 1 + 2i + (-1) = 2i$

```
(1+i)^2
            2i
■
```

25. $i^{23} = i^{22+1} = i^{22} \cdot i = \left(i^2\right)^{11} \cdot i = (-1)^{11}i = -i$

```
i^23
      3E-13-i
■
```

27. $i^{-15} = \dfrac{1}{i^{15}} = \dfrac{1}{i^{14+1}} = \dfrac{1}{i^{14} \cdot i} = \dfrac{1}{(i^2)^7 \cdot i} = \dfrac{1}{(-1)^7 i} = \dfrac{1}{-i} = \dfrac{1}{-i} \cdot \dfrac{i}{i} = \dfrac{i}{-i^2} = \dfrac{i}{-(-1)} = i$

```
i^-15
      5E-13+i
■
```

29. $i^6 - 5 = \left(i^2\right)^3 - 5 = (-1)^3 - 5 = -1 - 5 = -6$

```
i^6-5
            -6
■
```

31. $6i^3 - 4i^5 = i^3(6 - 4i^2) = i^2 \cdot i(6 - 4(-1)) = -1 \cdot i(10) = -10i$

```
6i^3-4i^5
            -10i
■
```

33. $(1+i)^3 = (1+i)(1+i)(1+i) = (1+2i+i^2)(1+i) = (1+2i-1)(1+i) = 2i(1+i)$
   $= 2i+2i^2 = 2i+2(-1) = -2+2i$

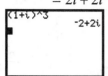

35. $i^7(1+i^2) = i^7(1+(-1)) = i^7(0) = 0$

37. $i^6 + i^4 + i^2 + 1 = \left(i^2\right)^3 + \left(i^2\right)^2 + i^2 + 1 = (-1)^3 + (-1)^2 + (-1) + 1 = -1+1-1+1 = 0$

39. $\sqrt{-4} = 2i$ 41. $\sqrt{-25} = 5i$

43. $\sqrt{(3+4i)(4i-3)} = \sqrt{12i-9+16i^2-12i} = \sqrt{-9+16(-1)} = \sqrt{-25} = 5i$

45. $x^2 + 4 = 0$
   $a = 1, b = 0, c = 4,\quad b^2 - 4ac = 0^2 - 4(1)(4) = -16$

   $x = \dfrac{-0 \pm \sqrt{-16}}{2(1)} = \dfrac{\pm 4i}{2} = \pm 2i$

   The solution set is $\{\pm 2i\}$.

47. $x^2 - 16 = 0$
   $(x+4)(x-4) = 0 \Rightarrow x = -4, x = 4$

   The solution set is $\{\pm 4\}$.

49. $x^2 - 6x + 13 = 0$
   $a = 1, b = -6, c = 13,$

   $b^2 - 4ac = (-6)^2 - 4(1)(13) = 36 - 52 = -16$

   $x = \dfrac{-(-6) \pm \sqrt{-16}}{2(1)} = \dfrac{6 \pm 4i}{2} = 3 \pm 2i$

   The solution set is $\{3 - 2i, 3 + 2i\}$.

51. $x^2 - 6x + 10 = 0$
$a = 1, b = -6, c = 10$

$b^2 - 4ac = (-6)^2 - 4(1)(10) = 36 - 40 = -4$

$x = \dfrac{-(-6) \pm \sqrt{-4}}{2(1)} = \dfrac{6 \pm 2i}{2} = 3 \pm i$

The solution set is $\{3 - i, 3 + i\}$.

53. $8x^2 - 4x + 1 = 0$
$a = 8, b = -4, c = 1$

$b^2 - 4ac = (-4)^2 - 4(8)(1) = 16 - 32 = -16$

$x = \dfrac{-(-4) \pm \sqrt{-16}}{2(8)} = \dfrac{4 \pm 4i}{16} = \dfrac{1}{4} \pm \dfrac{1}{4}i$

The solution set is $\left\{ \dfrac{1}{4} - \dfrac{1}{4}i, \ \dfrac{1}{4} + \dfrac{1}{4}i \right\}$.

55. $5x^2 + 2x + 1 = 0$
$a = 5, b = 2, c = 1$

$b^2 - 4ac = (2)^2 - 4(5)(1) = 4 - 20 = -16$

$x = \dfrac{-2 \pm \sqrt{-16}}{2(5)} = \dfrac{-2 \pm 4i}{10} = -\dfrac{1}{5} \pm \dfrac{2}{5}i$

The solution set is $\left\{ -\dfrac{1}{5} - \dfrac{2}{5}i, \ -\dfrac{1}{5} + \dfrac{2}{5}i \right\}$.

57. $x^2 + x + 1 = 0$
$a = 1, b = 1, c = 1, \quad b^2 - 4ac = 1^2 - 4(1)(1) = 1 - 4 = -3$

$x = \dfrac{-1 \pm \sqrt{-3}}{2(1)} = \dfrac{-1 \pm \sqrt{3}i}{2} = -\dfrac{1}{2} \pm \dfrac{\sqrt{3}}{2}i$

The solution set is $\left\{ -\dfrac{1}{2} - \dfrac{\sqrt{3}}{2}i, \ -\dfrac{1}{2} + \dfrac{\sqrt{3}}{2}i \right\}$.

59. $x^3 - 8 = 0$
$(x - 2)(x^2 + 2x + 4) = 0$

$$x - 2 = 0 \Rightarrow x = 2$$

$$x^2 + 2x + 4 = 0$$
$a = 1, b = 2, c = 4$

$b^2 - 4ac = 2^2 - 4(1)(4) = 4 - 16 = -12$

$x = \dfrac{-2 \pm \sqrt{-12}}{2(1)} = \dfrac{-2 \pm 2\sqrt{3}i}{2} = -1 \pm \sqrt{3}i$

The solution set is $\left\{ 2, \ -1 - \sqrt{3}i, \ -1 + \sqrt{3}i \right\}$.

61. $x^4 - 16 = 0$

$\left(x^2 - 4\right)\left(x^2 + 4\right) = 0 \Rightarrow (x-2)(x+2)\left(x^2 + 4\right) = 0$

$x - 2 = 0 \Rightarrow x = 2$

$x + 2 = 0 \Rightarrow x = -2$

$x^2 + 4 = 0 \Rightarrow x = \pm 2i$

The solution set is $\{-2,\ 2,\ -2i,\ 2i\}$.

63. $x^4 + 13x^2 + 36 = 0$

$\left(x^2 + 9\right)\left(x^2 + 4\right) = 0$

$x^2 + 9 = 0 \Rightarrow x = \pm 3i$

$x^2 + 4 = 0 \Rightarrow x = \pm 2i$

The solution set is $\{-3i,\ -2i,\ 2i,\ 3i\}$.

65. $3x^2 - 3x + 4 = 0$

$a = 3, b = -3, c = 4$

$b^2 - 4ac = (-3)^2 - 4(3)(4) = 9 - 48 = -39$

The equation has two complex conjugate solutions.

67. $2x^2 + 3x - 4 = 0$

$a = 2, b = 3, c = -4$

$b^2 - 4ac = 3^2 - 4(2)(-4) = 9 + 32 = 41$

The equation has two unequal real solutions.

69. $9x^2 - 12x + 4 = 0$

$a = 9, b = -12, c = 4$

$b^2 - 4ac = (-12)^2 - 4(9)(4) = 144 - 144 = 0$

The equation has a repeated real solution.

71. The other solution is the conjugate of $2 + 3i$, i.e. $2 - 3i$.

73. $z + \bar{z} = 3 - 4i + \overline{3 - 4i} = 3 - 4i + 3 + 4i = 6$

75. $z \cdot \bar{z} = (3 - 4i)(\overline{3 - 4i}) = (3 - 4i)(3 + 4i) = 9 + 12i - 12i - 16i^2 = 9 - 16(-1) = 25$

77. $z + \bar{z} = a + bi + \overline{a + bi} = a + bi + a - bi = 2a$

$z - \bar{z} = a + bi - (\overline{a + bi}) = a + bi - (a - bi) = a + bi - a + bi = 2bi$

79. $\overline{z + w} = \overline{(a + bi) + (c + di)} = \overline{(a + c) + (b + d)i} = (a + c) - (b + d)i$

$= (a - bi) + (c - di) = \overline{a + bi} + \overline{c + di} = \bar{z} + \bar{w}$

81 – 83.   Answers will vary.

Quadratic Functions and Models

3.R Chapter Review

1. $x^2 + 12x + 20 = 0$
$(x + 10)(x + 2) = 0$
$x = -10$ or $x = -2$
the solution set is $\{-10, -2\}$.

3. $x(1 - x) = 6 \Rightarrow x - x^2 = 6$
$0 = x^2 - x + 6; \quad a = 1, b = -1, c = 6$
The discriminant is given by:
$b^2 - 4ac = (-1)^2 - 4(1)(6) = -23 < 0$
Therefore, no real solution.

5. $(x - 1)(2x + 3) = 3$
$2x^2 + x - 3 = 3$
$2x^2 + x - 6 = 0$
$(2x - 3)(x + 2) = 0$
$x = \dfrac{3}{2}$ or $x = -2$
the solution set is $\left\{-2, \dfrac{3}{2}\right\}$.

7. $2x + 3 = 4x^2$
$0 = 4x^2 - 2x - 3$
$x = \dfrac{2 \pm \sqrt{4 + 48}}{8} = \dfrac{2 \pm \sqrt{52}}{8}$
$= \dfrac{2 \pm 2\sqrt{13}}{8} = \dfrac{1 \pm \sqrt{13}}{4}$
the solution set is $\left\{\dfrac{1 - \sqrt{13}}{4}, \dfrac{1 + \sqrt{13}}{4}\right\}$.

9. $x(x + 1) + 2 = 0$
$x^2 + x + 2 = 0$
$x = \dfrac{-1 \pm \sqrt{1 - 8}}{2} = \dfrac{-1 \pm \sqrt{-7}}{2}$
no real solutions

11. $x^4 - 5x^2 + 4 = 0$
$(x^2 - 4)(x^2 - 1) = 0$
$x^2 - 4 = 0$ or $x^2 - 1 = 0$
$x = \pm 2$ or $x = \pm 1$
the solution set is $\{-2, -1, 1, 2,\}$

13. $x^{-6} - 7x^{-3} - 8 = 0$
$\text{let } p = x^{-3} \Rightarrow p^2 = x^{-6}$
$p^2 - 7p - 8 = 0 \Rightarrow (p - 8)(p + 1) = 0 \Rightarrow p = 8 \quad \text{or} \quad p = -1$
$p = 8 \Rightarrow x^{-3} = 8 \Rightarrow \left(x^{-3}\right)^{-1/3} = (8)^{-1/3} \Rightarrow x = \dfrac{1}{2}$
$p = -1 \Rightarrow x^{-3} = -1 \Rightarrow \left(x^{-3}\right)^{-1/3} = (-1)^{-1/3} \Rightarrow x = -1$
Check:
$x = \dfrac{1}{2} : \left(\dfrac{1}{2}\right)^{-6} - 7(p)^{-3} - 8 = 0 \Rightarrow 64 - 56 - 8 = 0 \Rightarrow 0 = 0$
$x = -1 : (-1)^{-6} - 7(-1)^{-3} - 8 = 0 \Rightarrow 1 + 7 - 8 = 0 \Rightarrow 0 = 0$
The solution set is $\left\{\dfrac{1}{2}, -1\right\}$.

15. $(6+3i)-(2-4i)=(6-2)+(3-(-4))i=4+7i$

17. $4(3-i)+3(-5+2i)=12-4i-15+6i=-3+2i$

19. $\dfrac{3}{3+i}=\dfrac{3}{3+i}\cdot\dfrac{3-i}{3-i}=\dfrac{9-3i}{9-3i+3i-i^2}=\dfrac{9-3i}{10}=\dfrac{9}{10}-\dfrac{3}{10}i$

21. $i^{50}=i^{48}\cdot i^2=(i^4)^{12}\cdot i^2=1^{12}(-1)=-1$

23. $(2+3i)^3=(2+3i)^2(2+3i)=\left(4+12i+9i^2\right)(2+3i)=(-5+12i)(2+3i)$
$=-10-15i+24i+36i^2=-46+9i$

25. $x^2+x+1=0$
$a=1,b=1,c=1,\quad b^2-4ac=1^2-4(1)(1)=1-4=-3$
$x=\dfrac{-1\pm\sqrt{-3}}{2(1)}=\dfrac{-1\pm\sqrt{3}i}{2}=\dfrac{-1}{2}\pm\dfrac{\sqrt{3}}{2}i\Rightarrow$ The solution set is $\left\{\dfrac{-1}{2}-\dfrac{\sqrt{3}}{2}i,\ \dfrac{-1}{2}+\dfrac{\sqrt{3}}{2}i\right\}.$

27. $2x^2+x-2=0$
$a=2,b=1,c=-2,\quad b^2-4ac=1^2-4(2)(-2)=1+16=17$
$x=\dfrac{-1\pm\sqrt{17}}{2(2)}=\dfrac{-1\pm\sqrt{17}}{4}\quad\Rightarrow\quad$ The solution set is $\left\{\dfrac{-1-\sqrt{17}}{4},\ \dfrac{-1+\sqrt{17}}{4}\right\}.$

29. $x^2+3=x$
$x^2-x+3=0$
$a=1,b=-1,c=3,\quad b^2-4ac=(-1)^2-4(1)(3)=1-12=-11$
$x=\dfrac{-(-1)\pm\sqrt{-11}}{2(1)}=\dfrac{1\pm\sqrt{11}i}{2}=\dfrac{1}{2}\pm\dfrac{\sqrt{11}}{2}i\Rightarrow$ The solution set is $\left\{\dfrac{1}{2}-\dfrac{\sqrt{11}}{2}i,\ \dfrac{1}{2}+\dfrac{\sqrt{11}}{2}i\right\}.$

31. $x(1-x)=6$
$-x^2+x-6=0$
$a=-1,b=1,c=-6,\quad b^2-4ac=1^2-4(-1)(-6)=1-24=-23$
$x=\dfrac{-1\pm\sqrt{-23}}{2(-1)}=\dfrac{-1\pm\sqrt{23}i}{-2}=\dfrac{1}{2}\pm\dfrac{\sqrt{23}}{2}i\Rightarrow$ The solution set is $\left\{\dfrac{1}{2}-\dfrac{\sqrt{23}}{2}i,\ \dfrac{1}{2}+\dfrac{\sqrt{23}}{2}i\right\}.$

33. $f(x)=\dfrac{1}{4}x^2-16,\ a=\dfrac{1}{4},b=0,c=-16.$ Since $a=\dfrac{1}{4}>0$, the graph opens up.

The x-coordinate of the vertex is $x=\dfrac{-b}{2a}=\dfrac{-0}{2(1/4)}=\dfrac{0}{(1/2)}=0.$

The y-coordinate of the vertex is $f\left(\dfrac{-b}{2a}\right)=f(0)=\dfrac{1}{4}(0)^2-16=-16.$

Thus, the vertex is $(0,-16)$.
The axis of symmetry is the line $x=0$.

The discriminant is:

$$b^2 - 4ac = (0)^2 - 4\left(\frac{1}{4}\right)(-16) = 16 > 0,$$

so the graph has two x-intercepts.
The x-intercepts are found by solving:

$$\frac{1}{4}x^2 - 16 = 0$$

$$x^2 - 64 = 0 \Rightarrow x^2 = 64 \Rightarrow x = 8 \ \text{ or } \ x = -8$$

The x-intercepts are –8 and 8.
The y-intercept is $f(0) = -16$.
Domain: $(-\infty, \infty)$.
Range: $[-16, \infty)$.
f is increasing on $(0, \infty)$
f is decreasing on $(-\infty, 0)$

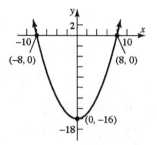

35. $f(x) = -4x^2 + 4x$, $a = -4$, $b = 4$, $c = 0$. Since $a = -4 < 0$, the graph opens down.

The x-coordinate of the vertex is $x = \dfrac{-b}{2a} = \dfrac{-4}{2(-4)} = \dfrac{-4}{-8} = \dfrac{1}{2}$.

The y-coordinate of the vertex is $f\left(\dfrac{-b}{2a}\right) = f\left(\dfrac{1}{2}\right) = -4\left(\dfrac{1}{2}\right)^2 + 4\left(\dfrac{1}{2}\right) = -1 + 2 = 1$.

Thus, the vertex is $\left(\dfrac{1}{2}, 1\right)$.

The axis of symmetry is the line $x = \dfrac{1}{2}$.

The discriminant is:

$$b^2 - 4ac = 4^2 - 4(-4)(0) = 16 > 0,$$

so the graph has two x-intercepts.
The x-intercepts are found by solving:
$-4x^2 + 4x = 0 \Rightarrow -4x(x - 1) = 0 \Rightarrow x = 0 \ \text{ or } \ x = 1$
The x-intercepts are 0 and 1.
The y-intercept is $f(0) = -4(0)^2 + 4(0) = 0$.
Domain: $(-\infty, \infty)$.
Range: $(-\infty, 1]$.

f is increasing on $\left(-\infty, \dfrac{1}{2}\right)$

f is decreasing on $\left(\dfrac{1}{2}, \infty\right)$

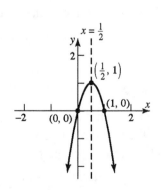

37. $f(x) = \dfrac{9}{2}x^2 + 3x + 1$, $a = \dfrac{9}{2}$, $b = 3$, $c = 1$. Since $a = \dfrac{9}{2} > 0$, the graph opens up.

The x-coordinate of the vertex is $x = \dfrac{-b}{2a} = \dfrac{-(3)}{2(9/2)} = -\dfrac{1}{3}$.

The y-coordinate of the vertex is $f\left(\dfrac{-b}{2a}\right) = f\left(-\dfrac{1}{3}\right) = \dfrac{9}{2}\left(-\dfrac{1}{3}\right)^2 + 3\left(-\dfrac{1}{3}\right) + 1 = \dfrac{1}{2} - 1 + 1 = \dfrac{1}{2}$.

Thus, the vertex is $\left(-\dfrac{1}{3}, \dfrac{1}{2}\right)$.

The axis of symmetry is the line $x = -\dfrac{1}{3}$.

The discriminant is:

$$b^2 - 4ac = 3^2 - 4\left(\dfrac{9}{2}\right)(1) = -9 < 0,$$

so the graph has no x-intercepts.

The y-intercept is $f(x) = \dfrac{9}{2}(0)^2 + 3(0) + 1 = 1$.

Domain: $(-\infty, \infty)$.

Range: $\left[\dfrac{1}{2}, \infty\right)$.

f is increasing on $\left(\dfrac{1}{2}, \infty\right)$

f is decreasing on $\left(-\infty, \dfrac{1}{2}\right)$

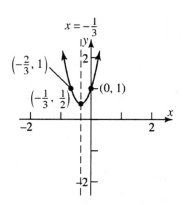

39. $f(x) = 3x^2 + 4x - 1$, $a = 3, b = 4, c = -1$. Since $a = 3 > 0$, the graph opens up.

The x-coordinate of the vertex is $x = \dfrac{-b}{2a} = \dfrac{-4}{2(3)} = \dfrac{-4}{6} = -\dfrac{2}{3}$.

The y-coordinate of the vertex is $f\left(\dfrac{-b}{2a}\right) = f\left(-\dfrac{2}{3}\right) = 3\left(-\dfrac{2}{3}\right)^2 + 4\left(-\dfrac{2}{3}\right) - 1 = \dfrac{4}{3} - \dfrac{8}{3} - 1 = -\dfrac{7}{3}$.

Thus, the vertex is $\left(-\dfrac{2}{3}, -\dfrac{7}{3}\right)$.

The axis of symmetry is the line $x = -\dfrac{2}{3}$.

The discriminant is: $b^2 - 4ac = (4)^2 - 4(3)(-1) = 16 + 12 = 28 > 0$,
so the graph has two x-intercepts.

The x-intercepts are found by solving: $3x^2 + 4x - 1 = 0$

$$x = \dfrac{-b \pm \sqrt{b^2 - 4ac}}{2a} = \dfrac{-4 \pm \sqrt{28}}{2(3)} = \dfrac{-4 \pm 2\sqrt{7}}{6} = \dfrac{-2 \pm \sqrt{7}}{3} \approx \dfrac{-2 \pm 2.646}{3}$$

The x-intercepts are approximately 0.22 and −1.55.
The y-intercept is $f(0) = 3(0)^2 + 4(0) - 1 = -1$.
Domain: $(-\infty, \infty)$.

Range: $\left[-\dfrac{7}{3}, \infty\right)$.

f is increasing on $\left(-\dfrac{2}{3}, \infty\right)$

f is decreasing on $\left(-\infty, -\dfrac{2}{3}\right)$

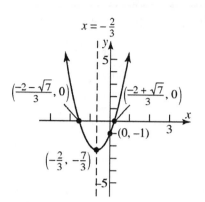

41. $f(x) = x^2 - 4x + 6$, $a = 1, b = -4, c = 6$. Since $a = 1 > 0$, the graph opens up.

The x-coordinate of the vertex is $x = \dfrac{-b}{2a} = \dfrac{-(-4)}{2(1)} = \dfrac{4}{2} = 2$.

The y-coordinate of the vertex is $f\left(\dfrac{-b}{2a}\right) = f(2) = (2)^2 - 4(2) + 6 = 4 - 8 + 6 = 2$.

Thus, the vertex is $(2, 2)$.

The axis of symmetry is the line $x = 2$.
The discriminant is:
$$b^2 - 4ac = (-4)^2 - 4(1)(6) = 16 - 24 = -8 < 0,$$
so the graph has no x-intercepts.
The y-intercept is $f(0) = (0)^2 - 4(0) + 6 = 6$.
Domain: $(-\infty, \infty)$.
Range: $[2, \infty)$.
f is increasing on $(2, \infty)$
f is decreasing on $(-\infty, 2)$

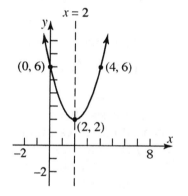

43. $f(x) = 3x^2 - 6x + 4$, $a = 3, b = -6, c = 4$. Since $a = 3 > 0$, the graph opens up, so the

vertex is a minimum point. The minimum occurs at $x = \dfrac{-b}{2a} = \dfrac{-(-6)}{2(3)} = \dfrac{6}{6} = 1$. The

minimum value is $f\left(\dfrac{-b}{2a}\right) = f(1) = 3(1)^2 - 6(1) + 4 = 3 - 6 + 4 = 1$.

45. $f(x) = -x^2 + 8x - 4$, $a = -1, b = 8, c = -4$. Since $a = -1 < 0$, the graph opens down, so

the vertex is a maximum point. The maximum occurs at $x = \dfrac{-b}{2a} = \dfrac{-8}{2(-1)} = \dfrac{-8}{-2} = 4$. The

maximum value is $f\left(\dfrac{-b}{2a}\right) = f(4) = -(4)^2 + 8(4) - 4 = -16 + 32 - 4 = 12$.

47. $f(x) = -3x^2 + 12x + 4$, $a = -3, b = 12, c = 4$. Since $a = -3 < 0$, the graph opens down, so

the vertex is a maximum point. The maximum occurs at $x = \dfrac{-b}{2a} = \dfrac{-12}{2(-3)} = \dfrac{-12}{-6} = 2$. The

maximum value is $f\left(\dfrac{-b}{2a}\right) = f(2) = -3(2)^2 + 12(2) + 4 = -12 + 24 + 4 = 16$.

49. $2x^2 + 5x - 12 < 0$ $f(x) = 2x^2 + 5x - 12$

$(x + 4)(2x - 3) < 0$ $x = -4, x = \dfrac{3}{2}$ are the zeros.

Interval	Test Number	$f(x)$	Positive/Negative
$-\infty < x < -4$	-5	13	Positive
$-4 < x < 3/2$	0	-12	Negative
$3/2 < x < \infty$	2	6	Positive

The solution set is $\left\{ x \middle| -4 < x < \dfrac{3}{2} \right\}$.

51. $3x^2 \geq 14x + 5 \Rightarrow 3x^2 - 14x - 5 \geq 0$ $f(x) = 3x^2 - 14x - 5$

$(3x + 1)(x - 5) \geq 0$ $x = -\dfrac{1}{3}, x = 5$ are the zeros.

Interval	Test Number	$f(x)$	Positive/Negative
$-\infty < x < -\dfrac{1}{3}$	-1	12	Positive
$-\dfrac{1}{3} < x < 5$	0	-5	Negative
$5 < x < \infty$	6	19	Positive

The solution set is $\left\{ x \middle| x \leq -\dfrac{1}{3} \text{ or } x \geq 5 \right\}$.

53. Let x represent the number of passengers over 20.
Then $20 + x$ represents the total number of passengers.
$15 - 0.1x$ represents the fare for each passenger.
Solving the equation for total cost ($482.40), we have:
$(20 + x)(15 - 0.1x) = 482.40$

$300 + 13x - 0.1x^2 = 482.40 \Rightarrow -0.1x^2 + 13x - 182.40 = 0$

$x^2 - 130x + 1824 = 0 \Rightarrow (x - 114)(x - 16) = 0 \Rightarrow x = 114$ or $x = 16$
Since the capacity of the bus is 44, we discard the 114. The total number of passengers is
20 + 16 = 36, and the ticket price per passenger is 15 – 0.1(16) = $13.40.
So 36 people went on the trip; each person paid $13.40.

55. length of $\text{leg}_1 = x$, length of $\text{leg}_2 = 17 - x$, by the Pythagorean Theorem we have
$x^2 + (17 - x)^2 = (13)^2 \Rightarrow x^2 + x^2 - 34x + 289 = 1692x^2 - 34x + 120 = 0$
$x^2 - 17x + 60 = 0 \Rightarrow (x - 12)(x - 5) = 0 \Rightarrow x = 12$ or $x = 5$
the legs are 5 cm and 12 cm long.

57. $C(x) = 4.9x^2 - 617.40x + 19,600$; $a = 4.9, b = -617.40, c = 19,600$. Since $a = 4.9 > 0$, the
graph opens up, so the vertex is a minimum point.

    (a) The minimum marginal cost occurs at $x = \dfrac{-b}{2a} = \dfrac{-(-617.40)}{2(4.9)} = \dfrac{617.40}{9.8} = 63$.

    (b) The minimum marginal cost is $C\left(\dfrac{-b}{2a}\right) = C(63) = 4.9(63)^2 - (617.40)(63) + 19600 = \$151.90$

59. Let x represent the length and y represent the width of the rectangle.
$2x + 2y = 200 \Rightarrow y = 100 - x$.
Area $= (\text{length}) \cdot (\text{width}) = x \cdot y = x \cdot (100 - x) = 100x - x^2$.
$A(x) = 100x - x^2$ is a quadratic function with $a = -1, b = 100, c = 0$. Since $a = -1 < 0$, the graph opens down, so the vertex is a maximum point.
The maximum area occurs when $x = \dfrac{-b}{2a} = \dfrac{-(100)}{2(-1)} = 50$.

So the dimensions that yield the maximum area are:
length = 50 feet and width = 100–50 = 50 feet.

61. The area function is: $A(x) = x(10 - x) = -x^2 + 10x$
The maximum value occurs at the vertex:
$$x = \frac{-b}{2a} = \frac{-10}{2(-1)} = \frac{-10}{-2} = 5$$
The maximum area is:
$A(5) = -(5)^2 + 10(5) = -25 + 50 = 25$ square units.

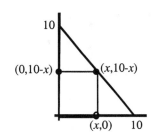

63. (a) Graphing, the data appear to be quadratic with $a < 0$.

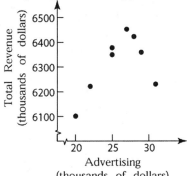

Advertising
(thousands of dollars)

(b) Using the QUADratic REGression program, the quadratic function of best fit is:
$R(A) = -7.760A^2 + 411.875A + 942.721$

(c) The maximum revenue occurs at $A = \dfrac{-b}{2a} = \dfrac{-(411.875)}{2(-7.76)} = \dfrac{-411.875}{-15.52}$
≈ 26.5 thousand dollars $\approx \$26,500$

(d) The maximum revenue is
$$R\left(\frac{-b}{2a}\right) = R(26.53866) = -7.76(26.5)^2 + (411.875)(26.5) + 942.721$$
≈ 6408 thousand dollars $\approx \$6,408,000$

(e) graphing:

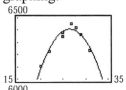

Quadratic Functions and Models

3.CR   Cumulative Review

1. $P = (1,3); Q = (-4,2);$ Distance between P and Q:

$$d(P,Q) = \sqrt{(-4-1)^2 + (2-3)^2} = \sqrt{(-5)^2 + (-1)^2} = \sqrt{25+1} = \sqrt{26}$$

3. $y = 3x^2 + 14x - 5$

y-intercept: $y = 3(0)^2 + 14(0) - 5 = -5$ x-intercepts: $y = 3x^2 + 14x - 5 = 0$

$$(3x-1)(x+5) = 0 \Rightarrow x = \frac{1}{3}, x = -5$$

5. $x^2 \geq x \Rightarrow x^2 - x \geq 0 \Rightarrow x(x-1) \geq 0$

     $x = 0, \; x = 1$ are the zeros. $f(x) = x^2 - x$

Interval	Test Number	$f(x)$	Positive/Negative
$-\infty < x < 0$	-1	2	Positive
$0 < x < 1$	0.5	-0.25	Negative
$1 < x < \infty$	2	2	Positive

The solution set is $\{x \mid x \leq 0 \text{ or } x \geq 1\}$.

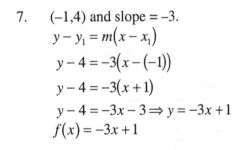

7. $(-1,4)$ and slope $= -3$.

$$y - y_1 = m(x - x_1)$$
$$y - 4 = -3(x - (-1))$$
$$y - 4 = -3(x + 1)$$
$$y - 4 = -3x - 3 \Rightarrow y = -3x + 1$$
$$f(x) = -3x + 1$$

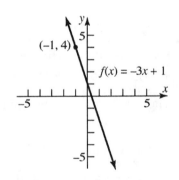

9. $y = x^3$

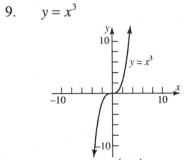

x-intercept : $(0,0)$;   y-intercept : $(0,0)$

11. $f(x) = 2x^2 + x$

    (a) $f(2) = 2(2)^2 + 2 = 8 + 2 = 10$

    (b) $f(x) + f(2) = 2x^2 + x + 10$

    (c) $f(-x) = 2(-x)^2 + (-x) = 2x^2 - x$

    (d) $-f(x) = -(2x^2 + x) = -2x^2 - x$

    (e) $f(x + 2) = 2(x + 2)^2 + (x + 2) = 2(x^2 + 4x + 4) + x + 2$
$$= 2x^2 + 8x + 8 + x + 2 = 2x^2 + 9x + 10$$

    (f) $\dfrac{f(x + h) - f(x)}{h} = \dfrac{2(x + h)^2 + x + h - (2x^2 + x)}{h}, h \neq 0$

$$= \dfrac{2(x^2 + 2xh + h^2) + x + h - 2x^2 - x}{h} = \dfrac{2x^2 + 4xh + 2h^2 + x + h - 2x^2 - x}{h}$$

$$= \dfrac{4xh + 2h^2 + h}{h} = \dfrac{h(4x + 2h + 1)}{h} = 4x + 2h + 1$$

13. Not a function, the graph fails the Vertical Line Test.

15. $f(x) = 3x^2 - 12x + 1$, $a = 3, b = -12, c = 1$. Since $a = 3 > 0$, the graph opens up, so the

    vertex is a minimum point. The minimum occurs at $x = \dfrac{-b}{2a} = \dfrac{-(-12)}{2(3)} = \dfrac{12}{6} = 2$.

    The minimum value is $f\left(\dfrac{-b}{2a}\right) = f(2) = 3(2)^2 - 12(2) + 1 = 12 - 24 + 1 = -11$.

17. (a) Scatter diagram with $x = $ year

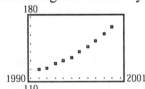

    (b) The scatter diagram for the data indicates a quadratic model.

    (c) Using QuadReg to obtain the quadratic function of best fit yields:
$$P(x) = 0.37x^2 - 1451.86x + 1443273.86$$

    (d) Answers will vary.

Chapter 4

Additional Functions and Models

4.1 Radical Equations; Absolute Value Equations; Absolute Value Inequalities

1.
$$\sqrt{x} = 3$$
$$\left(\sqrt{x}\right)^2 = 3^2$$
$$x = 9$$
Check: $\sqrt{9} = 3$
The solution is $x = 9$.

3.
$$\sqrt{y+3} = 5$$
$$\left(\sqrt{y+3}\right)^2 = 5^2$$
$$y + 3 = 25 \Rightarrow y = 22$$
Check: $\sqrt{22+3} = \sqrt{25} = 5$
The solution is $y = 22$.

5.
$$\sqrt{2t-1} = 1$$
$$\left(\sqrt{2t-1}\right)^2 = 1^2$$
$$2t - 1 = 1 \Rightarrow 2t = 2 \Rightarrow t = 1$$
Check: $\sqrt{2(1)-1} = \sqrt{1} = 1$
The solution is $t = 1$.

7. $\sqrt{3t+1} = -6$

Since the principal square root is always a non negative number, this equation has no real solution.

9.
$$\sqrt[3]{1-2x} - 3 = 0$$
$$\sqrt[3]{1-2x} = 3$$
$$\left(\sqrt[3]{1-2x}\right)^3 = 3^3$$
$$1 - 2x = 27 \Rightarrow -2x = 26 \Rightarrow x = -13$$
Check: $\sqrt[3]{1-2(-13)} - 3 = \sqrt[3]{27} - 3 = 0$
The solution is $x = -13$.

11.
$$x = 6\sqrt{x}$$
$$(x)^2 = \left(6\sqrt{x}\right)^2$$
$$x^2 = 36x \Rightarrow x^2 - 36x = 0$$
$$x(x-36) = 0 \Rightarrow x = 0 \text{ or } x = 36$$
Check
$x = 0$: $0 = 6\sqrt{0} \Rightarrow 0 = 0$
$x = 36$: $36 = 6\sqrt{36} \Rightarrow 36 = (6)(6) = 36$
The solution set is $\{0, 36\}$.

13.
$$\sqrt{15-2x} = x$$
$$\left(\sqrt{15-2x}\right)^2 = x^2$$
$$15 - 2x = x^2 \Rightarrow x^2 + 2x - 15 = 0$$
$$(x+5)(x-3) = 0 \Rightarrow x = -5 \text{ or } x = 3$$

Check $x = 5$: $\sqrt{15-2(-5)} = \sqrt{25}$
$$= 5 \neq -5$$
Check $x = 3$: $\sqrt{15-2(3)} = \sqrt{9} = 3 = 3$
The solution is $x = 3$.

15.
$$x = 2\sqrt{x-1}$$
$$x^2 = \left(2\sqrt{x-1}\right)^2$$
$$x^2 = 4(x-1) \Rightarrow x^2 = 4x - 4$$
$$x^2 - 4x + 4 = 0 \Rightarrow (x-2)^2 = 0 \Rightarrow x = 2$$

Check: $2 = 2\sqrt{2-1} \Rightarrow 2 = 2$
The solution is $x = 2$.

17.
$$\sqrt{x^2 - x - 4} = x + 2$$
$$\left(\sqrt{x^2 - x - 4}\right)^2 = (x+2)^2$$
$$x^2 - x - 4 = x^2 + 4x + 4$$
$$-8 = 5x \Rightarrow -\frac{8}{5} = x$$

Check

$$x = -\frac{8}{5} : \sqrt{\left(-\frac{8}{5}\right)^2 - \left(-\frac{8}{5}\right) - 4} = \left(-\frac{8}{5}\right) + 2$$

$$\sqrt{\frac{64}{25} + \frac{8}{5} - 4} = \frac{2}{5} \Rightarrow \sqrt{\frac{64 + 40 - 100}{25}} = \frac{2}{5}$$

$$\sqrt{\frac{4}{25}} = \frac{2}{5} \Rightarrow \frac{2}{5} = \frac{2}{5} \text{ , The solution is } x = -\frac{8}{5}.$$

19.
$$3 + \sqrt{3x+1} = x$$
$$\sqrt{3x+1} = x - 3$$
$$\left(\sqrt{3x+1}\right)^2 = (x-3)^2$$
$$3x + 1 = x^2 - 6x + 9$$
$$0 = x^2 - 9x + 8$$
$$(x-1)(x-8) = 0$$
$$x = 1 \text{ or } x = 8$$

Check $x = 1$: $3 + \sqrt{3(1)+1}$
$$= 3 + \sqrt{4} = 5 \neq 1$$
Check $x = 8$: $3 + \sqrt{3(8)+1}$
$$= 3 + \sqrt{25} = 8 = 8$$
The solution is $x = 8$.

21. $\sqrt{2x+3} - \sqrt{x+1} = 1$
$$\sqrt{2x+3} = 1 + \sqrt{x+1}$$
$$\left(\sqrt{2x+3}\right)^2 = \left(1 + \sqrt{x+1}\right)^2$$
$$2x + 3 = 1 + 2\sqrt{x+1} + x + 1$$
$$x + 1 = 2\sqrt{x+1}$$
$$(x+1)^2 = \left(2\sqrt{x+1}\right)^2$$
$$x^2 + 2x + 1 = 4(x+1)$$
$$x^2 + 2x + 1 = 4x + 4$$
$$x^2 - 2x - 3 = 0$$
$$(x+1)(x-3) = 0 \Rightarrow x = -1 \text{ or } x = 3$$

Check $x = 1$: $\sqrt{2(-1)+3} - \sqrt{-1+1}$
$$= \sqrt{1} - \sqrt{0} = 1 - 0 = 1 = 1$$
Check $x = 3$: $\sqrt{2(3)+3} - \sqrt{3+1}$
$$= \sqrt{9} - \sqrt{4} = 3 - 2 = 1 = 1$$
The solution is $x = -1$ or $x = 3$.

23. $\sqrt{3x+1} - \sqrt{x-1} = 2$

$\sqrt{3x+1} = 2 + \sqrt{x-1}$

$\left(\sqrt{3x+1}\right)^2 = \left(2 + \sqrt{x-1}\right)^2$

$3x + 1 = 4 + 4\sqrt{x-1} + x - 1$

$2x - 2 = 4\sqrt{x-1}$

$(2x-2)^2 = \left(4\sqrt{x-1}\right)^2$

$4x^2 - 8x + 4 = 16(x-1)$

$x^2 - 2x + 1 = 4x - 4$

$x^2 - 6x + 5 = 0$

$(x-1)(x-5) = 0 \Rightarrow x = 1 \ \text{ or } \ x = 5$

Check $x = 1$: $\sqrt{3(1)+1} - \sqrt{1-1}$

$= \sqrt{4} - \sqrt{0} = 2 - 0 = 2 = 2$

Check $x = 5$: $\sqrt{3(5)+1} - \sqrt{5-1}$

$= \sqrt{16} - \sqrt{4} = 4 - 2 = 2 = 2$

The solution is $x = 1$ or $x = 5$.

25. $\sqrt[3]{3x^2 - 11} = 1$

$\left(\sqrt[3]{3x^2 - 11}\right)^3 = 1^3$

$3x^2 - 11 = 1 \Rightarrow 3x^2 = 12$

$x^2 = 4 \Rightarrow x = -2 \ \text{ or } \ x = 2$

Check $x = -2$: $\sqrt[3]{3(-2)^2 - 11} = 1$

$\sqrt[3]{12 - 11} = \sqrt[3]{1} = 1$

Check $x = 2$: $\sqrt[3]{3(2)^2 - 11} = 1$

$\sqrt[3]{12 - 11} = \sqrt[3]{1} = 1$

The solution is $x = -2 \ \text{ or } \ x = 2$.

27. $\sqrt[5]{2x+1} - 2 = 0$

$\sqrt[5]{2x+1} = 2$

$\left(\sqrt[5]{2x+1}\right)^5 = 2^5$

$2x + 1 = 32 \Rightarrow 2x = 31$

$x = \dfrac{31}{2}$

Check $x = 15.5$: $\sqrt[5]{2(31/2)+1} - 2 = 0$

$\sqrt[5]{31+1} - 2 = \sqrt[5]{32} - 2$

$2 - 2 = 0$

The solution is $x = \dfrac{31}{2}$.

29. $(3x+1)^{1/2} = 4$

$\left((3x+1)^{1/2}\right)^2 = (4)^2$

$3x + 1 = 16 \Rightarrow 3x = 15 \Rightarrow x = 5$

Check

$x = 5$: $(3(5)+1)^{1/2} = 4$

$16^{1/2} = 4 \Rightarrow 4 = 4$

The solution is $x = 5$.

31. $(5x-2)^{1/3} = 2$

$\left((5x-2)^{1/3}\right)^3 = (2)^3$

$5x - 2 = 8 \Rightarrow 5x = 10 \Rightarrow x = 2$

Check

$x = 2$: $(5(2)-2)^{1/3} = 2$

$8^{1/3} = 2 \Rightarrow 2 = 2$

The solution is $x = 2$.

33. $\left(x^2+9\right)^{1/2}=5$

$$\left(\left(x^2+9\right)^{1/2}\right)^2=(5)^2$$

$$x^2+9=25 \Rightarrow x^2=16$$

$$x=-4 \ \text{or} \ x=4$$

Check

$x=-4: \ \left((-4)^2+9\right)^{1/2}=5$

$$25^{1/2}=5 \Rightarrow 5=5$$

$x=4: \ \left((4)^2+9\right)^{1/2}=5$

$$25^{1/2}=5 \Rightarrow 5=5$$

The solution set is $\{-4, 4\}$.

35. $|x|=6$

$x=6 \ \text{or} \ x=-6$

The solution set is $\{-6, 6\}$.

37. $|2x+3|=5$

$2x+3=5 \ \text{or} \ 2x+3=-5$

$2x=2 \ \text{or} \ \ \ \ 2x=-8$

$x=1 \ \text{or} \ \ \ \ \ \ x=-4$

The solution set is $\{-4, 1\}$.

39. $|1-4t|+8=13 \Rightarrow |1-4t|=5$

$1-4t=5 \ \text{or} \ 1-4t=-5$

$-4t=4 \ \text{or} \ \ \ \ -4t=-6$

$t=-1 \ \text{or} \ \ \ \ t=\dfrac{3}{2}$

The solution set is $\left\{-1, \dfrac{3}{2}\right\}$.

41. $|-2x|=8$

$-2x=8 \ \ \ \ \text{or} \ \ -2x=-8$

$x=-4 \ \ \text{or} \ \ \ \ \ x=4$

The solution set is $\{-4, 4\}$.

43. $4-|2x|=3 \Rightarrow |2x|=1$

$2x=1 \ \text{or} \ 2x=-1$

$x=\dfrac{1}{2} \ \text{or} \ x=-\dfrac{1}{2}$

The solution set is $\left\{-\dfrac{1}{2}, \dfrac{1}{2}\right\}$.

45. $\dfrac{2}{3}|x|=9$

$|x|=\dfrac{27}{2} \Rightarrow x=\dfrac{27}{2} \ \text{or} \ x=-\dfrac{27}{2}$

The solution set is $\left\{-\dfrac{27}{2}, \dfrac{27}{2}\right\}$.

47. $\left|\dfrac{x}{3}+\dfrac{2}{5}\right|=2$

$\dfrac{x}{3}+\dfrac{2}{5}=2 \ \ \text{or} \ \ \dfrac{x}{3}+\dfrac{2}{5}=-2$

$5x+6=30 \ \ \text{or} \ \ 5x+6=-30$

$5x=24 \ \ \text{or} \ \ \ \ \ \ 5x=-36$

$x=\dfrac{24}{5} \ \ \text{or} \ \ \ \ \ \ x=-\dfrac{36}{5}$

The solution set is $\left\{-\dfrac{36}{5}, \dfrac{24}{5}\right\}$.

49. $|u-2|=-\dfrac{1}{2}$

impossible, since absolute value always yields a non-negative number.

51. $|x^2-9|=0$

$x^2-9=0$

$x^2=9$

$x=\pm 3$

The solution set is $\{-3, 3\}$.

53. $\left|x^2 - 2x\right| = 3$

$x^2 - 2x = 3$ or $x^2 - 2x = -3$

$x^2 - 2x - 3 = 0$ or $x^2 - 2x + 3 = 0$

$(x-3)(x+1) = 0$ or $x = \dfrac{2 \pm \sqrt{4-12}}{2} = \dfrac{2 \pm \sqrt{-8}}{2} \Rightarrow$ no real solution

$x = 3$ or $x = -1$

The solution set is $\{-1, 3\}$.

55. $\left|x^2 + x - 1\right| = 1$

$x^2 + x - 1 = 1$ or $x^2 + x - 1 = -1$

$x^2 + x - 2 = 0$ or $x^2 + x = 0$

$(x-1)(x+2) = 0$ or $x(x+1) = 0$

$x = 1, x = -2$ or $x = 0, x = -1$

The solution set is $\{-2, -1, 0, 1\}$.

57. $\left|x\right| < 6$

$-6 < x < 6$

$\left\{x \middle| -6 < x < 6\right\}$ or $(-6, 6)$

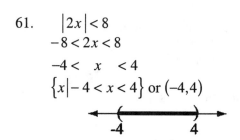

59. $\left|x\right| > 4$

$x < -4$ or $x > 4$

$\left\{x \middle| x < -4 \text{ or } x > 4\right\}$ or

$(-\infty, -4) \cup (4, +\infty)$

61. $\left|2x\right| < 8$

$-8 < 2x < 8$

$-4 <\ \ x\ \ < 4$

$\left\{x \middle| -4 < x < 4\right\}$ or $(-4, 4)$

63. $\left|3x\right| > 12$

$3x < -12$ or $3x > 12$

$x < -4$ or $x > 4$

$\left\{x \middle| x < -4 \text{ or } x > 4\right\}$ or $(-\infty, -4) \cup (4, \infty)$

65. $\left|x-2\right| + 2 < 3 \Rightarrow \left|x-2\right| < 1$

$-1 < x - 2 < 1$

$1 <\ \ x\ \ < 3$

$\left\{x \middle| 1 < x < 3\right\}$ or $(1, 3)$

67. $\left|3t - 2\right| \le 4$

$-4 \le 3t - 2 \le 4$

$-2 \le 3t \le 6 \Rightarrow -\dfrac{2}{3} \le t \le 2$

$\left\{t \middle| -\dfrac{2}{3} \le t \le 2\right\}$ or $\left[-\dfrac{2}{3}, 2\right]$

69. $\left|x - 3\right| \ge 2$

$x - 3 \le -2$ or $x - 3 \ge 2$

$x \le 1$ or $x \ge 5$

$\left\{x \middle| x \le 1 \text{ or } x \ge 5\right\}$ or

$(-\infty, 1] \cup [5, +\infty)$

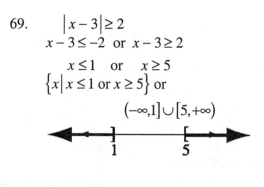

71. $|1-4x|-7<-2 \Rightarrow |1-4x|<5$
$-5<1-4x<5$

$-6<-4x<4$

$\dfrac{-6}{-4}>x>\dfrac{4}{-4}$

$\dfrac{3}{2}>x>-1 \Rightarrow -1<x<\dfrac{3}{2}$

$\left\{x \middle| -1<x<\dfrac{3}{2}\right\}$ or $\left(-1,\dfrac{3}{2}\right)$

73. $|1-2x|>|-3| \Rightarrow |1-2x|>3$
$1-2x<-3$ or $1-2x>3$

$-2x<-4$ or $-2x>2$

$x>2$ or $x<-1$
$\left\{x \middle| x<-1 \text{ or } x>2\right\}$ or $(-\infty,-1)\cup(2,\infty)$

75. $|2x+1|<-1$
No solution since absolute value is
always non-negative.

77. $|4x+1|<0.01$
$-0.01<4x+1<0.01$

$-1.01<4x<-0.99$

$\dfrac{-1.01}{4}<x<\dfrac{-0.99}{4}$

$-0.2525<x<-0.2475$

$\left\{x \middle| -0.2525<x<-0.2475\right\}$

or $(-0.2525,-0.2475)$

79. $|x+4|<0.001$
$-0.001<x+4<0.001$

$-4.001<x<-3.999$

$\left\{x \middle| -4.001<x<-3.999\right\}$

or $(-4.001,-3.999)$

81. $|x-1|<3 \Rightarrow -3<x-1<3$
$-2<x<4$

$2<x+4<8$

$\Rightarrow a=2, b=8$

83. $|x+4|\le 2 \Rightarrow -2\le x+4\le 2$
$-6\le x\le -2$

$-12\le 2x\le -4$

$-15\le 2x-3\le -7$

$\Rightarrow a=-15, b=-7$

85. $|x-2|\le 7 \Rightarrow -7\le x-2\le 7$
$-5\le x\le 9$

$-15\le x-10\le -1$

$-\dfrac{1}{15}\ge \dfrac{1}{x-10}\ge -1$

$-1\le \dfrac{1}{x-10}\le -\dfrac{1}{15}$

$\Rightarrow a=-1, b=-\dfrac{1}{15}$

87. $|x-2|<0.5$
$-0.5<x-2<0.5$
$-0.5+2<x<0.5+2$
$\dfrac{3}{2}<x<\dfrac{5}{2}$
Solution set: $\left\{x\bigg|\ \dfrac{3}{2}<x<\dfrac{5}{2}\right\}$

89. $|x-(-3)|>2$
$x-(-3)<-2$ or $x-(-3)>2$
$x+3<-2$ or $x+3>2$
$x<-5$ or $x>-1$
Solution set: $\{x|\ x<-5\ \text{or}\ x>-1\}$

91. $|x-100|\le 20$
$-20\le x-100\le 20$
$80\le x\le 120$
The range of IQ test scores is $80\le x\le120$.

93. A temperature x that differs from $98.6°\text{F}$ by at least $1.5°$
$|x-98.6°|\ge1.5°$
$x-98.6°\le-1.5°$ or $x-98.6°\ge1.5°$
$x\le97.1°$ or $x\ge100.1°$
The temperatures that are considered unhealthy are those that are less than $97.1°\text{F}$ or greater than $100.1°\text{F}$, inclusive.

95. Graph the equations and to find the x-coordinate of the points of intersection:

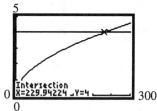

The distance to the water's surface is approximately 229.94 feet.

97. Show that $a\le|a|$.
We know that $0\le|a|$. So if $a<0$, then we have $a<0\le|a|\Rightarrow a\le|a|$
Now, if $a\ge0$, then $|a|=a$. So $a\le|a|$.

99. To prove $|a-b|\ge|a|-|b|$, consider the following:
$|a|=|(a-b)+b|\le|a-b|+|b|$ by the Triangle Inequality
so $|a|\le|a-b|+|b|\Rightarrow|a|-|b|\le|a-b|$, therefore $|a-b|\ge|a|-|b|$.

101. Given that $a>0$
$x^2>a\Rightarrow x^2-a>0\Rightarrow(x+\sqrt{a})(x-\sqrt{a})>0$
If $x<-\sqrt{a}$, then $x+\sqrt{a}<0$ and $x-\sqrt{a}<-2\sqrt{a}<0$
therefore $(x+\sqrt{a})(x-\sqrt{a})>0$
If $-\sqrt{a}<x<\sqrt{a}$, then $0<x+\sqrt{a}<2\sqrt{a}$ and $-2\sqrt{a}<x-\sqrt{a}<0$
therefore $(x+\sqrt{a})(x-\sqrt{a})<0$

If $x > \sqrt{a}$, then $x + \sqrt{a} > 2\sqrt{a} > 0$ and $x - \sqrt{a} > 0$

therefore $\left(x + \sqrt{a}\right)\left(x - \sqrt{a}\right) > 0$

So the solution set for $x^2 > a$ is $\left\{\text{real numbers } x \mid x < -\sqrt{a} \text{ or } x > \sqrt{a}\right\}$

103. $\left\{\text{real numbers } x \mid -2 < x < 2\right\}$

105. $\left\{\text{real numbers } x \mid x \le -1 \text{ or } x \ge 1\right\}$

107. $\left\{\text{real numbers } x \mid -3 \le x \le 3\right\}$

109. $\left\{\text{real numbers } x \mid x < -4 \text{ or } x > 4\right\}$

111. $\big|\, x + |3x - 2| \,\big| = 2$

$\Rightarrow x + |3x - 2| = 2 \text{ or } x + |3x - 2| = -2$

$x + |3x - 2| = 2 \Rightarrow |3x - 2| = 2 - x$

$\Rightarrow 3x - 2 = 2 - x \Rightarrow 3x - 2 = 2 - x \Rightarrow 4x = 4 \Rightarrow x = 1$

$\text{or } 3x - 2 = -(2 - x) \Rightarrow 3x - 2 = -2x + 1 \Rightarrow 5x = -3 \Rightarrow x = -\dfrac{3}{5}$

$x + |3x - 2| = -2 \Rightarrow |3x - 2| = -2 - x$

$\Rightarrow 3x - 2 = -2 - x \text{ or } 3x - 2 = -(-2 - x)$

$3x - 2 = -2 - x \Rightarrow 4x = 0 \Rightarrow x = 0$

$3x - 2 = -(-2 - x) \Rightarrow 3x - 2 = 2 + x \Rightarrow 2x = 4 \Rightarrow x = 2$

However, the only values that check in the original equation are $x = 0$ and $x = 1$.

113. The absolute value of a real number is always greater than or equal to zero.

115. $|x| > 0 \Rightarrow x < -0 \text{ or } x > 0$

$\Rightarrow x < 0 \text{ or } x > 0 \Rightarrow x \ne 0$

117. Answers will vary, one example is $x - \sqrt{x} - 2 = 0$

Additional Functions and Models

4.2   Library of Functions; Piecewise-Defined Functions

1.   C   3.   E   5.   B   7.   F

9. $f(x) = \sqrt[3]{x}$

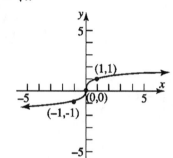

11. $f(x) = x^3$

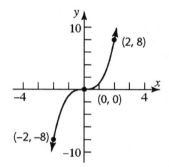

13. $f(x) = \dfrac{1}{x}$

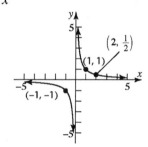

15.   (a) $f(-2) = (-2)^2 = 4$
       (b) $f(0) = 2$
       (c) $f(2) = 2(2) + 1 = 5$

17.   (a) $f(1.2) = \text{int}(2(1.2)) = \text{int}(2.4) = 2$
       (b) $f(1.6) = \text{int}(2(1.6)) = \text{int}(3.2) = 3$
       (c) $f(-1.8) = \text{int}(2(-1.8)) = \text{int}(-3.6) = -4$

19. $f(x) = \begin{cases} 2x & \text{if } x \neq 0 \\ 1 & \text{if } x = 0 \end{cases}$
       (a)   Domain: {Real Numbers}
       (b)   x-intercept: none
              y-intercept: (0,1)
       (c)

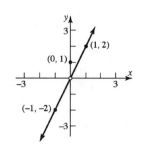

(d)   Range: $\left\{ y \mid y \neq 0 \right\}$
(e)   graphing utility:

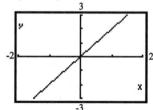

21. $f(x) = \begin{cases} -2x+3 & \text{if } x < 1 \\ 3x-2 & \text{if } x \geq 1 \end{cases}$

    (a)   Domain: {Real Numbers}

    (b)   x-intercept: none

            y-intercept: (0,3)

    (c)

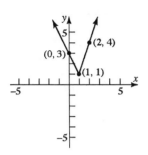

    (d)   Range: $\{y \mid y \geq 1\}$

    (e)   graphing utility:

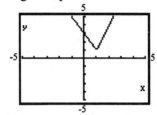

23. $f(x) = \begin{cases} x+3 & \text{if } -2 \leq x < 1 \\ 5 & \text{if } x = 1 \\ -x+2 & \text{if } x > 1 \end{cases}$

    (a)   Domain: $\{x \mid x \geq -2\}$

    (b)   x-intercept: (2, 0)

            y-intercept: (0, 3)

    (c)

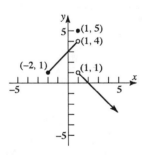

    (d)   Range: $\{y \mid y < 4\} \cup \{5\}$

    (e)   graphing utility:

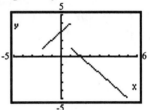

25. $f(x) = \begin{cases} 1+x & \text{if } x < 0 \\ x^2 & \text{if } x \geq 0 \end{cases}$

    (a)   Domain: {Real Numbers}

    (b)   x-intercept: (−1,0), (0,0)

            y-intercept: (0,0)

    (c)

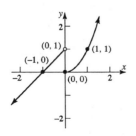

    (d)   Range: {Real Numbers}

    (e)   graphing utility:

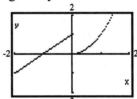

27. $f(x) = \begin{cases} |x| & \text{if } -2 \le x < 0 \\ 1 & \text{if } x = 0 \\ x^3 & \text{if } x > 0 \end{cases}$

(d) Range: $\{y \mid y > 0\}$

(e) graphing utility:

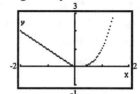

(a) Domain: $\{x \mid x \ge -2\}$

(b) x-intercept: none
    y-intercept: $(0, 1)$

(c)

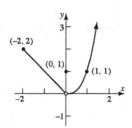

29. $h(x) = 2\,\text{int}(x)$

(a) Domain: {Real Numbers}

(b) x-intercept: all ordered pairs
    $(x, 0)$ when $0 \le x < 1$.
    y-intercept: $(0,0)$

(c)

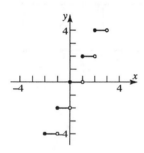

(d) Range: {Even Integers}

(e) graphing utility:

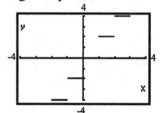

31. $f(x) = \begin{cases} -x & \text{if } -1 \le x \le 0 \\ \dfrac{1}{2}x & \text{if } 0 < x \le 2 \end{cases}$

33. $f(x) = \begin{cases} -x & \text{if } x \le 0 \\ -x + 2 & \text{if } 0 < x \le 2 \end{cases}$

35. Let x represent the number of anytime minutes and C be the monthly cost.

$C(x) = \begin{cases} 39.99 & \text{if } 0 < x \le 350 \\ 0.25x - 47.51 & \text{if } x > 350 \end{cases}$

(a) $C(200) = \$39.99$.

(b) $C(365) = 0.25 \cdot (365) - 47.51 = \$43.74$.

(c) $C(351) = 0.25 \cdot (351) - 47.51 = \$40.24$.

37. (a) $W = 10°C$

(b) $W = 33 - \dfrac{(10.45 + 10\sqrt{5} - 5)(33 - 10)}{22.04} = 3.98°C$

(c) $W = 33 - \dfrac{(10.45 + 10\sqrt{15} - 15)(33 - 10)}{22.04} = -2.67°C$

(d) $W = 33 - 1.5958(33 - 10) = -3.7°C$

(e)   When $0 \le v < 1.79$, the wind speed is so small that there is no effect on the temperature.

(f)   For each drop of 1° in temperature, the wind chill factor drops approximately 1.6°C. When the wind speed exceeds 20, there is a constant drop in temperature.

39.   Each graph is that of $y = x^2$, but shifted horizontally.

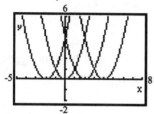

If $y = (x - k)^2$, $k > 0$, the shift is to the right k units; if $y = (x + k)^2$, $k > 0$, the shift is to the left k units. The graph of $y = (x + 4)^2$ is the same as the graph of $y = x^2$, but shifted to the left 4 units. The graph of $y = (x - 5)^2$ is the graph of $y = x^2$, but shifted to the right 5 units.

41.   The graph of $y = -x^2$ is the reflection of the graph of $y = x^2$ on the x-axis.

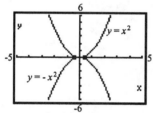

The graph of $y = -|x|$ is the reflection of the graph of $y = |x|$ on the x-axis.

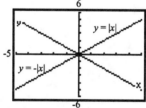

Multiplying a function by -1 causes the graph to be a reflection on the x-axis of the original function's graph.

43.   The graph of $y = (x - 1)^3 + 2$ is a shifting of the graph of $y = x^3$ one unit to the right and two units up.

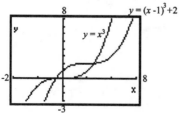

45. For the graph of $y = x^n$, n a positive odd integer, as n increases, the graph of the function increases at a greater rate for $|x| > 1$ and is closer to zero for $|x| < 1$. They have the same basic shape and pass through the points $(-1,1)$, $(0,0)$ and $(1,1)$.

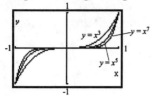

47. For $0 < x < 1$, the graph of $y = x^n$ flattens down toward the x-axis as n gets bigger. For $1 < x$, the graph of $y = x^n$ grows more steeply as n gets bigger.

Additional Functions and Models

4.3 Graphing Techniques; Transformations

1. B   3. H   5. I   7. L

9. F   11. G   13. C   15. B

17. $y = (x-4)^3$ 19. $y = x^3 + 4$ 21. $y = (-x)^3 = -x^3$ 23. $y = 4x^3$

25. (1) $y = \sqrt{x} + 2$
    (2) $y = -\left(\sqrt{x} + 2\right)$
    (3) $y = -\left(\sqrt{-x} + 2\right)$

27. (1) $y = -\sqrt{x}$
    (2) $y = -\sqrt{x} + 2$
    (3) $y = -\sqrt{x+3} + 2$

29. c

31. c

33. $f(x) = x^2 - 1$
Using the graph of $y = x^2$, vertically shift downward 1 unit.

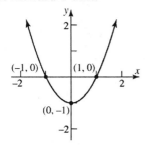

35. $g(x) = x^3 + 1$
Using the graph of $y = x^3$, vertically shift upward 1 unit.

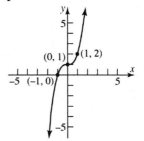

37. $h(x) = \sqrt{x-2}$
Using the graph of $y = \sqrt{x}$, horizontally shift to the right 2 units.

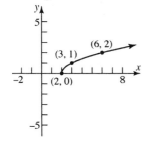

39. $f(x) = (x-1)^3 + 2$
Using the graph of $y = x^3$, horizontally shift to the right 1 unit, then vertically shift up 2 units.

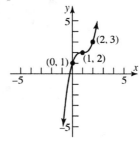

41. $g(x) = 4\sqrt{x}$

Using the graph of $y = \sqrt{x}$, vertically stretch by a factor of 4.

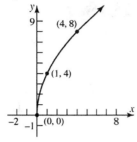

43. $h(x) = \dfrac{1}{2x} = \left(\dfrac{1}{2}\right)\left(\dfrac{1}{x}\right)$

Using the graph of $y = \dfrac{1}{x}$, vertically compress by a factor of $\dfrac{1}{2}$.

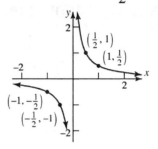

45. $f(x) = -\sqrt[3]{x}$

Reflect the graph of $y = \sqrt[3]{x}$, about the x-axis.

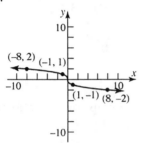

47. $g(x) = \left|-x\right|$

Reflect the graph of $y = |x|$, about the y-axis.

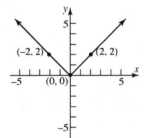

49. $h(x) = -x^3 + 2$

Reflect the graph of $y = x^3$ on the x-axis, vertically shift upward 2 units.

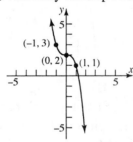

51. $f(x) = 2(x+1)^2 - 3$

Using the graph of $y = x^2$, horizontally shift to the left 1 unit, vertically stretch by a factor of 2, and vertically shift downward 3 units.

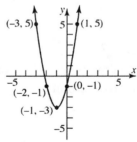

53. $g(x) = \sqrt{x-2} + 1$

Using the graph of $y = \sqrt{x}$, horizontally shift to the right 2 units and vertically shift upward 1 unit.

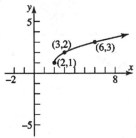

55. $h(x) = \sqrt{-x} - 2$

Reflect the graph of $y = \sqrt{x}$, about the y-axis and vertically shift downward 2 units.

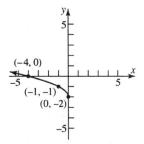

57. $f(x) = -(x+1)^3 - 1$

Using the graph of $y = x^3$, horizontally shift to the left 1 units, reflect the graph on the x-axis, and vertically shift downward 1 unit.

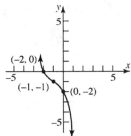

59. $g(x) = 2\left|1-x\right| = 2\left|-(-1+x)\right| = 2\left|x-1\right|$

Using the graph of $y = |x|$, horizontally shift to the right 1 unit, and vertically stretch by a factor or 2.

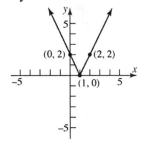

61. $h(x) = 2\operatorname{int}(x-1)$

Using the graph of $y = \operatorname{int}(x)$, horizontally shift to the right 1 unit, and vertically stretch by a factor of 2.

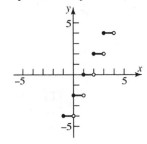

63. (a) $F(x) = f(x) + 3$
     Shift up 3 units.

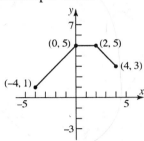

(0, 5) (2, 5)
(4, 3)
(−4, 1)

(b) $G(x) = f(x + 2)$
     Shift left 2 units.

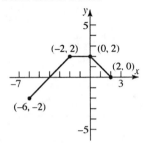

(−2, 2) (0, 2)
(2, 0)
(−6, −2)

(c) $P(x) = -f(x)$
     Reflect about the x-axis.

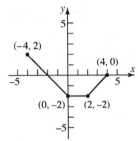

(−4, 2)
(4, 0)
(0, −2) (2, −2)

(d) $H(x) = f(x + 1) - 2$
     Shift left 1 unit and shift down 2 units.

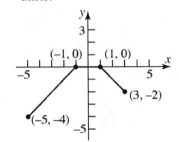

(−1, 0) (1, 0)
(3, −2)
(−5, −4)

(e) $Q(x) = \dfrac{1}{2} f(x)$

     Compress vertically by a factor of $\dfrac{1}{2}$.

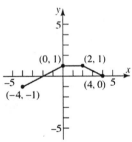

(0, 1) (2, 1)
(4, 0)
(−4, −1)

(f) $g(x) = f(-x)$
     Reflect about y-axis.

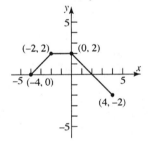

(−2, 2) (0, 2)
(−4, 0)
(4, −2)

(g) $h(x) = f(2x)$

     Compress horizontally by a factor of $\dfrac{1}{2}$.

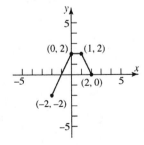

(0, 2) (1, 2)
(2, 0)
(−2, −2)

65. (a) $F(x) = f(x) + 3$
Shift up 3 units.

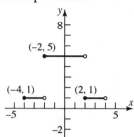

(b) $G(x) = f(x + 2)$
Shift left 2 units.

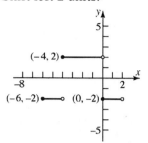

(c) $P(x) = -f(x)$
Reflect about the x-axis.

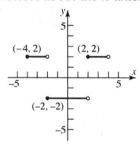

(d) $H(x) = f(x + 1) - 2$
Shift left 1 unit and shift down 2 units.

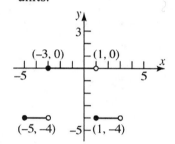

(e) $Q(x) = \dfrac{1}{2} f(x)$

Compress vertically by a factor of $\dfrac{1}{2}$.

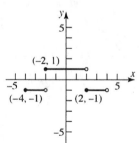

(f) $g(x) = f(-x)$
Reflect about y-axis.

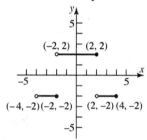

(g) $h(x) = f(2x)$

Compress horizontally by a factor of $\dfrac{1}{2}$.

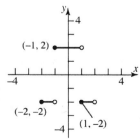

67.   (a) $F(x) = f(x) + 3$
             Shift up 3 units.

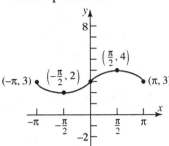

      (b) $G(x) = f(x + 2)$
             Shift left 2 units.

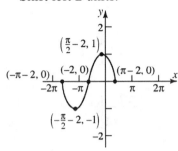

      (c) $P(x) = -f(x)$
             Reflect about the x-axis.

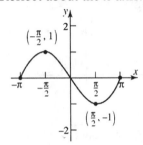

      (d) $H(x) = f(x + 1) - 2$
             Shift left 1 unit and shift down 2 units.

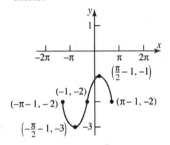

      (e) $Q(x) = \dfrac{1}{2} f(x)$

             Compress vertically by a factor of $\dfrac{1}{2}$.

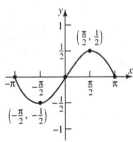

      (f) $g(x) = f(-x)$
             Reflect about y-axis.

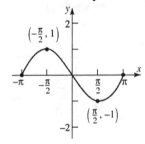

      (g) $h(x) = f(2x)$

             Compress horizontally by a factor of $\dfrac{1}{2}$.

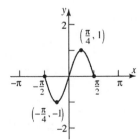

69. (a) $y = |x + 1|$

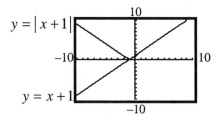

$y = x + 1$

(b) $y = |4 - x^2|$

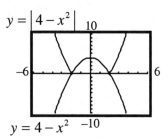

$y = 4 - x^2$

(c) $y = |x^3 + x|$

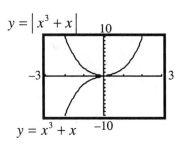

$y = x^3 + x$

(d)   Any part of the graph of $y = f(x)$ that lies below the x-axis is reflected about the x-axis to obtain the graph of $y = |f(x)|$.

71. (a) $y = |f(x)|$

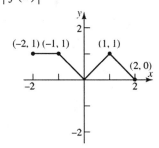

(b) $y = f(|x|)$

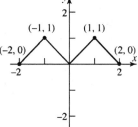

73. $f(x) = x^2 + 2x$
$f(x) = (x^2 + 2x + 1) - 1$
$f(x) = (x + 1)^2 - 1$
Using $f(x) = x^2$, shift left 1 unit and shift down 1 unit.

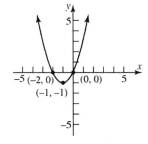

75. $f(x) = x^2 - 8x + 1$
$f(x) = (x^2 - 8x + 16) + 1 - 16$
$f(x) = (x - 4)^2 - 15$
Using $f(x) = x^2$, shift right 4 units and shift down 15 units.

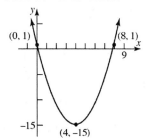

191

77. $f(x) = x^2 + x + 1$

$f(x) = \left(x^2 + x + \dfrac{1}{4}\right) + 1 - \dfrac{1}{4}$

$f(x) = \left(x + \dfrac{1}{2}\right)^2 + \dfrac{3}{4}$

Using $f(x) = x^2$, shift left $\dfrac{1}{2}$ unit and

shift up $\dfrac{3}{4}$ unit.

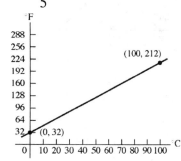

79. $y = (x - c)^2$

If $c = 0$, $y = x^2$.

If $c = 3$, $y = (x - 3)^2$; shift right 3 units.

If $c = -2$, $y = (x + 2)^2$; shift left 2 units.

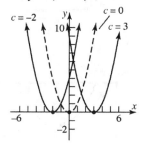

81. $F = \dfrac{9}{5}C + 32$

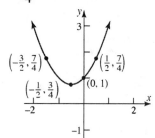

$F = \dfrac{9}{5}(K - 273) + 32$

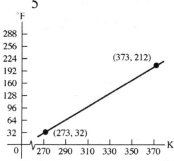

Shift the graph 273 units to the right.

83. (a)

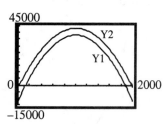

(b) Select the 10% tax since the profits are higher.

(c) The graph of Y1 is obtained by shifting the graph of $p(x)$ vertically down 10,000. The graph of Y2 is obtained by multiplying the y-coordinate of the graph of $p(x)$ by 0.9. Thus, Y2 is the graph of $p(x)$ vertically compressed by a factor of 0.9.

(d) Select the 10% tax since the graph of $Y1 = 0.9p(x) \geq Y2 = -0.05x^2 + 100x - 6800$ for all x in the domain.

85.   Given the graph of the function f, the graph of $y = 4f(x)$ is obtained by vertically stretching the graph of f by a factor of 4. The graph of $y = f(4x)$ is obtained by horizontally compressing the graph of f by a factor of 4.

Additional Functions and Models

4.4 Models Involving the Square Root Function and Piecewise-Defined Functions

1. (a) The distance d from P to the origin is $d = \sqrt{x^2 + y^2}$. Since P is a point on the graph of $y = x^2 - 8$, we have: $d(x) = \sqrt{x^2 + (x^2 - 8)^2} = \sqrt{x^4 - 15x^2 + 64}$

   (b) $d(0) = \sqrt{0^4 - 15(0)^2 + 64} = \sqrt{64} = 8$

   (c) $d(1) = \sqrt{(1)^4 - 15(1)^2 + 64} = \sqrt{1 - 15 + 64} = \sqrt{50} = 5\sqrt{2} \approx 7.07$

   (d) Graphing: $d(x) = \sqrt{x^4 - 15x^2 + 64}$

   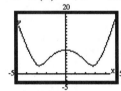

   (e) Using MINIMUM, d is smallest when $x \approx -2.74$ and when $x \approx 2.74$.

3. (a) The distance d from P to the point $(1, 0)$ is $d = \sqrt{(x - 1)^2 + y^2}$. Since P is a point on the graph of $y = \sqrt{x}$, we have: $d(x) = \sqrt{(x - 1)^2 + \left(\sqrt{x}\right)^2} = \sqrt{x^2 - x + 1}$

   (b) Graphing: $d(x) = \sqrt{x^2 - x + 1}$

   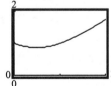

   (c) Using MINIMUM, d is smallest when x is 0.50.

5. (a) The total cost of installing the cable along the road is $10x$. If cable is installed x miles along the road, there are $5 - x$ miles left from the road to the house and where the cable ends.

   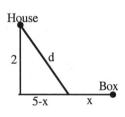

   $$d = \sqrt{(5 - x)^2 + 2^2} = \sqrt{25 - 10x + x^2 + 4}$$
   $$= \sqrt{x^2 - 10x + 29}$$

   The total cost of installing the cable is:
   $$C(x) = 100x + 140\sqrt{x^2 - 10x + 29}$$

   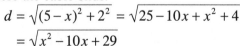

   Domain: $\left\{x \mid 0 \leq x \leq 5\right\}$

(b) $C(1) = 100(1) + 140\sqrt{1^2 - 10(1) + 29} = 100 + 140\sqrt{20} \approx \$726.10$

(c) $C(3) = 100(3) + 140\sqrt{3^2 - 10(3) + 29} = 300 + 140\sqrt{8} \approx \$695.98$

(d)   Graphing $C(x) = 100x + 140\sqrt{x^2 - 10x + 29}$ (e)

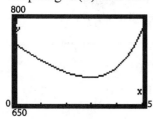

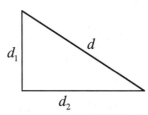

The table indicates that $x = 3$ miles results in the least cost.

(f)   Using MINIMUM, the graph indicates that $x = 2.96$ results in the least cost.

7. (a)

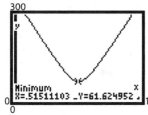

$d_1 = 200 - 475t;\ \ d_2 = 300 - 500t$

$d^2 = d_1^2 + d_2^2$

$d^2 = (200 - 475t)^2 + (300 - 500t)^2$

$d(t) = \sqrt{(200 - 475t)^2 + (300 - 500t)^2}$

(b)   Graphing: $d(t) = \sqrt{(200 - 475t)^2 + (300 - 500t)^2}$

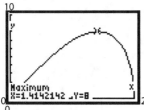

Using MINIMUM, the distance is smallest at $t \approx 0.52$ hours.
The planes come within approximately 61.6 miles of each other.

9.   (a) $A(x) = (2x)(2y) = 4x\sqrt{4 - x^2}$

(b) $p(x) = 2(2x) + 2(2y) = 4x + 4\sqrt{4 - x^2}$

(c)   Graphing: $A(x) = 4x\sqrt{4 - x^2}$ (d)   Graphing: $p(x) = 4x + 4\sqrt{4 - x^2}$

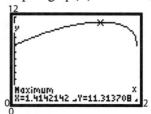

Using MAXIMUM , the area is largest when $x \approx 1.41$.

Using MAXIMUM , the perimeter is largest when $x \approx 1.41$.

11. For schedule X:

$$f(x) = \begin{cases} 0.10x & \text{if } 0 < x \le 6000 \\ 600.00 + 0.15(x - 6000) & \text{if } 6000 < x \le 27{,}950 \\ 3892.50 + 0.27(x - 27{,}950) & \text{if } 27{,}950 < x \le 67{,}700 \\ 14{,}625 + 0.30(x - 67{,}700) & \text{if } 67{,}700 < x \le 141{,}250 \\ 36{,}690 + 0.35(x - 141{,}250) & \text{if } 141{,}250 < x \le 307{,}050 \\ 94{,}720 + 0.386(x - 307{,}050) & \text{if } x > 307{,}050 \end{cases}$$

13. (a) Charge for 50 therms: $C = 9.45 + 0.36375(50) + 0.3128(50) = \$43.28$

(b) Charge for 500 therms:
$$C = 9.45 + 0.36375(50) + 0.11445(450) + 0.3128(500) = \$235.54$$

(c) The monthly charge function:

$$C = \begin{cases} 9.45 + 0.36375x + 0.3128x & \text{for } 0 \le x \le 50 \\ 9.45 + 0.36375(50) + 0.11445(x - 50) + 0.3128x & \text{for } x > 50 \end{cases}$$

$$= \begin{cases} 9.45 + 0.67655x & \text{for } 0 \le x \le 50 \\ 9.45 + 18.1875 + 0.11445x - 5.7225 + 0.3128x & \text{for } x > 50 \end{cases}$$

$$= \begin{cases} 9.45 + 0.67655x & \text{for } 0 \le x \le 50 \\ 21.915 + 0.42725x & \text{for } x > 50 \end{cases}$$

(d) Graphing:

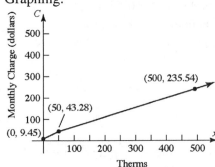

15. (a) Let x represent the number of miles and C be the cost of transportation.

$$C(x) = \begin{cases} 0.50x & \text{if } 0 \le x \le 100 \\ 0.50(100) + 0.40(x - 100) & \text{if } 100 < x \le 400 \\ 0.50(100) + 0.40(300) + 0.25(x - 400) & \text{if } 400 < x \le 800 \\ 0.50(100) + 0.40(300) + 0.25(400) + 0(x - 800) & \text{if } 800 < x \le 960 \end{cases}$$

$$C(x) = \begin{cases} 0.50x & \text{if } 0 \le x \le 100 \\ 10 + 0.40x & \text{if } 100 < x \le 400 \\ 70 + 0.25x & \text{if } 400 < x \le 800 \\ 270 & \text{if } 800 < x \le 960 \end{cases}$$

Graphing:

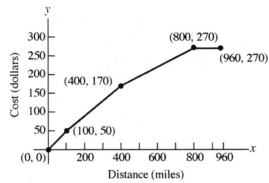

(b)   For hauls between 100 and 400 miles the cost is: $C(x) = 50 + 0.40(x - 100)$.

(c)   For hauls between 400 and 800 miles the cost is: $C(x) = 170 + 0.25(x - 400)$.

17.   Let x = the amount of the bill in dollars. The minimum payment due is given by

$$f(x) = \begin{cases} x & \text{if } 0 \le x < 10 \\ 10 & \text{if } 10 \le x < 500 \\ 30 & \text{if } 500 \le x < 1000 \\ 50 & \text{if } 1000 \le x < 1500 \\ 70 & \text{if } 1500 \le x \end{cases}$$

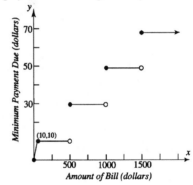

Additional Functions and Models

4.R   Chapter Review

1. $\sqrt[3]{x^2-1}=2$

   $\left(\sqrt[3]{x^2-1}\right)^3=(2)^3$

   $x^2-1=8$

   $x^2=9$

   $x=\pm3$

Check:

$x=-3$	$x=3$
$\sqrt[3]{(-3)^2-1}=2$	$\sqrt[3]{(3)^2-1}=2$
$\sqrt[3]{9-1}=2$	$\sqrt[3]{9-1}=2$
$\sqrt[3]{8}=2$	$\sqrt[3]{8}=2$
$2=2$	$2=2$

The solution set is $\{-3,3\}$.

3. $\sqrt{2x-3}+x=3$

   $\sqrt{2x-3}=3-x$

   $2x-3=9-6x+x^2$

   $x^2-8x+12=0$

   $(x-2)(x-6)=0$

   $x=2\ \text{ or }\ x=6$

Check $x=2$: $\sqrt{2(2)-3}+2=\sqrt{1}+2=3$

Check $x=6$: $\sqrt{2(6)-3}+6=\sqrt{9}+6$

   $=9\neq3$

The solution set is $\{2\}$.

5. $\sqrt{x+1}+\sqrt{x-1}=\sqrt{2x+1}$

   $\left(\sqrt{x+1}+\sqrt{x-1}\right)^2=\left(\sqrt{2x+1}\right)^2$

   $x+1+2\sqrt{x+1}\sqrt{x-1}+x-1=2x+1$

   $2x+2\sqrt{x+1}\sqrt{x-1}=2x+1$

   $2\sqrt{x+1}\sqrt{x-1}=1$

   $\left(2\sqrt{x+1}\sqrt{x-1}\right)^2=(1)^2$

   $4(x+1)(x-1)=1\Rightarrow4x^2-4=1$

   $4x^2=5\Rightarrow x^2=\dfrac{5}{4}\Rightarrow x=\pm\dfrac{\sqrt{5}}{2}$

Check:

$x=\dfrac{\sqrt{5}}{2}\Rightarrow\sqrt{\dfrac{\sqrt{5}}{2}+1}+\sqrt{\dfrac{\sqrt{5}}{2}-1}=\sqrt{2\left(\dfrac{\sqrt{5}}{2}\right)+1}$

$1.79890743995=1.79890743995$

$x=-\dfrac{\sqrt{5}}{2}\Rightarrow\sqrt{-\dfrac{\sqrt{5}}{2}+1}+\sqrt{-\dfrac{\sqrt{5}}{2}-1}=\sqrt{2\left(-\dfrac{\sqrt{5}}{2}\right)+1}$

impossible since $-\dfrac{\sqrt{5}}{2}-1<0$

The solution set is $\left\{\dfrac{\sqrt{5}}{2}\right\}$.

7. $\sqrt[3]{4x-5}-3=0$

$\sqrt[3]{4x-5}=3$

$\left(\sqrt[3]{4x-5}\right)^3=(3)^3$

$4x-5=27$

$4x=32$

$x=8$

Check $x=8$:

$\sqrt[3]{4(8)-5}-3=0$

$\sqrt[3]{32-5}-3=0$

$\sqrt[3]{27}-3=0$

$0=0$

The solution set is $\{8\}$.

9. $\sqrt{x^2+3x+7}-\sqrt{x^2-3x+9}+2=0$

$\sqrt{x^2+3x+7}=\sqrt{x^2-3x+9}-2 \Rightarrow \left(\sqrt{x^2+3x+7}\right)^2=\left(\sqrt{x^2-3x+9}-2\right)^2$

$x^2+3x+7=x^2-3x+9-4\sqrt{x^2-3x+9}+4$

$6x-6=-4\sqrt{x^2-3x+9}$

$\left(6(x-1)\right)^2=\left(-4\sqrt{x^2-3x+9}\right)^2 \Rightarrow 36\left(x^2-2x+1\right)=16\left(x^2-3x+9\right)$

$36x^2-72x+36=16x^2-48x+144$

$20x^2-24x-108=0$

$5x^2-6x-27=0$

$(5x+9)(x-3)=0 \Rightarrow x=-\dfrac{9}{5}$ or $x=3$

Check $x=-\dfrac{9}{5}$:

$\sqrt{\left(-\dfrac{9}{5}\right)^2+3\left(-\dfrac{9}{5}\right)+7}-\sqrt{\left(-\dfrac{9}{5}\right)^2-3\left(-\dfrac{9}{5}\right)+9}+2=0$

$\sqrt{\dfrac{81}{25}-\dfrac{27}{5}+7}-\sqrt{\dfrac{81}{25}+\dfrac{27}{5}+9}+2=0 \Rightarrow \sqrt{\dfrac{81-135+175}{25}}-\sqrt{\dfrac{81+135+225}{25}}+2=0$

$\sqrt{\dfrac{121}{25}}-\sqrt{\dfrac{441}{25}}+2=0 \Rightarrow \dfrac{11}{5}-\dfrac{21}{5}+2=0 \Rightarrow 0=0$

Check:

$x=3: \sqrt{(3)^2+3(3)+7}-\sqrt{(3)^2-3(3)+9}+2=0$

$\sqrt{9+9+7}-\sqrt{9-9+9}+2=0 \Rightarrow \sqrt{25}-\sqrt{9}+2=0 \Rightarrow 2+2=0 \Rightarrow 4 \neq 0$

The solution set is $\left\{-\dfrac{9}{5}\right\}$.

11. $|2x+3|=7$
$2x+3=7$ or $2x+3=-7$
$2x=4$ or $2x=-10$
$x=2$ or $x=-5$
The solution set is $\{-5, 2\}$.

13. $|2-3x|+2=9 \Rightarrow |2-3x|=7$
$2-3x=7$ or $2-3x=-7$
$3x=-5$ or $3x=9$
$x=-\dfrac{5}{3}$ or $x=3$
The solution set is $\left\{-\dfrac{5}{3},3\right\}$.

15. $|3x+4|<\dfrac{1}{2}$
$\dfrac{-1}{2}<3x+4<\dfrac{1}{2}$
$-\dfrac{9}{2}<\ \ 3x\ \ <-\dfrac{7}{2}$
$-\dfrac{3}{2}<\ \ x\ \ <-\dfrac{7}{6}$
$\left\{x\left|-\dfrac{3}{2}<x<-\dfrac{7}{6}\right.\right\}$ or $\left(-\dfrac{3}{2},-\dfrac{7}{6}\right)$

$-\dfrac{3}{2}$ $-\dfrac{7}{6}$

17. $|2x-5|\geq 9$
$2x-5\leq -9$ or $2x-5\geq 9$
$2x\leq -4$ or $2x\geq 14$
$x\leq -2$ or $x\geq 7$
$\{x\,|\,x\leq -2 \text{ or } x\geq 7\}$
or $(-\infty,-2]\cup[7,+\infty)$

-2 7

19. $2+|2-3x|\leq 4$
$|2-3x|\leq 2$
$-2\leq 2-3x\leq 2$
$-4\leq -3x\leq 0 \Rightarrow \dfrac{4}{3}\geq x\geq 0$
$0\leq x\leq \dfrac{4}{3}$
$\left\{x\left|0\leq x\leq \dfrac{4}{3}\right.\right\}$ or $\left[0,\dfrac{4}{3}\right]$

0 $\dfrac{4}{3}$

21. $1-|2-3x|>-4$
$-|2-3x|>-5 \Rightarrow |2-3x|<5$
$-5<2-3x<5$
$-7<-3x\ \ <3$
$\dfrac{-7}{-3}>x>\dfrac{3}{-3} \Rightarrow -1<x<\dfrac{7}{3}$
$\left\{x\left|-1<x<\dfrac{7}{3}\right.\right\}$ or $\left(-1,\dfrac{7}{3}\right)$

-1 $\dfrac{7}{3}$

23. $y = x^3$

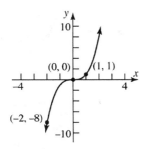

25. $f(x) = \begin{cases} 3x & \text{if } -2 < x \leq 1 \\ x+1 & \text{if } x > 1 \end{cases}$

(a)   Domain: $\{ x \mid x > -2 \}$

(b)   x-intercept: $(0,0)$
      y-intercept: $(0,0)$

(c)

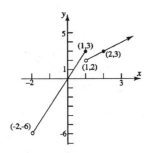

(d)   Range: $\{ y > -6 \}$

(e)   Graphing utility:

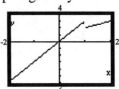

27. $f(x) = \begin{cases} x & \text{if } -4 \leq x < 0 \\ 1 & \text{if } x = 0 \\ 3x & \text{if } x > 0 \end{cases}$

(a)   Domain: $\{ x \mid x \geq -4 \}$

(b)   x-intercept: none
      y-intercept: $(0, 1)$

(c)

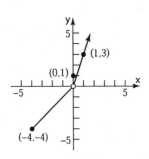

(d)   Range: $\{ y \mid y \geq -4, \, y \neq 0 \}$

(e)   Graphing utility:

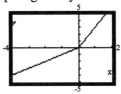

29. $F(x) = |x| - 4$

Using the graph of $y = |x|$, vertically shift the graph downward 4 units.

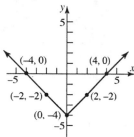

Intercepts: $(-4,0)$, $(4,0)$, $(0,-4)$
Domain: {Real Numbers}
Range: $\{y \mid y \geq -4\}$

31. $g(x) = -2|x|$

Reflect the graph of $y = |x|$ about the x-axis and vertically stretch the graph by a factor of 2.

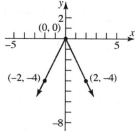

Intercepts: $(0,0)$
Domain: {Real Numbers}
Range: $\{y \mid y \leq 0\}$

33. $h(x) = \sqrt{x-1}$

Using the graph of $y = \sqrt{x}$, horizontally shift the graph to the right 1 unit.

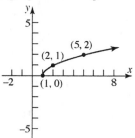

Intercepts: $(1,0)$
Domain: $\{x \mid x \geq 1\}$
Range: $\{y \mid y \geq 0\}$

35. $f(x) = \sqrt{1-x} = \sqrt{-1(x-1)}$

Reflect the graph of $y = \sqrt{x}$ about the y-axis and horizontally shift the graph to the right 1 unit..

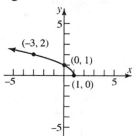

Intercepts: $(1,0)$, $(0,1)$
Domain: $\{x \mid x \leq 1\}$
Range: $\{y \mid y \geq 0\}$

37. $h(x) = (x-1)^2 + 2$

Using the graph of $y = x^2$, horizontally shift the graph to the right 1 unit and vertically shift the graph up 2 units.

Intercepts: $(0,3)$
Domain: {Real Numbers}
Range: $\{y \mid y \geq 2\}$

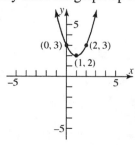

39. $g(x) = 3(x-1)^3 + 1$

Using the graph of $y = x^3$, horizontally shift the graph to the right 1 unit, vertically stretch the graph by a factor of 3, and vertically shift the graph up 1 unit.

Intercepts: $(0,-2)$, $\left(\sqrt[3]{-\dfrac{1}{3}} + 1, 0 \right)$

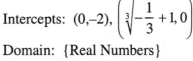

Domain: {Real Numbers}
Range: {Real Numbers}

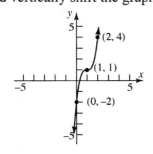

41. (a) $y = f(-x)$
Reflect about the y-axis.

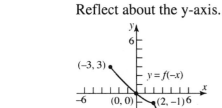

(b) $y = -f(x)$
Reflect about the x-axis.

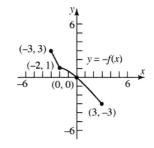

(c) $y = f(x+2)$
Horizontally shift left 2 units.

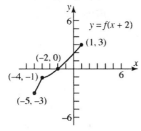

(d) $y = f(x) + 2$
Vertically shift up 2 units.

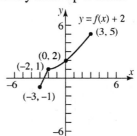

(e) $y = 2f(x)$
Vertical stretch by a factor of 2.

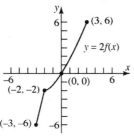

(f) $y = f(3x)$
Horizontal compression by $\dfrac{1}{3}$.

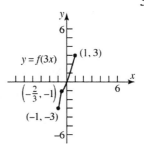

43.

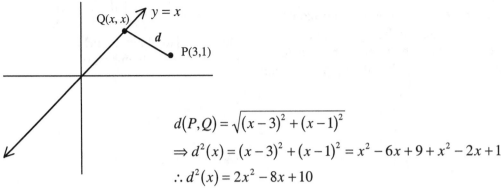

$$d(P,Q) = \sqrt{(x-3)^2 + (x-1)^2}$$
$$\Rightarrow d^2(x) = (x-3)^2 + (x-1)^2 = x^2 - 6x + 9 + x^2 - 2x + 1$$
$$\therefore d^2(x) = 2x^2 - 8x + 10$$

Use MINIMUM on the graph of $y_1 = 2x^2 - 8x + 10$ to determine that the minimum occurs when $x = 2$. Therefore the point Q on the line $y = x$ will be closest to the point $P = (3,1)$ when $Q = (2,2)$.

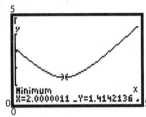

45. Let x = the number of minutes used in a month. Therefore, for the first 400 minutes, the monthly bill is 40 dollars.

Once the number of minutes exceeds 400 minutes (that is, when $x > 400$), the number of additional minutes is given by $x - 400$.

(a) Therefore, when $x > 400$, the total monthly cost is computed as follows:

Total cost $= ($cost of first 400 minutes$) + ($cost of each additional minute$)$
$$= 40 + (0.40)(x - 400) = 40 + 0.40x - 160 = 0.40x - 120$$

We can express the total monthly cost as a piecewise-defined function as follows:

$$C(x) = \begin{cases} \$40 & \text{for } 0 \le x \le 400 \\ \$0.40x - 120 & \text{for } x > 400 \end{cases}$$

(b) $C(423) = 0.40(423) - 120 = \$49.20$

Additional Functions and Models

4.CR   Cumulative Review

1. $x^3 - 6x^2 + 8x = 0$
    $x(x^2 - 6x + 8) = 0$
    $x(x-4)(x-2) = 0$
    $x = 0$ or $x = 4$ or $x = 2$

3. $x^2 + 4x + y^2 - 2y - 4 = 0$
    $(x^2 + 4x + 4) + (y^2 - 2y + 1) = 4 + 4 + 1$
    $\qquad (x+2)^2 + (y-1)^2 = 9$
    Center: $(-2,1)$
    Radius $= 3$

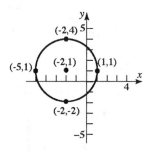

5. Perpendicular to $3x - 2y = 7 \Rightarrow y = \dfrac{3}{2}x - \dfrac{7}{2}$;

    Slope of perpendicular $= -\dfrac{2}{3}$ $\qquad$ Containing $(1,5)$

    $y - y_1 = m(x - x_1) \Rightarrow y - 5 = -\dfrac{2}{3}(x-1)$

    $y - 5 = -\dfrac{2}{3}x + \dfrac{2}{3} \Rightarrow y = -\dfrac{2}{3}x + \dfrac{17}{3}$

7. $f(x) = x^2 + 5x - 2$

    (a) $f(3) = 3^2 + 5 \cdot 3 - 2 = 9 + 15 - 2 = 22$

    (b) $f(-x) = (-x)^2 + 5(-x) - 2 = x^2 - 5x - 2$

    (c) $-f(x) = -(x^2 + 5x - 2) = -x^2 - 5x + 2$

    (d) $f(3x) = (3x)^2 + 5(3x) - 2 = 9x^2 + 15x - 2$

    (e) $\dfrac{f(x+h) - f(x)}{h} = \dfrac{(x+h)^2 + 5(x+h) - 2 - (x^2 + 5x - 2)}{h}$

    $\qquad = \dfrac{x^2 + 2xh + h^2 + 5x + 5h - 2 - x^2 - 5x + 2}{h} = \dfrac{2xh + h^2 + 5h}{h} = 2x + h + 5$

9. $f(x) = -3x + 7$

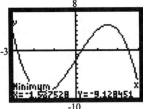

x-intercept: $\left(\dfrac{7}{3}, 0\right)$

y-intercept: $(0, 7)$

11. $f(x) = x^2 + 3x + 1$

$$\text{avg rate of change of } f \atop \text{from 1 to } x = \frac{f(x) - f(1)}{x - 1} = \frac{x^2 + 3x + 1 - \left(1^2 + 3 \cdot 1 + 1\right)}{x - 1}$$

$$= \frac{x^2 + 3x + 1 - 5}{x - 1} = \frac{x^2 + 3x - 4}{x - 1} = \frac{(x + 4)(x - 1)}{x - 1} = x + 4 = m_{\text{sec}}$$

when $x = 2$, $m_{\text{sec}} = 2 + 4 = 6$.

13. $f(x) = -x^3 + 7x - 2$, for $-3 < x < 3$

Use MAXIMUM and MINIMUM on the graph of $y_1 = -x^3 + 7x - 2$.

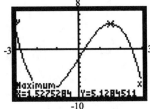

local maximum at: $(1.53, 5.13)$;

f is increasing on: $(-1.53, 1.53)$

local minimum at: $(-1.53, -9.13)$

f is decreasing on: $(-3, 1.53) \cup (1.53, 3)$

15. $f(x) = \begin{cases} 2x + 1 & \text{if } -3 < x < 2 \\ -3x + 4 & \text{if } x \geq 2 \end{cases}$

(a) Domain: $(-3, \infty)$

(b) x-intercept: $\left(-\dfrac{1}{2}, 0\right)$

      y-intercept: $(0, 1)$

(c)

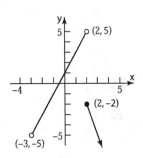

(d) Range: $\{y < 5\}$

(e) Graphing Utility:

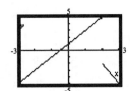

17. $f(x) = x^2 - 5x + 1$ $g(x) = -4x - 7$

(a) $(f + g)(x) = x^2 - 5x + 1 + (-4x - 7) = x^2 - 9x - 6$

The domain is all real numbers.

(b) $\left(\dfrac{f}{g}\right)(x) = \dfrac{f(x)}{g(x)} = \dfrac{x^2 - 5x + 1}{-4x - 7}$ The domain is all real numbers except $-\dfrac{7}{4}$.

19.   Let x = the number of minutes. Therefore, during the first 20 minutes, the call costs 0.99 dollars.

Once the call lasts longer than 20 minutes (that is, when $x > 20$), the number of additional minutes is given by $x - 20$.

Therefore, the total cost is computed as follows:

Total cost = (cost of first 20 minutes) + (cost of each additional minute)

$$= 0.99 + (0.07)(x - 20) = 0.99 + 0.07x - 1.4 = 0.07x - 0.41$$

We can express the total cost as a piecewise-defined function as follows:

$$C(x) = \begin{cases} 0.99 & \text{for} \quad 0 \le x \le 20 \\ 0.99 + 0.07(x - 20) & \text{for} \quad x > 20 \end{cases}$$

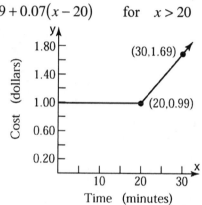

Polynomial and Rational Functions

5.1   Power Functions and Models

1. $f(x) = (x+1)^4$
Using the graph of $y = x^4$, shift the graph horizontally, 1 unit to the left.

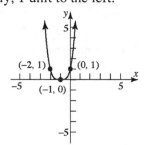

3. $f(x) = x^5 - 3$
Using the graph of $y = x^5$, shift the graph vertically, 3 units down.

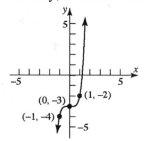

5. $f(x) = \dfrac{1}{2}x^4$
Using the graph of $y = x^4$, compress the graph vertically by a factor of $\dfrac{1}{2}$.

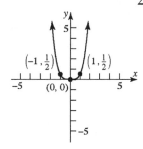

7. $f(x) = -x^5$
Using the graph of $y = x^5$, reflect the graph about the x-axis.

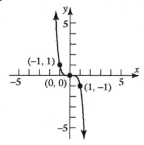

9. $f(x) = (x-1)^5 + 2$
Using the graph of $y = x^5$, shift the graph horizontally, 1 unit to the right, and shift vertically 2 units up.

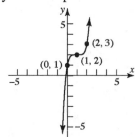

11. $f(x) = 2(x+1)^4 + 1$
Using the graph of $y = x^4$, shift the graph horizontally, 1 unit to the left, stretch vertically by a factor of 2, and shift vertically 1 unit up.

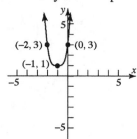

13. $f(x) = 4 - (x-2)^5 = -(x-2)^5 + 4$
     Using the graph of $y = x^5$, shift the graph
     horizontally, 2 units to the right, reflect about
     the x-axis, and shift vertically 4 units up.

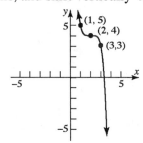

15. $f(x) = -\frac{1}{2}(x-2)^4 - 1$
     Using the graph of $y = x^4$, shift the
     graph horizontally, 2 units to the
     right, reflect about the x-axis,
     compress vertically by a factor
     of $\frac{1}{2}$ and shift vertically 1 unit down.

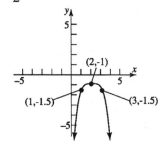

17. By definition, a triangle has area $A = \frac{1}{2}bh$, $b =$ base, $h =$ height. Because a vertex of the
     triangle is at the origin, we know that $b = x$ and $h = y$. Expressing the area of the triangle
     as a function of x, we have: $A(x) = \frac{1}{2}xy = \frac{1}{2}x(x^3) = \frac{1}{2}x^4$.

19. By definition, a right circular cylinder has volume $V = \pi r^2 h$, $r =$ radius, $h =$ height.
     The radius of the cylinder $= 4$ feet at every point along the height of the cylinder.
     Therefore, the volume of the water in the cylinder is given by:
     $$V = \pi r^2 h, \ r = \text{ radius of the water, } h = \text{ height of the water.}$$
     $$V(h) = \pi (4)^2 h = 16\pi h, \ 0 \le h \le 16$$

21. (a)

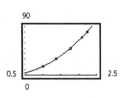

     (b) $s = 15.97274 t^{2.00182}$
     (c)

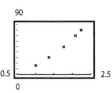

     (d)   Solve $s = 15.973 t^{2.002} = 100$ for t.
           $15.97274 t^{2.00182} = 100$

           $$t^{2.00182} = \frac{100}{15.97274}$$

           $$t \approx \left(\frac{100}{15.97274}\right)^{1/2.00182} \approx 2.5 \text{ seconds}$$

     (e) $s = 15.97274 t^2 = \frac{1}{2}gt^2$

           $$15.97274 = \frac{1}{2}g$$

           $$g = 31.9455 \ \text{ft}/s^2$$

           $$s = \left(\frac{1}{2}\right)(31.9455)t^2$$

Chapter 5

Polynomial and Rational Functions

5.2　Polynomial Functions and Models

1.　$f(x) = 4x + x^3$ is a polynomial function of degree 3.

3.　$g(x) = \dfrac{1 - x^2}{2} = \dfrac{1}{2} - \dfrac{1}{2}x^2$ is a polynomial function of degree 2.

5.　$f(x) = 1 - \dfrac{1}{x} = 1 - x^{-1}$ is not a polynomial function because it contains a negative exponent.

7.　$g(x) = x^{3/2} - x^2 + 2$ is not a polynomial function because it contains a fractional exponent.

9.　$F(x) = 5x^4 - \pi x^3 + \dfrac{1}{2}$ is a polynomial function of degree 4.

11.　$f(x) = a(x - (-1))(x - 1)(x - 3)$
　　　For $a = 1$: $f(x) = (x+1)(x-1)(x-3) = (x^2 - 1)(x-3) = x^3 - 3x^2 - x + 3$

13.　$f(x) = a(x - (-3))(x - 0)(x - 4)$
　　　For $a = 1$: $f(x) = (x+3)(x)(x-4)$
　　　　　　　　　$f(x) = (x^2 + 3x)(x - 4) = x^3 - 4x^2 + 3x^2 - 12x = x^3 - x^2 - 12x$

15.　$f(x) = a(x - (-4))(x - (-1))(x - 2)(x - 3)$
　　　For $a = 1$: $f(x) = (x+4)(x+1)(x-2)(x-3)$
　　　　　　　　　$f(x) = (x^2 + 5x + 4)(x^2 - 5x + 6)$
　　　　　　　　　　$f(x) = x^4 - 5x^3 + 6x^2 + 5x^3 - 25x^2 + 30x + 4x^2 - 20x + 24$
　　　　　　　　　　$f(x) = x^4 - 15x^2 + 10x + 24$

17.　$f(x) = a(x - (-1))(x - 3)^2$
　　　For $a = 1$: $f(x) = (x+1)(x-3)^2$
　　　　　　　　　$f(x) = (x+1)(x^2 - 6x + 9) = x^3 - 6x^2 + 9x + x^2 - 6x + 9 = x^3 - 5x^2 + 3x + 9$

19.　(a)　The real zeros of $f(x) = 3(x - 7)(x + 3)^2$ are: 7, with multiplicity one; and -3, with multiplicity two.
　　　(b)　The graph crosses the x-axis at 7 and touches it at -3.
　　　(c)　The function resembles $y = 3x^3$ for large values of $|x|$.

21. (a) The real zeros of $f(x) = 4(x^2 + 1)(x - 2)^3$ is: 2, with multiplicity three.
    $x^2 + 1 = 0$ has no real solution.
    (b) The graph crosses the x-axis at 2.
    (c) The function resembles $y = 4x^5$ for large values of $|x|$.

23. (a) The real zeros of $f(x) = -2\left(x + \dfrac{1}{2}\right)^2 (x^2 + 4)^2$ is: $-\dfrac{1}{2}$, with multiplicity two.
    $x^2 + 4 = 0$ has no real solution.
    (b) The graph touches the x-axis at $-\dfrac{1}{2}$.
    (c) The function resembles $y = -2x^6$ for large values of $|x|$.

25. (a) The real zeros of $f(x) = (x - 5)^3(x + 4)^2$ are: 5, with multiplicity three; and –4, with multiplicity two.
    (b) The graph crosses the x-axis at 5 and touches it at –4.
    (c) The function resembles $y = x^5$ for large values of $|x|$.

27. (a) $f(x) = 3(x^2 + 8)(x^2 + 9)^2$ has no real zeros. $x^2 + 8 = 0$ and $x^2 + 9 = 0$ have no real solutions.
    (b) The graph neither touches nor crosses the x-axis.
    (c) The function resembles $y = 3x^6$ for large values of $|x|$.

29. (a) The real zeros of $f(x) = -2x^2(x^2 - 2)$ are: $-\sqrt{2}$ and $\sqrt{2}$ with multiplicity one; and 0, with multiplicity two.
    (b) The graph touches the x-axis at 0 and crosses the x-axis at $-\sqrt{2}$ and $\sqrt{2}$.
    (c) The function resembles $y = -2x^4$ for large values of $|x|$.

31. $f(x) = (x - 1)^2$
    (a) Degree = 2; The function resembles $y = x^2$ for large values of $|x|$.
    (b) x-intercept: 1; y-intercept: 1
    (c) touches x-axis at x = 1
    (d) f is above the x-axis for $(-\infty, 1) \cup (1, \infty)$

X	Y1
-1	4
3	4

    Y1⊟(X−1)²

    (e) graphing utility:

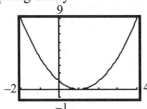

(f)   1 turning point; local minimum $(1,0)$

(g)   graphing by hand

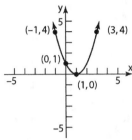

(h)   Domain of f: $\{$All real numbers$\}$; Range of f: $\{y|y \geq 0\}$.

(i) f is increasing on $(1,\infty)$; f is decreasing on $(-\infty,1)$

33. $f(x) = x^2(x-3)$

(a)   Degree $= 3$; The function resembles $y = x^3$ for large values of $|x|$.

(b)   x-intercepts: 0, 3; y-intercept: 0

(c)   touches x-axis at $x = 0$; crosses x-axis at $x = 3$

(d) f is below the x-axis for $(-\infty,0)\cup(0,3)$; f is above the x-axis for $(3,\infty)$

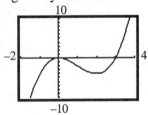

(e)   graphing utility:

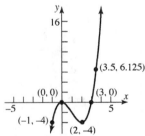

(f)   2 turning points; local maximum: (0, 0); local minimum: (2, –4)

(g)   graphing by hand

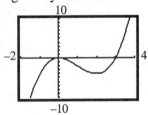

(h)   Domain of f: $\{$All real numbers$\}$; Range of f: $\{$All real numbers$\}$.

(i) f is increasing on $(-\infty,0)\cup(2,\infty)$; f is decreasing on $(0,2)$

35. $f(x) = 6x^3(x+4)$

(a)   Degree = 4; The function resembles $y = 6x^4$ for large values of $|x|$.

(b)   x-intercepts: –4, 0; y-intercept: 0   (c)   crosses x-axis at x = –4 and x = 0

(d) f is above the x-axis for $(-\infty,-4) \cup (0,\infty)$; f is below the x-axis for $(-4,0)$

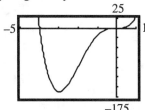

(e)   graphing utility:

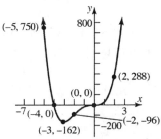

(f)   1 turning point; local minimum: $(-3, -162)$

(g)   graphing by hand

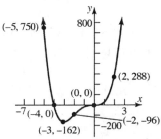

(h)   Domain of f: {All real numbers}; Range of f: $\{y | y \geq -162\}$.

(i) f is increasing on $(-3,\infty)$; f is decreasing on $(-\infty,-3)$

37. $f(x) = -4x^2(x+2)$

(a)   Degree = 3; The function resembles $y = -4x^3$ for large values of $|x|$.

(b)   x-intercepts: $0, -2$; y-intercept: 0

(c)   crosses x-axis at $x = -2$; touches x-axis at $x = 0$

(d) f is above the x-axis for $(-\infty,-2)$; f is below the x-axis for $(-2,0) \cup (0,\infty)$

(e)   graphing utility:

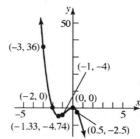

(f)   2 turning points;   local maximum: $(0, 0)$; local minimum: $(-1.33, -4.74)$

(g)   graphing by hand

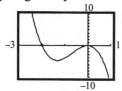

(h)   Domain of f: {All real numbers}; Range of f: {All real numbers}.

(i) f is increasing on $(-1.33, 0)$; f is decreasing on $(-\infty, -1.33) \cup (0, \infty)$

39. $f(x) = (x+1)(x-2)(x+4)$

(a)   Degree $= 3$; The function resembles $y = x^3$ for large values of $|x|$.

(b)   x-intercepts: $-1, 2, -4$; y-intercept: -8

(c)   crosses x-axis at $x = -1, 2, -4$

(d) f is above the x-axis for $(-4, -1) \cup (2, \infty)$; f is below the x-axis for $(-\infty, -4) \cup (-1, 2)$

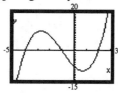

(e)   graphing utility:

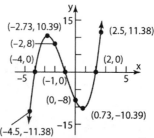

(f)   2 turning points; local maximum: $(-2.73, 10.39)$; local minimum: $(0.73, -10.39)$

(g)   graphing by hand

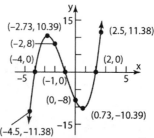

(h)   Domain of f: {All real numbers}; Range of f: {All real numbers}.

(i) f is increasing on $(-\infty, -2.73) \cup (0.73, \infty)$; f is decreasing on $(-2.73, 0.73)$

41. $f(x) = 4x - x^3 = x(4 - x^2) = x(2 + x)(2 - x)$

(a) Degree = 3; The function resembles $y = -x^3$ for large values of $|x|$.

(b) x-intercepts: $0, -2, 2$; y-intercept: 0

(c) crosses x-axis at $x = 0, x = -2, x = 2$

(d) f is above the x-axis for $(-\infty, -2) \cup (0, 2)$; f is below the x-axis for $(-2, 0) \cup (2, \infty)$

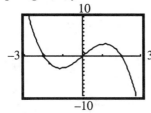

(e) graphing utility:

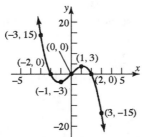

(f) 2 turning points; local maximum: $(1.15, 3.08)$;
    local minimum: $(-1.15, -3.08)$

(g) graphing by hand

(h) Domain of f: {All real numbers}; Range of f: {All real numbers}.

(i) f is increasing on $(-1.15, 1.15)$; f is decreasing on $(-\infty, -1.15) \cup (1.15, \infty)$

43. $f(x) = x^2(x - 2)(x + 2)$

(a) Degree = 4; The function resembles $y = x^4$ for large values of $|x|$.

(b) x-intercepts: $0, 2, -2$; y-intercept: 0

(c) crosses x-axis at $x = 2, x = -2$; touches x-axis at x = 0

(d) f is above the x-axis for $(-\infty, -2) \cup (2, \infty)$; f is below the x-axis for $(-2, 0) \cup (0, 2)$

(e)   graphing utility:

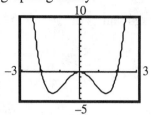

(f)   3 turning points; local maximum: $(0, 0)$; local minima: $(-1.41, -4)$, $(1.41, -4)$
(g)   graphing by hand

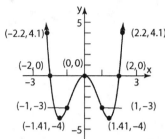

(h)   Domain of f: {All real numbers}; Range of f: $\{y | y \geq -4\}$.

(i) f is increasing on $(-1.41, 0) \cup (1.41, \infty)$; f is decreasing on $(-\infty, -1.41) \cup (0, 1.41)$

45. $f(x) = (x + 1)^2 (x - 2)^2$

(a)   Degree = 4; The function resembles $y = x^4$ for large values of $|x|$.
(b)   x-intercepts: $-1, 2$; y-intercept: 4
(c)   touches x-axis at $x = -1, x = 2$
(d) f is above the x-axis for $(-\infty, -1) \cup (-1, 2) \cup (2, \infty)$

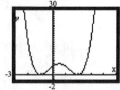

(e)   graphing utility:

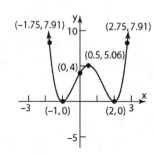

(f)   3 turning points; local maximum: $(0.5, 5.06)$; local minima: $(-1, 0), (2, 0)$
(g)   graphing by hand

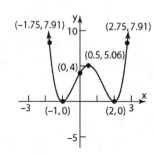

(h)   Domain of f: {All real numbers}; Range of f: $\{y|y \geq 0\}$.

(i) f is increasing on $(-1, 0.5) \cup (2, \infty)$; f is decreasing on $(-\infty, -1) \cup (0.5, 2)$

47. $f(x) = x^2(x-3)(x+1)$

(a)   Degree = 4; The function resembles $y = x^4$ for large values of $|x|$.

(b)   x-intercepts: $0, 3, -1$; y-intercept: 0

(c)   crosses x-axis at $x = -1, x = 3$; touches x-axis at $x = 0$

(d) f is above the x-axis for $(-\infty, -1) \cup (3, \infty)$; f is below the x-axis for $(-1, 0) \cup (0, 3)$

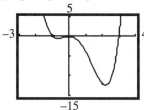

(e)   graphing utility:

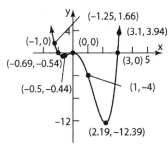

(f)   3 turning points; local maximum: (0, 0); local minima: (–0.69, –0.54), (2.19, –12.39)

(g)   graphing by hand

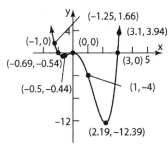

(h)   Domain of f: {All real numbers}; Range of f: $\{y|y \geq -12.39\}$.

(i) f is increasing on $(-0.69, 0) \cup (2.19, \infty)$; f is decreasing on $(-\infty, -0.69) \cup (0, 2.19)$

49. $f(x) = (x+2)^2(x-4)^2$

(a)   Degree = 4; The function resembles $y = x^4$ for large values of $|x|$.

(b)   x-intercepts: $-2, 4$; y-intercept: 64

(c)   touches x-axis at $x = -2, x = 4$

(d) f is above the x-axis for $(-\infty, -2) \cup (-2, 4) \cup (4, \infty)$

(e)   graphing utility:

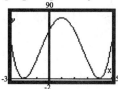

(f)   3 turning points; local maximum $(1,81)$; local minima $(-2,0)$ and $(4,0)$

(g)   graphing by hand

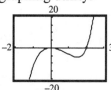

(h)   Domain of f: $\{$All real numbers$\}$; Range of f: $\{y|y \geq 0\}$.

(i) f is increasing on $(-2,1) \cup (4,\infty)$; f is decreasing on $(-\infty,-2) \cup (1,4)$

51. $f(x) = x^2(x-2)(x^2+3)$

(a)   Degree = 5; The function resembles $y = x^5$ for large values of $|x|$.

(b)   x-intercepts: 0, 2; y-intercept: 0

(c)   crosses x-axis at x = 2 ; touches x-axis at x = 0

(d) f is above the x-axis for $(2,\infty)$; f is below the x-axis for $(-\infty,0) \cup (0,2)$

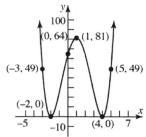

(e)   graphing utility:

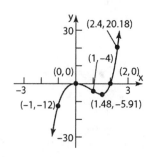

(f)   2 turning points; local maximum: (0, 0); local minimum: (1.48, –5.91)

(g)   graphing by hand

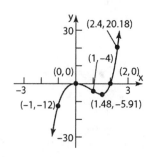

(h)   Domain of f: $\{$All real numbers$\}$; Range of f: $\{$All real numbers$\}$.

(i) f is increasing on $(-\infty,0)\cup(1.48,\infty)$; f is decreasing on $(0,1.48)$

53. $f(x)=-x^2(x^2-1)(x+1)=-x^2(x-1)(x+1)(x+1)=-x^2(x-1)(x+1)^2$

(a)   Degree $= 5$; The function resembles $y=-x^5$ for large values of $|x|$.

(b)   x-intercepts: $0,1,-1$; y-intercept: 0

(c)   crosses x-axis at $x=1$; touches x-axis at $x=0$ and $x=-1$

(d) f is above the x-axis for $(-\infty,-1)\cup(-1,0)\cup(0,1)$; f is below the x-axis for $(1,\infty)$

(e) graphing utility:

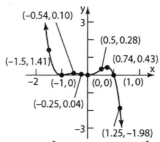

(f)   4 turning points; local maxima: $(-0.54,0.10),(0.74,0.43)$; local minima: $(-1,0),(0,0)$

(g)   graphing by hand

(h)   Domain of f: $\{$All real numbers$\}$; Range of f: $\{$All real numbers$\}$.

(i) f is increasing on $(-1,-0.54)\cup(0,0.74)$;

   f is decreasing on $(-\infty,-1)\cup(-0.54,0)\cup(0.74,\infty)$

55. $f(x) = x^3 + 0.2x^2 - 1.5876x - 0.31752$

(a) Degree = 3; The function resembles $y = x^3$ for large values of $|x|$.

(b) graphing utility:

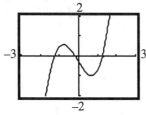

(c) x-intercepts: $-1.26, -0.2, 1.26$; y-intercept: -0.31752

(d)

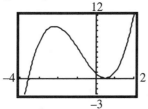

(e) 2 turning points; local maximum: $(-0.80, 0.57)$ local minimum: $(0.66, -0.99)$

(f) graphing by hand

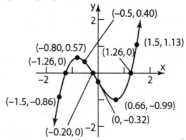

(g) Domain of f: {All real numbers}; Range of f: {All real numbers}.

(h) f is increasing on $(-\infty, -0.80) \cup (0.66, \infty)$; f is decreasing on $(-0.80, 0.66)$

57. $f(x) = x^3 + 2.56x^2 - 3.31x + 0.89$

(a) Degree = 3; The function resembles $y = x^3$ for large values of $|x|$.

(b) graphing utility

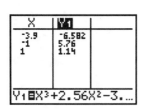

(c) x-intercepts: $-3.56, 0.50$; y-intercept: 0.89

(d)

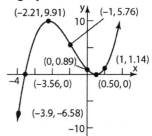

(e) 2 turning points; local maximum: $(-2.21, 9.91)$ local minimum: $(0.50, 0)$

(f) graphing by hand

(g) Domain of f: {All real numbers}; Range of f: {All real numbers}.

(h) f is increasing on $(-\infty, -2.21) \cup (0.50, \infty)$; f is decreasing on $(-2.21, 0.50)$

59. $f(x) = x^4 - 2.5x^2 + 0.5625$

(a) Degree = 4; The function resembles $y = x^4$ for large values of $|x|$.

(b) graphing utility:

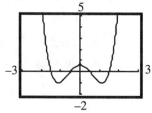

(c) x-intercepts: $-1.5, -0.5, 0.5, 1.5$; y-intercept: 0.5625

(d)
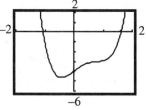

(e) 3 turning points:
local maximum: $(0, 0.56)$
local minima: $(-1.12, -1), (1.12, -1)$

(f) graphing by hand

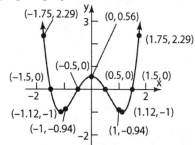

(g) Domain of f: {All real numbers};
Range of f: $\{y | y \geq -1\}$.

(h) f is increasing on $(-1.12, 0) \cup (1.12, \infty)$;
f is decreasing on $(-\infty, -1.12) \cup (0, 1.12)$

61. $f(x) = 2x^4 - \pi x^3 + \sqrt{5}x - 4$

(a) Degree = 4; The function resembles $y = 2x^4$ for large values of $|x|$.

(b) graphing utility:

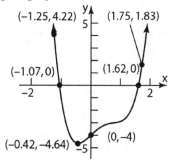

(c) x-intercepts: $-1.07, 1.62$; y-intercept: -4

(d)

(e) 1 turning point;
local minimum: $(-0.42, -4.64)$

(f) graphing by hand

(g) Domain of f: {All real numbers};
Range of f: $\{y | y \geq -4.62\}$.

(h) f is increasing on $(-0.42, \infty)$;
f is decreasing on $(-\infty, -0.42)$

63. $f(x) = -2x^5 - \sqrt{2}x^2 - x - \sqrt{2}$

(a)   Degree = 5; The function resembles $y = -2x^5$ for large values of $|x|$.

(b)   graphing utility:

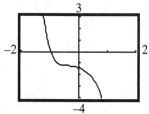

(c)   x-intercept: –0.98;
      y-intercept: $-\sqrt{2}$

(d)

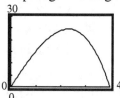

(e)   No turning points
      No local extrema

(f)   graphing by hand

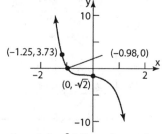

(g)   Domain of f: {All real numbers};
      Range of f: {All real numbers}.

(h) f is decreasing on $(-\infty, \infty)$

65.   Answers will vary. One possible answer is $f(x) = x(x-1)(x-2)$, since the graph crosses the x-axis at $x = 0, 1$ and 2.

67.   Answers will vary. One possible answer is $f(x) = -\dfrac{1}{2}(x+1)(x-1)(x-2)$, since the graph crosses the x-axis at $x = -1, 1$ and 2 and has a y-intercept at -1.

69.   (a) $A(x) = xy = x(16 - x^2) = -x^3 + 16x$

      (b)   Domain: $\{x \mid 0 < x < 4\}$

      (c)   Graphing: Using MAXIMUM, the area is largest when x is approximately 2.31.

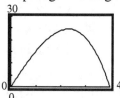

71.   (a)   length = $24 - 2x$; width = $24 - 2x$; height = x
            $V(x) = x(24 - 2x)(24 - 2x) = x(24 - 2x)^2$

      (b)   Since the length, width and height must all be > 0, we need $24 - 2x > 0$ and $x > 0$.
            Note that $24 - 2x > 0 \Rightarrow 24 > 2x \Rightarrow 12 > x$.
            Domain: $\{x \mid 0 < x < 12\}$

      (c) $V(3) = 3(24 - 2(3))^2 = 3(18)^2 = 3(324) = 972$ cu. in.

      (d) $V(10) = 10(24 - 2(10))^2 = 10(4)^2 = 10(16) = 160$ cu. in.

(e)

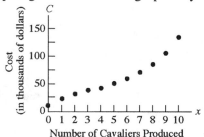

Using MAXIMUM, the volume is largest when $x \approx 4$ inches.

73. $r =$ radius of cylinder, $h =$ height of cylinder, $V =$ volume of cylinder

$$r^2 + \left(\frac{h}{2}\right)^2 = R^2 \Rightarrow r^2 + \frac{h^2}{4} = R^2$$

$$r^2 = R^2 - \frac{h^2}{4} \Rightarrow r^2 = \frac{4R^2 - h^2}{4}$$

$$V = \pi r^2 h \Rightarrow V(h) = \pi\left(\frac{4R^2 - h^2}{4}\right)h = \pi h\left(R^2 - \frac{h^2}{4}\right)$$

75.   (a)   Graphing, we see that the graph may be a cubic relation.

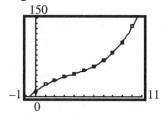

(b)   Average rate of change $= \dfrac{50 - 43}{5 - 4} = \dfrac{7}{1} = 7$ thousand dollars per car

(c)   Average rate of change $= \dfrac{105 - 85}{9 - 8} = \dfrac{20}{1} = 20$ thousand dollars per car

(d) $C(x) = 0.2156x^3 - 2.3473x^2 + 14.3275x + 10.2238$

(e) Graphing the cubic function of best fit:

(f) $C(11) \approx 170.7666$

The cost of manufacturing 11 Cavaliers in 1 hour would be approximately $171,00.

(g)   The y-intercept would indicate the fixed costs of approximately $10,200 before any cars are made.

77. (a)   Graphing, we see that the graph may be a cubic relation..

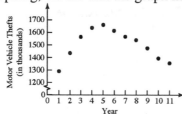

   (b) $T(x) = 1.5243x^3 - 39.8089x^2 + 282.2881x + 1035.5$

   (c)   Graphing the cubic function of best fit:

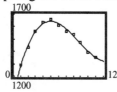

   (d) $T(12) \approx 1324.466$

         According to the function there would be approximately 1,324,000 motor vehicle thefts in 1998.

   (e)   Answers will vary

79.   The graph of a polynomial function $f(x) = a_0 + a_1x + a_2x^2 + \cdots + a_nx^n$ will always have a y-intercept since $f(0) = a_0 + a_1(0) + a_2(0)^2 + \cdots + a_n(0)^n = a_0$.

      The graph of a polynomial function $f(x) = a_0 + a_1x + a_2x^2 + \cdots + a_nx^n$ may have no x-intercepts. Consider $f(x) = x^2 + 1$, then $f(x) = x^2 + 1 = 0$ yields no real solution.

81.   Answers will vary, one such polynomial is $f(x) = x^2(x+1)(4-x)(x-2)^2$

83. $f(x) = \dfrac{1}{x}$ is smooth but not continuous; $g(x) = |x|$ is continuous but not smooth.

Chapter 5

Polynomial and Rational Functions

5.3   Rational Functions I

1. In $R(x) = \dfrac{4x}{x-3}$, the denominator, $q(x) = x - 3$, has a zero at 3. Thus, the domain of $R(x)$ is all real numbers except 3.

3. In $H(x) = \dfrac{-4x^2}{(x-2)(x+4)}$, the denominator, $q(x) = (x-2)(x+4)$, has zeros at 2 and –4. Thus, the domain of $H(x)$ is all real numbers except 2 and –4.

5. In $F(x) = \dfrac{3x(x-1)}{2x^2 - 5x - 3}$, the denominator, $q(x) = 2x^2 - 5x - 3 = (2x+1)(x-3)$, has zeros at $-\dfrac{1}{2}$ and 3. Thus, the domain of $F(x)$ is all real numbers except $-\dfrac{1}{2}$ and 3.

7. In $R(x) = \dfrac{x}{x^3 - 8}$, the denominator, $q(x) = x^3 - 8 = (x-2)(x^2 + 2x + 4)$, has a zero at 2. ($x^2 + 2x + 4$ has no real zeros.) Thus, the domain of $R(x)$ is all real numbers except 2.

9. In $H(x) = \dfrac{3x^2 + x}{x^2 + 4}$, the denominator, $q(x) = x^2 + 4$, has no real zeros. Thus, the domain of $H(x)$ is all real numbers.

11. In $R(x) = \dfrac{3(x^2 - x - 6)}{4(x^2 - 9)}$, the denominator, $q(x) = 4(x^2 - 9) = 4(x-3)(x+3)$, has zeros at 3 and –3. Thus, the domain of $R(x)$ is all real numbers except 3 and –3.

13. (a) Domain: $\{x \mid x \neq 2\}$; Range: $\{y \mid y \neq 1\}$
    (b) Intercept: $(0, 0)$
    (c) Horizontal Asymptote: $y = 1$
    (d) Vertical Asymptote: $x = 2$
    (e) Oblique Asymptote: none

15. (a) Domain: $\{x \mid x \neq 0\}$; Range: all real numbers
    (b) Intercepts: $(-1, 0), (1, 0)$
    (c) Horizontal Asymptote: none
    (d) Vertical Asymptote: $x = 0$
    (e) Oblique Asymptote: $y = 2x$

17. (a) Domain: $\{x \mid x \neq -2, x \neq 2\}$; Range: $\{y \mid y \leq 0 \text{ or } y > 1\}$
    (b) Intercept: $(0, 0)$
    (c) Horizontal Asymptote: $y = 1$
    (d) Vertical Asymptotes: $x = -2, x = 2$
    (e) Oblique Asymptote: none

19. (a) Domain: $\{x \mid x \neq -1\}$; Range: $\{y \mid y \neq 2\}$
     (b) Intercepts: $(-1.5, 0)$; $(0, 3)$ (c) Horizontal Asymptote: $y = 2$
     (d) Vertical Asymptote: $x = -1$ (e) Oblique Asymptote: none

21. (a) Domain: $\{x \mid x \neq -4, x \neq 3\}$; Range: all real numbers
     (b) Intercept: $(0, 0)$ (c) Horizontal Asymptote: $y = 0$
     (d) Vertical Asymptotes: $x = -4, x = 3$ (e) Oblique Asymptote: none

23. $R(x) = \dfrac{1}{(x-1)^2}$

Using the function, $y = \dfrac{1}{x^2}$, shift the graph horizontally 1 unit to the right.

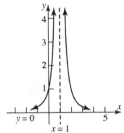

25. $H(x) = \dfrac{-2}{x+1} = -2\left(\dfrac{1}{x+1}\right)$

Using the function $y = \dfrac{1}{x}$, shift the graph horizontally 1 unit to the left, reflect about the x-axis, and stretch vertically by a factor of 2.

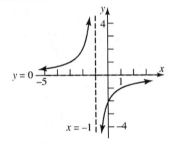

27. $R(x) = \dfrac{1}{x^2 + 4x + 4} = \dfrac{1}{(x+2)^2}$

$= \dfrac{1}{(x+2)^2}$

Using the function $y = \dfrac{1}{x^2}$, shift the graph horizontally 2 units to the left.

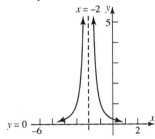

29. $F(x) = 1 - \dfrac{1}{x} = -\dfrac{1}{x} + 1$

Using the function, $y = \dfrac{1}{x}$, reflect the graph across the x-axis and then shift the graph vertically 1 unit up.

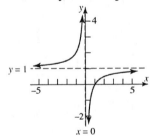

31. $R(x) = \dfrac{x^2 - 4}{x^2} = 1 - \dfrac{4}{x^2} = -4\left(\dfrac{1}{x^2}\right) + 1$

Using the function $y = \dfrac{1}{x^2}$, reflect about the x-axis, stretch vertically by a factor of 4 and shift vertically 1 unit up.

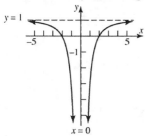

33. $G(x) = 1 + \dfrac{2}{(x-3)^2} = \dfrac{2}{(x-3)^2} + 1$
$= 2\left(\dfrac{1}{(x-3)^2}\right) + 1$

Using the function $y = \dfrac{1}{x^2}$, shift the graph 3 units right, stretch vertically by a factor of 2, and shift vertically 1 unit up.

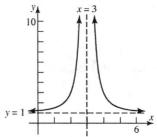

35. $R(x) = \dfrac{3x}{x+4}$

The degree of the numerator, $p(x) = 3x$, is $n = 1$. The degree of the denominator, $q(x) = x + 4$, is $m = 1$. Since $n = m$, the line $y = \dfrac{3}{1} = 3$ is a horizontal asymptote. The denominator is zero at $x = -4$, so $x = -4$ is a vertical asymptote.

37. $H(x) = \dfrac{x^4 + 2x^2 + 1}{x^2 - x + 1}$

The degree of the numerator, $p(x) = x^4 + 2x^2 + 1$, is $n = 4$. The degree of the denominator, $q(x) = x^2 - x + 1$, is $m = 2$. Since $n > m + 1$, there is no horizontal asymptote or oblique asymptote. The denominator has no real zeros, so there is no vertical asymptote.

39. $T(x) = \dfrac{x^3}{x^4 - 1}$

The degree of the numerator, $p(x) = x^3$, is $n = 3$. The degree of the denominator, $q(x) = x^4 - 1$ is $m = 4$. Since $n < m$, the line $y = 0$ is a horizontal asymptote. The denominator is zero at $x = -1$ and $x = 1$, so $x = -1$ and $x = 1$ are vertical asymptotes.

41. $Q(x) = \dfrac{5 - x^2}{3x^4}$

The degree of the numerator, $p(x) = 5 - x^2$, is $n = 2$. The degree of the denominator, $q(x) = 3x^4$ is $m = 4$. Since $n < m$, the line $y = 0$ is a horizontal asymptote. The denominator is zero at $x = 0$, so $x = 0$ is a vertical asymptote.

43. $R(x) = \dfrac{3x^4 - 4}{x^3 + 3x}$

The degree of the numerator, $p(x) = 3x^4 - 4$, is $n = 4$. The degree of the denominator, $q(x) = x^3 + 3x$ is $m = 3$. Since $n = m+1$, there is an oblique asymptote.
Dividing:

$$\begin{array}{r} 3x \\ x^3 + 3x \overline{)3x^4 + 0x^3 + 0x^2 + 0x - 4} \\ \underline{3x^4 + 9x^2 } \\ -9x^2 + 0x - 4 \end{array}$$

$$R(x) = 3x + \dfrac{-9x^2 - 4}{x^3 + 3x}$$

Thus, the oblique asymptote is $y = 3x$.
The denominator is zero at $x = 0$, so $x = 0$ is a vertical asymptote.

45. $G(x) = \dfrac{x^3 - 1}{x - x^2}, \; x \neq 1$

The degree of the numerator, $p(x) = x^3 - 1$, is $n = 3$. The degree of the denominator, $q(x) = x - x^2$ is $m = 2$. Since $n = m+1$, there is an oblique asymptote.
Dividing:

$$\begin{array}{r} -x - 1 \\ -x^2 + x \overline{)x^3 + 0x^2 + 0x - 1} \\ \underline{x^3 - x^2 } \\ x^2 + 0x \\ \underline{x^2 - x } \\ x - 1 \end{array}$$

$$G(x) = -x - 1 + \dfrac{x-1}{x-x^2} = -x - 1 - \dfrac{1}{x}, \; x \neq 1$$

Thus, the oblique asymptote is $y = -x - 1 = -(x+1)$

$G(x)$ must be in lowest terms to find the vertical asymptote:

$$G(x) = \dfrac{x^3 - 1}{x - x^2} = \dfrac{(x-1)(x^2 + x + 1)}{-x(x-1)} = \dfrac{x^2 + x + 1}{-x}$$

The denominator is zero at $x = 0$, so $x = 0$ is a vertical asymptotes.

47. $\lim\limits_{x \to \infty} R(x) = L$ means as we choose larger and large positive values for x, the corresponding function values $R(x)$ get closer and closer to the number L.

49. A rational function cannot have both a horizontal and an oblique asymptote since a horizontal asymptote occurs when the degree of the numerator is less than or equal to the degree of the denominator, while an oblique asymptote occurs when the degree of the numerator is exactly 1 less than the degree of the denominator.

51. If $R(x) = \dfrac{p(x)}{q(x)}$ has horizontal asymptote $y = 2$, then, as $x \to \pm\infty, \dfrac{p(x)}{q(x)} \to 2$.

In other words, eventually, $\dfrac{p(x)}{q(x)} \approx 2$. Therefore, as $x \to \pm\infty, p(x) \approx 2q(x)$. But this is only possible when the degree of $p(x) = $ the degree of $q(x)$.

Polynomial and Rational Functions

5.4 Rational Functions II: Analyzing Graphs

In problems 1–37, we will use the terminology: $R(x) = \dfrac{p(x)}{q(x)}$, *where the degree of* $p(x) = n$ *and the degree of* $q(x) = m$.

1. $R(x) = \dfrac{x+1}{x(x+4)}$ $p(x) = x+1$; $q(x) = x(x+4) = x^2 + 4x$; $n = 1$; $m = 2$

    Step 1:   Domain: $\{x \mid x \neq -4, \, x \neq 0\}$

    Step 2: $R(x) = \dfrac{x+1}{x(x+4)}$ is in lowest terms.

    Step 3:   (a)   The x-intercept is the zero of $p(x)$: -1
              (b)   There is no y-intercept; $R(0)$ is not defined, since $q(0) = 0$.

    Step 4: $R(-x) = \dfrac{-x+1}{-x(-x+4)} = \dfrac{-x+1}{x^2 - 4x}$; this is neither $R(x)$ nor $-R(x)$, so there is no symmetry.

    Step 5:   The vertical asymptotes are the zeros of $q(x)$: $x = -4$ and $x = 0$

    Step 6:   Since $n < m$, the line $y = 0$ is the horizontal asymptote.
              $R(x)$ intersects $y = 0$ at $(-1, 0)$.

    Step 7:

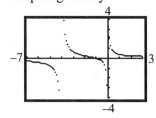

    Step 8:   Graphing Utility: Step 9:   Graphing by hand:

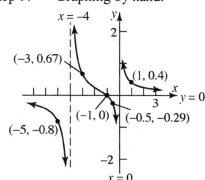

    f is decreasing on $(-\infty, -4) \cup (-4, 0) \cup (0, \infty)$

3. $R(x) = \dfrac{3x+3}{2x+4}$ $p(x) = 3x+3;\ q(x) = 2x+4;\ n = 1;\ m = 1$

Step 1:   Domain: $\{x \mid x \neq -2\}$

Step 2: $R(x) = \dfrac{3x+3}{2x+4}$ is in lowest terms.

Step 3:   (a)   The x-intercept is the zero of $p(x)$: -1

(b)   The y-intercept is $R(0) = \dfrac{3(0)+3}{2(0)+4} = \dfrac{3}{4}$.

Step 4: $R(-x) = \dfrac{3(-x)+3}{2(-x)+4} = \dfrac{-3x+3}{-2x+4} = \dfrac{3x-3}{2x-4}$; this is neither $R(x)$ nor $-R(x)$, so there

is no symmetry.

Step 5:   The vertical asymptote is the zero of $q(x)$: $x = -2$

Step 6:   Since $n = m$, the line $y = \dfrac{3}{2}$ is the horizontal asymptote.

$R(x)$ does not intersect $y = \dfrac{3}{2}$

Step 7:

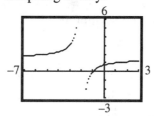

Step 8:   Graphing Utility:

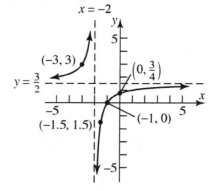

f is increasing on $(-\infty, -2) \cup (-2, \infty,)$

Step 9:   Graphing by hand:

5. $R(x) = \dfrac{3}{x^2 - 4}$ $p(x) = 3;\ q(x) = x^2 - 4;\ n = 0;\ m = 2$

Step 1:   Domain: $\{x \mid x \neq -2,\ x \neq 2\}$

Step 2: $R(x) = \dfrac{3}{x^2 - 4}$ is in lowest terms.

Step 3:   (a)   There is no x-intercept.

(b)   The y-intercept is $R(0) = \dfrac{3}{0^2 - 4} = \dfrac{3}{-4} = -\dfrac{3}{4}$.

Step 4: $R(-x) = \dfrac{3}{(-x)^2 - 4} = \dfrac{3}{x^2 - 4} = R(x)$; $R(x)$ is symmetric to the y-axis.

Step 5:   The vertical asymptotes are the zeros of $q(x)$: $x = -2$ and $x = 2$

Step 6:   Since $n < m$, the line $y = 0$ is the horizontal asymptote.

$R(x)$ does not intersect $y = 0$.

Step 7:

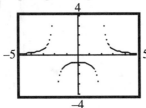

Step 8:   Graphing Utility:

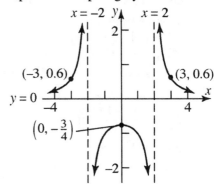

Using MAXIMUM and MINIMUM:
f is increasing on $(-\infty, -2) \cup (-2, 0)$
f is decreasing on $(0, 2) \cup (2, \infty)$

Step 9:   Graphing by hand:

7. $P(x) = \dfrac{x^4 + x^2 + 1}{x^2 - 1}$ $p(x) = x^4 + x^2 + 1$; $q(x) = x^2 - 1$; $n = 4$; $m = 2$

Step 1:   Domain: $\{x \mid x \neq -1, \, x \neq 1\}$

Step 2: $P(x) = \dfrac{x^4 + x^2 + 1}{x^2 - 1}$ is in lowest terms.

Step 3:   (a)   There is no x-intercept.

   (b)   The y-intercept is $P(0) = \dfrac{0^4 + 0^2 + 1}{0^2 - 1} = \dfrac{1}{-1} = -1$.

Step 4: $P(-x) = \dfrac{(-x)^4 + (-x)^2 + 1}{(-x)^2 - 1} = \dfrac{x^4 + x^2 + 1}{x^2 - 1} = P(x)$; $P(x)$ is symmetric to the y-axis.

Step 5:   The vertical asymptotes are the zeros of $q(x)$: $x = -1$ and $x = 1$

Step 6:   Since $n > m + 1$, there is no horizontal asymptote and no oblique asymptote.

Step 7:

Step 8:   Graphing Utility:

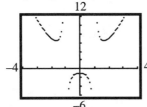

Step 9:   Graphing by hand:

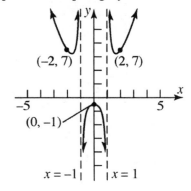

Using MAXIMUM and MINIMUM:

f is increasing on
$$(-1.653,-1)\cup(-1,0)\cup(1.653,\infty)$$

f is decreasing on
$$(-\infty,-1.653)\cup(0,1)\cup(1,1.653)$$

9. $H(x)=\dfrac{x^3-1}{x^2-9}$ $p(x)=x^3-1;\ \ q(x)=x^2-9;\ \ n=3;\ \ m=2$

Step 1:   Domain: $\{x\,|\,x\neq-3,\ x\neq3\}$

Step 2: $H(x)=\dfrac{x^3-1}{x^2-9}$ is in lowest terms.

Step 3:   (a)   The x-intercept is the zero of $p(x)$: 1.

(b)   The y-intercept is $H(0)=\dfrac{0^3-1}{0^2-9}=\dfrac{-1}{-9}=\dfrac{1}{9}$.

Step 4: $H(-x)=\dfrac{(-x)^3-1}{(-x)^2-9}=\dfrac{-x^3-1}{x^2-9}$; this is neither $H(x)$ nor $-H(x)$, so there is no symmetry.

Step 5:   The vertical asymptotes are the zeros of $q(x)$: $x=-3$ and $x=3$

Step 6:   Since $n=m+1$, there is an oblique asymptote. Dividing:

$$x^2-9\overline{\smash{)}\,x^3+0x^2+0x-1} \qquad H(x)=x+\dfrac{9x-1}{x^2-9}$$
$$\underline{\ x^3\qquad\ -9x}$$
$$9x-1$$

The oblique asymptote is $y=x$.

Solve to find intersection points:

$$\frac{x^3-1}{x^2-9}=x\Rightarrow x^3-1=x^3-9x\Rightarrow -1=-9x\Rightarrow x=\frac{1}{9}$$

The oblique asymptote intersects $H(x)$ at $\left(\dfrac{1}{9},\dfrac{1}{9}\right)$.

Step 7:

X	Y1
-4	-9.286
0	.11111
2	-1.4
4	9

$Y_1\boxminus(X^3-1)/(X^2-9)$

Step 8:   Graphing Utility:

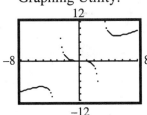

Step 9:   Graphing by hand:

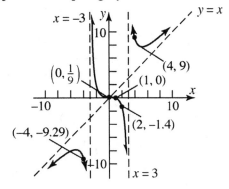

Using MAXIMUM and MINIMUM:

f is increasing on

$$(-\infty,-5.233)\cup(5.159,\infty)$$

f is decreasing on

$$(-5.233,-3)\cup(-3,3)\cup(3,5.159)$$

11. $R(x)=\dfrac{x^2}{x^2+x-6}=\dfrac{x^2}{(x+3)(x-2)}$ $p(x)=x^2$; $q(x)=x^2+x-6$; $n=2$; $m=2$

Step 1:   Domain: $\{x\,|\,x\neq-3,\ x\neq2\}$

Step 2: $R(x)=\dfrac{x^2}{x^2+x-6}$ is in lowest terms.

Step 3:   (a)   The x-intercept is the zero of $p(x)$: 0

(b)   The y-intercept is $R(0)=\dfrac{0^2}{0^2+0-6}=\dfrac{0}{-6}=0$.

Step 4: $R(-x)=\dfrac{(-x)^2}{(-x)^2+(-x)-6}=\dfrac{x^2}{x^2-x-6}$; this is neither $R(x)$ nor $-R(x)$, so there

is no symmetry.

Step 5:   The vertical asymptotes are the zeros of $q(x)$: $x=-3$ and $x=2$

Step 6:   Since $n=m$, the line $y=1$ is the horizontal asymptote.

$R(x)$ intersects $y=1$ at (6, 1), since:

$$\frac{x^2}{x^2+x-6}=1\Rightarrow x^2=x^2+x-6\Rightarrow 0=x-6\Rightarrow x=6$$

Step 7:

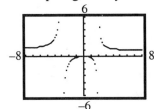

Step 8:   Graphing Utility:

Using MAXIMUM and MINIMUM:

f is increasing on $(-\infty,-3)\cup(-3,0)$

f is decreasing on $(0,2)\cup(2,\infty)$

Step 9:   Graphing by hand:

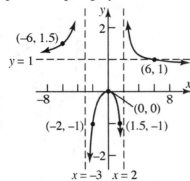

13. $G(x) = \dfrac{x}{x^2 - 4} = \dfrac{x}{(x+2)(x-2)}$ $p(x) = x;\ q(x) = x^2 - 4;\ n = 1;\ m = 2$

Step 1:   Domain: $\left\{x \mid x \neq -2,\ x \neq 2\right\}$

Step 2: $G(x) = \dfrac{x}{x^2 - 4}$ is in lowest terms.

Step 3:   (a)   The x-intercept is the zero of $p(x)$: 0

   (b)   The y-intercept is $G(0) = \dfrac{0}{0^2 - 4} = \dfrac{0}{-4} = 0$.

Step 4: $G(-x) = \dfrac{-x}{(-x)^2 - 4} = \dfrac{-x}{x^2 - 4} = -G(x);\ G(x)$ is symmetric to the origin.

Step 5:   The vertical asymptotes are the zeros of $q(x)$: $x = -2$ and $x = 2$

Step 6:   Since $n < m$, the line $y = 0$ is the horizontal asymptote.

   $G(x)$ intersects $y = 0$ at $(0, 0)$.

Step 7:

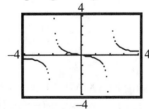

Step 8:   Graphing Utility:

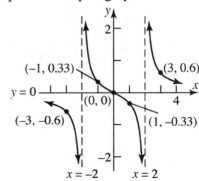

f is decreasing on $(-\infty, -2) \cup (-2, 2) \cup (2, \infty)$

Step 9:   Graphing by hand:

234

15. $R(x) = \dfrac{3}{(x-1)(x^2-4)} = \dfrac{3}{(x-1)(x+2)(x-2)}$ $p(x) = 3$; $q(x) = (x-1)(x^2-4)$;

$n = 0$; $m = 3$

Step 1: Domain: $\{x \mid x \neq -2,\ x \neq 1,\ x \neq 2\}$

Step 2: $R(x) = \dfrac{3}{(x-1)(x^2-4)}$ is in lowest terms.

Step 3: (a)   There is no x-intercept.

(b)   The y-intercept is $R(0) = \dfrac{3}{(0-1)(0^2-4)} = \dfrac{3}{4}$.

Step 4: $R(-x) = \dfrac{3}{(-x-1)\big((-x)^2-4\big)} = \dfrac{3}{(-x-1)(x^2-4)}$; this is neither $R(x)$ nor $-R(x)$,

so there is no symmetry.

Step 5: The vertical asymptotes are the zeros of $q(x)$: $x = -2$, $x = 1$, and $x = 2$

Step 6: Since $n < m$, the line $y = 0$ is the horizontal asymptote.

$R(x)$ does not intersect $y = 0$.

Step 7:

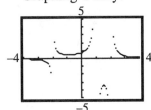

Step 8:   Graphing Utility:

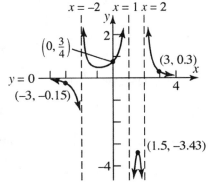

Using MAXIMUM and MINIMUM:

f is increasing on $(-0.868,1) \cup (1,1.535)$

f is decreasing on

$(-\infty,-2) \cup (-2,-0.868) \cup (1.535,2) \cup (2,\infty)$

Step 9:   Graphing by hand:

17. $H(x) = \dfrac{4(x-1)^2}{x^4-16} = \dfrac{4(x-1)^2}{(x^2+4)(x+2)(x-2)}$ $p(x) = 4(x-1)^2$; $q(x) = x^4-16$;

$n = 2$; $m = 4$

Step 1: Domain: $\{x \mid x \neq -2,\ x \neq 2\}$

Step 2: $H(x) = \dfrac{4(x-1)^2}{x^4-16}$ is in lowest terms.

Step 3: (a)   The x-intercepts are the zeros of $p(x)$: 1

(b)   The y-intercept is $H(0) = \dfrac{4(0-1)^2}{0^4-16} = \dfrac{4}{-16} = -\dfrac{1}{4}$.

Step 4: $H(-x) = \dfrac{4((-x)-1)^2}{(-x)^4 - 16} = \dfrac{4(-x-1)^2}{x^4 - 16} = \dfrac{4(-(x+1))^2}{x^4 - 16} = \dfrac{4(x+1)^2}{x^4 - 16}$. This is neither $H(x)$
nor $-H(x)$, so there is no symmetry. No symmetry.

Step 5: The vertical asymptotes are the zeros of $q(x)$: $x = -2$, and $x = 2$

Step 6: Since $n < m$, the line $y = 0$ is the horizontal asymptote.
$H(x)$ intersects $y = 0$ at $(1, 0)$.

Step 7:

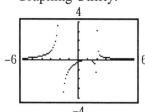

Step 8: Graphing Utility:

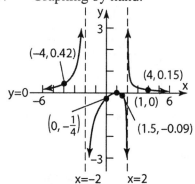

Using MAXIMUM and MINIMUM:
f is increasing on $(-\infty, -2) \cup (-2, 0)$
f is decreasing on $(0, 2) \cup (2, \infty)$

Step 9: Graphing by hand:

19. $F(x) = \dfrac{x^2 - 3x - 4}{x + 2} = \dfrac{(x+1)(x-4)}{x+2}$ $p(x) = x^2 - 3x - 4;\ q(x) = x + 2;\ n = 2;\ m = 1$

Step 1: Domain: $\{x \mid x \neq -2\}$

Step 2: $F(x) = \dfrac{x^2 - 3x - 4}{x + 2}$ is in lowest terms.

Step 3: (a) The x-intercepts are the zeros of $p(x)$: -1 and 4.

(b) The y-intercept is $F(0) = \dfrac{0^2 - 3(0) - 4}{0 + 2} = \dfrac{-4}{2} = -2$.

Step 4: $F(-x) = \dfrac{(-x)^2 - 3(-x) - 4}{-x + 2} = \dfrac{x^2 + 3x - 4}{-x + 2}$; this is neither $F(x)$ nor $-F(x)$, so
there is no symmetry.

Step 5: The vertical asymptote is the zero of $q(x)$: $x = -2$

Step 6: Since $n = m + 1$, there is an oblique asymptote.
Dividing:

$$\begin{array}{r} x - 5 \\ x + 2 \overline{)\, x^2 - 3x - 4} \\ \underline{x^2 + 2x} \\ -5x - 4 \\ \underline{-5x - 10} \\ 6 \end{array}$$

$F(x) = x - 5 + \dfrac{6}{x + 2}$

The oblique asymptote is $y = x - 5$.
Solve to find intersection points:
$$\frac{x^2 - 3x - 4}{x + 2} = x - 5 \Rightarrow x^2 - 3x - 4 = x^2 - 3x - 10 \Rightarrow -4 = -10$$
Since there is no solution, the oblique asymptote does not intersect $F(x)$.

Step 7:

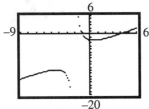

Step 8:   Graphing Utility:

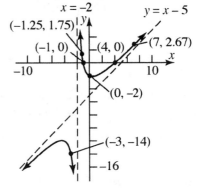

Using MAXIMUM and MINIMUM:
f is increasing on $(-\infty, -4.45) \cup (0.45, \infty)$
f is decreasing on $(-4.45, -2) \cup (0, 0.45)$

Step 9:   Graphing by hand:

21. $R(x) = \dfrac{x^2 + x - 12}{x - 4} = \dfrac{(x + 4)(x - 3)}{x - 4}$ $p(x) = x^2 + x - 12$; $q(x) = x - 4$; $n = 2$; $m = 1$

Step 1:   Domain: $\{x \mid x \neq 4\}$

Step 2: $R(x) = \dfrac{x^2 + x - 12}{x - 4}$ is in lowest terms.

Step 3:   (a)   The x-intercepts are the zeros of $p(x)$: -4 and 3.

(b)   The y-intercept is $R(0) = \dfrac{0^2 + 0 - 12}{0 - 4} = \dfrac{-12}{-4} = 3$.

Step 4: $R(-x) = \dfrac{(-x)^2 + (-x) - 12}{-x - 4} = \dfrac{x^2 - x - 12}{-x - 4}$; this is neither $R(x)$ nor $-R(x)$, so
there is no symmetry.

Step 5:   The vertical asymptote is the zero of $q(x)$: $x = 4$

Step 6:   Since $n = m + 1$, there is an oblique asymptote. Dividing:

$$\begin{array}{r}
x + 5 \\
x - 4 \overline{)\, x^2 +\ \ x - 12} \\
\underline{x^2 - 4x} \\
5x - 12 \\
\underline{5x - 20} \\
8
\end{array}$$

$R(x) = x + 5 + \dfrac{8}{x - 4}$

The oblique asymptote is $y = x + 5$.

Solve to find intersection points:

$$\frac{x^2 + x - 12}{x - 4} = x + 5$$
$$x^2 + x - 12 = x^2 + x - 20$$
$$-12 = -20$$

Since there is no solution, the oblique asymptote does not intersect $R(x)$.

Step 7:

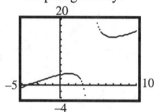

Step 8:   Graphing Utility:

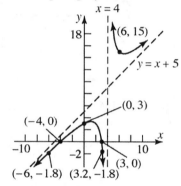

Using MAXIMUM and MINIMUM:

f is increasing on $(-\infty, 1.17) \cup (6.83, \infty)$

f is decreasing on $(1.17, 4) \cup (4, 6.83)$

Step 9:   Graphing by hand:

23. $F(x) = \dfrac{x^2 + x - 12}{x + 2} = \dfrac{(x + 4)(x - 3)}{x + 2}$ $p(x) = x^2 + x - 12;$ $q(x) = x + 2;$ $n = 2;$ $m = 1$

Step 1:   Domain: $\{x \mid x \neq -2\}$

Step 2: $F(x) = \dfrac{x^2 + x - 12}{x + 2}$ is in lowest terms.

Step 3:   (a)   The x-intercepts are the zeros of $p(x)$: -4 and 3.

  (b)   The y-intercept is $F(0) = \dfrac{0^2 + 0 - 12}{0 + 2} = \dfrac{-12}{2} = -6$.

Step 4: $F(-x) = \dfrac{(-x)^2 + (-x) - 12}{-x + 2} = \dfrac{x^2 - x - 12}{-x + 2}$; this is neither $F(x)$ nor $-F(x)$, so there is no symmetry.

Step 5:   The vertical asymptote is the zero of $q(x)$: $x = -2$

Step 6:   Since $n = m + 1$, there is an oblique asymptote.
  Dividing:

$$\begin{array}{r}
x - 1 \\
x + 2 \overline{)\, x^2 + x - 12} \\
\underline{x^2 + 2x } \\
-x - 12 \\
\underline{-x - 2 } \\
-10
\end{array}$$

$F(x) = x - 1 + \dfrac{-10}{x + 2}$

The oblique asymptote is $y = x - 1$.

238

Solve to find intersection points:
$$\frac{x^2 + x - 12}{x + 2} = x - 1 \Rightarrow x^2 + x - 12 = x^2 + x - 2 \Rightarrow -12 = -2$$
Since there is no solution, the oblique asymptote does not intersect $F(x)$.

Step 7:

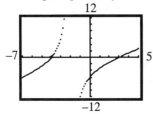

Step 8:   Graphing Utility:

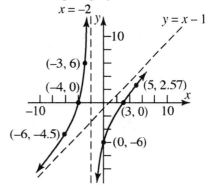

f is increasing on $(-\infty, -2) \cup (-2, \infty)$

Step 9:   Graphing by hand:

25. $R(x) = \dfrac{x(x-1)^2}{(x+3)^3}$ $p(x) = x(x-1)^2$; $q(x) = (x+3)^3$; $n = 3$; $m = 3$

Step 1:   Domain: $\{x \mid x \neq -3\}$

Step 2: $R(x) = \dfrac{x(x-1)^2}{(x+3)^3}$ is in lowest terms.

Step 3:   (a)   The x-intercepts are the zeros of $p(x)$: 0 and 1

   (b)   The y-intercept is $R(0) = \dfrac{0(0-1)^2}{(0+3)^3} = \dfrac{0}{27} = 0$.

Step 4: $R(-x) = \dfrac{-x(-x-1)^2}{(-x+3)^3}$; this is neither $R(x)$ nor $-R(x)$, so there is no symmetry.

Step 5:   The vertical asymptote is the zero of $q(x)$: $x = -3$

Step 6:   Since $n = m$, the line $y = 1$ is the horizontal asymptote.
Solve to find intersection points:
$$\frac{x(x-1)^2}{(x+3)^3} = 1$$
$$x^3 - 2x^2 + x = x^3 + 9x^2 + 27x + 27$$
$$0 = 11x^2 + 26x + 27$$
Since there is no real solution, $R(x)$ does not intersect $y = 1$.

Step 7:

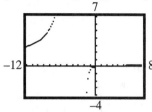

Step 8:   Graphing Utility: Step 9:   Graphing by hand:

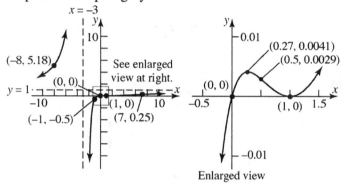

Using MAXIMUM and
MINIMUM:

f is increasing on

$(-\infty, -3) \cup (-3, 0.273) \cup (1, \infty)$

f is decreasing on $(0.273, 1)$

27. $R(x) = \dfrac{x^2 + x - 12}{x^2 - x - 6} = \dfrac{(x+4)(x-3)}{(x-3)(x+2)} = \dfrac{x+4}{x+2}$ $p(x) = x^2 + x - 12;\ q(x) = x^2 - x - 6;$

$n = 2;\ m = 2$

Step 1:   Domain: $\{x \mid x \neq -2,\ x \neq 3\}$

Step 2: $R(x) = \dfrac{x^2 + x - 12}{x^2 - x - 6} = \dfrac{(x+4)(x-3)}{(x-3)(x+2)} = \dfrac{x+4}{x+2}$ is in lowest terms.

Step 3:   (a)   The x-intercept is the zero of $p(x)$: -4 ; 3 is not a zero because reduced
form must be used to find the zeros.

(b)   The y-intercept is $R(0) = \dfrac{0^2 + 0 - 12}{0^2 - 0 - 6} = \dfrac{-12}{-6} = 2$.

Step 4: $R(-x) = \dfrac{(-x)^2 + (-x) - 12}{(-x)^2 - (-x) - 6} = \dfrac{x^2 - x - 12}{x^2 + x - 6}$; this is neither $R(x)$ nor $-R(x)$, so
there is no symmetry.

Step 5:   The vertical asymptote is the zero of $q(x)$: $x = -2$; $x = 3$ is not a vertical
asymptote because reduced form must be used to find the them. The graph

has a hole at $\left(3, \dfrac{7}{5}\right)$.

Step 6:   Since $n = m$, the line $y = 1$ is the horizontal asymptote.

$R(x)$ does not intersect $y = 1$ because $R(x)$ is not defined at $x = 3$.

$$\dfrac{x^2 + x - 12}{x^2 - x - 6} = 1$$

$$x^2 + x - 12 = x^2 - x - 6$$

$$2x = 6$$

$$x = 3$$

Step 7:

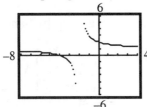

Step 8:   Graphing Utility:

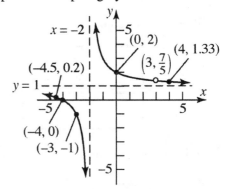

f is decreasing on
$$\left(-\infty,-2\right)\cup\left(-2,3\right)\cup\left(3,\infty\right)$$

Step 9:   Graphing by hand:

29. $R(x) = \dfrac{6x^2 - 7x - 3}{2x^2 - 7x + 6} = \dfrac{(3x+1)(2x-3)}{(2x-3)(x-2)} = \dfrac{3x+1}{x-2}$ $p(x) = 6x^2 - 7x - 3$;

$q(x) = 2x^2 - 7x + 6$; $n = 2$; $m = 2$

Step 1:   Domain: $\left\{x \,\middle|\, x \ne \dfrac{3}{2},\, x \ne 2\right\}$

Step 2: $R(x) = \dfrac{6x^2 - 7x - 3}{2x^2 - 7x + 6} = \dfrac{(3x+1)(2x-3)}{(2x-3)(x-2)} = \dfrac{3x+1}{x-2}$ is in lowest terms.

Step 3:   (a)   The x-intercept is the zero of $p(x)$: $-\dfrac{1}{3}$; $x = \dfrac{3}{2}$ is not a zero because

reduced form must be used to find the zeros.

(b)   The y-intercept is $R(0) = \dfrac{6(0)^2 - 7(0) - 3}{2(0)^2 - 7(0) + 6} = \dfrac{-3}{6} = -\dfrac{1}{2}$.

Step 4: $R(-x) = \dfrac{6(-x)^2 - 7(-x) - 3}{2(-x)^2 - 7(-x) + 6} = \dfrac{6x^2 + 7x - 3}{2x^2 + 7x + 6}$; this is neither $R(x)$ nor $-R(x)$, so

there is no symmetry.

Step 5:   The vertical asymptote is the zero of $q(x)$: $x = 2$; $x = \dfrac{3}{2}$ is not a vertical

asymptote because reduced form must be used to find the them. The graph

has a hole at $\left(\dfrac{3}{2}, -11\right)$.

Step 6:   Since $n = m$, the line $y = 3$ is the horizontal asymptote.

$$\dfrac{6x^2 - 7x - 3}{2x^2 - 7x + 6} = 3 \Rightarrow 6x^2 - 7x - 3 = 6x^2 - 21x + 18$$

$$14x = 21 \Rightarrow x = \dfrac{3}{2}$$

$R(x)$ does not intersect $y = 3$ because $R(x)$ is not defined at $x = \dfrac{3}{2}$.

Step 7:

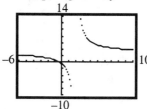

Step 8:   Graphing Utility:

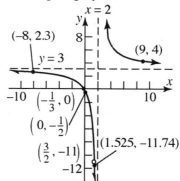

f is decreasing on

$$\left(-\infty, \frac{3}{2}\right) \cup \left(\frac{3}{2}, 2\right) \cup (2, \infty)$$

Step 9:   Graphing by hand:

31. $R(x) = \dfrac{x^2 + 5x + 6}{x + 3} = \dfrac{(x+2)(x+3)}{x + 3} = x + 2$ $p(x) = x^2 + 5x + 6$; $q(x) = x + 3$;
$$n = 2;\ m = 1$$

Step 1:   Domain: $\{x \mid x \neq -3\}$

Step 2: $R(x) = \dfrac{x^2 + 5x + 6}{x + 3} = \dfrac{(x+2)(x+3)}{x + 3} = x + 2$ is in lowest terms.

Step 3:   (a)   The x-intercept is the zero of $p(x)$: -2 ; -3 is not a zero because reduced
form must be used to find the zeros.

(b)   The y-intercept is $R(0) = \dfrac{0^2 + 5(0) + 6}{0 + 3} = \dfrac{6}{3} = 2$.

Step 4: $R(-x) = \dfrac{(-x)^2 + 5(-x) + 6}{-x + 3} = \dfrac{x^2 - 5x + 6}{-x + 3}$; this is neither $R(x)$ nor $-R(x)$, so
there is no symmetry.

Step 5:   There are no vertical asymptotes. $x = -3$ is not a vertical asymptote because
reduced form must be used to find them. The graph has a hole at $(-3, -1)$.

Step 6:   Since $n = m + 1$ there is a oblique asymptote. The line $y = x + 2$ is the oblique
asymptote. The oblique asymptote intersects $R(x)$ at every point of the
form $(x, x + 2)$ except $(-3, -1)$.

Step 7:

Step 8:   Graphing Utility:

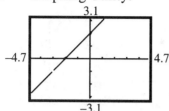

f is increasing on $(-\infty,-3)\cup(-3,\infty)$

Step 9:   Graphing by hand:

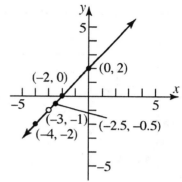

33. $f(x)=x+\dfrac{1}{x}=\dfrac{x^2+1}{x}$ $p(x)=x^2+1;\;q(x)=x;\;n=2;\;m=1$

Step 1:   Domain: $\{x\,|\,x\ne 0\}$

Step 2: $f(x)=x+\dfrac{1}{x}=\dfrac{x^2+1}{x}$ is in lowest terms.

Step 3:   (a)   There are no x-intercepts.
          (b)   There is no y-intercept because 0 is not in the domain.

Step 4: $f(-x)=\dfrac{(-x)^2+1}{-x}=\dfrac{x^2+1}{-x}=-f(x)$; The graph of $f(x)$ is symmetric to the origin.

Step 5:   The vertical asymptote is the zero of $q(x)$: $x=0$

Step 6   Since $n=m+1$, there is an oblique asymptote. Dividing:

$$\begin{array}{r} x \\ x\overline{)x^2+1} \\ \underline{x^2} \\ 1 \end{array}$$

$f(x)=x+\dfrac{1}{x}$

The oblique asymptote is $y=x$.

Solve to find intersection points:
$$\dfrac{x^2+1}{x}=x\Rightarrow x^2+1=x^2\Rightarrow 1=0$$

Since there is no solution, the oblique asymptote does not intersect $f(x)$.

Step 7:

X	Y1	
-3	-3.333	
3	3.3333	
Y1▪X+1/X		

Step 8:   Graphing Utility:

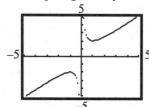

Step 9:   Graphing by hand:

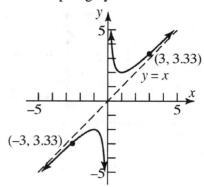

Using MAXIMUM and MINIMUM:
f is increasing on $(-\infty,-1)\cup(1,\infty)$
f is decreasing on $(-1,0)\cup(0,1)$

35. $f(x)=x^2+\dfrac{1}{x}=\dfrac{x^3+1}{x}$ $p(x)=x^3+1$; $q(x)=x$; $n=3$; $m=1$

Step 1:   Domain: $\{x\,|\,x\neq 0\}$

Step 2: $f(x)=x^2+\dfrac{1}{x}=\dfrac{x^3+1}{x}$ is in lowest terms.

Step 3:   (a)   The x-intercept is the zero of $p(x)$: -1
           (b)   There is no y-intercept because 0 is not in the domain.

Step 4: $f(-x)=\dfrac{(-x)^3+1}{-x}=\dfrac{-x^3+1}{-x}$; this is neither $f(x)$ nor $-f(x)$, so there is no symmetry.

Step 5:   The vertical asymptote is the zero of $q(x)$: $x=0$

Step 6:   Since $n>m+1$, there is no horizontal or oblique asymptote.

Step 7:

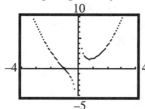

Step 8:   Graphing Utility:

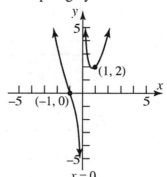

Step 9:   Graphing by hand:

Using MAXIMUM and MINIMUM:
f is increasing on $(0.794,\infty)$
f is decreasing on $(-\infty,0)\cup(0,0.794)$

37. $f(x) = x + \dfrac{1}{x^3} = \dfrac{x^4 + 1}{x^3}$ $p(x) = x^4 + 1;\ q(x) = x^3;\ n = 4;\ m = 3$

Step 1:   Domain: $\{x \mid x \neq 0\}$

Step 2: $f(x) = x + \dfrac{1}{x^3} = \dfrac{x^4 + 1}{x^3}$ is in lowest terms.

Step 3:   (a)   There are no x-intercepts.
           (b)   There is no y-intercept because 0 is not in the domain.

Step 4: $f(-x) = \dfrac{(-x)^4 + 1}{(-x)^3} = \dfrac{x^4 + 1}{-x^3} = -f(x)$; the graph of $f(x)$ is symmetric with respect to

the origin.

Step 5:   The vertical asymptote is the zero of $q(x)$: $x = 0$

Step 6:   Since $n = m + 1$, there is an oblique asymptote. Dividing:

$$f(x) = x + \frac{1}{x^3}$$ The oblique asymptote is $y = x$.

Solve to find intersection points: $\dfrac{x^4 + 1}{x^3} = x \Rightarrow x^4 + 1 = x^4 \Rightarrow 1 = 0$

Since there is no solution, the oblique asymptote does not intersect $f(x)$.

Step 7:

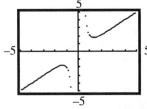

Step 8:   Graphing Utility:

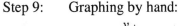

Using MAXIMUM and MINIMUM:
f is increasing on $(-\infty, -1.32) \cup (1.32, \infty)$
f is decreasing on $(-1.32, 0) \cup (0, 1.32)$

Step 9:   Graphing by hand:

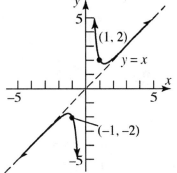

39. $f(x) = \dfrac{x^2}{x^2 - 4}$

41. $f(x) = \dfrac{(x-1)^3(x-3)}{(x+1)^2(x-2)^2}$

43. $g(h) = \dfrac{3.99 \times 10^{14}}{\left(6.374 \times 10^6 + h\right)^2}$

(a) $g(0) = \dfrac{3.99 \times 10^{14}}{\left(6.374 \times 10^6 + 0\right)^2} \approx 9.8208\ \text{m/s}^2$

(b) $g(443) = \dfrac{3.99 \times 10^{14}}{\left(6.374 \times 10^6 + 443\right)^2} \approx 9.8195 \ \text{m/s}^2$

(c) $g(8848) = \dfrac{3.99 \times 10^{14}}{\left(6.374 \times 10^6 + 8848\right)^2} \approx 9.7936 \ \text{m/s}^2$

(d) $g(h) = \dfrac{3.99 \times 10^{14}}{\left(6.374 \times 10^6 + h\right)^2} \approx \dfrac{3.99 \times 10^{14}}{h^2} \to 0 \ \text{as} \ h \to \infty$

$\therefore \ y = 0$ is the horizontal asymptote.

(e)

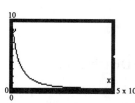

(f) $g(h) = \dfrac{3.99 \times 10^{14}}{\left(6.374 \times 10^6 + h\right)^2} = 0$, to solve this equation would require that

$3.99 \times 10^{14} = 0$, which is impossible. Therefore, there is no height above sea level at which $g = 0$. In other words, there is no point in the entire universe that is unaffected by the Earth's gravity!

45.   (a)   Graphing:

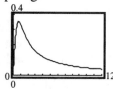

(b)   Using MAXIMUM, the concentration is highest when $t = 0.71$ hours.

(c) $C(t) = \dfrac{t}{2t^2 + 1} \approx \dfrac{t}{2t^2} = \dfrac{1}{2t} \to 0 \ \text{as} \ t \to \pm\infty$

therefore the horizontal asymptote is $y = 0$.

The concentration of the drug decreases to 0 as time increases.

47.   (a)   The average cost function is: $\overline{C}(x) = \dfrac{0.2x^3 - 2.3x^2 + 14.3x + 10.2}{x}$

(b) $\overline{C}(6) = \dfrac{0.2(6)^3 - 2.3(6)^2 + 14.3(6) + 10.2}{6} = \dfrac{56.4}{6} = 9.4$

The average cost of producing 6 Cavaliers per hour is \$9400 per car.

(c) $\overline{C}(9) = \dfrac{0.2(9)^3 - 2.3(9)^2 + 14.3(9) + 10.2}{9} = \dfrac{98.4}{9} = 10.933$

The average cost of producing 9 Cavaliers per hour is \$10,933 per car.

(d)   Graphing:

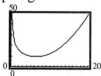

(e)   Using MINIMUM, the number of Cavaliers that should be produced per hour to minimize cost is 6.38 cars

(f)   The minimum average cost is

$$\overline{C}(6.38) = \frac{0.2(6.38)^3 - 2.3(6.38)^2 + 14.3(6.38) + 10.2}{6.38} \approx \$9366 \text{ per car.}$$

49. (a)   The surface area is the sum of the areas of the four sides plus the areas of the bottom and the top.

$$S = xy + xy + xy + xy + x^2 + x^2 = 4xy + 2x^2$$

The volume is $x \cdot x \cdot y = x^2 y = 10{,}000 \implies y = \dfrac{10000}{x^2}$

Thus, $S(x) = 4x\left(\dfrac{10000}{x^2}\right) + 2x^2 = 2x^2 + \dfrac{40000}{x}$

(b)   Graphing:

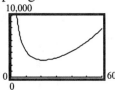

(c)   Using MINIMUM, the minimum surface area (amount of cardboard) is approximately 2784.95 square inches.

(d)   The surface area is a minimum when $x \approx 21.54$.

$$y \approx \frac{10000}{21.54^2} \approx 21.54$$

The dimensions of the box are: 21.54 in. by 21.54 in. by 21.54 in.

51. (a) $500 = \pi r^2 h \implies h = \dfrac{500}{\pi r^2}$

$$C(r) = 6(2\pi r^2) + 4(2\pi rh) = 12\pi r^2 + 8\pi r\left(\frac{500}{\pi r^2}\right) = 12\pi r^2 + \frac{4000}{r}$$

(b)   Graphing:

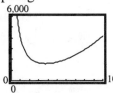

Using MINIMUM, the cost is least for $r \approx 3.76$ cm.

53. (a)   The surface area is the sum of the areas of the four sides plus the area of the bottom.

$$S = xy + xy + xy + xy + x^2 = 4xy + x^2$$

The volume is $x \cdot x \cdot y = x^2 y = 10 \implies y = \dfrac{10}{x^2}$

Thus, $S(x) = 4x\left(\dfrac{10}{x^2}\right) + x^2 = x^2 + \dfrac{40}{x}$

(b) $S(1) = \dfrac{1^3 + 40}{1} = \dfrac{41}{1} = 41$ square feet.   (c) $S(2) = \dfrac{2^3 + 40}{x} = \dfrac{48}{2} = 24$ square feet.

(d)   Graphing:

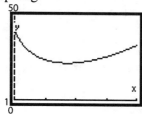

Using MINIMUM, the surface area is a minimum when $x \approx 2.71$ inches.

55.   Answers will vary, one example is $R(x) = \dfrac{2(x-3)(x+2)^2}{(x-1)^3}$.

57.   Answers will vary.

Polynomial and Rational Functions

5.5 Polynomial and Rational Inequalities

1. $x^2 + x > 12$ $f(x) = x^2 + x - 12$

    $x^2 + x - 12 > 0$

    $(x+4)(x-3) > 0$

    $x = -4$, $x = 3$ are the zeros.

Interval	Test Number	$f(x)$	Positive/Negative
$-\infty < x < -4$	-5	8	Positive
$-4 < x < 3$	0	-12	Negative
$3 < x < \infty$	4	8	Positive

    The solution set is $\left\{ x \mid x < -4 \text{ or } x > 3 \right\}$; $(-\infty, -4) \cup (3, \infty)$.

3. $2x^2 < 5x + 3$ $f(x) = 2x^2 - 5x - 3$

    $2x^2 - 5x - 3 < 0 \Rightarrow (2x+1)(x-3) < 0$

    $x = -\dfrac{1}{2}$, $x = 3$ are the zeros.

Interval	Test Number	$f(x)$	Positive/Negative
$-\infty < x < -1/2$	-1	4	Positive
$-1/2 < x < 3$	0	-3	Negative
$3 < x < \infty$	4	9	Positive

    The solution set is $\left\{ x \mid -\dfrac{1}{2} < x < 3 \right\}$; $\left(-\dfrac{1}{2}, 3 \right)$.

5. $x(x - 7) > 8$ $f(x) = x^2 - 7x - 8$

    $x^2 - 7x > 8 \Rightarrow x^2 - 7x - 8 > 0 \rightarrow (x+1)(x-8) > 0$

    $x = -1$, $x = 8$ are the zeros.

Interval	Test Number	$f(x)$	Positive/Negative
$-\infty < x < -1$	-2	10	Positive
$-1 < x < 8$	0	-8	Negative
$8 < x < \infty$	9	10	Positive

    The solution set is $\left\{ x \mid x < -1 \text{ or } x > 8 \right\}$; $(-\infty, -1) \cup (8, \infty)$.

7. $(x - 1)\left(x^2 + x + 1\right) > 0$ $f(x) = (x - 1)\left(x^2 + x + 1\right)$

    $x = 1$ is the zero. $x^2 + x + 1 = 0$ has no real zeros.

Interval	Test Number	$f(x)$	Positive/Negative
$-\infty < x < 1$	0	-1	Negative
$1 < x < \infty$	2	7	Positive

    The solution set is $\left\{ x \mid x > 1 \right\}$.

9. $(x-1)(x-2)(x-3) < 0$ $f(x) = (x-1)(x-2)(x-3)$
    $x = 1, x = 2, x = 3$ are the zeros.

Interval	Test Number	$f(x)$	Positive/Negative
$-\infty < x < 1$	0	–6	Negative
$1 < x < 2$	1.5	0.375	Positive
$2 < x < 3$	2.5	–0.375	Negative
$3 < x < \infty$	4	6	Positive

The solution set is $\{x \mid x < 1 \text{ or } 2 < x < 3\}$; $(-\infty, 1) \cup (2,3)$.

11. $x^3 - 2x^2 - 3x > 0$ $f(x) = x^3 - 2x^2 - 3x$
    $x(x^2 - 2x - 3) > 0$

    $x(x+1)(x-3) > 0$
    $x = -1, x = 0, x = 3$ are the zeros.

Interval	Test Number	$f(x)$	Positive/Negative
$-\infty < x < -1$	–2	–10	Negative
$-1 < x < 0$	–0.5	0.875	Positive
$0 < x < 3$	1	–4	Negative
$3 < x < \infty$	4	20	Positive

The solution set is $\{x \mid -1 < x < 0 \text{ or } x > 3\}$; $(-1,0) \cup (3,\infty)$.

13. $x^4 > x^2$ $f(x) = x^4 - x^2$
    $x^4 - x^2 > 0$

    $x^2(x^2 - 1) > 0$

    $x^2(x+1)(x-1) > 0$
    $x = -1, x = 0, x = 1$ are the zeros.

Interval	Test Number	$f(x)$	Positive/Negative
$-\infty < x < -1$	–2	12	Positive
$-1 < x < 0$	–0.5	–0.1875	Negative
$0 < x < 1$	0.5	–0.1875	Negative
$1 < x < \infty$	2	12	Positive

The solution set is $\{x \mid x < -1 \text{ or } x > 1\}$; $(-\infty, -1) \cup (1,\infty)$.

15. $x^3 > x^2$ $f(x) = x^3 - x^2$
    $x^3 - x^2 > 0 \Rightarrow x^2(x-1) > 0$
    $x = 0, x = 1$ are the zeros.

Interval	Test Number	$f(x)$	Positive/Negative
$-\infty < x < 0$	–1	–2	Negative
$0 < x < 1$	0.5	–0.125	Negative
$1 < x < \infty$	2	4	Positive

The solution set is $\{x \mid x > 1\}$; $(1,\infty)$.

17. $x^4 > 1$ $\qquad\qquad$ $f(x) = x^4 - 1$

$x^4 - 1 > 0 \Rightarrow (x^2 + 1)(x^2 - 1) > 0 \Rightarrow (x^2 + 1)(x+1)(x-1) > 0$

$x = -1, x = 1$ are the zeros.

Interval	Test Number	$f(x)$	Positive/Negative
$-\infty < x < -1$	-2	15	Positive
$-1 < x < 1$	0	-1	Negative
$1 < x < \infty$	2	15	Positive

The solution set is $\left\{ x \mid x < -1 \text{ or } x > 1 \right\};$ $(-\infty, -1) \cup (1, \infty)$.

19. $x^4 - 7x^3 - 8x^2 < 0$ $\qquad\qquad$ $f(x) = x^4 - 7x^3 - 8x^2$

$x^4 - 7x^3 - 8x^2 = x^2(x^2 - 7x - 8x) = x^2(x+1)(x-8) < 0$

$x = -1, x = 0, x = 8$ are the zeros.

Interval	Test Number	$f(x)$	Positive/Negative
$-\infty < x < -1$	-2	40	Positive
$-1 < x < 0$	-0.5	-1.0625	Negative
$0 < x < 8$	1	-14	Negative
$8 < x < \infty$	9	810	Positive

The solution set is $\left\{ x \mid -1 < x < 0 \text{ or } 0 < x < 8 \right\};$ $(-1, 0) \cup (0, 8)$.

21. Graph $f(x) = x^3 + x - 12$ and use ZERO to find the zero of the function.

$x = 2.14$ is the zero (rounded to two decimal places).

Interval	Test Number	$f(x)$	Positive/Negative
$-\infty < x < 2.14$	0	-12	Negative
$2.14 < x < \infty$	3	18	Positive

The solution set is $\left\{ x \mid x \geq 2.14 \right\};$ $[2.14, \infty)$.

23. $x^4 - 3x^2 - 4 > 0$ $\qquad\qquad$ $f(x) = x^4 - 3x^2 - 4$

$\left(x^2 - 4\right)\left(x^2 + 1\right) > 0$

$(x+2)(x-2)\left(x^2 + 1\right) > 0$

$x = -2, x = 2$ are the zeros.

Interval	Test Number	$f(x)$	Positive/Negative
$-\infty < x < -2$	-3	50	Positive
$-2 < x < 2$	0	-4	Negative
$2 < x < \infty$	3	50	Positive

The solution set is $\left\{ x \mid x < -2 \text{ or } x > 2 \right\};$ $(-\infty, -2) \cup (2, \infty)$.

25. $x^3 - 4 \geq 3x^2 + 5x - 3$ $\qquad\qquad$ $f(x) = x^3 - 3x^2 - 5x - 1$

$x^3 - 3x^2 - 5x - 1 \geq 0$

Do synthetic division by -1:

$$
\begin{array}{r|rrrr}
-1) & 1 & -3 & -5 & -1 \\
    &   & -1 & 4 & 1 \\
\hline
    & 1 & -4 & -1 & 0
\end{array}
$$

$x = -1$ is a solution. Solving the remaining factor $x^2 - 4x - 1 = 0$:

$$x = \frac{-(-4) \pm \sqrt{(-4)^2 - 4(1)(-1)}}{2(1)} = \frac{4 \pm \sqrt{20}}{2} = \frac{4 \pm 2\sqrt{5}}{2} = 2 \pm \sqrt{5}$$

$x = -1$, $x = 2 - \sqrt{5}$, $x = 2 + \sqrt{5}$ or $x = -1$, $x = -0.24$, $x = 4.24$ are the zeros.

Interval	Test Number	$f(x)$	Positive/Negative
$-\infty < x < -1$	-2	-11	Negative
$-1 < x < 2 - \sqrt{5}$	-0.5	0.625	Positive
$2 - \sqrt{5} < x < 2 + \sqrt{5}$	0	-1	Negative
$2 + \sqrt{5} < x < \infty$	5	24	Positive

The solution set is $\left\{ x \mid -1 \le x \le 2 - \sqrt{5} \text{ or } x \ge 2 + \sqrt{5} \right\}$; $\left[-1, 2 - \sqrt{5} \right] \cup \left[2 + \sqrt{5}, \infty \right)$.

27. $\dfrac{x+1}{x-1} > 0$ $\qquad f(x) = \dfrac{x+1}{x-1}$

The zeros and values where the expression is undefined are $x = -1$, and $x = 1$.

Interval	Test Number	$f(x)$	Positive/Negative
$-\infty < x < -1$	-2	$1/3$	Positive
$-1 < x < 1$	0	-1	Negative
$1 < x < \infty$	2	3	Positive

The solution set is $\left\{ x \mid x < -1 \text{ or } x > 1 \right\}$; $(-\infty, -1) \cup (1, \infty)$.

29. $\dfrac{(x-1)(x+1)}{x} < 0$ $\qquad f(x) = \dfrac{(x-1)(x+1)}{x}$

The zeros and values where the expression is undefined are $x = -1$, $x = 0$, and $x = 1$.

Interval	Test Number	$f(x)$	Positive/Negative
$-\infty < x < -1$	-2	-1.5	Negative
$-1 < x < 0$	-0.5	1.5	Positive
$0 < x < 1$	0.5	-1.5	Negative
$1 < x < \infty$	2	1.5	Positive

The solution set is $\left\{ x \mid x < -1 \text{ or } 0 < x < 1 \right\}$; $(-\infty, -1) \cup (0, 1)$.

31. $\dfrac{(x-2)^2}{x^2 - 1} \ge 0$ $\qquad f(x) = \dfrac{(x-2)^2}{x^2 - 1}$

$\dfrac{(x-2)^2}{(x+1)(x-1)} \ge 0$

The zeros and values where the expression is undefined are $x = -1$, $x = 1$, and $x = 2$.

Interval	Test Number	$f(x)$	Positive/Negative
$-\infty < x < -1$	-2	$16/3$	Positive
$-1 < x < 1$	0	-4	Negative
$1 < x < 2$	1.5	0.2	Positive
$2 < x < \infty$	3	0.125	Positive

The solution set is $\left\{ x \mid x < -1 \text{ or } x > 1 \right\}$; $(-\infty, -1) \cup (1, \infty)$.

33. $6x - 5 < \dfrac{6}{x}$ $\qquad f(x) = 6x - 5 - \dfrac{6}{x}$

$6x - 5 - \dfrac{6}{x} < 0$

$\dfrac{6x^2 - 5x - 6}{x} < 0 \Rightarrow \dfrac{(2x - 3)(3x + 2)}{x} < 0$

The zeros and values where the expression is undefined are $x = -\dfrac{2}{3}$, $x = 0$, and $x = \dfrac{3}{2}$.

Interval	Test Number	$f(x)$	Positive/Negative
$-\infty < x < -2/3$	-1	-5	Negative
$-2/3 < x < 0$	-0.5	4	Positive
$0 < x < 3/2$	1	-5	Negative
$3/2 < x < \infty$	2	4	Positive

The solution set is $\left\{ x \,\middle|\, x < -\dfrac{2}{3} \text{ or } 0 < x < \dfrac{3}{2} \right\}$; $\left(-\infty, -\dfrac{2}{3}\right) \cup \left(0, \dfrac{3}{2}\right)$.

35. $\dfrac{x + 4}{x - 2} \le 1$ $\qquad f(x) = \dfrac{x + 4}{x - 2} - 1$

$\dfrac{x + 4}{x - 2} - 1 \le 0 \Rightarrow \dfrac{x + 4 - (x - 2)}{x - 2} \le 0 \Rightarrow \dfrac{6}{x - 2} \le 0$

The value where the expression is undefined is $x = 2$.

Interval	Test Number	$f(x)$	Positive/Negative
$-\infty < x < 2$	0	-3	Negative
$2 < x < \infty$	3	6	Positive

The solution set is $\left\{ x \,\middle|\, x < 2 \right\}$; $(-\infty, 2)$.

37. $\dfrac{3x - 5}{x + 2} \le 2$ $\qquad f(x) = \dfrac{3x - 5}{x + 2} - 2$

$\dfrac{3x - 5}{x + 2} - 2 \le 0 \Rightarrow \dfrac{3x - 5 - 2(x + 2)}{x + 2} \le 0 \Rightarrow \dfrac{x - 9}{x + 2} \le 0$

The zeros and values where the expression is undefined are $x = -2$, and $x = 9$.

Interval	Test Number	$f(x)$	Positive/Negative
$-\infty < x < -2$	-3	12	Positive
$-2 < x < 9$	0	-4.5	Negative
$9 < x < \infty$	10	$1/12$	Positive

The solution set is $\left\{ x \,\middle|\, -2 < x \le 9 \right\}$; $(-2, 9]$.

39. $\dfrac{1}{x - 2} < \dfrac{2}{3x - 9}$ $\qquad f(x) = \dfrac{1}{x + 2} - \dfrac{2}{3x - 9}$

$\dfrac{1}{x - 2} - \dfrac{2}{3x - 9} < 0$

$\dfrac{3x - 9 - 2(x - 2)}{(x - 2)(3x - 9)} < 0$

$\dfrac{x - 5}{(x - 2)(3x - 9)} < 0$

The zeros and values where the expression is undefined are $x = 2$, $x = 3$, and $x = 5$.

Interval	Test Number	$f(x)$	Positive/Negative
$-\infty < x < 2$	0	$-5/18$	Negative
$2 < x < 3$	2.5	$10/3$	Positive
$3 < x < 5$	4	$-1/6$	Negative
$5 < x < \infty$	6	$1/36$	Positive

The solution set is $\left\{ x \mid x < 2 \text{ or } 3 < x < 5 \right\}$; $(-\infty, 2) \cup (3, 5)$.

41. $\dfrac{2x+5}{x+1} > \dfrac{x+1}{x-1}$ $f(x) = \dfrac{2x+5}{x+1} - \dfrac{x+1}{x-1}$

$$\frac{2x+5}{x+1} - \frac{x+1}{x-1} > 0$$

$$\frac{(2x+5)(x-1) - (x+1)(x+1)}{(x+1)(x-1)} > 0$$

$$\frac{2x^2 + 3x - 5 - \left(x^2 + 2x + 1\right)}{(x+1)(x-1)} > 0$$

$$\frac{x^2 + x - 6}{(x+1)(x-1)} > 0$$

$$\frac{(x+3)(x-2)}{(x+1)(x-1)} > 0$$

The zeros and values where the expression is undefined are
$x = -3$, $x = -1$, $x = 1$, and $x = 2$.

Interval	Test Number	$f(x)$	Positive/Negative
$-\infty < x < -3$	-4	$2/5$	Positive
$-3 < x < -1$	-2	$-4/3$	Negative
$-1 < x < 1$	0	6	Positive
$1 < x < 2$	1.5	$-9/5$	Negative
$2 < x < \infty$	3	$3/4$	Positive

The solution set is $\left\{ x \mid x < -3 \text{ or } -1 < x < 1 \text{ or } x > 2 \right\}$; $(-\infty, -3) \cup (-1, 1) \cup (2, \infty)$.

43. $\dfrac{x^2(3+x)(x+4)}{(x+5)(x-1)} > 0$ $f(x) = \dfrac{x^2(3+x)(x+4)}{(x+5)(x-1)}$

The zeros and values where the expression is undefined are
$x = -5$, $x = -4$, $x = -3$, $x = 0$ and $x = 1$.

Interval	Test Number	$f(x)$	Positive/Negative
$-\infty < x < -5$	-6	$216/7$	Positive
$-5 < x < -4$	-4.5	$-243/44$	Negative
$-4 < x < -3$	-3.5	$49/108$	Positive
$-3 < x < 0$	-1	$-3/4$	Negative
$0 < x < 1$	0.5	$-63/44$	Negative
$1 < x < \infty$	2	$120/7$	Positive

The solution set is $\left\{ x \mid x < -5 \text{ or } -4 < x < -3 \text{ or } x > 1 \right\}$; $(-\infty, -5) \cup (-4, -3) \cup (1, \infty)$.

45. $\dfrac{2x^2 - x - 1}{x - 4} \le 0$ $f(x) = \dfrac{2x^2 - x - 1}{x - 4}$

   $\dfrac{(2x+1)(x-1)}{x-4} \le 0$

The zeros and values where the expression is undefined are $x = -\dfrac{1}{2}$, $x = 1$, and $x = 4$.

Interval	Test Number	$f(x)$	Positive/Negative
$-\infty < x < -1/2$	-1	$-2/5$	Negative
$-1/2 < x < 1$	0	$1/4$	Positive
$1 < x < 4$	2	$-5/2$	Negative
$4 < x < \infty$	5	44	Positive

The solution set is $\left\{ x \,\middle|\, x \le -\dfrac{1}{2} \text{ or } 1 \le x < 4 \right\}$; $\left(-\infty, -\dfrac{1}{2}\right] \cup [1, 4)$.

47. $\dfrac{x^2 + 3x - 1}{x + 3} > 0$ $f(x) = \dfrac{x^2 + 3x - 1}{x + 3}$

   Solving the numerator: $x = \dfrac{-3 \pm \sqrt{3^2 - 4(1)(-1)}}{2(1)} = \dfrac{-3 \pm \sqrt{13}}{2}$

The zeros and values where the expression is undefined are

   $x = \dfrac{-3 - \sqrt{13}}{2}$, $x = \dfrac{-3 + \sqrt{13}}{2}$, and $x = -3$ or $x = -3.30$, $x = 0.30$, $x = -3$.

Interval	Test Number	$f(x)$	Positive/Negative
$-\infty < x < \dfrac{-3 - \sqrt{13}}{2}$	-4	-3	Negative
$\dfrac{-3 - \sqrt{13}}{2} < x < -3$	-3.2	$9/5$	Positive
$-3 < x < \dfrac{-3 + \sqrt{13}}{2}$	0	$-1/3$	Negative
$\dfrac{-3 + \sqrt{13}}{2} < x < \infty$	1	$3/4$	Positive

The solution set is

   $\left\{ x \,\middle|\, \dfrac{-3 - \sqrt{13}}{2} < x < -3 \text{ or } x > \dfrac{-3 + \sqrt{13}}{2} \right\}$; $\left(\dfrac{-3 - \sqrt{13}}{2}, -3 \right) \cup \left(\dfrac{-3 + \sqrt{13}}{2}, \infty \right)$.

49. Let x be the positive number. Then

   $x^3 > 4x^2 \Rightarrow x^3 - 4x^2 > 0 \Rightarrow x^2(x - 4) > 0$

The zeros are $x = 0$ and $x = 4$. $f(x) = x^3 - 4x^2$

Interval	Test Number	$f(x)$	Positive/Negative
$-\infty < x < 0$	-1	-5	Negative
$0 < x < 4$	1	-3	Negative
$4 < x < \infty$	5	25	Positive

The solution set is $\{ x \mid x > 4 \}$; $(4, \infty)$. All real numbers larger than 4 satisfy the condition.

51. The domain of the expression $f(x) = \sqrt{x^2 - x^3}$ consists of all values for which
$$x^2 - x^3 \geq 0 \Rightarrow x^2(1 - x) \geq 0$$
The zeros are $x = 0$ and $x = 1$. $p(x) = x^2 - x^3$

Interval	Test Number	$p(x)$	Positive/Negative
$-\infty < x < 0$	-1	2	Positive
$0 < x < 1$	0.5	0.125	Positive
$1 < x < \infty$	2	-4	Negative

The solution or domain is $\{x \mid x \leq 1\}$; $(-\infty, 1]$.

53. The domain of the expression $R(x) = \sqrt{\dfrac{x - 2}{x + 4}}$ consists of all values

for which $\dfrac{x - 2}{x + 4} \geq 0$.

The zeros and values where the expression is undefined are $x = -4$ and $x = 2$
$$p(x) = \frac{x - 2}{x + 4}$$

Interval	Test Number	$p(x)$	Positive/Negative
$-\infty < x < -4$	-5	7	Positive
$-4 < x < 2$	0	$-1/2$	Negative
$2 < x < \infty$	3	$1/7$	Positive

The solution or domain is $\{x \mid x < -4 \text{ or } x \geq 2\}$; $(-\infty, -4) \cup [2, \infty)$.

55. (a)   Profit = Revenue − Cost
$$x(40 - 0.2x) - 32x \geq 50 \Rightarrow 40x - 0.2x^2 - 32x \geq 50$$
$$-0.2x^2 + 8x - 50 \geq 0 \Rightarrow 2x^2 - 80x + 500 \leq 0 \Rightarrow x^2 - 40x + 250 \leq 0$$
The zeros are approximately $x = 7.75$ and $x = 32.25$.
$$f(x) = x^2 - 40x + 250$$

Interval	Test Number	$f(x)$	Positive/Negative
$0 < x < 7.75$	7	19	Positive
$7.75 < x < 32.25$	10	-50	Negative
$32.25 < x < \infty$	40	250	Positive

The profit is at least $50 when at least 8 and no more than 32 watches are sold, that is for $8 \leq x \leq 20$.

(b)   Graphing the revenue function: $R(x) = x(40 - 0.2x)$

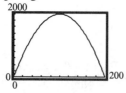

(c)   Using MAXIMUM, the maximum revenue is $2,000.

(d)   Using MAXIMUM, the company should sell 100 wristwatches to maximize revenue.

(e)   Graphing the profit function: $P(x) = x(40 - 0.2x) - 32x$

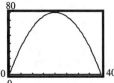

(f)   Using MAXIMUM, the maximum profit is $80.
(g)   Using MAXIMUM, the company should sell 20 watches for maximum profit.

57.   The cost of manufacturing x Chevy Cavaliers in a day was found to be:

$$C(x) = 0.216x^3 - 2.347x^2 + 14.328x + 10.224$$

Since the budget constraints require that the cost must be less than or equal to $97,000, we need to solve: $C(x) \le 97$ or

$$0.216x^3 - 2.347x^2 + 14.328x + 10.224 \le 97$$

Graphing $y_1 = 0.216x^3 - 2.347x^2 + 14.328x + 10.224$ and $y_2 = 97$:

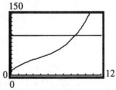

y_1 intersects y_2 at $x = 8.59$. $y_1 < y_2$ when $x < 8.59$. Chevy can produce at most eight Cavaliers in a day, assuming cars cannot be partially completed.

59.   Answers will vary, for example, $x^2 < 0$ has no real solution and $x^2 \le 0$ has exactly one real solution.

61.   Answers will vary.

Polynomial and Rational Functions

5.6   The Real Zeros of a Polynomial Function

1. $f(x) = 4x^3 - 3x^2 - 8x + 4;$ $c = 3$
     $f(3) = 4(3)^3 - 3(3)^2 - 8(3) + 4 = 108 - 27 - 24 + 4 = 61 \neq 0$
     Thus, 3 is not a zero of f $\therefore$ $x - 3$ is not a factor of f.

3. $f(x) = 3x^4 - 6x^3 - 5x + 10;$ $c = 1$
     $f(1) = 3(1)^4 - 6(1)^3 - 5(1) + 10 = 3 - 6 - 5 + 10 = 2 \neq 0$
     Thus, 1 is not a zero of f $\therefore$ $x - 1$ is not a factor of f.

5. $f(x) = 3x^6 + 2x^3 - 176;$ $c = -2$
     $f(-2) = 3(-2)^6 + 2(-2)^3 - 176 = 192 - 16 - 176 = 0$
     Thus, -2 is a zero of f $\therefore$ $x + 2$ is a factor of f. Use synthetic division to find the factors.

$$
\begin{array}{r|rrrrrrr}
-2 & 3 & 0 & 0 & 2 & 0 & 0 & -176 \\
   &   & -6 & 12 & -24 & 44 & -88 & 176 \\
\hline
   & 3 & -6 & 12 & -22 & 44 & -88 & 0 \\
\end{array}
$$

Factoring: $f(x) = (x + 2)\left(3x^5 - 6x^4 + 12x^3 - 22x^2 + 44x - 88\right)$.

7. $f(x) = 4x^6 - 64x^4 + x^2 - 16;$ $c = 4$
     $f(4) = 4(4)^6 - 64(4)^4 + (4)^2 - 16 = 16384 - 16384 + 16 - 16 = 0$
     Thus, 4 is a zero of f $\therefore$ $x - 4$ is a factor of f. Use synthetic division to find the factors.

$$
\begin{array}{r|rrrrrrr}
4 & 4 & 0 & -64 & 0 & 1 & 0 & -16 \\
  &   & 16 & 64 & 0 & 0 & 4 & 16 \\
\hline
  & 4 & 16 & 0 & 0 & 1 & 4 & 0 \\
\end{array}
$$

Factoring: $f(x) = (x - 4)\left(4x^5 + 16x^4 + x + 4\right)$.

9. $f(x) = 2x^4 - x^3 + 2x - 1;$ $c = -\dfrac{1}{2}$

$$f(-1/2) = 2(-1/2)^4 - (-1/2)^3 + 2(-1/2) - 1 = \frac{1}{8} + \frac{1}{8} - 1 - 1 = -\frac{7}{4} \neq 0$$

Thus, $-\dfrac{1}{2}$ is not a zero of f $\therefore$ $x + \dfrac{1}{2}$ is not a factor of f.

11. $f(x) = 3x^4 - 3x^3 + x^2 - x + 1$

The maximum number of zeros is the degree of the polynomial which is 4.

p must be a factor of 1: $p = \pm 1$; q must be a factor of 3: $q = \pm 1, \pm 3$

The possible rational zeros are: $\dfrac{p}{q} = \pm 1, \pm \dfrac{1}{3}$

13. $f(x) = x^5 - 6x^2 + 9x - 3$

The maximum number of zeros is the degree of the polynomial which is 5.

p must be a factor of -3: $p = \pm 1, \pm 3$; q must be a factor of 1: $q = \pm 1$

The possible rational zeros are: $\dfrac{p}{q} = \pm 1, \pm 3$

15. $f(x) = -4x^3 - x^2 + x + 2$

The maximum number of zeros is the degree of the polynomial which is 3.

p must be a factor of 2: $p = \pm 1, \pm 2$; q must be a factor of -4: $q = \pm 1, \pm 2, \pm 4$

The possible rational zeros are: $\dfrac{p}{q} = \pm 1, \pm 2, \pm \dfrac{1}{2}, \pm \dfrac{1}{4}$

17. $f(x) = 3x^4 - x^2 + 2$

The maximum number of zeros is the degree of the polynomial which is 4.

p must be a factor of 2: $p = \pm 1, \pm 2$; q must be a factor of 3: $q = \pm 1, \pm 3$

The possible rational zeros are: $\dfrac{p}{q} = \pm 1, \pm \dfrac{1}{3}, \pm 2, \pm \dfrac{2}{3}$

19. $f(x) = 2x^5 - x^3 + 2x^2 + 4$

The maximum number of zeros is the degree of the polynomial which is 5.

p must be a factor of 4: $p = \pm 1, \pm 2, \pm 4$; q must be a factor of 2: $q = \pm 1, \pm 2$

The possible rational zeros are: $\dfrac{p}{q} = \pm 1, \pm \dfrac{1}{2}, \pm 2, \pm 4$

21. $f(x) = 6x^4 + 2x^3 - x^2 + 2$

The maximum number of zeros is the degree of the polynomial which is 4.

p must be a factor of 2: $p = \pm 1, \pm 2$; q must be a factor of 6: $q = \pm 1, \pm 2, \pm 3, \pm 6$

The possible rational zeros are: $\dfrac{p}{q} = \pm 1, \pm \dfrac{1}{2}, \pm \dfrac{1}{3}, \pm \dfrac{1}{6}, \pm 2, \pm \dfrac{2}{3}$

23. $f(x) = 2x^3 + x^2 - 1 = 2\left(x^3 + \dfrac{1}{2}x^2 - \dfrac{1}{2} \right)$

Note: The leading coefficient must be 1.

$a_2 = \dfrac{1}{2}, a_1 = 0, a_0 = -\dfrac{1}{2}$

$Max\left\{ 1, \left| -\dfrac{1}{2} \right| + |\,0\,| + \left| \dfrac{1}{2} \right| \right\} = Max\left\{ 1, \dfrac{1}{2} + 0 + \dfrac{1}{2} \right\} = Max\{1, 1\} = 1$

$$1 + Max\left\{\left|-\frac{1}{2}\right|, |0|, \left|\frac{1}{2}\right|\right\} = 1 + Max\left\{\frac{1}{2}, 0, \frac{1}{2}\right\} = 1 + \frac{1}{2} = 1.5$$

The smaller of the two numbers is 1. Thus, every zero of f lies between -1 and 1.
Graphing using the bounds and ZOOM-FIT:

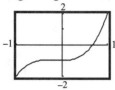

25. $f(x) = x^3 - 5x^2 - 11x + 11$
$a_2 = -5, a_1 = -11, a_0 = 11$

$Max\{1, |-5| + |-11| + |11|\} = Max\{1, 5 + 11 + 11\} = Max\{1, 27\} = 27$

$1 + Max\{|-5|, |-11|, |11|\} = 1 + Max\{1, 5, 11, 11\} = 1 + 11 = 12$

The smaller of the two numbers is 12. Thus, every zero of f lies between -12 and 12.
Graphing using the bounds and ZOOM-FIT: (Second graph has a better window.)

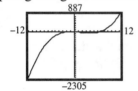 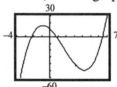

27. $f(x) = x^4 + 3x^3 - 5x^2 + 9$
$a_3 = 3, a_2 = -5, a_1 = 0, a_0 = 9$
$Max\{1, |9| + |0| + |-5| + |3|\} = Max\{1, 9 + 0 + 5 + 3\} = Max\{1, 17\} = 17$

$1 + Max\{|9|, |0|, |-5|, |3|\} = 1 + Max\{9, 0, 5, 3\} = 1 + 9 = 10$

The smaller of the two numbers is 10. Thus, every zero of f lies between -10 and 10.
Graphing using the bounds and ZOOM-FIT: (Second graph has a better window.)

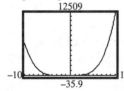 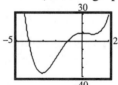

29. $f(x) = x^3 + 2x^2 - 5x - 6$
Step 1: $f(x)$ has at most 3 real zeros.
Step 2: Possible rational zeros:

$$p = \pm 1, \pm 2, \pm 3, \pm 6; \quad q = \pm 1; \quad \frac{p}{q} = \pm 1, \pm 2, \pm 3, \pm 6$$

Step 3: Using the Bounds on Zeros Theorem:
$a_2 = 2, \quad a_1 = -5, \quad a_0 = -6$
$Max \{1, |-6| + |-5| + |2|\} = Max \{1, 13\} = 13$
$1 + Max \{|-6|, |-5|, |2|\} = 1 + 6 = 7$

The smaller of the two numbers is 7. Thus, every zero of f lies between -7 and 7.

Graphing using the bounds and ZOOM-FIT: (Second graph has a better window.)

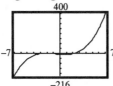

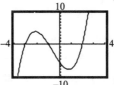

Step 4: (a)   From the graph it appears that there are x-intercepts at -3, -1, and 2.

       (b)   Using synthetic division:

$$-3\overline{)\begin{array}{rrrr} 1 & 2 & -5 & -6 \\ & -3 & 3 & 6 \end{array}}$$
$$\begin{array}{rrrr} 1 & -1 & -2 & 0 \end{array}$$

Since the remainder is 0, $x-(-3) = x+3$ is a factor. The other factor is the quotient: $x^2 - x - 2$.

       (c)   Thus, $f(x) = (x+3)(x^2 - x - 2) = (x+3)(x+1)(x-2)$.

The zeros are -3, -1, and 2.

31. $f(x) = 2x^3 - 13x^2 + 24x - 9$

Step 1: $f(x)$ has at most 3 real zeros.

Step 2:   Possible rational zeros:

$$p = \pm 1, \pm 3, \pm 9; \quad q = \pm 1, \pm 2; \quad \frac{p}{q} = \pm 1, \pm 3, \pm 9, \pm\frac{1}{2}, \pm\frac{3}{2}, \pm\frac{9}{2}$$

Step 3:   Using the Bounds on Zeros Theorem:

$$f(x) = 2\left(x^3 - 6.5x^2 + 12x - 4.5\right)$$

$$a_2 = -6.5, \quad a_1 = 12, \quad a_0 = -4.5$$

$$\text{Max}\left\{1, |-4.5| + |12| + |-6.5|\right\} = \text{Max}\left\{1, 23\right\} = 23$$

$$1 + \text{Max}\left\{|-4.5|, |12|, |-6.5|\right\} = 1 + 12 = 13$$

The smaller of the two numbers is 13. Thus, every zero of f lies between -13 and 13.

Graphing using the bounds and ZOOM-FIT: (Second graph has a better window.)

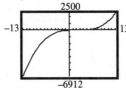

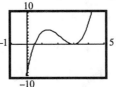

Step 4: (a)   From the graph it appears that there are x-intercepts at 0.5 and 3.

       (b)   Using synthetic division:

$$3\overline{)\begin{array}{rrrr} 2 & -13 & 24 & -9 \\ & 6 & -21 & 9 \end{array}}$$
$$\begin{array}{rrrr} 2 & -7 & 3 & 0 \end{array}$$

Since the remainder is 0, $x-3$ is a factor. The other factor is the quotient: $2x^2 - 7x + 3$.

(c)   Thus, $f(x) = (x - 3)(2x^2 - 7x + 3) = (x - 3)(2x - 1)(x - 3) = (x - 3)^2(2x - 1)$.
The zeros are 1/2 and 3 (multiplicity 2).

33. $f(x) = 3x^3 + 4x^2 + 4x + 1$
Step 1: $f(x)$ has at most 3 real zeros..
Step 2:   Possible rational zeros:

$$p = \pm 1; \quad q = \pm 1, \pm 3; \quad \frac{p}{q} = \pm 1, \pm \frac{1}{3}$$

Step 3:   Using the Bounds on Zeros Theorem:

$$f(x) = 3\left(x^3 + \frac{4}{3}x^2 + \frac{4}{3}x + \frac{1}{3} \right)$$

$$a_2 = \frac{4}{3}, \quad a_1 = \frac{4}{3}, \quad a_0 = \frac{1}{3}$$

$$\text{Max}\left\{ 1, \left|\frac{1}{3}\right| + \left|\frac{4}{3}\right| + \left|\frac{4}{3}\right| \right\} = \text{Max}\{1, 3\} = 3$$

$$1 + \text{Max}\left\{ \left|\frac{1}{3}\right|, \left|\frac{4}{3}\right|, \left|\frac{4}{3}\right| \right\} = 1 + \frac{4}{3} = \frac{7}{3}$$

The smaller of the two numbers is 7/3. Thus, every zero of f lies
between –7/3 and 7/3.
Graphing using the bounds and ZOOM-FIT: (Second graph has a better window.)

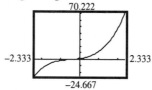 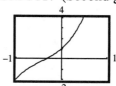

Step 4:   (a)   From the graph it appears that there is an x-intercepts at –1/3.
(b)   Using synthetic division:

$$-\frac{1}{3} \overline{)\begin{array}{cccc} 3 & 4 & 4 & 1 \\ & -1 & -1 & -1 \\ \hline 3 & 3 & 3 & 0 \end{array}}$$

Since the remainder is 0, $x - \left(-\frac{1}{3} \right) = x + \frac{1}{3}$ is a factor. The other factor is

the quotient: $3x^2 + 3x + 3$.

(c)   Thus, $f(x) = \left(x + \frac{1}{3} \right)(3x^2 + 3x + 3) = (3x + 1)(x^2 + x + 1)$.

$x^2 + x + 1 = 0$ has no real solution.
The zero is –1/3.

35. $f(x) = x^3 - 8x^2 + 17x - 6$
Step 1: $f(x)$ has at most 3 real zeros.
Step 2:   Possible rational zeros:

$$p = \pm 1, \pm 2, \pm 3, \pm 6; \quad q = \pm 1; \quad \frac{p}{q} = \pm 1, \pm 2, \pm 3, \pm 6$$

Step 3:   Using the Bounds on Zeros Theorem:

$$a_2 = -8, \quad a_1 = 17, \quad a_0 = -6$$

$$\text{Max} \left\{1, |-6| + |17| + |-8| \right\} = \text{Max} \left\{1, 31\right\} = 31$$

$$1 + \text{Max} \left\{|-6|, |17|, |-8| \right\} = 1 + 17 = 18$$

The smaller of the two numbers is 18. Thus, every zero of f lies between -18 and 18.

Graphing using the bounds and ZOOM-FIT: (Second graph has a better window.)

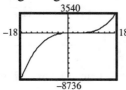 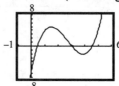

Step 4:   (a)   From the graph it appears that there are x-intercepts at 0.5, 3, and 4.5.

(b)   Using synthetic division:

$$\begin{array}{r|rrrr} 3 & 1 & -8 & 17 & -6 \\ & & 3 & -15 & 6 \\ \hline & 1 & -5 & 2 & 0 \end{array}$$

Since the remainder is 0, $x - 3$ is a factor. The other factor is the quotient: $x^2 - 5x + 2$.

(c)   Thus, $f(x) = (x - 3)(x^2 - 5x + 2)$. Using the quadratic formula to find the solutions of the depressed equation $x^2 - 5x + 2 = 0$:

$$x = \frac{-(-5) \pm \sqrt{(-5)^2 - 4(1)(2)}}{2(1)} = \frac{5 \pm \sqrt{17}}{2}$$

Thus, $f(x) = (x - 3)\left(x - \left(\frac{5 + \sqrt{17}}{2}\right)\right)\left(x - \left(\frac{5 - \sqrt{17}}{2}\right)\right)$.

The zeros are 3, $\dfrac{5 + \sqrt{17}}{2}$, and $\dfrac{5 - \sqrt{17}}{2}$ or 3, 4.56, and 0.44.

37. $f(x) = x^4 + x^3 - 3x^2 - x + 2$

Step 1: $f(x)$ has at most 4 real zeros.

Step 2:   Possible rational zeros:

$$p = \pm 1, \pm 2; \quad q = \pm 1; \quad \frac{p}{q} = \pm 1, \pm 2$$

Step 3:   Using the Bounds on Zeros Theorem:

$$a_3 = 1, \quad a_2 = -3, \quad a_1 = -1, \quad a_0 = 2$$

$$\text{Max} \left\{1, |2| + |-1| + |-3| + |1| \right\} = \text{Max} \left\{1, 7\right\} = 7$$

$$1 + \text{Max} \left\{|2|, |-1|, |-3|, |1| \right\} = 1 + 3 = 4$$

The smaller of the two numbers is 4. Thus, every zero of f lies between -4 and 4.

Graphing using the bounds and ZOOM-FIT: (Second graph has a better window.)

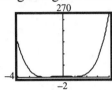 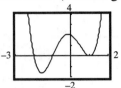

Step 4: (a) From the graph it appears that there are x-intercepts at –2, –1, and 1.

(b) Using synthetic division:

$$-2 \overline{)\begin{array}{rrrr} 1 & 1 & -3 & -1 & 2 \\ & -2 & 2 & 2 & -2 \\ \hline 1 & -1 & -1 & 1 & 0 \end{array}}$$

$$-1 \overline{)\begin{array}{rrrr} 1 & -1 & -1 & 1 \\ & -1 & 2 & -1 \\ \hline 1 & -2 & 1 & 0 \end{array}}$$

Since the remainder is 0, $x+2$ and $x+1$ are factors. The other factor is the quotient: $x^2 - 2x + 1$.

(c) Thus, $f(x) = (x+2)(x+1)(x-1)^2$.

The zeros are –2, –1, and 1 (multiplicity 2).

39. $f(x) = 2x^4 + 17x^3 + 35x^2 - 9x - 45$

Step 1: $f(x)$ has at most 4 real zeros.

Step 2: Possible rational zeros:

$p = \pm 1, \pm 3, \pm 5, \pm 9, \pm 15, \pm 45; \quad q = \pm 1, \pm 2;$

$\frac{p}{q} = \pm 1, \pm 3, \pm 5, \pm 9, \pm 15, \pm 45, \pm \frac{1}{2}, \pm \frac{3}{2}, \pm \frac{5}{2}, \pm \frac{9}{2}, \pm \frac{15}{2}, \pm \frac{45}{2}$

Step 3: Using the Bounds on Zeros Theorem:

$f(x) = 2\left(x^4 + 8.5x^3 + 17.5x^2 - 4.5x - 22.5\right)$

$a_3 = 8.5, \quad a_2 = 17.5, \quad a_1 = -4.5, \quad a_0 = -22.5$

$\text{Max}\{1, |-22.5| + |-4.5| + |17.5| + |8.5|\} = \text{Max}\{1, 53\} = 53$

$1 + \text{Max}\{|-22.5|, |-4.5|, |17.5|, |8.5|\} = 1 + 22.5 = 23.5$

The smaller of the two numbers is 23.5. Thus, every zero of f lies between –23.5 and 23.5.

Graphing using the bounds and ZOOM-FIT: (Second graph has a better window.)

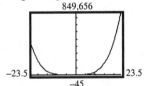 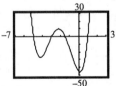

Step 4: (a) From the graph it appears that there are x-intercepts at –5, –3, –3/2, and 1.

(b) Using synthetic division:

$$-5 \overline{)\begin{array}{rrrr} 2 & 17 & 35 & -9 & -45 \\ & -10 & -35 & 0 & 45 \\ \hline 2 & 7 & 0 & -9 & 0 \end{array}}$$

$$-3 \overline{)\begin{array}{rrrr} 2 & 7 & 0 & -9 \\ & -6 & -3 & 9 \\ \hline 2 & 1 & -3 & 0 \end{array}}$$

Since the remainder is 0, $x+5$ and $x+3$ are factors. The other factor is the quotient: $2x^2 + x - 3$.

(c)   Thus, $f(x) = (x+5)(x+3)(2x+3)(x-1)$.
The zeros are $-5, -3, -1.5$ and 1.

41. $f(x) = 2x^4 - 3x^3 - 21x^2 - 2x + 24$
Step 1: $f(x)$ has at most 4 real zeros.
Step 2:   Possible rational zeros:

$$p = \pm 1, \pm 2, \pm 3, \pm 4, \pm 6, \pm 8, \pm 12, \pm 24; \quad q = \pm 1, \pm 2;$$

$$\frac{p}{q} = \pm 1, \pm 2, \pm 3, \pm 4, \pm 6, \pm 8, \pm 12, \pm 24, \pm \frac{1}{2}, \pm \frac{3}{2}$$

Step 3:   Using the Bounds on Zeros Theorem:

$$f(x) = 2\left(x^4 - 1.5x^3 - 10.5x^2 - x + 12\right)$$

$$a_3 = -1.5, \quad a_2 = -10.5, \quad a_1 = -1, \quad a_0 = 12$$

$$\text{Max} \left\{1, |12| + |-1| + |-10.5| + |-1.5|\right\} = \text{Max} \left\{1, 25\right\} = 25$$

$$1 + \text{Max} \left\{|12|, |-1|, |-10.5|, |-1.5|\right\} = 1 + 12 = 13$$

The smaller of the two numbers is 13. Thus, every zero of f lies
between -13 and 13.
Graphing using the bounds and ZOOM-FIT: (Second graph has a better window.)

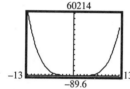   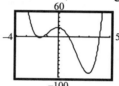

Step 4:   (a)   From the graph it appears that there are x-intercepts at $-2, -3/2, 1$,
and 4.
(b)   Using synthetic division:

$$
\begin{array}{r}
-2)\overline{\begin{array}{rrrrr} 2 & -3 & -21 & -2 & 24 \\ & -4 & 14 & 14 & -24 \end{array}} \\
\hline
\begin{array}{rrrrr} 2 & -7 & -7 & 12 & 0 \end{array}
\end{array}
\qquad
\begin{array}{r}
4)\overline{\begin{array}{rrrr} 2 & -7 & -7 & 12 \\ & & 8 & 4 & -12 \end{array}} \\
\hline
\begin{array}{rrrr} 2 & 1 & -3 & 0 \end{array}
\end{array}
$$

Since the remainder is 0, $x + 2$ and $x - 4$ are factors. The other factor is the
quotient: $2x^2 + x - 3$.
(c)   Thus, $f(x) = (x+2)(2x+3)(x-1)(x-4)$.
The zeros are $-2, -3/2, 1$ and 4.

43. $f(x) = 4x^4 + 7x^2 - 2$
Step 1: $f(x)$ has at most 4 real zeros.
Step 2:   Possible rational zeros:

$$p = \pm 1, \pm 2; \quad q = \pm 1, \pm 2, \pm 4; \quad \frac{p}{q} = \pm 1, \pm 2, \pm \frac{1}{2}, \pm \frac{1}{4}$$

Step 3:   Using the Bounds on Zeros Theorem:

$$f(x) = 4\left(x^4 + 1.75x^2 - 0.5\right)$$

$$a_3 = 0, \quad a_2 = 1.75, \quad a_1 = 0, \quad a_0 = -0.5$$

$$\text{Max} \left\{1, |-0.5| + |0| + |1.75| + |0|\right\} = \text{Max} \left\{1, 2.25\right\} = 2.25$$

$$1 + \text{Max} \left\{|-0.5|, |0|, |1.75|, |0|\right\} = 1 + 1.75 = 2.75$$

The smaller of the two numbers is 2.25. Thus, every zero of f lies between –2.25 and 2.25.

Graphing using the bounds and ZOOM-FIT: (Second graph has a better window.)

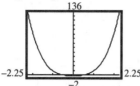   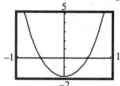

Step 4: (a) From the graph it appears that there are x-intercepts at –1/2, and 1/2.

(b) Using synthetic division:

$$-1/2\overline{)4 \quad 0 \quad 7 \quad 0 \quad -2}$$
$$ -2 \quad 1 \quad -4 \quad 2$$
$$\overline{4 \quad -2 \quad 8 \quad -4 \quad 0}$$

$$1/2\overline{)4 \quad -2 \quad 8 \quad -4}$$
$$ 2 \quad 0 \quad 4$$
$$\overline{4 \quad 0 \quad 8 \quad 0}$$

Since the remainder is 0, $x+1/2$ and $x-1/2$ are factors. The other factor is the quotient: $4x^2 + 8$.

(c) Thus, $f(x) = 4(x+1/2)(x-1/2)(x^2+2) = (2x+1)(2x-1)(x^2+2)$.

The depressed equation has no real zeros.

The zeros are –1/2, and 1/2.

45. $f(x) = 4x^5 - 8x^4 - x + 2$

Step 1: $f(x)$ has at most 5 real zeros.

Step 2: Possible rational zeros:

$$p = \pm1, \pm2; \quad q = \pm1, \pm2, \pm4; \quad \frac{p}{q} = \pm1, \pm2, \pm\frac{1}{2}, \pm\frac{1}{4}$$

Step 3: Using the Bounds on Zeros Theorem:

$$f(x) = 4\left(x^5 - 2x^4 - 0.25x + 0.5\right)$$

$$a_4 = -2, \ a_3 = 0, \ a_2 = 0, \ a_1 = -0.25, \ a_0 = 0.5$$

$$\text{Max}\left\{1, |0.5| + |-0.25| + |0| + |0| + |-2|\right\} = \text{Max}\left\{1, 2.75\right\} = 2.75$$

$$1 + \text{Max}\left\{|0.5|, |-0.25|, |0|, |0|, |-2|\right\} = 1 + 2 = 3$$

The smaller of the two numbers is 2.75. Thus, every zero of f lies between –2.75 and 2.75.

Graphing using the bounds and ZOOM-FIT: (Second graph has a better window.)

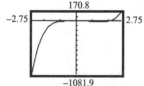   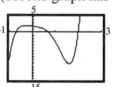

Step 4: (a) From the graph it appears that there are x-intercepts at –0.7, 0.7 and 2.

(b) Using synthetic division:

$$2\overline{)4 \quad -8 \quad 0 \quad 0 \quad -1 \quad 2}$$
$$ 8 \quad 0 \quad 0 \quad 0 \quad -2$$
$$\overline{4 \quad 0 \quad 0 \quad 0 \quad -1 \quad 0}$$

Since the remainder is 0, $x-2$ is a factor. The other factor is the quotient: $4x^4 - 1$.

(c) Factoring,
$$f(x) = (x-2)\left(4x^4 - 1\right) = (x-2)(2x^2 - 1)(2x^2 + 1)$$
$$= (x-2)\left(\sqrt{2}x - 1\right)\left(\sqrt{2}x + 1\right)\left(2x^2 + 1\right)$$
The zeros are $-\dfrac{\sqrt{2}}{2}, \dfrac{\sqrt{2}}{2}$, and 2 or $-0.71, -0.71$, and 2.

47. $f(x) = x^3 + 3.2x^2 - 16.83x - 5.31$
$f(x)$ has at most 3 real zeros.
Solving by graphing (using ZERO):

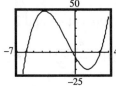

The zeros are approximately $-5.9, -0.3$, and 3.

49. $f(x) = x^4 - 1.4x^3 - 33.71x^2 + 23.94x + 292.41$
$f(x)$ has at most 4 real zeros.
Solving by graphing (using ZERO):

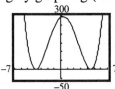

The zeros are approximately -3.8 and 4.5. These zeros are each of multiplicity 2.

51. $f(x) = x^3 + 19.5x^2 - 1021x + 1000.5$
$f(x)$ has at most 3 real zeros.
Solving by graphing (using ZERO):

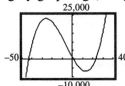

The zeros are approximately $-43.5, 1$, and 23.

53. $x^4 - x^3 + 2x^2 - 4x - 8 = 0$
The solutions of the equation are the zeros of $f(x) = x^4 - x^3 + 2x^2 - 4x - 8$.
Step 1: $f(x)$ has at most 4 real zeros.
Step 2: Possible rational zeros:
$$p = \pm 1, \pm 2, \pm 4, \pm 8; \quad q = \pm 1; \quad \frac{p}{q} = \pm 1, \pm 2, \pm 4, \pm 8$$

Step 3:   Using the Bounds on Zeros Theorem:

$$a_3 = -1, \quad a_2 = 2, \quad a_1 = -4, \quad a_0 = -8$$

$$\text{Max}\left\{1, |-8| + |-4| + |2| + |-1|\right\} = \text{Max}\left\{1, 15\right\} = 15$$

$$1 + \text{Max}\left\{|-8|, |-4|, |2|, |-1|\right\} = 1 + 8 = 9$$

The smaller of the two numbers is 9. Thus, every zero of f lies between -9 and 9.

Graphing using the bounds and ZOOM-FIT: (Second graph has a better window.)

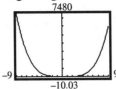   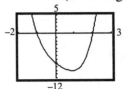

Step 4:   (a)   From the graph it appears that there are x-intercepts at -1 and 2.

(b)   Using synthetic division:

$$\begin{array}{r|rrrr} -1 & 1 & -1 & 2 & -4 & -8 \\ & & -1 & 2 & -4 & 8 \\ \hline & 1 & -2 & 4 & -8 & 0 \end{array}$$

$$\begin{array}{r|rrrr} 2 & 1 & -2 & 4 & -8 \\ & & 2 & 0 & 8 \\ \hline & 1 & 0 & 4 & 0 \end{array}$$

Since the remainder is 0, $x + 1$ and $x - 2$ are factors. The other factor is the quotient: $x^2 + 4$.

(c)   The zeros are -1 and 2. ($x^2 + 4 = 0$ has no real solutions.)

55. $3x^3 + 4x^2 - 7x + 2 = 0$

The solutions of the equation are the zeros of $f(x) = 3x^3 + 4x^2 - 7x + 2$.

Step 1: $f(x)$ has at most 3 real zeros.

Step 2:   Possible rational zeros:

$$p = \pm 1, \pm 2; \quad q = \pm 1, \pm 3; \quad \frac{p}{q} = \pm 1, \pm 2, \pm\frac{1}{3}, \pm\frac{2}{3}$$

Step 3:   Using the Bounds on Zeros Theorem:

$$f(x) = 3\left(x^3 + \frac{4}{3}x^2 - \frac{7}{3}x + \frac{2}{3}\right)$$

$$a_2 = \frac{4}{3}, \quad a_1 = -\frac{7}{3}, \quad a_0 = \frac{2}{3}$$

$$\text{Max}\left\{1, \left|\frac{2}{3}\right| + \left|-\frac{7}{3}\right| + \left|\frac{4}{3}\right|\right\} = \text{Max}\left\{1, \frac{13}{3}\right\} = \frac{13}{3} \approx 4.333$$

$$1 + \text{Max}\left\{\left|\frac{2}{3}\right|, \left|-\frac{7}{3}\right|, \left|\frac{4}{3}\right|\right\} = 1 + \frac{7}{3} = \frac{10}{3} \approx 3.333$$

The smaller of the two numbers is 3.33. Thus, every zero of f lies between -3.33 and 3.33.

Graphing using the bounds and ZOOM-FIT: (Second graph has a better window.)

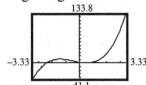 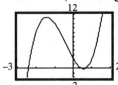

Step 4: (a) From the graph it appears that there are x-intercepts at $\dfrac{1}{3}, \dfrac{2}{3}$, and -2.4.

(b) Using synthetic division:

$$\dfrac{2}{3}\overline{)\begin{array}{rrr} 3 & 4 & -7 & 2 \\ & 2 & 4 & -2 \\ \hline 3 & 6 & -3 & 0 \end{array}}$$

Since the remainder is 0, $x - \dfrac{2}{3}$ is a factor. The other factor is the

quotient: $3x^2 + 6x - 3$.

$$f(x) = \left(x - \dfrac{2}{3}\right)\left(3x^2 + 6x - 3\right) = 3\left(x - \dfrac{2}{3}\right)\left(x^2 + 2x - 1\right)$$

Using the quadratic formula to solve $x^2 + 2x - 1 = 0$:

$$x = \dfrac{-2 \pm \sqrt{4 - 4(1)(-1)}}{2(1)} = \dfrac{-2 \pm \sqrt{8}}{2} = \dfrac{-2 \pm 2\sqrt{2}}{2} = -1 \pm \sqrt{2}$$

(c) The zeros are $\dfrac{2}{3}, -1 + \sqrt{2}$, and $-1 - \sqrt{2}$ or $0.67, 0.41$, and -2.41.

57. $3x^3 - x^2 - 15x + 5 = 0$

Solving by factoring: $x^2(3x - 1) - 5(3x - 1) = 0 \Rightarrow (3x - 1)\left(x^2 - 5\right) = 0$

$$(3x - 1)\left(x - \sqrt{5}\right)\left(x + \sqrt{5}\right) = 0$$

The solutions of the equation are $\dfrac{1}{3}, \sqrt{5}$, and $-\sqrt{5}$ or $0.33, 2.24$, and -2.24.

59. $x^4 + 4x^3 + 2x^2 - x + 6 = 0$

The solutions of the equation are the zeros of $f(x) = x^4 + 4x^3 + 2x^2 - x + 6$.

Step 1: $f(x)$ has at most 4 real zeros.

Step 2: Possible rational zeros:

$$p = \pm 1, \pm 2, \pm 3, \pm 6; \quad q = \pm 1; \quad \dfrac{p}{q} = \pm 1, \pm 2, \pm 3, \pm 6$$

Step 3: Using the Bounds on Zeros Theorem:

$$a_3 = 4, \ a_2 = 2, \ a_1 = -1, \ a_0 = 6$$

$$\text{Max} \left\{1, |6| + |-1| + |2| + |4|\right\} = \text{Max} \left\{1, 13\right\} = 13$$

$$1 + \text{Max} \left\{|6|, |-1|, |2|, |4|\right\} = 1 + 6 = 7$$

The smaller of the two numbers is 7. Thus, every zero of f lies between -7 and 7.

Graphing using the bounds and ZOOM-FIT: (Second graph has a better window.)

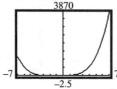 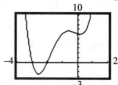

Step 4:   (a)   From the graph it appears that there are x-intercepts at –3 and –2.
          (b)   Using synthetic division:

$$-3\overline{)\begin{array}{rrrrr} 1 & 4 & 2 & -1 & 6 \\ & -3 & -3 & 3 & -6 \\ \hline 1 & 1 & -1 & 2 & 0 \end{array}}$$
$$-2\overline{)\begin{array}{rrrr} 1 & 1 & -1 & 2 \\ & -2 & 2 & -2 \\ \hline 1 & -1 & 1 & 0 \end{array}}$$

          Since the remainder is 0, $x+3$ and $x+2$ are factors. The other factor is the
          quotient: $x^2 - x + 1$.
          (c)   The zeros are –3 and –2. ($x^2 - x + 1 = 0$ has no real solutions.)

61. $x^3 - \dfrac{2}{3}x^2 + \dfrac{8}{3}x + 1 = 0$

The solutions of the equation are the zeros of $f(x) = x^3 - \dfrac{2}{3}x^2 + \dfrac{8}{3}x + 1 = 0$.

Step 1: $f(x)$ has at most 3 real zeros.

Step 2:   Use the equivalent equation $3x^3 - 2x^2 + 8x + 3 = 0$ to find the possible rational
          zeros:

$$p = \pm 1, \pm 3; \quad q = \pm 1, \pm 3; \quad \frac{p}{q} = \pm 1, \pm 3, \pm \frac{1}{3}$$

Step 3:   Using the Bounds on Zeros Theorem:

$$a_2 = -\frac{2}{3}, \quad a_1 = \frac{8}{3}, \quad a_0 = 1$$

$$\text{Max}\left\{1, |1| + \left|\frac{8}{3}\right| + \left|-\frac{2}{3}\right|\right\} = \text{Max}\left\{1, \frac{13}{3}\right\} = \frac{13}{3} \approx 4.333$$

$$1 + \text{Max}\left\{|1|, \left|\frac{8}{3}\right|, \left|-\frac{2}{3}\right|\right\} = 1 + \frac{8}{3} = \frac{11}{3} \approx 3.667$$

The smaller of the two numbers is 3.67. Thus, every zero of f lies
between –3.67 and 3.67.

Graphing using the bounds and ZOOM-FIT: (Second graph has a better window.)

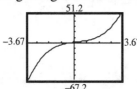 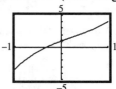

Step 4:   (a)   From the graph it appears that there is an x-intercepts at $-\dfrac{1}{3}$.

(b)   Using synthetic division:

$$-\frac{1}{2}\overline{\big)\,1 \quad -\frac{2}{3} \quad \frac{8}{2} \quad 1\,}$$

$$\underline{\quad\quad -\frac{1}{3} \quad \frac{1}{3} \quad -1\,}$$

$$1 \quad -1 \quad 3 \quad 0$$

Since the remainder is 0, $x + \dfrac{1}{3}$ is a factor. The other factor is the quotient: $x^2 - x + 3$.

(c)   The real zero is $-\dfrac{1}{3}$. ($x^2 - x + 3 = 0$ has no real solutions.)

63.   Using the TABLE feature to show that there is a zero in the interval:

$$f(x) = 8x^4 - 2x^2 + 5x - 1; \quad [0,1]$$

X	Y_1
-1	0
0	-1
1	10
2	129
3	644
4	2035
5	4974

X=-1

$f(0) = -1 < 0$ and $f(1) = 10 > 0$
Since one is positive and one is negative, there is a zero in the interval.

Using the TABLE feature to approximate the zero to two decimal places:

X	Y_1
.213	-.0093
.214	-.0048
.215	-4E-4
.216	.0041
.217	.00856
.218	.01302
	.01748

X=.219

The zero is approximately 0.22.

65.   Using the TABLE feature to show that there is a zero in the interval:

$$f(x) = 2x^3 + 6x^2 - 8x + 2; \quad [-5, -4]$$

X	Y_1
-8	-574
-7	-334
-6	-166
-5	-58
-4	2
-3	26
-2	26

$Y_1 \equiv 2X\wedge3+6X^2-8X+2$

$f(-5) = -58 < 0$ and $f(-4) = 2 > 0$
Since one is positive and one is negative, there is a zero in the interval.

Using the TABLE feature to approximate the zero to two decimal places:

X	Y_1
-4.052	-.129
-4.051	-.0871
-4.05	-.0453
-4.049	-.0035
-4.048	.03831
-4.047	.08003
-4.046	.12172

$Y_1 \equiv 2X\wedge3+6X^2-8X+2$ The zero is approximately –4.05.

67. Using the TABLE feature to show that there is a zero in the interval:
$$f(x) = x^5 - x^4 + 7x^3 - 7x^2 - 18x + 18; \quad [1.4,\ 1.5]$$

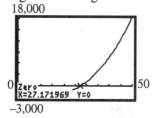

X	Y1
1.3	-.9942
1.4	-.1754
1.5	1.4063
1.6	3.8842
1.7	7.4075
1.8	12.142
1.9	18.272

Y1∎X^5−X^4+7X^3...

$f(1.4) = -0.17536 < 0$ and $f(1.5) = 1.40625 > 0$
Since one is positive and one is negative,
there is a zero in the interval.

Using the TABLE feature to approximate the zero to two decimal places:

X	Y1
1.411	-.041
1.412	-.0283
1.413	-.0156
1.414	-.0028
1.415	.01016
1.416	.02315
1.417	.03621

Y1∎X^5−X^4+7X^3... The zero is approximately 1.41.

69. $C(x) = 3000$

$0.216x^3 - 2.347x^2 + 14.328x + 10.224 = 3000 \Rightarrow 0.216x^3 - 2.347x^2 + 14.328x - 2989.776 = 0$
There are at most 3 solutions.
Graphing and solving:

18,000

0 ⌐Zero   50
X=27.171969 Y=0

−3,000

About 27 Cavaliers can be manufactured.

71. $x - 2$ is a factor of $f(x) = x^3 - kx^2 + kx + 2$ only if the remainder that results when $f(x)$ is divided by $x - 2$ is 0. Dividing, we have:

$$
\begin{array}{r|rrrr}
2) & 1 & -k & k & 2 \\
 & & 2 & -2k+4 & -2k+8 \\
\hline
 & 1 & -k+2 & -k+4 & -2k+10
\end{array}
$$

Since we want the remainder to equal 0, set the remainder equal to zero and solve:
$$-2k + 10 = 0 \Rightarrow -2k = -10 \Rightarrow k = 5$$

73. By the Remainder Theorem we know that the remainder from synthetic division by c is equal to $f(c)$. Thus the easiest way to find the remainder is to evaluate:
$$f(1) = 2(1)^{20} - 8(1)^{10} + 1 - 2 = 2 - 8 + 1 - 2 = -7$$
The remainder is –7.

75. Let x be the length of a side of the original cube.
After removing the 1 inch slice, one dimension will be $x - 1$.
The volume of the new solid will be:
$$(x - 1) \cdot x \cdot x = 294 \Rightarrow x^3 - x^2 = 294 \Rightarrow x^3 - x^2 - 294 = 0$$
The possible rational zeros are:
$$p = \pm 1,\ \pm 2,\ \pm 3,\ \pm 6,\ \pm 7,\ \pm 14,\ \pm 21,\ \pm 42,\ \pm 49,\ \pm 98,\ \pm 147,\ \pm 294; \quad q = \pm 1$$

The rational zeros are the same as the values for p.
Using synthetic division:

$$7{\overline{)}}\begin{array}{rrrr} 1 & -1 & 0 & -294 \\ & 7 & 42 & 294 \\ \hline 1 & 6 & 42 & 0 \end{array}$$

7 is a zero, so the length of the original edge of the cube was 7 inches.

77. $f(x) = 2x^6 - 5x^4 + x^3 - x + 1$
By the Rational Zero Theorem, the only possible rational zeros are:
$$\frac{p}{q} = \pm 1, \pm \frac{1}{2}$$

Since $\dfrac{3}{5}$ is not in the list of possible rational zeros, it is not a zero of $f(x)$.

Chapter 5

Polynomial and Rational Functions

5.7 Complex Zeros; Fundamental Theorem of Algebra

1. Since complex zeros appear in conjugate pairs, $4+i$, the conjugate of $4-i$, is the remaining zero of f.

3. Since complex zeros appear in conjugate pairs, $-i$, the conjugate of i, and $1-i$, the conjugate of $1+i$, are the remaining zeros of f.

5. Since complex zeros appear in conjugate pairs, $-i$, the conjugate of i, and $-2i$, the conjugate of $2i$, are the remaining zeros of f.

7. Since complex zeros appear in conjugate pairs, $-i$, the conjugate of i, is the remaining zero of f.

9. Since complex zeros appear in conjugate pairs, $2-i$, the conjugate of $2+i$, and $-3+i$, the conjugate of $-3-i$, are the remaining zeros of f.

11. Since $3+2i$ is a zero, its conjugate $3-2i$ is also a zero of f.
     Finding the function with $a=1$:
     $$f(x) = (x-4)(x-4)\big(x-(3+2i)\big)\big(x-(3-2i)\big) = \big(x^2-8x+16\big)\big((x-3)-2i\big)\big((x-3)+2i\big)$$
     $$= \big(x^2-8x+16\big)\big(x^2-6x+9-4i^2\big) = \big(x^2-8x+16\big)\big(x^2-6x+13\big)$$
     $$= x^4-6x^3+13x^2-8x^3+48x^2-104x+16x^2-96x+208$$
     $$= x^4-14x^3+77x^2-200x+208$$

13. Since $-i$ is a zero, its conjugate i is also a zero, and since $1+i$ is a zero, its conjugate $1-i$ is also a zero of f. Finding the function with $a=1$:
     $$f(x) = (x-2)(x+i)(x-i)\big(x-(1+i)\big)\big(x-(1-i)\big) = (x-2)\big(x^2-i^2\big)\big((x-1)-i\big)\big((x-1)+i\big)$$
     $$= (x-2)\big(x^2+1\big)\big(x^2-2x+1-i^2\big) = \big(x^3-2x^2+x-2\big)\big(x^2-2x+2\big)$$
     $$= x^5-2x^4+2x^3-2x^4+4x^3-4x^2+x^3-2x^2+2x-2x^2+4x-4$$
     $$= x^5-4x^4+7x^3-8x^2+6x-4$$

15. Since $-i$ is a zero, its conjugate i is also a zero of f. Finding the function with $a=1$:
     $$f(x) = (x-3)(x-3)(x+i)(x-i) = \big(x^2-6x+9\big)\big(x^2-i^2\big)$$
     $$= \big(x^2-6x+9\big)\big(x^2+1\big) = x^4+x^2-6x^3-6x+9x^2+9$$
     $$= x^4-6x^3+10x^2-6x+9$$

17. Since $2i$ is a zero, its conjugate $-2i$ is also a zero of f. $x - 2i$ and $x + 2i$ are factors of f. Thus, $(x - 2i)(x + 2i) = x^2 + 4$ is a factor of f. Using division to find the other factor:

$$
\begin{array}{r}
x - 4 \\
x^2 + 4 \overline{\smash{\big)}\ x^3 - 4x^2 + 4x - 16} \\
\underline{x^3 \qquad\quad + 4x} \\
-4x^2 \qquad\ -16 \\
\underline{-4x^2 \qquad\ -16}
\end{array}
$$

$x - 4$ is a factor and the remaining zero is 4. The zeros of f are $4, 2i, -2i$.

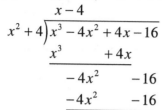

19. Since $-2i$ is a zero, its conjugate $2i$ is also a zero of f. $x - 2i$ and $x + 2i$ are factors of f. Thus, $(x - 2i)(x + 2i) = x^2 + 4$ is a factor of f. Using division to find the other factor:

$$
\begin{array}{r}
2x^2 + 5x - 3 \\
x^2 + 4 \overline{\smash{\big)}\ 2x^4 + 5x^3 + 5x^2 + 20x - 12} \\
\underline{2x^4 \qquad\quad + 8x^2} \\
5x^3 - 3x^2 + 20x \\
\underline{5x^3 \qquad\ + 20x} \\
-3x^2 \qquad\ -12 \\
\underline{-3x^2 \qquad\ -12}
\end{array}
$$

$2x^2 + 5x - 3 = (2x - 1)(x + 3)$ are factors and the remaining zeros are $\dfrac{1}{2}$ and -3. The zeros of f are $2i, -2i, -3, \dfrac{1}{2}$.

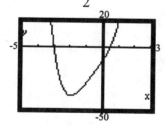

21. Since $3 - 2i$ is a zero, its conjugate $3 + 2i$ is also a zero of h. $x - (3 - 2i)$ and $x - (3 + 2i)$ are factors of h. Thus,
$(x - (3 - 2i))(x - (3 + 2i)) = ((x - 3) + 2i)((x - 3) - 2i) = x^2 - 6x + 9 - 4i^2 = x^2 - 6x + 13$ is a factor of h.

Using division to find the other factor:

$$
\begin{array}{r}
x^2 - 3x - 10 \\
x^2 - 6x + 13 \overline{\smash{)}\, x^4 - 9x^3 + 21x^2 + 21x - 130} \\
\underline{x^4 - 6x^3 + 13x^2} \\
-3x^3 + 8x^2 + 21x \\
\underline{-3x^3 + 18x^2 - 39x} \\
-10x^2 + 60x - 130 \\
\underline{-10x^2 + 60x - 130}
\end{array}
$$

$x^2 - 3x - 10 = (x+2)(x-5)$ are factors and the remaining zeros are -2 and 5.

The zeros of h are $3 - 2i, 3 + 2i, -2, 5$.

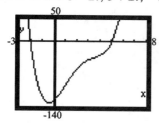

23. Since $-4i$ is a zero, its conjugate $4i$ is also a zero of h. $x - 4i$ and $x + 4i$ are factors of h.
Thus, $(x - 4i)(x + 4i) = x^2 + 16$ is a factor of h. Using division to find the other factor:

$$
\begin{array}{r}
3x^3 + 2x^2 - 33x - 22 \\
x^2 + 16 \overline{\smash{)}\, 3x^5 + 2x^4 + 15x^3 + 10x^2 - 528x - 352} \\
\underline{3x^5 \qquad + 48x^3} \\
2x^4 - 33x^3 + 10x^2 \\
\underline{2x^4 \qquad + 32x^2} \\
-33x^3 - 22x^2 - 528x \\
\underline{-33x^3 \qquad - 528x} \\
-22x^2 \qquad - 352 \\
\underline{-22x^2 \qquad - 352}
\end{array}
$$

$3x^3 + 2x^2 - 33x - 22 = x^2(3x + 2) - 11(3x + 2) = (3x + 2)(x^2 - 11)$

$= (3x + 2)\left(x - \sqrt{11}\right)\left(x + \sqrt{11}\right)$ are factors and the remaining zeros are $-\dfrac{2}{3}, \sqrt{11}$, and $-\sqrt{11}$.

The zeros of h are $4i, -4i, -\sqrt{11}, \sqrt{11}, -\dfrac{2}{3}$.

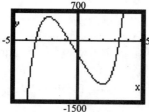

25. $f(x) = x^3 - 1 = (x-1)(x^2 + x + 1)$ The zeros of $x^2 + x + 1 = 0$ are:

$$x = \frac{-1 \pm \sqrt{1^2 - 4(1)(1)}}{2(1)} = \frac{-1 \pm \sqrt{-3}}{2} = -\frac{1}{2} + \frac{\sqrt{3}}{2}i \text{ or } -\frac{1}{2} - \frac{\sqrt{3}}{2}i$$

The zeros are: $1, -\frac{1}{2} + \frac{\sqrt{3}}{2}i, -\frac{1}{2} - \frac{\sqrt{3}}{2}i$.

Evaluating f at each zero:

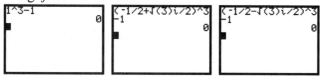

27. $f(x) = x^3 - 8x^2 + 25x - 26$

Step 1: $f(x)$ has 3 complex zeros.

Step 2: Possible rational zeros:

$$p = \pm 1, \pm 2, \pm 13, \pm 26; \quad q = \pm 1; \quad \frac{p}{q} = \pm 1, \pm 2, \pm 13, \pm 26$$

Step 3: Using synthetic division:

$$\begin{array}{r|rrrr} 2) & 1 & -8 & 25 & -26 \\ & & 2 & -12 & 26 \\ \hline & 1 & -6 & 13 & 0 \end{array}$$

Since the remainder is 0, $x - 2$ is a factor. The other factor is the
quotient: $x^2 - 6x + 13$.

Using the quadratic formula to find the zeros of $x^2 - 6x + 13 = 0$:

$$x = \frac{-(-6) \pm \sqrt{(-6)^2 - 4(1)(13)}}{2(1)} = \frac{6 \pm \sqrt{-16}}{2} = \frac{6 \pm 4i}{2} = 3 \pm 2i.$$

The complex zeros are $2, 3 - 2i, 3 + 2i$.

Evaluating f at each zero:

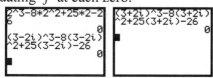

29. $f(x) = x^4 + 5x^2 + 4 = (x^2 + 4)(x^2 + 1) = (x + 2i)(x - 2i)(x + i)(x - i)$

The zeros are: $-2i, -i, i, 2i$.

Evaluating f at each zero:

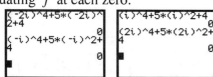

31. $f(x) = x^4 + 2x^3 + 22x^2 + 50x - 75$

     Step 1: $f(x)$ has 4 complex zeros.

     Step 2:   Possible rational zeros:
$$p = \pm 1, \pm 3, \pm 5, \pm 15, \pm 25, \pm 75; \quad q = \pm 1;$$
$$\frac{p}{q} = \pm 1, \pm 3, \pm 5, \pm 15, \pm 25, \pm 75$$

     Step 3:   Using synthetic division:

$$-3\overline{)\begin{array}{rrrrr} 1 & 2 & 22 & 50 & -75 \\ & -3 & 3 & -75 & 75 \\ \hline 1 & -1 & 25 & -25 & 0 \end{array}}$$

     Since the remainder is 0, $x + 3$ is a factor. The other factor is the quotient:
$$x^3 - x^2 + 25x - 25 = x^2(x - 1) + 25(x - 1) = (x - 1)\left(x^2 + 25\right)$$
$$= (x - 1)(x + 5i)(x - 5i)$$

     The complex zeros are $-3, \ 1, \ -5i, \ 5i$.

     Evaluating f at each zero:

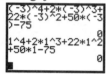 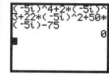 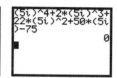

33. $f(x) = 3x^4 - x^3 - 9x^2 + 159x - 52$

     Step 1: $f(x)$ has 4 complex zeros.

     Step 2:   Possible rational zeros:
$$p = \pm 1, \pm 2, \pm 4, \pm 13, \pm 26, \pm 52; \quad q = \pm 1, \pm 3;$$
$$\frac{p}{q} = \pm 1, \pm 2, \pm 4, \pm 13, \pm 26, \pm 52, \pm \frac{1}{3}, \pm \frac{2}{3}, \pm \frac{4}{3}, \pm \frac{13}{3}, \pm \frac{26}{3}, \pm \frac{52}{3}$$

     Step 3:   Using synthetic division:

$$-4\overline{)\begin{array}{rrrrr} 3 & -1 & -9 & 159 & -52 \\ & -12 & 52 & -172 & 52 \\ \hline 3 & -13 & 43 & -13 & 0 \end{array}} \qquad \frac{1}{3}\overline{)\begin{array}{rrrr} 3 & -13 & 43 & -13 \\ & 1 & -4 & 13 \\ \hline 3 & -12 & 39 & 0 \end{array}}$$

     Since the remainder is 0, $x + 4$ and $x - \dfrac{1}{3}$ are factors. The other factor is the

     quotient: $3x^2 - 12x + 39 = 3\left(x^2 - 4x + 13\right)$.

     Using the quadratic formula to find the zeros of $x^2 - 4x + 13 = 0$:
$$x = \frac{-(-4) \pm \sqrt{(-4)^2 - 4(1)(13)}}{2(1)} = \frac{4 \pm \sqrt{-36}}{2} = \frac{4 \pm 6i}{2} = 2 \pm 3i.$$

     The complex zeros are $-4, \ \dfrac{1}{3}, \ 2 - 3i, \ 2 + 3i$.

     Evaluating f at each zero:

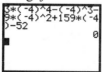 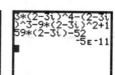 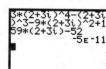

35. If the coefficients are real numbers and $2 + i$ is a zero, then $2 - i$ would also be a zero. This would then require a polynomial of degree 4.

37. Since complex zeros appear in conjugate pairs, if the remaining zero were a complex number, its conjugate would also be a zero, which would mean that the fourth degree polynomial has five zeros. But this is impossible. Therefore, the remaining zero must be a real number.

Polynomial and Rational Functions

5.R Chapter Review

1. $f(x) = 4x^5 - 3x^2 + 5x - 2$ is a polynomial function of degree 5.

3. $f(x) = 3x^2 + 5x^{1/2} - 1$ is not a polynomial function because there is a fractional exponent on the variable.

5. $f(x) = (x+2)^3$
   Using the graph of $y = x^3$, shift the graph horizontally, 2 units to the left.

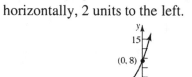

7. $f(x) = -(x-1)^4$
   Using the graph of $y = x^4$, shift the graph horizontally, 1 unit right, and reflect about the x-axis.

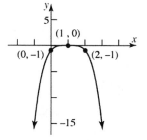

9. $f(x) = (x-1)^4 + 2$
   Using the graph of $y = x^4$, shift the graph horizontally, 1 unit to the right, and shift vertically 2 units up.

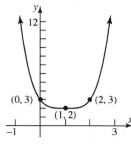

11. $f(x) = x(x+2)(x+4)$

(a)   Degree = 3; The function resembles $y = x^3$ for large values of $|x|$.

(b)   x-intercepts: –4, –2, 0;   y-intercept: 0   (c)   crosses x axis at x = –4, –2, 0

(d)   Graph of f is above the x-axis for $(-4,-2) \cup (0,\infty)$
        Graph of f is below the x-axis for $(-\infty,-4) \cup (-2,0)$

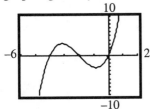

(e)   graphing utility

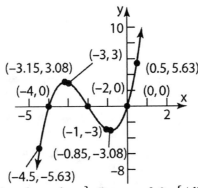

(f)   2 turning points; local maximum: (–3.15, 3.08)
        local minimum: (–0.85, –3.08)

(g)   graphing by hand

(h)   Domain of f: {All real numbers}; Range of f: {All real numbers}.

(i) f is increasing on $(-\infty,-3.15) \cup (-0.85,\infty)$; f is decreasing on $(-3.15,-0.85)$

13. $f(x) = (x-2)^2(x+4)$

(a)   Degree = 3; The function resembles $y = x^3$ for large values of $|x|$.

(b)   x-intercepts: –4, 2;   y-intercept: 16

(c)   crosses x axis at x = –4 and touches the x axis at x = 2

(d)   Graph of f is above the x-axis for $(-4,2) \cup (2,\infty)$;
        Graph of f is below the x-axis for $(-\infty,-4)$

(e)   graphing utility

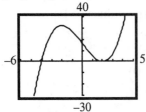

(f)   2 turning points; local maximum: (–2, 32)
      local minimum: (2, 0)

(g)   graphing by hand

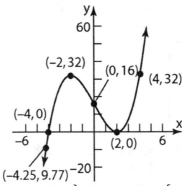

(h)   Domain of f: {All real numbers}; Range of f: {All real numbers}.

(i) f is increasing on $(-\infty,-2)\cup(2,\infty)$; f is decreasing on $(-2,2)$

15. $f(x)=x^3-4x^2=x^2(x-4)$

(a)   Degree = 3; The function resembles $y=x^3$ for large values of $|x|$.

(b)   x-intercepts: 0, 4;   y-intercept: 0

(c)   crosses x axis at x = 4 and touches the x axis at x = 0

(d)   Graph of f is above the x-axis for $(4,\infty)$;
      Graph of f is below the x-axis for $(-\infty,0)\cup(0,4)$

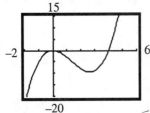

(e)   graphing utility

(f)   2 turning points; local maximum: (0, 0)
      local minimum: (2.67, –9.48)

(g)   graphing by hand

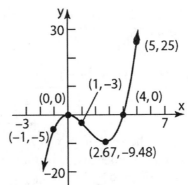

(h)   Domain of f: {All real numbers}; Range of f: {All real numbers}.

(i) f is increasing on $(-\infty,0)\cup(2.67,\infty)$; f is decreasing on $(0,2.67)$

17. $f(x)=(x-1)^2(x+3)(x+1)$

(a)   Degree = 4; The function resembles $y = x^4$ for large values of $|x|$.

(b)   x-intercepts: −3, −1, 1;   y-intercept: 3

(c)   crosses x axis at x = −3, −1 and touches x-axis at x = 1

(d)   Graph of f is above the x-axis for $(-\infty,-3)\cup(-1,1)\cup(1,\infty)$

Graph of f is below the x-axis for $(-3,-1)$

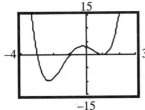

(e)   graphing utility

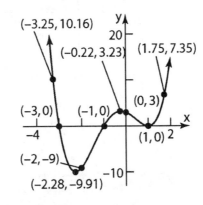

(f)   3 turning points; local maximum: (−0.22, 3.23)
local minima: (−2.28, −9.91), (1,0)

(g)   graphing by hand

(h)   Domain of f: $\{$All real numbers$\}$; Range of f: $\{y | y \geq -9.91\}$.

(i) f is increasing on $(-2.28, -0.22) \cup (1, \infty)$;

  f is decreasing on $(-\infty, -2.28) \cup (-0.22, 1)$

19. $R(x) = \dfrac{2x - 6}{x}$ $p(x) = 2x - 6$; $q(x) = x$; $n = 1$; $m = 1$

Step 1:   Domain: $\{x | x \neq 0\}$

Step 2: R is in lowest terms.

Step 3:   (a)   The x-intercept is the zero of $p(x)$: 3

  (b)   There is no y-intercept because 0 is not in the domain.

Step 4: $R(-x) = \dfrac{2(-x) - 6}{-x} = \dfrac{-2x - 6}{-x} = \dfrac{2x + 6}{x}$; this is neither $R(x)$ nor $-R(x)$, so there

  is no symmetry.

Step 5:   The vertical asymptote is the zero of $q(x)$: $x = 0$

Step 6:   Since $n = m$, the line $y = 2$ is the horizontal asymptote.

  $R(x)$ does not intersect $y = 2$.

Step 7:

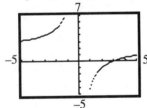

Step 8:   Graphing utility:

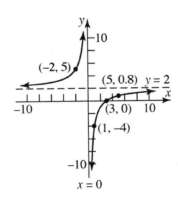

  f is increasing on $(-\infty, 0) \cup (0, \infty)$;

Step 9:   Graphing by hand

21. $H(x) = \dfrac{x+2}{x(x-2)}$ $p(x) = x+2;\; q(x) = x(x-2) = x^2 - 2x;\; n = 1;\; m = 2$

Step 1:   Domain: $\{x \mid x \neq 0,\, x \neq 2\}$

Step 2: H is in lowest terms.

Step 3:   (a)   The x-intercept is the zero of $p(x)$: -2

         (b)   There is no y-intercept because 0 is not in the domain.

Step 4: $H(-x) = \dfrac{-x+2}{-x(-x-2)} = \dfrac{-x+2}{x^2+2x}$; this is neither $H(x)$ nor $-H(x)$, so there is no

        symmetry.

Step 5:   The vertical asymptotes are the zeros of $q(x)$: $x = 0$ and $x = 2$

Step 6:   Since $n < m$, the line $y = 0$ is the horizontal asymptote.

        $R(x)$ intersects $y = 0$ at $(-2, 0)$.

Step 7:

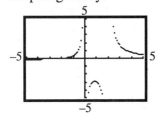

Step 8:   Graphing utility:

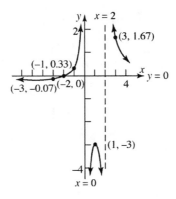

        Using MAXIMUM and MINIMUM:
        f is increasing on $(-\infty, 0) \cup (0, 0.823)$;
        f is decreasing on $(0.823, 2) \cup (2, \infty)$

Step 9:   Graphing by hand:

23. $R(x) = \dfrac{x^2+x-6}{x^2-x-6} = \dfrac{(x+3)(x-2)}{(x-3)(x+2)}$ $p(x) = x^2+x-6;\; q(x) = x^2-x-6;$

$$n = 2;\; m = 2$$

Step 1:   Domain: $\{x \mid x \neq -2,\, x \neq 3\}$

Step 2: R is in lowest terms.

Step 3: (a) The x-intercepts are the zeros of $p(x)$: -3 and 2

(b) The y-intercept is $R(0) = \dfrac{0^2 + 0 - 6}{0^2 - 0 - 6} = \dfrac{-6}{-6} = 1$.

Step 4: $R(-x) = \dfrac{(-x)^2 + (-x) - 6}{(-x)^2 - (-x) - 6} = \dfrac{x^2 - x - 6}{x^2 + x - 6}$; this is neither $R(x)$ nor $-R(x)$, so there is no symmetry.

Step 5: The vertical asymptotes are the zeros of $q(x)$: $x = -2$ and $x = 3$

Step 6: Since $n = m$, the line $y = 1$ is the horizontal asymptote.

$R(x)$ intersects $y = 1$ at $(0, 1)$, since:

$$\frac{x^2 + x - 6}{x^2 - x - 6} = 1 \Rightarrow x^2 + x - 6 = x^2 - x - 6$$

$$2x = 0 \Rightarrow x = 0$$

Step 7:

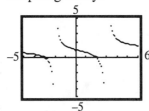

Step 8: Graphing utility:

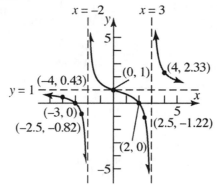

f is decreasing on $(-\infty, -2) \cup (-2, 3) \cup (3, \infty)$

Step 9: Graphing by hand:

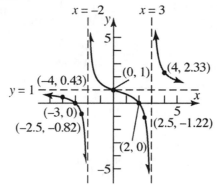

25. $F(x) = \dfrac{x^3}{x^2 - 4}$ $p(x) = x^3$; $q(x) = x^2 - 4$; $n = 3$; $m = 2$

Step 1: Domain: $\{x \mid x \neq -2,\ x \neq 2\}$

Step 2: F is in lowest terms.

Step 3: (a) The x-intercept is the zero of $p(x)$: 0.

(b) The y-intercept is $F(0) = \dfrac{0^3}{0^2 - 4} = \dfrac{0}{-4} = 0$.

Step 4: $F(-x) = \dfrac{(-x)^3}{(-x)^2 - 4} = \dfrac{-x^3}{x^2 - 4} = -F(x)$; $F(x)$ is symmetric to the origin.

Step 5:   The vertical asymptotes are the zeros of $q(x)$: $x = -2$ and $x = 2$

Step 6:   Since $n = m + 1$, there is an oblique asymptote. Dividing:

$$\begin{array}{r} x \\ x^2 - 4 \overline{\smash{\big)}\, x^3 + 0x^2 + 0x + 0} \\ \underline{x^3 \qquad\quad -4x} \\ 4x \end{array} \qquad F(x) = x + \dfrac{4x}{x^2 - 4}$$

The oblique asymptote is $y = x$.

Solve to find intersection points:

$$\dfrac{x^3}{x^2 - 4} = x \Rightarrow x^3 = x^3 - 4x \Rightarrow 0 = -4x \Rightarrow x = 0$$

The oblique asymptote intersects $F(x)$ at $(0, 0)$.

Step 7:

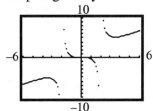

Step 8:   Graphing utility:

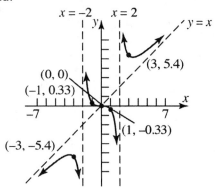

Using MAXIMUM and MINIMUM:

f is increasing on $(-\infty, -3.46) \cup (3.46, \infty)$;

f is decreasing on $(-3.46, -2) \cup (-2, 2) \cup (2, 3.46)$

Step 9:   Graphing by hand:

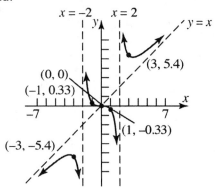

27. $R(x) = \dfrac{2x^4}{(x-1)^2}$ $p(x) = 2x^4$; $q(x) = (x-1)^2$; $n = 4$; $m = 2$

Step 1:   Domain: $\{x \mid x \neq 1\}$

Step 2: R is in lowest terms.

Step 3:   (a)   The x-intercept is the zero of $p(x)$: 0

(b)   The y-intercept is $R(0) = \dfrac{2(0)^4}{(0-1)^2} = \dfrac{0}{1} = 0.$

Step 4: $R(-x) = \dfrac{2(-x)^4}{(-x-1)^2} = \dfrac{2x^4}{(x+1)^2}$; this is neither $R(x)$ nor $-R(x)$, so there is no symmetry.

Step 5:   The vertical asymptote is the zero of $q(x)$: $x = 1$

Step 6:   Since $n > m+1$, there is no horizontal asymptote and no oblique asymptote.

Step 7:

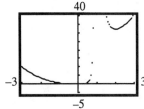

Step 8:   Graphing utility:

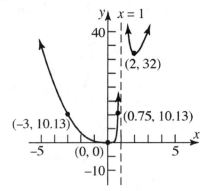

Using MAXIMUM and MINIMUM:
f is increasing on $(0,1) \cup (2,\infty)$;
f is decreasing on $(-\infty,0) \cup (1,2)$

Step 9: Graphing by hand:

29. $G(x) = \dfrac{x^2-4}{x^2-x-2}$ $p(x) = x^2 - 4$; $q(x) = x^2 - x - 2$;

$n = 2$; $m = 2$

Step 1:   Domain: $\{x \mid x \neq -1, x \neq 2\}$

Step 2:   Write G in lowest terms: $G(x) = \dfrac{x^2 - 4}{x^2 - x - 2} = \dfrac{(x+2)(x-2)}{(x-2)(x+1)} = \dfrac{x+2}{x+1}$

Step 3:   (a)   The x-intercept is the zero of $p(x)$: -2 ; 2 is not a zero because reduced
form must be used to find the zeros.

(b)   The y-intercept is $G(0) = \dfrac{0^2 - 4}{0^2 - 0 - 2} = \dfrac{-4}{-2} = 2$.

Step 4: $G(-x) = \dfrac{(-x)^2 - 4}{(-x)^2 - (-x) - 2} = \dfrac{x^2 - 4}{x^2 + x - 2}$; this is neither $G(x)$ nor $-G(x)$, so there
is no symmetry.

Step 5:   The vertical asymptote is the zero of $q(x)$: $x = -1$; $x = 2$ is not a vertical
asymptote
because reduced form must be used to find the them.

The graph has a hole at $\left(2, \dfrac{4}{3}\right)$.

Step 6:   Since $n = m$, the line $y = 1$ is the horizontal asymptote.

$G(x)$ does not intersect $y = 1$ because $G(x)$ is not defined at $x = 2$.

$\dfrac{x^2 - 4}{x^2 - x - 2} = 1 \Rightarrow x^2 - 4 = x^2 - x - 2 \Rightarrow -2 = -x \Rightarrow x = 2$

Step 7:

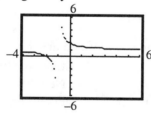

Step 8:   Graphing utility:

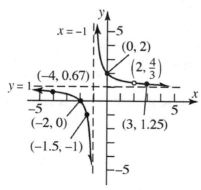

f is decreasing on $(-\infty, -1) \cup (1, 2) \cup (2, \infty)$

Step 9:   Graphing by hand:

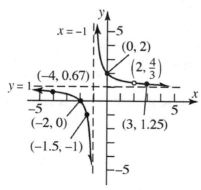

289

31. $x^3 - x^2 - 2x \le 0$ $f(x) = x^3 - x^2 - 2x$

$x^3 - x^2 - 2x = x(x^2 - x - 2) = x(x-2)(x+1) \le 0$

$x = -1, x = 0, x = 2$ are the zeros.

Interval	Test Number	$f(x)$	Positive/Negative
$-\infty < x < -1$	-2	-8	Negative
$-1 < x < 0$	-0.5	0.625	Positive
$0 < x < 2$	1	-2	Negative
$2 < x < \infty$	3	12	Positive

The solution set is $\left\{ x \mid x \le -1 \text{ or } 0 \le x \le 2 \right\}$; $(-\infty, -1] \cup [0, 2]$.

33. $x^4 - 5x^2 + 4 > 0$ $f(x) = x^4 - 5x^2 + 4$

$x^4 - 5x^2 + 4 = (x^2 - 4)(x^2 - 1) = (x-2)(x+2)(x-1)(x+1) > 0$

$x = -2, x = -1, x = 1, x = 2$ are the zeros.

Interval	Test Number	$f(x)$	Positive/Negative
$-\infty < x < -2$	-3	40	Positive
$-2 < x < -1$	-1.5	-2.1875	Negative
$-1 < x < 1$	0	4	Positive
$1 < x < 2$	1.5	-2.1875	Negative
$2 < x < \infty$	3	40	Positive

The solution set is $\left\{ x \mid x < -3 \text{ or } -1 < x < 1 \text{ or } x > 2 \right\}$; $(-\infty, -3) \cup (-1, 1) \cup (2, \infty)$.

35. $\dfrac{6}{x+3} \ge 1$ $f(x) = \dfrac{6}{x+3} - 1$

$\dfrac{6}{x+3} - 1 \ge 0 \Rightarrow \dfrac{6 - 1(x+3)}{x+3} \ge 0 \Rightarrow \dfrac{-x+3}{x+3} \ge 0$

The zeros and values where the expression is undefined are $x = -3$, and $x = 3$.

Interval	Test Number	$f(x)$	Positive/Negative
$-\infty < x < -3$	-4	-7	Negative
$-3 < x < 3$	0	1	Positive
$3 < x < \infty$	4	$-1/7$	Negative

The solution set is $\left\{ x \mid -3 < x \le 3 \right\}$; $(-3, 3]$.

37. $\dfrac{2x-6}{1-x} < 2$ $f(x) = \dfrac{2x-6}{1-x} - 2$

$\dfrac{2x-6}{1-x} - 2 < 0 \Rightarrow \dfrac{2x - 6 - 2(1-x)}{1-x} < 0 \Rightarrow \dfrac{4x-8}{1-x} < 0$

The zeros and values where the expression is undefined are $x = 1$, and $x = 2$.

Interval	Test Number	$f(x)$	Positive/Negative
$-\infty < x < 1$	0	-8	Negative
$1 < x < 2$	1.5	4	Positive
$2 < x < \infty$	3	-2	Negative

The solution set is $\left\{ x \mid x < 1 \text{ or } x > 2 \right\}$; $(-\infty, 1) \cup (2, \infty)$.

39. $\dfrac{(x-2)(x-1)}{x-3} > 0$ $\qquad$ $f(x) = \dfrac{(x-2)(x-1)}{x-3}$

The zeros and values where the expression is undefined are $x = 1$, $x = 2$, and $x = 3$.

Interval	Test Number	$f(x)$	Positive/Negative
$-\infty < x < 1$	0	$-2/3$	Negative
$1 < x < 2$	1.5	$1/6$	Positive
$2 < x < 3$	2.5	$-3/2$	Negative
$3 < x < \infty$	4	6	Positive

The solution set is $\{x \mid 1 < x < 2 \ \text{or} \ x > 3\}$; $(1,2) \cup (3,\infty)$.

41. $\dfrac{x^2 - 8x + 12}{x^2 - 16} > 0$ $\qquad$ $f(x) = \dfrac{x^2 - 8x + 12}{x^2 - 16}$

$\dfrac{(x-2)(x-6)}{(x+4)(x-4)} > 0$

The zeros and values where the expression is undefined are

$x = -4$, $x = 2$, $x = 4$, and $x = 6$.

Interval	Test Number	$f(x)$	Positive/Negative
$-\infty < x < -4$	-5	$77/9$	Positive
$-4 < x < 2$	0	$-3/4$	Negative
$2 < x < 4$	3	$3/7$	Positive
$4 < x < 6$	5	$-1/3$	Negative
$6 < x < \infty$	7	$5/33$	Positive

The solution set is $\{x \mid x < -4 \ \text{or} \ 2 < x < 4 \ \text{or} \ x > 6\}$; $(-\infty,-4) \cup (2,4) \cup (6,\infty)$.

43. Use synthetic division: $\qquad$ Quotient: $8x^2 + 5x + 6$ $\qquad$ Remainder: $10 \neq 0$

$$1 \overline{)\ 8 \quad -3 \quad 1 \quad 4}$$
$$\underline{\quad\quad 8 \quad 5 \quad 6}$$
$$\quad\ 8 \quad 5 \quad 6 \quad 10$$

Therefore, g is not a factor of f.

45. Use synthetic division: $\qquad$ Quotient: $x^3 - 4x^2 + 8x - 1$ $\qquad$ Remainder: 0

$$-2 \overline{)\ 1 \quad -2 \quad 0 \quad 15 \quad -2}$$
$$\underline{\quad\quad -2 \quad 8 \quad -16 \quad 2}$$
$$\quad\ 1 \quad -4 \quad 8 \quad -1 \quad 0$$

Therefore, g is a factor of f.

47. $f(x) = 2x^8 - x^7 + 8x^4 - 2x^3 + x + 3$

Step 1: $f(x)$ has at most 8 real zeros.

Step 2: Possible rational zeros:

p must be a factor of 3: $p = \pm 1, \pm 3$

q must be a factor of 2: $q = \pm 1, \pm 2$

The possible rational zeros are: $\dfrac{p}{q} = \pm 1, \pm \dfrac{1}{2}, \pm 3, \pm \dfrac{3}{2}$

49. $f(x) = x^3 - 3x^2 - 6x + 8$

Step 1: $f(x)$ has at most 3 real zeros.

Step 2:   Possible rational zeros:

$$p = \pm 1, \pm 2, \pm 4, \pm 8; \quad q = \pm 1; \quad \frac{p}{q} = \pm 1, \pm 2, \pm 4, \pm 8$$

Step 3:   Using the Bounds on Zeros Theorem:

$$a_2 = -3, \quad a_1 = -6, \quad a_0 = 8$$

$$\text{Max}\left\{1, |8| + |-6| + |-3|\right\} = \text{Max}\left\{1, 17\right\} = 17$$

$$1 + \text{Max}\left\{|8|, |-6|, |-3|\right\} = 1 + 8 = 9$$

The smaller of the two numbers is 9. Thus, every zero of f lies between –9 and 9.

Graphing using the bounds and ZOOM-FIT: (Second graph has a better window.)

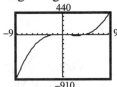 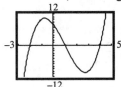

Step 4:   (a)   From the graph it appears that there are x-intercepts at –2, 1, and 4.

(b)   Using synthetic division:

$$-2)\overline{\begin{array}{cccc} 1 & -3 & -6 & 8 \\ & -2 & 10 & -8 \\ \hline 1 & -5 & 4 & 0 \end{array}}$$

Since the remainder is 0, $x - (-2) = x + 2$ is a factor. The other factor is the quotient: $x^2 - 5x + 4$.

(c)   Thus, $f(x) = (x + 2)(x^2 - 5x + 4) = (x + 2)(x - 1)(x - 4)$.

The zeros are –2, 1, and 4.

51. $f(x) = 4x^3 + 4x^2 - 7x + 2$

Step 1: $f(x)$ has at most 3 real zeros.

Step 2:   Possible rational zeros:

$$p = \pm 1, \pm 2; \quad q = \pm 1, \pm 2, \pm 4; \quad \frac{p}{q} = \pm 1, \pm 2, \pm \frac{1}{2}, \pm \frac{1}{4}$$

Step 3:   Using the Bounds on Zeros Theorem:

$$f(x) = 4\left(x^3 + x^2 - 1.75x + 0.5\right)$$

$$a_2 = 1, \quad a_1 = -1.75, \quad a_0 = 0.5$$

$$\text{Max}\left\{1, |0.5| + |-1.75| + |1|\right\} = \text{Max}\left\{1, 3.25\right\} = 3.25$$

$$1 + \text{Max}\left\{|0.5|, |-1.75|, |1|\right\} = 1 + 1.75 = 2.75$$

The smaller of the two numbers is 2.75. Thus, every zero of f lies between –2.75 and 2.75.

Graphing using the bounds and ZOOM-FIT: (Second graph has a better window.)

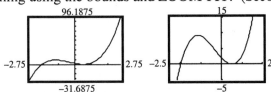

Step 4: (a) From the graph it appears that there are x-intercepts at –2 and 1/2.
    (b) Using synthetic division:

$$-2\overline{)\begin{array}{cccc} 4 & 4 & -7 & 2 \\ & -8 & 8 & -2 \end{array}}$$
$$\begin{array}{cccc} 4 & -4 & 1 & 0 \end{array}$$

    Since the remainder is 0, $x-(-2) = x+2$ is a factor. The other factor is the quotient: $4x^2 - 4x + 1$.
    (c) Thus, $f(x) = (x+2)(4x^2 - 4x + 1) = (x+2)(2x-1)^2$.
    The zeros are –2 and 1/2 (multiplicity 2).

53. $f(x) = x^4 - 4x^3 + 9x^2 - 20x + 20$
    Step 1: $f(x)$ has at most 4 real zeros.
    Step 2: Possible rational zeros:
    $p = \pm 1, \pm 2, \pm 4, \pm 5, \pm 10, \pm 20; \quad q = \pm 1;$

    $\dfrac{p}{q} = \pm 1, \pm 2, \pm 4, \pm 5, \pm 10, \pm 20$

    Step 3: Using the Bounds on Zeros Theorem:
    $a_3 = -4, \ a_2 = 9, \ a_1 = -20, \ a_0 = 20$
    $\text{Max}\left\{1, |20| + |-20| + |9| + |-4|\right\} = \text{Max}\left\{1, 53\right\} = 53$
    $1 + \text{Max}\left\{|20|, |-20|, |9|, |-4|\right\} = 1 + 20 = 21$

    The smaller of the two numbers is 21. Thus, every zero of f lies between –21 and 21.

    Graphing using the bounds and ZOOM-FIT: (Second graph has a better window.)

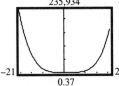
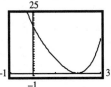

Step 4: (a) From the graph it appears that there is an x-intercept at 2.
    (b) Using synthetic division:

$$2\overline{)\begin{array}{ccccc} 1 & -4 & 9 & -20 & 20 \\ & 2 & -4 & 10 & -20 \end{array}}$$
$$\begin{array}{ccccc} 1 & -2 & 5 & -10 & 0 \end{array}$$

$$2\overline{)\begin{array}{cccc} 1 & -2 & 5 & -10 \\ & 2 & 0 & 10 \end{array}}$$
$$\begin{array}{cccc} 1 & 0 & 5 & 0 \end{array}$$

    Since the remainder is 0, $x - 2$ is a factor twice. The other factor is the quotient: $x^2 + 5$.
    (c) Thus, $f(x) = (x-2)(x-2)(x^2+5) = (x-2)^2(x^2+5)$.
    The zero is 2 (multiplicity 2). ($x^2 + 5 = 0$ has no real solutions.)

55. $f(x) = 2x^3 - 11.84x^2 - 9.116x + 82.46$
      $f(x)$ has at most 3 real zeros.
      Solving by graphing (using ZERO):

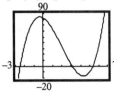

The zeros are approximately –2.5, 3.1, and 5.32.

57. $g(x) = 15x^4 - 21.5x^3 - 1718.3x^2 + 5308x + 3796.8$
      $g(x)$ has at most 4 real zeros. Solving by graphing (using ZERO):

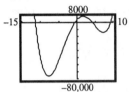

The zeros are approximately –11.3, –0.6, 4, and 9.33.

59. $2x^4 + 2x^3 - 11x^2 + x - 6 = 0$
      The solutions of the equation are the zeros of $f(x) = 2x^4 + 2x^3 - 11x^2 + x - 6$.
      Step 1: $f(x)$ has at most 4 real zeros.
      Step 2:   Possible rational zeros:

$$p = \pm 1, \pm 2, \pm 3, \pm 6; \quad q = \pm 1, \pm 2; \quad \frac{p}{q} = \pm 1, \pm 2, \pm 3, \pm 6, \pm \frac{1}{2}, \pm \frac{3}{2}$$

      Step 3:   Using the Bounds on Zeros Theorem:

$$f(x) = 2\left(x^4 + x^3 - 5.5x^2 + 0.5x - 3\right)$$
$$a_3 = 1, \ a_2 = -5.5, \ a_1 = 0.5, \ a_0 = -3$$
$$\text{Max}\left\{1, |-3| + |0.5| + |-5.5| + |1|\right\} = \text{Max}\left\{1, 10\right\} = 10$$
$$1 + \text{Max}\left\{|-3|, |0.5|, |-5.5|, |1|\right\} = 1 + 5.5 = 6.5$$

The smaller of the two numbers is 6.5. Thus, every zero of f lies
between –6.5 and 6.5.
Graphing using the bounds and ZOOM-FIT: (Second graph has a better window.)

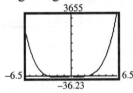 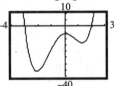

      Step 4:   (a)   From the graph it appears that there are x-intercepts at –3 and 2.
                (b)   Using synthetic division:

```
-3)2    2   -11    1   -6          2)2   -4    1   -2
        -6   12   -3    6               4    0    2
     ─────────────────────          ──────────────────
     2   -4    1   -2    0          2    0    1    0
```

Since the remainder is 0, $x + 3$ and $x - 2$ are factors. The other factor is the
quotient: $2x^2 + 1$.
                (c)   The zeros are –3 and 2. ($2x^2 + 1 = 0$ has no real solutions.)

61. $2x^4 + 7x^3 + x^2 - 7x - 3 = 0$

The solutions of the equation are the zeros of $f(x) = 2x^4 + 7x^3 + x^2 - 7x - 3$.

Step 1: $f(x)$ has at most 4 real zeros.

Step 2: Possible rational zeros:

$$p = \pm 1, \pm 3; \quad q = \pm 1, \pm 2; \quad \frac{p}{q} = \pm 1, \pm 3, \pm \frac{1}{2}, \pm \frac{3}{2}$$

Step 3: Using the Bounds on Zeros Theorem:

$$f(x) = 2\left(x^4 + 3.5x^3 + 0.5x^2 - 3.5x - 1.5\right)$$

$$a_3 = 3.5, \ a_2 = 0.5, \ a_1 = -3.5, \ a_0 = -1.5$$

$$\text{Max}\left\{1, |-1.5| + |-3.5| + |0.5| + |3.5|\right\} = \text{Max}\left\{1, 9\right\} = 9$$

$$1 + \text{Max}\left\{|-1.5|, |-3.5|, |0.5|, |3.5|\right\} = 1 + 3.5 = 4.5$$

The smaller of the two numbers is 4.5. Thus, every zero of f lies between –4.5 and 4.5.

Graphing using the bounds and ZOOM-FIT: (Second graph has a better window.)

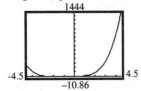 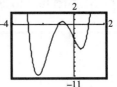

Step 4: (a)   From the graph it appears that there are x-intercepts at –3, –1, –1/2, and 1.

(b)   Using synthetic division:

$$\begin{array}{r} -3\overline{)2 \quad 7 \quad 1 \quad -7 \quad -3} \\ \underline{-6 \quad -3 \quad 6 \quad 3} \\ 2 \quad 1 \quad -2 \quad -1 \quad 0 \end{array} \qquad \begin{array}{r} -1\overline{)2 \quad 1 \quad -2 \quad -1} \\ \underline{-2 \quad 1 \quad 1} \\ 2 \quad -1 \quad -1 \quad 0 \end{array}$$

Since the remainder is 0, $x + 3$ and $x + 1$ are factors. The other factor is the quotient: $2x^2 - x - 1$.

(c)   Thus, $f(x) = (x + 3)(x + 1)\left(2x^2 - x - 1\right) = (x + 3)(x + 1)(2x + 1)(x - 1)$.

The zeros are –3, –1, –1/2, and 1.

63. $f(x) = x^3 - x^2 - 4x + 2$

$a_2 = -1, \ a_1 = -4, \ a_0 = 2$

$\text{Max}\left\{1, |2| + |-4| + |-1|\right\} = \text{Max}\left\{1, 7\right\} = 7$

$1 + \text{Max}\left\{|2|, |-4|, |-1|\right\} = 1 + 4 = 5$

The smaller of the two numbers is 5. Thus, every zero of f lies between –5 and 5.

Graphing using the bounds and ZOOM-FIT: (Second graph has a better window.)

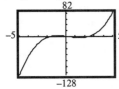 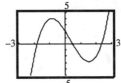

65. $f(x) = 2x^3 - 7x^2 - 10x + 35 = 2(x^3 - 3.5x^2 - 5x + 17.5)$

$a_2 = -3.5, \quad a_1 = -5, \quad a_0 = 17.5$

$\text{Max}\{1, |17.5| + |-5| + |-3.5|\} = \text{Max}\{1, 26\} = 26$

$1 + \text{Max}\{|17.5|, |-5|, |-3.5|\} = 1 + 17.5 = 18.5$

The smaller of the two numbers is 37/2. Thus, every zero of f lies between –37/2 and 37/2.

Graphing using the bounds and ZOOM-FIT: (Second graph has a better window.)

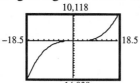

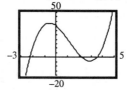

67.   Using the TABLE feature to show that there is a zero in the interval:

$f(x) = 3x^3 - x - 1; \quad [0, 1]$

X	Y1
-2	-23
-1	-3
0	-1
1	1
2	21
3	77
4	187

Y1■3X^3–X–1

$f(0) = -1 < 0$ and $f(1) = 1 > 0$

Since one is positive and one is negative, there is a zero in the interval.

Using the TABLE feature to approximate the zero to two decimal places:

X	Y1
.82	-.1659
.83	-.1146
.84	-.0619
.85	-.0076
.86	.04817
.87	.10551
.88	.16442

Y1■3X^3–X–1

The zero is approximately 0.85.

69.   Using the TABLE feature to show that there is a zero in the interval:

$f(x) = 8x^4 - 4x^3 - 2x - 1; \quad [0, 1]$

X	Y1
-2	163
-1	13
0	-1
1	1
2	91
3	533
4	1783

Y1■8X^4–4X^3–2X…

$f(0) = -1 < 0$ and $f(1) = 1 > 0$
Since one is positive and one is negative, there is a zero in the interval.

Using the TABLE feature to approximate the zero to two decimal places:

X	Y1
.9	-.4672
.91	-.3483
.92	-.2236
.93	-.093
.94	.04366
.95	.18655
.96	.33583

Y1■8X^4–4X^3–2X… The zero is approximately 0.94.

71. Since complex zeros appear in conjugate pairs, $4-i$, the conjugate of $4+i$, is the remaining zero of f.

$$f(x) = (x-6)(x-(4-i))(x-(4+i)) = (x-6)(x-4+i)(x-4-i)$$
$$= (x-6)((x-4)^2 - i^2) = (x-6)((x-4)^2 + 1)$$
$$= (x-6)(x^2 - 8x + 16 + 1) = (x-6)(x^2 - 8x + 17)$$
$$= x^3 - 8x^2 + 17x - 6x^2 + 48x - 102$$

$$f(x) = x^3 - 14x^2 + 65x - 102$$

73. Since complex zeros appear in conjugate pairs, $-i$, the conjugate of i, and $1-i$, the conjugate of $1+i$, are the remaining zeros of f.

$$f(x) = (x-i)(x+i)(x-(1-i))(x-(1+i)) = (x^2 - i^2)(x-1+i)(x-1-i)$$
$$= (x^2 + 1)((x-1)^2 - i^2) = (x^2 + 1)((x-1)^2 + 1)$$
$$= (x^2 + 1)(x^2 - 2x + 1 + 1) = (x^2 + 1)(x^2 - 2x + 2)$$
$$= x^4 - 2x^3 + 2x^2 + x^2 - 2x + 2$$

$$f(x) = x^4 - x^3 - 2x^3 + 3x^2 - 2x + 2$$

75. $x^4 + 2x^2 - 8 = 0$
$$(x^2 + 4)(x^2 - 2) = 0 \Rightarrow x^2 + 4 = 0 \text{ or } x^2 - 2 = 0$$
$$x^2 = -4 \text{ or } x^2 = 2 \Rightarrow x = \pm 2i \text{ or } x = \pm\sqrt{2}$$
The solution set is $\left\{ -2i, \ 2i, \ -\sqrt{2}, \ \sqrt{2} \right\}$.

77. $x^3 - x^2 - 8x + 12 = 0$
The solutions of the equation are the zeros of the function $f(x) = x^3 - x^2 - 8x + 12$.
Step 1: $f(x)$ has 3 complex zeros.
Step 2:   Possible rational zeros:
$$p = \pm 1, \pm 2, \pm 3, \pm 4, \pm 6, \pm 12; \quad q = \pm 1; \quad \frac{p}{q} = \pm 1, \pm 2, \pm 3, \pm 4, \pm 6, \pm 12$$
Step 3:   Graphing the function:

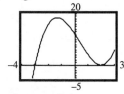

From the graph it appears that there are x-intercepts at –3 and 2.
Step 4:   Using synthetic division:

$$2\overline{)1 \quad -1 \quad -8 \quad \quad 12}$$
$$\underline{\quad \quad \quad 2 \quad \quad 2 \quad -12}$$
$$1 \quad \quad 1 \quad -6 \quad \quad 0$$

Since the remainder is 0, $x-2$ is a factor. The other factor is the quotient:
$$x^2 + x - 6 = (x+3)(x-2).$$
The complex zeros are –3, 2 (multiplicity 2).

79. $3x^4 - 4x^3 + 4x^2 - 4x + 1 = 0$

The solutions of the equation are the zeros of the function
$$f(x) = 3x^4 - 4x^3 + 4x^2 - 4x + 1$$

Step 1: $f(x)$ has 4 complex zeros.

Step 2: Possible rational zeros:
$$p = \pm 1; \quad q = \pm 1, \pm 3; \quad \frac{p}{q} = \pm 1, \pm \frac{1}{3}$$

Step 3: Graphing the function:

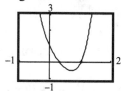

From the graph it appears that there are x-intercepts at $\frac{1}{3}$ and 1.

Step 4: Using synthetic division:

$$\begin{array}{r|rrrrr} 1 & 3 & -4 & 4 & -4 & 1 \\ & & 3 & -1 & 3 & -1 \\ \hline & 3 & -1 & 3 & -1 & 0 \end{array} \qquad \begin{array}{r|rrrr} \frac{1}{3} & 3 & -1 & 3 & -1 \\ & & 1 & 0 & 1 \\ \hline & 3 & 0 & 3 & 0 \end{array}$$

Since the remainder is 0, $x - 1$ and $x - \frac{1}{3}$ are factors. The other factor is the

quotient: $3x^2 + 3 = 3(x^2 + 1)$.

Solving $x^2 + 1 = 0$:
$$x^2 = -1 \Rightarrow x = \pm i$$

The complex zeros are $1, \frac{1}{3}, -i, i$.

81. (a) Graphing:

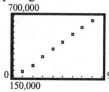

(b) $A(t) = -212.0076t^3 + 2429.1320t^2 + 59568.8539t + 130003.1429$

(c) Graphing the cubic function of best fit:

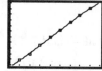

(d) In the year 2000, $t = 11$. $A(11) \approx 797{,}000$ cases.

(e) Answers will vary.

83. Answers will vary, one example is $p(x) = -5(x^2 + 1)(x + 1)^3 \left(x - \frac{3}{5}\right)$

85. (a)   The degree is even.
    (b)   The leading coefficient is positive.
    (c)   The function is even - it is symmetric to the y-axis.
    (d) x^2 is a factor because the curve touches the x-axis at the origin.
    (e)   The minimum degree is 8.
    (f)   Answers will vary, 5 possibilities are:

$$p_1(x) = x^2(x+3)(x+2)(x+1)(x-1)(x-2)(x-3)$$
$$p_2(x) = x^4(x+3)(x+2)(x+1)(x-1)(x-2)(x-3)$$
$$p_3(x) = x^6(x+3)(x+2)(x+1)(x-1)(x-2)(x-3)$$
$$p_4(x) = x^8(x+3)(x+2)(x+1)(x-1)(x-2)(x-3)$$
$$p_5(x) = x^{10}(x+3)(x+2)(x+1)(x-1)(x-2)(x-3)$$

Polynomial and Rational Functions

5.CR   Cumulative Review

1. $4x^2 + 2x = 5 \Rightarrow 4x^2 + 2x - 5 = 0$
     $a = 4, b = 2, c = -5$

$$x = \frac{-b \pm \sqrt{b^2 - 4ac}}{2a} = \frac{-2 \pm \sqrt{2^2 - 4(4)(-5)}}{2(4)} = \frac{-2 \pm \sqrt{4 + 80}}{8}$$

$$= \frac{-2 \pm \sqrt{84}}{8} = \frac{-2 \pm 2\sqrt{21}}{8} = \frac{-1 \pm \sqrt{21}}{4}$$

The solution set is $\left\{ \dfrac{-1 - \sqrt{21}}{4}, \dfrac{-1 + \sqrt{21}}{4} \right\}$.

3. $3x - 4y = 5 \Rightarrow y = \dfrac{3}{4}x - \dfrac{5}{4} \Rightarrow \text{slope} = \dfrac{3}{4}$

$4x + 3y = 10 \Rightarrow y = -\dfrac{4}{3}x + \dfrac{10}{3} \Rightarrow \text{slope} = -\dfrac{4}{3}$

Therefore, the lines are perpendicular since their slopes are negative reciprocals.

5. $g(t) = -16t^2 + 100t + 100 \Rightarrow g(4) = -16(4)^2 + 100(4) + 10 = -256 + 400 + 10 = 154$

7. $f(x) = -2(x + 3)^2 + 5$

Using the graph of $y = x^2$, shift the graph horizontally, 3 units to the left, reflect about the x-axis, stretch vertically by a factor of 2 and shift vertically 3 units up.

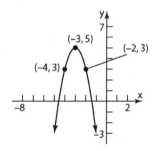

9. $f(x) = 0.2x^3 + x^2 + 1$

Use MAXIMUM and MINIMUM on the graph of $y_1 = 0.2x^3 + x^2 + 1$.

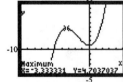   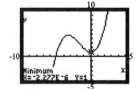

local maximum at: $(-3.33, 4.70)$;   local minimum at: $(0,1)$

f is increasing on: $(-\infty, -3.33) \cup (0, \infty)$; f is decreasing on: $(-3.33, 0)$

11. $f(x) = (x+3)(x-4)^2$

(a)   Degree = 3; The function resembles $y = x^3$ for large values of $|x|$.

(b)   x-intercepts: –3, 4;   y-intercept: 48

(c)   crosses x axis at x = –3, touches x-axis at $x = 4$

(d)   Graph of f is above the x-axis for $(-3,4) \cup (4,\infty)$

Graph of f is below the x-axis for $(-\infty,-3)$

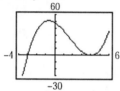

(e)   graphing utility

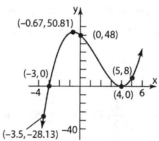

(f)   2 turning points; Local maximum: (–0.67, 50.81); Local minimum: (4, 0)

(g)   graphing by hand

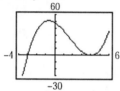

(h) f is increasing on $(-\infty,-0.67) \cup (4,\infty)$; f is decreasing on $(-0.67,4)$

(i) $f(x) = (x+3)(x-4)^2 \geq 0$

From the graph in part (h), we can see that $f(x) = (x+3)(x-4)^2 \geq 0$ when $x \geq -3$. So the solution set is $\{x | x \geq -3\}$.

Chapter 6

Exponential and Logarithmic Functions

6.1 Composite Functions

1. (a) $(f \circ g)(1) = f(g(1)) = f(0) = -1$
   (b) $(f \circ g)(-1) = f(g(-1)) = f(0) = -1$
   (c) $(g \circ f)(-1) = g(f(-1)) = g(-3) = 8$
   (d) $(g \circ f)(0) = g(f(0)) = g(-1) = 0$
   (e) $(g \circ g)(-2) = g(g(-2)) = g(3) = 8$
   (f) $(f \circ f)(-1) = f(f(-1)) = f(-3) = -7$

3. $f(x) = 2x \qquad g(x) = 3x^2 + 1$
   (a) $(f \circ g)(4) = f(g(4)) = f(3(4)^2 + 1) = f(49) = 2(49) = 98$
   (b) $(g \circ f)(2) = g(f(2)) = g(2 \cdot 2) = g(4) = 3(4)^2 + 1 = 48 + 1 = 49$
   (c) $(f \circ f)(1) = f(f(1)) = f(2(1)) = f(2) = 2(2) = 4$
   (d) $(g \circ g)(0) = g(g(0)) = g(3(0)^2 + 1) = g(1) = 3(1)^2 + 1 = 4$

5. $f(x) = 4x^2 - 3 \qquad g(x) = 3 - \frac{1}{2}x^2$
   (a) $(f \circ g)(4) = f(g(4)) = f\left(3 - \frac{1}{2}(4)^2\right) = f(-5) = 4(-5)^2 - 3 = 97$
   (b) $(g \circ f)(2) = g(f(2)) = g(4(2)^2 - 3) = g(13) = 3 - \frac{1}{2}(13)^2 = 3 - \frac{169}{2} = -\frac{163}{2}$
   (c) $(f \circ f)(1) = f(f(1)) = f(4(1)^2 - 3) = f(1) = 4(1)^2 - 3 = 1$
   (d) $(g \circ g)(0) = g(g(0)) = g\left(3 - \frac{1}{2}(0)^2\right) = g(3) = 3 - \frac{1}{2}(3)^2 = 3 - \frac{9}{2} = -\frac{3}{2}$

7. $f(x) = \sqrt{x} \qquad g(x) = 2x$
   (a) $(f \circ g)(4) = f(g(4)) = f(2(4)) = f(8) = \sqrt{8} = 2\sqrt{2}$
   (b) $(g \circ f)(2) = g(f(2)) = g(\sqrt{2}) = 2\sqrt{2}$
   (c) $(f \circ f)(1) = f(f(1)) = f(\sqrt{1}) = f(1) = \sqrt{1} = 1$
   (d) $(g \circ g)(0) = g(g(0)) = g(2(0)) = g(0) = 2(0) = 0$

9. $f(x) = |x| \qquad g(x) = \frac{1}{x^2 + 1}$
   (a) $(f \circ g)(4) = f(g(4)) = f\left(\frac{1}{4^2 + 1}\right) = f\left(\frac{1}{17}\right) = \left|\frac{1}{17}\right| = \frac{1}{17}$
   (b) $(g \circ f)(2) = g(f(2)) = g(|2|) = g(2) = \frac{1}{2^2 + 1} = \frac{1}{5}$

(c) $(f \circ f)(1) = f(f(1)) = f(|1|) = f(1) = |1| = 1$

(d) $(g \circ g)(0) = g(g(0)) = g\left(\dfrac{1}{0^2 + 1}\right) = g(1) = \dfrac{1}{1^2 + 1} = \dfrac{1}{2}$

11. $f(x) = \dfrac{3}{x+1}$ $g(x) = \sqrt[3]{x}$

(a) $(f \circ g)(4) = f(g(4)) = f\left(\sqrt[3]{4}\right) = \dfrac{3}{\sqrt[3]{4} + 1}$

(b) $(g \circ f)(2) = g(f(2)) = g\left(\dfrac{3}{2+1}\right) = g\left(\dfrac{3}{3}\right) = \sqrt[3]{1} = 1$

(c) $(f \circ f)(1) = f(f(1)) = f\left(\dfrac{3}{1+1}\right) = f\left(\dfrac{3}{2}\right) = \dfrac{3}{\left(\dfrac{3}{2}\right)+1} = \dfrac{3}{\left(\dfrac{5}{2}\right)} = \dfrac{6}{5}$

(d) $(g \circ g)(0) = g(g(0)) = g\left(\sqrt{0}\right) = g(0) = \sqrt{0} = 0$

13.   The domain of g is $\{x \,|\, x \neq 0\}$. The domain of f is $\{x \,|\, x \neq 1\}$.
Thus, $g(x) \neq 1$, so we solve:
$$g(x) = 1$$
$$\dfrac{2}{x} = 1 \qquad \text{Thus, } x \neq 2; \text{ so the domain of } f \circ g \text{ is } \{x \,|\, x \neq 0, \, x \neq 2\}.$$
$$x = 2$$

15.   The domain of g is $\{x \,|\, x \neq 0\}$. The domain of f is $\{x \,|\, x \neq 1\}$.
Thus, $g(x) \neq 1$, so we solve:
$$g(x) = 1$$
$$-\dfrac{4}{x} = 1 \qquad \text{Thus, } x \neq -4; \text{ so the domain of } f \circ g \text{ is } \{x \,|\, x \neq -4, \, x \neq 0\}.$$
$$x = -4$$

17.   The domain of g is $\{\text{Real Numbers}\}$. The domain of f is $\{x \,|\, x \geq 0\}$.
Thus, $g(x) \geq 0$, so we solve:
$$g(x) \geq 0$$
$$2x + 3 \geq 0 \qquad \text{Thus, the domain of } f \circ g \text{ is } \left\{x \,\middle|\, x \geq -\dfrac{3}{2}\right\}.$$
$$x \geq -\dfrac{3}{2}$$

19.   The domain of g is $\{x \,|\, x \geq 1\}$. The domain of f is $\{\text{Real Numbers}\}$.
Thus, the domain of $f \circ g$ is $\{x \,|\, x \geq 1\}$.

21. $f(x) = 2x + 3$ $g(x) = 3x$
The domain of f is all real numbers. The domain of g is all real numbers.

(a) $(f \circ g)(x) = f(g(x)) = f(3x) = 2(3x) + 3 = 6x + 3$
Domain: All real numbers.

(b) $(g \circ f)(x) = g(f(x)) = g(2x + 3) = 3(2x + 3) = 6x + 9$
     Domain: All real numbers.

(c) $(f \circ f)(x) = f(f(x)) = f(2x + 3) = 2(2x + 3) + 3 = 4x + 6 + 3 = 4x + 9$
     Domain: All real numbers.

(d) $(g \circ g)(x) = g(g(x)) = g(3x) = 3(3x) = 9x$ Domain: All real numbers.

23. $f(x) = 3x + 1$ $g(x) = x^2$
     The domain of f is all real numbers. The domain of g is all real numbers.

(a) $(f \circ g)(x) = f(g(x)) = f(x^2) = 3x^2 + 1$ Domain: All real numbers.

(b) $(g \circ f)(x) = g(f(x)) = g(3x + 1) = (3x + 1)^2 = 9x^2 + 6x + 1$
     Domain: All real numbers.

(c) $(f \circ f)(x) = f(f(x)) = f(3x + 1) = 3(3x + 1) + 1 = 9x + 3 + 1 = 9x + 4$
     Domain: All real numbers.

(d) $(g \circ g)(x) = g(g(x)) = g(x^2) = (x^2)^2 = x^4$ Domain: All real numbers.

25. $f(x) = x^2$ $g(x) = x^2 + 4$
     The domain of f is all real numbers. The domain of g is all real numbers.

(a) $(f \circ g)(x) = f(g(x)) = f(x^2 + 4) = (x^2 + 4)^2 = x^4 + 8x^2 + 16$
     Domain: All real numbers.

(b) $(g \circ f)(x) = g(f(x)) = g(x^2) = (x^2)^2 + 4 = x^4 + 4$ Domain: All real numbers.

(c) $(f \circ f)(x) = f(f(x)) = f(x^2) = (x^2)^2 = x^4$ Domain: All real numbers.

(d) $(g \circ g)(x) = g(g(x)) = g(x^2 + 4) = (x^2 + 4)^2 + 4 = x^4 + 8x^2 + 16 + 4$
     $= x^4 + 8x^2 + 20$ Domain: All real numbers.

27. $f(x) = \dfrac{3}{x - 1}$ $g(x) = \dfrac{2}{x}$ The domain of f is $\{x \mid x \neq 1\}$.
     The domain of g is $\{x \mid x \neq 0\}$.

(a) $(f \circ g)(x) = f(g(x)) = f\left(\dfrac{2}{x}\right) = \dfrac{3}{\left(\dfrac{2}{x} - 1\right)} = \dfrac{3}{\left(\dfrac{2 - x}{x}\right)} = \dfrac{3x}{2 - x}$
     Domain of $f \circ g$ is $\{x \mid x \neq 0, \, x \neq 2\}$.

(b) $(g \circ f)(x) = g(f(x)) = g\left(\dfrac{3}{x - 1}\right) = \dfrac{2}{\left(\dfrac{3}{x - 1}\right)} = \dfrac{2(x - 1)}{3}$
     Domain of $g \circ f$ is $\{x \mid x \neq 1\}$

(c) $(f \circ f)(x) = f(f(x)) = f\left(\dfrac{3}{x - 1}\right) = \dfrac{3}{\left(\dfrac{3}{x - 1} - 1\right)} = \dfrac{3}{\left(\dfrac{3 - (x - 1)}{x - 1}\right)} = \dfrac{3(x - 1)}{4 - x}$
     Domain of $f \circ f$ is $\{x \mid x \neq 1, \, x \neq 4\}$.

(d) $(g \circ g)(x) = g(g(x)) = g\left(\dfrac{2}{x}\right) = \dfrac{2}{\left(\dfrac{2}{x}\right)} = \dfrac{2x}{2} = x$;   Domain of $g \circ g$ is $\{x \mid x \neq 0\}$.

29. $f(x) = \dfrac{x}{x-1}$ $g(x) = -\dfrac{4}{x}$

The domain of f is $\{x \mid x \neq 1\}$. The domain of g is $\{x \mid x \neq 0\}$.

(a) $(f \circ g)(x) = f(g(x)) = f\left(-\dfrac{4}{x}\right) = \dfrac{\left(-\dfrac{4}{x}\right)}{\left(-\dfrac{4}{x}-1\right)} = \dfrac{\left(-\dfrac{4}{x}\right)}{\left(\dfrac{-4-x}{x}\right)} = \dfrac{-4}{-4-x} = \dfrac{4}{4+x}$

Domain of $f \circ g$ is $\{x \mid x \neq -4, x \neq 0\}$.

(b) $(g \circ f)(x) = g(f(x)) = g\left(\dfrac{x}{x-1}\right) = -\dfrac{4}{\left(\dfrac{x}{x-1}\right)} = \dfrac{-4(x-1)}{x}$

Domain of $g \circ f$ is $\{x \mid x \neq 0, x \neq 1\}$.

(c) $(f \circ f)(x) = f(f(x)) = f\left(\dfrac{x}{x-1}\right) = \dfrac{\left(\dfrac{x}{x-1}\right)}{\left(\dfrac{x}{x-1}-1\right)} = \dfrac{\left(\dfrac{x}{x-1}\right)}{\left(\dfrac{x-(x-1)}{x-1}\right)} = \dfrac{x}{1} = x$

Domain of $f \circ f$ is $\{x \mid x \neq 1\}$.

(d) $(g \circ g)(x) = g(g(x)) = g\left(\dfrac{-4}{x}\right) = -\dfrac{4}{\left(-\dfrac{4}{x}\right)} = \dfrac{-4x}{-4} = x$

Domain of $g \circ g$ is $\{x \mid x \neq 0\}$.

31. $f(x) = \sqrt{x}$ $g(x) = 2x + 3$

The domain of f is $\{x \mid x \geq 0\}$. The domain of g is {Real Numbers}.

(a) $(f \circ g)(x) = f(g(x)) = f(2x+3) = \sqrt{2x+3}$ Domain of $f \circ g$ is $\left\{x \mid x \geq -\dfrac{3}{2}\right\}$.

(b) $(g \circ f)(x) = g(f(x)) = g\left(\sqrt{x}\right) = 2\sqrt{x} + 3$ Domain of $g \circ f$ is $\{x \mid x \geq 0\}$.

(c) $(f \circ f)(x) = f(f(x)) = f\left(\sqrt{x}\right) = \sqrt{\sqrt{x}} = x^{1/4} = \sqrt[4]{x}$

Domain of $f \circ f$ is $\{x \mid x \geq 0\}$.

(d) $(g \circ g)(x) = g(g(x)) = g(2x+3) = 2(2x+3) + 3 = 4x + 6 + 3 = 4x + 9$

Domain of $g \circ g$ is {Real Numbers}.

33. $f(x) = x^2 + 1$ $g(x) = \sqrt{x-1}$

The domain of f is {Real Numbers}. The domain of g is $\{x \mid x \geq 1\}$.

(a) $(f \circ g)(x) = f(g(x)) = f\left(\sqrt{x-1}\right) = \left(\sqrt{x-1}\right)^2 + 1 = x - 1 + 1 = x$

Domain of $f \circ g$ is $\{x \mid x \geq 1\}$.

(b) $(g \circ f)(x) = g(f(x)) = g\left(x^2 + 1\right) = \sqrt{x^2 + 1 - 1} = \sqrt{x^2} = |x|$

Domain of $g \circ f$ {Real Numbers}.

(c) $(f \circ f)(x) = f(f(x)) = f(x^2 + 1) = (x^2 + 1)^2 + 1 = x^4 + 2x^2 + 1 + 1 = x^4 + 2x^2 + 2$
     Domain of $f \circ f$ is {Real Numbers}.

(d) $(g \circ g)(x) = g(g(x)) = g(\sqrt{x-1}) = \sqrt{\sqrt{x-1}-1}$ Domain of $g \circ g$ is $\{x \mid x \geq 2\}$.

35. $f(x) = ax + b$ $g(x) = cx + d$ The domain of f is {Real Numbers}.
           The domain of g is {Real Numbers}.

(a) $(f \circ g)(x) = f(g(x)) = f(cx + d) = a(cx + d) + b = acx + ad + b$
     Domain of $f \circ g$ is {Real Numbers}.

(b) $(g \circ f)(x) = g(f(x)) = g(ax + b) = c(ax + b) + d = acx + bc + d$
     Domain of $g \circ f$ is {Real Numbers}.

(c) $(f \circ f)(x) = f(f(x)) = f(ax + b) = a(ax + b) + b = a^2 x + ab + b$
     Domain of $f \circ f$ is {Real Numbers}.

(d) $(g \circ g)(x) = g(g(x)) = g(cx + d) = c(cx + d) + d = c^2 x + cd + d$
     Domain of $g \circ g$ is {Real Numbers}.

37. $(f \circ g)(x) = f(g(x)) = f\left(\dfrac{1}{2}x\right) = 2\left(\dfrac{1}{2}x\right) = x$

     $(g \circ f)(x) = g(f(x)) = g(2x) = \dfrac{1}{2}(2x) = x$

39. $(f \circ g)(x) = f(g(x)) = f(\sqrt[3]{x}) = (\sqrt[3]{x})^3 = x$

     $(g \circ f)(x) = g(f(x)) = g(x^3) = \sqrt[3]{x^3} = x$

41. $(f \circ g)(x) = f(g(x)) = f\left(\dfrac{1}{2}(x + 6)\right) = 2\left(\dfrac{1}{2}(x + 6)\right) - 6 = x + 6 - 6 = x$

     $(g \circ f)(x) = g(f(x)) = g(2x - 6) = \dfrac{1}{2}((2x - 6) + 6) = \dfrac{1}{2}(2x) = x$

43. $(f \circ g)(x) = f(g(x)) = f\left(\dfrac{1}{a}(x - b)\right) = a\left(\dfrac{1}{a}(x - b)\right) + b = x - b + b = x$

     $(g \circ f)(x) = g(f(x)) = g(ax + b) = \dfrac{1}{a}((ax + b) - b) = \dfrac{1}{a}(ax) = x$

45. $H(x) = (2x + 3)^4$ $f(x) = x^4, \quad g(x) = 2x + 3$

47. $H(x) = \sqrt{x^2 + 1}$ $f(x) = \sqrt{x}, \quad g(x) = x^2 + 1$

49. $H(x) = |2x + 1|$ $f(x) = |x|, \quad g(x) = 2x + 1$

51. $f(x) = 2x^3 - 3x^2 + 4x - 1$ $g(x) = 2$
     $(f \circ g)(x) = f(g(x)) = f(2) = 2(2)^3 - 3(2)^2 + 4(2) - 1 = 16 - 12 + 8 - 1 = 11$
     $(g \circ f)(x) = g(f(x)) = g(2x^3 - 3x^2 + 4x - 1) = 2$

53. $f(x) = 2x^2 + 5 \qquad g(x) = 3x + a$
$(f \circ g)(x) = f(g(x)) = f(3x + a) = 2(3x + a)^2 + 5$
When $x = 0$, $(f \circ g)(0) = 23$
Solving: $2(3 \cdot 0 + a)^2 + 5 = 23 \Rightarrow 2a^2 + 5 = 23 \Rightarrow 2a^2 = 18 \Rightarrow a^2 = 9 \Rightarrow a = -3$ or 3

55. $S(r) = 4\pi r^2 \qquad r(t) = \dfrac{2}{3} t^3,\ t \geq 0$

$S(r(t)) = S\left(\dfrac{2}{3} t^3\right) = 4\pi \left(\dfrac{2}{3} t^3\right)^2 = 4\pi \left(\dfrac{4}{9} t^6\right) = \dfrac{16}{9} \pi t^6$

57. $N(t) = 100t - 5t^2,\ 0 \leq t \leq 10 \qquad C(N) = 15000 + 8000 N$
$C(N(t)) = C\left(100t - 5t^2\right) = 15000 + 8000\left(100t - 5t^2\right)$
$\qquad\qquad = 15{,}000 + 800{,}000t - 40{,}000t^2$

59. $p = -\dfrac{1}{4} x + 100 \qquad 0 \leq x \leq 400$

$\dfrac{1}{4} x = 100 - p \Rightarrow x = 4(100 - p)$

$C = \dfrac{\sqrt{x}}{25} + 600 = \dfrac{\sqrt{4(100 - p)}}{25} + 600 = \dfrac{2\sqrt{100 - p}}{25} + 600, \quad 0 \leq p \leq 100$

61. $V = \pi r^2 h \qquad h = 2r \qquad \Rightarrow V(r) = \pi r^2 (2r) = 2\pi r^3$

63. $f(x) =$ number of Euros bought for x dollars; $g(x) =$ number of Yen bought for x Euros
(a) $f(x) = 1.136235x$
(b) $g(x) = 109.846x$
(c) $g(f(x)) = 109.846(1.136235x) \approx 124.81087x$
(d) $g(f(1000)) = 124.81087(1000) = 124810.867$ Yen

65. Given that f is odd and g is even, we know that
$f(-x) = -f(x)$ and $g(-x) = g(x)$ for all x in the domain of f and g respectively.
The composite function $f \circ g = f(g(x))$ has the following property:
$\quad f(g(-x)) = f(g(x))$ since g is even, $\therefore f \circ g$ is even
The composite function $g \circ f = g(f(x))$ has the following property:
$\quad g(f(-x)) = g(-f(x))$ since f is odd
$\quad = g(f(x))$ since g is even, $\therefore g \circ f$ is even

Exponential and Logarithmic Functions

6.2   Inverse Functions

1.   (a)
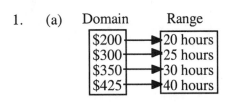

(b)   Inverse is a function.

3.   (a)
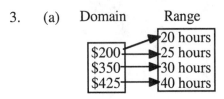

(b)   Inverse is not a function since $200 corresponds to two elements in the range.

5.   (a) $\{(6,2), (6,-3), (9,4), (10,1)\}$

(b)   Inverse is not a function since 6 corresponds to 2 and –3.

7.   (a) $\{(0,0), (1,1), (16,2), (81,3)\}$

(b)   Inverse is a function.

9.   Every horizontal line intersects the graph of f at exactly one point. One-to-One.

11.   There are horizontal lines that intersect the graph of f at more than one point. Not One-to-One.

13.   Every horizontal line intersects the graph of f at exactly one point. One-to-One.

15.   Graphing the inverse:

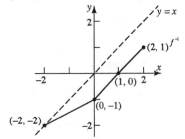

17.   Graphing the inverse:

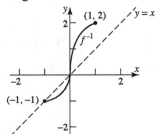

19. Graphing the inverse:

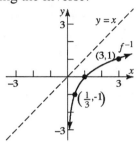

21. $f(x) = 3x + 4, \qquad g(x) = \dfrac{1}{3}(x - 4)$

$f(g(x)) = f\left(\dfrac{1}{3}(x - 4)\right) = 3\left(\dfrac{1}{3}(x - 4)\right) + 4 = (x - 4) + 4 = x$

$g(f(x)) = g(3x + 4) = \dfrac{1}{3}\big((3x + 4) - 4\big) = \dfrac{1}{3}(3x) = x$

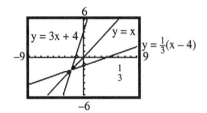

23. $f(x) = 4x - 8, \qquad g(x) = \dfrac{x}{4} + 2$

$f(g(x)) = f\left(\dfrac{x}{4} + 2\right) = 4\left(\dfrac{x}{4} + 2\right) - 8 = (x + 8) - 8 = x$

$g(f(x)) = g(4x - 8) = \dfrac{4x - 8}{4} + 2 = x - 2 + 2 = x$

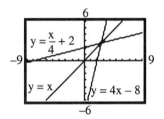

25. $f(x) = x^3 - 8, \qquad g(x) = \sqrt[3]{x + 8}$

$f(g(x)) = f\left(\sqrt[3]{x + 8}\right) = \left(\sqrt[3]{x + 8}\right)^3 - 8 = (x + 8) - 8 = x$

$g(f(x)) = g(x^3 - 8) = \sqrt[3]{(x^3 - 8) + 8} = \sqrt[3]{x^3} = x$

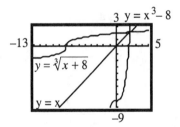

27. $f(x) = \dfrac{1}{x}, \qquad g(x) = \dfrac{1}{x}$

$f(g(x)) = f\left(\dfrac{1}{x}\right) = \dfrac{1}{(1/x)} = x$

$g(f(x)) = g\left(\dfrac{1}{x}\right) = \dfrac{1}{(1/x)} = x$

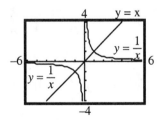

29. $f(x) = \dfrac{2x + 3}{x + 4}, \qquad g(x) = \dfrac{4x - 3}{2 - x}$

$f(g(x)) = f\left(\dfrac{4x - 3}{2 - x}\right) = \dfrac{2\left(\dfrac{4x - 3}{2 - x}\right) + 3}{\left(\dfrac{4x - 3}{2 - x}\right) + 4} = \dfrac{\left(\dfrac{8x - 6 + 6 - 3x}{2 - x}\right)}{\left(\dfrac{4x - 3 + 8 - 4x}{2 - x}\right)} = \dfrac{\left(\dfrac{5x}{2 - x}\right)}{\left(\dfrac{5}{2 - x}\right)} = \dfrac{5x}{2 - x} \cdot \dfrac{2 - x}{5} = x$

$$g(f(x)) = g\left(\frac{2x+3}{x+4}\right) = \frac{4\left(\frac{2x+3}{x+4}\right)-3}{2-\left(\frac{2x+3}{x+4}\right)} = \frac{\left(\frac{8x+12-3x-12}{x+4}\right)}{\left(\frac{2x+8-2x-3}{x+4}\right)} = \frac{\left(\frac{5x}{x+4}\right)}{\left(\frac{5}{x+4}\right)} = \frac{5x}{x+4}\cdot\frac{x+4}{5} = x$$

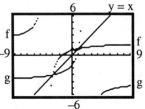

31.　$f(x) = 3x$

　　$y = 3x$

　　$x = 3y$　Inverse

　　$y = \frac{x}{3} \Rightarrow f^{-1}(x) = \frac{1}{3}x$

　　Verify: $f\left(f^{-1}(x)\right) = f\left(\frac{1}{3}x\right) = 3\left(\frac{1}{3}x\right) = x$

　　　　　$f^{-1}\left(f(x)\right) = f^{-1}(3x) = \frac{1}{3}(3x) = x$

Domain of f = range of $f^{-1} = (-\infty, \infty)$

Range of f = domain of $f^{-1} = (-\infty, \infty)$

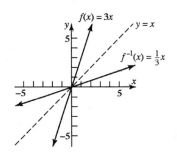

33.　$f(x) = 4x + 2$

　　$y = 4x + 2$

　　$x = 4y + 2$　Inverse

　　$4y = x - 2$

　　$y = \frac{x-2}{4}$

　　$f^{-1}(x) = \frac{x-2}{4} = \frac{x}{4} - \frac{1}{2}$

Domain of f = range of $f^{-1} = (-\infty, \infty)$

Range of f = domain of $f^{-1} = (-\infty, \infty)$

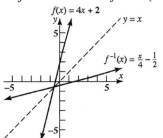

　　Verify: $f\left(f^{-1}(x)\right) = f\left(\frac{x}{4} - \frac{1}{2}\right) = 4\left(\frac{x}{4} - \frac{1}{2}\right) + 2 = x - 2 + 2 = x$

　　　　　$f^{-1}\left(f(x)\right) = f^{-1}(4x+2) = \frac{4x+2}{4} - \frac{1}{2} = \frac{x}{4} + \frac{1}{2} - \frac{1}{2} = x$

35. $f(x) = x^3 - 1$

   $y = x^3 - 1$

   $x = y^3 - 1$ Inverse

   $y^3 = x + 1$

   $y = \sqrt[3]{x+1}$

   $f^{-1}(x) = \sqrt[3]{x+1}$

Domain of f = range of $f^{-1} = (-\infty, \infty)$

Range of f = domain of $f^{-1} = (-\infty, \infty)$

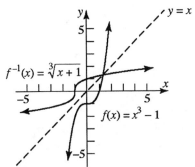

Verify: $f\left(f^{-1}(x)\right) = f\left(\sqrt[3]{x+1}\right) = \left(\sqrt[3]{x+1}\right)^3 - 1 = x + 1 - 1 = x$

   $f^{-1}(f(x)) = f^{-1}\left(x^3 - 1\right) = \sqrt[3]{\left(x^3 - 1\right) + 1} = \sqrt[3]{x^3} = x$

37. $f(x) = x^2 + 4, \ x \geq 0$

   $y = x^2 + 4 \ \ x \geq 0$

   $x = y^2 + 4 \ \ y \geq 0$ Inverse

   $y^2 = x - 4 \ \ y \geq 0$

   $y = \sqrt{x-4} \rightarrow f^{-1}(x) = \sqrt{x-4}$

Verify:

   $f\left(f^{-1}(x)\right) = f\left(\sqrt{x-4}\right) =$

   $\left(\sqrt{x-4}\right)^2 + 4 = x - 4 + 4 = x$

   $f^{-1}(f(x)) = f^{-1}\left(x^2 + 4\right) = \sqrt{\left(x^2 + 4\right) - 4}$

   $= \sqrt{x^2} = |x| = x, \ x \geq 0$

Domain of f = range of $f^{-1} = [0, \infty)$

Range of f = domain of $f^{-1} = [4, \infty)$

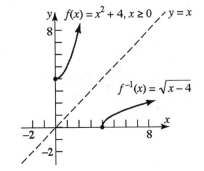

39. $f(x) = \dfrac{4}{x}$

$y = \dfrac{4}{x}$

$x = \dfrac{4}{y}$ Inverse

$xy = 4$

$y = \dfrac{4}{x}$

$f^{-1}(x) = \dfrac{4}{x}$

Domain of f = range of f^{-1}
= all real numbers except 0

Range of f = domain of f^{-1}
= all real numbers except 0

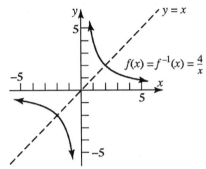

Verify: $f\left(f^{-1}(x)\right) = f\left(\dfrac{4}{x}\right) = \dfrac{4}{(4/x)} = 4 \cdot \left(\dfrac{x}{4}\right) = x$

$f^{-1}\left(f(x)\right) = f^{-1}\left(\dfrac{4}{x}\right) = \dfrac{4}{(4/x)} = 4 \cdot \left(\dfrac{x}{4}\right) = x$

41. $f(x) = \dfrac{1}{x-2}$

$y = \dfrac{1}{x-2}$

$x = \dfrac{1}{y-2}$ Inverse

$x(y-2) = 1$

$xy - 2x = 1$

$xy = 2x + 1$

$y = \dfrac{2x+1}{x}$

$f^{-1}(x) = \dfrac{2x+1}{x}$

Domain of f = range of f^{-1}
= all real numbers except 2

Range of f = domain of f^{-1}
= all real numbers except 0

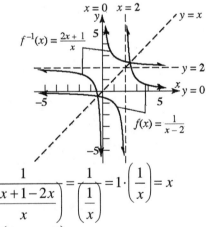

Verify: $f\left(f^{-1}(x)\right) = f\left(\dfrac{2x+1}{x}\right) = \dfrac{1}{\left(\dfrac{2x+1}{x} - 2\right)} = \dfrac{1}{\left(\dfrac{2x+1-2x}{x}\right)} = \dfrac{1}{\left(\dfrac{1}{x}\right)} = 1 \cdot \left(\dfrac{1}{x}\right) = x$

$f^{-1}\left(f(x)\right) = f^{-1}\left(\dfrac{1}{x-2}\right) = \dfrac{2\left(\dfrac{1}{x-2}\right)+1}{\left(\dfrac{1}{x-2}\right)} = \dfrac{\left(\dfrac{2+x-2}{x-2}\right)}{\left(\dfrac{1}{x-2}\right)} = \left(\dfrac{x}{x-2}\right) \cdot \left(\dfrac{x-2}{1}\right) = x$

43. $f(x) = \dfrac{2}{3+x}$

   $y = \dfrac{2}{3+x}$

   $x = \dfrac{2}{3+y}$ Inverse

   $x(3+y) = 2$

   $3x + xy = 2$

   $xy = 2 - 3x$

   $y = \dfrac{2-3x}{x}$

   $f^{-1}(x) = \dfrac{2-3x}{x}$

Domain of f =
range of f^{-1} = all real numbers except -3

Range of f =
domain of f^{-1} = all real numbers except 0

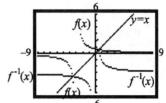

Verify: $f\left(f^{-1}(x)\right) = f\left(\dfrac{2-3x}{x}\right) = \dfrac{2}{3+\left(\dfrac{2-3x}{x}\right)} = \dfrac{2}{\left(\dfrac{3x+2-3x}{x}\right)} = \dfrac{2}{\left(\dfrac{2}{x}\right)} = 2 \cdot \left(\dfrac{x}{2}\right) = x$

$f^{-1}\left(f(x)\right) = f^{-1}\left(\dfrac{2}{3+x}\right) = \dfrac{2 - 3\left(\dfrac{2}{3+x}\right)}{\left(\dfrac{2}{3+x}\right)} = \dfrac{\left(\dfrac{6+2x-6}{3+x}\right)}{\left(\dfrac{2}{3+x}\right)} = \left(\dfrac{2x}{3+x}\right) \cdot \left(\dfrac{3+x}{2}\right) = x$

45. $f(x) = (x+2)^2, \ x \ge -2$

   $y = (x+2)^2 \quad x \ge -2$

   $x = (y+2)^2 \quad y \ge -2$ Inverse

   $\sqrt{x} = y + 2, \quad x \ge 0$

   $y = \sqrt{x} - 2, \quad x \ge 0$

   $f^{-1}(x) = \sqrt{x} - 2, \quad x \ge 0$

Domain of f = range of f^{-1} = $[-2, \infty)$
Range of f = domain of f^{-1} = $[0, \infty)$

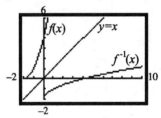

Verify: $f\left(f^{-1}(x)\right) = f\left(\sqrt{x} - 2\right) = \left(\sqrt{x} - 2 + 2\right)^2 = \left(\sqrt{x}\right)^2 = x$

   $f^{-1}\left(f(x)\right) = f^{-1}\left((x+2)^2\right) = \sqrt{(x+2)^2} - 2 = x + 2 - 2 = x, \ x \ge -2$

47. $f(x) = \dfrac{2x}{x-1}$

$y = \dfrac{2x}{x-1}$

$x = \dfrac{2y}{y-1}$ Inverse

$x(y-1) = 2y \Rightarrow xy - x = 2y$

$xy - 2y = x \Rightarrow y(x-2) = x$

$y = \dfrac{x}{x-2} \Rightarrow f^{-1}(x) = \dfrac{x}{x-2}$

Domain of f = range of f^{-1}
= all real numbers except 1
Range of f = domain of f^{-1}
= all real numbers except 2

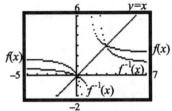

Verify: $f\big(f^{-1}(x)\big) = f\left(\dfrac{x}{x-2}\right) = \dfrac{2\left(\dfrac{x}{x-2}\right)}{\left(\dfrac{x}{x-2}\right)-1} = \dfrac{\left(\dfrac{2x}{x-2}\right)}{\left(\dfrac{x-x+2}{x-2}\right)} = \dfrac{\left(\dfrac{2x}{x-2}\right)}{\left(\dfrac{2}{x-2}\right)} = \left(\dfrac{2x}{x-2}\right)\cdot\left(\dfrac{x-2}{2}\right) = x$

$f^{-1}\big(f(x)\big) = f^{-1}\left(\dfrac{2x}{x-1}\right) = \dfrac{\left(\dfrac{2x}{x-1}\right)}{\left(\dfrac{2x}{x-1}\right)-2} = \dfrac{\left(\dfrac{2x}{x-1}\right)}{\left(\dfrac{2x-2x+2}{x-1}\right)} = \left(\dfrac{2x}{x-1}\right)\cdot\left(\dfrac{x-1}{2}\right) = x$

49. $f(x) = \dfrac{3x+4}{2x-3}$

$y = \dfrac{3x+4}{2x-3}$

$x = \dfrac{3y+4}{2y-3}$ Inverse

$x(2y-3) = 3y+4$

$2xy - 3x = 3y + 4$

$2xy - 3y = 3x + 4$

$y(2x-3) = 3x + 4$

$y = \dfrac{3x+4}{2x-3} \Rightarrow f^{-1}(x) = \dfrac{3x+4}{2x-3}$

Domain of f = range of f^{-1} = all real numbers except $\dfrac{3}{2}$

Range of f = domain of f^{-1} = all real numbers except $\dfrac{3}{2}$

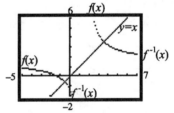

Verify:

$f\big(f^{-1}(x)\big) = f\left(\dfrac{3x+4}{2x-3}\right) = \dfrac{3\left(\dfrac{3x+4}{2x-3}\right)+4}{2\left(\dfrac{3x+4}{2x-3}\right)-3} = \dfrac{\left(\dfrac{9x+12+8x-12}{2x-3}\right)}{\left(\dfrac{6x+8-6x+9}{2x-3}\right)} = \dfrac{\left(\dfrac{17x}{2x-3}\right)}{\left(\dfrac{17}{2x-3}\right)}$

$= \dfrac{17x}{2x-3}\cdot\dfrac{2x-3}{17} = x$

$$f^{-1}(f(x)) = f^{-1}\left(\frac{3x+4}{2x-3}\right) = \frac{3\left(\dfrac{3x+4}{2x-3}\right)+4}{2\left(\dfrac{3x+4}{2x-3}\right)-3} = \frac{\left(\dfrac{9x+12+8x-12}{2x-3}\right)}{\left(\dfrac{6x+8-6x+9}{2x-3}\right)} = \frac{\left(\dfrac{17x}{2x-3}\right)}{\left(\dfrac{17}{2x-3}\right)}$$

$$= \frac{17x}{2x-3} \cdot \frac{2x-3}{17} = x$$

51. $f(x) = \dfrac{2x+3}{x+2}$

$y = \dfrac{2x+3}{x+2}$

$x = \dfrac{2y+3}{y+2}$ **Inverse**

$x(y+2) = 2y+3$

$xy + 2x = 2y + 3$

$xy - 2y = -2x + 3$

$y(x-2) = -2x + 3$

$y = \dfrac{-2x+3}{x-2}$

$f^{-1}(x) = \dfrac{-2x+3}{x-2}$

Domain of $f =$
range of f^{-1} = all real numbers except –2

Range of $f =$
domain of f^{-1} = all real numbers except 2

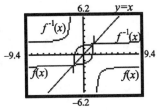

Verify:

$$f\left(f^{-1}(x)\right) = f\left(\frac{-2x+3}{x-2}\right) = \frac{2\left(\dfrac{-2x+3}{x-2}\right)+3}{\left(\dfrac{-2x+3}{x-2}\right)+2} = \frac{\left(\dfrac{-4x+6+3x-6}{x-2}\right)}{\left(\dfrac{-2x+3+2x-4}{x-2}\right)} = \frac{\left(\dfrac{-x}{x-2}\right)}{\left(\dfrac{-1}{x-2}\right)}$$

$$= \left(\frac{-x}{x-2}\right) \cdot \left(\frac{x-2}{-1}\right) = x$$

$$f^{-1}(f(x)) = f^{-1}\left(\frac{2x+3}{x+2}\right) = \frac{-2\left(\dfrac{2x+3}{x+2}\right)+3}{\left(\dfrac{2x+3}{x+2}\right)-2} = \frac{\left(\dfrac{-4x-6+3x+6}{x+2}\right)}{\left(\dfrac{2x+3-2x-4}{x+2}\right)} = \frac{\left(\dfrac{-x}{x+2}\right)}{\left(\dfrac{-1}{x+2}\right)}$$

$$= \left(\frac{-x}{x+2}\right) \cdot \left(\frac{x+2}{-1}\right) = x$$

53. $f(x) = 2\sqrt{x+1}, \quad x \geq -1$ Domain of f = range of $f^{-1} = [-1, \infty)$

$y = 2\sqrt{x+1}$

$x = 2\sqrt{y+1}$ Inverse   Range of f = domain of $f^{-1} = [0, \infty)$

$x^2 = 4(y+1) \Rightarrow \dfrac{x^2}{4} = y+1$

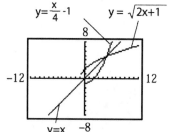

$y = \dfrac{x^2}{4} - 1$

$f^{-1}(x) = \dfrac{x^2}{4} - 1$

Verify: $f(f^{-1}(x)) = f\left(\dfrac{x^2}{4} - 1\right) = 2\sqrt{\dfrac{x^2}{4} - 1 + 1} = 2\sqrt{\dfrac{x^2}{4}} = 2\left(\dfrac{x}{2}\right) = x$

$f^{-1}(f(x)) = f^{-1}\left(2\sqrt{x+1}\right) = \dfrac{\left(2\sqrt{x+1}\right)^2}{4} - 1 = \dfrac{4(x+1)}{4} - 1 = x + 1 - 1 = x$

55. (a) $f(-1) = 0$ (b) $f(1) = 2$ (c) $f^{-1}(1) = 0$ (d) $f^{-1}(2) = 1$

57. $f(x) = mx + b, \quad m \neq 0$

$y = mx + b$

$x = my + b$ Inverse

$x - b = my$

$y = \dfrac{x-b}{m}$

$f^{-1}(x) = \dfrac{1}{m}(x - b), \quad m \neq 0$

59. f^{-1} lies in quadrant I. Whenever (a, b) is on f, then (b, a) is on f^{-1}. Since both coordinates of (a, b) are positive, both coordinates of (b, a) are positive and it is in quadrant I.

61. $f(x) = |x|, x \geq 0$ is one-to-one. Thus, $f(x) = x, x \geq 0$ and $f^{-1}(x) = x, x \geq 0$.

63. (a) $H(C) = 2.15C - 10.53$ 65. $p(x) = 300 - 50x, \quad x \geq 0$

$H = 2.15C - 10.53$ $p = 300 - 50x$

$H + 10.53 = 2.15C$ $50x = 300 - p$

$\dfrac{H + 10.53}{2.15} = C \Rightarrow C(H) = \dfrac{H + 10.53}{2.15}$ $x = \dfrac{300 - p}{50}$

(b) $C(26) = \dfrac{26 + 10.53}{2.15} \approx 16.99$ inches $x(p) = \dfrac{300 - p}{50}, \quad p \leq 300$

67. $f(x) = \dfrac{ax + b}{cx + d}$

(a)   domain of f is all real numbers except $-\dfrac{d}{c}$.

(b) $y = \dfrac{ax + b}{cx + d}$

$x = \dfrac{ay + b}{cy + d}$ Inverse

$x(cy + d) = ay + b \Rightarrow cxy + dx = ay + b \Rightarrow cxy - ay = b - dx$

$y(cx - a) = b - dx \Rightarrow y = \dfrac{b - dx}{cx - a} \Rightarrow f^{-1}(x) = \dfrac{-dx + b}{cx - a}$

Therefore, $f = f^{-1}$ if $\dfrac{ax + b}{cx + d} = \dfrac{-dx + b}{cx - a}$, this is true if $a = -d$.

69. Answers will vary.

71. The only way the function $y = f(x)$ can be both even and one-to-one is if the domain of $y = f(x)$ is $\{x | x = 0\}$. Otherwise, its graph will fail the Horizontal Line Test.

73. If the graph of a function and its inverse intersect, they must intersect at a point on the line $y = x$. However, the graphs do not have to intersect.

Exponential and Logarithmic Functions

6.3   Exponential Functions

1.   (a) $3^{2.2} \approx 11.212$ (b) $3^{2.23} \approx 11.587$ (c) $3^{2.236} \approx 11.664$ (d) $3^{\sqrt{5}} \approx 11.665$

3.   (a) $2^{3.14} \approx 8.815$ (b) $2^{3.141} \approx 8.821$ (c) $2^{3.1415} \approx 8.824$ (d) $2^{\pi} \approx 8.825$

5.   (a) $3.1^{2.7} \approx 21.217$ (b) $3.14^{2.71} \approx 22.217$
     (c) $3.141^{2.718} \approx 22.440$ (d) $\pi^{e} \approx 22.459$

7. $e^{1.2} \approx 3.320$ 9. $e^{-0.85} \approx 0.427$

11.

x	$y = f(x)$	$\dfrac{f(x+1)}{f(x)}$
-1	3	$\dfrac{6}{3} = 2$
0	6	$\dfrac{12}{6} = 2$
1	12	$\dfrac{18}{12} = \dfrac{3}{2}$
2	18	
3	30	

Not an exponential function since the ratio of consecutive terms is not constant.

13.

x	$y = f(x)$	$\dfrac{f(x+1)}{f(x)}$
-1	$\dfrac{1}{4}$	$\dfrac{1}{(1/4)} = 4$
0	1	$\dfrac{4}{1} = 4$
1	4	$\dfrac{16}{4} = 4$
2	16	$\dfrac{64}{16} = 4$
3	64	

Yes, an exponential function since the ratio of consecutive terms is constant with $a = 4$. So $f(x) = a^x = 4^x$.

15.

x	$y = f(x)$	$\dfrac{f(x+1)}{f(x)}$
-1	$\dfrac{3}{2}$	$\dfrac{3}{(3/2)} = 2$
0	3	$\dfrac{6}{3} = 2$
1	6	$\dfrac{12}{6} = 2$
2	12	$\dfrac{24}{12} = 2$
3	24	

Yes, an exponential function since the ratio of consecutive terms is constant with $a = 2$. So $f(x) = a^x = 2^x$.

17.

x	$y = f(x)$	$\dfrac{f(x+1)}{f(x)}$
-1	2	$\dfrac{4}{2} = 2$
0	4	$\dfrac{6}{4} = \dfrac{3}{2}$
1	6	
2	8	
3	10	

Not an exponential function since the ratio of consecutive terms is not constant.

19. B   21. D   23. A   25. E

27. $f(x) = 2^x + 1$
   Using the graph of $y = 2^x$, shift the graph up 1 unit.
   Domain: $(-\infty, \infty)$
   Range: $(1, \infty)$
   Horizontal Asymptote: $y = 1$

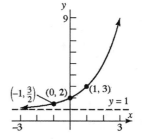

29. $f(x) = 3^{-x} - 2$
   Using the graph of $y = 3^x$, reflect the graph about the y-axis, and shift down 2 units.
   Domain: $(-\infty, \infty)$
   Range: $(-2, \infty)$
   Horizontal Asymptote: $y = -2$

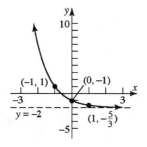

31. $f(x) = 3(4^x)$

Using the graph of $y = 4^x$, stretch the graph vertically by a factor of 3.
Domain: $(-\infty, \infty)$
Range: $(0, \infty)$
Horizontal Asymptote: $y = 0$

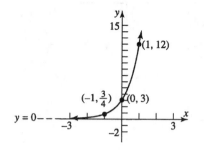

33. $f(x) = 3^{x/2}$

Using the graph of $y = 3^x$, stretch the graph horizontally by a factor of 2.
Domain: $(-\infty, \infty)$
Range: $(0, \infty)$
Horizontal Asymptote: $y = 0$

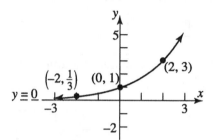
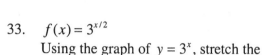

35. $f(x) = 5 - 2(3^{(x+1)}) = -2(3^{(x+1)}) + 5$

Using the graph of $y = 3^x$, shift the graph one unit to the left, stretch vertically by a factor of 2, reflect on the x-axis, and shift up 5 units.
Domain: $(-\infty, \infty)$
Range: $(-\infty, 5)$
Horizontal Asymptote: $y = 5$

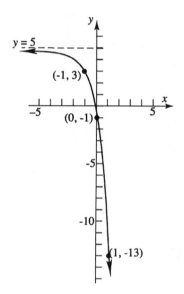

37. $f(x) = e^{-x}$

Using the graph of $y = e^x$, reflect the graph about the y-axis.
Domain: $(-\infty, \infty)$
Range: $(0, \infty)$
Horizontal Asymptote: $y = 0$

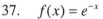
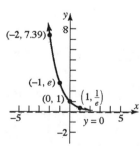

39. $f(x) = e^{x+2}$
Using the graph of $y = e^x$, shift the graph
2 units to the left.
Domain: $(-\infty, \infty)$
Range: $(0, \infty)$
Horizontal Asymptote: $y = 0$

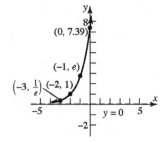

41. $f(x) = 5 + e^{-x} = e^{-x} + 5$
Using the graph of $y = e^x$, reflect the
graph about the y-axis and shift up 5
units.
Domain: $(-\infty, \infty)$
Range: $(5, \infty)$
Horizontal Asymptote: $y = 5$

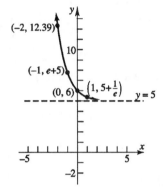

43. $f(x) = 2 - e^{x/2} = -e^{x/2} + 2$
Using the graph of $y = e^x$, stretch
horizontally by a factor of 2, reflect about
the x-axis, and shift up 2 units.
Domain: $(-\infty, \infty)$
Range: $(-\infty, 2)$
Horizontal Asymptote: $y = 2$

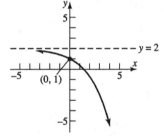

45. We need a function of the form $f(x) = k \cdot a^{p \cdot x}$, with $a > 0, a \neq 1$.

The graph contains the points $\left(-1, \dfrac{1}{3}\right)$, $(0,1)$, $(1,3)$ and $(2,9)$.

In other words, $f(-1) = \dfrac{1}{3}, f(0) = 1, f(1) = 3$ and $f(2) = 9$.

Therefore, $f(0) = k \cdot a^{p \cdot (0)} = k \cdot a^0 = k \cdot 1 = k \Rightarrow k = 1$.

and $f(1) = a^{p \cdot (1)} = a^p \Rightarrow a^p = 3$.

Let's choose $a = 3, p = 1$. Then $f(x) = 3^x$.

Now we need to verify that this function yields the other known points on the graph.

$$f(-1) = 3^{-1} = \frac{1}{3}; \qquad f(2) = 3^2 = 9$$

So we have the function $f(x) = 3^x$.

47. We need a function of the form $f(x) = k \cdot a^{p \cdot x}$, with $a > 0, a \neq 1$.

The graph contains the points $\left(-1, \frac{1}{2}\right)$, $(0,2)$, $(1,8)$ and $(2,32)$.

In other words, $f(-1) = \frac{1}{2}, f(0) = 2, f(1) = 8$ and $f(2) = 32$.

Therefore, $f(0) = k \cdot a^{p \cdot (0)} = k \cdot a^0 = k \cdot 1 = k \Rightarrow k = 2$.

and $f(1) = 2a^{p \cdot (1)} = 2a^p \Rightarrow 2a^p = 8 \Rightarrow a^p = 4$.

Let's choose $a = 4, p = 1$. Then $f(x) = 2 \cdot 4^x$.

Now we need to verify that this function yields the other known points on the graph.

$$f(-1) = 2 \cdot 4^{-1} = 2 \cdot \frac{1}{4} = \frac{1}{2}; \quad f(2) = 2 \cdot 4^2 = 2 \cdot 16 = 32$$

So we have the function $f(x) = 2 \cdot 4^x$.

49. We need a function of the form $f(x) = k \cdot a^{p \cdot x}$, with $a > 0, a \neq 1$.

The graph contains the points $\left(-1, -\frac{1}{6}\right)$, $(0,-1)$, $(1,-6)$ and $(2,-36)$.

In other words, $f(-1) = -\frac{1}{6}, f(0) = -1, f(1) = -6$ and $f(2) = -36$.

Therefore, $f(0) = k \cdot a^{p \cdot (0)} = k \cdot a^0 = k \cdot 1 = k \Rightarrow k = -1$.

and $f(1) = -a^{p \cdot (1)} = -a^p \Rightarrow -a^p = -6 \Rightarrow a^p = 6$.

Let's choose $a = 6, p = 1$. Then $f(x) = -6^x$.

Now we need to verify that this function yields the other known points on the graph.

$$f(-1) = -6^{-1} = -\frac{1}{6}; \quad f(2) = -6^2 = -36$$

So we have the function $f(x) = -6^x$.

51. $2^{2x+1} = 4$
$2^{2x+1} = 2^2$

$2x + 1 = 2 \Rightarrow 2x = 1 \Rightarrow x = \frac{1}{2}$

The solution set is $\left\{\frac{1}{2}\right\}$.

53. $3^{x^3} = 9^x$
$3^{x^3} = \left(3^2\right)^x \Rightarrow 3^{x^3} = 3^{2x}$

$x^3 = 2x \Rightarrow x^3 - 2x = 0 \Rightarrow x(x^2 - 2) = 0$

$x = 0$ or $x^2 = 2$

$x = 0$ or $x = \pm\sqrt{2}$

The solution set is $\left\{-\sqrt{2}, \ 0, \ \sqrt{2}\right\}$.

55. $8^{x^2-2x} = \frac{1}{2}$

$\left(2^3\right)^{x^2-2x} = 2^{-1} \Rightarrow 2^{3x^2-6x} = 2^{-1} \Rightarrow 3x^2 - 6x = -1 \Rightarrow 3x^2 - 6x + 1 = 0$

$$x = \frac{-(-6) \pm \sqrt{(-6)^2 - 4(3)(1)}}{2(3)} = \frac{6 \pm \sqrt{24}}{6} = \frac{6 \pm 2\sqrt{6}}{6} = \frac{3 \pm \sqrt{6}}{3}$$

The solution set is $\left\{1 - \frac{\sqrt{6}}{3}, \ 1 + \frac{\sqrt{6}}{3}\right\}$.

57. $2^x \cdot 8^{-x} = 4^x$

$2^x \cdot \left(2^3\right)^{-x} = \left(2^2\right)^x$

$2^x \cdot 2^{-3x} = 2^{2x}$

$2^{-2x} = 2^{2x}$

$-2x = 2x \Rightarrow -4x = 0 \Rightarrow x = 0$

The solution set is $\{0\}$.

59. $\left(\dfrac{1}{5}\right)^{2-x} = 25$

$\left(5^{-1}\right)^{2-x} = 5^2$

$5^{x-2} = 5^2$

$x - 2 = 2 \Rightarrow x = 4$

The solution set is $\{4\}$.

61. $4^x = 8$

$\left(2^2\right)^x = 2^3$

$2^{2x} = 2^3 \Rightarrow 2x = 3 \Rightarrow x = \dfrac{3}{2}$

The solution set is $\left\{\dfrac{3}{2}\right\}$.

63. $e^{x^2} = e^{3x} \cdot \dfrac{1}{e^2}$

$e^{x^2} = e^{3x-2} \Rightarrow x^2 = 3x - 2$

$x^2 - 3x + 2 = 0$

$(x-1)(x-2) = 0 \Rightarrow x = 1 \text{ or } x = 2$

The solution set is $\{1, 2\}$.

65. $4^x = 7$

$\left(4^x\right)^{-2} = 7^{-2} \Rightarrow 4^{-2x} = \dfrac{1}{7^2} = \dfrac{1}{49}$

67. $3^{-x} = 2$

$(3^{-x})^{-2} = 2^{-2} \Rightarrow 3^{2x} = \dfrac{1}{2^2} = \dfrac{1}{4}$

69. $p(n) = 100(0.97)^n$

(a) $p(10) = 100(0.97)^{10} \approx 100(0.7374) \approx 74\% \text{ of light}$

(b) $p(25) = 100(0.97)^{25} \approx 100(0.4670) = 46.70\% \text{ of light}$

71. $p(x) = 16,630(0.90)^x$

(a) $p(3) = 16,630(0.90)^3 \approx 16,630(0.729) \approx \$12,123$

(b) $p(9) = 16,630(0.90)^9 \approx 16,630(0.387) = \$6442.80$

73. $D(h) = 5e^{-0.4h}$

$D(1) = 5e^{-0.4(1)} = 5e^{-0.4} \approx 5(0.670) = 3.35 \text{ milligrams}$

$D(6) = 5e^{-0.4(6)} = 5e^{-2.4} \approx 5(0.091) = 0.45 \text{ milligrams}$

75. $F(t) = 1 - e^{-0.1t}$

(a) $F(10) = 1 - e^{-0.1(10)} = 1 - e^{-1} \approx 1 - 0.368 = 0.632 = 63.2\%$

(b) $F(40) = 1 - e^{-0.1(40)} = 1 - e^{-4} \approx 1 - 0.018 = 0.982 = 98.2\%$

(c)   as $t \to +\infty$, $F(t) = 1 - e^{-0.1t} \to 1 - 0 = 1$

(d)   Graphing the function:

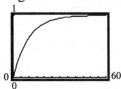

77. $P(x) = \dfrac{20^x e^{-20}}{x!}$

(a) $P(15) = \dfrac{20^{15} e^{-20}}{15!} \approx 0.052 = 5.2\%$ The probability that 15 cars will arrive between 5:00 p.m. and 6:00 p.m. is 5.2%.

(b) $P(20) = \dfrac{20^{20} e^{-20}}{20!} \approx 0.0888 = 8.88\%$ The probability that 20 cars will arrive between 5:00 p.m. and 6:00 p.m. is 8.88%.

79. $R = 10^{\left(\frac{4221}{T+459.4} - \frac{4221}{D+459.4} + 2\right)}$

(a) $R = 10^{\left(\frac{4221}{50+459.4} - \frac{4221}{41+459.4} + 2\right)} \approx 10^{1.851} \approx 70.95\%$

(b) $R = 10^{\left(\frac{4221}{68+459.4} - \frac{4221}{59+459.4} + 2\right)} \approx 10^{1.861} \approx 72.62\%$

(c) $R = 10^{\left(\frac{2345}{x} - \frac{2345}{x} + 2\right)} = 10^2 = 100\%$

81. $I = \dfrac{E}{R}\left[1 - e^{-\left(\frac{R}{L}\right)t}\right]$

(a) $I = \dfrac{120}{10}\left[1 - e^{-\left(\frac{10}{5}\right)0.3}\right] = 12\left[1 - e^{-0.6}\right] \approx 5.414$ amperes after 0.3 second

   $I = \dfrac{120}{10}\left[1 - e^{-\left(\frac{10}{5}\right)0.5}\right] = 12\left[1 - e^{-1}\right] \approx 7.585$ amperes after 0.5 second

   $I = \dfrac{120}{10}\left[1 - e^{-\left(\frac{10}{5}\right)1}\right] = 12\left[1 - e^{-2}\right] \approx 10.376$ amperes after 1 second

(b)   As $t \to \infty$, $e^{-\left(\frac{10}{5}\right)t} \to 0$. Therefore, the maximum current is 12 amperes.

(c), (f) Graphing the function:

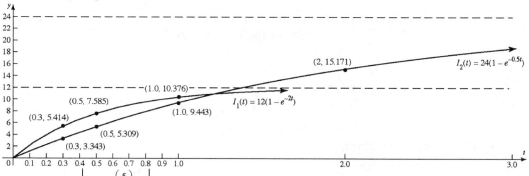

(d) $I = \dfrac{120}{5}\left[1 - e^{-\left(\frac{5}{10}\right)0.3}\right] = 24\left[1 - e^{-0.15}\right] \approx 3.343$ amperes after 0.3 second

   $I = \dfrac{120}{5}\left[1 - e^{-\left(\frac{5}{10}\right)0.5}\right] = 24\left[1 - e^{-0.25}\right] \approx 5.309$ amperes after 0.5 second

$$I = \frac{120}{5}\left[1 - e^{-\left(\frac{5}{10}\right)1}\right] = 24\left[1 - e^{-0.5}\right] \approx 9.443 \text{ amperes after 1 second}$$

(e)   As $t \to \infty$, $e^{-\left(\frac{5}{10}\right)t} \to 0$. Therefore, the maximum current is 24 amperes.

83. $2 + \dfrac{1}{2!} + \dfrac{1}{3!} + \dfrac{1}{4!} + \ldots + \dfrac{1}{n!}$

$n = 4$; $2 + \dfrac{1}{2!} + \dfrac{1}{3!} + \dfrac{1}{4!} \approx 2.7083$

$n = 6$; $2 + \dfrac{1}{2!} + \dfrac{1}{3!} + \dfrac{1}{4!} + \dfrac{1}{5!} + \dfrac{1}{6!} \approx 2.7181$

$n = 8$; $2 + \dfrac{1}{2!} + \dfrac{1}{3!} + \dfrac{1}{4!} + \dfrac{1}{5!} + \dfrac{1}{6!} + \dfrac{1}{7!} + \dfrac{1}{8!} \approx 2.7182788$

$n = 10$; $2 + \dfrac{1}{2!} + \dfrac{1}{3!} + \dfrac{1}{4!} + \dfrac{1}{5!} + \dfrac{1}{6!} + \dfrac{1}{7!} + \dfrac{1}{8!} + \dfrac{1}{9!} + \dfrac{1}{10!} \approx 2.7182818$

$e \approx 2.718281828$

85. $f(x) = a^x$

$\dfrac{f(x+h) - f(x)}{h} = \dfrac{a^{x+h} - a^x}{h} = \dfrac{a^x a^h - a^x}{h} = \dfrac{a^x\left(a^h - 1\right)}{h} = a^x\left(\dfrac{a^h - 1}{h}\right)$

87. $f(x) = a^x$

$f(-x) = a^{-x} = \dfrac{1}{a^x} = \dfrac{1}{f(x)}$

89. $\sinh x = \dfrac{1}{2}\left(e^x - e^{-x}\right)$

(a) $f(-x) = \sinh(-x) = \dfrac{1}{2}\left(e^{-x} - e^x\right) = -\dfrac{1}{2}\left(e^x - e^{-x}\right) = -\sinh x = -f(x)$

Therefore, $f(x) = \sinh x$ is an odd function.

(b)   Graphing:

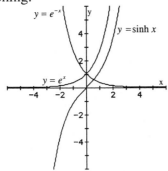

91. $f(x) = 2^{(2^x)} + 1$

$f(1) = 2^{(2^1)} + 1 = 2^2 + 1 = 4 + 1 = 5$

$f(2) = 2^{(2^2)} + 1 = 2^4 + 1 = 16 + 1 = 17$

$f(3) = 2^{(2^3)} + 1 = 2^8 + 1 = 256 + 1 = 257$

$f(4) = 2^{(2^4)} + 1 = 2^{16} + 1 = 65536 + 1 = 65537$

$f(5) = 2^{(2^5)} + 1 = 2^{32} + 1 = 4,294,967,296 + 1 = 4,294,967,297$

$4,294,967,297 = 641 \times 6,700,417$

93. Answers will vary.

95. Given the function $f(x) = a^x$, with $a > 1$,
   - if $x > 0$, the graph becomes steeper as a increases.
   - if $x < 0$, the graph becomes less steep as a increases.

Chapter 6

Exponential and Logarithmic Functions

6.4　Logarithmic Functions

1.　$9 = 3^2$ is equivalent to $2 = \log_3 9$

3.　$a^2 = 1.6$ is equivalent to $2 = \log_a 1.6$

5.　$1.1^2 = M$ is equivalent to $2 = \log_{1.1} M$

7.　$2^x = 7.2$ is equivalent to $x = \log_2 7.2$

9.　$x^{\sqrt{2}} = \pi$ is equivalent to $\sqrt{2} = \log_x \pi$

11.　$e^x = 8$ is equivalent to $x = \ln 8$

13.　$\log_2 8 = 3$ is equivalent to $2^3 = 8$

15.　$\log_a 3 = 6$ is equivalent to $a^6 = 3$

17.　$\log_3 2 = x$ is equivalent to $3^x = 2$

19.　$\log_2 M = 1.3$ is equivalent to $2^{1.3} = M$

21.　$\log_{\sqrt{2}} \pi = x$ is equivalent to $\left(\sqrt{2}\right)^x = \pi$

23.　$\ln 4 = x$ is equivalent to $e^x = 4$

25.　$\log_2 1 = 0$ since $2^0 = 1$

27.　$\log_5 25 = 2$ since $5^2 = 25$

29.　$\log_{\frac{1}{2}} 16 = -4$ since $\left(\dfrac{1}{2}\right)^{-4} = 2^4 = 16$

31.　$\log_{10} \sqrt{10} = \dfrac{1}{2}$ since $10^{1/2} = \sqrt{10}$

33.　$\log_{\sqrt{2}} 4 = 4$ since $\left(\sqrt{2}\right)^4 = 4$

35.　$\ln \sqrt{e} = \dfrac{1}{2}$ since $e^{1/2} = \sqrt{e}$

37.　The domain of $f(x) = \ln(x - 3)$ is:
$$x - 3 > 0 \Rightarrow x > 3$$
$$\{x \mid x > 3\}$$

39.　The domain of $F(x) = \log_2 x^2$ is:
$$x^2 > 0$$
$$\{x \mid x \neq 0\}$$

41.　The domain of $h(x) = \log_{\frac{1}{2}}\left(x^2 - 2x + 1\right)$ is:
$$x^2 - 2x + 1 > 0 \Rightarrow (x - 1)^2 > 0$$
$$\{x \mid x \neq 1\}$$

43.　The domain of $f(x) = \ln\left(\dfrac{1}{x+1}\right)$ is:
$$\dfrac{1}{x+1} > 0 \Rightarrow x + 1 > 0$$
$$x > -1$$
$$\{x \mid x > -1\}$$

45.   The domain of $g(x) = \log_5\left(\dfrac{x+1}{x}\right)$ requires that $\dfrac{x+1}{x} > 0$.

The expression is zero or undefined when $x = -1$ or $x = 0$.

Interval	Test Number	$f(x) = \dfrac{x+1}{x}$	Positive/Negative
$-\infty < x < -1$	-2	0.5	Positive
$-1 < x < 0$	-0.5	-1	Negative
$0 < x < \infty$	1	2	Positive

The domain is $\{x \mid x < -1 \text{ or } x > 0\}$

47. $\ln\left(\dfrac{5}{3}\right) \approx 0.511$

49. $\dfrac{\ln(10/3)}{0.04} \approx 30.099$

51.   For $f(x) = \log_a x$, find a so that $f(2) = \log_a 2 = 2$ or $a^2 = 2$ or $a = \sqrt{2}$.
(The base a must be positive by definition.)

53.   B   55.   D   57.   A   59.   E

61. $f(x) = \ln(x+4)$
Using the graph of $y = \ln x$, shift the
graph 4 units to the left.
Domain: $(-4, \infty)$
Range: $(-\infty, \infty)$
Vertical Asymptote: $x = -4$

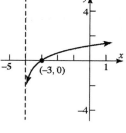

63. $f(x) = 2 + \ln(x) = \ln(x) + 2$
Using the graph of $y = \ln x$, shift up 2
units.
Domain: $(0, \infty)$
Range: $(-\infty, \infty)$
Vertical Asymptote: $x = 0$

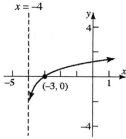

65. $g(x) = \ln(2x)$
Using the graph of $y = \ln x$, compress the
graph horizontally by a factor of $\dfrac{1}{2}$.
Domain: $(0, \infty)$
Range: $(-\infty, \infty)$
Vertical Asymptote: $x = 0$

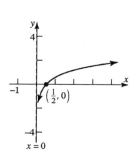

67. $f(x) = 3\ln x$
Using the graph of $y = \ln x$, stretch the
graph vertically by a factor of 3.
Domain: $(0, \infty)$
Range: $(-\infty, \infty)$
Vertical Asymptote: $x = 0$

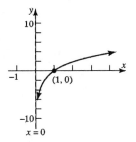

69. $g(x) = \ln(3 - x) = \ln(-(x - 3))$
Using the graph of $y = \ln x$, reflect the
graph about the y-axis, and shift 3 units to
the right.
Domain: $(-\infty, 3)$
Range: $(-\infty, \infty)$
Vertical Asymptote: $x = 3$

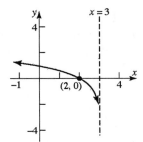

71. $f(x) = -\ln(x - 1)$
Using the graph of $y = \ln x$, shift the
graph 1 unit to the right, and reflect about
the x-axis.
Domain: $(1, \infty)$
Range: $(-\infty, \infty)$
Vertical Asymptote: $x = 1$

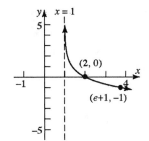

73. $f(x) = \log(x - 4)$
Using the graph of $y = \log x$, shift 4 units
to the right.
Domain: $(4, \infty)$
Range: $(-\infty, \infty)$
Vertical Asymptote: $x = 4$

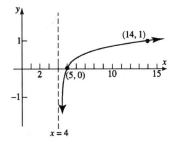

75. $h(x) = 4\log x$
Using the graph of $y = \log x$, stretch the
graph vertically by a factor of 4.
Domain: $(0, \infty)$
Range: $(-\infty, \infty)$
Vertical Asymptote: $x = 0$

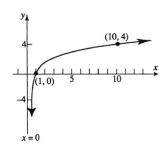

77. $f(x) = \log(2x)$
Using the graph of $y = \log x$, compress
the graph horizontally by a factor of $\dfrac{1}{2}$.
Domain: $(0, \infty)$
Range: $(-\infty, \infty)$
Vertical Asymptote: $x = 0$

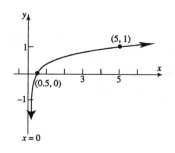

79. $f(x) = 2\log(x + 3)$
Using the graph of $y = \log x$, shift 3 units
to the left and stretch vertically by a
factor of 2.
Domain: $(-3, \infty)$
Range: $(-\infty, \infty)$
Vertical Asymptote: $x = -3$

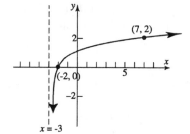

81. $f(x) = 3 + \log(x + 2) = \log(x + 2) + 3$
Using the graph of $y = \log x$, shift 2 units
to the left, and shift up 3 units.
Domain: $(-2, \infty)$
Range: $(-\infty, \infty)$
Vertical Asymptote: $x = -2$

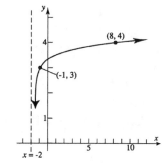

83. $f(x) = \log(2 - x) = \log(-(x - 2))$
Using the graph of $y = \log x$, reflect the
graph about the y-axis, and shift 2 units to
the right.
Domain: $(-\infty, 2)$
Range: $(-\infty, \infty)$
Vertical Asymptote: $x = 2$

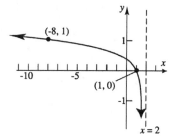

85. $\log_3 x = 2$
$\quad x = 3^2 \Rightarrow x = 9$

87. $\log_2(2x + 1) = 3$
$\quad 2x + 1 = 2^3 \Rightarrow 2x + 1 = 8$
$\quad 2x = 7 \Rightarrow x = \dfrac{7}{2}$

89. $\log_x 4 = 2$
$\quad x^2 = 4$
$\quad x = 2 \quad (x \neq -2, \text{ base is positive})$

91. $\ln e^x = 5$
$\quad e^x = e^5 \Rightarrow x = 5$

93. $\log_4 64 = x$

$$4^x = 64 \Rightarrow 4^x = 4^3 \Rightarrow x = 3$$

95. $\log_3 243 = 2x + 1$

$$3^{2x+1} = 243$$
$$3^{2x+1} = 3^5$$
$$2x + 1 = 5 \Rightarrow 2x = 4 \Rightarrow x = 2$$

97. $e^{3x} = 10$

$$3x = \ln(10) \Rightarrow x = \frac{\ln(10)}{3}$$

99. $e^{2x+5} = 8$

$$2x + 5 = \ln(8)$$
$$2x = -5 + \ln(8) \Rightarrow x = \frac{\ln(8) - 5}{2}$$

101. $\log_3(x^2 + 1) = 2$

$$x^2 + 1 = 3^2$$
$$x^2 + 1 = 9 \Rightarrow x^2 = 8$$
$$x = \pm\sqrt{8} = \pm 2\sqrt{2}$$
$$x = -2\sqrt{2} \text{ or } x = 2\sqrt{2}$$

103. $\log_2 8^x = -3$

$$8^x = 2^{-3}$$
$$8^x = \frac{1}{8} \Rightarrow 8^x = 8^{-1} \Rightarrow x = -1$$

105. (a)   Graphing $f(x) = 2^x$:

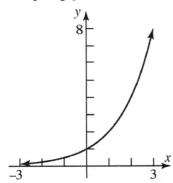

Domain: $(-\infty, \infty)$
Range: $(0, \infty)$
Horizontal asymptote: $y = 0$

(b)   Finding the inverse:
$$f(x) = 2^x$$
$$y = 2^x$$
$$x = 2^y \quad \text{Inverse}$$
$$y = \log_2 x$$
$$f^{-1}(x) = \log_2 x$$

(c)   Graphing the inverse:

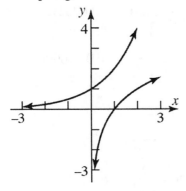

Domain: $(0, \infty)$
Range: $(-\infty, \infty)$
Vertical asymptote: $x = 0$

107. (a)   Graphing $f(x) = 2^{x+3}$:

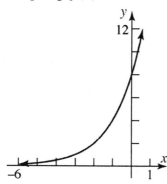

Domain: $(-\infty, \infty)$
Range: $(0, \infty)$
Horizontal asymptote: $y = 0$

(b)   Finding the inverse:
$$f(x) = 2^{x+3}$$
$$y = 2^{x+3}$$
$$x = 2^{y+3} \quad \text{Inverse}$$
$$y + 3 = \log_2 x$$
$$y = -3 + \log_2 x$$
$$f^{-1}(x) = -3 + \log_2 x$$

(c)   Graphing the inverse:

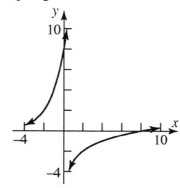

Domain: $(0, \infty)$
Range: $(-\infty, \infty)$
Vertical asymptote: $x = 0$

109. $pH = -\log_{10}[H^+]$

(a) $pH = -\log_{10}[0.1] = -(-1) = 1$
(b) $pH = -\log_{10}[0.01] = -(-2) = 2$
(c) $pH = -\log_{10}[0.001] = -(-3) = 3$
(d)   As the H^+ decreases, the pH increases.
(e) $3.5 = -\log_{10}[H^+] \implies -3.5 = \log_{10}[H^+] \implies [H^+] = 10^{-3.5}$

$$= 3.16 \times 10^{-4} = 0.000316$$

(f) $7.4 = -\log_{10}[H^+] \implies -7.4 = \log_{10}[H^+] \implies [H^+] = 10^{-7.4}$

$$\approx 3.981 \times 10^{-8} = 0.00000003981$$

111. $p = 760e^{-0.145h}$

(a) $320 = 760e^{-0.145h}$
$$\frac{320}{760} = e^{-0.145h}$$
$$\ln(320/760) = -0.145n$$
$$h = \frac{\ln(320/760)}{-0.145} \approx 5.97 \text{ km}$$

(b) $667 = 760e^{-0.145h}$
$$\frac{667}{760} = e^{-0.145h}$$
$$\ln\left(\frac{667}{760}\right) = -0.145h$$
$$h = \frac{\ln(667/760)}{-0.145} \approx 0.90 \text{ km}$$

113. $F(t) = 1 - e^{-0.1t}$

(a) $0.5 = 1 - e^{-0.1t}$

$-0.5 = -e^{-0.1t}$

$0.5 = e^{-0.1t} \Rightarrow \ln(0.5) = -0.1t$

$t = \dfrac{\ln(0.5)}{-0.1} \approx 6.93$

(b) $0.8 = 1 - e^{-0.1t}$

$-0.2 = -e^{-0.1t}$

$0.2 = e^{-0.1t} \Rightarrow \ln(0.2) = -0.1t$

$t = \dfrac{\ln(0.2)}{-0.1} \approx 16.09$

(c)   It is impossible for the probability to reach 100% because $e^{-0.1t}$ will never equal zero; thus, $F(t) = 1 - e^{-0.1t}$ will never equal 1.

115. $D = 5e^{-0.4h}$

$2 = 5e^{-0.4h}$

$0.4 = e^{-0.4h}$

$\ln(0.4) = -0.4h$

$h = \dfrac{\ln(0.4)}{-0.4} \approx 2.29$ hours

117. $I = \dfrac{E}{R}\left[1 - e^{-\left(\frac{R}{L}\right)t}\right]$

0.5 ampere:

$0.5 = \dfrac{12}{10}\left[1 - e^{-\left(\frac{10}{5}\right)t}\right]$

$0.4167 = 1 - e^{-2t} \Rightarrow e^{-2t} = 0.5833$

$-2t = \ln(0.5833)$

$t = \dfrac{\ln(0.5833)}{-2} \approx 0.2695$ seconds

1.0 ampere:

$1.0 = \dfrac{12}{10}\left[1 - e^{-\left(\frac{10}{5}\right)t}\right]$

$0.8333 = 1 - e^{-2t} \Rightarrow e^{-2t} = 0.1667$

$-2t = \ln(0.1667)$

$t = \dfrac{\ln(0.1667)}{-2} \approx 0.8959$ seconds

Graphing:

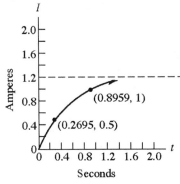

333

119. $L(10^{-7}) = 10 \log\left(\dfrac{10^{-7}}{10^{-12}}\right) = 10 \log\left(10^5\right) = 10 \cdot 5 = 50$ decibels

121. $L(10^{-1}) = 10 \log\left(\dfrac{10^{-1}}{10^{-12}}\right) = 10 \log\left(10^{11}\right) = 10 \cdot 11 = 110$ decibels

123. $M(125,892) = \log\left(\dfrac{125,892}{10^{-3}}\right) = 8.1$

125. $R = 3e^{kx}$

    (a) $10 = 3e^{k(0.06)}$

             $3.3333 = e^{0.06k}$

             $\ln(3.3333) = 0.06k$

             $k = \dfrac{\ln(3.3333)}{0.06}$

             $k \approx 20.07$

    (b) $R = 3e^{20.066\,(0.17)}$

             $R = 3e^{3.41122}$

             $R \approx 91\%$

    (c) $100 = 3e^{20.066\,x}$

             $33.3333 = e^{20.066x}$

             $\ln(33.3333) = 20.066x$

             $x = \dfrac{\ln(33.3333)}{20.07}$

             $x \approx 0.175$

    (d) $15 = 3e^{20.066\,x}$

             $5 = e^{20.066x}$

             $\ln(5) = 20.066x$

             $x = \dfrac{\ln(5)}{20.066}$

             $x \approx 0.08$

127.   If the base of a logarithmic function equals 1, we would have the following:

           $f(x) = \log_1(x) \Rightarrow f^{-1}(x) = 1^x = 1$ for every real number x.

    In other words, f^{-1} would be a constant function and, therefore, f^{-1} would not be one-to-one.

Exponential and Logarithmic Functions

6.5 Properties of Logarithms

1. $\log_3 3^{71} = 71$ 3. $\ln e^{-4} = -4$ 5. $2^{\log_2 7} = 7$

7. $\log_8 2 + \log_8 4 = \log_8(4 \cdot 2) = \log_8(8) = 1$

9. $\log_6 18 - \log_6 3 = \log_6\left(\dfrac{18}{3}\right) = \log_6(6) = 1$

11. $\log_2 6 \cdot \log_6 4$

     $= \log_6\left(4^{\log_2 6}\right) = \log_6\left(\left(2^2\right)^{\log_2 6}\right)$

     $= \log_6\left((2)^{2\log_2 6}\right) = \log_6\left((2)^{\log_2 6^2}\right) = \log_6\left(6^2\right) = 2$

13. $3^{\log_3 5 - \log_3 4} = 3^{\log_3\left(\frac{5}{4}\right)} = \dfrac{5}{4}$

15. $e^{\log_{e^2} 16}$

     Simplify the exponent:

         Let $a = \log_{e^2} 16$

$$\left(e^2\right)^a = 16$$

$$e^{2a} = 16 = 4^2$$

$$e^a = 4 \Rightarrow a = \ln 4$$

        Thus, $e^{\log_{e^2} 16} = e^{\ln 4} = 4$

17. $\ln 6 = \ln(3 \cdot 2) = \ln 3 + \ln 2 = b + a$

19. $\ln(1.5) = \ln\left(\dfrac{3}{2}\right) = \ln 3 - \ln 2 = b - a$

21. $\ln 8 = \ln 2^3 = 3 \cdot \ln 2 = 3a$

23. $\ln\left(\sqrt[5]{6}\right) = \ln\left(6^{1/5}\right) = \dfrac{1}{5} \cdot \ln 6 = \dfrac{1}{5} \cdot \ln(2 \cdot 3) = \dfrac{1}{5} \cdot (\ln 2 + \ln 3) = \dfrac{1}{5} \cdot (a + b)$

25. $\log_5(25x) = \log_5(25) + \log_5(x) = 2 + \log_5(x)$

27. $\log_2\left(z^3\right) = 3\log_2(z)$

29. $\ln(ex) = \ln e + \ln x = 1 + \ln x$

31. $\ln\left(xe^x\right) = \ln x + \ln e^x = \ln x + x$

33. $\log_a\left(u^2 v^3\right) = \log_a u^2 + \log_a v^3 = 2\log_a u + 3\log_a v$

35. $\ln\left(x^2\sqrt{1-x}\right) = \ln x^2 + \ln\sqrt{1-x} = \ln x^2 + \ln(1-x)^{1/2} = 2\ln x + \dfrac{1}{2}\ln(1-x)$

37. $\log_2\left(\dfrac{x^3}{x-3}\right) = \log_2 x^3 - \log_2(x-3) = 3\log_2 x - \log_2(x-3)$

39. $\log\left|\dfrac{x(x+2)}{(x+3)^2}\right| = \log(x(x+2)) - \log(x+3)^2 = \log x + \log(x+2) - 2\log(x+3)$

41. $\ln\left[\dfrac{x^2 - x - 2}{(x+4)^2}\right]^{1/3} = \dfrac{1}{3}\ln\left[\dfrac{(x-2)(x+1)}{(x+4)^2}\right] = \dfrac{1}{3}\left[\ln(x-2)(x+1) - \ln(x+4)^2\right]$

$= \dfrac{1}{3}\left[\ln(x-2) + \ln(x+1) - 2\ln(x+4)\right] = \dfrac{1}{3}\ln(x-2) + \dfrac{1}{3}\ln(x+1) - \dfrac{2}{3}\ln(x+4)$

43. $\ln\left(\dfrac{5x\sqrt{1-3x}}{(x-4)^3}\right) = \ln\left(5x\sqrt{1-3x}\right) - \ln(x-4)^3 = \ln 5 + \ln x + \ln\sqrt{1-3x} - 3\ln(x-4)$

$= \ln 5 + \ln x + \ln(1-3x)^{1/2} - 3\ln(x-4) = \ln 5 + \ln x + \dfrac{1}{2}\ln(1-3x) - 3\ln(x-4)$

45. $3\log_5 u + 4\log_5 v = \log_5 u^3 + \log_5 v^4 = \log_5(u^3 v^4)$

47. $\log_3 \sqrt{x} - \log_3 x^3 = \log_3\left(\dfrac{\sqrt{x}}{x^3}\right) = \log_3\left(\dfrac{x^{1/2}}{x^3}\right) = \log_3\left(x^{-5/2}\right) = -\dfrac{5}{2}\log_3 x$

49. $\log_4\left(x^2 - 1\right) - 5\log_4(x+1) = \log_4\left(x^2 - 1\right) - \log_4(x+1)^5 = \log_4\left(\dfrac{x^2 - 1}{(x+1)^5}\right)$

$= \log_4\left(\dfrac{(x+1)(x-1)}{(x+1)^5}\right) = \log_4\left(\dfrac{x-1}{(x+1)^4}\right)$

51. $\ln\left(\dfrac{x}{x-1}\right) + \ln\left(\dfrac{x+1}{x}\right) - \ln\left(x^2 - 1\right) = \ln\left|\dfrac{x}{x-1} \cdot \dfrac{x+1}{x}\right| - \ln\left(x^2 - 1\right) = \ln\left|\dfrac{x+1}{x-1} \div \left(x^2 - 1\right)\right|$

$= \ln\left|\dfrac{x+1}{(x-1)(x-1)(x+1)}\right| = \ln\left(\dfrac{1}{(x-1)^2}\right) = \ln(x-1)^{-2} = -2\ln(x-1)$

53. $8\log_2 \sqrt{3x-2} - \log_2\left(\dfrac{4}{x}\right) + \log_2 4 = \log_2\left(\sqrt{3x-2}\right)^8 - \left(\log_2 4 - \log_2 x\right) + \log_2 4$

$$= \log_2 (3x-2)^4 - \log_2 4 + \log_2 x + \log_2 4 = \log_2\left[x(3x-2)^4\right]$$

55. $2\log_a\left(5x^3\right) - \dfrac{1}{2}\log_a(2x+3) = \log_a\left(5x^3\right)^2 - \log_a(2x+3)^{1/2} = \log_a\left[\dfrac{25x^6}{\sqrt{2x+3}}\right]$

57. $2\log_2(x+1) - \log_2(x+3) - \log_2(x-1) = \log_2(x+1)^2 - \log_2(x+3) - \log_2(x-1)$

$$= \log_2\left(\dfrac{(x+1)^2}{(x+3)}\right) - \log_2(x-1) = \log_2\left(\dfrac{\dfrac{(x+1)^2}{(x+3)}}{(x-1)}\right) = \log_2\left(\dfrac{(x+1)^2}{(x+3)(x-1)}\right)$$

59. $y = ab^x$

$\log(y) = \log\left(ab^x\right) = \log(a) + \log\left(b^x\right) = \log(a) + x\log(b)$

61. $\log_3 21 = \dfrac{\log 21}{\log 3} \approx \dfrac{1.32222}{0.47712} \approx 2.771$

63. $\log_{\frac{1}{3}} 71 = \dfrac{\log 71}{\log(1/3)} = \dfrac{\log 71}{-\log 3} \approx \dfrac{1.85126}{-0.47712} \approx -3.880$

65. $\log_{\sqrt{2}} 7 = \dfrac{\log 7}{\log\sqrt{2}} = \dfrac{\log 7}{\log 2^{1/2}} = \dfrac{\log 7}{\left(\dfrac{1}{2}\log 2\right)} \approx \dfrac{0.84510}{0.5(0.30103)} \approx 5.615$

67. $\log_\pi e = \dfrac{\ln e}{\ln \pi} \approx \dfrac{1}{1.14473} \approx 0.874$

69. $y = \log_4 x = \dfrac{\ln x}{\ln 4}$ or $y = \dfrac{\log x}{\log 4}$

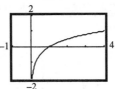

71. $y = \log_2(x+2) = \dfrac{\ln(x+2)}{\ln 2}$

or $y = \dfrac{\log(x+2)}{\log 2}$

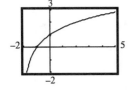

73. $y = \log_{x-1}(x+1) = \dfrac{\ln(x+1)}{\ln(x-1)}$

or $y = \dfrac{\log(x+1)}{\log(x-1)}$

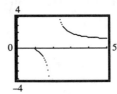

75. $\ln y = \ln x + \ln C$
$\ln y = \ln(xC)$
$\quad y = Cx$

77. $\ln y = \ln x + \ln(x+1) + \ln C$
$\ln y = \ln\big(x(x+1)C\big)$
$\quad y = Cx(x+1)$

79. $\ln y = 3x + \ln C$
$\ln y = \ln e^{3x} + \ln C$
$\ln y = \ln(Ce^{3x})$
$\quad y = Ce^{3x}$

81. $\ln(y-3) = -4x + \ln C$
$\ln(y-3) = \ln e^{-4x} + \ln C$
$\ln(y-3) = \ln\big(Ce^{-4x}\big)$
$\quad y - 3 = Ce^{-4x} \Rightarrow y = Ce^{-4x} + 3$

83. $3\ln y = \dfrac{1}{2}\ln(2x+1) - \dfrac{1}{3}\ln(x+4) + \ln C$

$\ln y^3 = \ln(2x+1)^{1/2} - \ln(x+4)^{1/3} + \ln C$

$\ln y^3 = \ln\left[\dfrac{C(2x+1)^{1/2}}{(x+4)^{1/3}}\right]$

$y^3 = \dfrac{C(2x+1)^{1/2}}{(x+4)^{1/3}}$

$y = \left[\dfrac{C(2x+1)^{1/2}}{(x+4)^{\frac{1}{3}}}\right]^{1/3}$

$y = \dfrac{\sqrt[3]{C}(2x+1)^{1/6}}{(x+4)^{1/9}}$

85. $\log_2 3 \cdot \log_3 4 \cdot \log_4 5 \cdot \log_5 6 \cdot \log_6 7 \cdot \log_7 8$

$= \dfrac{\log 3}{\log 2} \cdot \dfrac{\log 4}{\log 3} \cdot \dfrac{\log 5}{\log 4} \cdot \dfrac{\log 6}{\log 5} \cdot \dfrac{\log 7}{\log 6} \cdot \dfrac{\log 8}{\log 7} = \dfrac{\log 8}{\log 2} = \dfrac{\log 2^3}{\log 2} = \dfrac{3\log 2}{\log 2} = 3$

87. $\log_2 3 \cdot \log_3 4 \cdot \ldots \cdot \log_n (n+1) \cdot \log_{n+1} 2$

$= \dfrac{\log 3}{\log 2} \cdot \dfrac{\log 4}{\log 3} \cdot \ldots \cdot \dfrac{\log(n+1)}{\log n} \cdot \dfrac{\log 2}{\log(n+1)} = \dfrac{\log 2}{\log 2} = 1$

89. Verifying:

$\log_a\left(x + \sqrt{x^2-1}\right) + \log_a\left(x - \sqrt{x^2-1}\right) = \log_a\left[\left(x+\sqrt{x^2-1}\right)\left(x-\sqrt{x^2-1}\right)\right]$

$= \log_a\left[x^2 - \left(x^2-1\right)\right] = \log_a\left[x^2 - x^2 + 1\right] = \log_a 1 = 0$

91. Verifying:

$2x + \ln\left(1 + e^{-2x}\right) = \ln e^{2x} + \ln\left(1 + e^{-2x}\right) = \ln\left(e^{2x}\left(1 + e^{-2x}\right)\right) = \ln\left(e^{2x} + e^0\right) = \ln\left(e^{2x} + 1\right)$

93. $f(x) = \log_a x$

$$x = a^{f(x)} \implies x^{-1} = a^{-f(x)} = \left(a^{-1}\right)^{f(x)} = \left(\frac{1}{a}\right)^{f(x)}$$

$$\log_{\frac{1}{a}} x^{-1} = f(x) \implies -\log_{\frac{1}{a}} x = f(x) \implies -f(x) = \log_{\frac{1}{a}} x$$

95. $f(x) = \log_a x$

$$a^{f(x)} = x \implies \frac{1}{a^{f(x)}} = \frac{1}{x} \implies a^{-f(x)} = \frac{1}{x} \implies -f(x) = \log_a\left(\frac{1}{x}\right) = f\left(\frac{1}{x}\right)$$

97.   If $A = \log_a M$ and $B = \log_a N$, then $a^A = M$ and $a^B = N$.

$$\log_a\left(\frac{M}{N}\right) = \log_a\left(\frac{a^A}{a^B}\right) = \log_a a^{A-B} = A - B = \log_a M - \log_a N$$

99. $y_1 = \log(x^2)$ $y_2 = 2\log(x)$

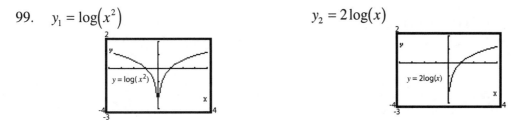

These graphs are not equivalent because $\log(x^2) = 2\log(x)$ only if $x > 0$.

Exponential and Logarithmic Functions

6.6   Logarithmic and Exponential Equations

1. $\log_4(x+2) = \log_4 8$
    $$x+2 = 8 \Rightarrow x = 6$$

3. $\dfrac{1}{2}\log_3 x = 2\log_3 2$
    $$\log_3 x^{1/2} = \log_3 2^2$$
    $$x^{1/2} = 4 \Rightarrow x = 16$$

5. $2\log_5 x = 3\log_5 4$
    $$\log_5 x^2 = \log_5 4^3$$
    $$x^2 = 64$$
    $$x = \pm 8$$
    Since $\log_5(-8)$ is undefined, the
    only solution is $x = 8$.

7. $3\log_2(x-1) + \log_2 4 = 5$
    $$\log_2(x-1)^3 + \log_2 4 = 5$$
    $$\log_2\left(4(x-1)^3\right) = 5$$
    $$4(x-1)^3 = 2^5$$
    $$(x-1)^3 = \frac{32}{4}$$
    $$(x-1)^3 = 8$$
    $$x-1 = 2$$
    $$x = 3$$

9. $\log x + \log(x+15) = 2$
    $$\log\left(x(x+15)\right) = 2$$
    $$x(x+15) = 10^2$$
    $$x^2 + 15x - 100 = 0 \Rightarrow (x+20)(x-5) = 0$$
    $$x = -20 \text{ or } x = 5$$
    Since $\log(-20)$ is undefined, the only solution is $x = 5$.

11. $\ln x + \ln(x+2) = 4$
    $$\ln\left(x(x+2)\right) = 4$$
    $$x(x+2) = e^4 \Rightarrow x^2 + 2x - e^4 = 0$$
    $$x = \frac{-2 \pm \sqrt{2^2 - 4(1)(-e^4)}}{2(1)} = \frac{-2 \pm \sqrt{4 + 4e^4}}{2} = \frac{-2 \pm 2\sqrt{1+e^4}}{2} = -1 \pm \sqrt{1+e^4}$$
    Since $\ln\left(-1 - \sqrt{1+e^4}\right)$ is undefined, the only solution is $x = -1 + \sqrt{1+e^4} \approx 6.456$.

13. $2^{2x} + 2^x - 12 = 0$

$$\left(2^x\right)^2 + 2^x - 12 = 0$$

$$\left(2^x - 3\right)\left(2^x + 4\right) = 0$$

$\qquad 2^x - 3 = 0 \qquad$ or $\quad 2^x + 4 = 0$

$\qquad\qquad 2^x = 3 \qquad$ or $\qquad 2^x = -4$

$\qquad\qquad x = \log_2 3 \qquad\qquad$ No solution

$$x = \frac{\ln 3}{\ln 2}$$

$\qquad\qquad x \approx 1.585$

The only solution is $x = \log_2 3 \approx 1.585$.

15. $3^{2x} + 3^{x+1} - 4 = 0$

$$\left(3^x\right)^2 + 3 \cdot 3^x - 4 = 0$$

$$\left(3^x - 1\right)\left(3^x + 4\right) = 0$$

$\qquad 3^x - 1 = 0 \quad$ or $\qquad 3^x + 4 = 0$

$\qquad\quad 3^x = 1 \quad$ or $\qquad 3^x = -4$

$\qquad\qquad x = 0 \qquad\qquad$ No solution

The only solution is $x = 0$.

17. $2^x = 10$, using base 10 logarithm

$$\log\left(2^x\right) = \log 10$$

$$x \log 2 = 1$$

$$x = \frac{1}{\log 2} \approx 3.322$$

19. $8^{-x} = 1.2$, using base 10 logarithm

$$\log\left(8^{-x}\right) = \log(1.2)$$

$$-x \log 8 = \log(1.2)$$

$$x = \frac{\log(1.2)}{-\log 8} \approx -0.088$$

21. $3^{1-2x} = 4^x$, using base 10 logarithm

$$\log\left(3^{1-2x}\right) = \log\left(4^x\right)$$

$$(1 - 2x)\log 3 = x \log 4$$

$$\log 3 - 2x \log 3 = x \log 4$$

$$\log 3 = x \log 4 + 2x \log 3$$

$$\log 3 = x(\log 4 + 2\log 3)$$

$$x = \frac{\log 3}{\log 4 + 2\log 3} \approx 0.307$$

23. $\left(\dfrac{3}{5}\right)^x = 7^{1-x}$, using base 10 logarithm

$$\log\left(\left(\frac{3}{5}\right)^x\right) = \log\left(7^{1-x}\right)$$

$$x \log(3/5) = (1 - x)\log 7$$

$$x(\log 3 - \log 5) = \log 7 - x \log 7$$

$$x \log 3 - x \log 5 + x \log 7 = \log 7$$

$$x(\log 3 - \log 5 + \log 7) = \log 7$$

$$x = \frac{\log 7}{\log 3 - \log 5 + \log 7} \approx 1.356$$

25. $1.2^x = (0.5)^{-x}$, using base 10 logarithm

$$\log 1.2^x = \log(0.5)^{-x}$$
$$x\log(1.2) = -x\log(0.5)$$
$$x\log(1.2) + x\log(0.5) = 0$$
$$x(\log(1.2) + \log(0.5)) = 0$$
$$x = 0$$

27. $\pi^{1-x} = e^x$, using base e logarithm

$$\ln \pi^{1-x} = \ln e^x$$
$$(1-x)\ln \pi = x$$
$$\ln \pi - x\ln \pi = x$$
$$\ln \pi = x + x\ln \pi$$
$$\ln \pi = x(1 + \ln \pi)$$
$$x = \frac{\ln \pi}{1 + \ln \pi} \approx 0.534$$

29. $5\left(2^{3x}\right) = 8$, using base 10 logarithm

$$2^{3x} = \frac{8}{5}$$
$$\log 2^{3x} = \log\left(\frac{8}{5}\right)$$
$$3x\log 2 = \log 8 - \log 5$$
$$x = \frac{\log 8 - \log 5}{3\log 2} \approx 0.226$$

31. $\log_a(x-1) - \log_a(x+6) = \log_a(x-2) - \log_a(x+3)$

$$\log_a\left(\frac{x-1}{x+6}\right) = \log_a\left(\frac{x-2}{x+3}\right) \Rightarrow a^{\left(\log_a\left(\frac{x-1}{x+6}\right)\right)} = a^{\left(\log_a\left(\frac{x-2}{x+3}\right)\right)}$$

so

$$\frac{x-1}{x+6} = \frac{x-2}{x+3} \Rightarrow (x-1)(x+3) = (x-2)(x+6)$$

$$x^2 + 2x - 3 = x^2 + 4x - 12 \Rightarrow 2x - 3 = 4x - 12 \Rightarrow 9 = 2x \Rightarrow x = \frac{9}{2}$$

Since each of the original logarithms is defined for $x = \frac{9}{2}$, the solution is $x = \frac{9}{2}$.

33. $\log_{\frac{1}{3}}(x^2 + x) - \log_{\frac{1}{3}}(x^2 - x) = -1$

$$\log_{\frac{1}{3}}\left(\frac{x^2 + x}{x^2 - x}\right) = -1$$

$$\frac{x^2 + x}{x^2 - x} = \left(\frac{1}{3}\right)^{-1}$$

$$\frac{x(x+1)}{x(x-1)} = 3 \Rightarrow x + 1 = 3(x-1)$$

$$x + 1 = 3x - 3 \Rightarrow -2x = -4 \Rightarrow x = 2$$

35. $\log_2(x+1) - \log_4 x = 1$

$\log_2(x+1) - \dfrac{\log_2 x}{\log_2 4} = 1$

$\log_2(x+1) - \dfrac{\log_2 x}{2} = 1$

$2\log_2(x+1) - \log_2 x = 2$

$\log_2(x+1)^2 - \log_2 x = 2$

$\log_2\left(\dfrac{(x+1)^2}{x}\right) = 2$

$\dfrac{(x+1)^2}{x} = 2^2$

$x^2 + 2x + 1 = 4x$

$x^2 - 2x + 1 = 0$

$(x-1)^2 = 0$

$x - 1 = 0$

$x = 1$

37. $\log_{16} x + \log_4 x + \log_2 x = 7$

$\dfrac{\log_2 x}{\log_2 16} + \dfrac{\log_2 x}{\log_2 4} + \log_2 x = 7$

$\dfrac{\log_2 x}{4} + \dfrac{\log_2 x}{2} + \log_2 x = 7$

$\log_2 x + 2\log_2 x + 4\log_2 x = 28$

$7\log_2 x = 28$

$\log_2 x = 4$

$x = 2^4 = 16$

39. $\left(\sqrt[3]{2}\right)^{2-x} = 2^{x^2}$

$\left(2^{1/3}\right)^{2-x} = 2^{x^2} \Rightarrow 2^{\frac{1}{3}(2-x)} = 2^{x^2}$

$\dfrac{1}{3}(2-x) = x^2 \Rightarrow 2 - x = 3x^2$

$3x^2 + x - 2 = 0 \Rightarrow (3x-2)(x+1) = 0$

$x = \dfrac{2}{3}$ or $x = -1$

41. $\dfrac{e^x + e^{-x}}{2} = 1$

$e^x + e^{-x} = 2$

$e^x\left(e^x + e^{-x}\right) = 2e^x$

$e^{2x} + 1 = 2e^x$

$(e^x)^2 - 2e^x + 1 = 0$

$\left(e^x - 1\right)^2 = 0$

$e^x - 1 = 0$

$e^x = 1$

$x = 0$

43. $\dfrac{e^x - e^{-x}}{2} = 2$

$e^x - e^{-x} = 4 \Rightarrow e^x\left(e^x - e^{-x}\right) = 4e^x \Rightarrow e^{2x} - 1 = 4e^x \Rightarrow (e^x)^2 - 4e^x - 1 = 0$

$e^x = \dfrac{-(-4) \pm \sqrt{(-4)^2 - 4(1)(-1)}}{2(1)} = \dfrac{4 \pm \sqrt{20}}{2} = \dfrac{4 \pm 2\sqrt{5}}{2} = 2 \pm \sqrt{5}$

$x = \ln\left(2 + \sqrt{5}\right) \approx 1.444$

Since $\ln\left(2 - \sqrt{5}\right)$ is undefined; it is not a solution.

45. Using INTERSECT to solve:
$y_1 = \ln(x) / \ln(5) + \ln(x) / \ln(3)$
$y_2 = 1$

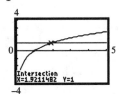

The solution is 1.92.

47. Using INTERSECT to solve:
$y_1 = \ln(x + 1) / \ln(5) - \ln(x - 2) / \ln(4)$
$y_2 = 1$

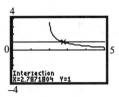

The solution is 2.79.

49. Using INTERSECT to solve:
$y_1 = e^x; \ \ y_2 = -x$

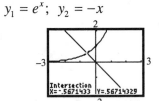

The solution is –0.57.

51. Using INTERSECT to solve:
$y_1 = e^x; \ \ y_2 = x^2$

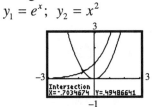

The solution is –0.70.

53. Using INTERSECT to solve:
$y_1 = \ln x; \ \ y_2 = -x$

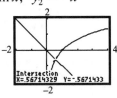

The solution is 0.57.

55. Using INTERSECT to solve:
$y_1 = \ln x; \ \ y_2 = x^3 - 1$

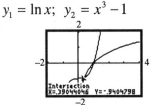

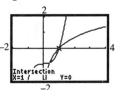

The solutions are 0.39, 1.00.

57. Using INTERSECT to solve:
$y_1 = e^x + \ln x; \ \ y_2 = 4$

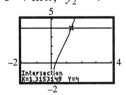

The solution is 1.32.

59. Using INTERSECT to solve:
$y_1 = e^{-x}; \ \ y_2 = \ln x$

The solution is 1.31.

Chapter 6

Exponential and Logarithmic Functions

6.7 Compound Interest

1. $P = \$100,\ r = 0.04,\ n = 4,\ t = 2$

$$A = P\left(1 + \frac{r}{n}\right)^{nt} = 100\left(1 + \frac{0.04}{4}\right)^{(4)(2)} \approx \$108.29$$

3. $P = \$500,\ r = 0.08,\ n = 4,\ t = 2.5$

$$A = P\left(1 + \frac{r}{n}\right)^{nt} = 500\left(1 + \frac{0.08}{4}\right)^{(4)(2.5)} \approx \$609.50$$

5. $P = \$600,\ r = 0.05,\ n = 365,\ t = 3$

$$A = P\left(1 + \frac{r}{n}\right)^{nt} = 600\left(1 + \frac{0.05}{365}\right)^{(365)(3)} \approx \$697.09$$

7. $P = \$10,\ r = 0.11,\ t = 2$

$$A = Pe^{rt} = 10e^{(0.11)(2)} \approx \$12.46$$

9. $P = \$100,\ r = 0.10,\ t = 2.25$

$$A = Pe^{rt} = 100e^{(0.10)(2.25)} \approx \$125.23$$

11. $A = \$100,\ r = 0.06,\ n = 12,\ t = 2$

$$P = A\left(1 + \frac{r}{n}\right)^{-nt} = 100\left(1 + \frac{0.06}{12}\right)^{(-12)(2)} \approx \$88.72$$

13. $A = \$1000,\ r = 0.06,\ n = 365,\ t = 2.5$

$$P = A\left(1 + \frac{r}{n}\right)^{-nt} = 1000\left(1 + \frac{0.06}{365}\right)^{(-365)(2.5)} \approx \$860.72$$

15. $A = \$600,\ r = 0.04,\ n = 4,\ t = 2$

$$P = A\left(1 + \frac{r}{n}\right)^{-nt} = 600\left(1 + \frac{0.04}{4}\right)^{(-4)(2)} \approx \$554.09$$

17. $A = \$80,\ r = 0.09,\ t = 3.25$

$$P = Ae^{-rt} = 80e^{(-0.09)(3.25)} \approx \$59.71$$

19. $A = \$400,\ r = 0.10,\ t = 1$

$$P = Ae^{-rt} = 400e^{(-0.10)(1)} \approx \$361.93$$

21. $r_e = \left(1 + \dfrac{r}{n}\right)^n - 1 = \left(1 + \dfrac{0.0525}{4}\right)^4 - 1 \approx 1.0535 - 1 = 0.0535 = 5.35\%$

23. $2P = P(1 + r)^3$

    $2 = (1 + r)^3$

    $\sqrt[3]{2} = 1 + r$

    $r = \sqrt[3]{2} - 1 \approx 1.26 - 1 = 0.26 = 26\%$

25. 6% compounded quarterly:

    $$A = 10,000\left(1 + \dfrac{0.06}{4}\right)^{(4)(1)} \approx \$10,613.64$$

    $6\frac{1}{4}\%$ compounded annually:

    $$A = 10,000(1 + 0.0625)^1 \approx \$10,625$$

    $6\frac{1}{4}\%$ compounded annually yields the larger amount.

27. 9% compounded monthly:

    $$A = 10,000\left(1 + \dfrac{0.09}{12}\right)^{(12)(1)} \approx \$10,938.07$$

    8.8% compounded daily:

    $$A = 10,000\left(1 + \dfrac{0.088}{365}\right)^{365} \approx \$10,919.77$$

    9% compounded monthly yields the larger amount.

29. Compounded monthly:

    $$2P = P\left(1 + \dfrac{0.08}{12}\right)^{12t}$$

    $$2 \approx (1.00667)^{12t}$$

    $$\ln(2) \approx 12t \ln(1.00667)$$

    $$t \approx \dfrac{\ln(2)}{12 \ln(1.00667)} \approx 8.6932 \text{ years}$$

    $$\approx 104.32 \text{ months}$$

    Compounded continuously:

    $$2P = Pe^{0.08t}$$

    $$2 = e^{0.08t}$$

    $$\ln(2) = 0.08t$$

    $$t = \dfrac{\ln(2)}{0.08} \approx 8.6643 \text{ years}$$

    $$\approx 103.92 \text{ months}$$

31. Compounded monthly:

    $$150 = 100\left(1 + \dfrac{0.08}{12}\right)^{12t}$$

    $$1.5 \approx (1.00667)^{12t}$$

    $$\ln(1.5) \approx 12t \ln(1.00667)$$

    $$t \approx \dfrac{\ln(1.5)}{12 \ln(1.00667)} \approx 5.0852 \text{ years}$$

    $$\approx 61.02 \text{ months}$$

    Compounded continuously:

    $$150 = 100e^{0.08t}$$

    $$1.5 = e^{0.08t}$$

    $$\ln(1.5) = 0.08t$$

    $$t = \dfrac{\ln(1.5)}{0.08} \approx 5.0683 \text{ years}$$

    $$\approx 60.82 \text{ months}$$

33. $25,000 = 10,000e^{0.06t}$
      $2.5 = e^{0.06t}$

   $\ln(2.5) = 0.06t$

   $t = \dfrac{\ln(2.5)}{0.06} \approx 15.27$ years

35. $A = 90,000(1+0.03)^5 \approx \$104,335$

37. $P = 15,000e^{(-0.05)(3)} \approx \$12,910.62$

39. $A = 1500(1+0.15)^5$
      $= 1500(1.15)^5 \approx \$3017$

41. $850,000 = 650,000(1+r)^3$

   $\dfrac{85}{65} = (1+r)^3$

   $\sqrt[3]{\dfrac{85}{65}} = 1+r \Rightarrow r \approx \sqrt[3]{1.3077} - 1 \approx 0.0935 = 9.35\%$

43. 5.6% compounded continuously:
      $A = 1000e^{(0.056)(1)} \approx \$1057.60$
      Jim does not have enough money to buy the computer.
      5.9% compounded monthly:

   $A = 1000\left(1 + \dfrac{0.059}{12}\right)^{12} \approx \$1060.62$

   The second bank offers the better deal.

45. Will - 9% compounded semiannually:

   $A = 2000\left(1 + \dfrac{0.09}{2}\right)^{(2)(20)} \approx \$11,632.73$

   Henry - 8.5% compounded continuously:
      $A = 2000e^{(0.085)(20)} \approx \$10,947.89$
   Will has more money after 20 years.

47. $P = 50,000$; $t = 5$
   (a) Simple interest at 12% per annum:
         $A = 50,000 + 50,000(0.12)(5) = \$80,000$
   (b) 11.5% compounded monthly:

   $A = 50,000\left(1 + \dfrac{0.115}{12}\right)^{(12)(5)} \approx \$88,613.59$

   (c) 11.25% compounded continuously:
         $A = 50,000e^{(0.1125)(5)} \approx \$87,752.73$
         Subtract $50,000 from each to get the amount of interest:
            (a) \$30,000   (b) \$38,613.59   (c) \$37.752.73
   Option (a) results in the least interest.

49. (a) $A = \$10,000$, $r = 0.10$, $n = 12$, $t = 20$ (compounded monthly)

   $P = 10,000\left(1 + \dfrac{0.10}{12}\right)^{(-12)(20)} \approx \$1364.62$

(b) $A = \$10{,}000$, $r = 0.10$, $t = 20$ (compounded continuously)
$$P = 10{,}000e^{(-0.10)(20)} \approx \$1353.35$$

51. $A = \$10{,}000$, $r = 0.08$, $n = 1$, $t = 10$ (compounded annually)
$$P = 10{,}000\left(1 + \frac{0.08}{1}\right)^{(-1)(10)} \approx \$4631.93$$

53.   Answers will vary.

55.   (a) $y = \dfrac{\ln(2)}{1 \cdot \ln\left(1 + \dfrac{0.12}{1}\right)} = \dfrac{\ln(2)}{\ln(1.12)} \approx 6.12$ years

(b) $y = \dfrac{\ln(3)}{4 \cdot \ln\left(1 + \dfrac{0.06}{4}\right)} = \dfrac{\ln(3)}{4\ln(1.015)} \approx 18.45$ years

(c) $mP = P\left(1 + \dfrac{r}{n}\right)^{nt}$

$m = \left(1 + \dfrac{r}{n}\right)^{nt} \;\Rightarrow\; \ln(m) = nt \cdot \ln\left(1 + \dfrac{r}{n}\right) \;\Rightarrow\; t = \dfrac{\ln(m)}{n \cdot \ln\left(1 + \dfrac{r}{n}\right)}$

57.   Answers will vary.

Chapter 6

Exponential and Logarithmic Functions

6.8   Exponential Growth and Decay

1. $P(t) = 500e^{0.02t}$

   (a) $P(0) = 500e^{(0.02)\cdot(0)} = 500$ flies

   (b)   growth rate = 2 %

   (c)   graphing:

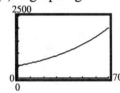

   (d) $P(10) = 500e^{(0.02)\cdot(10)} \approx 611$ flies

   (e)   Find t when $P = 800$:

$$800 = 500e^{0.02t}$$

$$1.6 = e^{0.02t}$$

$$\ln(1.6) = 0.02t$$

$$t = \frac{\ln(1.6)}{0.02} \approx 23.5 \text{ days}$$

   (f)   Find t when $P = 1000$:

$$1000 = 500e^{0.02t}$$

$$2 = e^{0.02t}$$

$$\ln(2) = 0.02t$$

$$t = \frac{\ln(2)}{0.02} \approx 34.7 \text{ days}$$

3. $A(t) = A_0 e^{-0.0244t} = 500e^{-0.0244t}$

   (a)   decay rate = 2.44 %

   (b)   graphing

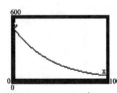

   (c) $A(10) = 500e^{(-0.0244)(10)} \approx 391.7$ grams

   (d)   Find t when $A = 400$:

$$400 = 500e^{-0.0244t}$$

$$0.8 = e^{-0.0244t}$$

$$\ln(0.8) = -0.0244t$$

$$t = \frac{\ln(0.8)}{-0.0244} \approx 9.1 \text{ years}$$

   (e)   Find t when $A = 250$:

$$250 = 500e^{-0.0244t}$$

$$0.5 = e^{-0.0244t}$$

$$\ln(0.5) = -0.0244t$$

$$t = \frac{\ln(0.5)}{-0.0244} \approx 28.4 \text{ years}$$

5. Use $N(t) = N_0 e^{kt}$ and solve for k:

$$1800 = 1000e^{k(1)}$$

$$1.8 = e^k \Rightarrow k = \ln(1.8)$$

When $t = 3$:

$$N(3) = 1000e^{(\ln(1.8))(3)} = 5832 \text{ mosquitos}$$

Find t when $N(t) = 10,000$:

$$10,000 = 1000e^{(\ln(1.8))\,t} \Rightarrow 10 = e^{(\ln(1.8))\,t}$$

$$\ln(10) = (\ln(1.8))t \Rightarrow t = \frac{\ln(10)}{(\ln(1.8))} \approx 3.9 \text{ days}$$

7. Use $P(t) = P_0 e^{kt}$ and solve for k:

$$2P_0 = P_0 e^{k(1.5)} \Rightarrow 2 = e^{1.5k}$$

$$\ln(2) = 1.5k \Rightarrow k = \frac{\ln(2)}{1.5}$$

When $t = 2$:

$$P(2) = 10,000e^{\left(\frac{\ln(2)}{1.5}\right)(2)} \approx 25,198 \text{ is the population 2 years from now.}$$

9. Use $A = A_0 e^{kt}$ and solve for k:

$$0.5A_0 = A_0 e^{k(1690)} \Rightarrow 0.5 = e^{1690k}$$

$$\ln(0.5) = 1690k \Rightarrow k = \frac{\ln(0.5)}{1690}$$

When $A_0 = 10$ and $t = 50$: $A = 10e^{\left(\frac{\ln(0.5)}{1690}\right)(50)} \approx 9.797 \text{ grams}$

11. Use $A = A_0 e^{kt}$ and solve for k:

half-life $= 5600$ years   (b) graphing $y_1 = e^{\left(\frac{\ln(0.5)}{5600}\right)x}$

$$\Rightarrow 0.5A_0 = A_0 e^{k(5600)}$$

$$0.5 = e^{5600\,k}$$

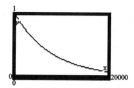

$$\ln(0.5) = 5600k \Rightarrow k = \frac{\ln(0.5)}{5600}$$

(a) Solve for t when $A = 0.3A_0$:

$$0.3A_0 = A_0 e^{kt}$$

$$0.3 = e^{kt}$$

$$\ln(0.3) = kt$$

$$t = \frac{\ln(0.3)}{k} = \frac{\ln(0.3)}{\left(\frac{\ln(0.5)}{5600}\right)}$$

$$\approx 9727 \text{ years ago}$$

(c) Using INTERSECT with $y_1 = e^{\left(\frac{\ln(0.5)}{5600}\right)x}$
and $y_2 = 0.5$
$t \approx 5600$ years

(d) Using INTERSECT with $y_1 = e^{\left(\frac{\ln(0.5)}{5600}\right)x}$
and $y_2 = 0.3$
$x \approx 9727$ years

13.   (a)   Using $u = T + (u_0 - T)e^{kt}$ where $t = 5$,

$T = 70,\ u_0 = 450,\ u = 300$:

$$300 = 70 + (450 - 70)e^{k(5)}$$

$$230 = 380e^{5k}$$

$$23/38 = e^{5k}$$

$$5k = \ln(23/38)$$

$$k = \frac{\ln(23/38)}{5}$$

$T = 70,\ u_0 = 450,\ u = 135$:

$$135 = 70 + (450 - 70)e^{\left(\frac{\ln(23/38)}{5}\right)t}$$

$$65 = 380e^{\left(\frac{\ln(23/38)}{5}\right)t}$$

$$65/380 = e^{\left(\frac{\ln(23/38)}{5}\right)t}$$

$$\left(\frac{\ln(23/38)}{5}\right)t = \ln(65/380)$$

$$t = \frac{\ln(65/380)}{\left(\frac{\ln(23/38)}{5}\right)} \approx 17.6 \text{ minutes}$$

The pizza will be cool enough to eat at approximately 5:18 p.m.

(b) graphing: $y_1 = 70 + 380e^{\left(\frac{\ln(23/38)}{5}\right)x}$

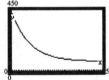

(c) Using INTERSECT with $y_1 = 70 + 380e^{\left(\frac{\ln(23/38)}{5}\right)x}$ and $y_2 = 160$

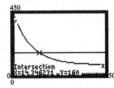
The pizza will be 160°F after about 14.3 minutes.

(d)   Use TRACE with $y_1 = 70 + 380e^{\left(\frac{\ln(23/38)}{5}\right)x}$

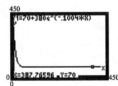
As time passes the temperature gets closer to 70°F.

15.   (a)   Using $u = T + (u_0 - T)e^{kt}$ where $t = 3$,

$T = 35,\ u_0 = 8,\ u = 15$:

$$15 = 35 + (8 - 35)e^{k(3)} \Rightarrow -20 = -27e^{3k} \Rightarrow 20/27 = e^{3k}$$

$$3k = \ln(20/27) \Rightarrow k = \frac{\ln(20/27)}{3}$$

At $t = 5$:

$$u = 35 + (8-35)e^{\left(\frac{\ln(20/27)}{3}\right)(5)} \approx 18.63°C$$

At $t = 10$:

$$u = 35 + (8-35)e^{\left(\frac{\ln(20/27)}{3}\right)(10)} \approx 25.1°C$$

(b)   graphing $y_1 = 35 - 27e^{\left(\frac{\ln(20/27)}{3}\right)x}$

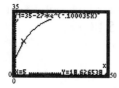

Use TRACE on the graph of $y_1 = 35 - 27e^{\left(\frac{\ln(20/27)}{3}\right)x}$:

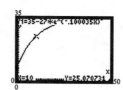

17.   Use $A = A_0 e^{kt}$ and solve for k:

$$15 = 25e^{k(10)}$$

$$0.6 = e^{10k} \Rightarrow \ln(0.6) = 10k \Rightarrow k = \frac{\ln(0.6)}{10}$$

When $A_0 = 25$ and $t = 24$:

$$A = 25e^{\left(\frac{\ln(0.6)}{10}\right)(24)} \approx 7.34 \text{ kilograms}$$

Find t when $A = 0.5A_0$:

$$0.5 = 25e^{\left(\frac{\ln(0.6)}{10}\right)t}$$

$$0.02 = e^{\left(\frac{\ln(0.6)}{10}\right)t} \Rightarrow \ln(0.02) = \left(\frac{\ln(0.6)}{10}\right)t \Rightarrow t = \frac{\ln(0.02)}{\left(\frac{\ln(0.6)}{10}\right)} \approx 76.6 \text{ hours}$$

19.   Use $A = A_0 e^{kt}$ and solve for k:

$$0.5A_0 = A_0 e^{k(8)}$$

$$0.5 = e^{8k} \Rightarrow \ln(0.5) = 8k$$

$$k = \frac{\ln(0.5)}{8}$$

Find t when $A = 0.1A_0$:

$$0.1A_0 = A_0 e^{\left(\frac{\ln(0.5)}{8}\right)t}$$

$$0.1 = e^{\left(\frac{\ln(0.5)}{8}\right)t} \Rightarrow \ln(0.1) = \left(\frac{\ln(0.5)}{8}\right)t$$

$$t = \frac{\ln(0.1)}{\left(\frac{\ln(0.5)}{8}\right)} \approx 26.6 \text{ days}$$

The farmers need to wait about 27 days before using the hay.

Exponential and Logarithmic Functions

6.9   Logistic Growth and Decay

1.   (a)   The maximum proportion is the carrying capacity, $0.9 = 90\%$.

(b) $P(0) = \dfrac{0.9}{1 + 6e^{-0.32(0)}} = \dfrac{0.9}{1 + 6 \cdot 1} = \dfrac{0.9}{7} \approx 0.1286 = 12.86\%$

(c) graphing:

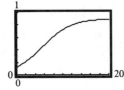

(d) $P(15) = \dfrac{0.9}{1 + 6e^{-0.32(15)}} \approx 0.8577$, so 85.77% owned a VCR in 1999.

(e) $$0.8 = \dfrac{0.9}{1 + 6e^{-0.32t}}$$
$$0.8\left(1 + 6e^{-0.32t}\right) = 0.9 \Rightarrow 1 + 6e^{-0.32t} = 1.125 \Rightarrow 6e^{-0.32t} = 0.125$$
$$e^{-0.32t} = 0.020833 \Rightarrow -0.32t = \ln(0.020833)$$
$$t = \dfrac{\ln(0.020833)}{-0.32} \approx 12.1$$

80% of households will own VCR's in 1996 (t = 12).

(f) $$0.45 = \dfrac{0.9}{1 + 6e^{-0.32t}}$$
$$0.45\left(1 + 6e^{-0.32t}\right) = 0.9 \Rightarrow 1 + 6e^{-0.32t} = 2 \Rightarrow 6e^{-0.32t} = 1$$
$$e^{-0.32t} = \dfrac{1}{6} \Rightarrow -0.32t = \ln(1/6)$$
$$t = \dfrac{\ln(1/6)}{-0.32} \approx 5.60 \text{ years}$$

45% of households will own VCR's in 1990 (t = 6).

3.   (a)   As $t \to \infty$, $e^{-0.439t} \to 0$. Thus, $P(t) \to 1000$. The carrying capacity is 1000g.

      (b)   Growth rate = 43.9%.

      (c) $P(0) = \dfrac{1000}{1 + 32.33e^{-0.439(0)}} = \dfrac{1000}{33.33} = 30$ g

      (d)   graphing:

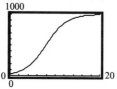

      (e) $P(9) = \dfrac{1000}{1 + 32.33e^{-0.439(9)}} \approx 616.6$ g

      (f) $700 = \dfrac{1000}{1 + 32.33e^{-0.439t}}$

$$700\left(1 + 32.33e^{-0.439t}\right) = 1000 \Rightarrow 1 + 32.33e^{-0.439t} = \frac{1000}{700} = \frac{10}{7}$$

$$32.33e^{-0.439t} = \frac{3}{7} \Rightarrow e^{-0.439t} = \frac{(3/7)}{32.33}$$

$$-0.439t = \ln\left(\frac{(3/7)}{32.33}\right) \Rightarrow t = \frac{\ln\left(\dfrac{(3/7)}{32.33}\right)}{-0.439} \approx 9.85 \text{ hours}$$

      (g)   To reach half-carrying capacity, we need

$$500 = \frac{1000}{1 + 32.33e^{-0.439t}}$$

$$500\left(1 + 32.33e^{-0.439t}\right) = 1000 \Rightarrow 1 + 32.33e^{-0.439t} = 2$$

$$32.33e^{-0.439t} = 1 \Rightarrow e^{-0.439t} = \frac{1}{32.33}$$

$$-0.439t = \ln\left(\frac{1}{32.33}\right) \Rightarrow t = \frac{\ln(1/32.33)}{-0.439} \approx 7.9 \text{ hours}$$

5.   (a) $y = \dfrac{6}{1 + e^{-(5.085 - 0.1156(100))}} \approx 0.0092 \approx 0$ O-rings

      (b) $y = \dfrac{6}{1 + e^{-(5.085 - 0.1156(60))}} \approx 0.81 \approx 1$ O-rings

      (c) $y = \dfrac{6}{1 + e^{-(5.085 - 0.1156(30))}} \approx 5.01 \approx 5$ O-rings

      (d)   Graphing:

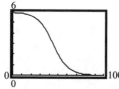

At 57.91°F, there would be 1 leaky O-ring.

At 43.99°F, there would be 3 leaky O-rings.

At 30.07°F, there would be 5 leaky O-rings.

7.   (a) $P(0) = \dfrac{95.4993}{1 + 0.0405e^{0.1968(0)}} = \dfrac{95.4993}{1 + 0.0405} \approx 91.8\%.$

Thus, in 1984, approximately 91.8% of households did not own a computer.

(b)   graphing:

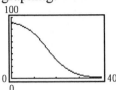

(c) $P(11) = \dfrac{95.4993}{1 + 0.0405e^{0.1968(11)}} \approx 70.6\%$

(d)   Find t such that $P = 20$:

$$20 = \dfrac{95.4993}{1 + 0.0405e^{0.1968(11)}}$$

$$20\left(1 + 0.0405e^{0.1968(t)}\right) = 95.4993 \Rightarrow 1 + 0.0405e^{0.1968(t)} = \dfrac{95.4993}{20}$$

$$0.0405e^{0.1968(t)} = \dfrac{95.4993}{20} - 1 \Rightarrow e^{0.1968(t)} = \dfrac{\left(\dfrac{95.4993}{20} - 1\right)}{0.0405}$$

$$0.1968t = \ln\left(\dfrac{\left(\dfrac{95.4993}{20} - 1\right)}{0.0405}\right) \Rightarrow t = \dfrac{\ln\left(\dfrac{\left(\dfrac{95.4993}{20} - 1\right)}{0.0405}\right)}{0.1968} \approx 23 \text{ years}$$

The percentage reached 20% in 2027.

9.   (a)   graphing:

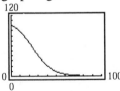

(b) $P(15) = \dfrac{113.3198}{1 + 0.115e^{0.0912(15)}} \approx 78\%$

(c)   Find n such that $P = 10$:

$$10 = \dfrac{113.3198}{1 + 0.115e^{0.0912n}}$$

$$10\left(1 + 0.115e^{0.0912n}\right) = 113.3198 \Rightarrow 1 + 0.115e^{0.0912n} = 11.33198$$

$$0.115e^{0.0912n} = 10.33198 \Rightarrow e^{0.0912n} = \dfrac{10.33198}{0.115}$$

$$0.0912n = \ln\left(\dfrac{10.33198}{0.115}\right) \Rightarrow n = \dfrac{\ln\left(\dfrac{10.33198}{0.115}\right)}{0.0912} \approx 50 \text{ people}$$

(e)   As $n \to \infty$, $e^{0.0912n} \to \infty$. Thus, $P(n) \to \dfrac{113.3198}{\infty} \to 0$.

This means that, as the number of people in the room increases, the probability that no two people share the same birthday approaches zero. In other words, the more people there are in the room, the more likely it becomes that two people **do** share the same birthday.

Exponential and Logarithmic Functions

6.10 Fitting Data to Exponential, Logarithmic and Logistic Functions

1.   (a)   scatter diagram

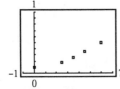

(b)   Using EXPonential REGression on the data yields: $y = (0.0903)(1.3384)^x$

(c) $y = (0.0903)(1.3384)^x = (0.0903)\left(e^{\ln(1.3384)}\right)^x = (0.0903)\left(e^{\ln(1.3384)x}\right)$

      $N(t) = (0.0903)\left(e^{\ln(1.3384)t}\right) = (0.0903)\left(e^{0.2915t}\right)$

(d)   graphing: $y_1 = (0.0903)\left(e^{0.2915x}\right)$

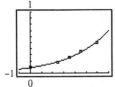

(e) $N(7) = (0.0903)\left(e^{(0.2915)\cdot 7}\right) \approx 0.69$ bacteria

(f)   Find t when $N(t) = 0.75$

$$(0.0903)\left(e^{(0.2915)\cdot t}\right) = 0.75$$

$$\left(e^{(0.2915)\cdot t}\right) = \frac{0.75}{0.0903}$$

$$(0.2915)\cdot t = \ln\left(\frac{0.75}{0.0903}\right)$$

$$t \approx \frac{\ln\left(\dfrac{0.75}{0.0903}\right)}{0.2915} \approx 7.26 \text{ hours}$$

3.   (a)   scatter diagram

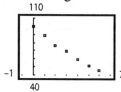

     (b)   Using EXPonential REGression on the data yields: $y = (100.326)(0.8769)^x$

     (c) $y = (100.3262)(0.8769)^x = (100.326)\left(e^{\ln(0.8769)}\right)^x = (100.326)\left(e^{\ln(0.8769)x}\right)$

$$A(t) = (100.326)\left(e^{(-0.1314)t}\right)$$

     (d)   graphing: $y_1 = (100.326)\left(e^{(-0.1314)x}\right)$

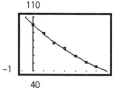

     (e)   Find t when $A(t) = 0.5 \cdot A_0$

$$(100.326)\left(e^{(-0.1314)t}\right) = (0.5)(100.326)$$

$$\left(e^{(-0.1314)t}\right) = 0.5$$

$$(-0.1314)t = \ln(0.5)$$

$$t = \frac{\ln(0.5)}{-0.1314} \approx 5.3 \text{ weeks}$$

     (f) $A(50) = (100.326)\left(e^{(-0.1314)\cdot 50}\right) \approx 0.14$ grams

     (g)   Find t when $A(t) = 20$

$$(100.326)\left(e^{(-0.1314)t}\right) = 20$$

$$\left(e^{(-0.1314)t}\right) = \frac{20}{100.326}$$

$$(-0.1314)t = \ln\left(\frac{20}{100.326}\right)$$

$$t = \frac{\ln\left(\dfrac{20}{100.326}\right)}{-0.1314} \approx 12.3 \text{ weeks}$$

5.   (a)   Scatter diagram with $x =$ year:

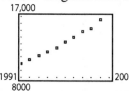

     (b)   Using EXPonential REGression on the data yields:

$$y = (2.7018 \times 10^{-44})(1.056554737)^x$$

     (c)   The average annual rate of return over the past 10 years is given by $056554737 \approx 5.66\%$.

(d)   In the year 2021, $y = \left(2.7018 \times 10^{-44}\right)(1.056554737)^{(2021)} \approx \$52{,}166$.

(e)   Find x when $y = 50000$

$$\left(2.7018 \times 10^{-44}\right)(1.056554737)^{x} = 50000$$

$$(1.056554737)^{x} = \frac{50000}{2.7018 \times 10^{-44}}$$

$$x\ln(1.056554737) = \ln\left(\frac{50000}{2.7018 \times 10^{-44}}\right) \Rightarrow x = \frac{\ln\left(\dfrac{50000}{2.7018 \times 10^{-44}}\right)}{\ln(1.056554737)} \approx 2020$$

The account will be worth \$50,000 in the year 2020.

7.   (a)   scatter diagram

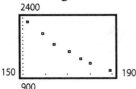

(b)   Using LnREGression on the data yields: $y = 32741.02 - 6070.96\ln(x)$

(c)   graphing $y_1 = 32741.02 - 6070.96\ln(x)$

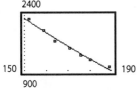

(d)   find x when $y = 1650$:

$$1650 = 32741.02 - 6070.96\ln(x)$$

$$-31091.02 = -6070.96\ln(x)$$

$$\frac{-31091.02}{-6070.96} = \ln(x)$$

$$\Rightarrow x = e^{\left(\frac{31091.02}{6070.96}\right)} \approx 168 \text{ computers}$$

9.   (a)   Scatter diagram with $x = $ year:

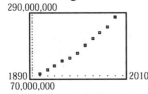

(b)   Using LOGISTIC REGression on the data yields:

$$y = \frac{799475916.5}{1 + \left(1.56344 \times 10^{14}\right)e^{-0.0160x}}$$

(c)　graphing $y_1 = \dfrac{799475916.5}{1+\left(1.56344 \times 10^{14}\right)e^{-0.0160x}}$:

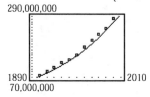

(d)　as $x \to \infty$,

$$y = \dfrac{799475916.5}{1+\left(1.56344 \times 10^{14}\right)e^{-0.0160x}} \to \dfrac{799475916.5}{1} = 799475916.5$$

Therefore, the carrying capacity of the United States is approximately 799,475,916 people.

(e)　in the year 2001,

$$y = \dfrac{799475916.5}{1+\left(1.56344 \times 10^{14}\right)e^{-0.0160(2001)}} \approx 271,143,076 \text{ people}$$

(f)　Find x when $y = 300,000,000$

$$\dfrac{799475916.5}{1+\left(1.56344 \times 10^{14}\right)e^{-0.0160x}} = 300000000$$

$$799475916.5 = 300000000\left(1+\left(1.56344 \times 10^{14}\right)e^{-0.0160x}\right)$$

$$\dfrac{799475916.5}{300000000} = 1+\left(1.56344 \times 10^{14}\right)e^{-0.0160x}$$

$$\dfrac{799475916.5}{300000000} - 1 = \left(1.56344 \times 10^{14}\right)e^{-0.0160x}$$

$$\dfrac{\left(\dfrac{799475916.5}{300000000} - 1\right)}{1.56344 \times 10^{14}} = e^{-0.0160x} \Rightarrow \ln\left(\dfrac{\left(\dfrac{799475916.5}{300000000} - 1\right)}{1.56344 \times 10^{14}}\right) = -0.0160x$$

$$x = \dfrac{\ln\left(\dfrac{\left(\dfrac{799475916.5}{300000000} - 1\right)}{1.56344 \times 10^{14}}\right)}{-0.0160} \approx 2011$$

$$\ln\left(\dfrac{799475916.5}{300000000\left(1+1.56344 \times 10^{14}\right)}\right) \approx -0.1603x$$

$$\dfrac{\ln\left(\dfrac{799475916.5}{300000000\left(1+1.56344 \times 10^{14}\right)}\right)}{-0.1603} = x \Rightarrow x \approx 2011$$

Therefore, the United States population will be 300,000,000 in the year 2011.

11. (a)   Scatter diagram with x = year:

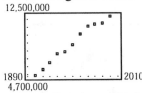

(b)   Using LOGISTIC REGression on the data yields:

$$y = \frac{14471245.24}{1+\left(3.860\times10^{20}\right)e^{-0.0246x}}$$

(c)   graphing $y_1 = \dfrac{14471245.24}{1+\left(3.860\times10^{20}\right)e^{-0.0246x}}$:

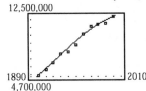

(d)   as $x \to \infty$, $y = \dfrac{14471245.24}{1+\left(3.860\times10^{20}\right)e^{-0.0246x}} \to \dfrac{14471245.24}{1+0} = 14471245.24$

Therefore, the carrying capacity of Illinois is approximately 14,471,245 people.

(e)   in the year 2010, $x = 11$, so $y = \dfrac{14471245.24}{1+\left(3.860\times10^{20}\right)e^{-0.0246(2010)}} \approx 12,811,429$ people

Exponential and Logarithmic Functions

6.R   Chapter Review

1. $f(x) = 3x - 5 \qquad g(x) = 1 - 2x^2$
    (a) $(f \circ g)(2) = f(g(2)) = f\left(1 - 2(2)^2\right) = f(-7) = 3(-7) - 5 = -26$
    (b) $(g \circ f)(-2) = g(f(-2)) = g(3(-2) - 5) = g(-11) = 1 - 2(-11)^2 = -241$
    (c) $(f \circ f)(4) = f(f(4)) = f(3(4) - 5) = f(7) = 3(7) - 5 = 16$
    (d) $(g \circ g)(-1) = g(g(-1)) = g\left(1 - 2(-1)^2\right) = g(-1) = 1 - 2(-1)^2 = -1$

3. $f(x) = \sqrt{x + 2} \qquad g(x) = 2x^2 + 1$
    (a) $(f \circ g)(2) = f(g(2)) = f\left(2(2)^2 + 1\right) = f(9) = \sqrt{9 + 2} = \sqrt{11}$
    (b) $(g \circ f)(-2) = g(f(-2)) = g\left(\sqrt{-2 + 2}\right) = g(0) = 2(0)^2 + 1 = 1$
    (c) $(f \circ f)(4) = f(f(4)) = f\left(\sqrt{4 + 2}\right) = f\left(\sqrt{6}\right) = \sqrt{\sqrt{6} + 2}$
    (d) $(g \circ g)(-1) = g(g(-1)) = g\left(2(-1)^2 + 1\right) = g(3) = 2(3)^2 + 1 = 19$

5. $f(x) = e^x \qquad g(x) = 3x - 2$
    (a) $(f \circ g)(2) = f(g(2)) = f(3(2) - 2) = f(4) = e^4$
    (b). $(g \circ f)(-2) = g(f(-2)) = g\left(e^{-2}\right) = 3e^{-2} - 2$
    (c) $(f \circ f)(4) = f(f(4)) = f\left(e^4\right) = e^{e^4}$
    (d) $(g \circ g)(-1) = g(g(-1)) = g(3(-1) - 2) = g(-5) = 3(-5) - 2 = -17$

7. $f(x) = 2 - x \qquad g(x) = 3x + 1$
    The domain of f is all real numbers. The domain of g is all real numbers.
    (a) $(f \circ g)(x) = f(g(x)) = f(3x + 1) = 2 - (3x + 1) = 2 - 3x - 1 = 1 - 3x$
             Domain: All real numbers.
    (b) $(g \circ f)(x) = g(f(x)) = g(2 - x) = 3(2 - x) + 1 = 6 - 3x + 1 = 7 - 3x$
             Domain: All real numbers.
    (c) $(f \circ f)(x) = f(f(x)) = f(2 - x) = 2 - (2 - x) = 2 - 2 + x = x$
             Domain: All real numbers.
    (d) $(g \circ g)(x) = g(g(x)) = g(3x + 1) = 3(3x + 1) + 1 = 9x + 3 + 1 = 9x + 4$
             Domain: All real numbers.

9. $f(x) = 3x^2 + x + 1 \qquad g(x) = |3x|$
    The domain of f is all real numbers. The domain of g is all real numbers.
    (a) $(f \circ g)(x) = f(g(x)) = f(|3x|) = 3(|3x|)^2 + (|3x|) + 1 = 27x^2 + 3|x| + 1$
             Domain: All real numbers.

(b) $(g \circ f)(x) = g(f(x)) = g(3x^2 + x + 1) = |3(3x^2 + x + 1)| = 3|3x^2 + x + 1|$
Domain: All real numbers.

(c) $(f \circ f)(x) = f(f(x)) = f(3x^2 + x + 1) = 3(3x^2 + x + 1)^2 + (3x^2 + x + 1) + 1$
$= 3(3x^2 + x + 1)^2 + 3x^2 + x + 2$
Domain: All real numbers.

(d) $(g \circ g)(x) = g(g(x)) = g(|3x|) = |3|3x|| = 9|x|$ Domain: All real numbers.

11. $f(x) = \dfrac{x+1}{x-1} \qquad g(x) = \dfrac{1}{x}$
The domain of f is $\{x \mid x \neq 1\}$. The domain of g is $\{x \mid x \neq 0\}$.

(a) $(f \circ g)(x) = f(g(x)) = f\left(\dfrac{1}{x}\right) = \dfrac{\left(\dfrac{1}{x}+1\right)}{\left(\dfrac{1}{x}-1\right)} = \dfrac{\left(\dfrac{1+x}{x}\right)}{\left(\dfrac{1-x}{x}\right)} = \left(\dfrac{1+x}{x}\right)\left(\dfrac{x}{1-x}\right) = \left(\dfrac{1+x}{1-x}\right)$
Domain of $f \circ g$ is $\{x \mid x \neq 0, \ x \neq 1\}$.

(b) $(g \circ f)(x) = g(f(x)) = g\left(\dfrac{x+1}{x-1}\right) = \dfrac{1}{\left(\dfrac{x+1}{x-1}\right)} = \left(\dfrac{x-1}{x+1}\right)$
Domain of $g \circ f$ is $\{x \mid x \neq -1, \ x \neq 1\}$.

(c) $(f \circ f)(x) = f(f(x)) = f\left(\dfrac{x+1}{x-1}\right) = \dfrac{\left(\dfrac{x+1}{x-1}+1\right)}{\left(\dfrac{x+1}{x-1}-1\right)} = \dfrac{\left(\dfrac{x+1+1(x-1)}{x-1}\right)}{\left(\dfrac{x+1-1(x-1)}{x-1}\right)}$

$= \dfrac{\left(\dfrac{x+1+x-1}{x-1}\right)}{\left(\dfrac{x+1-x+1}{x-1}\right)} = \dfrac{\left(\dfrac{2x}{x-1}\right)}{\left(\dfrac{2}{x-1}\right)} = \left(\dfrac{2x}{x-1}\right)\left(\dfrac{x-1}{2}\right) = x$
Domain of $f \circ f$ is $\{x \mid x \neq 1\}$.

(d) $(g \circ g)(x) = g(g(x)) = g\left(\dfrac{1}{x}\right) = \dfrac{1}{(1/x)} = x$, Domain of $g \circ g$ is $\{x \mid x \neq 0\}$.

13. inverse $\{(2,1),(5,3),(8,5),(10,6)\}$ is a function

15.

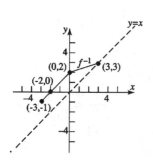

17. $f(x) = \dfrac{2x+3}{5x-2}$

$\qquad y = \dfrac{2x+3}{5x-2}$

$\qquad x = \dfrac{2y+3}{5y-2}$ Inverse

$\qquad x(5y-2) = 2y+3$

$\qquad 5xy - 2x = 2y + 3$

$\qquad 5xy - 2y = 2x + 3$

$\qquad y(5x-2) = 2x + 3$

$\qquad y = \dfrac{2x+3}{5x-2} \Rightarrow f^{-1}(x) = \dfrac{2x+3}{5x-2}$

Verify:

Domain of $f =$

range of f^{-1} = all real numbers except $\dfrac{2}{5}$.

Range of $f =$

domain of f^{-1} = all real numbers except $\dfrac{2}{5}$.

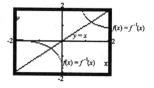

$$f\left(f^{-1}(x)\right) = f\left(\frac{2x+3}{5x-2}\right) = \frac{2\left(\dfrac{2x+3}{5x-2}\right)+3}{5\left(\dfrac{2x+3}{5x-2}\right)-2} = \frac{\left(\dfrac{4x+6+15x-6}{5x-2}\right)}{\left(\dfrac{10x+15-10x+4}{5x-2}\right)} = \frac{\left(\dfrac{19x}{5x-2}\right)}{\left(\dfrac{19}{5x-2}\right)} = \left(\frac{19x}{5x-2}\right)\left(\frac{5x-2}{19}\right) = x$$

$$f^{-1}\left(f(x)\right) = f^{-1}\left(\frac{2x+3}{5x-2}\right) = \frac{2\left(\dfrac{2x+3}{5x-2}\right)+3}{5\left(\dfrac{2x+3}{5x-2}\right)-2} = \frac{\left(\dfrac{4x+6+15x-6}{5x-2}\right)}{\left(\dfrac{10x+15-10x+4}{5x-2}\right)} = \frac{\left(\dfrac{19x}{5x-2}\right)}{\left(\dfrac{19}{5x-2}\right)} = \left(\frac{19x}{5x-2}\right)\left(\frac{5x-2}{19}\right) = x$$

19. $f(x) = \dfrac{1}{x-1}$

$\qquad y = \dfrac{1}{x-1}$

$\qquad x = \dfrac{1}{y-1}$ Inverse

$\qquad x(y-1) = 1$

$\qquad xy - x = 1 \Rightarrow xy = x + 1$

$\qquad y = \dfrac{x+1}{x} \Rightarrow f^{-1}(x) = \dfrac{x+1}{x}$

Domain of $f =$

range of f^{-1} = all real numbers except 1

Range of $f =$

domain of f^{-1} = all real numbers except 0

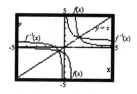

Verify:

$$f\left(f^{-1}(x)\right) = f\left(\frac{x+1}{x}\right) = \frac{1}{\left(\dfrac{x+1}{x}\right)-1} = \frac{1}{\left(\dfrac{x+1-x}{x}\right)} = \frac{1}{\left(\dfrac{1}{x}\right)} = (1)\left(\frac{x}{1}\right) = x$$

$$f^{-1}\left(f(x)\right) = f^{-1}\left(\frac{1}{x-1}\right) = \frac{\left(\dfrac{1}{x-1}\right)+1}{\left(\dfrac{1}{x-1}\right)} = \frac{\left(\dfrac{1+x-1}{x-1}\right)}{\left(\dfrac{1}{x-1}\right)} = \frac{\left(\dfrac{x}{x-1}\right)}{\left(\dfrac{1}{x-1}\right)} = \left(\frac{x}{x-1}\right)\left(\frac{x-1}{1}\right) = x$$

21. $f(x) = \dfrac{3}{x^{1/3}}$

$y = \dfrac{3}{x^{1/3}}$

$x = \dfrac{3}{y^{1/3}}$ Inverse

$xy^{1/3} = 3 \Rightarrow y^{1/3} = \dfrac{3}{x}$

$y = \dfrac{27}{x^3} \Rightarrow f^{-1}(x) = \dfrac{27}{x^3}$

Domain of f =
range of f^{-1} = all real numbers except 0
Range of f =
domain of f^{-1} = all real numbers except 0

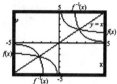

Verify:

$$f\left(f^{-1}(x)\right) = f\left(\dfrac{27}{x^3}\right) = \dfrac{3}{\left(\dfrac{27}{x^3}\right)^{1/3}} = \dfrac{3}{\left(\dfrac{3}{x}\right)} = 3\left(\dfrac{x}{3}\right) = x$$

$$f^{-1}\left(f(x)\right) = f^{-1}\left(\dfrac{3}{x^{1/3}}\right) = \dfrac{27}{\left(\dfrac{3}{x^{1/3}}\right)^3} = \dfrac{27}{\left(\dfrac{27}{x}\right)} = 27\left(\dfrac{x}{27}\right) = x$$

23. (a) $f(4) = 3^4 = 81$

(b) $g(9) = \log_3(9) = \log_3\left(3^2\right) = 2$

(c) $f(-2) = 3^{-2} = \dfrac{1}{9}$

(d) $g\left(\dfrac{1}{27}\right) = \log_3\left(\dfrac{1}{27}\right) = \log_3\left(3^{-3}\right) = -3$

25. $5^2 = z$ is equivalent to $2 = \log_5 z$

27. $\log_5 u = 13$ is equivalent to $5^{13} = u$

29. The domain of $y = \log(3x - 2)$ is:

$3x - 2 > 0 \Rightarrow x > \dfrac{2}{3}$

$\left\{x \,\middle|\, x > \dfrac{2}{3}\right\}$

31. The domain of
$y = \log_2\left(x^2 - 3x + 2\right)$ is:

$x^2 - 3x + 2 > 0$

$(x - 2)(x - 1) > 0$

$x > 2$ or $x < 1$

$\left\{x \,\middle|\, x < 1 \text{ or } x > 2\right\}$

33. $\log_2\left(\dfrac{1}{8}\right) = \log_2 2^{-3} = -3\log_2 2 = -3$

35. $\ln e^{\sqrt{2}} = \sqrt{2}$

37. $2^{\log_2 0.4} = 0.4$

39. $\log_3\left(\dfrac{uv^2}{w}\right) = \log_3 uv^2 - \log_3 w = \log_3 u + \log_3 v^2 - \log_3 w = \log_3 u + 2\log_3 v - \log_3 w$

41. $\log\left(x^2\sqrt{x^3 + 1}\right) = \log x^2 + \log\left(x^3 + 1\right)^{1/2} = 2\log x + \dfrac{1}{2}\log\left(x^3 + 1\right)$

43. $\ln\left(\dfrac{x\sqrt[3]{x^2+1}}{x-3}\right) = \ln\left(x\sqrt[3]{x^2+1}\right) - \ln(x-3) = \ln x + \ln\left(x^2+1\right)^{1/3} - \ln(x-3)$

$$= \ln x + \frac{1}{3}\ln\left(x^2+1\right) - \ln(x-3)$$

45. $3\log_4 x^2 + \dfrac{1}{2}\log_4 \sqrt{x} = \log_4\left(x^2\right)^3 + \log_4\left(x^{1/2}\right)^{1/2} = \log_4 x^6 + \log_4 x^{1/4} = \log_4 x^6 \cdot x^{1/4}$

$$= \log_4 x^{25/4} = \frac{25}{4}\log_4 x$$

47. $\ln\left(\dfrac{x-1}{x}\right) + \ln\left(\dfrac{x}{x+1}\right) - \ln\left(x^2-1\right) = \ln\left(\dfrac{x-1}{x}\cdot\dfrac{x}{x+1}\right) - \ln\left(x^2-1\right) = \ln\left[\dfrac{\left|\dfrac{x-1}{x+1}\right|}{x^2-1}\right]$

$$= \ln\left(\frac{x-1}{x+1}\cdot\frac{1}{(x-1)(x+1)}\right) = \ln\frac{1}{(x+1)^2} = \ln(x+1)^{-2} = -2\ln(x+1)$$

49. $2\log 2 + 3\log x - \dfrac{1}{2}\left[\log(x+3) + \log(x-2)\right] = \log 2^2 + \log x^3 - \dfrac{1}{2}\log\left[(x+3)(x-2)\right]$

$$= \log 4x^3 - \log\left((x+3)(x-2)\right)^{1/2} = \log\left[\frac{4x^3}{\left((x+3)(x-2)\right)^{1/2}}\right]$$

51. $\log_4 19 = \dfrac{\log 19}{\log 4} \approx 2.124$

53. $y = \log_3(x) = \dfrac{\ln(x)}{\ln(3)}$

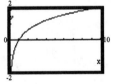

55. $f(x) = 2^{x-3}$

Using the graph of $y = 2^x$, shift the graph 3 units to the right.

Domain: $(-\infty, \infty)$

Range: $(0, \infty)$

Horizontal Asymptote: $y = 0$

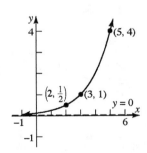

57. $f(x) = \dfrac{1}{2} \cdot 3^{-x}$

Using the graph of $y = 3^x$, reflect the
graph about the y-axis, and shrink

vertically by a factor of $\dfrac{1}{2}$.

Domain: $(-\infty, \infty)$
Range: $(0, \infty)$
Horizontal Asymptote: $y = 0$

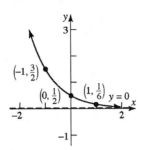

59. $f(x) = 1 - e^x$

Using the graph of $y = e^x$, reflect about
the x-axis, and shift up 1 unit.
Domain: $(-\infty, \infty)$
Range: $(-\infty, 1)$
Horizontal Asymptote: $y = 1$

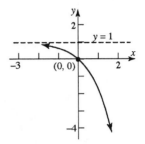

61. $f(x) = \dfrac{1}{2} \ln x$

Using the graph of $y = \ln x$, shrink

vertically by a factor of $\dfrac{1}{2}$.

Domain: $(0, \infty)$
Range: $(-\infty, \infty)$
Vertical Asymptote: $x = 0$

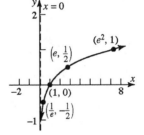

63. $f(x) = 3 - e^{-x}$

Using the graph of $y = e^x$, reflect the
graph about the y-axis, reflect about the
x-axis, and shift up 3 units.
Domain: $(-\infty, \infty)$
Range: $(-\infty, 3)$
Horizontal Asymptote: $y = 3$

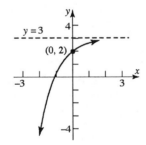

65. $\quad 4^{1-2x} = 2$

$\quad \left(2^2\right)^{1-2x} = 2$

$\quad 2^{2-4x} = 2^1$

$\quad 2 - 4x = 1 \Rightarrow -4x = -1 \Rightarrow x = \dfrac{1}{4}$

67. $3^{x^2+x} = \sqrt{3}$

$3^{x^2+x} = 3^{1/2}$

$x^2 + x = \dfrac{1}{2} \Rightarrow 2x^2 + 2x - 1 = 0 \Rightarrow x = \dfrac{-2 \pm \sqrt{4 - 4(2)(-1)}}{2(2)} = \dfrac{-2 \pm \sqrt{12}}{4} = \dfrac{-2 \pm 2\sqrt{3}}{4} = \dfrac{-1 \pm \sqrt{3}}{2}$

$x = \dfrac{-1 - \sqrt{3}}{2}$ or $x = \dfrac{-1 + \sqrt{3}}{2}$

69. $\log_x 64 = -3$

$x^{-3} = 64$

$\left(x^{-3}\right)^{-1/3} = 64^{-1/3} \Rightarrow x = \dfrac{1}{\sqrt[3]{64}} = \dfrac{1}{4}$

71. $5^x = 3^{x+2}$ using base 10 logarithm

$\log\left(5^x\right) = \log\left(3^{x+2}\right)$

$x \log 5 = (x + 2)\log 3$

$x \log 5 = x \log 3 + 2 \log 3$

$x \log 5 - x \log 3 = 2 \log 3$

$x(\log 5 - \log 3) = 2 \log 3$

$x = \dfrac{2 \log 3}{\log 5 - \log 3}$

$x \approx 4.301$

73. $9^{2x} = 27^{3x-4}$

$\left(3^2\right)^{2x} = \left(3^3\right)^{3x-4}$

$3^{4x} = 3^{9x-12}$

$4x = 9x - 12 \Rightarrow -5x = -12$

$x = \dfrac{12}{5}$

75. $\log_3 \sqrt{x - 2} = 2$

$\sqrt{x - 2} = 3^2$

$x - 2 = 9^2 \Rightarrow x - 2 = 81 \Rightarrow x = 83$

77. $8 = 4^{x^2} \cdot 2^{5x}$

$2^3 = \left(2^2\right)^{x^2} \cdot 2^{5x}$

$2^3 = 2^{2x^2 + 5x}$

$3 = 2x^2 + 5x \Rightarrow 0 = 2x^2 + 5x - 3$

$0 = (2x - 1)(x + 3) \Rightarrow x = \dfrac{1}{2}$ or $x = -3$

79. $\log_6 (x + 3) + \log_6 (x + 4) = 1$

$\log_6 (x + 3)(x + 4) = 1$

$(x + 3)(x + 4) = 6^1$

$x^2 + 7x + 12 = 6$

$x^2 + 7x + 6 = 0$

$(x + 6)(x + 1) = 0$

$x = -6$ or $x = -1$

The logarithms are undefined when $x = -6$, so $x = -1$ is the only solution.

81. $e^{1-x} = 5$

$1 - x = \ln 5$

$-x = -1 + \ln 5$

$x = 1 - \ln 5 \approx -0.609$

83. $2^{3x} = 3^{2x+1}$

$\ln 2^{3x} = \ln 3^{2x+1}$

$3x \ln 2 = (2x + 1)\ln 3$

$3x \ln 2 = 2x \ln 3 + \ln 3$

$3x \ln 2 - 2x \ln 3 = \ln 3$

$x(3 \ln 2 - 2 \ln 3) = \ln 3$

$x = \dfrac{\ln 3}{3 \ln 2 - 2 \ln 3}$

$x \approx -9.327$

85. $h(300) = (30(0) + 8000)\log\left(\dfrac{760}{300}\right) \approx 8000\log(2.53333) \approx 3229.5$ meters

87. $P = 25e^{0.1d}$

     (a) $P = 25e^{0.1(4)}$

           $= 25e^{0.4}$

           ≈ 37.3 watts

     (b) $50 = 25e^{0.1d}$

           $2 = e^{0.1d}$

        $\ln(2) = (0.1)d$

           $d = \dfrac{\ln(2)}{0.1} \approx 6.9$ decibels

89.   (a) $n = \dfrac{\log(10000) - \log(90000)}{\log(1 - 0.20)} \approx 9.85$ years

     (b) $n = \dfrac{\log(0.5i) - \log(i)}{\log(1 - 0.15)} = \dfrac{\log\left(\dfrac{0.5i}{i}\right)}{\log(0.85)} = \dfrac{\log(0.5)}{\log(0.85)} \approx 4.27$ years

91. $P = A\left(1 + \dfrac{r}{n}\right)^{-nt} = 85000\left(1 + \dfrac{0.04}{2}\right)^{-2(18)} = \$41{,}668.97$

93. $A = A_0 e^{kt}$

     $0.5A_0 = A_0 e^{k(5600)}$

       $0.5 = e^{5600k} \Rightarrow \ln(0.5) = 5600k \Rightarrow k = \dfrac{\ln(0.5)}{5600}$

       $0.05A_0 = A_0 e^{\left(\frac{\ln(0.5)}{5600}\right)t}$

         $0.05 = e^{\left(\frac{\ln(0.5)}{5600}\right)t} \Rightarrow \ln(0.05) = \left(\dfrac{\ln(0.5)}{5600}\right)t \Rightarrow t = \dfrac{\ln(0.05)}{\left(\dfrac{\ln(0.5)}{5600}\right)} \approx 24{,}203$ years ago

95. $P = P_0 e^{kt} = 5{,}840{,}445{,}216 e^{0.0133(3)} \approx 6{,}078{,}190{,}457$

97.   (a) $P(0) = \dfrac{0.8}{1 + 1.67e^{-0.16(0)}} = \dfrac{0.8}{1 + 1.67} \approx 0.3$

     (b)   0.8

     (c)   Graphing:

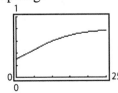

     (d)   Using INTERSECT we have:

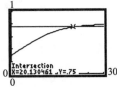

           75% use Windows 98 in 2018, that is, after approximately 20.1 years.

99.   (a)   scatter diagram

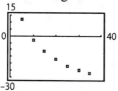

(b)   Using LnREGression on the data yields: $y = 44.198 - 20.331\ln(x)$

(c)   graphing $y_1 = 44.198 - 20.331\ln(x)$

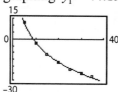

(d)   if $x = 23$, $y = 44.198 - 20.331\ln(23) \approx -20°F$.

Chapter 6

Exponential and Logarithmic Functions

6.CR Cumulative Review

1. The graph represents a function since it passes the Vertical Line Test. The function is not a one-to-one function since the graph fails the Horizontal Line Test.

3. $x^2 + y^2 = 1$

   (a) $\left(\dfrac{1}{2}\right)^2 + \left(\dfrac{1}{2}\right)^2 = \dfrac{1}{4} + \dfrac{1}{4} = \dfrac{1}{2} \neq 1; \left(\dfrac{1}{2}, \dfrac{1}{2}\right)$ is not on the graph.

   (b) $\left(\dfrac{1}{2}\right)^2 + \left(\dfrac{\sqrt{3}}{2}\right)^2 = \dfrac{1}{4} + \dfrac{3}{4} = 1; \left(\dfrac{1}{2}, \dfrac{\sqrt{3}}{2}\right)$ is on the graph.

5. $2x - 4y = 16$

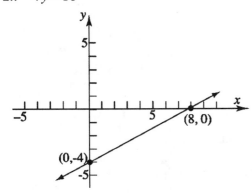

7. Given that the graph of $f(x) = ax^2 + bx + c$ has vertex $(4, -8)$ and passes through the point $(0, 24)$, we can conclude

$$\frac{-b}{2a} = 4, \qquad f(4) = -8, \qquad \text{and} \qquad f(0) = 24$$

Notice that $f(0) = 24 \Rightarrow a(0)^2 + b(0) + c = 24 \Rightarrow c = 24$

Therefore $f(x) = ax^2 + bx + c = ax^2 + bx + 24$.

Furthermore, $\dfrac{-b}{2a} = 4 \Rightarrow b = -8a$

and $f(4) = -8 \Rightarrow a(4)^2 + b(4) + 24 = -8 \Rightarrow 16a + 4b + 24 = -8 \Rightarrow 16a + 4b = -32$

$$\Rightarrow 4a + b = -8$$

Replacing b with $-8a$ in this equation yields

$4a - 8a = -8 \Rightarrow -4a = -8 \Rightarrow a = 2$.

So $b = -8a = -8(2) = -16$.

Therefore, we have the function $f(x) = 2x^2 - 16x + 24$.

9. $f(x) = x^2 + 2$ $g(x) = \dfrac{2}{x-3}$

$$(f \circ g)(x) = f(g(x)) = f\left(\dfrac{2}{x-3}\right) = \left(\dfrac{2}{x-3}\right)^2 + 2 = \dfrac{4}{(x-3)^2} + 2$$

The domain of g is $\{x \mid x \neq 3\}$. The domain of f is $\{\text{Real Numbers}\}$
So the domain of $f \circ g$ is $\{x \mid x \neq 3\}$.

11.   (a) $g(x) = 3^x + 2$
Using the graph of $y = 3^x$, shift vertically
3 units up.
Domain: $(-\infty, \infty)$
Range: $(2, \infty)$
Horizontal Asymptote: $y = 2$

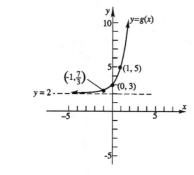

(b) $g(x) = 3^x + 2$

$\qquad y = 3^x + 2$

$\qquad x = 3^y + 2$ Inverse

$\qquad x - 2 = 3^y$

$\qquad \ln(x-2) = \ln\left(3^y\right)$

$\qquad \ln(x-2) = y \cdot \ln(3)$

$\qquad \dfrac{\ln(x-2)}{\ln(3)} = y$

$\qquad g^{-1}(x) = \dfrac{\ln(x-2)}{\ln(3)} = \log_3(x-2)$

(c)

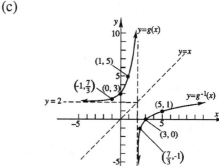

Domain: $(2, \infty)$
Range: $(-\infty, \infty)$
Vertical Asymptote: $x = 2$

13. $\log_3(x+1) + \log_3(2x-3) = 1$

$\qquad \log_3(x+1)(2x-3) = 1$

$\qquad\qquad (x+1)(2x-3) = 3^1$

$\qquad\qquad\quad 2x^2 - x - 3 = 3$

$\qquad\qquad\quad 2x^2 - x - 6 = 0$

$\qquad\qquad (2x+3)(x-2) = 0$

$$x = -\dfrac{3}{2} \ \text{ or } \ x = 2$$

The logarithms are undefined when
$x = -\dfrac{3}{2}$, so $x = 2$ is the only solution.

15.   (a) Scatter diagram:

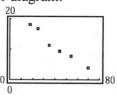

(b)   Answers will vary.

Analytic Geometry
7.2 The Parabola

1. B   3. E   5. H   7. C

9. E   11. D   13. C

15. The focus is $(4, 0)$ and the vertex is $(0, 0)$. Both lie
on the horizontal line $y = 0$. $a = 4$ and since $(4, 0)$
is to the right of $(0, 0)$, the parabola opens to the
right. The equation of the parabola is:
$$y^2 = 4ax$$
$$y^2 = 4 \cdot 4 \cdot x$$
$$y^2 = 16x$$
Letting $x = 4$, we find $y^2 = 64$ or $y = \pm 8$.
The points $(4, 8)$ and $(4, -8)$ define the latus rectum.

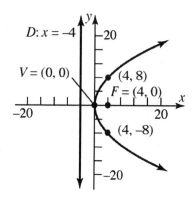

17. The focus is $(0, -3)$ and the vertex is $(0, 0)$. Both lie
on the vertical line $x = 0$. $a = 3$ and since $(0, -3)$ is
below $(0, 0)$, the parabola opens down. The
equation of the parabola is:
$$x^2 = -4ay$$
$$x^2 = -4 \cdot 3 \cdot y$$
$$x^2 = -12y$$
Letting $y = -3$, we find $x^2 = 36$ or $x = \pm 6$.
The points $(6, 3)$ and $(6, -3)$ define the latus rectum.

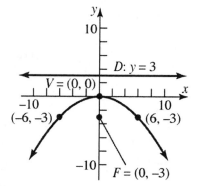

19. The focus is $(-2, 0)$ and the directrix is $x = 2$. The
vertex is $(0, 0)$. $a = 2$ and since $(-2, 0)$ is to the left
of $(0, 0)$, the parabola opens to the left. The
equation of the parabola is:
$$y^2 = -4ax$$
$$y^2 = -4 \cdot 2 \cdot x$$
$$y^2 = -8x$$
Letting $x = -2$, we find $y^2 = 16$ or $y = \pm 4$. The
points $(-2, 4)$ and $(-2, -4)$ define the latus rectum.

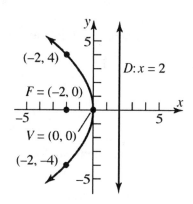

21. The directrix is $y = -\dfrac{1}{2}$ and the vertex is (0, 0). The

focus is $\left(0, \dfrac{1}{2}\right)$. $a = \dfrac{1}{2}$ and since $\left(0, \dfrac{1}{2}\right)$ is above

(0, 0), the parabola opens up. The equation of the
parabola is:

$$x^2 = 4ay$$

$$x^2 = 4 \cdot \dfrac{1}{2} \cdot y \Rightarrow x^2 = 2y$$

Letting $y = \dfrac{1}{2}$, we find $x^2 = 1$ or $x = \pm 1$.

The points $\left(1, \dfrac{1}{2}\right)$ and $\left(-1, \dfrac{1}{2}\right)$ define the latus

rectum.

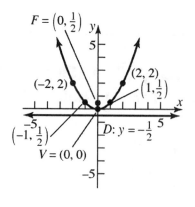

23. The focus is (2, –5) and the vertex is (2, –3). Both
lie on the vertical line $x = 2$. $a = 2$ and since
(2, –5) is below (2, –3), the parabola opens down.
The equation of the parabola is:

$$(x - h)^2 = -4a(y - k)$$

$$(x - 2)^2 = -4 \cdot 2 \cdot (y - (-3))$$

$$(x - 2)^2 = -8(y + 3)$$

Letting $y = -5$, we find $(x - 2)^2 = 16$ or $x - 2 = \pm 4$.
So, $x = 6$ or $x = -2$. The points (6, –5) and
(–2, –5) define the latus rectum.

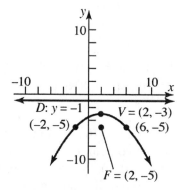

25. Vertex: (0,0). Since the axis of symmetry is
vertical, the parabola opens up or down. Since
(2, 3) is above (0, 0), the parabola opens up. The
equation has the form $x^2 = 4ay$. Substitute the
coordinates of (2, 3) into the equation to find a:

$$2^2 = 4a \cdot 3 \Rightarrow 4 = 12a \Rightarrow a = \dfrac{1}{3}$$

The equation of the parabola is: $x^2 = \dfrac{4}{3}y$. The

focus is $\left(0, \dfrac{1}{3}\right)$. Letting $y = \dfrac{1}{3}$,

we find $x^2 = \dfrac{4}{9}$ or $x = \pm \dfrac{2}{3}$. The points $\left(\dfrac{2}{3}, \dfrac{1}{3}\right)$ and

$\left(-\dfrac{2}{3}, \dfrac{1}{3}\right)$ define the latus rectum.

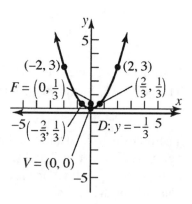

27. The directrix is $y = 2$ and the focus is $(-3, 4)$. This is a vertical case, so the vertex is $(-3, 3)$. $a = 1$ and since $(-3, 4)$ is above $y = 2$, the parabola opens up. The equation of the parabola is:
$$(x - h)^2 = 4a(y - k)$$
$$(x - (-3))^2 = 4 \cdot 1 \cdot (y - 3)$$
$$(x + 3)^2 = 4(y - 3)$$
Letting $y = 4$, we find $(x + 3)^2 = 4$ or $x + 3 = \pm 2$. So, $x = -1$ or $x = -5$. The points $(-1, 4)$ and $(-5, 4)$ define the latus rectum.

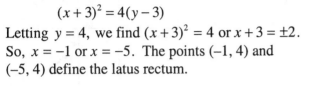

29. The directrix is $x = 1$ and the focus is $(-3, -2)$. This is a horizontal case, so the vertex is $(-1, -2)$. $a = 2$ and since $(-3, -2)$ is to the left of $x = 1$, the parabola opens to the left. The equation of the parabola is: $(y - k)^2 = -4a(x - h)$
$$(y - (-2))^2 = -4 \cdot 2 \cdot (x - (-1))$$
$$(y + 2)^2 = -8(x + 1)$$
Letting $x = -3$, we find $(y + 2)^2 = 16$ or $y + 2 = \pm 4$. So, $y = 2$ or $y = -6$. The points $(-3, 2)$ and $(-3, -6)$ define the latus rectum.

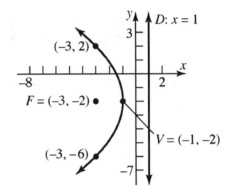

31. The equation $x^2 = 4y$ is in the form $x^2 = 4ay$ where $4a = 4$ or $a = 1$. Thus, we have:

Vertex: $(0, 0)$
Focus: $(0, 1)$
Directrix: $y = -1$

To graph, enter: $y_1 = x^2 / 4$

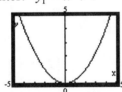

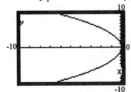

33. The equation $y^2 = -16x$ is in the form $y^2 = -4ax$ where $-4a = -16$ or $a = 4$. Thus, we have:

Vertex: $(0, 0)$
Focus: $(-4, 0)$
Directrix: $x = 4$

To graph, enter: $y_1 = \sqrt{-16x}$; $y_2 = -\sqrt{-16x}$

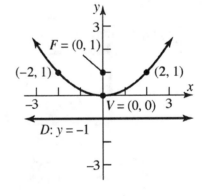

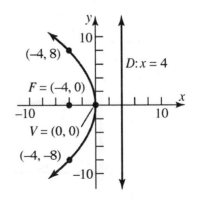

35. The equation $(y-2)^2 = 8(x+1)$ is in the form
$(y-k)^2 = 4a(x-h)$ where $4a = 8$ or $a = 2$,
$h = -1$, and $k = 2$. Thus, we have:

  Vertex: $(-1, 2)$
  Focus: $(1, 2)$
  Directrix: $x = -3$

To graph, enter: $y_1 = 2 + \sqrt{8(x+1)}$;
  $y_2 = 2 - \sqrt{8(x+1)}$

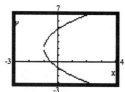

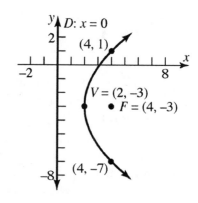

37. The equation $(x-3)^2 = -(y+1)$ is in the form
$(x-h)^2 = -4a(y-k)$ where $-4a = -1$ or $a = \dfrac{1}{4}$,
$h = 3$, and $k = -1$. Thus, we have:

  Vertex: $(3, -1)$
  Focus: $\left(3, -\dfrac{5}{4}\right)$
  Directrix: $y = -\dfrac{3}{4}$

To graph, enter: $y_1 = -1 - (x-3)^2$

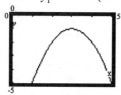

39. The equation $(y+3)^2 = 8(x-2)$ is in the form
$(y-k)^2 = 4a(x-h)$ where $4a = 8$ or $a = 2$,
$h = 2$, and $k = -3$. Thus, we have:

  Vertex: $(2, -3)$
  Focus: $(4, -3)$
  Directrix: $x = 0$

To graph, enter:
  $y_1 = -3 + \sqrt{8(x-2)}$; $y_2 = -3 - \sqrt{8(x-2)}$

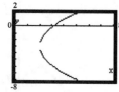

41. Complete the square to put in standard form:
$$y^2 - 4y + 4x + 4 = 0$$

$$y^2 - 4y + 4 = -4x \Rightarrow (y-2)^2 = -4x$$

The equation is in the form $(y-k)^2 = -4a(x-h)$
where $-4a = -4$ or $a = 1$, $h = 0$, and $k = 2$.
Thus, we have:
Vertex: $(0, 2)$; Focus: $(-1, 2)$; Directrix: $x = 1$
To graph, enter: $y_1 = 2 + \sqrt{-4x}$; $y_2 = 2 - \sqrt{-4x}$

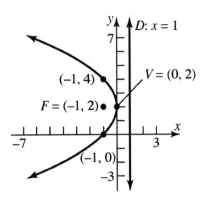

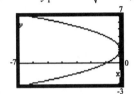

43. Complete the square to put in standard form:
$$x^2 + 8x = 4y - 8$$

$$x^2 + 8x + 16 = 4y - 8 + 16$$

$$(x+4)^2 = 4(y+2)$$

The equation is in the form $(x-h)^2 = 4a(y-k)$
where $4a = 4$ or $a = 1$, $h = -4$, and $k = -2$.
Thus, we have:
Vertex: $(-4, -2)$; Focus: $(-4, -1)$
Directrix: $y = -3$
To graph, enter: $y_1 = -2 + (x+4)^2 / 4$

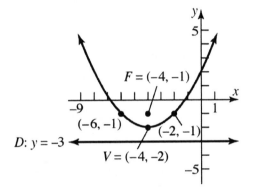

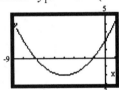

45. Complete the square to put in standard form:
$$y^2 + 2y - x = 0$$

$$y^2 + 2y + 1 = x + 1 \Rightarrow (y+1)^2 = x + 1$$

The equation is in the form $(y-k)^2 = 4a(x-h)$ where $4a = 1$ or $a = \dfrac{1}{4}$,

$h = -1$, and $k = -1$.
Thus, we have:

Vertex: $(-1, -1)$

Focus: $\left(-\dfrac{3}{4}, -1\right)$

Directrix: $x = -\dfrac{5}{4}$

To graph, enter:
$$y_1 = -1 + \sqrt{x+1}; \; y_2 = -1 - \sqrt{x+1}$$

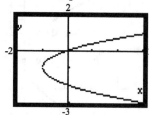

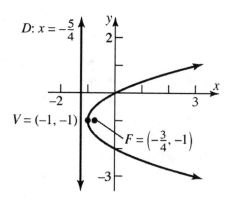

47.   Complete the square to put in standard form:
$$x^2 - 4x = y + 4$$
$$x^2 - 4x + 4 = y + 4 + 4$$
$$(x-2)^2 = y + 8$$

The equation is in the form $(x-h)^2 = 4a(y-k)$ where $4a = 1$ or $a = \dfrac{1}{4}$, $h = 2$, and $k = -8$.

Thus, we have:

Vertex: $(2, -8)$

Focus: $\left(2, -\dfrac{31}{4}\right)$

Directrix: $y = -\dfrac{33}{4}$

To graph, enter: $y_1 = -8 + (x-2)^2$

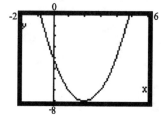

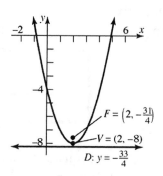

49. $(y-1)^2 = 4a(x-0)$
$(y-1)^2 = 4ax$
$(2-1)^2 = 4a(1) \Rightarrow 1 = 4a$
$(y-1)^2 = x$

51. $(y-1)^2 = 4a(x-2)$
$(0-1)^2 = 4a(1-2)$
$1 = -4a \Rightarrow 4a = -1$
$(y-1)^2 = -(x-2)$

53. $(x-0)^2 = 4a(y-1)$
$(2-0)^2 = 4a(2-1) \Rightarrow 4 = 4a$
$x^2 = 4(y-1)$

55. $(y-0)^2 = 4a(x-(-2))$
$y^2 = c(x+2)$
$1^2 = 4a(0+2) \Rightarrow 1 = 8a \Rightarrow 4a = \dfrac{1}{2}$
$y^2 = \dfrac{1}{2}(x+2)$

57. Set up the problem so that the vertex of the parabola is at (0, 0) and it opens up. Then the equation of the parabola has the form: $x^2 = 4ay$. Since the parabola is 10 feet across and 4 feet deep, the points (5, 4) and (–5, 4) are on the parabola.

Substitute and solve for a: $5^2 = 4a(4) \Rightarrow 25 = 16a \Rightarrow a = \dfrac{25}{16}$

a is the distance from the vertex to the focus. Thus, the receiver (located at the focus) is $\dfrac{25}{16} = 1.5625$ feet, or 18.75 inches from the base of the dish, along the axis of the parabola.

59. Set up the problem so that the vertex of the parabola is at (0, 0) and it opens up. Then the equation of the parabola has the form: $x^2 = 4ay$. Since the parabola is 4 inches across and 1 inch deep, the points (2, 1) and (–2, 1) are on the parabola.
Substitute and solve for a: $2^2 = 4a(1) \Rightarrow 4 = 4a \Rightarrow a = 1$, a is the distance from the vertex to the focus. Thus, the bulb (located at the focus) should be 1 inch, from the vertex.

61. Set up the problem so that the vertex of the parabola is at (0, 0) and it opens up. Then the equation of the parabola has the form: $x^2 = 4ay$.
The point (300, 80) is a point on the parabola.
Solve for $4a$ and find the equation:

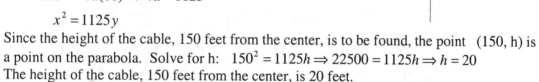

$$300^2 = 4a(80) \Rightarrow 4a = 1125$$

$$x^2 = 1125y$$

Since the height of the cable, 150 feet from the center, is to be found, the point (150, h) is a point on the parabola. Solve for h: $150^2 = 1125h \Rightarrow 22500 = 1125h \Rightarrow h = 20$
The height of the cable, 150 feet from the center, is 20 feet.

63. Set up the problem so that the vertex of the parabola is at (0, 0) and it opens up. Then the equation of the parabola has the form: $x^2 = 4ay$. a is the distance from the vertex to the focus (where the source is located), so $a = 2$. Since the opening is 5 feet across, there is a point (2.5, y) on the parabola.
Solve for y: $x^2 = 8y \Rightarrow 2.5^2 = 8y \Rightarrow 6.25 = 8y \Rightarrow y = 0.78125$ feet
The depth of the searchlight should be 0.78125 feet.

65. Set up the problem so that the vertex of the parabola is at (0, 0) and it opens up. Then the equation of the parabola has the form: $x^2 = 4ay$. Since the parabola is 20 feet across and 6 feet deep, the points (10, 6) and (–10, 6) are on the parabola.
Substitute and solve for a: $10^2 = 4a(6) \Rightarrow 100 = 24a \Rightarrow a \approx 4.17$ feet
The heat source will be concentrated 4.17 feet from the base, along the axis of symmetry.

67. Set up the problem so that the vertex of the parabola is at (0, 0) and it opens down. Then the equation of the parabola has the form: $x^2 = 4ay$.
The point (60, –25) is a point on the parabola.
Solve for $4a$ and find the equation:

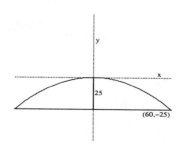

$$60^2 = 4a(-25) \Rightarrow 4a = -144$$

$$x^2 = -144y$$

To find the height of the bridge, 10 feet from the center, the point $(10, y)$ is a point on the parabola. Solve for y: $10^2 = -144y \Rightarrow 100 = -144y \Rightarrow y = -0.69$
The height of the bridge, 10 feet from the center, is $25 - 0.69 = 24.31$ feet.
To find the height of the bridge, 30 feet from the center, the point $(30, y)$ is a point on the parabola. Solve for y: $30^2 = -144y \Rightarrow 900 = -144y \Rightarrow y = -6.25$
The height of the bridge, 30 feet from the center, is $25 - 6.25 = 18.75$ feet.
To find the height of the bridge, 50 feet from the center, the point $(50, y)$ is a point on the parabola. Solve for y: $50^2 = -144y \Rightarrow 2500 = -144y \Rightarrow y = -17.36$
The height of the bridge, 50 feet from the center, is $25 - 17.36 = 7.64$ feet.

69. $Ax^2 + Ey = 0 \quad A \neq 0, \ E \neq 0$

$$Ax^2 = -Ey \Rightarrow x^2 = -\frac{E}{A}y$$

This is the equation of a parabola with vertex at $(0, 0)$ and axis of symmetry being the y-axis. The focus is $\left(0, -\dfrac{E}{4A}\right)$. The directrix is $y = \dfrac{E}{4A}$.

The parabola opens up if $-\dfrac{E}{A} > 0$ and down if $-\dfrac{E}{A} < 0$.

71. $Ax^2 + Dx + Ey + F = 0 \quad A \neq 0$

   (a)   If $E \neq 0$, then: $Ax^2 + Dx = -Ey - F \Rightarrow A\left(x^2 + \dfrac{D}{A}x + \dfrac{D^2}{4A^2}\right) = -Ey - F + \dfrac{D^2}{4A}$

$$\left(x + \frac{D}{2A}\right)^2 = \frac{1}{A}\left(-Ey - F + \frac{D^2}{4A}\right) \Rightarrow \left(x + \frac{D}{2A}\right)^2 = -\frac{E}{A}\left(y + \frac{F}{E} - \frac{D^2}{4AE}\right)$$

$$\left(x + \frac{D}{2A}\right)^2 = -\frac{E}{A}\left(y - \frac{D^2 - 4AF}{4AE}\right)$$

This is the equation of a parabola whose vertex is $\left(-\dfrac{D}{2A}, \dfrac{D^2 - 4AF}{4AE}\right)$ and axis of symmetry parallel to the y-axis.

   (b)   If $E = 0$, then $Ax^2 + Dx + F = 0 \Rightarrow x = \dfrac{-D \pm \sqrt{D^2 - 4AF}}{2A}$

       If $D^2 - 4AF = 0$, then $x = -\dfrac{D}{2A}$ is a single vertical line.

   (c)   If $E = 0$, then $Ax^2 + Dx + F = 0 \Rightarrow x = \dfrac{-D \pm \sqrt{D^2 - 4AF}}{2A}$

       If $D^2 - 4AF > 0$,

       then $x = \dfrac{-D + \sqrt{D^2 - 4AF}}{2A}$ or $x = \dfrac{-D - \sqrt{D^2 - 4AF}}{2A}$ are two vertical lines.

   (d)   If $E = 0$, then $Ax^2 + Dx + F = 0 \Rightarrow x = \dfrac{-D \pm \sqrt{D^2 - 4AF}}{2A}$

       If $D^2 - 4AF < 0$, there is no real solution. The graph contains no points.

Analytic Geometry

7.3   The Ellipse

1.   C   3.   B   5.   C   7.   D

9. $\dfrac{x^2}{25} + \dfrac{y^2}{4} = 1$

The center of the ellipse is at the origin.
$a = 5,\ b = 2$. The vertices are $(5, 0)$ and
$(-5, 0)$. Find the value of c:
$$c^2 = a^2 - b^2 = 25 - 4 = 21 \Rightarrow c = \sqrt{21}$$
The foci are $\left(\sqrt{21}, 0\right)$ and $\left(-\sqrt{21}, 0\right)$.

To graph, enter:
$$y_1 = 2\sqrt{(1 - x^2 / 25)};\quad y_1 = -2\sqrt{(1 - x^2 / 25)}$$

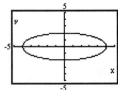

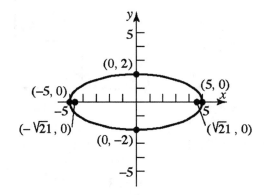

11. $\dfrac{x^2}{9} + \dfrac{y^2}{25} = 1$

The center of the ellipse is at the origin.
$a = 5,\ b = 3$. The vertices are $(0, 5)$ and $(0, -5)$.
Find the value of c:
$$c^2 = a^2 - b^2 = 25 - 9 = 16$$
$$c = 4$$
The foci are $(0, 4)$ and $(0, -4)$.

To graph, enter:
$$y_1 = 5\sqrt{(1 - x^2 / 9)};\quad y_1 = -5\sqrt{(1 - x^2 / 9)}$$

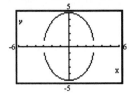

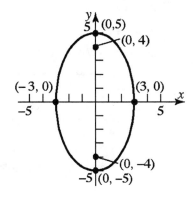

13. $4x^2 + y^2 = 16$

Divide by 16 to put in standard form:

$$\frac{4x^2}{16} + \frac{y^2}{16} = \frac{16}{16} \quad \Rightarrow \quad \frac{x^2}{4} + \frac{y^2}{16} = 1$$

The center of the ellipse is at the origin. $a = 4, \ b = 2$.

The vertices are $(0, 4)$ and $(0, -4)$. Find the value of c:

$$c^2 = a^2 - b^2 = 16 - 4 = 12$$

$$c = \sqrt{12} = 2\sqrt{3}$$

The foci are $\left(0, 2\sqrt{3}\right)$ and $\left(0, -2\sqrt{3}\right)$.

To graph, enter:

$$y_1 = \sqrt{(16 - 4x^2)}; \ y_1 = -\sqrt{(16 - 4x^2)}$$

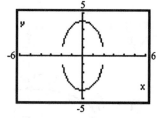

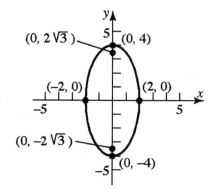

15. $4y^2 + x^2 = 8$

Divide by 8 to put in standard form:

$$\frac{4y^2}{8} + \frac{x^2}{8} = \frac{8}{8} \quad \Rightarrow \quad \frac{x^2}{8} + \frac{y^2}{2} = 1$$

The center of the ellipse is at the origin. $a = \sqrt{8} = 2\sqrt{2}, \ b = \sqrt{2}$.

The vertices are $\left(2\sqrt{2}, 0\right)$ and $\left(-2\sqrt{2}, 0\right)$. Find the value of c:

$$c^2 = a^2 - b^2 = 8 - 2 = 6$$

$$c = \sqrt{6}$$

The foci are $\left(\sqrt{6}, 0\right)$ and $\left(-\sqrt{6}, 0\right)$.

To graph, enter:

$$y_1 = \sqrt{(2 - x^2/4)}; \ y_1 = -\sqrt{(2 - x^2/4)}$$

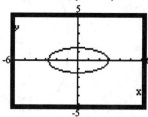

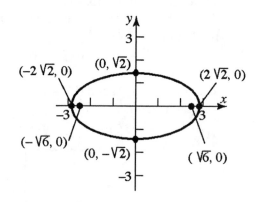

17. $x^2 + y^2 = 16$
This is the equation of a circle whose center
is at $(0, 0)$ and radius $= 4$.
Vertices: $(-4,0)$, $(4,0)$, $(0,-4)$, $(0,4)$
Focus: $(0,0)$
To graph, enter: $y_1 = \sqrt{(16 - x^2)}$; $y_1 = -\sqrt{(16 - x^2)}$

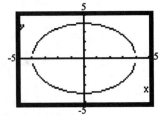

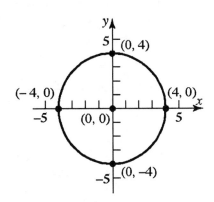

19.   Center: $(0, 0)$; Focus: $(3, 0)$; Vertex: $(5, 0)$;
Major axis is the x-axis; $a = 5$; $c = 3$. Find b:
$$b^2 = a^2 - c^2 = 25 - 9 = 16$$
$$b = 4$$
Write the equation: $\dfrac{x^2}{25} + \dfrac{y^2}{16} = 1$

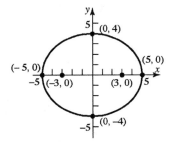

21.   Center: $(0, 0)$; Focus: $(0, -4)$; Vertex: $(0, 5)$;
Major axis is the y-axis; $a = 5$; $c = 4$. Find b:
$$b^2 = a^2 - c^2 = 25 - 16 = 9$$
$$b = 3$$
Write the equation: $\dfrac{x^2}{9} + \dfrac{y^2}{25} = 1$

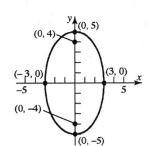

23.   Foci: $(\pm 2, 0)$; Length of major axis is 6.
Center: $(0, 0)$; Major axis is the x-axis;
$a = 3$; $c = 2$. Find b:
$$b^2 = a^2 - c^2 = 9 - 4 = 5$$
$$b = \sqrt{5}$$
Write the equation: $\dfrac{x^2}{9} + \dfrac{y^2}{5} = 1$

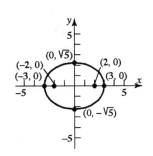

25. Foci: $(0, \pm 3)$; x-intercepts are ± 2. Center: $(0, 0)$;
    Major axis is the y-axis; $c = 3$; $b = 2$. Find a:

    $$a^2 = b^2 + c^2 = 4 + 9 = 13$$

    $$a = \sqrt{13}$$

    Write the equation: $\dfrac{x^2}{4} + \dfrac{y^2}{13} = 1$

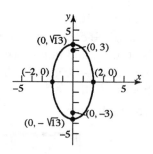

27. Center: $(0, 0)$; Vertex: $(0, 4)$; $b = 1$; Major axis is
    the y-axis; $a = 4$; $b = 1$.

    Write the equation: $\dfrac{x^2}{1} + \dfrac{y^2}{16} = 1$

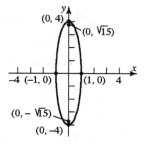

29. $\dfrac{(x+1)^2}{4} + \dfrac{(y-1)^2}{1} = 1$ 31. $\dfrac{(x-1)^2}{1} + \dfrac{y^2}{4} = 1$

33. The equation $\dfrac{(x-3)^2}{4} + \dfrac{(y+1)^2}{9} = 1$ is in the form $\dfrac{(x-h)^2}{b^2} + \dfrac{(y-k)^2}{a^2} = 1$
    (major axis parallel to the y-axis) where $a = 3$, $b = 2$, $h = 3$, and $k = -1$.
    Solving for c: $c^2 = a^2 - b^2 = 9 - 4 = 5 \Rightarrow c = \sqrt{5}$
    Thus, we have:

    Center: $(3, -1)$
    Foci: $\left(3, -1 + \sqrt{5}\right), \left(3, -1 - \sqrt{5}\right)$
    Vertices: $(3, 2), (3, -4)$

    To graph, enter: $y_1 = -1 + 3\sqrt{1 - (x-3)^2 / 4}$;

    $$y_2 = -1 - 3\sqrt{1 - (x-3)^2 / 4}$$

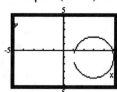

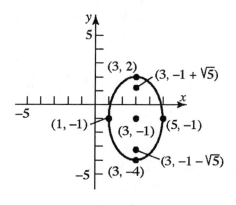

35. Divide by 16 to put the equation in standard form:

    $$(x+5)^2 + 4(y-4)^2 = 16 \Rightarrow \dfrac{(x+5)^2}{16} + \dfrac{4(y-4)^2}{16} = \dfrac{16}{16} \Rightarrow \dfrac{(x+5)^2}{16} + \dfrac{(y-4)^2}{4} = 1$$

    The equation is in the form $\dfrac{(x-h)^2}{a^2} + \dfrac{(y-k)^2}{b^2} = 1$ (major axis parallel to the x-axis) where
    $a = 4$, $b = 2$, $h = -5$, and $k = 4$.
    Solving for c: $c^2 = a^2 - b^2 = 16 - 4 = 12 \Rightarrow c = \sqrt{12} = 2\sqrt{3}$

Thus, we have:

    Center: $(-5, 4)$

    Foci: $\left(-5 - 2\sqrt{3}, 4\right), \left(-5 + 2\sqrt{3}, 4\right)$

    Vertices: $(-9, 4), (-1, 4)$

To graph, enter:

$y_1 = 4 + 2\sqrt{1 - (x + 5)^2 / 16}$;

$\quad y_2 = 4 - 2\sqrt{1 - (x + 5)^2 / 16}$

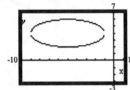

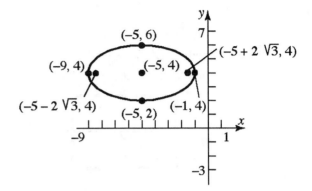

37.   Complete the square to put the equation in standard form:

$$x^2 + 4x + 4y^2 - 8y + 4 = 0$$

$$(x^2 + 4x + 4) + 4(y^2 - 2y + 1) = -4 + 4 + 4 \Rightarrow (x + 2)^2 + 4(y - 1)^2 = 4$$

$$\frac{(x + 2)^2}{4} + \frac{4(y - 1)^2}{4} = \frac{4}{4} \Rightarrow \frac{(x + 2)^2}{4} + \frac{(y - 1)^2}{1} = 1$$

The equation is in the form $\dfrac{(x - h)^2}{a^2} + \dfrac{(y - k)^2}{b^2} = 1$ (major axis parallel to the x-axis) where

$a = 2, \; b = 1, \; h = -2,$ and $k = 1.$

Solving for c: $\; c^2 = a^2 - b^2 = 4 - 1 = 3 \Rightarrow c = \sqrt{3}$

Thus, we have:

    Center: $(-2, 1)$;   Foci: $\left(-2 - \sqrt{3}, 1\right), \left(-2 + \sqrt{3}, 1\right)$; Vertices: $(-4, 1), (0, 1)$

To graph, enter: $y_1 = 1 + \sqrt{1 - (x + 2)^2 / 4}$;

$\qquad\qquad\quad y_2 = 1 - \sqrt{1 - (x + 2)^2 / 4}$

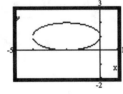

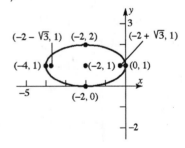

39.   Complete the square to put the equation in standard form:

$$2x^2 + 3y^2 - 8x + 6y + 5 = 0 \Rightarrow 2(x^2 - 4x) + 3(y^2 + 2y) = -5$$

$$2(x^2 - 4x + 4) + 3(y^2 + 2y + 1) = -5 + 8 + 3 \Rightarrow 2(x - 2)^2 + 3(y + 1)^2 = 6$$

$$\frac{2(x - 2)^2}{6} + \frac{3(y + 1)^2}{6} = \frac{6}{6} \Rightarrow \frac{(x - 2)^2}{3} + \frac{(y + 1)^2}{2} = 1$$

The equation is in the form $\dfrac{(x - h)^2}{a^2} + \dfrac{(y - k)^2}{b^2} = 1$ (major axis parallel to the x-axis) where

$a = \sqrt{3}, \; b = \sqrt{2}, \; h = 2,$ and $k = -1.$

Solving for c: $c^2 = a^2 - b^2 = 3 - 2 = 1 \implies c = 1$

Thus, we have:
    Center: $(2, -1)$
    Foci: $(1, -1),\ (3, -1)$
    Vertices: $\left(2 - \sqrt{3}, -1\right),\ \left(2 + \sqrt{3}, -1\right)$

To graph, enter: $y_1 = -1 + \sqrt{2 - 2(x-2)^2 / 3}$;
        $y_2 = -1 - \sqrt{2 - 2(x-2)^2 / 3}$

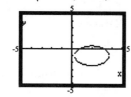

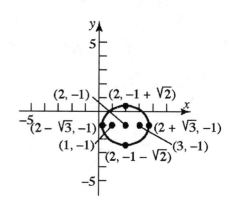

41.   Complete the square to put the equation in standard form:
$$9x^2 + 4y^2 - 18x + 16y - 11 = 0 \implies 9(x^2 - 2x) + 4(y^2 + 4y) = 11$$
$$9(x^2 - 2x + 1) + 4(y^2 + 4y + 4) = 11 + 9 + 16 \implies 9(x-1)^2 + 4(y+2)^2 = 36$$
$$\frac{9(x-1)^2}{36} + \frac{4(y+2)^2}{36} = \frac{36}{36} \implies \frac{(x-1)^2}{4} + \frac{(y+2)^2}{9} = 1$$

The equation is in the form $\dfrac{(x-h)^2}{b^2} + \dfrac{(y-k)^2}{a^2} = 1$ (major axis parallel to the y-axis) where
$a = 3,\ b = 2,\ h = 1,$ and $k = -2$.
Solving for c: $c^2 = a^2 - b^2 = 9 - 4 = 5 \implies c = \sqrt{5}$
Thus, we have:
    Center: $(1, -2)$
    Foci: $\left(1, -2 + \sqrt{5}\right),\ \left(1, -2 - \sqrt{5}\right)$
    Vertices: $(1, 1),\ (1, -5)$

To graph, enter: $y_1 = -2 + 3\sqrt{1 - (x-1)^2 / 4}$;
        $y_2 = -2 - 3\sqrt{1 - (x-1)^2 / 4}$

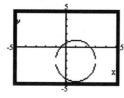

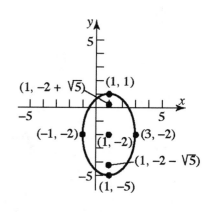

43.   Complete the square to put the equation in standard form:
$$4x^2 + y^2 + 4y = 0 \implies 4x^2 + y^2 + 4y + 4 = 4$$
$$4x^2 + (y+2)^2 = 4 \implies \frac{4x^2}{4} + \frac{(y+2)^2}{4} = \frac{4}{4} \implies \frac{x^2}{1} + \frac{(y+2)^2}{4} = 1$$

The equation is in the form $\dfrac{(x-h)^2}{b^2} + \dfrac{(y-k)^2}{a^2} = 1$ (major axis parallel to the y-axis) where
$a = 2,\ b = 1,\ h = 0,$ and $k = -2$.
Solving for c: $c^2 = a^2 - b^2 = 4 - 1 = 3 \implies c = \sqrt{3}$

Thus, we have:

Center: $(0, -2)$

Foci: $\left(0, -2 + \sqrt{3}\right),\ \left(0, -2 - \sqrt{3}\right)$

Vertices: $(0, 0),\ (0, -4)$

To graph, enter: $y_1 = -2 + 2\sqrt{1 - x^2}$;

$y_2 = -2 - 2\sqrt{1 - x^2}$

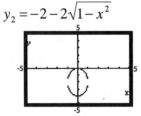

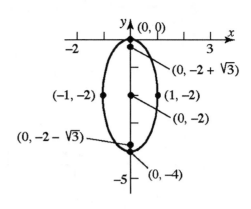

45. Center: $(2, -2)$; Vertex: $(7, -2)$;
Focus: $(4, -2)$; Major axis parallel
to the x-axis; $a = 5$; $c = 2$.
Find b:

$$b^2 = a^2 - c^2 = 25 - 4 = 21$$

$$b = \sqrt{21}$$

Write the equation:

$$\frac{(x-2)^2}{25} + \frac{(y+2)^2}{21} = 1$$

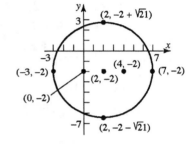

47. Vertices: $(4, 3),\ (4, 9)$; Focus: $(4, 8)$;
Center: $(4, 6)$; Major axis parallel to the
y-axis; $a = 3$; $c = 2$.
Find b:

$$b^2 = a^2 - c^2 = 9 - 4 = 5$$

$$b = \sqrt{5}$$

Write the equation: $\dfrac{(x-4)^2}{5} + \dfrac{(y-6)^2}{9} = 1$

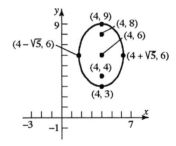

49. Foci: $(5, 1),\ (-1, 1)$; length of the major axis = 8;
Center: $(2, 1)$; Major axis parallel to the x-axis;
$a = 4$; $c = 3$.   Find b:

$$b^2 = a^2 - c^2 = 16 - 9 = 7$$

$$b = \sqrt{7}$$

Write the equation: $\dfrac{(x-2)^2}{16} + \dfrac{(y-1)^2}{7} = 1$

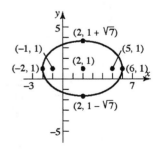

51. Center: $(1, 2)$; Focus: $(4, 2)$; contains the point $(1, 3)$; Major axis parallel to the   x-axis; $c = 3$.

The equation has the form:

$$\frac{(x-1)^2}{a^2} + \frac{(y-2)^2}{b^2} = 1$$

Since the point $(1, 3)$ is on the curve:

387

$$\frac{0}{a^2} + \frac{1}{b^2} = 1$$

$$\frac{1}{b^2} = 1 \Rightarrow b^2 = 1 \Rightarrow b = 1$$

Find a:

$$a^2 = b^2 + c^2 = 1 + 9 = 10 \Rightarrow a = \sqrt{10}$$

Write the equation: $\dfrac{(x-1)^2}{10} + \dfrac{(y-2)^2}{1} = 1$

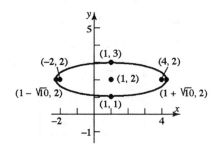

53. Center: $(1, 2)$; Vertex: $(4, 2)$; contains the point $(1, 3)$; Major axis parallel to the x-axis; $a = 3$.

The equation has the form:

$$\frac{(x-1)^2}{a^2} + \frac{(y-2)^2}{b^2} = 1$$

Since the point $(1, 3)$ is on the curve:

$$\frac{0}{9} + \frac{1}{b^2} = 1$$

$$\frac{1}{b^2} = 1 \Rightarrow b^2 = 1 \Rightarrow b = 1$$

Write the equation: $\dfrac{(x-1)^2}{9} + \dfrac{(y-2)^2}{1} = 1$

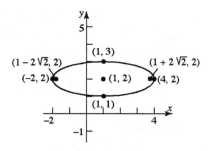

55. Rewrite the equation:

$$y = \sqrt{16 - 4x^2}$$
$$y^2 = 16 - 4x^2, \quad y \geq 0$$
$$4x^2 + y^2 = 16, \quad\quad y \geq 0$$
$$\frac{x^2}{4} + \frac{y^2}{16} = 1, \quad\quad y \geq 0$$

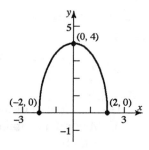

57. Rewrite the equation:

$$y = -\sqrt{64 - 16x^2}$$
$$y^2 = 64 - 16x^2, \quad y \leq 0$$
$$16x^2 + y^2 = 64, \quad\quad y \leq 0$$
$$\frac{x^2}{4} + \frac{y^2}{64} = 1, \quad\quad y \leq 0$$

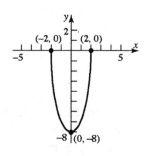

59. The center of the ellipse is $(0, 0)$. The length of the major axis is 20, so $a = 10$. The length of half the minor axis is 6, so $b = 6$. The ellipse is situated with its major axis on the x-axis. The equation is: $\dfrac{x^2}{100} + \dfrac{y^2}{36} = 1$.

61. Assume that the half ellipse formed by the gallery is centered at $(0, 0)$. Since the hall is 100 feet long, $2a = 100$ or $a = 50$. The distance from the center to the foci is 25 feet, so $c = 25$. Find the height of the gallery which is b:
$$b^2 = a^2 - c^2 = 2500 - 625 = 1875 \implies b = \sqrt{1875} \approx 43.3$$
The ceiling will be 43.3 feet high in the center.

63. Place the semielliptical arch so that the x-axis coincides with the water and the y-axis passes through the center of the arch. Since the bridge has a span of 120 feet, the length of the major axis is 120, or $2a = 120$ or $a = 60$. The maximum height of the bridge is 25 feet, so $b = 25$. The equation is: $\dfrac{x^2}{3600} + \dfrac{y^2}{625} = 1$.
The height 10 feet from the center:
$$\frac{10^2}{3600} + \frac{y^2}{625} = 1 \implies \frac{y^2}{625} = 1 - \frac{100}{3600} \implies y^2 = 625 \cdot \frac{3500}{3600} \implies y \approx 24.65 \text{ feet}$$
The height 30 feet from the center:
$$\frac{30^2}{3600} + \frac{y^2}{625} = 1 \implies \frac{y^2}{625} = 1 - \frac{900}{3600} \implies y^2 = 625 \cdot \frac{2700}{3600} \implies y \approx 21.65 \text{ feet}$$
The height 50 feet from the center:
$$\frac{50^2}{3600} + \frac{y^2}{625} = 1 \implies \frac{y^2}{625} = 1 - \frac{2500}{3600} \implies y^2 = 625 \cdot \frac{1100}{3600} \implies y \approx 13.82 \text{ feet}$$

65. Place the semielliptical arch so that the x-axis coincides with the major axis and the y-axis passes through the center of the arch. Since the ellipse is 40 feet wide, the length of the major axis is 40, or $2a = 40$ or $a = 20$. The height is 15 feet at the center, so $b = 15$. The equation is: $\dfrac{x^2}{400} + \dfrac{y^2}{225} = 1$.
The height 10 feet either side of the center:
$$\frac{10^2}{400} + \frac{y^2}{225} = 1 \implies \frac{y^2}{225} = 1 - \frac{100}{400} \implies y^2 = 225 \cdot \frac{3}{4} \implies y \approx 12.99 \text{ feet}$$
The height 20 feet either side of the center:
$$\frac{20^2}{400} + \frac{y^2}{225} = 1 \implies \frac{y^2}{225} = 1 - \frac{400}{400} \implies y^2 = 225 \cdot 0 \implies y \approx 0 \text{ feet}$$

67. Since the mean distance is 93 million miles, $a = 93$ million. The length of the major axis is 186 million. The perihelion is 186 million $-$ 94.5 million $=$ 91.5 million miles. The distance from the center of the ellipse to the sun (focus) is 93 million $-$ 91.5 million $=$ 1.5 million miles; therefore, $c = 1.5$ million. Find b:
$$b^2 = a^2 - c^2 = \left(93 \times 10^6\right)^2 - \left(1.5 \times 10^6\right)^2 = 8.64675 \times 10^{15} \implies b = 92.99 \times 10^6$$
The equation of the orbit is: $\dfrac{x^2}{\left(93 \times 10^6\right)^2} + \dfrac{y^2}{\left(92.99 \times 10^6\right)^2} = 1$.

69.   The mean distance is 507 million – 23.2 million = 483.8 million miles.
The perihelion is 483.8 million – 23.2 million = 460.6 million miles.
Since $a = 483.8 \times 10^6$ and $c = 23.2 \times 10^6$, we can find b:
$$b^2 = a^2 - c^2 = \left(483.8 \times 10^6\right)^2 - \left(23.2 \times 10^6\right)^2 = 2.335242 \times 10^{17} \implies b = 483.2 \times 10^6$$
The equation of the orbit of Jupiter is: $\dfrac{x^2}{\left(483.8 \times 10^6\right)^2} + \dfrac{y^2}{\left(483.2 \times 10^6\right)^2} = 1$.

71.   If the x-axis is placed along the 100 foot length and the y-axis is placed along the 50 foot
length, the equation for the ellipse is: $\dfrac{x^2}{50^2} + \dfrac{y^2}{25^2} = 1$.
Find y when x = 40:
$$\frac{40^2}{50^2} + \frac{y^2}{25^2} = 1 \implies \frac{y^2}{625} = 1 - \frac{1600}{2500} \implies y^2 = 625 \cdot \frac{9}{25} \implies y \approx 15 \text{ feet}$$
The width 10 feet from the side is 30 feet.

73.   (a)   Put the equation in standard ellipse form:
$$Ax^2 + Cy^2 + F = 0 \qquad A \neq 0, \, C \neq 0, \, F \neq 0$$
$$Ax^2 + Cy^2 = -F$$
$$\frac{Ax^2}{-F} + \frac{Cy^2}{-F} = 1$$
$$\frac{x^2}{(-F/A)} + \frac{y^2}{(-F/C)} = 1 \qquad \text{where } -F/A \text{ and } -F/C \text{ are positive}$$
This is the equation of an ellipse with center at (0, 0).
(b)   If $A = C$, the equation becomes:
$$Ax^2 + Ay^2 = -F \implies x^2 + y^2 = -\frac{F}{A}$$

This is the equation of a circle with center at (0, 0) and radius of $\sqrt{-\dfrac{F}{A}}$.

75.   Answers will vary.

Chapter 7

Analytic Geometry
7.4   The Hyperbola

1.   B   3.   A   5.   B   7.   C

9.   Center: $(0, 0)$; Focus: $(3, 0)$; Vertex: $(1, 0)$;
     Transverse axis is the x-axis; $a = 1$; $c = 3$.
     Find b:
     $$b^2 = c^2 - a^2 = 9 - 1 = 8$$
     $$b = \sqrt{8} = 2\sqrt{2}$$
     Write the equation: $\dfrac{x^2}{1} - \dfrac{y^2}{8} = 1$

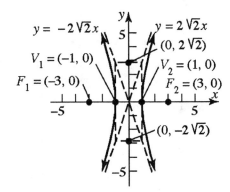

11. Center: $(0, 0)$; Focus: $(0, -6)$; Vertex: $(0, 4)$
     Transverse axis is the y-axis; $a = 4$; $c = 6$.
     Find b:
     $$b^2 = c^2 - a^2 = 36 - 16 = 20$$
     $$b = \sqrt{20} = 2\sqrt{5}$$
     Write the equation: $\dfrac{y^2}{16} - \dfrac{x^2}{20} = 1$

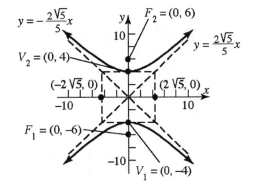

13. Foci: $(-5, 0)$, $(5, 0)$; Vertex: $(3, 0)$
     Center: $(0, 0)$; Transverse axis is the
     x-axis; $a = 3$; $c = 5$. Find b:
     $$b^2 = c^2 - a^2 = 25 - 9 = 16 \Rightarrow b = 4$$
     Write the equation: $\dfrac{x^2}{9} - \dfrac{y^2}{16} = 1$

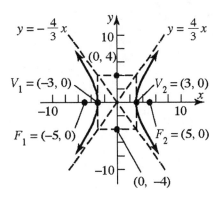

15. Vertices: $(0, -6), (0, 6)$; Asymptote: $y = 2x$;
Center: $(0, 0)$; Transverse axis is the y-axis;
$a = 6$. Find b using the slope of the
asymptote: $\dfrac{a}{b} = \dfrac{6}{b} = 2 \Rightarrow 2b = 6 \Rightarrow b = 3$

Write the equation: $\dfrac{y^2}{36} - \dfrac{x^2}{9} = 1$

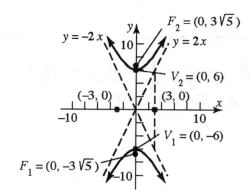

17. Foci: $(-4, 0), (4, 0)$; Asymptote: $y = -x$;
Center: $(0, 0)$; Transverse axis is the
x-axis; $c = 4$. Using the slope of the
asymptote: $-\dfrac{b}{a} = -1 \Rightarrow -b = -a \Rightarrow b = a$

Find b:
$$b^2 = c^2 - a^2 \rightarrow a^2 + b^2 = c^2 \quad (c = 4)$$
$$b^2 + b^2 = 16 \rightarrow 2b^2 = 16 \rightarrow b^2 = 8$$
$$b = \sqrt{8} = 2\sqrt{2}$$
$$a = \sqrt{8} = 2\sqrt{2} \quad (a = b)$$

Write the equation: $\dfrac{x^2}{8} - \dfrac{y^2}{8} = 1$

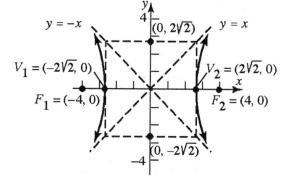

19. $\dfrac{x^2}{25} - \dfrac{y^2}{9} = 1$

The center of the hyperbola is at $(0, 0)$.
$a = 5$, $b = 3$. The vertices are $(5, 0)$ and
$(-5, 0)$. Find the value of c:
$c^2 = a^2 + b^2 = 25 + 9 = 34 \Rightarrow c = \sqrt{34}$
The foci are $\left(\sqrt{34}, 0\right)$ and $\left(-\sqrt{34}, 0\right)$.
The transverse axis is the x-axis.

The asymptotes are $y = \dfrac{3}{5}x$; $y = -\dfrac{3}{5}x$.

To graph, enter:
$$y_1 = 3\sqrt{(x^2/25 - 1)}; \quad y_2 = -3\sqrt{(x^2/25 - 1)}$$

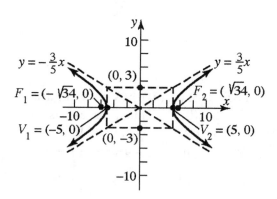

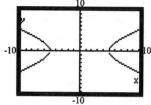

21. $4x^2 - y^2 = 16$

Divide both sides by 16 to put in standard form: $\dfrac{4x^2}{16} - \dfrac{y^2}{16} = \dfrac{16}{16} \Rightarrow \dfrac{x^2}{4} - \dfrac{y^2}{16} = 1$

The center of the hyperbola is at $(0, 0)$. $a = 2$, $b = 4$.

The vertices are $(2, 0)$ and $(-2, 0)$.

Find the value of c:

$\qquad c^2 = a^2 + b^2 = 4 + 16 = 20$

$\qquad c = \sqrt{20} = 2\sqrt{5}$

The foci are $\left(2\sqrt{5}, 0\right)$ and $\left(-2\sqrt{5}, 0\right)$.

The transverse axis is the x-axis.

The asymptotes are $y = 2x$; $y = -2x$.

To graph, enter:

$y_1 = 4\sqrt{(x^2/4 - 1)}$; $y_2 = -4\sqrt{(x^2/4 - 1)}$

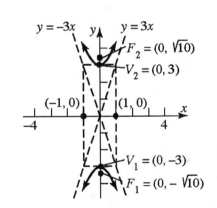

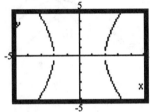

23. $y^2 - 9x^2 = 9$

Divide both sides by 9 to put in standard form: $\dfrac{y^2}{9} - \dfrac{9x^2}{9} = \dfrac{9}{9} \Rightarrow \dfrac{y^2}{9} - \dfrac{x^2}{1} = 1$

The center of the hyperbola is at $(0, 0)$. $a = 3$, $b = 1$.

The vertices are $(0, 3)$ and $(0, -3)$.

Find the value of c:

$\qquad c^2 = a^2 + b^2 = 9 + 1 = 10$

$\qquad c = \sqrt{10}$

The foci are $\left(0, \sqrt{10}\right)$ and $\left(0, -\sqrt{10}\right)$.

The transverse axis is the y-axis.

The asymptotes are $y = 3x$; $y = -3x$.

To graph, enter:

$y_1 = \sqrt{(9x^2 + 9)}$; $y_2 = -\sqrt{(9x^2 + 9)}$

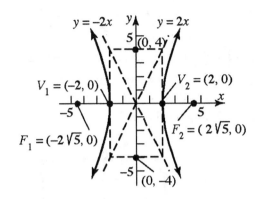

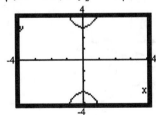

25. $y^2 - x^2 = 25$

Divide both sides by 25 to put in standard form: $\dfrac{y^2}{25} - \dfrac{x^2}{25} = 1$

The center of the hyperbola is at $(0, 0)$. $a = 5$, $b = 5$. The vertices are $(0, 5)$ and $(0, -5)$.

Find the value of c:

$$c^2 = a^2 + b^2 = 25 + 25 = 50$$

$$c = \sqrt{50} = 5\sqrt{2}$$

The foci are $\left(0, 5\sqrt{2}\right)$ and $\left(0, -5\sqrt{2}\right)$.

The transverse axis is the y-axis.

The asymptotes are $y = x$; $y = -x$.

To graph, enter:

$$y_1 = \sqrt{(x^2 + 25)}; \ \ y_2 = -\sqrt{(x^2 + 25)}$$

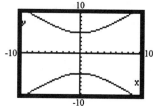

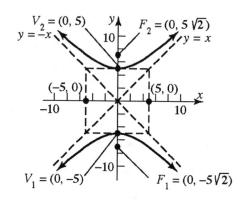

27. $x^2 - y^2 = 1$

29. $\dfrac{y^2}{36} - \dfrac{x^2}{9} = 1$

31. Center: $(4, -1)$; Focus: $(7, -1)$;
Vertex: $(6, -1)$; Transverse axis is
parallel to the x-axis; $a = 2$; $c = 3$.
Find b:

$$b^2 = c^2 - a^2 = 9 - 4 = 5 \Rightarrow b = \sqrt{5}$$

Write the equation:

$$\frac{(x-4)^2}{4} - \frac{(y+1)^2}{5} = 1$$

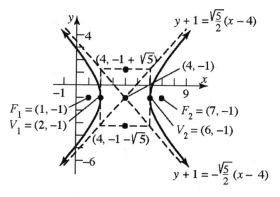

33. Center: $(-3, -4)$;
Focus: $(-3, -8)$;
Vertex: $(-3, -2)$;
Transverse axis is parallel to the
y-axis; $a = 2$; $c = 4$.
Find b:

$$b^2 = c^2 - a^2 = 16 - 4 = 12$$

$$b = \sqrt{12} = 2\sqrt{3}$$

Write the equation:

$$\frac{(y+4)^2}{4} - \frac{(x+3)^2}{12} = 1$$

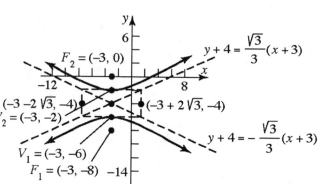

35. Foci: $(3, 7), (7, 7)$; Vertex: $(6, 7)$;
Center: $(5, 7)$; Transverse axis is parallel to
the x-axis; $a = 1$; $c = 2$.
Find b:
$$b^2 = c^2 - a^2 = 4 - 1 = 3$$
$$b = \sqrt{3}$$
Write the equation: $\dfrac{(x-5)^2}{1} - \dfrac{(y-7)^2}{3} = 1$

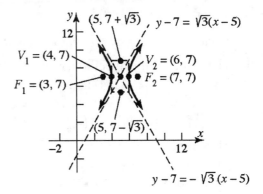

37. Vertices: $(-1, -1), (3, -1)$;
Center: $(1, -1)$; Transverse
axis is parallel to the x-axis;
$a = 2$.

Asymptote: $\dfrac{x-1}{2} = \dfrac{y+1}{3}$

Using the slope of the
asymptote:
$$\frac{b}{a} = \frac{b}{2} = \frac{3}{2} \Rightarrow b = 3$$
Write the equation:
$$\frac{(x-1)^2}{4} - \frac{(y+1)^2}{9} = 1$$

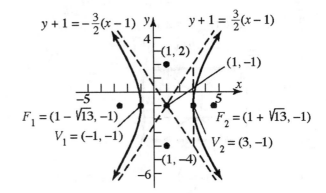

39. $\dfrac{(x-2)^2}{4} - \dfrac{(y+3)^2}{9} = 1$

The center of the hyperbola is at $(2, -3)$. $a = 2$, $b = 3$.
The vertices are $(0, -3)$ and $(4, -3)$. Find the value of c:
$$c^2 = a^2 + b^2 = 4 + 9 = 13 \Rightarrow c = \sqrt{13}$$
Foci: $\left(2 - \sqrt{13}, -3\right)$ and $\left(2 + \sqrt{13}, -3\right)$.
Transverse axis: $y = -3$,
parallel to the x-axis.

Asymptotes: $y + 3 = \dfrac{3}{2}(x-2)$;

$$y + 3 = -\frac{3}{2}(x-2).$$

To graph, enter:
$$y_1 = -3 + 3\sqrt{((x-2)^2/4 - 1)};$$
$$y_2 = -3 - 3\sqrt{((x-2)^2/4 - 1)}$$

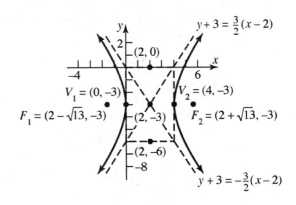

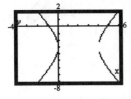

41. $(y-2)^2 - 4(x+2)^2 = 4$

Divide both sides by 4 to put in standard form: $\dfrac{(y-2)^2}{4} - \dfrac{(x+2)^2}{1} = 1$

The center of the hyperbola is at $(-2, 2)$. $a = 2$, $b = 1$.

The vertices are $(-2, 4)$ and $(-2, 0)$.   Find the value of c:
$$c^2 = a^2 + b^2 = 4 + 1 = 5 \Rightarrow c = \sqrt{5}$$

Foci: $\left(-2, 2 - \sqrt{5}\right)$ and $\left(-2, 2 + \sqrt{5}\right)$.

Transverse axis: $x = -2$,
parallel to the y-axis.

Asymptotes:
$y - 2 = 2(x+2)$; $y - 2 = -2(x+2)$.

To graph, enter: $y_1 = 2 + 2\sqrt{((x+2)^2 + 1)}$;

$\quad y_2 = 2 - 2\sqrt{((x+2)^2 + 1)}$

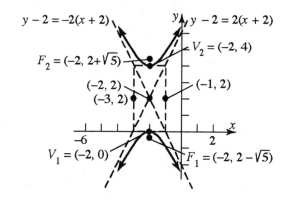

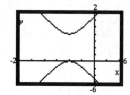

43. $(x+1)^2 - (y+2)^2 = 4$

Divide both sides by 4 to put in standard form: $\dfrac{(x+1)^2}{4} - \dfrac{(y+2)^2}{4} = 1$

The center of the hyperbola is
at $(-1, -2)$. $a = 2$, $b = 2$.

The vertices are $(-3, -2)$ and $(1, -2)$.

Find the value of c:
$$c^2 = a^2 + b^2 = 4 + 4 = 8$$
$$c = \sqrt{8} = 2\sqrt{2}$$

Foci: $\left(-1 - 2\sqrt{2}, -2\right)$ and $\left(-1 + 2\sqrt{2}, -2\right)$.

Transverse axis: $y = -2$, parallel to the x-axis.

Asymptotes: $y + 2 = x + 1$;
$$y + 2 = -(x+1).$$

To graph, enter:
$$y_1 = -2 + 2\sqrt{((x+1)^2 / 4 - 1)};$$
$$y_2 = -2 - 2\sqrt{((x+1)^2 / 4 - 1)}$$

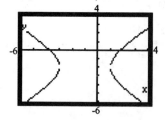

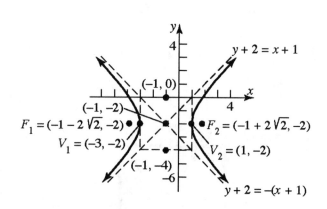

45. Complete the square to put in standard form:

$x^2 - y^2 - 2x - 2y - 1 = 0 \Rightarrow (x^2 - 2x + 1) - (y^2 + 2y + 1) = 1 + 1 - 1$

$(x-1)^2 - (y+1)^2 = 1$

The center of the hyperbola is at $(1, -1)$. $a = 1$, $b = 1$.

The vertices are $(0, -1)$ and $(2, -1)$.

Find the value of c:

$$c^2 = a^2 + b^2 = 1 + 1 = 2 \Rightarrow c = \sqrt{2}$$

Foci: $\left(1 - \sqrt{2}, -1\right)$ and $\left(1 + \sqrt{2}, -1\right)$.

Transverse axis: $y = -1$, parallel to the x-axis.

Asymptotes: $y + 1 = x - 1$; $y + 1 = -(x - 1)$.

To graph, enter:

$y_1 = -1 + \sqrt{((x-1)^2 - 1)}$;

$\quad y_2 = -1 - \sqrt{((x-1)^2 - 1)}$

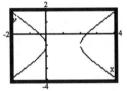

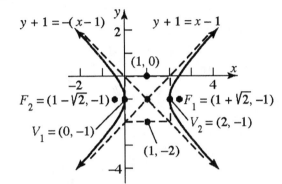

47. Complete the square to put in standard form:

$y^2 - 4x^2 - 4y - 8x - 4 = 0 \Rightarrow (y^2 - 4y + 4) - 4(x^2 + 2x + 1) = 4 + 4 - 4$

$$(y-2)^2 - 4(x+1)^2 = 4 \Rightarrow \frac{(y-2)^2}{4} - \frac{(x+1)^2}{1} = 1$$

The center of the hyperbola is at $(-1, 2)$. $a = 2$, $b = 1$.

The vertices are $(-1, 4)$ and $(-1, 0)$. Find the value of c:

$c^2 = a^2 + b^2 = 4 + 1 = 5 \Rightarrow c = \sqrt{5}$

Foci: $\left(-1, 2 - \sqrt{5}\right)$ and $\left(-1, 2 + \sqrt{5}\right)$.

Transverse axis: $x = -1$, parallel to the y-axis.

Asymptotes: $y - 2 = 2(x + 1)$; $y - 2 = -2(x + 1)$

To graph, enter: $y_1 = 2 + 2\sqrt{((x+1)^2 + 1)}$;

$\quad y_2 = 2 - 2\sqrt{((x+1)^2 + 1)}$

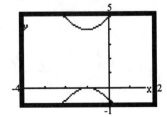

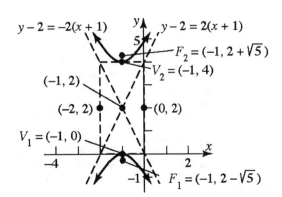

49.   Complete the square to put in standard form:

$$4x^2 - y^2 - 24x - 4y + 16 = 0 \Rightarrow 4(x^2 - 6x + 9) - (y^2 + 4y + 4) = -16 + 36 - 4$$

$$4(x-3)^2 - (y+2)^2 = 16 \Rightarrow \frac{(x-3)^2}{4} - \frac{(y+2)^2}{16} = 1$$

The center of the hyperbola is at $(3, -2)$. $a = 2$, $b = 4$.
The vertices are $(1, -2)$
and $(5, -2)$. Find the value of c:

$$c^2 = a^2 + b^2 = 4 + 16 = 20$$

$$c = \sqrt{20} = 2\sqrt{5}$$

Foci:

$$\left(3 - 2\sqrt{5}, -2\right) \text{ and } \left(3 + 2\sqrt{5}, -2\right).$$

Transverse axis: $y = -2$,
parallel to the x-axis.

Asymptotes: $y + 2 = 2(x-3)$;
$y + 2 = -2(x-3)$

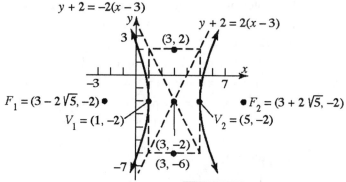

To graph, enter: $y_1 = -2 + 4\sqrt{((x-3)^2 / 4 - 1)}$;

$$y_2 = -2 - 4\sqrt{((x-3)^2 / 4 - 1)}$$

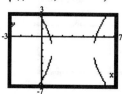

51.   Complete the square to put in standard form:

$$y^2 - 4x^2 - 16x - 2y - 19 = 0 \Rightarrow (y^2 - 2y + 1) - 4(x^2 + 4x + 4) = 19 + 1 - 16$$

$$(y-1)^2 - 4(x+2)^2 = 4 \Rightarrow \frac{(y-1)^2}{4} - \frac{(x+2)^2}{1} = 1$$

The center of the hyperbola is at $(-2, 1)$. $a = 2$, $b = 1$.
The vertices are $(-2, 3)$ and $(-2, -1)$. Find the value of c:

$$c^2 = a^2 + b^2 = 4 + 1 = 5 \Rightarrow c = \sqrt{5}$$

Foci: $\left(-2, 1 - \sqrt{5}\right)$ and $\left(-2, 1 + \sqrt{5}\right)$.

Transverse axis: $x = -2$, parallel to the y-axis.
Asymptotes: $y - 1 = 2(x+2); y - 1 = -2(x+2)$.
To graph, enter:

$$y_1 = 1 + 2\sqrt{((x+2)^2 + 1)};$$

$$y_2 = 1 - 2\sqrt{((x+2)^2 + 1)}$$

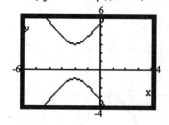

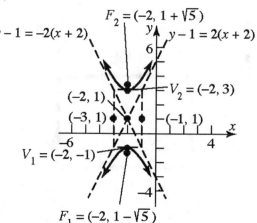

53. Rewrite the equation:
$$y = \sqrt{16 + 4x^2}$$
$$y^2 = 16 + 4x^2, \quad y \ge 0$$
$$y^2 - 4x^2 = 16, \quad y \ge 0$$
$$\frac{y^2}{16} - \frac{x^2}{4} = 1, \quad y \ge 0$$

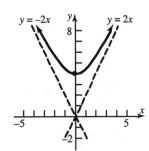

55. Rewrite the equation:
$$y = -\sqrt{-25 + x^2}$$
$$y^2 = -25 + x^2, \quad y \le 0$$
$$x^2 - y^2 = 25, \quad y \le 0$$
$$\frac{x^2}{25} - \frac{y^2}{25} = 1, \quad y \le 0$$

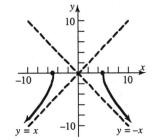

57. (a) Set up a coordinate system so that the two stations lie on the x-axis and the origin is midway between them. The ship lies on a hyperbola whose foci are the locations of the two stations. Since the time difference is 0.00038 seconds and the speed of the signal is 186,000 miles per second, the difference in the distances of the ships from each station is: $(186{,}000)(0.00038) \approx 70.68$ miles

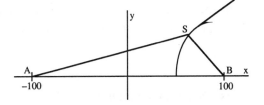

The difference of the distances from the ship to each station, 70.68, equals $2a$, so $a = 35.34$ and the vertex of the corresponding hyperbola is at $(35.34, 0)$. Since the focus is at $(100, 0)$, following this hyperbola, the ship would reach shore 64.66 miles from the master station.

(b) The ship should follow a hyperbola with a vertex at $(80, 0)$. For this hyperbola, $a = 80$, so the constant difference of the distances from the ship to each station is 160. The time difference the ship should look for is:
$$\text{time} = \frac{160}{186{,}000} \approx 0.00086 \text{ seconds}$$

(c) Find the equation of the hyperbola with vertex at $(80, 0)$ and a focus at $(100, 0)$. The form of the equation of the hyperbola is: $\dfrac{x^2}{a^2} - \dfrac{y^2}{b^2} = 1$ where $a = 80$.

Since $c = 100$ and $b^2 = c^2 - a^2 \Rightarrow b^2 = 100^2 - 80^2 = 3600$.

The equation of the hyperbola is: $\dfrac{x^2}{6400} - \dfrac{y^2}{3600} = 1$.

Since the ship is 50 miles off shore, we have $y = 50$. Solve the equation for x:
$$\frac{x^2}{6400} - \frac{50^2}{3600} = 1 \Rightarrow \frac{x^2}{6400} = 1 + \frac{2500}{3600} = \frac{61}{36} \Rightarrow x^2 = 6400 \cdot \frac{61}{36} \Rightarrow x \approx 104 \text{ miles}$$
The ship's location is $(104, 50)$.

59. (a) Set up a rectangular coordinate system so that the two devices lie on the x-axis and the origin is midway between them. The devices serve as foci to the hyperbola so $c = \dfrac{2000}{2} = 1000$. Since the explosion occurs 200 feet from point B, the vertex of the hyperbola is $(800, 0)$; therefore, $a = 800$. Finding b:
$$b^2 = c^2 - a^2 \;\Rightarrow\; b^2 = 1000^2 - 800^2 = 360000 \;\Rightarrow\; b = 600$$
The equation of the hyperbola is: $\dfrac{x^2}{800^2} - \dfrac{y^2}{600^2} = 1$

If $x = 1000$, find y:
$$\dfrac{1000^2}{800^2} - \dfrac{y^2}{600^2} = 1 \;\Rightarrow\; \dfrac{y^2}{600^2} = \dfrac{1000^2}{800^2} - 1 = \dfrac{600^2}{800^2}$$
$$y^2 = 600^2 \cdot \dfrac{600^2}{800^2} \;\Rightarrow\; y = 450 \text{ feet}$$
The second detonation should take place 450 feet north of point B.

61. If the eccentricity is close to 1, then $c \approx a$ and $b \approx 0$. When b is close to 0, the hyperbola is very narrow, because the slopes of the asymptotes are close to 0.
If the eccentricity is very large, then c is much larger than a and b is very large. The result is a hyperbola that is very wide.

63. $\dfrac{x^2}{4} - y^2 = 1 \quad (a = 2,\ b = 1)$
is a hyperbola with horizontal transverse axis, centered at $(0, 0)$ and has asymptotes: $y = \pm\dfrac{1}{2}x$

$y^2 - \dfrac{x^2}{4} = 1 \quad (a = 1,\ b = 2)$
is a hyperbola with vertical transverse axis, centered at $(0, 0)$ and has asymptotes: $y = \pm\dfrac{1}{2}x$

Since the two hyperbolas have the same asymptotes, they are conjugate.

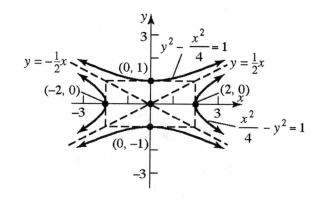

65. Put the equation in standard hyperbola form:
$$Ax^2 + Cy^2 + F = 0 \qquad A \neq 0,\ C \neq 0,\ F \neq 0$$
$$Ax^2 + Cy^2 = -F \Rightarrow \dfrac{Ax^2}{-F} + \dfrac{Cy^2}{-F} = 1 \Rightarrow \dfrac{x^2}{-F/A} + \dfrac{y^2}{-F/C} = 1$$
Since $-F/A$ and $-F/C$ have opposite signs, this is a hyperbola with center at $(0, 0)$.
The transverse axis is the x-axis if $-F/A > 0$.
The transverse axis is the y-axis if $-F/A < 0$.

Analytic Geometry

7.R Chapter Review

1. $y^2 = -16x$
   This is a parabola.

   $a = 4$
   Vertex: $(0, 0)$
   Focus: $(-4, 0)$
   Directrix: $x = 4$

3. $\dfrac{x^2}{25} - y^2 = 1$
   This is a hyperbola.
   $a = 5, \quad b = 1.$

   Find the value of c:
   $$c^2 = a^2 + b^2 = 25 + 1 = 26$$
   $$c = \sqrt{26}$$
   Center: $(0, 0)$
   Vertices: $(5, 0), (-5, 0)$
   Foci: $\left(\sqrt{26}, 0\right), \left(-\sqrt{26}, 0\right)$
   Asymptotes: $y = \dfrac{1}{5}x; \quad y = -\dfrac{1}{5}x$

5. $\dfrac{y^2}{25} + \dfrac{x^2}{16} = 1$
   This is an ellipse.
   $a = 5, \quad b = 4.$

   Find the value of c:
   $$c^2 = a^2 - b^2 = 25 - 16 = 9$$
   $$c = 3$$
   Center: $(0, 0)$
   Vertices: $(0, 5), (0, -5)$
   Foci: $(0, 3), (0, -3)$

7. $x^2 + 4y = 4$
   This is a parabola.
   Write in standard form:
   $$x^2 = -4y + 4$$
   $$x^2 = -4(y - 1)$$

   $a = 1$
   Vertex: $(0, 1)$
   Focus: $(0, 0)$
   Directrix: $y = 2$

9. $4x^2 - y^2 = 8$
   This is a hyperbola.
   Write in standard form:
   $$\dfrac{x^2}{2} - \dfrac{y^2}{8} = 1$$
   $a = \sqrt{2}, \quad b = \sqrt{8} = 2\sqrt{2}.$

   Find the value of c:
   $$c^2 = a^2 + b^2 = 2 + 8 = 10$$
   $$c = \sqrt{10}$$
   Center: $(0, 0)$
   Vertices: $\left(-\sqrt{2}, 0\right), \left(\sqrt{2}, 0\right)$
   Foci: $\left(-\sqrt{10}, 0\right), \left(\sqrt{10}, 0\right)$
   Asymptotes: $y = 2x; \quad y = -2x$

11. $x^2 - 4x = 2y$
This is a parabola.
Write in standard form:
$$x^2 - 4x + 4 = 2y + 4$$
$$(x-2)^2 = 2(y+2)$$

$a = \dfrac{1}{2}$

Vertex: $(2, -2)$

Focus: $\left(2, -\dfrac{3}{2}\right)$

Directrix: $y = -\dfrac{5}{2}$

13. $y^2 - 4y - 4x^2 + 8x = 4$
This is a hyperbola.
Write in standard form:
$$(y^2 - 4y + 4) - 4(x^2 - 2x + 1) = 4 + 4 - 4$$
$$(y-2)^2 - 4(x-1)^2 = 4$$
$$\dfrac{(y-2)^2}{4} - \dfrac{(x-1)^2}{1} = 1$$
$a = 2, \ b = 1.$

Find the value of c :
$$c^2 = a^2 + b^2 = 4 + 1 = 5$$
$$c = \sqrt{5}$$
Center: $(1, 2)$
Vertices: $(1, 0), (1, 4)$
Foci: $\left(1, 2 - \sqrt{5}\right), \left(1, 2 + \sqrt{5}\right)$
Asymptotes:
$$y - 2 = 2(x - 1); \quad y - 2 = -2(x - 1)$$

15. $4x^2 + 9y^2 - 16x - 18y = 11$
This is an ellipse.
Write in standard form:
$$4x^2 + 9y^2 - 16x - 18y = 11$$
$$4(x^2 - 4x + 4) + 9(y^2 - 2y + 1) = 11 + 16 + 9$$
$$4(x-2)^2 + 9(y-1)^2 = 36$$
$$\dfrac{(x-2)^2}{9} + \dfrac{(y-1)^2}{4} = 1$$
$a = 3, \ b = 2.$

Find the value of c:
$$c^2 = a^2 - b^2 = 9 - 4 = 5$$
$$c = \sqrt{5}$$
Center: $(2, 1)$
Vertices: $(-1, 1), (5, 1)$
Foci: $\left(2 - \sqrt{5}, 1\right), \left(2 + \sqrt{5}, 1\right)$

17. $4x^2 - 16x + 16y + 32 = 0$
This is a parabola.
Write in standard form:
$$4(x^2 - 4x + 4) = -16y - 32 + 16$$
$$4(x-2)^2 = -16(y+1)$$
$$(x-2)^2 = -4(y+1)$$

$a = -1$
Vertex: $(2, -1)$
Focus: $(2, -2)$
Directrix: $y = 0$

19. $9x^2 + 4y^2 - 18x + 8y = 23$
This is an ellipse.
Write in standard form:
$$9(x^2 - 2x + 1) + 4(y^2 + 2y + 1) = 23 + 9 + 4$$
$$9(x-1)^2 + 4(y+1)^2 = 36$$
$$\dfrac{(x-1)^2}{4} + \dfrac{(y+1)^2}{9} = 1$$
$a = 3, \ b = 2.$

Find the value of c:
$$c^2 = a^2 - b^2 = 9 - 4 = 5$$
$$c = \sqrt{5}$$
Center: $(1, -1)$
Vertices: $(1, -4), (1, 2)$
Foci: $\left(1, -1 - \sqrt{5}\right), \left(1, -1 + \sqrt{5}\right)$

21. Parabola: The focus is (–2, 0) and the directrix is
$x = 2$. The vertex is (0, 0). $a = 2$ and since (–2, 0)
is to the left of (0, 0), the parabola opens to the left.
The equation of the parabola is:
$$y^2 = -4ax$$
$$y^2 = -4 \cdot 2 \cdot x$$
$$y^2 = -8x$$

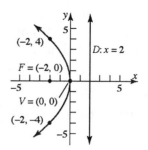

23. Hyperbola: Center: (0, 0);
Focus: (0, 4);   Vertex: (0, –2);
Transverse axis is the y-axis;
$a = 2;\ c = 4$.
Find b:
$$b^2 = c^2 - a^2 = 16 - 4 = 12$$
$$b = \sqrt{12} = 2\sqrt{3}$$
Write the equation: $\dfrac{y^2}{4} - \dfrac{x^2}{12} = 1$

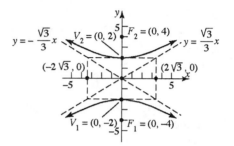

25. Ellipse: Foci: (–3, 0), (3, 0); Vertex: (4, 0);
Center: (0, 0); Major axis is the x-axis;
$a = 4;\ c = 3$. Find b:
$$b^2 = a^2 - c^2 = 16 - 9 = 7$$
$$b = \sqrt{7}$$
Write the equation: $\dfrac{x^2}{16} + \dfrac{y^2}{7} = 1$

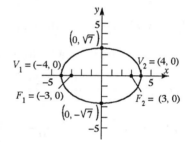

27. Parabola: The focus is (2, –4) and the vertex is
(2, –3). Both lie on the vertical line $x = 2$. $a = 1$
and since (2, –4) is below (2, –3), the parabola
opens down. The equation of the parabola is:
$$(x - h)^2 = -4a(y - k)$$
$$(x - 2)^2 = -4 \cdot 1 \cdot (y - (-3))$$
$$(x - 2)^2 = -4(y + 3)$$

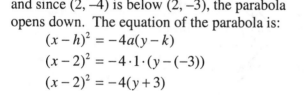

29. Hyperbola: Center: (–2, –3); Focus: (–4, –3);
Vertex: (–3, –3); Transverse axis is parallel to the
x-axis; $a = 1;\ c = 2$. Find b:
$$b^2 = c^2 - a^2 = 4 - 1 = 3$$
$$b = \sqrt{3}$$
Write the equation: $\dfrac{(x + 2)^2}{1} - \dfrac{(y + 3)^2}{3} = 1$

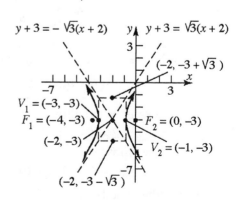

31. Ellipse: Foci: $(-4, 2)$, $(-4, 8)$; Vertex: $(-4, 10)$;
     Center: $(-4, 5)$; Major axis is parallel to the y-axis;
     $a = 5$; $c = 3$. Find b:
$$b^2 = a^2 - c^2 = 25 - 9 = 16$$
$$b = 4$$
Write the equation: $\dfrac{(x+4)^2}{16} + \dfrac{(y-5)^2}{25} = 1$

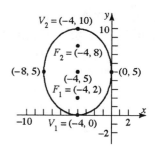

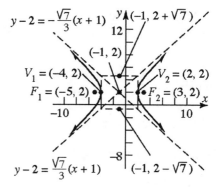

33. Hyperbola: Center: $(-1, 2)$;
     $a = 3$; $c = 4$; Transverse axis parallel to
     the x-axis;
     Find b:
$$b^2 = c^2 - a^2 = 16 - 9 = 7$$
$$b = \sqrt{7}$$
Write the equation:
$$\dfrac{(x+1)^2}{9} - \dfrac{(y-2)^2}{7} = 1$$

35. Hyperbola: Vertices: $(0, 1)$, $(6, 1)$; Asymptote: $3y + 2x - 9 = 0$; Center: $(3, 1)$;

Transverse axis is parallel to the x-axis; $a = 3$; The slope of the asymptote is $-\dfrac{2}{3}$;

Find b: $\dfrac{-b}{a} = \dfrac{-b}{3} = \dfrac{-2}{3} \Rightarrow -3b = -6 \Rightarrow b = 2$

Write the equation: $\dfrac{(x-3)^2}{9} - \dfrac{(y-1)^2}{4} = 1$

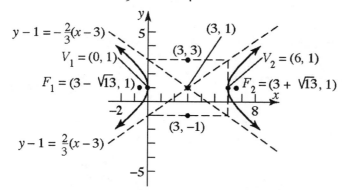

37. Write the equation in standard form:
$$4x^2 + 9y^2 = 36 \Rightarrow \dfrac{x^2}{9} + \dfrac{y^2}{4} = 1$$
The center of the ellipse is $(0, 0)$. The major axis is the x-axis.
$a = 3$; $b = 2$; $c^2 = a^2 - b^2 = 9 - 4 = 5 \Rightarrow c = \sqrt{5}$.
For the ellipse:
        Vertices: $(-3, 0)$, $(3, 0)$;   Foci: $\left(-\sqrt{5}, 0\right), \left(\sqrt{5}, 0\right)$
For the hyperbola:

Foci: $(-3, 0), (3, 0)$;   Vertices: $\left(-\sqrt{5}, 0\right), \left(\sqrt{5}, 0\right)$;   Center: $(0, 0)$

$a = \sqrt{5}; \ c = 3; \ b^2 = c^2 - a^2 = 9 - 5 = 4 \Rightarrow b = 2$

The equation of the hyperbola is: $\dfrac{x^2}{5} - \dfrac{y^2}{4} = 1$

39. Let (x, y) be any point in the collection of points.

The distance from (x, y) to $(3, 0) = \sqrt{(x-3)^2 + y^2}$.

The distance from (x, y) to the line $x = \dfrac{16}{3}$ is $\left| x - \dfrac{16}{3} \right|$.

Relating the distances, we have:

$$\sqrt{(x-3)^2 + y^2} = \frac{3}{4} \left| x - \frac{16}{3} \right| \Rightarrow (x-3)^2 + y^2 = \frac{9}{16} \left(x - \frac{16}{3} \right)^2$$

$$x^2 - 6x + 9 + y^2 = \frac{9}{16} \left(x^2 - \frac{32}{3} x + \frac{256}{9} \right)$$

$$16x^2 - 96x + 144 + 16y^2 = 9x^2 - 96x + 256$$

$$7x^2 + 16y^2 = 112 \Rightarrow \frac{7x^2}{112} + \frac{16y^2}{112} = 1 \Rightarrow \frac{x^2}{16} + \frac{y^2}{7} = 1$$

The set of points is an ellipse.

41. Locate the parabola so that the vertex is at $(0, 0)$ and opens up. It then has the equation:
$x^2 = 4ay$. Since the light source is located at the focus and is 1 foot from the base, $a = 1$.
The diameter is 2, so the point $(1, y)$ is located on the parabola. Solve for y:

$$1^2 = 4(1)y \Rightarrow 1 = 4y \Rightarrow y = 1/4 \text{ feet}$$

The mirror should be 1/4 feet deep or 3 inches deep.

43. Place the semielliptical arch so that the x-axis coincides with the water and the y-axis
passes through the center of the arch. Since the bridge has a span of 60 feet, the length of
the major axis is 60, or $2a = 60$ or $a = 30$. The maximum height of the bridge is 20 feet,

so $b = 20$. The equation is: $\dfrac{x^2}{900} + \dfrac{y^2}{400} = 1$.

The height 5 feet from the center:

$$\frac{5^2}{900} + \frac{y^2}{400} = 1 \Rightarrow \frac{y^2}{400} = 1 - \frac{25}{900} \Rightarrow y^2 = 400 \cdot \frac{875}{900} \Rightarrow y \approx 19.72 \text{ feet}$$

The height 10 feet from the center:

$$\frac{10^2}{900} + \frac{y^2}{400} = 1 \Rightarrow \frac{y^2}{400} = 1 - \frac{100}{900} \Rightarrow y^2 = 400 \cdot \frac{800}{900} \Rightarrow y \approx 18.86 \text{ feet}$$

The height 20 feet from the center:

$$\frac{20^2}{900} + \frac{y^2}{400} = 1 \Rightarrow \frac{y^2}{400} = 1 - \frac{400}{900} \Rightarrow y^2 = 400 \cdot \frac{500}{900} \Rightarrow y \approx 14.91 \text{ feet}$$

45. (a) Set up a coordinate system so that the two stations lie on the x-axis and the origin is midway between them. The ship lies on a hyperbola whose foci are the locations of the two stations. Since the time difference is 0.00032 seconds and the speed of the signal is 186,000 miles per second, the difference in the distances of the ships from each station is: $(186{,}000)(0.00032) = 59.52$ miles

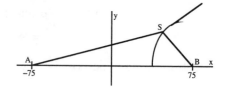

The difference of the distances from the ship to each station, 59.52, equals $a = 29.76$ and the vertex of the corresponding hyperbola is at $(29.76, 0)$. Since the focus is at $(75, 0)$, following this hyperbola, the ship would reach shore 45.24 miles from the master station.

(b) The ship should follow a hyperbola with a vertex at $(60, 0)$. For this hyperbola, $a = 60$, so the constant difference of the distances from the ship to each station is 120. The time difference the ship should look for is:

$$\text{time} = \frac{120}{186{,}000} = 0.000645 \text{ seconds}$$

(c) Find the equation of the hyperbola with vertex at $(60, 0)$ and a focus at $(75, 0)$. The form of the equation of the hyperbola is:

$$\frac{x^2}{a^2} - \frac{y^2}{b^2} = 1 \quad \text{where } a = 60.$$

Since $c = 75$ and $b^2 = c^2 - a^2 \Rightarrow b^2 = 75^2 - 60^2 = 2025$.

The equation of the hyperbola is: $\dfrac{x^2}{3600} - \dfrac{y^2}{2025} = 1$.

Since the ship is 20 miles off shore, we have $y = 20$.

Solve the equation for x:

$$\frac{x^2}{3600} - \frac{20^2}{2025} = 1 \Rightarrow \frac{x^2}{3600} = 1 + \frac{400}{2025} = \frac{97}{81} \Rightarrow x^2 = 3600 \cdot \frac{97}{81}$$

$$x \approx 66 \text{ miles}$$

The ship's location is $(66, 20)$.

Chapter 7

Analytic Geometry

7.CR   Cumulative Review

1. $f(x) = \dfrac{x}{x^2 - 4}$

   f will be defined provided $x^2 - 4 \neq 0$.

   $x^2 - 4 = 0 \Rightarrow (x+2)(x-2) = 0 \Rightarrow x \pm 2$

   The domain of $f(x) = \dfrac{x}{x^2 - 4}$ is $\{x \mid x \neq \pm 2\}$.

3. $f(x) = 3^x + 2$

   (a) Domain = {all real numbers}. Range = $\{y \mid y > 2\}$.

   (b) $f(x) = 3^x + 2$

   $\quad f(x) = 3^x + 2$ Domain of f^{-1} = range of $f = \{x \mid x > 2\}$.

   $\quad y = 3^x + 2$ Range of f^{-1} = domain of f

   $\quad x = 3^y + 2$ Inverse   = {all real numbers}.

   $\quad x - 2 = 3^y$

   $\quad \log_3(x - 2) = y \Rightarrow f^{-1}(x) = \log_3(x - 2)$

5. $6 - x \geq x^2 \Rightarrow 0 \geq x^2 + x - 6 \Rightarrow x^2 + x - 6 \leq 0$

   $x^2 + x - 6 \leq 0 \Rightarrow (x + 3)(x - 2) \leq 0$

   $x = -3, x = 2$ are the zeros. $g(x) = x^2 + x - 6$

Interval	Test Number	$g(x)$	Positive/Negative
$-\infty < x < -3$	-4	6	Positive
$-3 < x < 2$	0	-6	Negative
$2 < x < \infty$	3	6	Positive

   The solution set is $\{x \mid -3 \leq x \leq 2\}$.

7. $f(x) = \log_4(x - 2)$

   (a) $f(x) = \log_4(x - 2) = 2$ (b) $f(x) = \log_4(x - 2) \leq 2$

   $\quad\quad x - 2 = 4^2$ $x - 2 \leq 4^2$ and $x - 2 > 0$

   $\quad\quad x - 2 = 16$ $x - 2 \leq 16$ and $x > 2$

   $\quad\quad\quad x = 18$ $x \leq 18$ and $x > 2$

                                         $2 < x \leq 18$

                                           $(2, 18]$

Chapter 8

Systems of Equations and Inequalities

8.1 Systems of Linear Equations: Substitution and Elimination

1. Substituting the values of the variables:
$$\begin{cases} 2x - y = 5 & \Rightarrow \quad 2(2) - (-1) = 4 + 1 = 5 \\ 5x + 2y = 8 & \Rightarrow \quad 5(2) + 2(-1) = 10 - 2 = 8 \end{cases}$$
Each equation is satisfied, so $x = 2$, $y = -1$ is a solution to the system of equations.

3. Substituting the values of the variables:
$$\begin{cases} 3x - 4y = 4 & \Rightarrow \quad 3(2) - 4\left(\dfrac{1}{2}\right) = 6 - 2 = 4 \\ \dfrac{1}{2}x - 3y = -\dfrac{1}{2} & \Rightarrow \quad \dfrac{1}{2}(2) - 3\left(\dfrac{1}{2}\right) = 1 - \dfrac{3}{2} = -\dfrac{1}{2} \end{cases}$$
Each equation is satisfied, so $x = 2$, $y = \dfrac{1}{2}$ is a solution to the system of equations.

5. Substituting the values of the variables:
$$\begin{cases} x - y = 3 & \Rightarrow \quad 4 - 1 = 3 \\ \dfrac{1}{2}x + y = 3 & \Rightarrow \quad \dfrac{1}{2}(4) + 1 = 2 + 1 = 3 \end{cases}$$
Each equation is satisfied, so $x = 4$, $y = 1$ is a solution to the system of equations.

7. Substituting the values of the variables:
$$\begin{cases} 3x + 3y + 2z = 4 & \Rightarrow 3(1) + 3(-1) + 2(2) = 3 - 3 + 4 = 4 \\ x - y - z = 0 & \Rightarrow 1 - (-1) - 2 = 1 + 1 - 2 = 0 \\ 2y - 3z = -8 & \Rightarrow 2(-1) - 3(2) = -2 - 6 = -8 \end{cases}$$
Each equation is satisfied, so $x = 1$, $y = -1, z = 2$ is a solution to the system.

9. Substituting the values of the variables:
$$\begin{cases} 3x + 3y + 2z = 4 & \Rightarrow \quad 3(2) + 3(-2) + 2(2) = 6 - 6 + 4 = 4 \\ x - 3y + z = 10 & \Rightarrow \quad 2 - 3(-2) + 2 = 2 + 6 + 2 = 10 \\ 5x - 2y - 3z = 8 & \Rightarrow \quad 5(2) - 2(-2) - 3(2) = 10 + 4 - 6 = 8 \end{cases}$$
Each equation is satisfied, so $x = 2$, $y = -2, z = 2$ is a solution to the system of equations.

11. Solve the first equation for y, substitute into the second equation and solve:

$$\begin{cases} x+y=8 & \Rightarrow \quad y=8-x \\ x-y=4 \end{cases}$$

$$x-(8-x)=4 \Rightarrow x-8+x=4$$

$$2x=12 \Rightarrow x=6$$

Since $x=6$, $y=8-6=2$

The solution of the system is $x=6$, $y=2$.

13. Multiply each side of the first equation by 3 and add the equations:

$$\begin{cases} 5x-y=13 & \xrightarrow{\;3\;} & 15x-3y=39 \\ 2x+3y=12 & \longrightarrow & \underline{2x+3y=12} \end{cases}$$

$$17x \qquad =51 \Rightarrow x=3$$

Substitute and solve for y:

$$5(3)-y=13 \Rightarrow 15-y=13 \Rightarrow -y=-2 \Rightarrow y=2$$

The solution of the system is $x=3$, $y=2$.

15. Solve the first equation for x and substitute into the second equation:

$$\begin{cases} 3x & =24 & \Rightarrow & x=8 \\ x+2y= & 0 \end{cases}$$

$$8+2y=0 \Rightarrow 2y=-8 \Rightarrow y=-4$$

The solution of the system is $x=8$, $y=-4$.

17. Multiply each side of the first equation by 2 and each side of the second equation by 3 to eliminate y:

$$\begin{cases} 3x-6y=2 & \xrightarrow{\;2\;} & 6x-12y=4 \\ 5x+4y=1 & \xrightarrow{\;3\;} & \underline{15x+12y=3} \end{cases}$$

$$21x \qquad =7 \Rightarrow x=\frac{1}{3}$$

Substitute and solve for y:

$$3(1/3)-6y=2 \Rightarrow 1-6y=2 \Rightarrow -6y=1 \Rightarrow y=-\frac{1}{6}$$

The solution of the system is $x=\dfrac{1}{3}$, $y=-\dfrac{1}{6}$.

19. Solve the first equation for y, substitute into the second equation and solve:

$$\begin{cases} 2x+y=1 & \Rightarrow \quad y=1-2x \\ 4x+2y=3 \end{cases}$$

$$4x+2(1-2x)=3 \Rightarrow 4x+2-4x=3 \Rightarrow 0x=1$$

This has no solution, so the system is inconsistent.

21. Solve the first equation for y, substitute into the second equation and solve:

$$\begin{cases} 2x - y = 0 \;\Rightarrow\; 2x = y \\ 3x + 2y = 7 \end{cases}$$

$$3x + 2(2x) = 7 \Rightarrow 3x + 4x = 7 \Rightarrow 7x = 7 \Rightarrow x = 1$$

Since $x = 1$, $y = 2(1) = 2$ The solution of the system is $x = 1$, $y = 2$.

23. Solve the first equation for x, substitute into the second equation and solve:

$$\begin{cases} x + 2y = 4 \;\Rightarrow\; x = 4 - 2y \\ 2x + 4y = 8 \end{cases}$$

$$2(4 - 2y) + 4y = 8 \Rightarrow 8 - 4y + 4y = 8 \Rightarrow 0y = 0$$

These equations are dependent. Any real number is a solution for y.
The solution of the system is $x = 4 - 2y$, where y is any real number.

25. Multiply each side of the first equation by –5, and add the equations to eliminate x:

$$\begin{cases} 2x - 3y = -1 \;\xrightarrow{-5}\; -10x + 15y = 5 \\ 10x + y = 11 \;\xrightarrow{}\; \underline{10x + y = 11} \end{cases}$$

$$16y = 16 \Rightarrow y = 1$$

Substitute and solve for x:

$$2x - 3(1) = -1 \Rightarrow 2x - 3 = -1 \Rightarrow 2x = 2 \Rightarrow x = 1$$

The solution of the system is $x = 1$, $y = 1$.

27. Solve the second equation for x, substitute into the first equation and solve:

$$\begin{cases} 2x + 3y = 6 \\ x - y = \dfrac{1}{2} \;\Rightarrow\; x = y + \dfrac{1}{2} \end{cases}$$

$$2\left(y + \frac{1}{2}\right) + 3y = 6 \Rightarrow 2y + 1 + 3y = 6 \Rightarrow 5y = 5 \Rightarrow y = 1$$

Since $y = 1$, $x = 1 + \dfrac{1}{2} = \dfrac{3}{2}$, the solution of the system is $x = \dfrac{3}{2}$, $y = 1$.

29. Multiply each side of the first equation by –6 and each side of the second equation by 12 to eliminate x:

$$\begin{cases} \dfrac{1}{2}x + \dfrac{1}{3}y = 3 \;\xrightarrow{-6}\; -3x - 2y = -18 \\ \dfrac{1}{4}x - \dfrac{2}{3}y = -1 \;\xrightarrow{12}\; \underline{3x - 8y = -12} \end{cases}$$

$$-10y = -30 \Rightarrow y = 3$$

Substitute and solve for x:

$$\frac{1}{2}x + \frac{1}{3}(3) = 3 \Rightarrow \frac{1}{2}x + 1 = 3 \Rightarrow \frac{1}{2}x = 2 \Rightarrow x = 4$$

The solution of the system is $x = 4$, $y = 3$.

31.　Add the equations to eliminate y and solve for x:

$$\begin{cases} 3x - 5y = 3 \\ 15x + 5y = 21 \end{cases}$$

$$\overline{18x \qquad = 24} \Rightarrow x = \frac{4}{3}$$

Substitute and solve for y:　　$3\left(\dfrac{4}{3}\right) - 5y = 3 \Rightarrow 4 - 5y = 3 \Rightarrow -5y = -1 \Rightarrow y = \dfrac{1}{5}$

The solution of the system is $x = \dfrac{4}{3}$, $y = \dfrac{1}{5}$.

33.　Rewrite letting $a = \dfrac{1}{x}$, $b = \dfrac{1}{y}$:

$$\begin{cases} \dfrac{1}{x} + \dfrac{1}{y} = 8 \\ \dfrac{3}{x} - \dfrac{5}{y} = 0 \end{cases} \quad\begin{aligned} &\Rightarrow \quad a + b = 8 \\ &\Rightarrow \quad 3a - 5b = 0 \end{aligned}$$

Solve the first equation for a, substitute into the second equation and solve:

$$\begin{cases} a + b = 8 \quad \Rightarrow \quad a = 8 - b \\ 3a - 5b = 0 \end{cases}$$

$$3(8 - b) - 5b = 0 \Rightarrow 24 - 3b - 5b = 0 \Rightarrow -8b = -24 \Rightarrow b = 3$$

Since $b = 3$, $a = 8 - 3 = 5$.　　Thus, $x = \dfrac{1}{a} = \dfrac{1}{5}$, $y = \dfrac{1}{b} = \dfrac{1}{3}$

The solution of the system is $x = \dfrac{1}{5}$, $y = \dfrac{1}{3}$.

35.　Multiply each side of the first equation by –2 and add to the second equation to eliminate x:

$$\begin{cases} x - y = 6 \\ 2x - 3z = 16 \\ 2y + z = 4 \end{cases} \quad \begin{aligned} &\xrightarrow{-2} \quad -2x + 2y \qquad = -12 \\ &\xrightarrow{} \quad \underline{2x \qquad - 3z = \quad 16} \\ &\qquad\qquad 2y - 3z = \quad 4 \end{aligned}$$

Multiply each side of the result by –1 and add to the original third equation to eliminate y:

$$\begin{aligned} 2y - 3z = 4 \quad &\xrightarrow{-1} \quad -2y + 3z = -4 \\ 2y + z = 4 \quad &\xrightarrow{} \quad \underline{2y + z = \quad 4} \\ &\qquad\qquad\quad 4z = \quad 0 \\ &\qquad\qquad\quad\ z = 0 \end{aligned}$$

Substituting and solving for the other variables:

$$\begin{aligned} 2y + 0 &= 4 & 2x - 3(0) &= 16 \\ 2y &= 4 & 2x &= 16 \\ y &= 2 & x &= 8 \end{aligned}$$

The solution is $x = 8$, $y = 2$, $z = 0$.

37. Multiply each side of the first equation by –2 and add to the second equation to eliminate x; and multiply each side of the first equation by 3 and add to the third equation to eliminate x:

$$\begin{cases} x - 2y + 3z = 7 \\ 2x + y + z = 4 \\ -3x + 2y - 2z = -10 \end{cases}$$

$\xrightarrow{-2}$
$$\begin{array}{r} -2x + 4y - 6z = -14 \\ 2x + y + z = 4 \\ \hline 5y - 5z = -10 \end{array} \xrightarrow{1/5} \quad y - z = -2$$

$\xrightarrow{3}$
$$\begin{array}{r} 3x - 6y + 9z = 21 \\ -3x + 2y - 2z = -10 \\ \hline -4y + 7z = 11 \end{array}$$

Multiply each side of the first result by 4 and add to the second result to eliminate y:

$$\begin{array}{r} y - z = -2 \\ -4y + 7z = 11 \end{array} \xrightarrow{4} \begin{array}{r} 4y - 4z = -8 \\ -4y + 7z = 11 \\ \hline 3z = 3 \Rightarrow z = 1 \end{array}$$

Substituting and solving for the other variables:

$$\begin{array}{l} y - 1 = -2 \\ y = -1 \end{array} \qquad \begin{array}{l} x - 2(-1) + 3(1) = 7 \\ x + 2 + 3 = 7 \Rightarrow x = 2 \end{array}$$

The solution is $x = 2$, $y = -1$, $z = 1$.

39. Add the first and second equations to eliminate z:

$$\begin{cases} x - y - z = 1 \\ 2x + 3y + z = 2 \\ 3x + 2y = 0 \end{cases} \Rightarrow \begin{array}{r} x - y - z = 1 \\ 2x + 3y + z = 2 \\ \hline 3x + 2y = 3 \end{array}$$

Multiply each side of the result by –1 and add to the original third equation to eliminate y:

$$\begin{array}{r} 3x + 2y = 3 \\ 3x + 2y = 0 \end{array} \xrightarrow{-1} \begin{array}{r} -3x - 2y = -3 \\ 3x + 2y = 0 \\ \hline 0 = -3 \end{array}$$

This result has no solution, so the system is inconsistent.

41. Add the first and second equations to eliminate x; and multiply the first equation by –3 and add to the third equation to eliminate x:

$$\begin{cases} x - y - z = 1 \\ -x + 2y - 3z = -4 \\ 3x - 2y - 7z = 0 \end{cases} \Rightarrow \begin{array}{r} x - y - z = 1 \\ -x + 2y - 3z = -4 \\ \hline y - 4z = -3 \end{array}$$

$\xrightarrow{-3}$
$$\begin{array}{r} -3x + 3y + 3z = -3 \\ 3x - 2y - 7z = 0 \\ \hline y - 4z = -3 \end{array}$$

Multiply each side of the first result by -1 and add to the second result to eliminate y:

$$y - 4z = -3 \quad \xrightarrow{-1} \quad -y + 4z = 3$$
$$y - 4z = -3 \quad \longrightarrow \quad \underline{y - 4z = -3}$$
$$0 = 0$$

The system is dependent. If z is any real number, then $y = 4z - 3$.
Solving for x in terms of z in the first equation:

$$x - (4z - 3) - z = 1$$
$$x - 4z + 3 - z = 1$$
$$x - 5z + 3 = 1$$
$$x = 5z - 2$$

The solution is $x = 5z - 2$, $y = 4z - 3$, z is any real number.

43. Multiply the first equation by -2 and add to the second equation to eliminate x; and add the first and third equations to eliminate x:

$$\begin{cases} 2x - 2y + 3z = 6 \\ 4x - 3y + 2z = 0 \\ -2x + 3y - 7z = 1 \end{cases}$$

$$\begin{aligned} \xrightarrow{-2} \quad & -4x + 4y - 6z = -12 \\ \longrightarrow \quad & \underline{4x - 3y + 2z = 0} \\ & y - 4z = -12 \end{aligned}$$

$$\begin{aligned} \longrightarrow \quad & 2x - 2y + 3z = 6 \\ \longrightarrow \quad & \underline{-2x + 3y - 7z = 1} \\ & y - 4z = 7 \end{aligned}$$

Multiply each side of the first result by -1 and add to the second result to eliminate y:

$$y - 4z = -12 \quad \xrightarrow{-1} \quad -y + 4z = 12$$
$$y - 4z = 7 \quad \longrightarrow \quad \underline{y - 4z = 7}$$
$$0 = 19$$

This result has no solution, so the system is inconsistent.

45. Add the first and second equations to eliminate z; and multiply the second equation by 2 and add to the third equation to eliminate z:

$$\begin{cases} x + y - z = 6 \\ 3x - 2y + z = -5 \\ x + 3y - 2z = 14 \end{cases}$$

$$\begin{aligned} \longrightarrow \quad & x + y - z = 6 \\ \longrightarrow \quad & \underline{3x - 2y + z = -5} \\ & 4x - y = 1 \end{aligned}$$

$$\begin{aligned} \xrightarrow{2} \quad & 6x - 4y + 2z = -10 \\ \longrightarrow \quad & \underline{x + 3y - 2z = 14} \\ & 7x - y = 4 \end{aligned}$$

Multiply each side of the first result by -1 and add to the second result to eliminate y:

$$4x - y = 1 \quad \xrightarrow{-1} \quad -4x + y = -1$$
$$7x - y = 4 \quad \longrightarrow \quad \underline{7x - y = 4}$$
$$3x = 3$$
$$x = 1$$

Substituting and solving for the other variables:

$$4(1) - y = 1 \qquad\qquad 3(1) - 2(3) + z = -5$$
$$-y = -3 \qquad\qquad 3 - 6 + z = -5$$
$$y = 3 \qquad\qquad z = -2$$

The solution is $x = 1$, $y = 3$, $z = -2$.

47.   Add the first and second equations to eliminate z; and multiply the second equation by 3 and add to the third equation to eliminate z:

$$\begin{cases} x + 2y - z = -3 \\ 2x - 4y + z = -7 \\ -2x + 2y - 3z = 4 \end{cases}$$

$$\begin{array}{c} x + 2y - z = -3 \\ \underline{2x - 4y + z = -7} \\ 3x - 2y = -10 \end{array}$$

$$\xrightarrow{3} \quad 6x - 12y + 3z = -21$$
$$\xrightarrow{} \quad \underline{-2x + 2y - 3z = 4}$$
$$4x - 10y = -17$$

Multiply each side of the first result by –5 and add to the second result to eliminate y:

$$3x - 2y = -10 \xrightarrow{-5} -15x + 10y = 50$$
$$4x - 10y = -17 \longrightarrow \underline{4x - 10y = -17}$$
$$-11x = 33 \Rightarrow x = -3$$

Substituting and solving for the other variables:

$$3(-3) - 2y = -10 \qquad\qquad -3 + 2\left(\frac{1}{2}\right) - z = -3$$
$$-9 - 2y = -10 \qquad\qquad -3 + 1 - z = -3$$
$$-2y = -1 \qquad\qquad -z = -1$$
$$y = \frac{1}{2} \qquad\qquad z = 1$$

The solution is $x = -3$, $y = \frac{1}{2}$, $z = 1$.

49.   Let l be the length of the rectangle and w be the width of the rectangle. Then:
$$2l + 2w = 90 \Rightarrow l = 2w$$
Solve by substitution:
$$2(2w) + 2w = 90 \Rightarrow 4w + 2w = 90 \Rightarrow 6w = 90 \Rightarrow w = 15 \text{ feet}$$
$$l = 2(15) = 30 \text{ feet}$$
The dimensions of the floor are 15 feet by 30 feet.

51.   Let x = the cost of one cheeseburger and y = the cost of one shake. Then:
$$4x + 2y = 790 \Rightarrow 2y = x + 15$$
Solve by substitution:
$$4x + x + 15 = 790 \Rightarrow 5x = 775 \Rightarrow x = 155$$
$$2y = 155 + 15 \Rightarrow 2y = 170 \Rightarrow y = 85$$
A cheeseburger cost \$1.55 and a shake costs \$0.85.

53.   Let x = the number of pounds of cashews.
Then $x + 30$ is the number of pounds in the mixture.
The value of the cashews is $5x$.
The value of the peanuts is $1.50(30) = 45$.
The value of the mixture is $3(x + 30)$.
Setting up a value equation:
$$5x + 45 = 3(x + 30) \Rightarrow 5x + 45 = 3x + 90$$
$$2x = 45 \Rightarrow x = 22.5$$
22.5 pounds of cashews should be used in the mixture.

55.   Let x = the plane's air speed and y = the wind speed.

	Rate	Time	Distance
With Wind	$x + y$	3	600
Against	$x - y$	4	600

$$(x + y)(3) = 600 \quad \Rightarrow \quad x + y = 200$$
$$(x - y)(4) = 600 \quad \Rightarrow \quad x - y = 150$$
Solving by elimination:
$$2x = 350 \Rightarrow x = 175$$
$$y = 200 - x = 200 - 175 = 25$$
The airspeed of the plane is 175 mph, and the wind speed is 25 mph.

57.   Let x = the number of one design.
Let y = the number of the second design.
Then $x + y$ = the total number of sets of dishes.
$25x + 45y$ = the cost of the dishes.
Setting up the equations and solving by substitution:
$$\begin{cases} x + \quad y = \ 200 \quad \Rightarrow \quad y = 200 - x \\ 25x + 45y = 7400 \end{cases}$$
$$25x + 45(200 - x) = 7400$$
$$25x + 9000 - 45x = 7400$$
$$-20x = -1600 \Rightarrow x = 80$$
$$y = 200 - 80 = 120$$
80 sets of the \$25 dishes and 120 sets of the \$45 dishes should be ordered.

59.   Let x = the cost per package of bacon.
Let y = the cost of a carton of eggs.
Set up a system of equations for the problem:
$$\begin{cases} 3x + 2y = 7.45 \\ 2x + 3y = 6.45 \end{cases}$$
Multiply each side of the first equation by 3 and each side of the second equation by –2 and solve by elimination:
$$\begin{cases} 3x + 2y = 7.45 \ \xrightarrow{\ 3\ } \quad 9x + 6y = \ 22.35 \\ 2x + 3y = 6.45 \ \xrightarrow{\ -2\ } \ \underline{-4x - 6y = -12.90} \end{cases}$$
$$5x \quad = \quad 9.45 \Rightarrow x = 1.89$$

Substitute and solve for y:
$$3(1.89) + 2y = 7.45$$
$$5.67 + 2y = 7.45 \Rightarrow 2y = 1.78 \Rightarrow y = 0.89$$
A package of bacon costs \$1.89 and a carton of eggs cost \$0.89.
The refund for 2 packages of bacon and 2 cartons of eggs will be \$5.56.

61. Let x = the # of mg of liquid 1.
Let y = the # of mg of liquid 2.
Setting up the equations and solving by substitution:
$$\begin{cases} 0.2x + 0.4y = 40 & \text{vitamin C} \\ 0.3x + 0.2y = 30 & \text{vitamin D} \end{cases}$$
multiplying each equation by 10 yields
$$\begin{cases} 2x + 4y = 400 \longrightarrow 2x + 4y = 400 \\ 3x + 2y = 300 \overset{2}{\longrightarrow} 6x + 4y = 600 \end{cases}$$
subtracting the bottom equation from the top equation yields
$$2x + 4y - (6x + 4y) = -200$$
$$2x - 6x = -200 \Rightarrow -4x = -200 \Rightarrow x = 50$$
$$\Rightarrow 2(50) + 4y = 400 \Rightarrow 100 + 4y = 400$$
$$\Rightarrow 4y = 300 \Rightarrow y = \frac{300}{4} = 75$$
So 50 mg of liquid 1 should be mixed with 75 mg of liquid 2.

63. $y = ax^2 + bx + c$
At (−1, 4) the equation becomes:
$$4 = a(-1)^2 + b(-1) + c$$
$$4 = a - b + c \Rightarrow a - b + c = 4$$
At (2, 3) the equation becomes:
$$3 = a(2)^2 + b(2) + c$$
$$3 = 4a + 2b + c \Rightarrow 4a + 2b + c = 3$$
At (0, 1) the equation becomes:
$$1 = a(0)^2 + b(0) + c$$
$$c = 1$$
The system of equations is:
$$\begin{cases} a - b + c = 4 \\ 4a + 2b + c = 3 \\ \qquad c = 1 \end{cases}$$
Substitute $c = 1$ into the first and second equations and simplify:
$$\begin{cases} a - b + 1 = 4 \Rightarrow a - b = 3 \Rightarrow a = b + 3 \\ 4a + 2b + 1 = 3 \Rightarrow 4a + 2b = 2 \end{cases}$$

Solve the first equation for a, substitute into the second equation and solve:
$$4(b+3)+2b = 2$$

$$4b+12+2b = 2 \Rightarrow 6b = -10 \Rightarrow b = -\frac{5}{3}$$

$$a = -\frac{5}{3}+3 = \frac{4}{3}$$

The solution is $a = \frac{4}{3}$, $b = -\frac{5}{3}$, $c = 1$. So the equation is $y = \frac{4}{3}x^2 - \frac{5}{3}x + 1$.

65.   Substitute the expression for I_2 into the second and third equations and simplify:

$$\begin{cases} I_2 = I_1 + I_3 \\ 5 - 3I_1 - 5I_2 = 0 \quad \rightarrow \quad 5 - 3I_1 - 5(I_1 + I_3) = 0 \quad \rightarrow \quad -8I_1 - 5I_3 = -5 \\ 10 - 5I_2 - 7I_3 = 0 \quad \rightarrow \quad 10 - 5(I_1 + I_3) - 7I_3 = 0 \quad \rightarrow \quad -5I_1 - 12I_3 = -10 \end{cases}$$

Multiply both sides of the second equation by 5 and multiply both sides of the third equation by –8 to eliminate I_1:

$$-8I_1 - 5I_3 = -5 \xrightarrow{\ 5\ } -40I_1 - 25I_3 = -25$$

$$-5I_1 - 12I_3 = -10 \xrightarrow{\ -8\ } \underline{\ 40I_1 + 96I_3 = \ \ 80\ }$$

$$71I_3 = \ \ 55 \Rightarrow I_3 = \frac{55}{71}$$

Substituting and solving for the other variables:

$$-8I_1 - 5\left(\frac{55}{71}\right) = -5 \qquad\qquad I_2 = \frac{10}{71} + \frac{55}{71}$$

$$-8I_1 - \frac{275}{71} = -5 \qquad\qquad I_2 = \frac{65}{71}$$

$$-8I_1 = -\frac{80}{71}$$

$$I_1 = \frac{10}{71}$$

The solution is $I_1 = \frac{10}{71}$, $I_2 = \frac{65}{71}$, $I_3 = \frac{55}{71}$.

67.   Let x = the number of orchestra seats.
Let y = the number of main seats.
Let z = the number of balcony seats.
Since the total number of seats is 500, $x + y + z = 500$.
Since the total revenue is \$17,100 if all seats are sold, $50x + 35y + 25z = 17,100$.
If only half of the orchestra seats are sold, the revenue is \$14,600. So,

$$50\left(\frac{1}{2}x\right) + 35y + 25z = 14,600.$$

Multiply each side of the first equation by –25 and add to the second equation to eliminate z; and multiply each side of the third equation by –1 and add to the second equation to eliminate z:

$$\begin{cases} x + \ \ y + \ \ z = \ \ 500 \\ 50x + 35y + 25z = 17100 \\ 25x + 35y + 25z = 14600 \end{cases}$$

$$\xrightarrow{\ -25\ } \quad \begin{aligned} -25x - 25y - 25z &= -12500 \\ 50x + 35y + 25z &= \ \ 17100 \\ \hline 25x + 10y \qquad\quad &= \ \ \ 4600 \end{aligned}$$

$$\xrightarrow{} \quad 50x + 35y + 25z = 17100$$
$$\xrightarrow{-1} \quad -25x - 35y - 25z = -14600$$

$$25x \qquad\qquad = 2500 \Rightarrow x = 100$$

Substituting and solving for the other variables:

$$25(100) + 10y = 4600 \qquad\qquad 100 + 210 + z = 500$$
$$2500 + 10y = 4600 \qquad\qquad\qquad 310 + z = 500$$
$$10y = 2100 \qquad\qquad\qquad\qquad z = 190$$
$$y = 210$$

There are 100 orchestra seats, 210 main seats, and 190 balcony seats.

69. Let x = the number of servings of chicken.
Let y = the number of servings of corn.
Let z = the number of servings of 2% milk.
Protein equation: $30x + 3y + 9z = 66$
Carbohydrate equation: $35x + 16y + 13z = 94.5$
Calcium equation: $200x + 10y + 300z = 910$
Multiply each side of the first equation by −16 and multiply each side of the second equation by 3 and add them to eliminate y; and multiply each side of the second equation by −5 and multiply each side of the third equation by 8 and add to eliminate y:

$$\begin{cases} 30x + 3y + 9z = 66 \\ 35x + 16y + 13z = 94.5 \\ 200x + 10y + 300z = 910 \end{cases}$$

$$\xrightarrow{-16} \quad -480x - 48y - 144z = -1056$$
$$\xrightarrow{3} \quad 105x + 48y + 39z = 283.5$$
$$\overline{-375x \qquad\quad -105z = -772.5}$$

$$\xrightarrow{-5} \quad -175x - 80y - 65z = -472.5$$
$$\xrightarrow{8} \quad 1600x + 80y + 2400z = 7280$$
$$\overline{1425x \qquad\quad + 2335z = 6807.5}$$

Multiply each side of the first result by 19 and multiply each side of the second result by 5 to eliminate x:

$$-375x - 105z = -772.5 \quad \xrightarrow{19} \quad -7125x - 1995z = -14677.5$$
$$1425x + 2335z = 6807.5 \quad \xrightarrow{5} \quad 7125x + 11675z = 34037.5$$
$$\overline{\quad 9680z = 19360 \Rightarrow z = 2}$$

Substituting and solving for the other variables:

$$-375x - 105(2) = -772.5 \qquad\qquad 30(1.5) + 3y + 9(2) = 66$$
$$-375x - 210 = -772.5 \qquad\qquad\qquad 45 + 3y + 18 = 66$$
$$-375x = -562.5 \qquad\qquad\qquad\qquad 3y = 3$$
$$x = 1.5 \qquad\qquad\qquad\qquad\qquad y = 1$$

The dietitian should serve 1.5 servings of chicken, 1 serving of corn, and 2 servings of 2% milk.

71. Let x = the price of 1 hamburger.
Let y = the price of 1 order of fries.
Let z = the price of 1 drink.
We can construct the system
$$\begin{cases} 8x + 6y + 6z = 26.10 \\ 10x + 6y + 8z = 31.60 \end{cases}$$
A system involving only 2 equations that contain 3 or more unknowns cannot be solved uniquely. In other words, we can create as many solutions as we want by choosing a specific value for one of the variables and then solving the resulting 2 x 2 system.
For example, suppose we know that
$$\$1.75 < \text{hamburger price} < \$2.25$$
$$\$0.75 < \text{fries price} < \$1.00$$
$$\$0.60 < \text{fries price} < \$0.90$$

Pick a specific value for x, y or z	2x2 system	Solution
$x = \$2.00$	$\begin{cases} 8(2) + 6y + 6z = 26.10 \\ 10(2) + 6y + 8z = 31.60 \end{cases}$	$x = \$2.00$
	$\Downarrow$	$y = \$0.93$
	$\begin{cases} 16 + 6y + 6z = 26.10 \\ 20 + 6y + 8z = 31.60 \end{cases}$	$z = \$0.75$
	$\Downarrow$	
	$\begin{cases} 6y + 6z = 10.10 \\ 6y + 8z = 11.60 \end{cases}$	

Pick a specific value for x, y or z	2x2 system	Solution
$y = \$0.90$	$\begin{cases} 8x + 6(0.9) + 6z = 26.10 \\ 10x + 6(0.9) + 8z = 31.60 \end{cases}$	$x = \$2.00$
	$\Downarrow$	$y = \$0.90$
	$\begin{cases} 8x + 5.4 + 6z = 26.10 \\ 10x + 5.4 + 8z = 31.60 \end{cases}$	$z = \$0.65$
	$\Downarrow$	
	$\begin{cases} 8x + 6z = 20.7 \\ 10x + 8z = 26.2 \end{cases}$	

Pick a specific value for x, y or z	2x2 system	Solution
$z = \$0.80$	$\begin{cases} 8x + 6y + 6(.8) = 26.10 \\ 10x + 6y + 8(.8) = 31.60 \end{cases}$	$x = \$1.95$
	$\Downarrow$	$y = \$0.95$
	$\begin{cases} 8x + 6y + 4.8 = 26.10 \\ 10x + 6y + 6.4 = 31.60 \end{cases}$	$z = \$0.80$
	$\Downarrow$	
	$\begin{cases} 8x + 6y = 21.3 \\ 10x + 6y = 25.2 \end{cases}$	

73. Let x = Beth's time working alone.
Let y = Bill's time working alone.
Let z = Edie's time working alone.
We can use the following tables to organize our work:

	Beth	Bill	Edie	Together
Hours to do job	x	y	z	10
Part of job done in 1 hour	$\dfrac{1}{x}$	$\dfrac{1}{y}$	$\dfrac{1}{z}$	$\dfrac{1}{10}$

Equation: $\dfrac{1}{x} + \dfrac{1}{y} + \dfrac{1}{z} = \dfrac{1}{10}$

	Bill	Edie	Together
Hours to do job	y	z	15
Part of job done in 1 hour	$\dfrac{1}{y}$	$\dfrac{1}{z}$	$\dfrac{1}{15}$

Equation: $\dfrac{1}{y} + \dfrac{1}{z} = \dfrac{1}{15}$

	Beth	Bill	Edie	All three	Beth and Bill
Hours to do job	x	y	z	4	8
Part of job done in 1 hour	$\dfrac{1}{x}$	$\dfrac{1}{y}$	$\dfrac{1}{z}$	$\dfrac{1}{4}$	$\dfrac{1}{8}$

Equation: $4\left(\dfrac{1}{x} + \dfrac{1}{y} + \dfrac{1}{z}\right) + 8\left(\dfrac{1}{x} + \dfrac{1}{y}\right) = 1 \Rightarrow \dfrac{12}{x} + \dfrac{12}{y} + \dfrac{4}{z} = 1$

We can construct the system

$$\begin{cases} \dfrac{1}{x}+\dfrac{1}{y}+\dfrac{1}{z}=\dfrac{1}{10} \\[2mm] \dfrac{1}{y}+\dfrac{1}{z}=\dfrac{1}{15} \\[2mm] \dfrac{12}{x}+\dfrac{12}{y}+\dfrac{4}{z}=1 \end{cases}\longrightarrow$$

subtracting the second equation from the first equation yields

$$\dfrac{1}{x}+\dfrac{1}{y}+\dfrac{1}{z}=\dfrac{1}{10}$$

$$\underline{\dfrac{1}{y}+\dfrac{1}{z}=\dfrac{1}{15}}$$

$$\dfrac{1}{x}=\dfrac{1}{10}-\dfrac{1}{15}$$

$$\Rightarrow \dfrac{1}{x}=\dfrac{1}{30}\Rightarrow x=30$$

Plugging $x = 30$ into the original system yields

$$\begin{cases} \dfrac{1}{30}+\dfrac{1}{y}+\dfrac{1}{z}=\dfrac{1}{10}\Rightarrow \dfrac{1}{y}+\dfrac{1}{z}=\dfrac{1}{10}-\dfrac{1}{30}\Rightarrow \dfrac{1}{y}+\dfrac{1}{z}=\dfrac{1}{15} \\[2mm] \dfrac{12}{30}+\dfrac{12}{y}+\dfrac{4}{z}=1\Rightarrow \dfrac{12}{y}+\dfrac{4}{z}=1-\dfrac{12}{30}\Rightarrow \dfrac{12}{y}+\dfrac{4}{z}=\dfrac{3}{5} \end{cases}$$

Now consider the system

$$\begin{cases} \dfrac{1}{y}+\dfrac{1}{z}=\dfrac{1}{15}\xrightarrow{-12}\dfrac{-12}{y}+\dfrac{-12}{z}=\dfrac{-12}{15} \\[2mm] \dfrac{12}{y}+\dfrac{4}{z}=\dfrac{3}{5}\longrightarrow \dfrac{12}{y}+\dfrac{4}{z}=\dfrac{3}{5} \end{cases}$$

adding these 2 equations yields

$$\dfrac{-12}{y}+\dfrac{-12}{z}=\dfrac{-12}{15}$$

$$\underline{\dfrac{12}{y}+\dfrac{4}{z}\qquad=\dfrac{3}{5}}$$

$$\dfrac{-12}{z}+\dfrac{4}{z}=\dfrac{-12}{15}+\dfrac{3}{5}$$

$$\Rightarrow \dfrac{-8}{z}=\dfrac{-3}{15}\Rightarrow \dfrac{8}{z}=\dfrac{1}{5}\Rightarrow z=40$$

plugging $z = 40$ into the equation

$$\dfrac{12}{y}+\dfrac{4}{z}=\dfrac{3}{5}\Rightarrow \dfrac{12}{y}+\dfrac{4}{40}=\dfrac{3}{5}$$

$$\dfrac{12}{y}+\dfrac{1}{10}=\dfrac{3}{5}\Rightarrow \dfrac{12}{y}=\dfrac{3}{5}-\dfrac{1}{10}\Rightarrow \dfrac{12}{y}=\dfrac{1}{2}\Rightarrow y=24$$

So, working alone, it would take Beth 30 hours, Bill 24 hours and Edie 40 hours to finish the job.

75. Answers will vary.

Systems of Equations and Inequalities

8.2   Systems of Linear Equations: Matrices

1.   Writing the augmented matrix for the system of equations:

$$\begin{cases} x - 5y = 5 \\ 4x + 3y = 6 \end{cases} \rightarrow \begin{bmatrix} 1 & -5 & | & 5 \\ 4 & 3 & | & 6 \end{bmatrix}$$

3.   Writing the augmented matrix for the system of equations:

$$\begin{cases} 2x + 3y - 6 = 0 \\ 4x - 6y + 2 = 0 \end{cases} \rightarrow \begin{cases} 2x + 3y = 6 \\ 4x - 6y = -2 \end{cases} \rightarrow \begin{bmatrix} 2 & 3 & | & 6 \\ 4 & -6 & | & -2 \end{bmatrix}$$

5.   Writing the augmented matrix for the system of equations:

$$\begin{cases} 0.01x - 0.03y = 0.06 \\ 0.13x + 0.10y = 0.20 \end{cases} \rightarrow \begin{bmatrix} 0.01 & -0.03 & | & 0.06 \\ 0.13 & 0.10 & | & 0.20 \end{bmatrix}$$

7.   Writing the augmented matrix for the system of equations:

$$\begin{cases} x - y + z = 10 \\ 3x + 3y \quad\;\; = 5 \\ x + y + 2z = 2 \end{cases} \rightarrow \begin{vmatrix} 1 & -1 & 1 & | & 10 \\ 3 & 3 & 0 & | & 5 \\ 1 & 1 & 2 & | & 2 \end{vmatrix}$$

9.   Writing the augmented matrix for the system of equations:

$$\begin{cases} x + y - z = 2 \\ 3x - 2y \quad\;\; = 2 \\ 5x + 3y - z = 1 \end{cases} \rightarrow \begin{bmatrix} 1 & 1 & -1 & | & 2 \\ 3 & -2 & 0 & | & 2 \\ 5 & 3 & -1 & | & 1 \end{bmatrix}$$

11.   Writing the augmented matrix for the system of equations:

$$\begin{cases} x - y - z = 10 \\ 2x + y + 2z = -1 \\ -3x + 4y = 5 \\ 4x - 5y + z = 0 \end{cases} \rightarrow \begin{vmatrix} 1 & -1 & -1 & | & 10 \\ 2 & 1 & 2 & | & -1 \\ -3 & 4 & 0 & | & 5 \\ 4 & -5 & 1 & | & 0 \end{vmatrix}$$

13. $\begin{vmatrix} 1 & -3 & | & -2 \\ 2 & -5 & | & 5 \end{vmatrix} \rightarrow \begin{vmatrix} 1 & -3 & | & -2 \\ 0 & 1 & | & 9 \end{vmatrix}$

$$R_2 = -2r_1 + r_2$$

15. $\begin{bmatrix} 1 & -3 & 4 & | & 3 \\ 2 & -5 & 6 & | & 6 \\ -3 & 3 & 4 & | & 6 \end{bmatrix} \rightarrow \begin{bmatrix} 1 & -3 & 4 & | & 3 \\ 0 & 1 & -2 & | & 0 \\ -3 & 3 & 4 & | & 6 \end{bmatrix}$

(a) $R_2 = -2r_1 + r_2$

$\begin{bmatrix} 1 & -3 & 4 & | & 3 \\ 2 & -5 & 6 & | & 6 \\ -3 & 3 & 4 & | & 6 \end{bmatrix} \rightarrow \begin{bmatrix} 1 & -3 & 4 & | & 3 \\ 2 & -5 & 6 & | & 6 \\ 0 & -6 & 16 & | & 15 \end{bmatrix}$

(b) $R_3 = 3r_1 + r_3$

17. $\begin{bmatrix} 1 & -3 & 2 & | & -6 \\ 2 & -5 & 3 & | & -4 \\ -3 & -6 & 4 & | & 6 \end{bmatrix} \rightarrow \begin{bmatrix} 1 & -3 & 2 & | & -6 \\ 0 & 1 & -1 & | & 8 \\ -3 & -6 & 4 & | & 6 \end{bmatrix}$

(a) $R_2 = -2r_1 + r_2$

$\begin{bmatrix} 1 & -3 & 2 & | & -6 \\ 2 & -5 & 3 & | & -4 \\ -3 & -6 & 4 & | & 6 \end{bmatrix} \rightarrow \begin{bmatrix} 1 & -3 & 2 & | & -6 \\ 2 & -5 & 3 & | & -4 \\ 0 & -15 & 10 & | & -12 \end{bmatrix}$

(b) $R_3 = 3r_1 + r_3$

19. $\begin{bmatrix} 1 & -3 & 1 & | & -2 \\ 2 & -5 & 6 & | & -2 \\ -3 & 1 & 4 & | & 6 \end{bmatrix} \rightarrow \begin{bmatrix} 1 & -3 & 1 & | & -2 \\ 0 & 1 & 4 & | & 2 \\ -3 & 1 & 4 & | & 6 \end{bmatrix}$

(a) $R_2 = -2r_1 + r_2$

$\begin{bmatrix} 1 & -3 & 1 & | & -2 \\ 2 & -5 & 6 & | & -2 \\ -3 & 1 & 4 & | & 6 \end{bmatrix} \rightarrow \begin{bmatrix} 1 & -3 & 1 & | & -2 \\ 2 & -5 & 6 & | & -2 \\ 0 & -8 & 7 & | & 0 \end{bmatrix}$

(b) $R_3 = 3r_1 + r_3$

21. $\begin{cases} x = 5 \\ y = -1 \end{cases}$ consistent $x = 5, y = -1$

23. $\begin{cases} x = 1 \\ y = 2 \\ 0 = 3 \end{cases}$ inconsistent

25. $\begin{cases} x + 2z = -1 \\ y - 4z = -2 \\ \quad\; 0 = 0 \end{cases}$ consistent $x = -1 - 2z, y = -2 + 4z, z$ is any real number

27.

$$\begin{cases} x_1 = 1 \\ x_2 + x_4 = 2 \\ x_3 + 2x_4 = 3 \end{cases}$$
consistent $x_1 = 1, x_2 = 2 - x_4, x_3 = 3 - 2x_4, x_4$ is any real number

29.

$$\begin{cases} x_1 + 4x_4 = 2 \\ x_2 + x_3 + 3x_4 = 3 \\ 0 = 0 \end{cases}$$
consistent $x_1 = 2 - 4x_4, x_2 = 3 - x_3 - 3x_4,$
x_3, x_4 are any real numbers

31.

$$\begin{cases} x_1 + x_4 = -2 \\ x_2 + 2x_4 = 2 \\ x_3 - x_4 = 0 \\ 0 = 0 \end{cases}$$
consistent $x_1 = -2 - x_4, x_2 = 2 - 2x_4, x_3 = x_4,$
x_4 is any real number

33. $\begin{cases} x + y = 8 \\ x - y = 4 \end{cases}$ can be written as: $\begin{bmatrix} 1 & 1 & | & 8 \\ 1 & -1 & | & 4 \end{bmatrix}$

$$\rightarrow \begin{bmatrix} 1 & 1 & | & 8 \\ 0 & -2 & | & -4 \end{bmatrix} \rightarrow \begin{bmatrix} 1 & 1 & | & 8 \\ 0 & 1 & | & 2 \end{bmatrix} \rightarrow \begin{bmatrix} 1 & 0 & | & 6 \\ 0 & 1 & | & 2 \end{bmatrix}$$

$\quad R_2 = -r_1 + r_2 \quad R_2 = -\frac{1}{2}r_2 \quad R_1 = -r_2 + r_1$

The solution is $x = 6, y = 2$.

35. $\begin{cases} 2x - 4y = -2 \\ 3x + 2y = 3 \end{cases}$ can be written as: $\begin{bmatrix} 2 & -4 & | & -2 \\ 3 & 2 & | & 3 \end{bmatrix}$

$$\rightarrow \begin{bmatrix} 1 & -2 & | & -1 \\ 3 & 2 & | & 3 \end{bmatrix} \rightarrow \begin{bmatrix} 1 & -2 & | & -1 \\ 0 & 8 & | & 6 \end{bmatrix} \rightarrow \begin{bmatrix} 1 & -2 & | & -1 \\ 0 & 1 & | & \frac{3}{4} \end{bmatrix} \rightarrow \begin{bmatrix} 1 & 0 & | & \frac{1}{2} \\ 0 & 1 & | & \frac{3}{4} \end{bmatrix}$$

$\quad R_1 = \frac{1}{2}r_1 \quad R_2 = -3r_1 + r_2 \quad R_2 = \frac{1}{8}r_2 \quad R_1 = 2r_2 + r_1$

The solution is $x = \dfrac{1}{2}, y = \dfrac{3}{4}$.

37. $\begin{cases} x + 2y = 4 \\ 2x + 4y = 8 \end{cases}$ can be written as: $\begin{bmatrix} 1 & 2 & | & 4 \\ 2 & 4 & | & 8 \end{bmatrix}$

$$\rightarrow \begin{bmatrix} 1 & 2 & | & 4 \\ 0 & 0 & | & 0 \end{bmatrix}$$

$\quad R_2 = -2r_1 + r_2$

This is a dependent system and the solution is $x = 4 - 2y, y$ is any real number.

39. $\begin{cases} 2x+3y=6 \\ x-y=\dfrac{1}{2} \end{cases}$ can be written as: $\begin{bmatrix} 2 & 3 & | & 6 \\ 1 & -1 & | & \frac{1}{2} \end{bmatrix}$

$\rightarrow \begin{bmatrix} 1 & \frac{3}{2} & | & 3 \\ 1 & -1 & | & \frac{1}{2} \end{bmatrix} \rightarrow \begin{bmatrix} 1 & \frac{3}{2} & | & 3 \\ 0 & -\frac{5}{2} & | & -\frac{5}{2} \end{bmatrix} \rightarrow \begin{bmatrix} 1 & \frac{3}{2} & | & 3 \\ 0 & 1 & | & 1 \end{bmatrix} \rightarrow \begin{bmatrix} 1 & 0 & | & \frac{3}{2} \\ 0 & 1 & | & 1 \end{bmatrix}$

$R_1 = \frac{1}{2}r_1 \qquad R_2 = -r_1 + r_2 \qquad R_2 = -\frac{2}{5}r_2 \qquad R_1 = -\frac{3}{2}r_2 + r_1$

The solution is $x = \dfrac{3}{2},\ y = 1$.

41. $\begin{cases} 3x-5y=\ 3 \\ 15x+5y=21 \end{cases}$ can be written as: $\begin{bmatrix} 3 & -5 & | & 3 \\ 15 & 5 & | & 21 \end{bmatrix}$

$\rightarrow \begin{bmatrix} 1 & -\frac{5}{3} & | & 1 \\ 15 & 5 & | & 21 \end{bmatrix} \rightarrow \begin{bmatrix} 1 & -\frac{5}{3} & | & 1 \\ 0 & 30 & | & 6 \end{bmatrix} \rightarrow \begin{bmatrix} 1 & -\frac{5}{3} & | & 1 \\ 0 & 1 & | & \frac{1}{5} \end{bmatrix} \rightarrow \begin{bmatrix} 1 & 0 & | & \frac{4}{3} \\ 0 & 1 & | & \frac{1}{5} \end{bmatrix}$

$R_1 = \frac{1}{3}r_1 \qquad R_2 = -15r_1 + r_2 \qquad R_2 = \frac{1}{30}r_2 \qquad R_1 = \frac{5}{3}r_2 + r_1$

The solution is $x = \dfrac{4}{3},\ y = \dfrac{1}{5}$.

43. $\begin{cases} x-y\ \ \ \ =\ 6 \\ 2x\ \ \ \ -3z=16 \\ \ \ \ \ 2y+z=4 \end{cases}$ can be written as: $\begin{bmatrix} 1 & -1 & 0 & | & 6 \\ 2 & 0 & -3 & | & 16 \\ 0 & 2 & 1 & | & 4 \end{bmatrix}$

$\rightarrow \begin{bmatrix} 1 & -1 & 0 & | & 6 \\ 0 & 2 & -3 & | & 4 \\ 0 & 2 & 1 & | & 4 \end{bmatrix} \rightarrow \begin{bmatrix} 1 & -1 & 0 & | & 6 \\ 0 & 1 & -\frac{3}{2} & | & 2 \\ 0 & 2 & 1 & | & 4 \end{bmatrix} \rightarrow \begin{bmatrix} 1 & 0 & -\frac{3}{2} & | & 8 \\ 0 & 1 & -\frac{3}{2} & | & 2 \\ 0 & 0 & 4 & | & 0 \end{bmatrix} \rightarrow \begin{bmatrix} 1 & 0 & -\frac{3}{2} & | & 8 \\ 0 & 1 & -\frac{3}{2} & | & 2 \\ 0 & 0 & 1 & | & 0 \end{bmatrix}$

$R_2 = -2r_1 + r_2 \qquad R_2 = \frac{1}{2}r_2 \qquad R_1 = r_2 + r_1 \qquad R_3 = \frac{1}{4}r_3$

$R_3 = -2r_2 + r_3$

$\rightarrow \begin{bmatrix} 1 & 0 & 0 & | & 8 \\ 0 & 1 & 0 & | & 2 \\ 0 & 0 & 1 & | & 0 \end{bmatrix}$

$R_1 = \frac{3}{2}r_3 + r_1$

$R_2 = \frac{3}{2}r_3 + r_2$

The solution is $x = 8,\ y = 2,\ z = 0$.

45. $\begin{cases} x-2y+3z=\ 7 \\ 2x+y+z=\ 4 \\ -3x+2y-2z=-10 \end{cases}$ can be written as: $\begin{bmatrix} 1 & -2 & 3 & | & 7 \\ 2 & 1 & 1 & | & 4 \\ -3 & 2 & -2 & | & -10 \end{bmatrix}$

$$\rightarrow \begin{bmatrix} 1 & -2 & 3 & | & 7 \\ 0 & 5 & -5 & | & -10 \\ 0 & -4 & 7 & | & 11 \end{bmatrix} \rightarrow \begin{bmatrix} 1 & -2 & 3 & | & 7 \\ 0 & 1 & -1 & | & -2 \\ 0 & -4 & 7 & | & 11 \end{bmatrix} \rightarrow \begin{bmatrix} 1 & 0 & 1 & | & 3 \\ 0 & 1 & -1 & | & -2 \\ 0 & 0 & 3 & | & 3 \end{bmatrix}$$

$$R_2 = -2r_1 + r_2 \qquad R_2 = \tfrac{1}{5}r_2 \qquad\qquad R_1 = 2r_2 + r_1$$
$$R_3 = 3r_1 + r_3 \qquad\qquad\qquad\qquad\qquad R_3 = 4r_2 + r_3$$

$$\rightarrow \begin{bmatrix} 1 & 0 & 1 & | & 3 \\ 0 & 1 & -1 & | & -2 \\ 0 & 0 & 1 & | & 1 \end{bmatrix} \rightarrow \begin{bmatrix} 1 & 0 & 0 & | & 2 \\ 0 & 1 & 0 & | & -1 \\ 0 & 0 & 1 & | & 1 \end{bmatrix}$$

$$R_3 = \tfrac{1}{3}r_3 \qquad\qquad R_1 = -r_3 + r_1$$
$$R_2 = r_3 + r_2$$

The solution is $x = 2$, $y = -1$, $z = 1$.

47. $\begin{cases} 2x - 2y - 2z = 2 \\ 2x + 3y + z = 2 \\ 3x + 2y = 0 \end{cases}$ can be written as: $\begin{bmatrix} 2 & -2 & -2 & | & 2 \\ 2 & 3 & 1 & | & 2 \\ 3 & 2 & 0 & | & 0 \end{bmatrix}$

$$\rightarrow \begin{bmatrix} 1 & -1 & -1 & | & 1 \\ 2 & 3 & 1 & | & 2 \\ 3 & 2 & 0 & | & 0 \end{bmatrix} \rightarrow \begin{bmatrix} 1 & -1 & -1 & | & 1 \\ 0 & 5 & 3 & | & 0 \\ 0 & 5 & 3 & | & -3 \end{bmatrix} \rightarrow \begin{bmatrix} 1 & -1 & -1 & | & 1 \\ 0 & 5 & 3 & | & 0 \\ 0 & 0 & 0 & | & -3 \end{bmatrix}$$

$$R_1 = \tfrac{1}{2}r_1 \qquad\qquad R_2 = -2r_1 + r_2 \qquad R_3 = -r_2 + r_3$$
$$R_3 = -3r_1 + r_3$$

There is no solution. The system is inconsistent.

49. $\begin{cases} -x + y + z = -1 \\ -x + 2y - 3z = -4 \\ 3x - 2y - 7z = 0 \end{cases}$ can be written as: $\begin{bmatrix} -1 & 1 & 1 & | & -1 \\ -1 & 2 & -3 & | & -4 \\ 3 & -2 & -7 & | & 0 \end{bmatrix}$

$$\rightarrow \begin{bmatrix} 1 & -1 & -1 & | & 1 \\ -1 & 2 & -3 & | & -4 \\ 3 & -2 & -7 & | & 0 \end{bmatrix} \rightarrow \begin{bmatrix} 1 & -1 & -1 & | & 1 \\ 0 & 1 & -4 & | & -3 \\ 0 & 1 & -4 & | & -3 \end{bmatrix} \rightarrow \begin{bmatrix} 1 & 0 & -5 & | & -2 \\ 0 & 1 & -4 & | & -3 \\ 0 & 0 & 0 & | & 0 \end{bmatrix} \rightarrow \begin{array}{l} x - 5z = -2 \\ y - 4z = -3 \end{array}$$

$$R_1 = -r_1 \qquad\qquad R_2 = r_1 + r_2 \qquad\qquad R_1 = r_2 + r_1$$
$$R_3 = -3r_1 + r_3 \qquad R_3 = -r_2 + r_3$$

The solution is $x = 5z - 2$, $y = 4z - 3$, z is any real number.

51. $\begin{cases} 2x - 2y + 3z = 6 \\ 4x - 3y + 2z = 0 \\ -2x + 3y - 7z = 1 \end{cases}$ can be written as: $\begin{bmatrix} 2 & -2 & 3 & | & 6 \\ 4 & -3 & 2 & | & 0 \\ -2 & 3 & -7 & | & 1 \end{bmatrix}$

$$\rightarrow \begin{bmatrix} 1 & -1 & \tfrac{3}{2} & | & 3 \\ 4 & -3 & 2 & | & 0 \\ -2 & 3 & -7 & | & 1 \end{bmatrix} \rightarrow \begin{bmatrix} 1 & -1 & \tfrac{3}{2} & | & 3 \\ 0 & 1 & -4 & | & -12 \\ 0 & 1 & -4 & | & 7 \end{bmatrix} \rightarrow \begin{bmatrix} 1 & 0 & -\tfrac{5}{2} & | & -9 \\ 0 & 1 & -4 & | & -12 \\ 0 & 0 & 0 & | & 19 \end{bmatrix}$$

$$R_1 = \tfrac{1}{2}r_1 \qquad\qquad R_2 = -4r_1 + r_2 \qquad R_1 = r_2 + r_1$$
$$R_3 = 2r_1 + r_3 \qquad\qquad R_3 = -r_2 + r_3$$

There is no solution. The system is inconsistent.

53. $\begin{cases} x+ y- z = 6 \\ 3x - 2y + z = -5 \\ x + 3y - 2z = 14 \end{cases}$ can be written as: $\begin{bmatrix} 1 & 1 & -1 & | & 6 \\ 3 & -2 & 1 & | & -5 \\ 1 & 3 & -2 & | & 14 \end{bmatrix}$

$$\rightarrow \begin{bmatrix} 1 & 1 & -1 & | & 6 \\ 0 & -5 & 4 & | & -23 \\ 0 & 2 & -1 & | & 8 \end{bmatrix} \rightarrow \begin{bmatrix} 1 & 1 & -1 & | & 6 \\ 0 & 1 & -\frac{4}{5} & | & \frac{23}{5} \\ 0 & 2 & -1 & | & 8 \end{bmatrix} \rightarrow \begin{bmatrix} 1 & 0 & -\frac{1}{5} & | & \frac{7}{5} \\ 0 & 1 & -\frac{4}{5} & | & \frac{23}{5} \\ 0 & 0 & \frac{3}{5} & | & -\frac{6}{5} \end{bmatrix}$$

$R_2 = -3r_1 + r_2$ $R_2 = -\frac{1}{5}r_2$ $R_1 = -r_2 + r_1$
$R_3 = -r_1 + r_3$ $R_3 = -2r_2 + r_3$

$$\rightarrow \begin{bmatrix} 1 & 0 & -\frac{1}{5} & | & \frac{7}{5} \\ 0 & 1 & -\frac{4}{5} & | & \frac{23}{5} \\ 0 & 0 & 1 & | & -2 \end{bmatrix} \rightarrow \begin{bmatrix} 1 & 0 & 0 & | & 1 \\ 0 & 1 & 0 & | & 3 \\ 0 & 0 & 1 & | & -2 \end{bmatrix}$$

$\qquad R_3 = \frac{5}{3}r_3$ $R_1 = \frac{1}{5}r_3 + r_1$
$\qquad\qquad\qquad\qquad R_2 = \frac{4}{5}r_3 + r_2$

The solution is $x = 1, y = 3, z = -2$.

55. $\begin{cases} x + 2y - z = -3 \\ 2x - 4y + z = -7 \\ -2x + 2y - 3z = 4 \end{cases}$ can be written as: $\begin{bmatrix} 1 & 2 & -1 & | & -3 \\ 2 & -4 & 1 & | & -7 \\ -2 & 2 & -3 & | & 4 \end{bmatrix}$

$$\rightarrow \begin{bmatrix} 1 & 2 & -1 & | & -3 \\ 0 & -8 & 3 & | & -1 \\ 0 & 6 & -5 & | & -2 \end{bmatrix} \rightarrow \begin{bmatrix} 1 & 2 & -1 & | & -3 \\ 0 & 1 & -\frac{3}{8} & | & \frac{1}{8} \\ 0 & 6 & -5 & | & -2 \end{bmatrix} \rightarrow \begin{bmatrix} 1 & 0 & -\frac{1}{4} & | & -\frac{13}{4} \\ 0 & 1 & -\frac{3}{8} & | & \frac{1}{8} \\ 0 & 0 & -\frac{11}{4} & | & -\frac{11}{4} \end{bmatrix}$$

$R_2 = -2r_1 + r_2$ $R_2 = -\frac{1}{8}r_2$ $R_1 = -2r_2 + r_1$
$R_3 = 2r_1 + r_3$ $R_3 = -6r_2 + r_3$

$$\rightarrow \begin{bmatrix} 1 & 0 & -\frac{1}{4} & | & -\frac{13}{4} \\ 0 & 1 & -\frac{3}{8} & | & \frac{1}{8} \\ 0 & 0 & 1 & | & 1 \end{bmatrix} \rightarrow \begin{bmatrix} 1 & 0 & 0 & | & -3 \\ 0 & 1 & 0 & | & \frac{1}{2} \\ 0 & 0 & 1 & | & 1 \end{bmatrix}$$

$\qquad R_3 = -\frac{4}{11}r_3$ $R_1 = \frac{1}{4}r_3 + r_1$
$\qquad\qquad\qquad\qquad R_2 = \frac{3}{8}r_3 + r_2$

The solution is $x = -3, y = \dfrac{1}{2}, z = 1$.

57. $\begin{cases} 3x+ y- z = \dfrac{2}{3} \\ 2x - y + z = 1 \\ 4x + 2y = \dfrac{8}{3} \end{cases}$ can be written as : $\begin{bmatrix} 3 & 1 & -1 & | & \frac{2}{3} \\ 2 & -1 & 1 & | & 1 \\ 4 & 2 & 0 & | & \frac{8}{3} \end{bmatrix}$

$$\rightarrow \begin{vmatrix} 1 & \frac{1}{3} & -\frac{1}{3} & \frac{2}{9} \\ 2 & -1 & 1 & 1 \\ 4 & 2 & 0 & \frac{8}{3} \end{vmatrix} \rightarrow \begin{vmatrix} 1 & \frac{1}{3} & -\frac{1}{3} & \frac{2}{9} \\ 0 & -\frac{5}{3} & \frac{5}{3} & \frac{5}{9} \\ 0 & \frac{2}{3} & \frac{4}{3} & \frac{16}{9} \end{vmatrix} \rightarrow \begin{vmatrix} 1 & \frac{1}{3} & -\frac{1}{3} & \frac{2}{9} \\ 0 & 1 & -1 & -\frac{1}{3} \\ 0 & \frac{2}{3} & \frac{4}{3} & \frac{16}{9} \end{vmatrix} \rightarrow \begin{bmatrix} 1 & 0 & 0 & \frac{1}{3} \\ 0 & 1 & -1 & -\frac{1}{3} \\ 0 & 0 & 2 & 2 \end{bmatrix}$$

$R_1 = \frac{1}{3} r_1$ $R_2 = -2r_1 + r_2$ $R_2 = -\frac{3}{5} r_2$ $R_1 = -\frac{1}{3} r_2 + r_1$

$R_3 = -4r_1 + r_3$ $R_3 = -\frac{2}{3} r_2 + r_3$

$$\rightarrow \begin{vmatrix} 1 & 0 & 0 & \frac{1}{3} \\ 0 & 1 & -1 & -\frac{1}{3} \\ 0 & 0 & 1 & 1 \end{vmatrix} \rightarrow \begin{vmatrix} 1 & 0 & 0 & \frac{1}{3} \\ 0 & 1 & 0 & \frac{2}{3} \\ 0 & 0 & 1 & 1 \end{vmatrix}$$

$R_3 = \frac{1}{2} r_3$ $R_2 = r_3 + r_2$ The solution is $x = \dfrac{1}{3}, \; y = \dfrac{2}{3}, \; z = 1$.

59. $\begin{cases} x + y + z + w = 4 \\ 2x - y + z = 0 \\ 3x + 2y + z - w = 6 \\ x - 2y - 2z + 2w = -1 \end{cases}$ can be written as: $\begin{bmatrix} 1 & 1 & 1 & 1 & 4 \\ 2 & -1 & 1 & 0 & 0 \\ 3 & 2 & 1 & -1 & 6 \\ 1 & -2 & -2 & 2 & -1 \end{bmatrix}$

$$\rightarrow \begin{vmatrix} 1 & 1 & 1 & 1 & 4 \\ 0 & -3 & -1 & -2 & -8 \\ 0 & -1 & -2 & -4 & -6 \\ 0 & -3 & -3 & 1 & -5 \end{vmatrix} \rightarrow \begin{vmatrix} 1 & 1 & 1 & 1 & 4 \\ 0 & -1 & -2 & -4 & -6 \\ 0 & -3 & -1 & -2 & -8 \\ 0 & -3 & -3 & 1 & -5 \end{vmatrix} \rightarrow \begin{vmatrix} 1 & 1 & 1 & 1 & 4 \\ 0 & 1 & 2 & 4 & 6 \\ 0 & -3 & -1 & -2 & -8 \\ 0 & -3 & -3 & 1 & -5 \end{vmatrix}$$

$R_2 = -2r_1 + r_2$ Interchange r_2 and r_3 $R_2 = -r_2$

$R_3 = -3r_1 + r_3$

$R_4 = -r_1 + r_4$

$$\rightarrow \begin{vmatrix} 1 & 0 & -1 & -3 & -2 \\ 0 & 1 & 2 & 4 & 6 \\ 0 & 0 & 5 & 10 & 10 \\ 0 & 0 & 3 & 13 & 13 \end{vmatrix} \rightarrow \begin{vmatrix} 1 & 0 & -1 & -3 & -2 \\ 0 & 1 & 2 & 4 & 6 \\ 0 & 0 & 1 & 2 & 2 \\ 0 & 0 & 3 & 13 & 13 \end{vmatrix} \rightarrow \begin{bmatrix} 1 & 0 & 0 & -1 & 0 \\ 0 & 1 & 0 & 0 & 2 \\ 0 & 0 & 1 & 2 & 2 \\ 0 & 0 & 0 & 7 & 7 \end{bmatrix}$$

$R_1 = -r_2 + r_1$ $R_3 = \frac{1}{5} r_3$ $R_1 = r_3 + r_1$

$R_3 = 3r_2 + r_3$ $R_2 = -2r_3 + r_2$

$R_4 = 3r_2 + r_4$ $R_4 = -3r_3 + r_4$

$$\rightarrow \begin{vmatrix} 1 & 0 & 0 & -1 & 0 \\ 0 & 1 & 0 & 0 & 2 \\ 0 & 0 & 1 & 2 & 2 \\ 0 & 0 & 0 & 1 & 1 \end{vmatrix} \rightarrow \begin{vmatrix} 1 & 0 & 0 & 0 & 1 \\ 0 & 1 & 0 & 0 & 2 \\ 0 & 0 & 1 & 0 & 0 \\ 0 & 0 & 0 & 1 & 1 \end{vmatrix}$$

$R_4 = \frac{1}{7} r_4$ $R_1 = r_4 + r_1$

$R_3 = -2r_4 + r_3$

The solution is $x = 1, \; y = 2, \; z = 0, \; w = 1$.

61. $\begin{cases} x+2y+\ z=1 \\ 2x-\ y+2z=2 \\ 3x+\ y+3z=3 \end{cases}$ can be written as: $\begin{bmatrix} 1 & 2 & 1 & | & 1 \\ 2 & -1 & 2 & | & 2 \\ 3 & 1 & 3 & | & 3 \end{bmatrix}$

$\rightarrow \begin{bmatrix} 1 & 2 & 1 & | & 1 \\ 0 & -5 & 0 & | & 0 \\ 0 & -5 & 0 & | & 0 \end{bmatrix} \rightarrow \begin{bmatrix} 1 & 2 & 1 & | & 1 \\ 0 & -5 & 0 & | & 0 \\ 0 & 0 & 0 & | & 0 \end{bmatrix} \rightarrow \begin{matrix} x+2y+z=1 \\ -5y\ \ =0 \end{matrix}$

$R_2 = -2r_1 + r_2 \quad R_3 = -r_2 + r_3$
$R_3 = -3r_1 + r_3$

Substitute and solve:
$$y = 0$$
$$x + 2(0) + z = 1$$
$$x + z = 1 \Rightarrow z = 1 - x$$

The solution is $y = 0$, $z = 1 - x$, x is any real number.

63. $\begin{cases} x-y+z=5 \\ 3x+2y-2z=0 \end{cases}$ can be written as: $\begin{vmatrix} 1 & -1 & 1 & | & 5 \\ 3 & 2 & -2 & | & 0 \end{vmatrix}$

$\rightarrow \begin{vmatrix} 1 & -1 & 1 & | & 5 \\ 0 & 5 & -5 & | & -15 \end{vmatrix} \rightarrow \begin{vmatrix} 1 & -1 & 1 & | & 5 \\ 0 & 1 & -1 & | & -3 \end{vmatrix} \rightarrow \begin{vmatrix} 1 & 0 & 0 & | & 2 \\ 0 & 1 & -1 & | & -3 \end{vmatrix}$

$R_2 = -3r_1 + r_2 \qquad R_2 = \frac{1}{5}r_2 \qquad R_1 = r_2 + r_1$

The matrix in the third step represents the system $\begin{cases} x=2 \\ y-z=-3 \end{cases}$

Therefore the solution is $x = 2; y = -3 + z;\ z$ is any real number

or

$$x = 2; z = y + 3;\ y \text{ is any real number}$$

65. $\begin{cases} 2x+3y-z=3 \\ x-y-z=0 \\ -x+y+z=0 \\ x+y+3z=5 \end{cases}$ can be written as: $\begin{vmatrix} 2 & 3 & -1 & | & 3 \\ 1 & -1 & -1 & | & 0 \\ -1 & 1 & 1 & | & 0 \\ 1 & 1 & 3 & | & 5 \end{vmatrix}$

$\rightarrow \begin{vmatrix} 1 & -1 & -1 & | & 0 \\ 2 & 3 & -1 & | & 3 \\ -1 & 1 & 1 & | & 0 \\ 1 & 1 & 3 & | & 5 \end{vmatrix} \longrightarrow \begin{vmatrix} 1 & -1 & -1 & | & 0 \\ 0 & 5 & 1 & | & 3 \\ 0 & 0 & 0 & | & 0 \\ 0 & 2 & 4 & | & 5 \end{vmatrix} \rightarrow \begin{vmatrix} 1 & -1 & -1 & | & 0 \\ 0 & 5 & 1 & | & 3 \\ 0 & 2 & 4 & | & 5 \\ 0 & 0 & 0 & | & 0 \end{vmatrix}$

interchange r_1 and r_2 $\qquad R_2 = -2r_1 + r_2 \qquad$ interchange r_3 and r_4
$\qquad\qquad\qquad\qquad\qquad R_3 = r_1 + r_3$
$\qquad\qquad\qquad\qquad\qquad R_4 = -r_1 + r_4$

429

$$\rightarrow \begin{vmatrix} 1 & -1 & -1 & 0 \\ 0 & 1 & -7 & -7 \\ 0 & 2 & 4 & 5 \\ 0 & 0 & 0 & 0 \end{vmatrix} \longrightarrow \begin{vmatrix} 1 & 0 & -8 & -7 \\ 0 & 1 & -7 & -7 \\ 0 & 1 & 18 & 19 \\ 0 & 0 & 0 & 0 \end{vmatrix} \rightarrow \begin{vmatrix} 1 & 0 & -8 & -7 \\ 0 & 1 & -7 & -7 \\ 0 & 0 & 1 & \frac{19}{18} \\ 0 & 0 & 0 & 0 \end{vmatrix}$$

$$R_2 = -2r_3 + r_2 \qquad\qquad R_1 = r_2 + r_1 \qquad\qquad R_3 = \tfrac{1}{18} r_3$$

$$R_3 = -2r_2 + r_3$$

The matrix in the last step represents the system $\begin{cases} x - 8z = -7 \\ y - 7z = -7 \\ \quad z = \dfrac{19}{18} \end{cases}$

Therefore the solution is

$$z = \frac{19}{18}; \quad x = -7 + 8z = -7 + 8\left(\frac{19}{18}\right) = \frac{13}{9}; \quad y = -7 + 7z = -7 + 7\left(\frac{19}{18}\right) = \frac{7}{18}$$

67. $\begin{cases} 4x + y + z - w = 4 \\ x - y + 2z + 3w = 3 \end{cases}$ can be written as: $\begin{vmatrix} 4 & 1 & 1 & -1 & 4 \\ 1 & -1 & 2 & 3 & 3 \end{vmatrix}$

$$\rightarrow \begin{vmatrix} 1 & -1 & 2 & 3 & 3 \\ 4 & 1 & 1 & -1 & 4 \end{vmatrix} \longrightarrow \begin{vmatrix} 1 & -1 & 2 & 3 & 3 \\ 0 & 5 & -7 & -13 & -8 \end{vmatrix}$$

interchange r_1 and r_2 $R_2 = -4r_1 + r_2$

The matrix in the last step represents the system $\begin{cases} x - y + 2z + 3w = 3 \\ 5y - 7z - 13w = -8 \end{cases}$

The second equation yields

$$5y - 7z - 13w = -8 \Rightarrow 5y = -8 + 7z + 13w \Rightarrow y = -\frac{8}{5} + \frac{7}{5}z + \frac{13}{5}w$$

The first equation yields

$$x - y + 2z + 3w = 3 \Rightarrow x = 3 + y - 2z - 3w$$

substituting for y

$$x = 3 + \left(-\frac{8}{5} + \frac{7}{5}z + \frac{13}{5}w\right) - 2z - 3w$$

$$x = -\frac{3}{5}z - \frac{2}{5}w + \frac{7}{5}$$

Therefore the solution is

$$x = -\frac{3}{5}z - \frac{2}{5}w + \frac{7}{5}; \quad y = -\frac{8}{5} + \frac{7}{5}z + \frac{13}{5}w$$

z and w are any real numbers

69. Each of the points must satisfy the equation $y = ax^2 + bx + c$.

    $(1,2)$: $2 = a + b + c$

    $(-2,-7)$: $-7 = 4a - 2b + c$

    $(2,-3)$: $-3 = 4a + 2b + c$

Set up a matrix and solve:

$$\begin{bmatrix} 1 & 1 & 1 & | & 2 \\ 4 & -2 & 1 & | & -7 \\ 4 & 2 & 1 & | & -3 \end{bmatrix} \rightarrow \begin{bmatrix} 1 & 1 & 1 & | & 2 \\ 0 & -6 & -3 & | & -15 \\ 0 & -2 & -3 & | & -11 \end{bmatrix} \rightarrow \begin{bmatrix} 1 & 1 & 1 & | & 2 \\ 0 & 1 & \frac{1}{2} & | & \frac{5}{2} \\ 0 & -2 & -3 & | & -11 \end{bmatrix} \rightarrow \begin{bmatrix} 1 & 0 & \frac{1}{2} & | & -\frac{1}{2} \\ 0 & 1 & \frac{1}{2} & | & \frac{5}{2} \\ 0 & 0 & -2 & | & -6 \end{bmatrix}$$

$$\begin{array}{cccc} R_2 = -4r_1 + r_2 & R_2 = -\frac{1}{6}r_2 & R_1 = -r_2 + r_1 \\ R_3 = -4r_1 + r_3 & & R_3 = 2r_2 + r_3 \end{array}$$

$$\rightarrow \begin{bmatrix} 1 & 0 & \frac{1}{2} & | & -\frac{1}{2} \\ 0 & 1 & \frac{1}{2} & | & \frac{5}{2} \\ 0 & 0 & 1 & | & 3 \end{bmatrix} \rightarrow \begin{bmatrix} 1 & 0 & 0 & | & -2 \\ 0 & 1 & 0 & | & 1 \\ 0 & 0 & 1 & | & 3 \end{bmatrix}$$

$$\begin{array}{cc} R_3 = -\frac{1}{2}r_3 & R_1 = -\frac{1}{2}r_3 + r_1 \\ & R_2 = -\frac{1}{2}r_3 + r_2 \end{array}$$

The solution is $a = -2$, $b = 1$, $c = 3$; so the equation is $y = -2x^2 + x + 3$.

71. Each of the points must satisfy the equation $f(x) = ax^3 + bx^2 + cx + d$.

    $f(-3) = -112$: $\Rightarrow$ $-27a + 9b - 3c + d = -112$

    $f(-1) = -2$: $\Rightarrow$ $-a + b - c + d = -2$

    $f(1) = 4$: $\Rightarrow$ $a + b + c + d = 4$

    $f(2) = 13$: $\Rightarrow$ $8a + 4b + 2c + d = 13$

Set up a matrix and solve:

$$\begin{vmatrix} -27 & 9 & -3 & 1 & | & -112 \\ -1 & 1 & -1 & 1 & | & -2 \\ 1 & 1 & 1 & 1 & | & 4 \\ 8 & 4 & 2 & 1 & | & 13 \end{vmatrix} \rightarrow \begin{bmatrix} 1 & 1 & 1 & 1 & | & 4 \\ -1 & 1 & -1 & 1 & | & -2 \\ -27 & 9 & -3 & 1 & | & -112 \\ 8 & 4 & 2 & 1 & | & 13 \end{bmatrix} \rightarrow \begin{bmatrix} 1 & 1 & 1 & 1 & | & 4 \\ 0 & 2 & 0 & 2 & | & 2 \\ 0 & 36 & 24 & 28 & | & -4 \\ 0 & -4 & -6 & -7 & | & -19 \end{bmatrix}$$

$$\begin{array}{ccc} \text{Interchange } r_3 \text{ and } r_1 & R_2 = r_1 + r_2 \\ & R_3 = 27 r_1 + r_3 \\ & R_4 = -8 r_1 + r_4 \end{array}$$

$$\rightarrow \begin{vmatrix} 1 & 1 & 1 & 1 & | & 4 \\ 0 & 1 & 0 & 1 & | & 1 \\ 0 & 36 & 24 & 28 & | & -4 \\ 0 & -4 & -6 & -7 & | & -19 \end{vmatrix} \rightarrow \begin{bmatrix} 1 & 0 & 1 & 0 & | & 3 \\ 0 & 1 & 0 & 1 & | & 1 \\ 0 & 0 & 24 & -8 & | & -40 \\ 0 & 0 & -6 & -3 & | & -15 \end{bmatrix} \rightarrow \begin{bmatrix} 1 & 0 & 1 & 0 & | & 3 \\ 0 & 1 & 0 & 1 & | & 1 \\ 0 & 0 & 1 & -\frac{1}{3} & | & -\frac{5}{3} \\ 0 & 0 & -6 & -3 & | & -15 \end{bmatrix}$$

$$\begin{array}{ccc} R_2 = \frac{1}{2}r_2 & R_1 = -r_2 + r_1 & R_3 = \frac{1}{24}r_3 \\ & R_3 = -36 r_2 + r_3 \\ & R_4 = 4 r_2 + r_4 \end{array}$$

$$\rightarrow \begin{bmatrix} 1 & 0 & 0 & \frac{1}{3} & \frac{14}{3} \\ 0 & 1 & 0 & 1 & 1 \\ 0 & 0 & 1 & -\frac{1}{3} & -\frac{5}{3} \\ 0 & 0 & 0 & -5 & -25 \end{bmatrix} \rightarrow \begin{bmatrix} 1 & 0 & 0 & \frac{1}{3} & \frac{14}{3} \\ 0 & 1 & 0 & 1 & 1 \\ 0 & 0 & 1 & -\frac{1}{3} & -\frac{5}{3} \\ 0 & 0 & 0 & 1 & 5 \end{bmatrix} \rightarrow \begin{bmatrix} 1 & 0 & 0 & 0 & 3 \\ 0 & 1 & 0 & 0 & -4 \\ 0 & 0 & 1 & 0 & 0 \\ 0 & 0 & 0 & 1 & 5 \end{bmatrix}$$

$$\begin{array}{ccc} R_1 = -r_3 + r_1 & R_4 = -\frac{1}{5}r_4 & R_1 = -\frac{1}{3}r_4 + r_1 \\ R_4 = 6r_3 + r_4 & & R_2 = -r_4 + r_2 \\ & & R_3 = \frac{1}{3}r_4 + r_3 \end{array}$$

The solution is $a = 3$, $b = -4$, $c = 0$, $d = 5$; so the equation is $f(x) = 3x^3 - 4x^2 + 5$.

73. Let x = the number of servings of salmon steak.
    Let y = the number of servings of baked eggs.
    Let z = the number of servings of acorn squash.
    Protein equation: $30x + 15y + 3z = 78$
    Carbohydrate equation: $20x + 2y + 25z = 59$
    Vitamin A equation: $2x + 20y + 32z = 75$
    Set up a matrix and solve:

$$\begin{bmatrix} 30 & 15 & 3 & 78 \\ 20 & 2 & 25 & 59 \\ 2 & 20 & 32 & 75 \end{bmatrix} \rightarrow \begin{bmatrix} 2 & 20 & 32 & 75 \\ 20 & 2 & 25 & 59 \\ 30 & 15 & 3 & 78 \end{bmatrix} \rightarrow \begin{bmatrix} 1 & 10 & 16 & 37.5 \\ 20 & 2 & 25 & 59 \\ 30 & 15 & 3 & 78 \end{bmatrix}$$

Interchange r_3 and r_1 $R_1 = \frac{1}{2}r_1$

$$\rightarrow \begin{bmatrix} 1 & 10 & 16 & 37.5 \\ 0 & -198 & -295 & -691 \\ 0 & -285 & -477 & -1047 \end{bmatrix} \rightarrow \begin{bmatrix} 1 & 10 & 16 & 37.5 \\ 0 & -198 & -295 & -691 \\ 0 & 0 & -\frac{3457}{66} & -\frac{3457}{66} \end{bmatrix}$$

$$\begin{array}{cc} R_2 = -20r_1 + r_2 & R_3 = -\frac{95}{66}r_2 + r_3 \\ R_3 = -30r_1 + r_3 & \end{array}$$

$$\rightarrow \begin{bmatrix} 1 & 10 & 16 & 37.5 \\ 0 & -198 & -295 & -691 \\ 0 & 0 & 1 & 1 \end{bmatrix}$$

$$R_3 = -\frac{66}{3457}r_3$$

Substitute $z = 1$ and solve:

$$\begin{array}{ll} -198y - 295(1) = -691 & x + 10(2) + 16(1) = 37.5 \\ \quad\quad -198y = -396 & \quad\quad x + 36 = 37.5 \\ \quad\quad\quad\quad y = 2 & \quad\quad\quad\quad x = 1.5 \end{array}$$

The dietitian should serve 1.5 servings of salmon steak, 2 servings of baked eggs, and 1 serving of acorn squash.

75. Let x = the amount invested in Treasury bills.
    Let y = the amount invested in Treasury bonds.
    Let z = the amount invested in corporate bonds.
    Total investment equation: $x + y + z = 10000$
    Annual income equation: $0.06x + 0.07y + 0.08z = 680$
    Condition on investment equation: $z = 0.5x$

Set up a matrix and solve:

$$\begin{bmatrix} 1 & 1 & 1 & | & 10000 \\ 0.06 & 0.07 & 0.08 & | & 680 \\ 1 & 0 & -2 & | & 0 \end{bmatrix} \rightarrow \begin{bmatrix} 1 & 1 & 1 & | & 10000 \\ 0 & 0.01 & 0.02 & | & 80 \\ 0 & -1 & -3 & | & -10000 \end{bmatrix} \rightarrow \begin{bmatrix} 1 & 1 & 1 & | & 10000 \\ 0 & 1 & 2 & | & 8000 \\ 0 & -1 & -3 & | & -10000 \end{bmatrix}$$

$$R_2 = -0.06\,r_1 + r_2 \qquad\qquad R_2 = 100\,r_2$$
$$R_3 = -r_1 + r_3$$

$$\rightarrow \begin{bmatrix} 1 & 0 & -1 & | & 2000 \\ 0 & 1 & 2 & | & 8000 \\ 0 & 0 & -1 & | & -2000 \end{bmatrix} \rightarrow \begin{bmatrix} 1 & 0 & -1 & | & 2000 \\ 0 & 1 & 2 & | & 8000 \\ 0 & 0 & 1 & | & 2000 \end{bmatrix} \rightarrow \begin{bmatrix} 1 & 0 & 0 & | & 4000 \\ 0 & 1 & 0 & | & 4000 \\ 0 & 0 & 1 & | & 2000 \end{bmatrix}$$

$$R_1 = -r_2 + r_1 \qquad R_3 = -r_3 \qquad R_1 = r_3 + r_1$$
$$R_3 = r_2 + r_3 \qquad\qquad\qquad R_2 = -2r_3 + r_2$$

Carletta should invest \$4000 in Treasury bills, \$4000 in Treasury bonds, and \$2000 in corporate bonds.

77. Let x = the number of Deltas produced.
Let y = the number of Betas produced.
Let z = the number of Sigmas produced.
Painting equation: $10x + 16y + 8z = 240$
Drying equation: $3x + 5y + 2z = 69$
Polishing equation: $2x + 3y + z = 41$
Set up a matrix and solve:

$$\begin{bmatrix} 10 & 16 & 8 & | & 240 \\ 3 & 5 & 2 & | & 69 \\ 2 & 3 & 1 & | & 41 \end{bmatrix} \rightarrow \begin{bmatrix} 1 & 1 & 2 & | & 33 \\ 3 & 5 & 2 & | & 69 \\ 2 & 3 & 1 & | & 41 \end{bmatrix} \rightarrow \begin{bmatrix} 1 & 1 & 2 & | & 33 \\ 0 & 2 & -4 & | & -30 \\ 0 & 1 & -3 & | & -25 \end{bmatrix} \rightarrow \begin{bmatrix} 1 & 1 & 2 & | & 33 \\ 0 & 1 & -2 & | & -15 \\ 0 & 1 & -3 & | & -25 \end{bmatrix}$$

$$R_1 = -3r_2 + r_1 \quad R_2 = -3r_1 + r_2 \quad R_2 = \tfrac{1}{2}r_2$$
$$R_3 = -2r_1 + r_3$$

$$\rightarrow \begin{bmatrix} 1 & 0 & 4 & | & 48 \\ 0 & 1 & -2 & | & -15 \\ 0 & 0 & -1 & | & -10 \end{bmatrix} \rightarrow \begin{bmatrix} 1 & 0 & 4 & | & 48 \\ 0 & 1 & -2 & | & -15 \\ 0 & 0 & 1 & | & 10 \end{bmatrix} \rightarrow \begin{bmatrix} 1 & 0 & 0 & | & 8 \\ 0 & 1 & 0 & | & 5 \\ 0 & 0 & 1 & | & 10 \end{bmatrix}$$

$$R_1 = -r_2 + r_1 \qquad R_3 = -r_3 \qquad R_1 = -4r_3 + r_1$$
$$R_3 = -r_2 + r_3 \qquad\qquad\qquad R_2 = 2r_3 + r_2$$

The company should produce 8 Deltas, 5 Betas, and 10 Sigmas.

79. Rewrite the system as set up and solve the matrix:

$$\begin{cases} -4 + 8 - 2I_2 = 0 \\ 8 = 5I_4 + I_1 \\ 4 = 3I_3 + I_1 \\ I_3 + I_4 = I_1 \end{cases} \rightarrow \begin{cases} 2I_2 = 4 \\ I_1 + 5I_4 = 8 \\ I_1 + 3I_3 = 4 \\ I_1 - I_3 - I_4 = 0 \end{cases}$$

$$
\left[\begin{array}{cccc|c}
0 & 2 & 0 & 0 & 4 \\
1 & 0 & 0 & 5 & 8 \\
1 & 0 & 3 & 0 & 4 \\
1 & 0 & -1 & -1 & 0
\end{array}\right]
\rightarrow
\left[\begin{array}{cccc|c}
1 & 0 & 0 & 5 & 8 \\
0 & 2 & 0 & 0 & 4 \\
1 & 0 & 3 & 0 & 4 \\
1 & 0 & -1 & -1 & 0
\end{array}\right]
\rightarrow
\left[\begin{array}{cccc|c}
1 & 0 & 0 & 5 & 8 \\
0 & 1 & 0 & 0 & 2 \\
0 & 0 & 3 & -5 & -4 \\
0 & 0 & -1 & -6 & -8
\end{array}\right]
$$

Interchange r_2 and r_1 $R_2 = \frac{1}{2} r_2$

$$R_3 = -r_1 + r_3$$

$$R_4 = -r_1 + r_4$$

$$
\rightarrow
\left[\begin{array}{cccc|c}
1 & 0 & 0 & 5 & 8 \\
0 & 1 & 0 & 0 & 2 \\
0 & 0 & -1 & -6 & -8 \\
0 & 0 & 3 & -5 & -4
\end{array}\right]
\rightarrow
\left[\begin{array}{cccc|c}
1 & 0 & 0 & 5 & 8 \\
0 & 1 & 0 & 0 & 2 \\
0 & 0 & 1 & 6 & 8 \\
0 & 0 & 0 & -23 & -28
\end{array}\right]
\rightarrow
\left[\begin{array}{cccc|c}
1 & 0 & 0 & 5 & 8 \\
0 & 1 & 0 & 0 & 2 \\
0 & 0 & 1 & 6 & 8 \\
0 & 0 & 0 & 1 & \frac{28}{23}
\end{array}\right]
$$

Interchange r_3 and r_4 $R_3 = -r_3$ $R_4 = -\frac{1}{23} r_4$

$$R_4 = -3 r_3 + r_4$$

$$
\rightarrow
\left[\begin{array}{cccc|c}
1 & 0 & 0 & 0 & \frac{44}{23} \\
0 & 1 & 0 & 0 & 2 \\
0 & 0 & 1 & 0 & \frac{16}{23} \\
0 & 0 & 0 & 1 & \frac{28}{23}
\end{array}\right]
$$

$$R_1 = -5 r_4 + r_1$$

$$R_3 = -6 r_4 + r_3$$

The solution is $I_1 = \dfrac{44}{23}$, $I_2 = 2$, $I_3 = \dfrac{16}{23}$, $I_4 = \dfrac{28}{23}$.

81. Let x = the amount invested in Treasury bills.
Let y = the amount invested in Treasury bonds.
Let z = the amount invested in corporate bonds.

(a) Total investment equation: $x + y + z = 20000$

Annual income equation: $0.07x + 0.09y + 0.11z = 2000$

Set up a matrix and solve:

$$
\left[\begin{array}{ccc|c}
1 & 1 & 1 & 20000 \\
.07 & .09 & .11 & 2000
\end{array}\right]
\rightarrow
\left[\begin{array}{ccc|c}
1 & 1 & 1 & 20000 \\
7 & 9 & 11 & 200000
\end{array}\right]
\rightarrow
\left[\begin{array}{ccc|c}
1 & 1 & 1 & 20000 \\
0 & 2 & 4 & 60000
\end{array}\right]
$$

$$R_2 = 100 r_2 \qquad\qquad R_2 = r_2 - 7 r_1$$

$$
\rightarrow
\left[\begin{array}{ccc|c}
1 & 1 & 1 & 20000 \\
0 & 1 & 2 & 30000
\end{array}\right]
\rightarrow
\left[\begin{array}{ccc|c}
1 & 0 & -1 & -10000 \\
0 & 1 & 2 & 30000
\end{array}\right]
$$

$$R_2 = \tfrac{1}{2} r_2 \qquad\qquad R_1 = r_1 - r_2$$

The matrix in the last step represents the system $\begin{cases} x - z = -10000 \\ y + 2z = 30000 \end{cases}$

Therefore the solution is

$$x = -10000 + z; \ \ y = 30000 - 2z; \ \ z \text{ is any real number}$$

Possible investment strategies:

	Amount invested at	
7%	9%	11%
0	10000	10000
1000	8000	11000
2000	6000	12000
3000	4000	13000
4000	2000	14000
5000	0	15000

(b)   Total investment equation: $x + y + z = 25000$

Annual income equation: $0.07x + 0.09y + 0.11z = 2000$

Set up a matrix and solve:

$$\begin{bmatrix} 1 & 1 & 1 & | & 25000 \\ .07 & .09 & .11 & | & 2000 \end{bmatrix} \rightarrow \begin{bmatrix} 1 & 1 & 1 & | & 25000 \\ 7 & 9 & 11 & | & 200000 \end{bmatrix} \rightarrow \begin{bmatrix} 1 & 1 & 1 & | & 25000 \\ 0 & 2 & 4 & | & 25000 \end{bmatrix}$$

$$\qquad\qquad R_2 = 100r_2 \qquad\qquad R_2 = r_2 - 7r_1$$

$$\rightarrow \begin{bmatrix} 1 & 1 & 1 & | & 25000 \\ 0 & 1 & 2 & | & 12500 \end{bmatrix} \rightarrow \begin{bmatrix} 1 & 0 & -1 & | & 12500 \\ 0 & 1 & 2 & | & 12500 \end{bmatrix}$$

$$\quad R_2 = \tfrac{1}{2}r_2 \qquad\qquad R_1 = r_1 - r_2$$

The matrix in the last step represents the system $\begin{cases} x - z = 12500 \\ y + 2z = 12500 \end{cases}$

Therefore the solution is $x = 12500 + z; \ y = 12500 - 2z; \ z$ is any real number,

Possible investment strategies:

	Amount invested at	
7%	9%	11%
12500	12500	0
14500	8500	2000
16500	4500	4000
18750	0	6250

(c)   Total investment equation: $x + y + z = 30000$

Annual income equation: $0.07x + 0.09y + 0.11z = 2000$

Set up a matrix and solve:

$$\begin{bmatrix} 1 & 1 & 1 & | & 30000 \\ .07 & .09 & .11 & | & 2000 \end{bmatrix} \rightarrow \begin{bmatrix} 1 & 1 & 1 & | & 30000 \\ 7 & 9 & 11 & | & 200000 \end{bmatrix} \rightarrow \begin{bmatrix} 1 & 1 & 1 & | & 30000 \\ 0 & 2 & 4 & | & -10000 \end{bmatrix}$$

$$\qquad\qquad R_2 = 100r_2 \qquad\qquad R_1 = r_2 - 7r_1$$

$$\rightarrow \begin{bmatrix} 1 & 1 & 1 & | & 30000 \\ 0 & 1 & 2 & | & -5000 \end{bmatrix} \rightarrow \begin{bmatrix} 1 & 0 & -1 & | & 35000 \\ 0 & 1 & 2 & | & -5000 \end{bmatrix}$$

$$\quad R_2 = \tfrac{1}{2}r_2 \qquad\qquad R_1 = r_1 - r_2$$

The matrix in the last step represents the system $\begin{cases} x - z = 35000 \\ y + 2z = -5000 \end{cases}$

Therefore the solution is $x = 35000 + z; \ y = -5000 - 2z; \ z$ is any real number

One possible investment strategy

Amount invested at

7%	9%	11%
30000	0	0

This will yield ($30000)(.07) = $2100, which is more than the required income.

83.   Let x = the amount of liquid 1.
Let y = the amount of liquid 2.
Let z = the amount of liquid 3.
$$.20x + .40y + .30z = 40 \quad \text{Vitamin C}$$
$$.30x + .20y + .50z = 30 \quad \text{Vitamin D}$$
multiplying each equation by 10 yields
$$2x + 4y + 3z = 400$$
$$3x + 2y + 5z = 300$$

Set up a matrix and solve: $\begin{bmatrix} 2 & 4 & 3 & | & 400 \\ 3 & 2 & 5 & | & 300 \end{bmatrix} \rightarrow \begin{bmatrix} 1 & 2 & \frac{3}{2} & | & 200 \\ 3 & 2 & 5 & | & 300 \end{bmatrix} \rightarrow \begin{bmatrix} 1 & 2 & \frac{3}{2} & | & 200 \\ 0 & -4 & \frac{1}{2} & | & -300 \end{bmatrix}$

$$R_1 = \tfrac{1}{2}r_1 \qquad\qquad R_2 = r_2 - 3r_1$$

$\rightarrow \begin{vmatrix} 1 & 2 & \frac{3}{2} & | & 200 \\ 0 & 1 & -\frac{1}{8} & | & 75 \end{vmatrix} \rightarrow \begin{vmatrix} 1 & 0 & \frac{7}{4} & | & 50 \\ 0 & 1 & -\frac{1}{8} & | & 75 \end{vmatrix}$

$$R_2 = -\tfrac{1}{4}r_2 \qquad R_1 = r_1 - 2r_2$$

The matrix in the last step represents the system $\begin{cases} x + \frac{7}{4}z = 50 \\ y - \frac{1}{8}z = 75 \end{cases}$

Therefore the solution is $x = 50 - \dfrac{7}{4}z; \ y = 75 + \dfrac{1}{8}z; \ z$ is any real number

Possible combinations:

Liquid 1	Liquid 2	Liquid 3
50mg	75mg	0mg
36mg	76mg	8mg
22mg	77mg	16mg
8mg	78mg	24mg

85 – 87.   Answers will vary.

Systems of Equations and Inequalities

8.3 Systems of Linear Equations: Determinants

1. (a) Evaluating the determinant: $\begin{vmatrix} 3 & 1 \\ 4 & 2 \end{vmatrix} = 3(2) - 4(1) = 6 - 4 = 2$

   (b) Use MATRIX EDIT to create the matrix $\quad$ Then compute det([A]):

   $A = \begin{bmatrix} 3 & 1 \\ 4 & 2 \end{bmatrix}$

   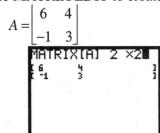

   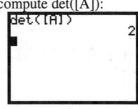

3. (a) Evaluating the determinant: $\begin{vmatrix} 6 & 4 \\ -1 & 3 \end{vmatrix} = 6(3) - (-1)(4) = 18 + 4 = 22$

   (b) Use MATRIX EDIT to create the matrix $\qquad$ Then compute det([A]):

   $A = \begin{bmatrix} 6 & 4 \\ -1 & 3 \end{bmatrix}$

   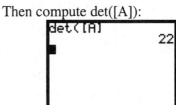

5. (a) Evaluating the determinant: $\begin{vmatrix} -3 & -1 \\ 4 & 2 \end{vmatrix} = -3(2) - 4(-1) = -6 + 4 = -2$

   (b) Use MATRIX EDIT to create the matrix $\qquad$ Then compute det([A]):

   $A = \begin{bmatrix} -3 & -1 \\ 4 & 2 \end{bmatrix}$

   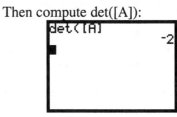

   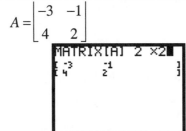

7. (a) Evaluating the determinant:

$$\begin{vmatrix} 3 & 4 & 2 \\ 1 & -1 & 5 \\ 1 & 2 & -2 \end{vmatrix} = 3\begin{vmatrix} -1 & 5 \\ 2 & -2 \end{vmatrix} - 4\begin{vmatrix} 1 & 5 \\ 1 & -2 \end{vmatrix} + 2\begin{vmatrix} 1 & -1 \\ 1 & 2 \end{vmatrix}$$

$$= 3\left[(-1)(-2) - 2(5)\right] - 4\left[1(-2) - 1(5)\right] + 2\left[1(2) - 1(-1)\right]$$

$$= 3(2-10) - 4(-2-5) + 2(2+1) = 3(-8) - 4(-7) + 2(3) = -24 + 28 + 6 = 10$$

(b) Use MATRIX EDIT to create the matrix

$$A = \begin{bmatrix} 3 & 4 & 2 \\ 1 & -1 & 5 \\ 1 & 2 & -2 \end{bmatrix}$$

Then compute det([A]):

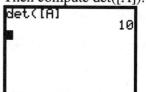

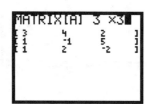

9. (a) Evaluating the determinant:

$$\begin{vmatrix} 4 & -1 & 2 \\ 6 & -1 & 0 \\ 1 & -3 & 4 \end{vmatrix} = 4\begin{vmatrix} -1 & 0 \\ -3 & 4 \end{vmatrix} - (-1)\begin{vmatrix} 6 & 0 \\ 1 & 4 \end{vmatrix} + 2\begin{vmatrix} 6 & -1 \\ 1 & -3 \end{vmatrix}$$

$$= 4\left[-1(4) - 0(-3)\right] + 1\left[6(4) - 1(0)\right] + 2\left[6(-3) - 1(-1)\right]$$

$$= 4(-4) + 1(24) + 2(-17) = -16 + 24 - 34 = -26$$

(b) Use MATRIX EDIT to create the matrix

$$A = \begin{bmatrix} 4 & -1 & 2 \\ 6 & -1 & 0 \\ 1 & -3 & 4 \end{bmatrix}$$

Then compute det([A]):

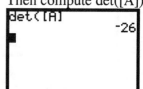

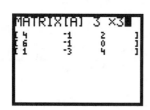

11. (a) Set up and evaluate the determinants to use Cramer's Rule:

$$\begin{cases} x + y = 8 \\ x - y = 4 \end{cases}$$

$$D = \begin{vmatrix} 1 & 1 \\ 1 & -1 \end{vmatrix} = -1 - 1 = -2; D_x = \begin{vmatrix} 8 & 1 \\ 4 & -1 \end{vmatrix} = -8 - 4 = -12; \quad D_y = \begin{vmatrix} 1 & 8 \\ 1 & 4 \end{vmatrix} = 4 - 8 = -4$$

Find the solutions by Cramer's Rule:

$$x = \frac{D_x}{D} = \frac{-12}{-2} = 6 \qquad y = \frac{D_y}{D} = \frac{-4}{-2} = 2$$

(b) Use MATRIX EDIT to create the matrices

$$A = \begin{vmatrix} 1 & 1 \\ 1 & -1 \end{vmatrix}; \quad B = \begin{vmatrix} 8 & 1 \\ 4 & -1 \end{vmatrix}; \quad C = \begin{vmatrix} 1 & 8 \\ 1 & 4 \end{vmatrix}$$

Then compute

$$x = \det([B])/\det([A]);$$

$$y = \det([C])/\det([A])$$

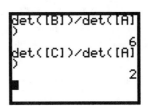

13. (a) Set up and evaluate the determinants to use Cramer's Rule:

$$\begin{cases} 5x - y = 13 \\ 2x + 3y = 12 \end{cases}$$

$$D = \begin{vmatrix} 5 & -1 \\ 2 & 3 \end{vmatrix} = 15 + 2 = 17; D_x = \begin{vmatrix} 13 & -1 \\ 12 & 3 \end{vmatrix} = 39 + 12 = 51; D_y = \begin{vmatrix} 5 & 13 \\ 2 & 12 \end{vmatrix} = 60 - 26 = 34$$

Find the solutions by Cramer's Rule:

$$x = \frac{D_x}{D} = \frac{51}{17} = 3 \qquad y = \frac{D_y}{D} = \frac{34}{17} = 2$$

(b) Use MATRIX EDIT to create the matrices

$$A = \begin{vmatrix} 5 & -1 \\ 2 & 3 \end{vmatrix}; \quad B = \begin{vmatrix} 13 & -1 \\ 12 & 3 \end{vmatrix}; \quad C = \begin{vmatrix} 5 & 13 \\ 2 & 12 \end{vmatrix}$$

Then compute

$$x = \det([B])/\det([A]);$$

$$y = \det([C])/\det([A])$$

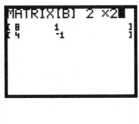

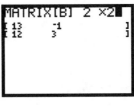

15. (a) Set up and evaluate the determinants to use Cramer's Rule:

$$\begin{cases} 3x \quad\;\; = 24 \\ x + 2y = \;\; 0 \end{cases}$$

$$D = \begin{vmatrix} 3 & 0 \\ 1 & 2 \end{vmatrix} = 6 - 0 = 6; D_x = \begin{vmatrix} 24 & 0 \\ 0 & 2 \end{vmatrix} = 48 - 0 = 48; \quad D_y = \begin{vmatrix} 3 & 24 \\ 1 & 0 \end{vmatrix} = 0 - 24 = -24$$

Find the solutions by Cramer's Rule:

$$x = \frac{D_x}{D} = \frac{48}{6} = 8 \qquad y = \frac{D_y}{D} = \frac{-24}{6} = -4$$

(b) Use MATRIX EDIT to create the matrices

$$A = \begin{vmatrix} 3 & 0 \\ 1 & 2 \end{vmatrix}; \quad B = \begin{vmatrix} 24 & 0 \\ 0 & 2 \end{vmatrix}; \quad C = \begin{vmatrix} 3 & 24 \\ 1 & 0 \end{vmatrix}$$

Then compute

$x = \det([B])/\det([A]);$

$y = \det([C])/\det([A])$

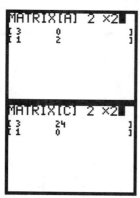
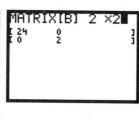
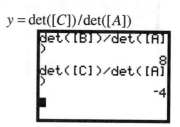

17. (a) Set up and evaluate the determinants to use Cramer's Rule:

$$\begin{cases} 3x - 6y = 24 \\ 5x + 4y = 12 \end{cases}$$

$$D = \begin{vmatrix} 3 & -6 \\ 5 & 4 \end{vmatrix} = 12 - (-30) = 42; D_x = \begin{vmatrix} 24 & -6 \\ 12 & 4 \end{vmatrix} = 96 - (-72) = 168; D_y = \begin{vmatrix} 3 & 24 \\ 5 & 12 \end{vmatrix} = 36 - 120 = -84$$

Find the solutions by Cramer's Rule:

$$x = \frac{D_x}{D} = \frac{168}{42} = 4 \qquad y = \frac{D_y}{D} = \frac{-84}{42} = -2$$

(b) Use MATRIX EDIT to create the matrices

$$A = \begin{vmatrix} 3 & -6 \\ 5 & 4 \end{vmatrix}; \quad B = \begin{vmatrix} 24 & -6 \\ 12 & 4 \end{vmatrix}; \quad C = \begin{vmatrix} 3 & 24 \\ 5 & 12 \end{vmatrix}$$

Then compute
$x = \det([B])/\det([A]);$
$y = \det([C])/\det([A])$

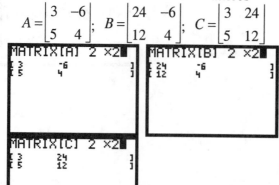
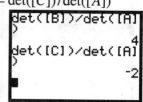

19. (a) Set up and evaluate the determinants to use Cramer's Rule:

$$\begin{cases} 3x - 2y = 4 \\ 6x - 4y = 0 \end{cases}$$

$$D = \begin{vmatrix} 3 & -2 \\ 6 & -4 \end{vmatrix} = -12 - (-12) = 0$$

Since $D = 0$, Cramer's Rule does not apply.

(b) Use MATRIX EDIT to create the matrix

$$A = \begin{vmatrix} 3 & -2 \\ 6 & -4 \end{vmatrix}$$

Then compute det([A]):

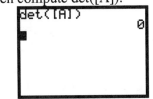

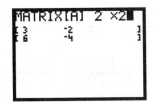

Cramer's Rule does not apply.

21. Set up and evaluate the determinants to use Cramer's Rule:

$$\begin{cases} 2x - 4y = -2 \\ 3x + 2y = 3 \end{cases}$$

$$D = \begin{vmatrix} 2 & -4 \\ 3 & 2 \end{vmatrix} = 4 - (-12) = 16$$

$$D_x = \begin{vmatrix} -2 & -4 \\ 3 & 2 \end{vmatrix} = -4 - (-12) = 8; \quad D_y = \begin{vmatrix} 2 & -2 \\ 3 & 3 \end{vmatrix} = 6 - (-6) = 12$$

Find the solutions by Cramer's Rule:

$$x = \frac{D_x}{D} = \frac{8}{16} = \frac{1}{2} \qquad y = \frac{D_y}{D} = \frac{12}{16} = \frac{3}{4}$$

(b) Use MATRIX EDIT to create the matrices

$$A = \begin{vmatrix} 2 & -4 \\ 3 & 2 \end{vmatrix}; \quad B = \begin{vmatrix} -2 & -4 \\ 3 & 2 \end{vmatrix}; \quad C = \begin{vmatrix} 2 & -2 \\ 3 & 3 \end{vmatrix}$$

Then compute

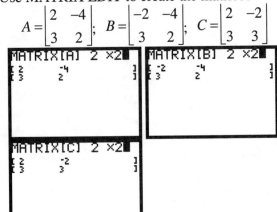

$x = \det([B])/\det([A]);$

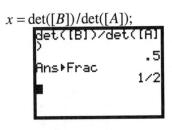

$y = \det([C])/\det([A])$

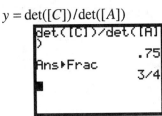

23.   (a) Set up and evaluate the determinants to use Cramer's Rule:

$$\begin{cases} 2x - 3y = -1 \\ 10x + 10y = 5 \end{cases}$$

$$D = \begin{vmatrix} 2 & -3 \\ 10 & 10 \end{vmatrix} = 20 - (-30) = 50$$

$$D_x = \begin{vmatrix} -1 & -3 \\ 5 & 10 \end{vmatrix} = -10 - (-15) = 5; D_y = \begin{vmatrix} 2 & -1 \\ 10 & 5 \end{vmatrix} = 10 - (-10) = 20$$

Find the solutions by Cramer's Rule:

$$x = \frac{D_x}{D} = \frac{5}{50} = \frac{1}{10} \qquad y = \frac{D_y}{D} = \frac{20}{50} = \frac{2}{5}$$

(b) Use MATRIX EDIT to create the matrices   Then compute

$$A = \begin{vmatrix} 2 & -3 \\ 10 & 10 \end{vmatrix}; \quad B = \begin{vmatrix} -1 & -3 \\ 5 & 10 \end{vmatrix}; \quad C = \begin{vmatrix} 2 & -1 \\ 10 & 5 \end{vmatrix}$$

$$x = \det([B])/\det([A]);$$

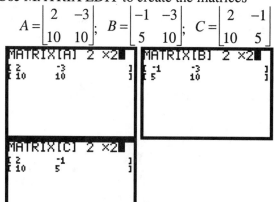

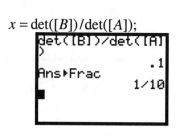

$$y = \det([C])/\det([A])$$

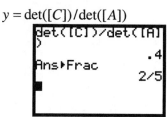

25.   (a) Set up and evaluate the determinants to use Cramer's Rule:

$$\begin{cases} 2x + 3y = 6 \\ x - y = \dfrac{1}{2} \end{cases}$$

$$D = \begin{vmatrix} 2 & 3 \\ 1 & -1 \end{vmatrix} = -2 - 3 = -5$$

$$D_x = \begin{vmatrix} 6 & 3 \\ \frac{1}{2} & -1 \end{vmatrix} = -6 - \frac{3}{2} = -\frac{15}{2}; \quad D_y = \begin{vmatrix} 2 & 6 \\ 1 & \frac{1}{2} \end{vmatrix} = 1 - 6 = -5$$

Find the solutions by Cramer's Rule:

$$x = \frac{D_x}{D} = \frac{\left(-\dfrac{15}{2}\right)}{-5} = \frac{3}{2} \qquad y = \frac{D_y}{D} = \frac{-5}{-5} = 1$$

(b) Use MATRIX EDIT to create the matrices

$$A = \begin{vmatrix} 2 & 3 \\ 1 & -1 \end{vmatrix}; \quad B = \begin{vmatrix} 6 & 3 \\ \frac{1}{2} & -1 \end{vmatrix}; \quad C = \begin{vmatrix} 2 & 6 \\ 1 & \frac{1}{2} \end{vmatrix}$$

Then compute

$$x = \det([B])/\det([A]);$$

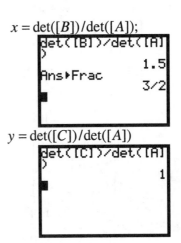

$$y = \det([C])/\det([A])$$

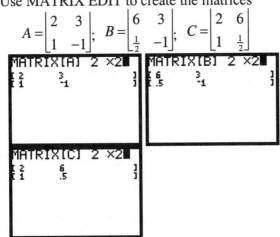

27. Set up and evaluate the determinants to use Cramer's Rule:

$$\begin{cases} 3x - 5y = 3 \\ 15x + 5y = 21 \end{cases}$$

$$D = \begin{vmatrix} 3 & -5 \\ 15 & 5 \end{vmatrix} = 15 - (-75) = 90$$

$$D_x = \begin{vmatrix} 3 & -5 \\ 21 & 5 \end{vmatrix} = 15 - (-105) = 120; \quad D_y = \begin{vmatrix} 3 & 3 \\ 15 & 21 \end{vmatrix} = 63 - 45 = 18$$

Find the solutions by Cramer's Rule:

$$x = \frac{D_x}{D} = \frac{120}{90} = \frac{4}{3} \qquad y = \frac{D_y}{D} = \frac{18}{90} = \frac{1}{5}$$

(b) Use MATRIX EDIT to create the matrices

$$A = \begin{vmatrix} 3 & -5 \\ 15 & 5 \end{vmatrix}; \quad B = \begin{vmatrix} 3 & -5 \\ 21 & 5 \end{vmatrix}; \quad C = \begin{vmatrix} 3 & 3 \\ 15 & 21 \end{vmatrix}$$

Then compute

$$x = \det([B])/\det([A]);$$

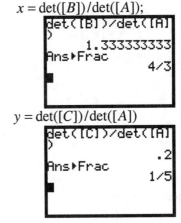

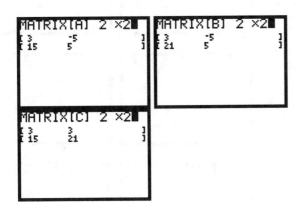

$$y = \det([C])/\det([A])$$

29. Set up and evaluate the determinants to use Cramer's Rule:

$$\begin{cases} x + y - z = 6 \\ 3x - 2y + z = -5 \\ x + 3y - 2z = 14 \end{cases}$$

$$D = \begin{vmatrix} 1 & 1 & -1 \\ 3 & -2 & 1 \\ 1 & 3 & -2 \end{vmatrix} = 1\begin{vmatrix} -2 & 1 \\ 3 & -2 \end{vmatrix} - 1\begin{vmatrix} 3 & 1 \\ 1 & -2 \end{vmatrix} + (-1)\begin{vmatrix} 3 & -2 \\ 1 & 3 \end{vmatrix}$$

$$= 1(4-3) - 1(-6-1) - 1(9+2) = 1 + 7 - 11 = -3$$

$$D_x = \begin{vmatrix} 6 & 1 & -1 \\ -5 & -2 & 1 \\ 14 & 3 & -2 \end{vmatrix} = 6\begin{vmatrix} -2 & 1 \\ 3 & -2 \end{vmatrix} - 1\begin{vmatrix} -5 & 1 \\ 14 & -2 \end{vmatrix} + (-1)\begin{vmatrix} -5 & -2 \\ 14 & 3 \end{vmatrix}$$

$$= 6(4-3) - 1(10-14) - 1(-15+28) = 6 + 4 - 13 = -3$$

$$D_y = \begin{vmatrix} 1 & 6 & -1 \\ 3 & -5 & 1 \\ 1 & 14 & -2 \end{vmatrix} = 1\begin{vmatrix} -5 & 1 \\ 14 & -2 \end{vmatrix} - 6\begin{vmatrix} 3 & 1 \\ 1 & -2 \end{vmatrix} + (-1)\begin{vmatrix} 3 & -5 \\ 1 & 14 \end{vmatrix}$$

$$= 1(10-14) - 6(-6-1) - 1(42+5) = -4 + 42 - 47 = -9$$

$$D_z = \begin{vmatrix} 1 & 1 & 6 \\ 3 & -2 & -5 \\ 1 & 3 & 14 \end{vmatrix} = 1\begin{vmatrix} -2 & -5 \\ 3 & 14 \end{vmatrix} - 1\begin{vmatrix} 3 & -5 \\ 1 & 14 \end{vmatrix} + 6\begin{vmatrix} 3 & -2 \\ 1 & 3 \end{vmatrix}$$

$$= 1(-28+15) - 1(42+5) + 6(9+2) = -13 - 47 + 66 = 6$$

Find the solutions by Cramer's Rule:

$$x = \frac{D_x}{D} = \frac{-3}{-3} = 1 \qquad y = \frac{D_y}{D} = \frac{-9}{-3} = 3 \qquad z = \frac{D_z}{D} = \frac{6}{-3} = -2$$

(b) Use MATRIX EDIT to create the matrices

$$A = \begin{bmatrix} 1 & 1 & -1 \\ 3 & -2 & 1 \\ 1 & 3 & -2 \end{bmatrix}; \quad B = \begin{bmatrix} 6 & 1 & -1 \\ -5 & -2 & 1 \\ 14 & 3 & -2 \end{bmatrix};$$

$$C = \begin{bmatrix} 1 & 6 & -1 \\ 3 & -5 & 1 \\ 1 & 14 & -2 \end{bmatrix}; \quad D = \begin{bmatrix} 1 & 1 & 6 \\ 3 & -2 & -5 \\ 1 & 3 & 14 \end{bmatrix}$$

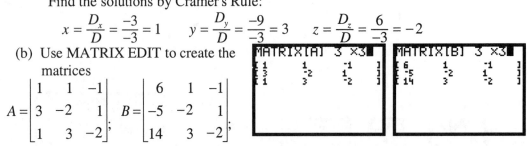

Then compute

$$x = \det([B])/\det([A]);$$
$$y = \det([C])/\det([A]);$$
$$z = \det([D])/\det([A])$$

31.   (a)   Set up and evaluate the determinants to use Cramer's Rule:

$$\begin{cases} x + 2y - z = -3 \\ 2x - 4y + z = -7 \\ -2x + 2y - 3z = 4 \end{cases}$$

$$D = \begin{vmatrix} 1 & 2 & -1 \\ 2 & -4 & 1 \\ -2 & 2 & -3 \end{vmatrix} = 1\begin{vmatrix} -4 & 1 \\ 2 & -3 \end{vmatrix} - 2\begin{vmatrix} 2 & 1 \\ -2 & -3 \end{vmatrix} + (-1)\begin{vmatrix} 2 & -4 \\ -2 & 2 \end{vmatrix}$$

$$= 1(12 - 2) - 2(-6 + 2) - 1(4 - 8) = 10 + 8 + 4 = 22$$

$$D_x = \begin{vmatrix} -3 & 2 & -1 \\ -7 & -4 & 1 \\ 4 & 2 & -3 \end{vmatrix} = -3\begin{vmatrix} -4 & 1 \\ 2 & -3 \end{vmatrix} - 2\begin{vmatrix} -7 & 1 \\ 4 & -3 \end{vmatrix} + (-1)\begin{vmatrix} -7 & -4 \\ 4 & 2 \end{vmatrix}$$

$$= -3(12 - 2) - 2(21 - 4) - 1(-14 + 16) = -30 - 34 - 2 = -66$$

$$D_y = \begin{vmatrix} 1 & -3 & -1 \\ 2 & -7 & 1 \\ -2 & 4 & -3 \end{vmatrix} = 1\begin{vmatrix} -7 & 1 \\ 4 & -3 \end{vmatrix} - (-3)\begin{vmatrix} 2 & 1 \\ -2 & -3 \end{vmatrix} + (-1)\begin{vmatrix} 2 & -7 \\ -2 & 4 \end{vmatrix}$$

$$= 1(21 - 4) + 3(-6 + 2) - 1(8 - 14) = 17 - 12 + 6 = 11$$

$$D_z = \begin{vmatrix} 1 & 2 & -3 \\ 2 & -4 & -7 \\ -2 & 2 & 4 \end{vmatrix} = 1\begin{vmatrix} -4 & -7 \\ 2 & 4 \end{vmatrix} - 2\begin{vmatrix} 2 & -7 \\ -2 & 4 \end{vmatrix} + (-3)\begin{vmatrix} 2 & -4 \\ -2 & 2 \end{vmatrix}$$

$$= 1(-16 + 14) - 2(8 - 14) - 3(4 - 8) = -2 + 12 + 12 = 22$$

Find the solutions by Cramer's Rule:

$$x = \frac{D_x}{D} = \frac{-66}{22} = -3 \qquad y = \frac{D_y}{D} = \frac{11}{22} = \frac{1}{2} \qquad z = \frac{D_z}{D} = \frac{22}{22} = 1$$

(b)   Use MATRIX EDIT to create the matrices

$$A = \begin{vmatrix} 1 & 2 & -1 \\ 2 & -4 & 1 \\ -2 & 2 & -3 \end{vmatrix}; B = \begin{vmatrix} -3 & 2 & -1 \\ -7 & -4 & 1 \\ 4 & 2 & -3 \end{vmatrix};$$

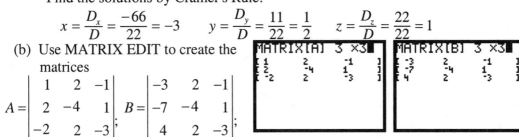

$$C = \begin{vmatrix} 1 & -3 & -1 \\ 2 & -7 & 1 \\ -2 & 4 & -3 \end{vmatrix}; D = \begin{vmatrix} 1 & 2 & -3 \\ 2 & -4 & -7 \\ -2 & 2 & 4 \end{vmatrix}$$

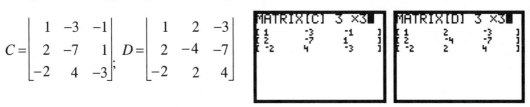

Then compute

$$x = \det([B])/\det([A]);$$
$$y = \det([C])/\det([A]);$$
$$z = \det([D])/\det([A])$$

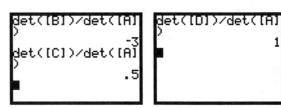

33. (a) Set up and evaluate the determinants to use Cramer's Rule:

$$\begin{cases} x - 2y + 3z = 1 \\ 3x + y - 2z = 0 \\ 2x - 4y + 6z = 2 \end{cases}$$

$$D = \begin{vmatrix} 1 & -2 & 3 \\ 3 & 1 & -2 \\ 2 & -4 & 6 \end{vmatrix} = 1\begin{vmatrix} 1 & -2 \\ -4 & 6 \end{vmatrix} - (-2)\begin{vmatrix} 3 & -2 \\ 2 & 6 \end{vmatrix} + 3\begin{vmatrix} 3 & 1 \\ 2 & -4 \end{vmatrix}$$

$$= 1(6 - 8) + 2(18 + 4) + 3(-12 - 2) = -2 + 44 - 42 = 0$$

Since $D = 0$, Cramer's Rule does not apply.

(b) Use MATRIX EDIT to create the   Then compute det([A]):
matrices

$$A = \begin{bmatrix} 1 & -2 & 3 \\ 3 & 1 & -2 \\ 2 & -4 & 6 \end{bmatrix}$$

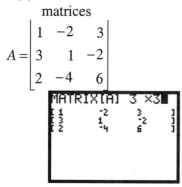

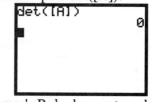

Cramer's Rule does not apply.

35. (a) Set up and evaluate the determinants to use Cramer's Rule:

$$\begin{cases} x + 2y - z = 0 \\ 2x - 4y + z = 0 \\ -2x + 2y - 3z = 0 \end{cases}$$

$$D = \begin{vmatrix} 1 & 2 & -1 \\ 2 & -4 & 1 \\ -2 & 2 & -3 \end{vmatrix} = 1\begin{vmatrix} -4 & 1 \\ 2 & -3 \end{vmatrix} - 2\begin{vmatrix} 2 & 1 \\ -2 & -3 \end{vmatrix} + (-1)\begin{vmatrix} 2 & -4 \\ -2 & 2 \end{vmatrix}$$

$$= 1(12 - 2) - 2(-6 + 2) - 1(4 - 8) = 10 + 8 + 4 = 22$$

$$D_x = \begin{vmatrix} 0 & 2 & -1 \\ 0 & -4 & 1 \\ 0 & 2 & -3 \end{vmatrix} = 0 \quad \text{(By Theorem 12)}$$

$$D_y = \begin{vmatrix} 1 & 0 & -1 \\ 2 & 0 & 1 \\ -2 & 0 & -3 \end{vmatrix} = 0 \quad \text{(By Theorem 12)}; \quad D_z = \begin{vmatrix} 1 & 2 & 0 \\ 2 & -4 & 0 \\ -2 & 2 & 0 \end{vmatrix} = 0 \quad \text{(By Theorem 12)}$$

Find the solutions by Cramer's Rule:

$$x = \frac{D_x}{D} = \frac{0}{22} = 0 \qquad y = \frac{D_y}{D} = \frac{0}{22} = 0 \qquad z = \frac{D_z}{D} = \frac{0}{22} = 0$$

(b) Use MATRIX EDIT to create the matrices

$$A = \begin{vmatrix} 1 & 2 & -1 \\ 2 & -4 & 1 \\ -2 & 2 & -3 \end{vmatrix}, \quad B = \begin{vmatrix} 0 & 2 & -1 \\ 0 & -4 & 1 \\ 0 & 2 & -3 \end{vmatrix};$$

$$C = \begin{vmatrix} 1 & 0 & -1 \\ 2 & 0 & 1 \\ -2 & 0 & -3 \end{vmatrix}, \quad D = \begin{vmatrix} 1 & 2 & 0 \\ 2 & -4 & 0 \\ -2 & 2 & 0 \end{vmatrix}$$

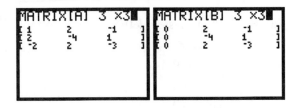

Then compute
$$x = \det([B])/\det([A]);$$
$$y = \det([C])/\det([A]);$$
$$z = \det([D])/\det([A])$$

37. (a) Set up and evaluate the determinants to use Cramer's Rule:

$$\begin{cases} x - 2y + 3z = 0 \\ 3x + y - 2z = 0 \\ 2x - 4y + 6z = 0 \end{cases}$$

$$D = \begin{vmatrix} 1 & -2 & 3 \\ 3 & 1 & -2 \\ 2 & -4 & 6 \end{vmatrix} = 1\begin{vmatrix} 1 & -2 \\ -4 & 6 \end{vmatrix} - (-2)\begin{vmatrix} 3 & -2 \\ 2 & 6 \end{vmatrix} + 3\begin{vmatrix} 3 & 1 \\ 2 & -4 \end{vmatrix}$$

$$= 1(6 - 8) + 2(18 + 4) + 3(-12 - 2) = -2 + 44 - 42 = 0$$

Since $D = 0$, Cramer's Rule does not apply.

(b) Use MATRIX EDIT to create the matrices

$$A = \begin{vmatrix} 1 & -2 & 3 \\ 3 & 1 & -2 \\ 2 & -4 & 6 \end{vmatrix}$$

Then compute det([A]):

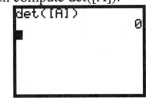

Cramer's Rule does not apply.

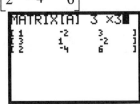

39. (a) Rewrite the system letting $u = \dfrac{1}{x}$ and $v = \dfrac{1}{y}$:

$$\begin{cases} \dfrac{1}{x} + \dfrac{1}{y} = 8 \\[2mm] \dfrac{3}{x} - \dfrac{5}{y} = 0 \end{cases} \Rightarrow \begin{cases} u + v = 8 \\ 3u - 5v = 0 \end{cases}$$

Set up and evaluate the determinants to use Cramer's Rule:

$$D = \begin{vmatrix} 1 & 1 \\ 3 & -5 \end{vmatrix} = -5 - 3 = -8$$

$$D_u = \begin{vmatrix} 8 & 1 \\ 0 & -5 \end{vmatrix} = -40 - 0 = -40; \quad D_v = \begin{vmatrix} 1 & 8 \\ 3 & 0 \end{vmatrix} = 0 - 24 = -24$$

Find the solutions by Cramer's Rule:

$$u = \frac{D_u}{D} = \frac{-40}{-8} = 5 \Rightarrow \frac{1}{x} = 5 \Rightarrow x = \frac{1}{5} \; ; \; v = \frac{D_v}{D} = \frac{-24}{-8} = 3 \Rightarrow \frac{1}{y} = 3 \Rightarrow y = \frac{1}{3}$$

The solutions are $x = \dfrac{1}{5}, \; y = \dfrac{1}{3}$.

(b) Use MATRIX EDIT to create the matrices   Then compute

$$A = \begin{bmatrix} 1 & 1 \\ 3 & -5 \end{bmatrix}; \quad B = \begin{bmatrix} 8 & 1 \\ 0 & -5 \end{bmatrix}; \quad C = \begin{bmatrix} 1 & 8 \\ 3 & 0 \end{bmatrix}$$

$u = \det([B])/\det([A]);$
$v = \det([C])/\det([A])$

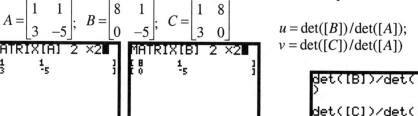

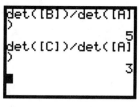

41. Solve for x:

$$\begin{vmatrix} x & x \\ 4 & 3 \end{vmatrix} = 3x - 4x = -x \Rightarrow -x = 5 \Rightarrow x = -5$$

43. Solve for x:

$$\begin{vmatrix} x & 1 & 1 \\ 4 & 3 & 2 \\ -1 & 2 & 5 \end{vmatrix} = x \begin{vmatrix} 3 & 2 \\ 2 & 5 \end{vmatrix} - 1 \begin{vmatrix} 4 & 2 \\ -1 & 5 \end{vmatrix} + 1 \begin{vmatrix} 4 & 3 \\ -1 & 2 \end{vmatrix}$$

$$= x(15 - 4) - (20 + 2) + (8 + 3) = 11x - 22 + 11 = 11x - 11$$

So, $11x - 11 = 2 \Rightarrow 11x = 13 \Rightarrow x = \dfrac{13}{11}$

45. Solve for x:

$$\begin{vmatrix} x & 2 & 3 \\ 1 & x & 0 \\ 6 & 1 & -2 \end{vmatrix} = x\begin{vmatrix} x & 0 \\ 1 & -2 \end{vmatrix} - 2\begin{vmatrix} 1 & 0 \\ 6 & -2 \end{vmatrix} + 3\begin{vmatrix} 1 & x \\ 6 & 1 \end{vmatrix}$$

$$= x(-2x-0) - 2(-2-0) + 3(1-6x)$$

$$= -2x^2 + 4 + 3 - 18x = -2x^2 - 18x + 7$$

So, $-2x^2 - 18x + 7 = 7$

$$-2x^2 - 18x = 0 \Rightarrow -2x(x+9) = 0 \Rightarrow x = 0 \ \text{ or } \ x = -9$$

47. Let $\begin{vmatrix} x & y & z \\ u & v & w \\ 1 & 2 & 3 \end{vmatrix} = 4$

Then $\begin{vmatrix} 1 & 2 & 3 \\ u & v & w \\ x & y & z \end{vmatrix} = -4$ by Theorem 11

The value of the determinant changes sign when two rows are interchanged.

Problems 49 – 53 use the Laws for Determinants in reverse order.

49. Let $\begin{vmatrix} x & y & z \\ u & v & w \\ 1 & 2 & 3 \end{vmatrix} = 4$

$$\begin{vmatrix} x & y & z \\ -3 & -6 & -9 \\ u & v & w \end{vmatrix} = -3\begin{vmatrix} x & y & z \\ 1 & 2 & 3 \\ u & v & w \end{vmatrix} = -3(-1)\begin{vmatrix} x & y & z \\ u & v & w \\ 1 & 2 & 3 \end{vmatrix} = 3(4) = 12$$

$$\underset{\text{Theorem 14}}{\hspace{3.5cm}} \underset{\text{Theorem 11}}{\hspace{1.5cm}}$$

51. Let $\begin{vmatrix} x & y & z \\ u & v & w \\ 1 & 2 & 3 \end{vmatrix} = 4$

$$\begin{vmatrix} 1 & 2 & 3 \\ x-3 & y-6 & z-9 \\ 2u & 2v & 2w \end{vmatrix} = 2\begin{vmatrix} 1 & 2 & 3 \\ x-3 & y-6 & z-9 \\ u & v & w \end{vmatrix} = 2(-1)\begin{vmatrix} x-3 & y-6 & z-9 \\ 1 & 2 & 3 \\ u & v & w \end{vmatrix}$$

$$\underset{\text{Theorem 14}}{\hspace{2.5cm}} \underset{\text{Theorem 11}}{\hspace{2.5cm}}$$

$$= 2(-1)(-1)\begin{vmatrix} x-3 & y-6 & z-9 \\ u & v & w \\ 1 & 2 & 3 \end{vmatrix} = 2(-1)(-1)\begin{vmatrix} x & y & z \\ u & v & w \\ 1 & 2 & 3 \end{vmatrix} = 2(-1)(-1)(4) = 8$$

$$\underset{\text{Theorem 11}}{\hspace{2cm}} \underset{\text{Theorem 15} \ (R_1 = -3r_3 + r_1)}{\hspace{3cm}}$$

53.   Let $\begin{vmatrix} x & y & z \\ u & v & w \\ 1 & 2 & 3 \end{vmatrix} = 4$

$$\begin{vmatrix} 1 & 2 & 3 \\ 2x & 2y & 2z \\ u-1 & v-2 & w-3 \end{vmatrix} = 2\begin{vmatrix} 1 & 2 & 3 \\ x & y & z \\ u-1 & v-2 & w-3 \end{vmatrix} = 2(-1)\begin{vmatrix} x & y & z \\ 1 & 2 & 3 \\ u-1 & v-2 & w-3 \end{vmatrix}$$

                  Theorem 14   Theorem 11

$$= 2(-1)(-1)\begin{vmatrix} x & y & z \\ u-1 & v-2 & w-3 \\ 1 & 2 & 3 \end{vmatrix} = 2(-1)(-1)\begin{vmatrix} x & y & z \\ u & v & w \\ 1 & 2 & 3 \end{vmatrix} = 2(-1)(-1)(4) = 8$$

          Theorem 11   Theorem 15 $(R_2 = -r_3 + r_2)$

55.   Expanding the determinant:

$$\begin{vmatrix} x & y & 1 \\ x_1 & y_1 & 1 \\ x_2 & y_2 & 1 \end{vmatrix} = x\begin{vmatrix} y_1 & 1 \\ y_2 & 1 \end{vmatrix} - y\begin{vmatrix} x_1 & 1 \\ x_2 & 1 \end{vmatrix} + 1\begin{vmatrix} x_1 & y_1 \\ x_2 & y_2 \end{vmatrix}$$

$$= x(y_1 - y_2) - y(x_1 - x_2) + (x_1 y_2 - x_2 y_1) = 0$$

$$x(y_1 - y_2) + y(x_2 - x_1) = x_2 y_1 - x_1 y_2$$

$$y(x_2 - x_1) = x_2 y_1 - x_1 y_2 + x(y_2 - y_1)$$

$$y(x_2 - x_1) - y_1(x_2 - x_1) = x_2 y_1 - x_1 y_2 + x(y_2 - y_1) - y_1(x_2 - x_1)$$

$$(x_2 - x_1)(y - y_1) = x(y_2 - y_1) + x_2 y_1 - x_1 y_2 - y_1 x_2 + y_1 x_1$$

$$(x_2 - x_1)(y - y_1) = (y_2 - y_1)x - (y_2 - y_1)x_1$$

$$(x_2 - x_1)(y - y_1) = (y_2 - y_1)(x - x_1)$$

$$(y - y_1) = \frac{(y_2 - y_1)}{(x_2 - x_1)}(x - x_1)$$

57.   Expanding the determinant:

$$\begin{vmatrix} x^2 & x & 1 \\ y^2 & y & 1 \\ z^2 & z & 1 \end{vmatrix} = x^2\begin{vmatrix} y & 1 \\ z & 1 \end{vmatrix} - x\begin{vmatrix} y^2 & 1 \\ z^2 & 1 \end{vmatrix} + 1\begin{vmatrix} y^2 & y \\ z^2 & z \end{vmatrix}$$

$$= x^2(y - z) - x(y^2 - z^2) + 1(y^2 z - z^2 y)$$

$$= x^2(y - z) - x(y - z)(y + z) + yz(y - z)$$

$$= (y - z)[x^2 - xy - xz + yz]$$

$$= (y - z)[x(x - y) - z(x - y)] = (y - z)(x - y)(x - z)$$

59. Evaluating the determinant to show the relationship:

$$\begin{vmatrix} a_{13} & a_{12} & a_{11} \\ a_{23} & a_{22} & a_{21} \\ a_{33} & a_{32} & a_{31} \end{vmatrix} = a_{13}\begin{vmatrix} a_{22} & a_{21} \\ a_{32} & a_{31} \end{vmatrix} - a_{12}\begin{vmatrix} a_{23} & a_{21} \\ a_{33} & a_{31} \end{vmatrix} + a_{11}\begin{vmatrix} a_{23} & a_{22} \\ a_{33} & a_{32} \end{vmatrix}$$

$$= a_{13}(a_{22}a_{31} - a_{21}a_{32}) - a_{12}(a_{23}a_{31} - a_{21}a_{33}) + a_{11}(a_{23}a_{32} - a_{22}a_{33})$$

$$= a_{13}a_{22}a_{31} - a_{13}a_{21}a_{32} - a_{12}a_{23}a_{31} + a_{12}a_{21}a_{33} + a_{11}a_{23}a_{32} - a_{11}a_{22}a_{33}$$

$$= -a_{11}a_{22}a_{33} + a_{11}a_{23}a_{32} + a_{12}a_{21}a_{33} - a_{12}a_{23}a_{31} - a_{13}a_{21}a_{32} + a_{13}a_{22}a_{31}$$

$$= -a_{11}(a_{22}a_{33} - a_{23}a_{32}) + a_{12}(a_{21}a_{33} - a_{23}a_{31}) - a_{13}(a_{21}a_{32} - a_{22}a_{31})$$

$$= -a_{11}\begin{vmatrix} a_{22} & a_{23} \\ a_{32} & a_{33} \end{vmatrix} + a_{12}\begin{vmatrix} a_{21} & a_{23} \\ a_{31} & a_{33} \end{vmatrix} - a_{13}\begin{vmatrix} a_{21} & a_{22} \\ a_{31} & a_{32} \end{vmatrix}$$

$$= -\left[a_{11}\begin{vmatrix} a_{22} & a_{23} \\ a_{32} & a_{33} \end{vmatrix} - a_{12}\begin{vmatrix} a_{21} & a_{23} \\ a_{31} & a_{33} \end{vmatrix} + a_{13}\begin{vmatrix} a_{21} & a_{22} \\ a_{31} & a_{32} \end{vmatrix} \right]$$

$$= -\begin{vmatrix} a_{11} & a_{12} & a_{13} \\ a_{21} & a_{22} & a_{23} \\ a_{31} & a_{32} & a_{33} \end{vmatrix}$$

61. Set up a 3 by 3 determinant in which the first column and third column are the same and evaluate:

$$\begin{vmatrix} a & b & a \\ c & d & c \\ e & f & e \end{vmatrix} = -b\begin{vmatrix} c & c \\ e & e \end{vmatrix} + d\begin{vmatrix} a & a \\ e & e \end{vmatrix} - f\begin{vmatrix} a & a \\ c & c \end{vmatrix}$$

$$= -b(ce - ce) + d(ae - ae) - f(ac - ac)$$

$$= -b(0) + d(0) - f(0) = 0$$

63. If the determinant of the coefficient matrix = 0, Cramer's Rule fails because it would require division by zero. In such a system, there may be infinitely many solutions or no solution. For example, consider the system:

$$\begin{cases} 3x + 2y = 1 \\ 6x + 4y = 2 \end{cases}$$

Computing the determinant of the coefficient matrix:

$$\begin{vmatrix} 3 & 2 \\ 6 & 4 \end{vmatrix} = (3)(4) - (2)(6) = 12 - 12 = 0$$

Solving the system by elimination:

$$\begin{cases} 3x + 2y = 1 \xrightarrow{2} 6x + 4y = 2 \\ 6x + 4y = 2 \longrightarrow \underline{6x + 4y = 2} \end{cases}$$
$$0 = 0$$

Therefore, the system is dependent and has infinitely many solutions where $y = \dfrac{1 - 3x}{2}$ and

x is any real number.

On the other hand, consider the system:

$$\begin{cases} 3x + 2y = 1 \\ 6x + 4y = 1 \end{cases}$$

Computing the determinant of the coefficient matrix:

$$\begin{vmatrix} 3 & 2 \\ 6 & 4 \end{vmatrix} = (3)(4) - (2)(6) = 12 - 12 = 0$$

Solving the system by elimination:

$$\begin{cases} 3x + 2y = 1 \xrightarrow{2} 6x + 4y = 2 \\ 6x + 4y = 2 \longrightarrow \underline{6x + 4y = 1} \end{cases}$$

$$0 \neq 1$$

Therefore, the system is inconsistent and has no solution.

Systems of Equations and Inequalities

8.4 Matrix Algebra

1.   (a) $A + B = \begin{vmatrix} 0 & 3 & -5 \\ 1 & 2 & 6 \end{vmatrix} + \begin{vmatrix} 4 & 1 & 0 \\ -2 & 3 & -2 \end{vmatrix} = \begin{vmatrix} 0+4 & 3+1 & -5+0 \\ 1+(-2) & 2+3 & 6+(-2) \end{vmatrix} = \begin{vmatrix} 4 & 4 & -5 \\ -1 & 5 & 4 \end{vmatrix}$

    (b) Use MATRIX EDIT to create the matrices   Then compute $[A]+[B]$:

$$A = \begin{vmatrix} 0 & 3 & -5 \\ 1 & 2 & 6 \end{vmatrix}; \quad B = \begin{vmatrix} 4 & 1 & 0 \\ -2 & 3 & -2 \end{vmatrix}$$

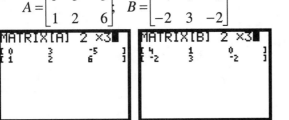
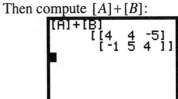

3.   (a) $4A = 4 \begin{bmatrix} 0 & 3 & -5 \\ 1 & 2 & 6 \end{bmatrix} = \begin{bmatrix} 4 \cdot 0 & 4 \cdot 3 & 4(-5) \\ 4 \cdot 1 & 4 \cdot 2 & 4 \cdot 6 \end{bmatrix} = \begin{bmatrix} 0 & 12 & -20 \\ 4 & 8 & 24 \end{bmatrix}$

    (b) Use MATRIX EDIT to create the matrix   Then compute $4*[A]$:

$$A = \begin{vmatrix} 0 & 3 & -5 \\ 1 & 2 & 6 \end{vmatrix}$$

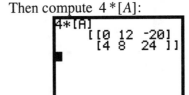

5.   (a) $3A - 2B = 3 \begin{bmatrix} 0 & 3 & -5 \\ 1 & 2 & 6 \end{bmatrix} - 2 \begin{bmatrix} 4 & 1 & 0 \\ -2 & 3 & -2 \end{bmatrix}$

$$= \begin{bmatrix} 0 & 9 & -15 \\ 3 & 6 & 18 \end{bmatrix} - \begin{bmatrix} 8 & 2 & 0 \\ -4 & 6 & -4 \end{bmatrix} = \begin{bmatrix} -8 & 7 & -15 \\ 7 & 0 & 22 \end{bmatrix}$$

    (b) Use MATRIX EDIT to create the matrices   Then compute $3*[A]-2*[B]$:

$$A = \begin{vmatrix} 0 & 3 & -5 \\ 1 & 2 & 6 \end{vmatrix}; \quad B = \begin{vmatrix} 4 & 1 & 0 \\ -2 & 3 & -2 \end{vmatrix}$$

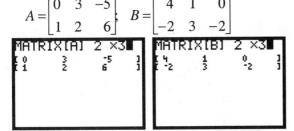
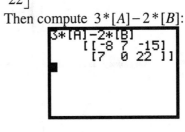

Chapter 8 Systems of Equations and Inequalities

7. (a) $AC = \begin{bmatrix} 0 & 3 & -5 \\ 1 & 2 & 6 \end{bmatrix} \cdot \begin{vmatrix} 4 & 1 \\ 6 & 2 \\ -2 & 3 \end{vmatrix} = \begin{bmatrix} 0(4)+3(6)+(-5)(-2) & 0(1)+3(2)+(-5)(3) \\ 1(4)+2(6)+6(-2) & 1(1)+2(2)+6(3) \end{bmatrix} = \begin{bmatrix} 28 & -9 \\ 4 & 23 \end{bmatrix}$

(b) Use MATRIX EDIT to create the matrices   Then compute $[A]*[C]$:

$A = \begin{bmatrix} 0 & 3 & -5 \\ 1 & 2 & 6 \end{bmatrix}; \quad C = \begin{vmatrix} 4 & 1 \\ 6 & 2 \\ -2 & 3 \end{vmatrix}$

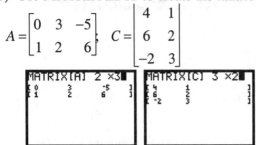

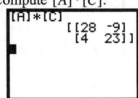

9. (a)

$CA = \begin{bmatrix} 4 & 1 \\ 6 & 2 \\ -2 & 3 \end{bmatrix} \cdot \begin{bmatrix} 0 & 3 & -5 \\ 1 & 2 & 6 \end{bmatrix} = \begin{bmatrix} 4(0)+1(1) & 4(3)+1(2) & 4(-5)+1(6) \\ 6(0)+2(1) & 6(3)+2(2) & 6(-5)+2(6) \\ -2(0)+3(1) & -2(3)+3(2) & -2(-5)+3(6) \end{bmatrix} = \begin{bmatrix} 1 & 14 & -14 \\ 2 & 22 & -18 \\ 3 & 0 & 28 \end{bmatrix}$

(b) Use MATRIX EDIT to create the matrices   Then compute $[C]*[A]$:

$A = \begin{bmatrix} 0 & 3 & -5 \\ 1 & 2 & 6 \end{bmatrix}; \quad C = \begin{vmatrix} 4 & 1 \\ 6 & 2 \\ -2 & 3 \end{vmatrix}$

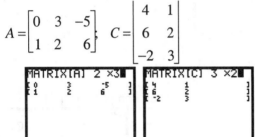

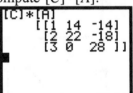

11. (a) $C(A+B) = \begin{vmatrix} 4 & 1 \\ 6 & 2 \\ -2 & 3 \end{vmatrix} \left(\begin{bmatrix} 0 & 3 & -5 \\ 1 & 2 & 6 \end{bmatrix} + \begin{bmatrix} 4 & 1 & 0 \\ -2 & 3 & -2 \end{bmatrix} \right) = \begin{bmatrix} 4 & 1 \\ 6 & 2 \\ -2 & 3 \end{bmatrix} \cdot \begin{bmatrix} 4 & 4 & -5 \\ -1 & 5 & 4 \end{bmatrix} = \begin{bmatrix} 15 & 21 & -16 \\ 22 & 34 & -22 \\ -11 & 7 & 22 \end{bmatrix}$

(b) Use MATRIX EDIT to create the matrices   Then compute $[C]*([A]+[B])$:

$A = \begin{bmatrix} 0 & 3 & -5 \\ 1 & 2 & 6 \end{bmatrix}; \quad B = \begin{bmatrix} 4 & 1 & 0 \\ -2 & 3 & -2 \end{bmatrix}; \quad C = \begin{vmatrix} 4 & 1 \\ 6 & 2 \\ -2 & 3 \end{vmatrix}$

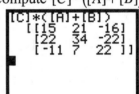

13. (a) $AC - 3I_2 = \begin{bmatrix} 0 & 3 & -5 \\ 1 & 2 & 6 \end{bmatrix} \cdot \begin{bmatrix} 4 & 1 \\ 6 & 2 \\ -2 & 3 \end{bmatrix} - 3\begin{bmatrix} 1 & 0 \\ 0 & 1 \end{bmatrix} = \begin{bmatrix} 28 & -9 \\ 4 & 23 \end{bmatrix} - \begin{bmatrix} 3 & 0 \\ 0 & 3 \end{bmatrix} = \begin{bmatrix} 25 & -9 \\ 4 & 20 \end{bmatrix}$

(b) Use MATRIX EDIT to create the matrices

$A = \begin{bmatrix} 0 & 3 & -5 \\ 1 & 2 & 6 \end{bmatrix}; \quad C = \begin{bmatrix} 4 & 1 \\ 6 & 2 \\ -2 & 3 \end{bmatrix}$

Then compute
$[A]*[C] - 3*\text{identity}(2):$

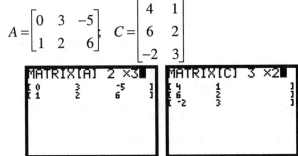

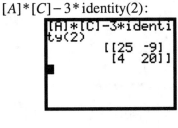

15. (a) $CA - CB = \begin{bmatrix} 4 & 1 \\ 6 & 2 \\ -2 & 3 \end{bmatrix} \cdot \begin{bmatrix} 0 & 3 & -5 \\ 1 & 2 & 6 \end{bmatrix} - \begin{bmatrix} 4 & 1 \\ 6 & 2 \\ -2 & 3 \end{bmatrix} \cdot \begin{bmatrix} 4 & 1 & 0 \\ -2 & 3 & -2 \end{bmatrix}$

$= \begin{bmatrix} 1 & 14 & -14 \\ 2 & 22 & -18 \\ 3 & 0 & 28 \end{bmatrix} - \begin{bmatrix} 14 & 7 & -2 \\ 20 & 12 & -4 \\ -14 & 7 & -6 \end{bmatrix} = \begin{bmatrix} -13 & 7 & -12 \\ -18 & 10 & -14 \\ 17 & -7 & 34 \end{bmatrix}$

(b) Use MATRIX EDIT to create the matrices

$A = \begin{bmatrix} 0 & 3 & -5 \\ 1 & 2 & 6 \end{bmatrix}; \quad B = \begin{bmatrix} 4 & 1 & 0 \\ -2 & 3 & -2 \end{bmatrix}; \quad C = \begin{bmatrix} 4 & 1 \\ 6 & 2 \\ -2 & 3 \end{bmatrix}$

Then compute $[C]*[A] - [C]*[B]:$

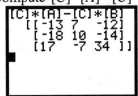

17. (a) $\begin{bmatrix} 2 & -2 \\ 1 & 0 \end{bmatrix}\begin{bmatrix} 2 & 1 & 4 & 6 \\ 3 & -1 & 3 & 2 \end{bmatrix}$

$= \begin{bmatrix} 2(2)+(-2)(3) & 2(1)+(-2)(-1) & 2(4)+(-2)(3) & 2(6)+(-2)(2) \\ 1(2)+0(3) & 1(1)+0(-1) & 1(4)+0(3) & 1(6)+0(2) \end{bmatrix}$

$= \begin{bmatrix} -2 & 4 & 2 & 8 \\ 2 & 1 & 4 & 6 \end{bmatrix}$

(b) Use MATRIX EDIT to create the matrices   Then compute $[A]*[B]$:

$$A = \begin{bmatrix} 2 & -2 \\ 1 & 0 \end{bmatrix}; \quad B = \begin{bmatrix} 2 & 1 & 4 & 6 \\ 3 & -1 & 3 & 2 \end{bmatrix}$$

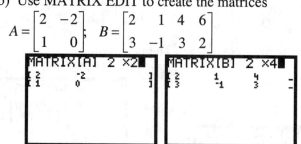

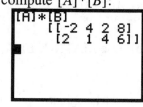

19. (a) $\begin{vmatrix} 1 & 0 & 1 \\ 2 & 4 & 1 \\ 3 & 6 & 1 \end{vmatrix} \begin{vmatrix} 1 & 3 \\ 6 & 2 \\ 8 & -1 \end{vmatrix} = \begin{vmatrix} 1(1)+0(6)+1(8) & 1(3)+0(2)+1(-1) \\ 2(1)+4(6)+1(8) & 2(3)+4(2)+1(-1) \\ 3(1)+6(6)+1(8) & 3(3)+6(2)+1(-1) \end{vmatrix} = \begin{vmatrix} 9 & 2 \\ 34 & 13 \\ 47 & 20 \end{vmatrix}$

(b) Use MATRIX EDIT to create the matrices   Then compute $[A]*[B]$:

$$A = \begin{bmatrix} 1 & 0 & 1 \\ 2 & 4 & 1 \\ 3 & 6 & 1 \end{bmatrix}; \quad B = \begin{bmatrix} 1 & 3 \\ 6 & 2 \\ 8 & -1 \end{bmatrix}$$

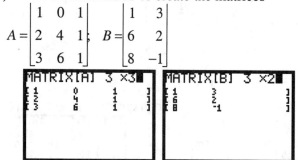

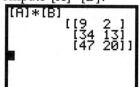

21. Augment the matrix with the identity and use row operations to find the inverse:

$$A = \begin{bmatrix} 2 & 1 \\ 1 & 1 \end{bmatrix} \rightarrow \begin{bmatrix} 2 & 1 & | & 1 & 0 \\ 1 & 1 & | & 0 & 1 \end{bmatrix}$$

$$\rightarrow \begin{bmatrix} 1 & 1 & | & 0 & 1 \\ 2 & 1 & | & 1 & 0 \end{bmatrix} \rightarrow \begin{bmatrix} 1 & 1 & | & 0 & 1 \\ 0 & -1 & | & 1 & -2 \end{bmatrix} \rightarrow \begin{bmatrix} 1 & 1 & | & 0 & 1 \\ 0 & 1 & | & -1 & 2 \end{bmatrix} \rightarrow \begin{bmatrix} 1 & 0 & | & 1 & -1 \\ 0 & 1 & | & -1 & 2 \end{bmatrix}$$

Interchange $R_2 = -2r_1 + r_2$ $R_2 = -r_2$ $R_1 = -r_2 + r_1$
r_1 and r_2

$$A^{-1} = \begin{bmatrix} 1 & -1 \\ -1 & 2 \end{bmatrix}$$

23. Augment the matrix with the identity and use row operations to find the inverse:

$$A = \begin{bmatrix} 6 & 5 \\ 2 & 2 \end{bmatrix} \rightarrow \begin{bmatrix} 6 & 5 & | & 1 & 0 \\ 2 & 2 & | & 0 & 1 \end{bmatrix}$$

$$\rightarrow \begin{bmatrix} 2 & 2 & | & 0 & 1 \\ 6 & 5 & | & 1 & 0 \end{bmatrix} \rightarrow \begin{bmatrix} 2 & 2 & | & 0 & 1 \\ 0 & -1 & | & 1 & -3 \end{bmatrix} \rightarrow \begin{bmatrix} 1 & 1 & | & 0 & \frac{1}{2} \\ 0 & 1 & | & -1 & 3 \end{bmatrix} \rightarrow \begin{bmatrix} 1 & 0 & | & 1 & -\frac{5}{2} \\ 0 & 1 & | & -1 & 3 \end{bmatrix}$$

Interchange $R_2 = -3r_1 + r_2$ $R_1 = \frac{1}{2}r_1$ $R_1 = -r_2 + r_1$
r_1 and r_2 $R_2 = -r_2$

$$A^{-1} = \begin{bmatrix} 1 & -\frac{5}{2} \\ -1 & 3 \end{bmatrix}$$

25. Augment the matrix with the identity and use row operations to find the inverse:

$A = \begin{bmatrix} 2 & 1 \\ a & a \end{bmatrix} \rightarrow \begin{bmatrix} 2 & 1 & | & 1 & 0 \\ a & a & | & 0 & 1 \end{bmatrix}$ where $a \neq 0$.

$\rightarrow \begin{bmatrix} 1 & \frac{1}{2} & | & \frac{1}{2} & 0 \\ a & a & | & 0 & 1 \end{bmatrix} \rightarrow \begin{bmatrix} 1 & \frac{1}{2} & | & \frac{1}{2} & 0 \\ 0 & \frac{1}{2}a & | & -\frac{1}{2}a & 1 \end{bmatrix} \rightarrow \begin{bmatrix} 1 & \frac{1}{2} & | & \frac{1}{2} & 0 \\ 0 & 1 & | & -1 & \frac{2}{a} \end{bmatrix} \rightarrow \begin{bmatrix} 1 & 0 & | & 1 & -\frac{1}{a} \\ 0 & 1 & | & -1 & \frac{2}{a} \end{bmatrix}$

$R_1 = \frac{1}{2}r_1 \qquad R_2 = -ar_1 + r_2 \qquad R_2 = \left(\frac{2}{a}\right)r_2 \qquad R_1 = -\frac{1}{2}r_2 + r_1$

$A^{-1} = \begin{bmatrix} 1 & -\frac{1}{a} \\ -1 & \frac{2}{a} \end{bmatrix}$

27. Augment the matrix with the identity and use row operations to find the inverse:

$A = \begin{bmatrix} 1 & -1 & 1 \\ 0 & -2 & 1 \\ -2 & -3 & 0 \end{bmatrix} \rightarrow \begin{bmatrix} 1 & -1 & 1 & | & 1 & 0 & 0 \\ 0 & -2 & 1 & | & 0 & 1 & 0 \\ -2 & -3 & 0 & | & 0 & 0 & 1 \end{bmatrix}$

$\rightarrow \begin{bmatrix} 1 & -1 & 1 & | & 1 & 0 & 0 \\ 0 & -2 & 1 & | & 0 & 1 & 0 \\ 0 & -5 & 2 & | & 2 & 0 & 1 \end{bmatrix} \rightarrow \begin{bmatrix} 1 & -1 & 1 & | & 1 & 0 & 0 \\ 0 & 1 & -\frac{1}{2} & | & 0 & -\frac{1}{2} & 0 \\ 0 & -5 & 2 & | & 2 & 0 & 1 \end{bmatrix} \rightarrow \begin{bmatrix} 1 & 0 & \frac{1}{2} & | & 1 & -\frac{1}{2} & 0 \\ 0 & 1 & -\frac{1}{2} & | & 0 & -\frac{1}{2} & 0 \\ 0 & 0 & -\frac{1}{2} & | & 2 & -\frac{5}{2} & 1 \end{bmatrix}$

$R_3 = 2r_1 + r_3 \qquad\qquad R_2 = -\frac{1}{2}r_2 \qquad\qquad R_1 = r_2 + r_1$

$\qquad\qquad\qquad\qquad\qquad\qquad\qquad\qquad\qquad\qquad R_3 = 5r_2 + r_3$

$\rightarrow \begin{bmatrix} 1 & 0 & \frac{1}{2} & | & 1 & -\frac{1}{2} & 0 \\ 0 & 1 & -\frac{1}{2} & | & 0 & -\frac{1}{2} & 0 \\ 0 & 0 & 1 & | & -4 & 5 & -2 \end{bmatrix} \rightarrow \begin{bmatrix} 1 & 0 & 0 & | & 3 & -3 & 1 \\ 0 & 1 & 0 & | & -2 & 2 & -1 \\ 0 & 0 & 1 & | & -4 & 5 & -2 \end{bmatrix}$

$R_3 = -2r_3 \qquad\qquad\qquad R_1 = -\frac{1}{2}r_3 + r_1$

$\qquad\qquad\qquad\qquad\qquad\quad R_2 = \frac{1}{2}r_3 + r_2$

$A^{-1} = \begin{bmatrix} 3 & -3 & 1 \\ -2 & 2 & -1 \\ -4 & 5 & -2 \end{bmatrix}$

29. Augment the matrix with the identity and use row operations to find the inverse:

$A = \begin{bmatrix} 1 & 1 & 1 \\ 3 & 2 & -1 \\ 3 & 1 & 2 \end{bmatrix} \rightarrow \begin{bmatrix} 1 & 1 & 1 & | & 1 & 0 & 0 \\ 3 & 2 & -1 & | & 0 & 1 & 0 \\ 3 & 1 & 2 & | & 0 & 0 & 1 \end{bmatrix}$

$\rightarrow \begin{bmatrix} 1 & 1 & 1 & | & 1 & 0 & 0 \\ 0 & -1 & -4 & | & -3 & 1 & 0 \\ 0 & -2 & -1 & | & -3 & 0 & 1 \end{bmatrix} \rightarrow \begin{bmatrix} 1 & 1 & 1 & | & 1 & 0 & 0 \\ 0 & 1 & 4 & | & 3 & -1 & 0 \\ 0 & -2 & -1 & | & -3 & 0 & 1 \end{bmatrix} \rightarrow \begin{bmatrix} 1 & 0 & -3 & | & -2 & 1 & 0 \\ 0 & 1 & 4 & | & 3 & -1 & 0 \\ 0 & 0 & 7 & | & 3 & -2 & 1 \end{bmatrix}$

$R_2 = -3r_1 + r_2 \qquad\qquad R_2 = -r_2 \qquad\qquad\qquad R_1 = -r_2 + r_1$

$R_3 = -3r_1 + r_3 \qquad\qquad\qquad\qquad\qquad\qquad\qquad R_3 = 2r_2 + r_3$

$$\rightarrow \begin{vmatrix} 1 & 0 & -3 & | & -2 & 1 & 0 \\ 0 & 1 & 4 & | & 3 & -1 & 0 \\ 0 & 0 & 1 & | & \frac{3}{7} & -\frac{2}{7} & \frac{1}{7} \end{vmatrix} \rightarrow \begin{vmatrix} 1 & 0 & 0 & | & -\frac{5}{7} & \frac{1}{7} & \frac{3}{7} \\ 0 & 1 & 0 & | & \frac{9}{7} & \frac{1}{7} & -\frac{4}{7} \\ 0 & 0 & 1 & | & \frac{3}{7} & -\frac{2}{7} & \frac{1}{7} \end{vmatrix}$$

$$R_3 = \tfrac{1}{7} r_3 \qquad\qquad R_1 = 3r_3 + r_1$$
$$R_2 = -4r_3 + r_2$$

$$A^{-1} = \begin{bmatrix} -\frac{5}{7} & \frac{1}{7} & \frac{3}{7} \\ \frac{9}{7} & \frac{1}{7} & -\frac{4}{7} \\ \frac{3}{7} & -\frac{2}{7} & \frac{1}{7} \end{bmatrix}$$

31. Rewrite the system of equations in matrix form:

$$\begin{cases} 2x + y = 8 \\ x + y = 5 \end{cases} \qquad A = \begin{bmatrix} 2 & 1 \\ 1 & 1 \end{bmatrix}, \quad X = \begin{bmatrix} x \\ y \end{bmatrix}, \quad B = \begin{bmatrix} 8 \\ 5 \end{bmatrix}$$

Find the inverse of A and solve $X = A^{-1}B$:

From Problem 21, $A^{-1} = \begin{bmatrix} 1 & -1 \\ -1 & 2 \end{bmatrix}$ and $X = A^{-1}B = \begin{bmatrix} 1 & -1 \\ -1 & 2 \end{bmatrix}\begin{bmatrix} 8 \\ 5 \end{bmatrix} = \begin{bmatrix} 3 \\ 2 \end{bmatrix}$.

The solution is $x = 3$, $y = 2$.

33. Rewrite the system of equations in matrix form:

$$\begin{cases} 2x + y = 0 \\ x + y = 5 \end{cases} \qquad A = \begin{bmatrix} 2 & 1 \\ 1 & 1 \end{bmatrix}, \quad X = \begin{bmatrix} x \\ y \end{bmatrix}, \quad B = \begin{bmatrix} 0 \\ 5 \end{bmatrix}$$

Find the inverse of A and solve $X = A^{-1}B$:

From Problem 21, $A^{-1} = \begin{bmatrix} 1 & -1 \\ -1 & 2 \end{bmatrix}$ and $X = A^{-1}B = \begin{bmatrix} 1 & -1 \\ -1 & 2 \end{bmatrix}\begin{bmatrix} 0 \\ 5 \end{bmatrix} = \begin{bmatrix} -5 \\ 10 \end{bmatrix}$.

The solution is $x = -5$, $y = 10$.

35. Rewrite the system of equations in matrix form:

$$\begin{cases} 6x + 5y = 7 \\ 2x + 2y = 2 \end{cases} \qquad A = \begin{bmatrix} 6 & 5 \\ 2 & 2 \end{bmatrix}, \quad X = \begin{bmatrix} x \\ y \end{bmatrix}, \quad B = \begin{bmatrix} 7 \\ 2 \end{bmatrix}$$

Find the inverse of A and solve $X = A^{-1}B$:

From Problem 23, $A^{-1} = \begin{bmatrix} 1 & -\frac{5}{2} \\ -1 & 3 \end{bmatrix}$ and $X = A^{-1}B = \begin{bmatrix} 1 & -\frac{5}{2} \\ -1 & 3 \end{bmatrix}\begin{bmatrix} 7 \\ 2 \end{bmatrix} = \begin{bmatrix} 2 \\ -1 \end{bmatrix}$.

The solution is $x = 2$, $y = -1$.

37. Rewrite the system of equations in matrix form:

$$\begin{cases} 6x + 5y = 13 \\ 2x + 2y = 5 \end{cases} \qquad A = \begin{bmatrix} 6 & 5 \\ 2 & 2 \end{bmatrix}, \quad X = \begin{bmatrix} x \\ y \end{bmatrix}, \quad B = \begin{bmatrix} 13 \\ 5 \end{bmatrix}$$

Find the inverse of A and solve $X = A^{-1}B$:

From Problem 23, $A^{-1} = \begin{bmatrix} 1 & -\frac{5}{2} \\ -1 & 3 \end{bmatrix}$ and $X = A^{-1}B = \begin{bmatrix} 1 & -\frac{5}{2} \\ -1 & 3 \end{bmatrix}\begin{bmatrix} 13 \\ 5 \end{bmatrix} = \begin{bmatrix} \frac{1}{2} \\ 2 \end{bmatrix}$.

The solution is $x = \dfrac{1}{2}$, $y = 2$.

39. Rewrite the system of equations in matrix form:

$$\begin{cases} 2x + y = -3 \\ ax + ay = -a \end{cases} \quad a \neq 0 \qquad A = \begin{bmatrix} 2 & 1 \\ a & a \end{bmatrix}, \quad X = \begin{bmatrix} x \\ y \end{bmatrix}, \quad B = \begin{bmatrix} -3 \\ -a \end{bmatrix}$$

Find the inverse of A and solve $X = A^{-1}B$:

From Problem 25, $A^{-1} = \begin{bmatrix} 1 & -\frac{1}{a} \\ -1 & \frac{2}{a} \end{bmatrix}$ and $X = A^{-1}B = \begin{bmatrix} 1 & -\frac{1}{a} \\ -1 & \frac{2}{a} \end{bmatrix}\begin{bmatrix} -3 \\ -a \end{bmatrix} = \begin{bmatrix} -2 \\ 1 \end{bmatrix}$.

The solution is $x = -2$, $y = 1$.

41. Rewrite the system of equations in matrix form:

$$\begin{cases} 2x + y = \dfrac{7}{a} \\ ax + ay = 5 \end{cases} \quad a \neq 0 \qquad A = \begin{bmatrix} 2 & 1 \\ a & a \end{bmatrix}, \quad X = \begin{bmatrix} x \\ y \end{bmatrix}, \quad B = \begin{bmatrix} \frac{7}{a} \\ 5 \end{bmatrix}$$

Find the inverse of A and solve $X = A^{-1}B$:

From Problem 25, $A^{-1} = \begin{bmatrix} 1 & -\frac{1}{a} \\ -1 & \frac{2}{a} \end{bmatrix}$ and $X = A^{-1}B = \begin{bmatrix} 1 & -\frac{1}{a} \\ -1 & \frac{2}{a} \end{bmatrix}\begin{bmatrix} \frac{7}{a} \\ 5 \end{bmatrix} = \begin{bmatrix} \frac{2}{a} \\ \frac{3}{a} \end{bmatrix}$.

The solution is $x = \dfrac{2}{a}$, $y = \dfrac{3}{a}$.

43. Rewrite the system of equations in matrix form:

$$\begin{cases} x - y + z = 0 \\ -2y + z = -1 \\ -2x - 3y = -5 \end{cases} \qquad A = \begin{bmatrix} 1 & -1 & 1 \\ 0 & -2 & 1 \\ -2 & -3 & 0 \end{bmatrix}, \quad X = \begin{bmatrix} x \\ y \\ z \end{bmatrix}, \quad B = \begin{bmatrix} 0 \\ -1 \\ -5 \end{bmatrix}$$

Find the inverse of A and solve $X = A^{-1}B$:

From Problem 27,

$$A^{-1} = \begin{bmatrix} 3 & -3 & 1 \\ -2 & 2 & -1 \\ -4 & 5 & -2 \end{bmatrix} \text{ and } X = A^{-1}B = \begin{bmatrix} 3 & -3 & 1 \\ -2 & 2 & -1 \\ -4 & 5 & -2 \end{bmatrix}\begin{bmatrix} 0 \\ -1 \\ -5 \end{bmatrix} = \begin{bmatrix} -2 \\ 3 \\ 5 \end{bmatrix}.$$

The solution is $x = -2$, $y = 3$, $z = 5$.

45. Rewrite the system of equations in matrix form:

$$\begin{cases} x - y + z = 2 \\ -2y + z = 2 \\ -2x - 3y = \dfrac{1}{2} \end{cases} \qquad A = \begin{bmatrix} 1 & -1 & 1 \\ 0 & -2 & 1 \\ -2 & -3 & 0 \end{bmatrix}, \quad X = \begin{bmatrix} x \\ y \\ z \end{bmatrix}, \quad B = \begin{bmatrix} 2 \\ 2 \\ \frac{1}{2} \end{bmatrix}$$

Find the inverse of A and solve $X = A^{-1}B$:

From Problem 27,

$$A^{-1} = \begin{bmatrix} 3 & -3 & 1 \\ -2 & 2 & -1 \\ -4 & 5 & -2 \end{bmatrix} \text{ and } X = A^{-1}B = \begin{bmatrix} 3 & -3 & 1 \\ -2 & 2 & -1 \\ -4 & 5 & -2 \end{bmatrix}\begin{bmatrix} 2 \\ 2 \\ \frac{1}{2} \end{bmatrix} = \begin{bmatrix} \frac{1}{2} \\ -\frac{1}{2} \\ 1 \end{bmatrix}.$$

The solution is $x = \dfrac{1}{2}$, $y = -\dfrac{1}{2}$, $z = 1$.

47. Rewrite the system of equations in matrix form:

$$\begin{cases} x+\ y+\ z=9 \\ 3x+2y-\ z=8 \\ 3x+\ y+2z=1 \end{cases} \qquad A=\begin{bmatrix} 1 & 1 & 1 \\ 3 & 2 & -1 \\ 3 & 1 & 2 \end{bmatrix}, \quad X=\begin{bmatrix} x \\ y \\ z \end{bmatrix}, \quad B=\begin{bmatrix} 9 \\ 8 \\ 1 \end{bmatrix}$$

Find the inverse of A and solve $X=A^{-1}B$:

From Problem 29,

$$A^{-1}=\begin{bmatrix} -\frac{5}{7} & \frac{1}{7} & \frac{3}{7} \\ \frac{9}{7} & \frac{1}{7} & -\frac{4}{7} \\ \frac{3}{7} & -\frac{2}{7} & \frac{1}{7} \end{bmatrix} \text{ and } X=A^{-1}B=\begin{bmatrix} -\frac{5}{7} & \frac{1}{7} & \frac{3}{7} \\ \frac{9}{7} & \frac{1}{7} & -\frac{4}{7} \\ \frac{3}{7} & -\frac{2}{7} & \frac{1}{7} \end{bmatrix}\begin{bmatrix} 9 \\ 8 \\ 1 \end{bmatrix}=\begin{bmatrix} -\frac{34}{7} \\ \frac{85}{7} \\ \frac{12}{7} \end{bmatrix}.$$

The solution is $x=-\dfrac{34}{7},\ y=\dfrac{85}{7},\ z=\dfrac{12}{7}$.

49. Rewrite the system of equations in matrix form:

$$\begin{cases} x+\ y+\ z=2 \\ 3x+2y-\ z=\dfrac{7}{3} \\ 3x+\ y+2z=\dfrac{10}{3} \end{cases} \qquad A=\begin{bmatrix} 1 & 1 & 1 \\ 3 & 2 & -1 \\ 3 & 1 & 2 \end{bmatrix}, \quad X=\begin{bmatrix} x \\ y \\ z \end{bmatrix}, \quad B=\begin{bmatrix} 2 \\ \frac{7}{3} \\ \frac{10}{3} \end{bmatrix}$$

Find the inverse of A and solve $X=A^{-1}B$:

From Problem 29,

$$A^{-1}=\begin{bmatrix} -\frac{5}{7} & \frac{1}{7} & \frac{3}{7} \\ \frac{9}{7} & \frac{1}{7} & -\frac{4}{7} \\ \frac{3}{7} & -\frac{2}{7} & \frac{1}{7} \end{bmatrix} \text{ and } X=A^{-1}B=\begin{bmatrix} -\frac{5}{7} & \frac{1}{7} & \frac{3}{7} \\ \frac{9}{7} & \frac{1}{7} & -\frac{4}{7} \\ \frac{3}{7} & -\frac{2}{7} & \frac{1}{7} \end{bmatrix}\begin{bmatrix} 2 \\ \frac{7}{3} \\ \frac{10}{3} \end{bmatrix}=\begin{bmatrix} \frac{1}{3} \\ 1 \\ \frac{2}{3} \end{bmatrix}.$$

The solution is $x=\dfrac{1}{3},\ y=1,\ z=\dfrac{2}{3}$.

51. Augment the matrix with the identity and use row operations to find the inverse:

$$A=\begin{bmatrix} 4 & 2 \\ 2 & 1 \end{bmatrix} \rightarrow \left[\begin{array}{cc|cc} 4 & 2 & 1 & 0 \\ 2 & 1 & 0 & 1 \end{array}\right]$$

$$\rightarrow \left[\begin{array}{cc|cc} 4 & 2 & 1 & 0 \\ 0 & 0 & -\frac{1}{2} & 1 \end{array}\right]\rightarrow\left[\begin{array}{cc|cc} 1 & \frac{1}{2} & \frac{1}{4} & 0 \\ 0 & 0 & -\frac{1}{2} & 1 \end{array}\right]$$

$$R_2=-\tfrac{1}{2}r_1+r_2 \qquad R_1=\tfrac{1}{4}r_1$$

There is no way to obtain the identity matrix on the left; thus, there is no inverse.

53. Augment the matrix with the identity and use row operations to find the inverse:

$$A=\begin{bmatrix} 15 & 3 \\ 10 & 2 \end{bmatrix}\rightarrow\left[\begin{array}{cc|cc} 15 & 3 & 1 & 0 \\ 10 & 2 & 0 & 1 \end{array}\right]\rightarrow\left[\begin{array}{cc|cc} 15 & 3 & 1 & 0 \\ 0 & 0 & -\frac{2}{3} & 1 \end{array}\right]\rightarrow\left[\begin{array}{cc|cc} 1 & \frac{1}{5} & \frac{1}{15} & 0 \\ 0 & 0 & -\frac{2}{3} & 1 \end{array}\right]$$

$$R_2=-\tfrac{2}{3}r_1+r_2 \qquad R_1=\tfrac{1}{15}r_1$$

There is no way to obtain the identity matrix on the left; thus, there is no inverse.

55. Augment the matrix with the identity and use row operations to find the inverse:

$$A=\begin{bmatrix} -3 & 1 & -1 \\ 1 & -4 & -7 \\ 1 & 2 & 5 \end{bmatrix}\rightarrow\left[\begin{array}{ccc|ccc} -3 & 1 & -1 & 1 & 0 & 0 \\ 1 & -4 & -7 & 0 & 1 & 0 \\ 1 & 2 & 5 & 0 & 0 & 1 \end{array}\right]$$

$$\rightarrow \begin{vmatrix} 1 & 2 & 5 & 0 & 0 & 1 \\ 1 & -4 & -7 & 0 & 1 & 0 \\ -3 & 1 & -1 & 1 & 0 & 0 \end{vmatrix} \rightarrow \begin{vmatrix} 1 & 2 & 5 & 0 & 0 & 1 \\ 0 & -6 & -12 & 0 & 1 & -1 \\ 0 & 7 & 14 & 1 & 0 & 3 \end{vmatrix} \rightarrow \begin{vmatrix} 1 & 2 & 5 & 0 & 0 & 1 \\ 0 & 1 & 2 & 0 & -\frac{1}{6} & \frac{1}{6} \\ 0 & 7 & 14 & 1 & 0 & 3 \end{vmatrix}$$

Interchange r_1 and r_3 $R_2 = -r_1 + r_2$ $R_2 = -\frac{1}{6}r_2$

$R_3 = 3r_1 + r_3$

$$\rightarrow \begin{vmatrix} 1 & 0 & 1 & 0 & \frac{1}{3} & \frac{2}{3} \\ 0 & 1 & 2 & 0 & -\frac{1}{6} & \frac{1}{6} \\ 0 & 0 & 0 & 1 & \frac{7}{6} & \frac{11}{6} \end{vmatrix}$$

$R_1 = -2r_2 + r_1$

$R_3 = -7r_2 + r_3$

There is no way to obtain the identity matrix on the left; thus, there is no inverse.

57. Use **MATRIX EDIT** to create the matrix

$$A = \begin{vmatrix} 25 & 61 & -12 \\ 18 & -2 & 4 \\ 8 & 35 & 21 \end{vmatrix}$$

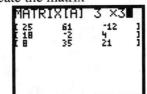

Then compute $[A]^{\wedge}(-1)$:

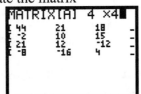

$$A^{-1} = \begin{vmatrix} 0.01 & 0.05 & -0.01 \\ 0.01 & -0.02 & 0.01 \\ -0.02 & 0.01 & 0.03 \end{vmatrix}$$

59. Use **MATRIX EDIT** to create the matrix

$$A = \begin{vmatrix} 44 & 21 & 18 & 6 \\ -2 & 10 & 15 & 5 \\ 21 & 12 & -12 & 4 \\ -8 & -16 & 4 & 9 \end{vmatrix}$$

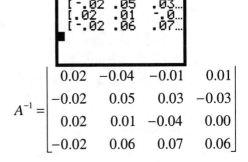

Then compute $[A]^{\wedge}(-1)$:

$$A^{-1} = \begin{vmatrix} 0.02 & -0.04 & -0.01 & 0.01 \\ -0.02 & 0.05 & 0.03 & -0.03 \\ 0.02 & 0.01 & -0.04 & 0.00 \\ -0.02 & 0.06 & 0.07 & 0.06 \end{vmatrix}$$

61. Use **MATRIX EDIT** to create the matrices

$$A = \begin{vmatrix} 25 & 61 & -12 \\ 18 & -12 & 7 \\ 3 & 4 & -1 \end{vmatrix} ; \quad B = \begin{vmatrix} 10 \\ -9 \\ 12 \end{vmatrix}$$

Then compute $\left([A]^{\wedge}(-1)\right) * [B]$:

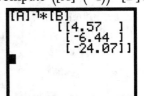

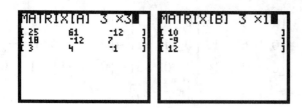

$x = 4.57,\ y = -6.44,\ z = -24.07$

63. Use MATRIX EDIT to create the matrices

$$A = \begin{vmatrix} 25 & 61 & -12 \\ 18 & -12 & 7 \\ 3 & 4 & -1 \end{vmatrix};\ B = \begin{vmatrix} 21 \\ 7 \\ -2 \end{vmatrix}$$

Then compute $\left([A]^{\wedge}(-1)\right)*[B]$:

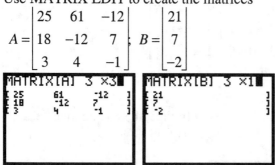
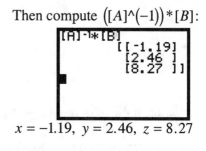

$x = -1.19,\ y = 2.46,\ z = 8.27$

65. (a) The rows of the 2 by 3 matrix represent stainless steel and aluminum. The columns represent 10-gallon, 5-gallon, and 1-gallon.

The 2 by 3 matrix is:

$$\begin{bmatrix} 500 & 350 & 400 \\ 700 & 500 & 850 \end{bmatrix}$$

The 3 by 2 matrix is:

$$\begin{bmatrix} 500 & 700 \\ 350 & 500 \\ 400 & 850 \end{bmatrix}$$

(b) The 3 by 1 matrix representing the amount of material is:

$$\begin{bmatrix} 15 \\ 8 \\ 3 \end{bmatrix}$$

(c) The days usage of materials is:

$$\begin{bmatrix} 500 & 350 & 400 \\ 700 & 500 & 850 \end{bmatrix} \cdot \begin{bmatrix} 15 \\ 8 \\ 3 \end{bmatrix} = \begin{bmatrix} 11,500 \\ 17,050 \end{bmatrix}$$

11,500 pounds of stainless steel and 17,050 pounds of aluminum are used each day.

(d) The 1 by 2 matrix representing cost is:

$$\begin{bmatrix} 0.10 & 0.05 \end{bmatrix}$$

(e) The total cost of the days production was:

$$\begin{bmatrix} 0.10 & 0.05 \end{bmatrix} \cdot \begin{bmatrix} 11,500 \\ 17,050 \end{bmatrix} = \begin{bmatrix} 2002.50 \end{bmatrix}$$

The total cost of the days production was $2,002.50.

67. Answers will vary.

69. A matrix A is singular if its determinant equals 0. Therefore, A^{-1} does not exist. If the determinant of the coefficient matrix of a system of linear equations = 0, there may be infinitely many solutions or no solution. For example, consider the system:

$$\begin{cases} 3x + 2y = 1 \\ 6x + 4y = 2 \end{cases}$$

Computing the determinant of the coefficient matrix:

$$\begin{vmatrix} 3 & 2 \\ 6 & 4 \end{vmatrix} = (3)(4) - (2)(6) = 12 - 12 = 0$$

Solving the system by elimination:

$$\begin{cases} 3x + 2y = 1 \xrightarrow{2} 6x + 4y = 2 \\ 6x + 4y = 2 \longrightarrow \underline{6x + 4y = 2} \end{cases}$$

$$0 = 0$$

Therefore, the system is dependent and has infinitely many solutions where $y = \dfrac{1 - 3x}{2}$ and

x is any real number.

On the other hand, consider the system:

$$\begin{cases} 3x + 2y = 1 \\ 6x + 4y = 1 \end{cases}$$

Computing the determinant of the coefficient matrix:

$$\begin{vmatrix} 3 & 2 \\ 6 & 4 \end{vmatrix} = (3)(4) - (2)(6) = 12 - 12 = 0$$

Solving the system by elimination:

$$\begin{cases} 3x + 2y = 1 \xrightarrow{2} 6x + 4y = 2 \\ 6x + 4y = 2 \longrightarrow \underline{6x + 4y = 1} \end{cases}$$

$$0 \neq 1$$

Therefore, the system is inconsistent and has no solution.

Systems of Equations and Inequalities

8.5   Partial Fraction Decomposition

1.   The rational expression $\dfrac{x}{x^2-1}$ is proper, since the degree of the numerator is less than the degree of the denominator.

3.   The rational expression $\dfrac{x^2+5}{x^2-4}$ is improper, so perform the division:

$$
\begin{array}{r}
1 \\
x^2-4 \overline{\smash{)}\, x^2+5} \\
\underline{x^2-4} \\
9
\end{array}
$$

The proper rational expression is:
$$\frac{x^2+5}{x^2-4}=1+\frac{9}{x^2-4}$$

5.   The rational expression $\dfrac{5x^3+2x-1}{x^2-4}$ is improper, so perform the division:

$$
\begin{array}{r}
5x \\
x^2-4 \overline{\smash{)}\, 5x^3+0x^2+\ 2x-1} \\
\underline{5x^3\qquad\ -20x} \\
22x-1
\end{array}
$$

The proper rational expression is:
$$\frac{5x^3+2x-1}{x^2-4}=5x+\frac{22x-1}{x^2-4}$$

7.   The rational expression $\dfrac{x(x-1)}{(x+4)(x-3)}=\dfrac{x^2-x}{x^2+x-12}$ is improper, so perform the division:

$$
\begin{array}{r}
1 \\
x^2+x-12 \overline{\smash{)}\, x^2-x+\ 0} \\
\underline{x^2+x-12} \\
-2x+12
\end{array}
$$

The proper rational expression is:
$$\frac{x(x-1)}{(x+4)(x-3)}=1+\frac{-2x+12}{x^2+x-12}=1+\frac{-2(x-6)}{(x+4)(x-3)}$$

9.   Find the partial fraction decomposition:
$$\frac{4}{x(x-1)}=\frac{A}{x}+\frac{B}{x-1}$$
$\qquad\qquad 4=A(x-1)+Bx \qquad$ (Multiply both sides by $x(x-1)$.)

Let $x=1$: then $4=A(0)+B \Rightarrow B=4$

Let $x=0$: then $4=A(-1)+B(0) \Rightarrow A=-4$

$$\frac{4}{x(x-1)}=\frac{-4}{x}+\frac{4}{x-1}$$

11. Find the partial fraction decomposition:
$$\frac{1}{x(x^2+1)} = \frac{A}{x} + \frac{Bx+C}{x^2+1}$$

$1 = A(x^2+1) + (Bx+C)x$ (Multiply both sides by $x(x^2+1)$.)

Let $x = 0$:   then $1 = A(1) + (B(0)+C)(0) \Rightarrow A = 1$

Let $x = 1$:   then $1 = A(1+1) + (B(1)+C)(1) \Rightarrow 1 = 2A+B+C$

so $1 = 2(1) + B + C \Rightarrow -1 = B + C$

Let $x = -1$: then $1 = A(1+1) + (B(-1)+C)(-1) \Rightarrow 1 = 2A+B-C$

so $1 = 2(1) + B - C \Rightarrow -1 = B - C$

Solve the system of equations:

$$\begin{aligned} B + C &= -1 \\ \underline{B - C} &= \underline{-1} \\ 2B &= -2 \qquad -1 + C = -1 \\ B &= -1 \qquad\quad C = 0 \end{aligned}$$

$$\frac{1}{x(x^2+1)} = \frac{1}{x} + \frac{-x}{x^2+1}$$

13. Find the partial fraction decomposition:
$$\frac{x}{(x-1)(x-2)} = \frac{A}{x-1} + \frac{B}{x-2}$$

$x = A(x-2) + B(x-1)$ (Multiply both sides by $(x-1)(x-2)$.)

Let $x = 1$: then $1 = A(1-2) + B(1-1) \Rightarrow 1 = -A \Rightarrow A = -1$

Let $x = 2$: then $2 = A(2-2) + B(2-1) \Rightarrow 2 = B \Rightarrow B = 2$

$$\frac{x}{(x-1)(x-2)} = \frac{-1}{x-1} + \frac{2}{x-2}$$

15. Find the partial fraction decomposition:
$$\frac{x^2}{(x-1)^2(x+1)} = \frac{A}{x-1} + \frac{B}{(x-1)^2} + \frac{C}{x+1}$$ (Multiply both sides by $(x-1)^2(x+1)$.)

$x^2 = A(x-1)(x+1) + B(x+1) + C(x-1)^2$

Let $x = 1$:   then $1^2 = A(1-1)(1+1) + B(1+1) + C(1-1)^2$

$$\Rightarrow 1 = 2B \Rightarrow B = \frac{1}{2}$$

Let $x = -1$:   then $(-1)^2 = A(-1-1)(-1+1) + B(-1+1) + C(-1-1)^2$

$$\Rightarrow 1 = 4C \Rightarrow C = \frac{1}{4}$$

Let $x = 0$:   then $0^2 = A(0-1)(0+1) + B(0+1) + C(0-1)^2$

$$\Rightarrow 0 = -A + B + C \Rightarrow A = \frac{1}{2} + \frac{1}{4} = \frac{3}{4}$$

$$\frac{x^2}{(x-1)^2(x+1)} = \frac{(3/4)}{x-1} + \frac{(1/2)}{(x-1)^2} + \frac{(1/4)}{x+1}$$

17. Find the partial fraction decomposition:

$$\frac{1}{x^3 - 8} = \frac{1}{(x-2)(x^2 + 2x + 4)} = \frac{A}{x-2} + \frac{Bx + C}{x^2 + 2x + 4}$$

(Multiply both sides by $(x-2)(x^2 + 2x + 4)$.)

$$1 = A(x^2 + 2x + 4) + (Bx + C)(x - 2)$$

Let $x = 2$:   then $1 = A\left(2^2 + 2(2) + 4\right) + (B(2) + C)(2 - 2)$

$$\Rightarrow 1 = 12A \Rightarrow A = \frac{1}{12}$$

Let $x = 0$:   then $1 = A\left(0^2 + 2(0) + 4\right) + (B(0) + C)(0 - 2)$

$$\Rightarrow 1 = 4A - 2C \Rightarrow 1 = 4(1/12) - 2C \Rightarrow -2C = \frac{2}{3} \Rightarrow C = -\frac{1}{3}$$

Let $x = 1$:   then $1 = A\left(1^2 + 2(1) + 4\right) + (B(1) + C)(1 - 2)$

$$\Rightarrow 1 = 7A - B - C \Rightarrow 1 = 7(1/12) - B + \frac{1}{3} \Rightarrow B = -\frac{1}{12}$$

$$\frac{1}{x^3 - 8} = \frac{(1/12)}{x-2} + \frac{-(1/12)x - 1/3}{x^2 + 2x + 4} = \frac{(1/12)}{x-2} + \frac{-(1/12)(x + 4)}{x^2 + 2x + 4}$$

19. Find the partial fraction decomposition:

$$\frac{x^2}{(x-1)^2(x+1)^2} = \frac{A}{x-1} + \frac{B}{(x-1)^2} + \frac{C}{x+1} + \frac{D}{(x+1)^2}$$

(Multiply both sides by $(x-1)^2(x+1)^2$.)

$$x^2 = A(x-1)(x+1)^2 + B(x+1)^2 + C(x-1)^2(x+1) + D(x-1)^2$$

Let $x = 1$:   then $1^2 = A(1-1)(1+1)^2 + B(1+1)^2 + C(1-1)^2(1+1) + D(1-1)^2$

$$\Rightarrow 1 = 4B \Rightarrow B = \frac{1}{4}$$

Let $x = -1$:   then

$$(-1)^2 = A(-1-1)(-1+1)^2 + B(-1+1)^2 + C(-1-1)^2(-1+1) + D(-1-1)^2$$

$$\Rightarrow 1 = 4D \Rightarrow D = \frac{1}{4}$$

Let $x = 0$:   then

$$0^2 = A(0-1)(0+1)^2 + B(0+1)^2 + C(0-1)^2(0+1) + D(0-1)^2$$

$$\Rightarrow 0 = -A + B + C + D \Rightarrow A - C = \frac{1}{4} + \frac{1}{4} = \frac{1}{2}$$

Let $x = 2$:   then

$$2^2 = A(2-1)(2+1)^2 + B(2+1)^2 + C(2-1)^2(2+1) + D(2-1)^2$$

$$\Rightarrow 4 = 9A + 9B + 3C + D \Rightarrow 9A + 3C = 4 - \frac{9}{4} - \frac{1}{4} = \frac{3}{2}$$

$$\Rightarrow 3A + C = \frac{1}{2}$$

Solve the system of equations:

$$A - C = \frac{1}{2}$$

$$3A + C = \frac{1}{2}$$

$$\overline{4A \quad = 1} \Rightarrow A = \frac{1}{4} \Rightarrow \frac{3}{4} + C = \frac{1}{2} \Rightarrow C = -\frac{1}{4}$$

$$\frac{x^2}{(x-1)^2(x+1)^2} = \frac{(1/4)}{x-1} + \frac{(1/4)}{(x-1)^2} + \frac{(-1/4)}{x+1} + \frac{(1/4)}{(x+1)^2}$$

21. Find the partial fraction decomposition:

$$\frac{x-3}{(x+2)(x+1)^2} = \frac{A}{x+2} + \frac{B}{x+1} + \frac{C}{(x+1)^2}$$

(Multiply both sides by $(x+2)(x+1)^2$.)

$$x - 3 = A(x+1)^2 + B(x+2)(x+1) + C(x+2)$$

Let $x = -2$: then $-2 - 3 = A(-2+1)^2 + B(-2+2)(-2+1) + C(-2+2)$

$$\Rightarrow -5 = A \Rightarrow A = -5$$

Let $x = -1$: then $-1 - 3 = A(-1+1)^2 + B(-1+2)(-1+1) + C(-1+2)$

$$\Rightarrow -4 = C \Rightarrow C = -4$$

Let $x = 0$: then

$$0 - 3 = A(0+1)^2 + B(0+2)(0+1) + C(0+2) \Rightarrow -3 = A + 2B + 2C$$

$$\Rightarrow -3 = -5 + 2B + 2(-4) \Rightarrow 2B = 10 \Rightarrow B = 5$$

$$\frac{x-3}{(x+2)(x+1)^2} = \frac{-5}{x+2} + \frac{5}{x+1} + \frac{-4}{(x+1)^2}$$

23. Find the partial fraction decomposition:

$$\frac{x+4}{x^2(x^2+4)} = \frac{A}{x} + \frac{B}{x^2} + \frac{Cx+D}{x^2+4}$$ (Multiply both sides by $x^2(x^2+4)$.)

$$x + 4 = Ax(x^2+4) + B(x^2+4) + (Cx+D)x^2$$

Let $x = 0$: then $0 + 4 = A(0)(0^2+4) + B(0^2+4) + (C0+D)(0)^2$

$$\Rightarrow 4 = 4B \Rightarrow B = 1$$

Let $x = 1$: then $1 + 4 = A(1)(1^2+4) + B(1^2+4) + (C(1)+D)(1)^2$

$$\Rightarrow 5 = 5A + 5B + C + D \Rightarrow 5 = 5A + 5 + C + D$$

$$\Rightarrow 5A + C + D = 0$$

Let $x = -1$: then

$$-1 + 4 = A(-1)((-1)^2+4) + B((-1)^2+4) + (C(-1)+D)(-1)^2$$

$$\Rightarrow 3 = -5A + 5B - C + D \Rightarrow 3 = -5A + 5 - C + D$$

$$\Rightarrow -5A - C + D = -2$$

Let $x = 2$: then $2 + 4 = A(2)(2^2+4) + B(2^2+4) + (C(2)+D)(2)^2$

$$\Rightarrow 6 = 16A + 8B + 8C + 4D \Rightarrow 6 = 16A + 8 + 8C + 4D$$

$$\Rightarrow 16A + 8C + 4D = -2$$

Solve the system of equations:

$$5A + C + D = 0$$
$$\underline{-5A - C + D = -2}$$

$$2D = -2 \qquad\qquad 5A + C - 1 = 0$$
$$D = -1 \qquad\qquad C = 1 - 5A$$

$$16A + 8(1 - 5A) + 4(-1) = -2$$
$$16A + 8 - 40A - 4 = -2$$

$$-24A = -6 \qquad\qquad C = 1 - 5(1/5)$$
$$C = 1 - 5/4 = -1/4$$
$$A = 1/4$$

$$\frac{x+4}{x^2(x^2+4)} = \frac{(1/4)}{x} + \frac{1}{x^2} + \frac{(-(1/4)x - 1)}{x^2+4} = \frac{(1/4)}{x} + \frac{1}{x^2} + \frac{-(1/4)(x+4)}{x^2+4}$$

25. Find the partial fraction decomposition:

$$\frac{x^2 + 2x + 3}{(x+1)(x^2 + 2x + 4)} = \frac{A}{x+1} + \frac{Bx + C}{x^2 + 2x + 4} \quad \text{(Multiply both sides by } (x+1)(x^2 + 2x + 4).)$$

$$x^2 + 2x + 3 = A(x^2 + 2x + 4) + (Bx + C)(x + 1)$$

Let $x = -1$:   then

$$(-1)^2 + 2(-1) + 3 = A((-1)^2 + 2(-1) + 4) + (B(-1) + C)(-1 + 1)$$

$$\Rightarrow 2 = 3A \Rightarrow A = \frac{2}{3}$$

Let $x = 0$:   then $0^2 + 2(0) + 3 = A(0^2 + 2(0) + 4) + (B(0) + C)(0 + 1)$

$$\Rightarrow 3 = 4A + C \Rightarrow 3 = 4(2/3) + C \Rightarrow C = \frac{1}{3}$$

Let $x = 1$:   then

$$1^2 + 2(1) + 3 = A(1^2 + 2(1) + 4) + (B(1) + C)(1 + 1)$$
$$\Rightarrow 6 = 7A + 2B + 2C \Rightarrow 6 = 7(2/3) + 2B + 2(1/3)$$

$$\Rightarrow 2B = 6 - \frac{14}{3} - \frac{2}{3} \Rightarrow 2B = 2/3 \Rightarrow B = 1/3$$

$$\frac{x^2 + 2x + 3}{(x+1)(x^2 + 2x + 4)} = \frac{(2/3)}{x+1} + \frac{((1/3)x + 1/3)}{x^2 + 2x + 4} = \frac{(2/3)}{x+1} + \frac{(1/3)(x+1)}{x^2 + 2x + 4}$$

27. Find the partial fraction decomposition:

$$\frac{x}{(3x - 2)(2x + 1)} = \frac{A}{3x - 2} + \frac{B}{2x + 1} \quad \text{(Multiply both sides by } (3x - 2)(2x + 1).)$$

$$x = A(2x + 1) + B(3x - 2)$$

Let $x = -\dfrac{1}{2}$:   then $-\dfrac{1}{2} = A(2(-1/2) + 1) + B(3(-1/2) - 2) \Rightarrow -\dfrac{1}{2} = -\dfrac{7}{2}B \Rightarrow B = \dfrac{1}{7}$

Let $x = \dfrac{2}{3}$:   then $\dfrac{2}{3} = A(2(2/3) + 1) + B(3(2/3) - 2) \Rightarrow \dfrac{2}{3} = \dfrac{7}{3}A \Rightarrow A = \dfrac{2}{7}$

$$\frac{x}{(3x - 2)(2x + 1)} = \frac{(2/7)}{3x - 2} + \frac{(1/7)}{2x + 1}$$

29. Find the partial fraction decomposition:

$$\frac{x}{x^2+2x-3} = \frac{x}{(x+3)(x-1)} = \frac{A}{x+3} + \frac{B}{x-1}$$

(Multiply both sides by $(x+3)(x-1)$.)

$$x = A(x-1) + B(x+3)$$

Let $x = 1$: then $1 = A(1-1) + B(1+3)$ $\Rightarrow$ $1 = 4B \Rightarrow B = \frac{1}{4}$

Let $x = -3$: then $-3 = A(-3-1) + B(-3+3)$ $\Rightarrow$ $-3 = -4A$ $\Rightarrow$ $A = \frac{3}{4}$

$$\frac{x}{x^2+2x-3} = \frac{(3/4)}{x+3} + \frac{(1/4)}{x-1}$$

31. Find the partial fraction decomposition:

$$\frac{x^2+2x+3}{(x^2+4)^2} = \frac{Ax+B}{x^2+4}$$ (Multiply both sides by $(x^2+4)^2$.)

$$x^2+2x+3 = (Ax+B)(x^2+4) + Cx + D$$

$$x^2+2x+3 = Ax^3 + Bx^2 + 4Ax + 4B + Cx + D$$

$$x^2+2x+3 = Ax^3 + Bx^2 + (4A+C)x + 4B + D$$

$$A = 0; B = 1$$

$$4A + C = 2 \Rightarrow 4(0) + C = 2 \Rightarrow C = 2$$

$$4B + D = 3 \Rightarrow 4(1) + D = 3 \Rightarrow D = -1$$

$$\frac{x^2+2x+3}{(x^2+4)^2} = \frac{1}{x^2+4} + \frac{2x-1}{(x^2+4)^2}$$

33. Find the partial fraction decomposition:

$$\frac{7x+3}{x^3-2x^2-3x} = \frac{7x+3}{x(x-3)(x+1)} = \frac{A}{x} + \frac{B}{x-3} + \frac{C}{x+1}$$

(Multiply both sides by $x(x-3)(x+1)$.)

$$7x+3 = A(x-3)(x+1) + Bx(x+1) + Cx(x-3)$$

Let $x = 0$: then $7(0) + 3 = A(0-3)(0+1) + B(0)(0+1) + C(0)(0-3)$

$$\Rightarrow 3 = -3A \Rightarrow A = -1$$

Let $x = 3$: then $7(3) + 3 = A(3-3)(3+1) + B(3)(3+1) + C(3)(3-3)$

$$\Rightarrow 24 = 12B \Rightarrow B = 2$$

Let $x = -1$: then

$$7(-1) + 3 = A(-1-3)(-1+1) + B(-1)(-1+1) + C(-1)(-1-3)$$

$$\Rightarrow -4 = 4C \Rightarrow C = -1$$

$$\frac{7x+3}{x^3-2x^2-3x} = \frac{-1}{x} + \frac{2}{x-3} + \frac{-1}{x+1}$$

35. Perform synthetic division to find a factor:

$$2\overline{)\begin{array}{rrrr} 1 & -4 & 5 & -2 \\ & 2 & -4 & 2 \end{array}}$$
$$\begin{array}{rrrr} 1 & -2 & 1 & 0 \end{array}$$

$$x^3 - 4x^2 + 5x - 2 = (x-2)(x^2 - 2x + 1) = (x-2)(x-1)^2$$

Find the partial fraction decomposition:

$$\frac{x^2}{x^3 - 4x^2 + 5x - 2} = \frac{x^2}{(x-2)(x-1)^2} = \frac{A}{x-2} + \frac{B}{x-1} + \frac{C}{(x-1)^2}$$

(Multiply both sides by $(x-2)(x-1)^2$.)

$$x^2 = A(x-1)^2 + B(x-2)(x-1) + C(x-2)$$

Let $x = 2$: then $2^2 = A(2-1)^2 + B(2-2)(2-1) + C(2-2)$

$$\Rightarrow 4 = A \Rightarrow A = 4$$

Let $x = 1$: then $1^2 = A(1-1)^2 + B(1-2)(1-1) + C(1-2)$

$$\Rightarrow 1 = -C \Rightarrow C = -1$$

Let $x = 0$: then $0^2 = A(0-1)^2 + B(0-2)(0-1) + C(0-2)$

$$\Rightarrow 0 = A + 2B - 2C \Rightarrow 0 = 4 + 2B - 2(-1)$$

$$\Rightarrow 2B = -6 \Rightarrow B = -3$$

$$\frac{x^2}{x^3 - 4x^2 + 5x - 2} = \frac{4}{x-2} + \frac{-3}{x-1} + \frac{-1}{(x-1)^2}$$

37. Find the partial fraction decomposition:

$$\frac{x^3}{(x^2+16)^3} = \frac{Ax+B}{x^2+16} + \frac{Cx+D}{(x^2+16)^2} + \frac{Ex+F}{(x^2+16)^3}$$

(Multiply both sides by $(x^2+16)^3$.)

$$x^3 = (Ax+B)(x^2+16)^2 + (Cx+D)(x^2+16) + Ex + F$$

$$x^3 = (Ax+B)(x^4 + 32x^2 + 256) + Cx^3 + Dx^2 + 16Cx + 16D + Ex + F$$

$$x^3 = Ax^5 + Bx^4 + 32Ax^3 + 32Bx^2 + 256Ax + 256B + Cx^3 + Dx^2$$
$$+ 16Cx + 16D + Ex + F$$

$$x^3 = Ax^5 + Bx^4 + (32A+C)x^3 + (32B+D)x^2 + (256A+16C+E)x$$
$$+ (256B+16D+F)$$

$$A = 0$$

$$B = 0$$

$$32A + C = 1 \Rightarrow 32(0) + C = 1 \Rightarrow C = 1$$

$$32B + D = 0 \Rightarrow 32(0) + D = 0 \Rightarrow D = 0$$

$$256A + 16C + E = 0 \Rightarrow 256(0) + 16(1) + E = 0 \Rightarrow E = -16$$

$$256B + 16D + F = 0 \Rightarrow 256(0) + 16(0) + F = 0 \Rightarrow F = 0$$

$$\frac{x^3}{(x^2+16)^3} = \frac{x}{(x^2+16)^2} + \frac{-16x}{(x^2+16)^3}$$

39. Find the partial fraction decomposition:

$$\frac{4}{2x^2 - 5x - 3} = \frac{4}{(x-3)(2x+1)} = \frac{A}{x-3} + \frac{B}{2x+1} \quad \text{(Multiply both sides by } (x-3)(2x+1).)$$

$$4 = A(2x+1) + B(x-3)$$

Let $x = -\dfrac{1}{2}$: then $4 = A\left(2(-1/2)+1\right) + B\left(-\dfrac{1}{2}-3\right) \Rightarrow 4 = -\dfrac{7}{2}B \Rightarrow B = -\dfrac{8}{7}$

Let $x = 3$: then $4 = A(2(3)+1) + B(3-3) \Rightarrow 4 = 7A \Rightarrow A = \dfrac{4}{7}$

$$\frac{4}{2x^2 - 5x - 3} = \frac{4}{(x-3)(2x+1)} = \frac{(4/7)}{x-3} + \frac{(-8/7)}{2x+1}$$

41. Find the partial fraction decomposition:

$$\frac{2x+3}{x^4 - 9x^2} = \frac{2x+3}{x^2(x-3)(x+3)} = \frac{A}{x} + \frac{B}{x^2} + \frac{C}{x-3} + \frac{D}{x+3}$$

$$\text{(Multiply both sides by } x^2(x-3)(x+3).)$$

$$2x+3 = Ax(x-3)(x+3) + B(x-3)(x+3) + Cx^2(x+3) + Dx^2(x-3)$$

Let $x = 0$: then

$$2 \cdot 0 + 3 = A \cdot 0(0-3)(0+3) + B(0-3)(0+3) + C \cdot 0^2(0+3) + D \cdot 0^2(0-3)$$

$$\Rightarrow 3 = -9B \Rightarrow B = -\frac{1}{3}$$

Let $x = 3$: then

$$2 \cdot 3 + 3 = A \cdot 3(3-3)(3+3) + B(3-3)(3+3) + C \cdot 3^2(3+3) + D \cdot 3^2(3-3)$$

$$\Rightarrow 9 = 54C \Rightarrow C = \frac{1}{6}$$

Let $x = -3$: then

$$2(-3) + 3 = A(-3)(-3-3)(-3+3) + B(-3-3)(-3+3) + C(-3)^2(-3+3)$$

$$+ D(-3)^2(-3-3)$$

$$\Rightarrow -3 = -54D \Rightarrow D = \frac{1}{18}$$

Let $x = 1$: then

$$2 \cdot 1 + 3 = A \cdot 1(1-3)(1+3) + B(1-3)(1+3) + C \cdot 1^2(1+3) + D \cdot 1^2(1-3)$$

$$\Rightarrow 5 = -8A - 8B + 4C - 2D$$

$$\Rightarrow 5 = -8A - 8(-1/3) + 4(1/6) - 2(1/18)$$

$$\Rightarrow 5 = -8A + \frac{8}{3} + \frac{2}{3} - \frac{1}{9} \Rightarrow -8A = \frac{16}{9} \Rightarrow A = -\frac{2}{9}$$

$$\frac{2x+3}{x^4 - 9x^2} = \frac{2x+3}{x^2(x-3)(x+3)} = \frac{(-2/9)}{x} + \frac{(-1/3)}{x^2} + \frac{(1/6)}{x-3} + \frac{(1/18)}{x+3}$$

Systems of Equations and Inequalities

8.6 Systems of Nonlinear Equations

1. $\begin{cases} y = x^2 + 1 \\ y = x + 1 \end{cases}$

Graph: $y_1 = x^2 + 1;\quad y_2 = x + 1$

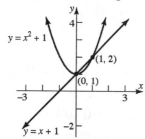

$(0, 1)$ and $(1, 2)$ are the intersection points.

Solve by substitution:
$$x^2 + 1 = x + 1$$
$$x^2 - x = 0$$
$$x(x - 1) = 0$$
$$x = 0 \text{ or } x = 1$$
$$y = 1 \qquad y = 2$$
Solutions: $(0, 1)$ and $(1, 2)$

3. $\begin{cases} y = \sqrt{36 - x^2} \\ y = 8 - x \end{cases}$

Graph: $y_1 = \sqrt{36 - x^2};\quad y_2 = 8 - x$

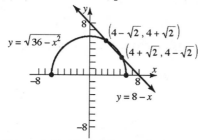

$(2.59, 5.41)$ and $(5.41, 2.59)$ are the intersection points.

Solve by substitution:
$$\sqrt{36 - x^2} = 8 - x$$
$$36 - x^2 = 64 - 16x + x^2$$
$$2x^2 - 16x + 28 = 0$$
$$x^2 - 8x + 14 = 0$$
$$x = \frac{8 \pm \sqrt{64 - 56}}{2}$$
$$x = \frac{8 \pm 2\sqrt{2}}{2}$$
$$x = 4 \pm \sqrt{2}$$
If $x = 4 + \sqrt{2}$, $y = 8 - \left(4 + \sqrt{2}\right) = 4 - \sqrt{2}$
If $x = 4 - \sqrt{2}$, $y = 8 - \left(4 - \sqrt{2}\right) = 4 + \sqrt{2}$
Solutions:
$$\left(4 + \sqrt{2}, 4 - \sqrt{2}\right) \text{ and } \left(4 - \sqrt{2}, 4 + \sqrt{2}\right)$$

5. $\begin{cases} y = \sqrt{x} \\ y = 2 - x \end{cases}$

Graph: $y_1 = \sqrt{x}; \quad y_2 = 2 - x$

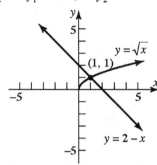

(1, 1) is the intersection point.

Solve by substitution:
$$\sqrt{x} = 2 - x$$
$$x = 4 - 4x + x^2$$
$$x^2 - 5x + 4 = 0$$
$$(x - 4)(x - 1) = 0$$
$$x = 4 \quad \text{or } x = 1$$
$$y = -2 \text{ or } y = 1$$
Eliminate (4, –2); it does not check.
Solution: (1, 1)

7. $\begin{cases} x = 2y \\ x = y^2 - 2y \end{cases}$

Solve each equation for y in order to enter it into the graphing utility:
$$y^2 - 2y + 1 = x + 1 \rightarrow (y - 1)^2 = x + 1 \rightarrow y - 1 = \pm\sqrt{x + 1} \rightarrow y = 1 \pm \sqrt{x + 1}$$

Graph: $y_1 = \dfrac{x}{2}; \quad y_2 = 1 + \sqrt{x + 1}; \quad y_3 = 1 - \sqrt{x + 1}$

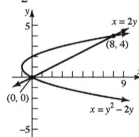

(0, 0) and (8, 4) are the intersection points.

Solve by substitution:
$$2y = y^2 - 2y$$
$$y^2 - 4y = 0$$
$$y(y - 4) = 0$$
$$y = 0 \quad \text{or } y = 4$$
$$x = 0 \quad \text{or } x = 8$$
Solutions: (0, 0) and (8, 4)

9. $\begin{cases} x^2 + y^2 = 4 \\ x^2 + 2x + y^2 = 0 \end{cases}$

Graph: $y_1 = \sqrt{4 - x^2}; \quad y_2 = -\sqrt{4 - x^2}; \quad y_3 = \sqrt{-x^2 - 2x}; \quad y_4 = -\sqrt{-x^2 - 2x}$

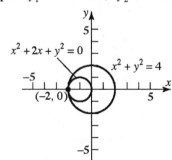

Substitute 4 for $x^2 + y^2$ in the second equation:
$$2x + 4 = 0$$
$$2x = -4$$
$$x = -2$$
$$y = \sqrt{4 - (-2)^2} = 0$$
Solution: (–2, 0)

(–2, 0) is the intersection point.   Note: This intersection point is impossible to find on your graphing utility unless you have just the right window and make an excellent guess.

11. $\begin{cases} y = 3x - 5 \\ x^2 + y^2 = 5 \end{cases}$

Graph: $y_1 = 3x - 5$; $y_2 = \sqrt{5 - x^2}$;
$$y_3 = -\sqrt{5 - x^2}$$

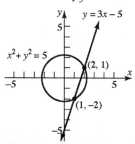

$(1, -2)$ and $(2, 1)$ are the intersection points.

Solve by substitution:
$$x^2 + (3x - 5)^2 = 5$$
$$x^2 + 9x^2 - 30x + 25 = 5$$
$$10x^2 - 30x + 20 = 0$$
$$x^2 - 3x + 2 = 0$$
$$(x - 1)(x - 2) = 0$$

$x = 1$ or $x = 2$

$y = 3(1) - 5$ $y = 3(2) - 5$

$y = -2$ $y = 1$

Solutions: $(1, -2)$ and $(2, 1)$

13. $\begin{cases} x^2 + y^2 = 4 \\ y^2 - x = 4 \end{cases}$

Graph: $y_1 = \sqrt{4 - x^2}$; $y_2 = -\sqrt{4 - x^2}$; $y_3 = \sqrt{x + 4}$; $y_4 = -\sqrt{x + 4}$

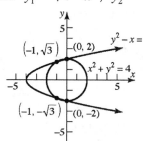

$(-1, 1.73)$, $(-1, -1.73)$, $(0, 2)$, and $(0, -2)$ are the intersection points.

Substitute $x + 4$ for y^2 in the first equation:
$$x^2 + x + 4 = 4$$
$$x^2 + x = 0$$
$$x(x + 1) = 0$$

$x = 0$ or $x = -1$

$y^2 = 4$ $y^2 = 3$

$y = \pm 2$ $y^2 = \pm\sqrt{3}$

Solutions:
$$(0, -2), (0, 2), \left(-1, \sqrt{3}\right), \left(-1, -\sqrt{3}\right)$$

15. $\begin{cases} xy = 4 \\ x^2 + y^2 = 8 \end{cases}$

Graph: $y_1 = \dfrac{4}{x}$; $y_2 = \sqrt{8 - x^2}$;
$$y_3 = -\sqrt{8 - x^2}$$

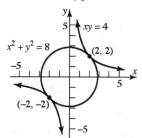

$(-2, -2)$ and $(2, 2)$ are the intersection points.

Solve by substitution:
$$x^2 + \left(\frac{4}{x}\right)^2 = 8$$
$$x^2 + \frac{16}{x^2} = 8$$
$$x^4 + 16 = 8x^2$$
$$x^4 - 8x^2 + 16 = 0$$
$$\left(x^2 - 4\right)^2 = 0$$
$$x^2 - 4 = 0$$
$$x^2 = 4$$

$x = 2$ or $x = -2$

$y = 2$ $y = -2$

Solutions: $(-2, -2)$ and $(2, 2)$

17. $\begin{cases} x^2 + y^2 = 4 \\ \quad\;\; y = x^2 - 9 \end{cases}$

Graph: $y_1 = x^2 - 9$; $y_2 = \sqrt{4 - x^2}$;
$$y_3 = -\sqrt{4 - x^2}$$

No solution; Inconsistent.

Solve by substitution:
$$x^2 + (x^2 - 9)^2 = 4$$
$$x^2 + x^4 - 18x^2 + 81 = 4$$
$$x^4 - 17x^2 + 77 = 0$$
$$x^2 = \frac{17 \pm \sqrt{289 - 4(77)}}{2}$$
$$x^2 = \frac{17 \pm \sqrt{-19}}{2}$$

There are no real solutions to this expression; Inconsistent.

19. $\begin{cases} y = x^2 - 4 \\ y = 6x - 13 \end{cases}$

Graph: $y_1 = x^2 - 4$; $\quad y_2 = 6x - 13$

(3,5) is the intersection point.

Solve by substitution:
$$x^2 - 4 = 6x - 13$$
$$x^2 - 6x + 9 = 0$$
$$(x - 3)^2 = 0$$
$$x - 3 = 0$$
$$x = 3$$
$$y = 6(3) - 13 = 5$$
Solutions: (3,5)

21. Solve the second equation for y, substitute into the first equation and solve:
$$\begin{cases} 2x^2 + y^2 = 18 \\ \quad xy = 4 \;\Rightarrow\; y = \dfrac{4}{x} \end{cases}$$
$$2x^2 + \left(\frac{4}{x}\right)^2 = 18$$
$$2x^2 + \frac{16}{x^2} = 18$$
$$2x^4 + 16 = 18x^2$$
$$2x^4 - 18x^2 + 16 = 0$$
$$x^4 - 9x^2 + 8 = 0$$
$$\left(x^2 - 8\right)\left(x^2 - 1\right) = 0$$
$$x^2 = 8 \;\Rightarrow\; x = \pm\sqrt{8} = \pm 2\sqrt{2}$$
$$\text{or}\;\; x^2 = 1 \Rightarrow x = \pm 1$$

$$\text{If } x = 2\sqrt{2}: \qquad y = \frac{4}{2\sqrt{2}} = \sqrt{2}$$

$$\text{If } x = -2\sqrt{2}: \qquad y = \frac{4}{-2\sqrt{2}} = -\sqrt{2}$$

$$\text{If } x = 1: \qquad y = \frac{4}{1} = 4$$

$$\text{If } x = -1: \qquad y = \frac{4}{-1} = -4$$

Solutions: $\left(2\sqrt{2}, \sqrt{2}\right), \left(-2\sqrt{2}, -\sqrt{2}\right), (1, 4), (-1, -4)$

23. Substitute the first equation into the second equation and solve:

$$\begin{cases} y = 2x + 1 \\ 2x^2 + y^2 = 1 \end{cases}$$

$$2x^2 + (2x+1)^2 = 1 \Rightarrow 2x^2 + 4x^2 + 4x + 1 = 1 \Rightarrow 6x^2 + 4x = 0 \Rightarrow 2x(3x+2) = 0$$

$$2x = 0 \Rightarrow x = 0$$

$$\text{or} \quad 3x + 2 = 0 \Rightarrow x = -\frac{2}{3}$$

$$\text{If } x = 0: \qquad y = 2(0) + 1 = 1$$

$$\text{If } x = -\frac{2}{3}: \qquad y = 2\left(-\frac{2}{3}\right) + 1 = -\frac{4}{3} + 1 = -\frac{1}{3}$$

Solutions: $(0, 1), \left(-\frac{2}{3}, -\frac{1}{3}\right)$

25. Solve the first equation for y, substitute into the second equation and solve:

$$\begin{cases} x + y + 1 = 0 \Rightarrow y = -x - 1 \\ x^2 + y^2 + 6y - x = -5 \end{cases}$$

$$x^2 + (-x-1)^2 + 6(-x-1) - x = -5 \Rightarrow x^2 + x^2 + 2x + 1 - 6x - 6 - x = -5$$

$$2x^2 - 5x = 0 \Rightarrow x(2x - 5) = 0 \Rightarrow x = 0 \quad \text{or} \quad x = \frac{5}{2}$$

$$\text{If } x = 0: \qquad y = -(0) - 1 = -1$$

$$\text{If } x = \frac{5}{2}: \qquad y = -\frac{5}{2} - 1 = -\frac{7}{2}$$

Solutions: $(0, -1), \left(\frac{5}{2}, -\frac{7}{2}\right)$

27. Solve the second equation for y, substitute into the first equation and solve:

$$\begin{cases} 4x^2 - 3xy + 9y^2 = 15 \\ \\ 2x + 3y = 5 \Rightarrow y = -\frac{2}{3}x + \frac{5}{3} \end{cases}$$

$$4x^2 - 3x\left(-\frac{2}{3}x + \frac{5}{3}\right) + 9\left(-\frac{2}{3}x + \frac{5}{3}\right)^2 = 15$$

$$4x^2 + 2x^2 - 5x + 4x^2 - 20x + 25 = 15$$

$$10x^2 - 25x + 10 = 0 \Rightarrow 2x^2 - 5x + 2 = 0$$

$$(2x - 1)(x - 2) = 0 \Rightarrow x = \frac{1}{2} \text{ or } x = 2$$

If $x = \frac{1}{2}$: $y = -\frac{2}{3}\left(\frac{1}{2}\right) + \frac{5}{3} = \frac{4}{3}$

If $x = 2$: $y = -\frac{2}{3}(2) + \frac{5}{3} = \frac{1}{3}$

Solutions: $\left(\frac{1}{2}, \frac{4}{3}\right), \left(2, \frac{1}{3}\right)$

29. Multiply each side of the second equation by 4 and add the equations to eliminate y:

$$\begin{cases} x^2 - 4y^2 = -7 \longrightarrow & x^2 - 4y^2 = -7 \\ 3x^2 + y^2 = 31 \xrightarrow{\;4\;} & 12x^2 + 4y^2 = 124 \end{cases}$$

$$13x^2 \qquad = 117 \Rightarrow x^2 = 9 \Rightarrow x = \pm 3$$

If $x = 3$: $3(3)^2 + y^2 = 31 \Rightarrow y^2 = 4 \Rightarrow y = \pm 2$

If $x = -3$: $3(-3)^2 + y^2 = 31 \Rightarrow y^2 = 4 \Rightarrow y = \pm 2$

Solutions: $(3, 2), (3, -2), (-3, 2), (-3, -2)$

31. Multiply each side of the first equation by 5 and each side of the second equation by 3 to eliminate y:

$$\begin{cases} 7x^2 - 3y^2 + 5 = 0 \to 7x^2 - 3y^2 = -5 \xrightarrow{\;5\;} & 35x^2 - 15y^2 = -25 \\ 3x^2 + 5y^2 = 12 \to \quad 3x^2 + 5y^2 = 12 \xrightarrow{\;3\;} & 9x^2 + 15y^2 = \quad 36 \end{cases}$$

$$44x^2 \qquad = \quad 11 \Rightarrow x^2 = \frac{1}{4} \Rightarrow x = \pm\frac{1}{2}$$

If $x = \frac{1}{2}$: $3\left(\frac{1}{2}\right)^2 + 5y^2 = 12 \Rightarrow 5y^2 = \frac{45}{4} \Rightarrow y^2 = \frac{9}{4} \Rightarrow y = \pm\frac{3}{2}$

If $x = -\frac{1}{2}$: $3\left(-\frac{1}{2}\right)^2 + 5y^2 = 12 \Rightarrow 5y^2 = \frac{45}{4} \Rightarrow y^2 = \frac{9}{4} \Rightarrow y = \pm\frac{3}{2}$

Solutions: $\left(\frac{1}{2}, \frac{3}{2}\right), \left(\frac{1}{2}, -\frac{3}{2}\right), \left(-\frac{1}{2}, \frac{3}{2}\right), \left(-\frac{1}{2}, -\frac{3}{2}\right)$

33. Multiply each side of the second equation by 2 and add to eliminate xy:

$$\begin{cases} x^2 + 2xy = 10 \longrightarrow & x^2 + 2xy = 10 \\ 3x^2 - xy = 2 \xrightarrow{\;2\;} & 6x^2 - 2xy = 4 \end{cases}$$

$$7x^2 \qquad = 14 \Rightarrow x^2 = 2 \Rightarrow x = \pm\sqrt{2}$$

If $x = \sqrt{2}$: $3\left(\sqrt{2}\right)^2 - \sqrt{2} \cdot y = 2 \Rightarrow -\sqrt{2} \cdot y = -4 \Rightarrow y = \frac{4}{\sqrt{2}} \Rightarrow y = 2\sqrt{2}$

If $x = -\sqrt{2}$: $3\left(-\sqrt{2}\right)^2 - \left(-\sqrt{2}\right)y = 2 \Rightarrow \sqrt{2} \cdot y = -4 \Rightarrow y = \frac{-4}{\sqrt{2}} \Rightarrow y = -2\sqrt{2}$

Solutions: $\left(\sqrt{2}, 2\sqrt{2}\right), \left(-\sqrt{2}, -2\sqrt{2}\right)$

35. Multiply each side of the first equation by 2 and add the equations to eliminate y:

$$\begin{cases} 2x^2 + y^2 = 2 \rightarrow 2x^2 + y^2 = 2 \xrightarrow{2} 4x^2 + 2y^2 = 4 \\ x^2 - 2y^2 + 8 = 0 \rightarrow x^2 - 2y^2 = -8 \longrightarrow \underline{x^2 - 2y^2 = -8} \end{cases}$$

$$5x^2 \qquad = -4 \Rightarrow x^2 = -\frac{4}{5}$$

No solution. The system is inconsistent.

37. Multiply each side of the second equation by 2 and add the equations to eliminate y:

$$\begin{cases} x^2 + 2y^2 = 16 \longrightarrow x^2 + 2y^2 = 16 \\ 4x^2 - y^2 = 24 \xrightarrow{2} \underline{8x^2 - 2y^2 = 48} \end{cases}$$

$$9x^2 \qquad = 64 \Rightarrow x^2 = \frac{64}{9} \Rightarrow x = \pm\frac{8}{3}$$

If $x = \frac{8}{3}$: $\left(\frac{8}{3}\right)^2 + 2y^2 = 16 \Rightarrow 2y^2 = \frac{80}{9} \Rightarrow y^2 = \frac{40}{9} \Rightarrow y = \pm\frac{2\sqrt{10}}{3}$

If $x = -\frac{8}{3}$: $\left(-\frac{8}{3}\right)^2 + 2y^2 = 16 \Rightarrow 2y^2 = \frac{80}{9} \Rightarrow y^2 = \frac{40}{9} \Rightarrow y = \pm\frac{2\sqrt{10}}{3}$

Solutions: $\left(\frac{8}{3}, \frac{2\sqrt{10}}{3}\right), \left(\frac{8}{3}, \frac{-2\sqrt{10}}{3}\right), \left(-\frac{8}{3}, \frac{2\sqrt{10}}{3}\right), \left(-\frac{8}{3}, \frac{-2\sqrt{10}}{3}\right)$

39. Multiply each side of the second equation by 2 and add the equations to eliminate y:

$$\begin{cases} \dfrac{5}{x^2} - \dfrac{2}{y^2} + 3 = 0 \rightarrow \dfrac{5}{x^2} - \dfrac{2}{y^2} = -3 \longrightarrow \dfrac{5}{x^2} - \dfrac{2}{y^2} = -3 \\ \dfrac{3}{x^2} + \dfrac{1}{y^2} = 7 \rightarrow \dfrac{3}{x^2} + \dfrac{1}{y^2} = 7 \xrightarrow{2} \dfrac{6}{x^2} + \dfrac{2}{y^2} = 14 \end{cases}$$

$$\dfrac{11}{x^2} \qquad = 11 \Rightarrow 11 = 11x^2 \Rightarrow x^2 = 1 \Rightarrow x = \pm 1$$

If $x = 1$: $\dfrac{3}{(1)^2} + \dfrac{1}{y^2} = 7 \Rightarrow \dfrac{1}{y^2} = 4 \Rightarrow y^2 = \dfrac{1}{4} \Rightarrow y = \pm\dfrac{1}{2}$

If $x = -1$: $\dfrac{3}{(-1)^2} + \dfrac{1}{y^2} = 7 \Rightarrow \dfrac{1}{y^2} = 4 \Rightarrow y^2 = \dfrac{1}{4} \Rightarrow y = \pm\dfrac{1}{2}$

Solutions: $\left(1, \dfrac{1}{2}\right), \left(1, -\dfrac{1}{2}\right), \left(-1, \dfrac{1}{2}\right), \left(-1, -\dfrac{1}{2}\right)$

41. Multiply each side of the first equation by –2 and add the equations to eliminate x:

$$\begin{cases} \dfrac{1}{x^4} + \dfrac{6}{y^4} = 6 \xrightarrow{-2} \dfrac{-2}{x^4} - \dfrac{12}{y^4} = -12 \\ \dfrac{2}{x^4} - \dfrac{2}{y^4} = 19 \longrightarrow \dfrac{2}{x^4} - \dfrac{2}{y^4} = 19 \end{cases}$$

$$\dfrac{-14}{y^4} \qquad = 7 \Rightarrow -14 = 7y^4 \Rightarrow y^4 = -2$$

There are no real solutions. The system is inconsistent.

43. Factor the first equation, solve for x, substitute into the second equation and solve:

$$\begin{cases} x^2 - 3xy + 2y^2 = 0 \implies (x - 2y)(x - y) = 0 \implies x = 2y \text{ or } x = y \\ x^2 + xy = 6 \end{cases}$$

Substitute $x = 2y$ and solve:

$$x^2 + xy = 6$$
$$(2y)^2 + (2y)y = 6$$
$$4y^2 + 2y^2 = 6 \implies 6y^2 = 6$$
$$y^2 = 1 \implies y = \pm 1$$

If $y = 1$: $x = 2 \cdot 1 = 2$
If $y = -1$: $x = 2(-1) = -2$

Substitute $x = y$ and solve:

$$x^2 + xy = 6$$
$$y^2 + y \cdot y = 6$$
$$y^2 + y^2 = 6 \implies 2y^2 = 6$$
$$y^2 = 3 \implies y = \pm\sqrt{3}$$

If $y = \sqrt{3}$: $x = \sqrt{3}$
If $y = -\sqrt{3}$: $x = -\sqrt{3}$

Solutions: $(2, 1), (-2, -1), \left(\sqrt{3}, \sqrt{3}\right), \left(-\sqrt{3}, -\sqrt{3}\right)$

45. Multiply each side of the second equation by $-y$ and add the equations to eliminate y:

$$\begin{cases} y^2 + y + x^2 - x - 2 = 0 \quad \longrightarrow \quad y^2 + y + x^2 - x - 2 = 0 \\ y + 1 + \dfrac{x-2}{y} = 0 \quad \xrightarrow{-y} \quad \underline{-y^2 - y \quad\quad - x + 2 = 0} \end{cases}$$

$$x^2 - 2x \quad = 0 \implies x(x - 2) = 0$$
$$x = 0 \text{ or } x = 2$$

If $x = 0$: $y^2 + y + 0^2 - 0 - 2 = 0 \implies y^2 + y - 2 = 0 \implies (y + 2)(y - 1) = 0$
$$\implies y = -2 \text{ or } y = 1$$

If $x = 2$: $y^2 + y + 2^2 - 2 - 2 = 0 \implies y^2 + y = 0 \implies y(y + 1) = 0$
$$\implies y = 0 \text{ or } y = -1 \quad \text{Note: } y \neq 0 \text{ because of division by zero.}$$

Solutions: $(0, -2), (0, 1), (2, -1)$

47. Rewrite each equation in exponential form:

$$\begin{cases} \log_x y = 3 \quad \rightarrow \quad y = x^3 \\ \log_x (4y) = 5 \quad \rightarrow \quad 4y = x^5 \end{cases}$$

Substitute the first equation into the second and solve:

$$4x^3 = x^5$$

$$x^5 - 4x^3 = 0 \implies x^3(x^2 - 4) = 0 \implies x^3 = 0 \text{ or } x^2 = 4 \implies x = 0 \text{ or } x = \pm 2$$

The base of a logarithm must be positive, thus $x \neq 0$ and $x \neq -2$.

If $x = 2$: $y = 2^3 = 8$

Solution: $(2, 8)$

49. Rewrite each equation in exponential form:

$$\begin{cases} \ln x = 4\ln y \implies x = e^{4\ln y} = e^{\ln y^4} = y^4 \\ \log_3 x = 2 + 2\log_3 y \implies x = 3^{2 + 2\log_3 y} = 3^2 \cdot 3^{2\log_3 y} = 3^2 \cdot 3^{\log_3 y^2} = 9y^2 \end{cases}$$

So we have the system

$$\begin{cases} x = y^4 \\ x = 9y^2 \end{cases}$$

Therefore we have : $9y^2 = y^4 \Rightarrow 9y^2 - y^4 = 0 \Rightarrow y^2(9 - y^2) = 0$

$$y^2(3 + y)(3 - y) = 0 \Rightarrow y = 0 \quad \text{or} \quad y = -3 \quad \text{or} \quad y = 3$$

Since $\ln y$ is undefined when $y \le 0$, the only solution is $y = 3$.

If $y = 3$: $x = y^4 \Rightarrow x = 3^4 = 81$

Solution: $(81, 3)$

51.   Solve the first equation for x, substitute into the second equation and solve:

$$\begin{cases} x + 2y = 0 \Rightarrow x = -2y \\ (x - 1)^2 + (y - 1)^2 = 5 \end{cases}$$

$$(-2y - 1)^2 + (y - 1)^2 = 5$$

$$4y^2 + 4y + 1 + y^2 - 2y + 1 = 5 \Rightarrow 5y^2 + 2y - 3 = 0$$

$$(5y - 3)(y + 1) = 0$$

$$y = \frac{3}{5} = 0.6 \quad \text{or} \quad y = -1$$

$$x = -\frac{6}{5} = -1.2 \quad \text{or} \quad x = 2$$

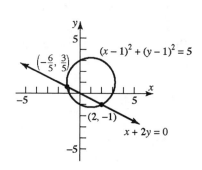

The points of intersection are $(-1.2, 0.6), (2, -1)$.

53.   Complete the square on the second equation, substitute into the first equation and solve:

$$\begin{cases} (x - 1)^2 + (y + 2)^2 = 4 \\ y^2 + 4y - x + 1 = 0 \Rightarrow y^2 + 4y + 4 = x - 1 + 4 \Rightarrow (y + 2)^2 = x + 3 \end{cases}$$

$$(x - 1)^2 + x + 3 = 4 \Rightarrow x^2 - 2x + 1 + x + 3 = 4$$

$$x^2 - x = 0 \Rightarrow x(x - 1) = 0 \Rightarrow x = 0 \quad \text{or} \quad x = 1$$

If $x = 0$: $(y + 2)^2 = 0 + 3$

$$y + 2 = \pm\sqrt{3} \Rightarrow y = -2 \pm \sqrt{3}$$

If $x = 1$: $(y + 2)^2 = 1 + 3$

$$y + 2 = \pm 2 \Rightarrow y = -2 \pm 2$$

The points of intersection are:

$\left(0, -2 - \sqrt{3}\right), \left(0, -2 + \sqrt{3}\right), (1, -4), (1, 0)$.

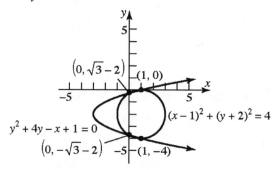

55. Solve the first equation for x, substitute into the second equation and solve:

$$\begin{cases} y = \dfrac{4}{x-3} \Rightarrow x-3 = \dfrac{4}{y} \Rightarrow x = \dfrac{4}{y}+3 \\ x^2 - 6x + y^2 + 1 = 0 \end{cases}$$

$$\left(\frac{4}{y}+3\right)^2 - 6\left(\frac{4}{y}+3\right) + y^2 + 1 = 0$$

$$\frac{16}{y^2} + \frac{24}{y} + 9 - \frac{24}{y} - 18 + y^2 + 1 = 0$$

$$\frac{16}{y^2} + y^2 - 8 = 0$$

$$16 + y^4 - 8y^2 = 0$$

$$y^4 - 8y^2 + 16 = 0$$

$$(y^2 - 4)^2 = 0$$

$$y^2 - 4 = 0$$

$$y^2 = 4$$

$$y = \pm 2$$

If $y = 2$: $x = \dfrac{4}{2} + 3 = 5$

If $y = -2$: $x = \dfrac{4}{-2} + 3 = 1$

The points of intersection are: $(1, -2), (5, 2)$.

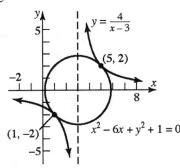

57. Graph: $y_1 = x \wedge (2/3)$; $y_2 = e \wedge (-x)$
Use INTERSECT to solve:

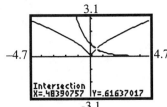

Solution: $(0.48, 0.62)$

59. Graph: $y_1 = \sqrt[3]{(2 - x^2)}$; $y_2 = 4/x^3$
Use INTERSECT to solve:

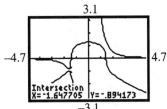

Solution: $(-1.65, -0.89)$

Chapter 8   Systems of Equations and Inequalities

61. Graph:
$$y_1 = \sqrt[4]{(12-x^4)}; \quad y_2 = -\sqrt[4]{(12-x^4)};$$
$$y_3 = \sqrt{2/x}; \quad y_4 = -\sqrt{2/x}$$
Use INTERSECT to solve:

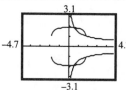

Solutions: $(0.58, 1.86)$, $(1.81, 1.05)$,
$(1.81, -1.05)$, $(0.58, -1.86)$

63. Graph: $y_1 = 2/x; \quad y_2 = \ln x$
Use INTERSECT to solve:

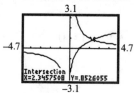

Solution: $(2.35, 0.85)$

65. Let x and y be the two numbers. The system of equations is:
$$\begin{cases} x - y = 2 \\ x^2 + y^2 = 10 \end{cases}$$
Solve the first equation for x, substitute into the second equation and solve:
$$(y+2)^2 + y^2 = 10 \Rightarrow y^2 + 4y + 4 + y^2 = 10$$
$$2y^2 + 4y - 6 = 0 \Rightarrow y^2 + 2y - 3 = 0 \Rightarrow (y+3)(y-1) = 0 \Rightarrow y = -3 \text{ or } y = 1$$
If $y = -3$: $x = -3 + 2 = -1$
If $y = 1$: $x = 1 + 2 = 3$
The two numbers are 1 and 3 or −1 and −3.

67. Let x and y be the two numbers. The system of equations is:
$$\begin{cases} xy = 4 \\ x^2 + y^2 = 8 \end{cases}$$
Solve the first equation for x, substitute into the second equation and solve:
$$\left(\frac{4}{y}\right)^2 + y^2 = 8 \Rightarrow \frac{16}{y^2} + y^2 = 8 \Rightarrow 16 + y^4 = 8y^2$$
$$y^4 - 8y^2 + 16 = 0 \Rightarrow (y^2 - 4)^2 = 0 \Rightarrow y^2 - 4 = 0 \Rightarrow y^2 = 4 \Rightarrow y = \pm 2$$
If $y = 2$: $x = \frac{4}{2} = 2$
If $y = -2$: $x = \frac{4}{-2} = -2$
The two numbers are 2 and 2 or −2 and −2.

69. Let x and y be the two numbers. The system of equations is:
$$\begin{cases} x - y = xy \\ \frac{1}{x} + \frac{1}{y} = 5 \end{cases}$$
Solve the first equation for x, substitute into the second equation and solve:
$$x - xy = y$$
$$x(1-y) = y \Rightarrow x = \frac{y}{1-y}$$

482

$$\frac{1}{\left(\dfrac{y}{1-y}\right)} + \frac{1}{y} = 5 \Rightarrow \frac{1-y}{y} + \frac{1}{y} = 5 \Rightarrow \frac{2-y}{y} = 5 \Rightarrow 2 - y = 5y \Rightarrow 6y = 2 \Rightarrow y = \frac{1}{3}$$

If $y = \dfrac{1}{3}$: $x = \dfrac{(1/3)}{\left(1-\dfrac{1}{3}\right)} = \dfrac{(1/3)}{(2/3)} = \dfrac{1}{2}$ $\therefore$ The two numbers are $\dfrac{1}{2}$ and $\dfrac{1}{3}$.

71. $\begin{cases} \dfrac{a}{b} = \dfrac{2}{3} \\ a + b = 10 \end{cases}$

Solve the second equation for a, substitute into the first equation and solve:

$$\frac{10-b}{b} = \frac{2}{3} \rightarrow 3(10-b) = 2b \Rightarrow 30 - 3b = 2b \Rightarrow 30 = 5b \Rightarrow b = 6 \Rightarrow a = 4$$

$a + b = 10;\ \ b - a = 2$ $\therefore$ The ratio of $a + b$ to $b - a$ is $\dfrac{10}{2} = 5$.

73. Let x = the width of the rectangle.
Let y = the length of the rectangle.

$\begin{cases} 2x + 2y = 16 \\ \quad\ xy = 15 \end{cases}$

Solve the first equation for y, substitute into the second equation and solve:

$$2x + 2y = 16 \Rightarrow 2y = 16 - 2x \Rightarrow y = 8 - x$$

$$x(8-x) = 15 \Rightarrow 8x - x^2 = 15 \Rightarrow x^2 - 8x + 15 = 0 \Rightarrow (x-5)(x-3) = 0$$

$$x = 5 \ \text{ or } \ x = 3$$

$$y = 3 \qquad y = 5$$

The dimensions of the rectangle are 3 inches by 5 inches.

75. Let x = the radius of the first circle.
Let y = the radius of the second circle.

$\begin{cases} 2\pi x + 2\pi y = 12\pi \\ \pi x^2 + \pi y^2 = 20\pi \end{cases}$

Solve the first equation for y, substitute into the second equation and solve:

$$\begin{aligned} 2\pi x + 2\pi y &= 12\pi \\ x + y &= 6 \\ y &= 6 - x \end{aligned} \qquad\qquad \begin{aligned} \pi x^2 + \pi y^2 &= 20\pi \\ x^2 + y^2 &= 20 \\ x^2 + (6-x)^2 &= 20 \end{aligned}$$

$$x^2 + 36 - 12x + x^2 = 20 \Rightarrow 2x^2 - 12x + 16 = 0$$

$$x^2 - 6x + 8 = 0 \Rightarrow (x-4)(x-2) = 0$$

$$x = 4 \ \text{ or } \ x = 2$$

$$y = 2 \qquad y = 4$$

The radii of the circles are 2 centimeters and 4 centimeters.

77.   The tortoise takes $9 + 3 = 12$ minutes or 0.2 hour longer to complete the race than the hare.
Let r = the rate of the hare.
Let t = the time for the hare to complete the race.
Then $t + 0.2$ = the time for the tortoise and $r - 0.5$ = the rate for the tortoise.
Since the length of the race is 21 meters, the distance equations are:
$$\begin{cases} rt = 21 \\ (r - 0.5)(t + 0.2) = 21 \end{cases}$$
Solve the first equation for r, substitute into the second equation and solve:
$$\left(\frac{21}{t} - 0.5\right)(t + 0.2) = 21 \Rightarrow 21 + \frac{4.2}{t} - 0.5t - 0.1 = 21$$

$$10t \cdot \left(21 + \frac{4.2}{t} - 0.5t - 0.1\right) = 10t \cdot (21)$$

$$210t + 42 - 5t^2 - t = 210t \Rightarrow 5t^2 + t - 42 = 0 \Rightarrow (5t - 14)(t + 3) = 0$$

$$t = \frac{14}{5} = 2.8 \ \text{ or } \ t = -3$$

$t = -3$ makes no sense, since time cannot be negative.
Solve for r:
$$r = \frac{21}{2.8} = 7.5$$
The average speed of the hare is 7.5 meters per hour, and the average speed for the tortoise is 7 meters per hour.

79.   Let x = the width of the cardboard. Let y = the length of the cardboard.
The width of the box will be $x - 4$, the length of the box will be $y - 4$, and the height is 2.
The volume is $V = (x - 4)(y - 4)(2)$.
Solve the system of equations:
$$\begin{cases} xy = 216 \\ 2(x - 4)(y - 4) = 224 \end{cases}$$
Solve the first equation for y, substitute into the second equation and solve:
$$(2x - 8)\left(\frac{216}{x} - 4\right) = 224 \Rightarrow 432 - 8x - \frac{1728}{x} + 32 = 224$$

$$432x - 8x^2 - 1728 + 32x = 224x \Rightarrow -8x^2 + 240x - 1728 = 0$$

$$x^2 - 30x + 216 = 0 \Rightarrow (x - 12)(x - 18) = 0$$

$$x = 12 \ \text{ or } \ x = 18$$

$$y = 18 \qquad y = 12$$

The cardboard should be 12 centimeters by 18 centimeters.

81. Find equations relating area and perimeter:
$$\begin{cases} x^2 + y^2 = 4500 \\ 3x + 3y + (x - y) = 300 \end{cases}$$
Solve the second equation for y, substitute into the first equation and solve:

$$4x + 2y = 300 \qquad\qquad x^2 + (150 - 2x)^2 = 4500$$
$$2y = 300 - 4x \qquad x^2 + 22500 - 600x + 4x^2 = 4500$$
$$y = 150 - 2x \qquad\qquad 5x^2 - 600x + 18000 = 0$$
$$x^2 - 120x + 3600 = 0$$
$$(x - 60)^2 = 0$$
$$x - 60 = 0$$
$$x = 60$$
$$y = 150 - 2(60) = 30$$

The sides of the squares are 30 feet and 60 feet.

83. Solve the system for l and w:
$$\begin{cases} 2l + 2w = P \\ lw = A \end{cases}$$
Solve the first equation for l, substitute into the second equation and solve:

$$2l = P - 2w \implies l = \frac{P}{2} - w$$

$$\left(\frac{P}{2} - w\right)w = A \implies \frac{P}{2}w - w^2 = A \implies w^2 - \frac{P}{2}w + A = 0$$

$$w = \frac{\left(\frac{P}{2} \pm \sqrt{\frac{P^2}{4} - 4A}\right)}{2} = \frac{\left(\frac{P}{2} \pm \sqrt{\frac{P^2 - 16A}{4}}\right)}{2} = \frac{\left(\frac{P}{2} \pm \frac{\sqrt{P^2 - 16A}}{2}\right)}{2}$$

$$w = \frac{P \pm \sqrt{P^2 - 16A}}{4}$$

If $w = \dfrac{P + \sqrt{P^2 - 16A}}{4}$ then $l = \dfrac{P}{2} - \dfrac{P + \sqrt{P^2 - 16A}}{4} = \dfrac{P - \sqrt{P^2 - 16A}}{4}$

If $w = \dfrac{P - \sqrt{P^2 - 16A}}{4}$ then $l = \dfrac{P}{2} - \dfrac{P - \sqrt{P^2 - 16A}}{4} = \dfrac{P + \sqrt{P^2 - 16A}}{4}$

If it is required that length be greater than width, then the solution is:

$$w = \frac{P - \sqrt{P^2 - 16A}}{4} \text{ and } l = \frac{P + \sqrt{P^2 - 16A}}{4}$$

85. Solve the equation: $m^2 - 4(2m - 4) = 0$

$$m^2 - 8m + 16 = 0 \implies (m - 4)^2 = 0 \implies m - 4 = 0 \implies m = 4$$

Use the point-slope equation with slope 4 and the point (2, 4) to obtain the equation of the tangent line: $y - 4 = 4(x - 2) \implies y - 4 = 4x - 8 \implies y = 4x - 4$

87. Solve the system:
$$\begin{cases} y = x^2 + 2 \\ y = mx + b \end{cases}$$
Solve the system by substitution:
$$x^2 + 2 = mx + b \Rightarrow x^2 - mx + 2 - b = 0$$
Note that the tangent line passes through (1, 3).
Find the relation between m and b: $3 = m(1) + b \Rightarrow b = 3 - m$
Substitute into the quadratic to eliminate b: $x^2 - mx + 2 - (3 - m) = 0 \Rightarrow x^2 - mx + (m - 1) = 0$
Find when the discriminant is 0:
$$(-m)^2 - 4(1)(m - 1) = 0 \Rightarrow m^2 - 4m + 4 = 0 \Rightarrow (m - 2)^2 = 0$$
$$m - 2 = 0 \Rightarrow m = 2 \Rightarrow b = 3 - 2 = 1$$
The equation of the tangent line is $y = 2x + 1$.

89. Solve the system:
$$\begin{cases} 2x^2 + 3y^2 = 14 \\ \qquad y = mx + b \end{cases}$$
Solve the system by substitution:
$$2x^2 + 3(mx + b)^2 = 14 \Rightarrow 2x^2 + 3m^2x^2 + 6mbx + 3b^2 = 14$$
$$(3m^2 + 2)x^2 + 6mbx + 3b^2 - 14 = 0$$
Note that the tangent line passes through (1, 2). Find the relation between m and b:
$$2 = m(1) + b \rightarrow b = 2 - m$$
Substitute into the quadratic to eliminate b:
$$(3m^2 + 2)x^2 + 6m(2 - m)x + 3(2 - m)^2 - 14 = 0$$
$$(3m^2 + 2)x^2 + (12m - 6m^2)x + 12 - 12m + 3m^2 - 14 = 0$$
$$(3m^2 + 2)x^2 + (12m - 6m^2)x + (3m^2 - 12m - 2) = 0$$
Find when the discriminant is 0:
$$(12m - 6m^2)^2 - 4(3m^2 + 2)(3m^2 - 12m - 2) = 0$$
$$144m^2 - 144m^3 + 36m^4 - 4(9m^4 - 36m^3 - 24m - 4) = 0$$
$$144m^2 - 144m^3 + 36m^4 - 36m^4 + 144m^3 + 96m + 16 = 0$$
$$144m^2 + 96m + 16 = 0$$
$$9m^2 + 6m + 1 = 0$$
$$(3m + 1)^2 = 0$$
$$3m + 1 = 0$$
$$m = -\frac{1}{3} \qquad b = 2 - \left(-\frac{1}{3}\right) = \frac{7}{3}$$
The equation of the tangent line is $y = -\frac{1}{3}x + \frac{7}{3}$.

91. Solve the system:
$$\begin{cases} x^2 - y^2 = 3 \\ \qquad y = mx + b \end{cases}$$
Solve the system by substitution:
$$x^2 - (mx + b)^2 = 3 \Rightarrow x^2 - m^2x^2 - 2mbx - b^2 = 3 \Rightarrow (1 - m^2)x^2 - 2mbx - b^2 - 3 = 0$$

Note that the tangent line passes through $(2, 1)$. Find the relation between m and b:
$$1 = m(2) + b \Rightarrow b = 1 - 2m$$
Substitute into the quadratic to eliminate b:
$$(1 - m^2)x^2 - 2m(1 - 2m)x - (1 - 2m)^2 - 3 = 0$$
$$(1 - m^2)x^2 + (-2m + 4m^2)x - 1 + 4m - 4m^2 - 3 = 0$$
$$(1 - m^2)x^2 + (-2m + 4m^2)x + (-4m^2 + 4m - 4) = 0$$
Find when the discriminant is 0:
$$(-2m + 4m^2)^2 - 4(1 - m^2)(-4m^2 + 4m - 4) = 0$$
$$4m^2 - 16m^3 + 16m^4 - 4(4m^4 - 4m^3 + 4m - 4) = 0$$
$$4m^2 - 16m^3 + 16m^4 - 16m^4 + 16m^3 - 16m + 16 = 0$$
$$4m^2 - 16m + 16 = 0 \Rightarrow m^2 - 4m + 4 = 0$$
$$(m - 2)^2 = 0 \Rightarrow m - 2 = 0 \Rightarrow m = 2 \Rightarrow b = 1 - 2(2) = -3$$
The equation of the tangent line is $y = 2x - 3$.

93. Solve for r_1 and r_2:
$$\begin{cases} r_1 + r_2 = -\dfrac{b}{a} \\ r_1 r_2 = \dfrac{c}{a} \end{cases}$$
Substitute and solve:
$$r_1 = -r_2 - \frac{b}{a} \Rightarrow \left(-r_2 - \frac{b}{a}\right) r_2 = \frac{c}{a} \Rightarrow -r_2{}^2 - \frac{b}{a}r_2 - \frac{c}{a} = 0 \Rightarrow ar_2{}^2 + br_2 + c = 0$$
$$r_2 = \frac{-b \pm \sqrt{b^2 - 4ac}}{2a}$$
$$r_1 = -r_2 - \frac{b}{a} = -\left(\frac{-b \pm \sqrt{b^2 - 4ac}}{2a}\right) - \frac{2b}{2a} = \frac{-b \mp \sqrt{b^2 - 4ac}}{2a}$$
The solutions are: $\dfrac{-b + \sqrt{b^2 - 4ac}}{2a}$ and $\dfrac{-b - \sqrt{b^2 - 4ac}}{2a}$.

95. Since the area of the square piece of sheet metal is 100 square feet, the sheet's dimensions are 10 feet by 10 feet. Let $x =$ the length of the cut.

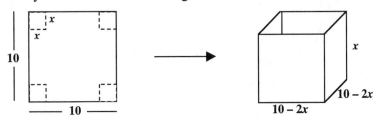

The dimensions of the box are length $= 10 - 2x$; width $= 10 - 2x$; height $= x$
Note that each of these expressions must be positive. So we must have
$$x > 0 \text{ and } 10 - 2x > 0 \Rightarrow x < 5, \text{ that is, } 0 < x < 5.$$

So the volume of the box is given by

$$V = (\text{length}) \cdot (\text{width}) \cdot (\text{height}) = (10-2x)(10-2x)(x) = (10-2x)^2(x)$$

(a) In order to get a volume equal to 9 cubic feet, we solve $(10-2x)^2(x) = 9$.

$$(10-2x)^2(x) = 9 \Rightarrow \left(100 - 40x + 4x^2\right)x = 9 \Rightarrow 100x - 40x^2 + 4x^3 = 9$$

So we need to solve the equation $4x^3 - 40x^2 + 100x - 9 = 0$.

Graphing the function $y_1 = 4x^3 - 40x^2 + 100x - 9$ on a calculator yields the graph

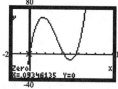 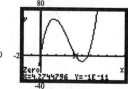 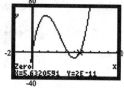

The graph indicates that there three real zeros on the interval [0,6].

Using the ZERO feature of a graphing calculator, we find that the three roots shown occur at $x \approx 0.09$, $x \approx 4.27$ and $x \approx 5.63$.

But we've already noted that we must have $0 < x < 5$, so the only practical values for the cut are $x \approx 0.09$ feet and $x \approx 4.27$ feet.

(b) If the sheet metal has dimensions k feet by k feet, then the volume equation becomes

$$V = (k-2x)(k-2x)(x) = (k-2x)^2(x) = 9$$

Solving for k we get the quadratic equation in the variable k.

$$xk^2 - 4x^2k + 4x^3 - 9 = 0$$

Using the quadratic formula we get:

$$k = \frac{-\left(-4x^2\right) \pm \sqrt{\left(-4x^2\right)^2 - 4(x)\left(4x^3 - 9\right)}}{2x} = \frac{4x^2 \pm \sqrt{16x^4 - 16x^4 + 36x}}{2x}$$

$$= \frac{4x^2 \pm \sqrt{36x}}{2x} = \frac{4x^2 \pm 6\sqrt{x}}{2x}$$

Therefore, we get a real solution for k provided $x > 0$ and $4x^2 \pm 6\sqrt{x} \geq 0$.

$$4x^2 \pm 6\sqrt{x} \geq 0 \Rightarrow 4x^2 \geq 6\sqrt{x} \Rightarrow 16x^4 \geq 36x$$

$$16x^4 - 36x \geq 0 \Rightarrow 4x\left(4x^3 - 9\right) \geq 0$$

This last inequality holds provided $x \geq \sqrt[3]{\dfrac{9}{4}}$.

Systems of Equations and Inequalities

8.7   Systems of Inequalities

1. $x \geq 0$
(a) Graph the line $x = 0$. Use a solid line since the inequality uses $\geq$.
     Choose a test point not on the line, such as $(2, 0)$.
     Since $2 \geq 0$ is true, shade the side of the line containing $(2, 0)$.

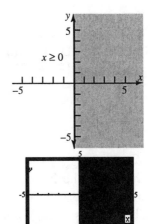

(b) Use the VERTICAL function and the SHADE function in the calculator's DRAW menu:

     Vertical 0

     Shade$(-5,5,0,2)$

3. $x \geq 4$
(a) Graph the line $x = 4$. Use a solid line since the inequality uses $\geq$.
     Choose a test point not on the line, such as $(5, 0)$.
     Since $5 \geq 0$ is true, shade the side of the line containing $(5, 0)$.

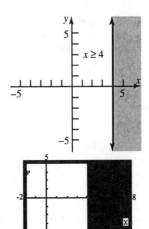

(b) Use the VERTICAL function and the SHADE function in the calculator's DRAW menu:
     Vertical 4

     Shade$(-5,5,4,8)$.

5. $x + y > 1$

(a) Graph the line $x + y = 1$. Use a dotted line since the inequality uses $>$.
     Choose a test point not on the line, such as $(0, 0)$.
     Since $0 + 0 > 1$ is false, shade the opposite side of the line from $(0, 0)$.

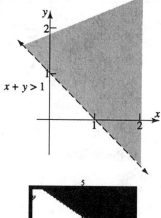

(b) Use the SHADE function in the calculator's DRAW menu: $\text{Shade}(-x + 1, 5)$.

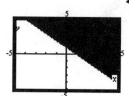

7. $2x + y \geq 6$

(a) Graph the line $2x + y = 6$. Use a solid line since the inequality uses $\geq$.
     Choose a test point not on the line, such as $(0, 0)$.
     Since $2(0) + 0 \geq 6$ is false, shade the opposite side of the line from $(0, 0)$.

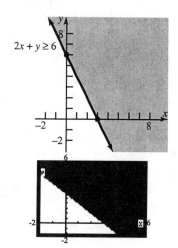

(b) Use the SHADE function in the calculator's DRAW menu: $\text{Shade}(-2x + 6, 6)$.

9. $x^2 + y^2 > 1$

Graph the circle $x^2 + y^2 > 1$. Use a dashed line since the inequality uses $>$.
Choose a test point not on the circle, such as $(0, 0)$.
Since $0^2 + 0^2 > 1$ is false, shade the opposite side of the circle from $(0, 0)$.

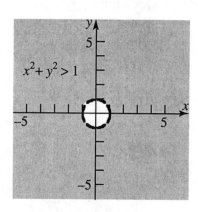

11. $y \le x^2 - 1$

Graph the parabola $y = x^2 - 1$. Use a solid line since the inequality uses $\le$.

Choose a test point not on the parabola, such as $(0, 0)$. Since $0 \le 0^2 - 1$ is false, shade the opposite side of the parabola from $(0, 0)$.

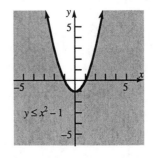

13. $y > |x| - 3$

Graph $y = |x| - 3$. Use a dashed line since the inequality uses $>$.

Choose a test point not on the graph, such as $(0, 0)$. Since $0 > 0 - 3$ is true, shade the same side of the graph as $(0, 0)$.

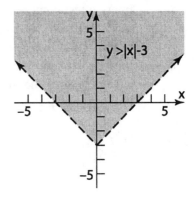

15. $xy \ge 4$

Graph the hyperbola $xy = 4$. Use a solid line since the inequality uses $\ge$.

Choose a test point not on the hyperbola, such as $(0, 0)$. Since $0 \cdot 0 \ge 4$ is false, shade the opposite side of the hyperbola from $(0, 0)$.

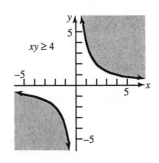

17. $\begin{cases} x + y \le 2 \\ 2x + y \ge 4 \end{cases}$

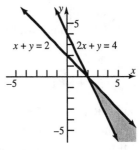

(a) Graph the line $x + y = 2$. Use a solid line since the inequality uses $\le$.
     Choose a test point not on the line, such as $(0, 0)$. Since $0 + 0 \le 2$ is true, shade the side of the line containing $(0, 0)$.

(b) Graph the line $2x + y = 4$. Use a solid line since the inequality uses $\ge$.
     Choose a test point not on the line, such as $(0, 0)$. Since $2(0) + 0 \ge 4$ is false, shade the opposite side of the line from $(0, 0)$.

(c) The overlapping region is the solution.

19. $\begin{cases} 2x - y \le 4 \\ 3x + 2y \ge -6 \end{cases}$

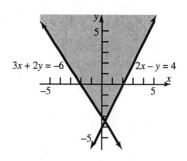

(a) Graph the line $2x - y = 4$. Use a solid line since the inequality uses $\le$.
Choose a test point not on the line, such as $(0, 0)$. Since $2(0) - 0 \le 4$ is true, shade the side of the line containing $(0, 0)$.

(b) Graph the line $3x + 2y = -6$. Use a solid line since the inequality uses $\ge$.
Choose a test point not on the line, such as $(0, 0)$. Since $3(0) + 2(0) \ge -6$ is true, shade the side of the line containing $(0, 0)$.

(c) The overlapping region is the solution.

21. $\begin{cases} 2x - 3y \le 0 \\ 3x + 2y \le 6 \end{cases}$

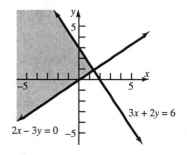

(a) Graph the line $2x - 3y = 0$. Use a solid line since the inequality uses $\le$.
Choose a test point not on the line, such as $(0, 3)$. Since $2(0) - 3(3) \le 0$ is true, shade the side of the line containing $(0, 3)$.

(b) Graph the line $3x + 2y = 6$. Use a solid line since the inequality uses $\le$.
Choose a test point not on the line, such as $(0, 0)$. Since $3(0) + 2(0) \le 6$ is true, shade the side of the line containing $(0, 0)$.

(c) The overlapping region is the solution.

23. $\begin{cases} x^2 + y^2 \le 9 \\ x + y \ge 3 \end{cases}$

(a) Graph the circle $x^2 + y^2 = 9$. Use a solid line since the inequality uses $\ge$. Choose a test point not on the circle, such as $(0, 0)$.
Since $0^2 + 0^2 \le 9$ is true, shade the same side of the circle as $(0, 0)$.

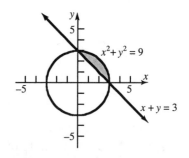

(b) Graph the line $x + y = 3$. Use a solid line since the inequality uses $\ge$. Choose a test point not on the line, such as $(0, 0)$. Since $0 + 0 \ge 3$ is false, shade the opposite side of the line from $(0, 0)$.

(c) The overlapping region is the solution.

25. $\begin{cases} y \geq x^2 - 4 \\ y \leq x - 2 \end{cases}$

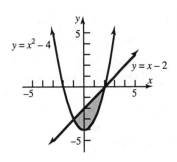

(a) Graph the parabola $y = x^2 - 4$.
Use a solid line since the inequality uses $\geq$. Choose a test point not on the parabola, such as $(0, 0)$. Since $0 \geq 0^2 - 4$ is true, shade the same side of the parabola as $(0, 0)$.

(b) Graph the line $y = x - 2$. Use a solid line since the inequality uses $\leq$. Choose a test point not on the line, such as $(0, 0)$. Since $0 \leq 0 - 2$ is false, shade the opposite side of the line from $(0, 0)$.

(c) The overlapping region is the solution.

27. $\begin{cases} xy \geq 4 \\ y \geq x^2 + 1 \end{cases}$

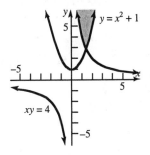

(a) Graph the hyperbola $xy = 4$.
Use a solid line since the inequality uses $\geq$. Choose a test point not on the parabola, such as $(0, 0)$. Since $0 \cdot 0 \geq 4$ is false, shade the opposite side of the hyperbola from $(0, 0)$.

(b) Graph the parabola $y = x^2 + 1$. Use a solid line since the inequality uses $\geq$. Choose a test point not on the parabola, such as $(0, 0)$. Since $0 \geq 0^2 + 1$ is false, shade the opposite side of the parabola from $(0, 0)$.

(c) The overlapping region is the solution.

29. $\begin{cases} x - 2y \leq 6 \\ 2x - 4y \geq 0 \end{cases}$

(a) Graph the line $x - 2y = 6$. Use a solid line since the inequality uses $\leq$. Choose a test point not on the line, such as $(0, 0)$. Since $0 - 2(0) \leq 6$ is true, shade the side of the line containing $(0, 0)$.

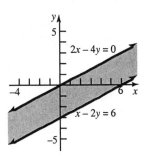

(b)   Graph the line $2x - 4y = 0$. Use a solid line since the inequality uses $\geq$.
Choose a test point not on the line, such as $(0, 2)$. Since $2(0) - 4(2) \geq 0$ is false,
shade the opposite side of the line from $(0, 2)$.

(c)   The overlapping region is the solution.

31. $\begin{cases} 2x + y \geq -2 \\ 2x + y \geq 2 \end{cases}$

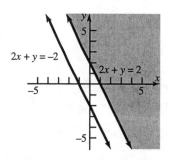

(a)   Graph the line $2x + y = -2$. Use a solid line since the inequality uses $\geq$.
Choose a test point not on the line, such as $(0, 0)$. Since $2(0) + 0 \geq -2$ is true, shade
the side of the line containing $(0, 0)$.

(b)   Graph the line $2x + y = 2$. Use a solid line since the inequality uses $\geq$.
Choose a test point not on the line, such as $(0, 0)$. Since $2(0) + 0 \geq 2$ is false, shade
the opposite side of the line from $(0, 0)$.

(c)   The overlapping region is the solution.

33. $\begin{cases} 2x + 3y \geq 6 \\ 2x + 3y \leq 0 \end{cases}$

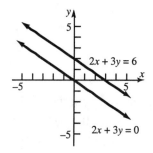

(a)   Graph the line $2x + 3y = 6$. Use a solid line since the inequality uses $\geq$.
Choose a test point not on the line, such as $(0, 0)$. Since $2(0) + 3(0) \geq 6$ is false,
shade the opposite side of the line from $(0, 0)$.

(b)   Graph the line $2x + 3y = 0$. Use a solid line since the inequality uses $\leq$.
Choose a test point not on the line, such as $(0, 2)$. Since $2(0) + 3(2) \leq 0$ is false,
shade the opposite side of the line from $(0, 2)$.

(c)   Since the regions do not overlap, the solution is an empty set.

35.   Graph the system of linear inequalities:

$$\begin{cases} x \geq 0 \\ y \geq 0 \\ 2x + y \leq 6 \\ x + 2y \leq 6 \end{cases}$$

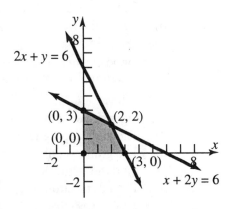

(a)   Graph $x \geq 0$; $y \geq 0$. Shaded region is the first quadrant.

(b)   Graph the line $2x + y = 6$. Use a solid line since the inequality uses $\leq$.
       Choose a test point not on the line, such as $(0, 0)$. Since $2(0) + 0 \leq 6$ is true, shade the side of the line containing $(0, 0)$.

(c)   Graph the line $x + 2y = 6$. Use a solid line since the inequality uses $\leq$.
       Choose a test point not on the line, such as $(0, 0)$. Since $0 + 2(0) \leq 6$ is true, shade the side of the line containing $(0, 0)$.

(d)   The overlapping region is the solution.

(e)   The graph is bounded.

(f)   Find the vertices:
       The x-axis and y-axis intersect at $(0, 0)$.
       The intersection of $x + 2y = 6$ and the y-axis is $(0, 3)$.
       The intersection of $2x + y = 6$ and the x-axis is $(3, 0)$.
       To find the intersection of $x + 2y = 6$ and $2x + y = 6$, solve the system:

$$\begin{cases} x + 2y = 6 \implies x = 6 - 2y \\ 2x + y = 6 \end{cases}$$

Substitute and solve:

$$2(6 - 2y) + y = 6 \implies 12 - 4y + y = 6 \implies -3y = -6 \implies y = 2$$
$$x = 6 - 2(2) = 6 - 4 = 2$$

The point of intersection is $(2, 2)$.
The four corner points are $(0, 0)$, $(0, 3)$, $(3, 0)$, and $(2, 2$

37.   Graph the system of linear inequalities:

$$\begin{cases} x \geq 0 \\ y \geq 0 \\ x + y \geq 2 \\ 2x + y \geq 4 \end{cases}$$

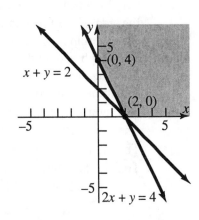

(a)   Graph $x \geq 0$; $y \geq 0$. Shaded region is the first quadrant.

(b)   Graph the line $x + y = 2$. Use a solid line since the inequality uses $\geq$.
      Choose a test point not on the line, such as $(0, 0)$. Since $0 + 0 \geq 2$ is false, shade the opposite side of the line from $(0, 0)$.

(c)   Graph the line $2x + y = 4$. Use a solid line since the inequality uses $\geq$.
      Choose a test point not on the line, such as $(0, 0)$. Since $2(0) + 0 \geq 4$ is false, shade the opposite side of the line from $(0, 0)$.

(d)   The overlapping region is the solution.

(e)   The graph is unbounded.

(f)   Find the vertices:
      The intersection of $x + y = 2$ and the x-axis is $(2, 0)$.
      The intersection of $2x + y = 4$ and the y-axis is $(0, 4)$.
      The two corner points are $(2, 0)$, and $(0, 4)$.

39.   Graph the system of linear inequalities:

$$\begin{cases} x \geq 0 \\ y \geq 0 \\ x + y \geq 2 \\ 2x + 3y \leq 12 \\ 3x + y \leq 12 \end{cases}$$

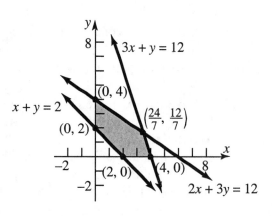

(a)   Graph $x \geq 0$; $y \geq 0$. Shaded region is the first quadrant.

(b)   Graph the line $x + y = 2$. Use a solid line since the inequality uses $\geq$.
      Choose a test point not on the line, such as $(0, 0)$. Since $0 + 0 \geq 2$ is false, shade the opposite side of the line from $(0, 0)$.

(c)   Graph the line $2x + 3y = 12$. Use a solid line since the inequality uses $\leq$.
      Choose a test point not on the line, such as $(0, 0)$. Since $2(0) + 3(0) \leq 12$ is true, shade the side of the line containing $(0, 0)$.

(d)   Graph the line $3x + y = 12$. Use a solid line since the inequality uses $\leq$.
      Choose a test point not on the line, such as $(0, 0)$. Since $3(0) + 0 \leq 12$ is true, shade the side of the line containing $(0, 0)$.

(e)   The overlapping region is the solution.

(f)   The graph is bounded.

(g)   Find the vertices:
      The intersection of $x + y = 2$ and the y-axis is $(0, 2)$.
      The intersection of $x + y = 2$ and the x-axis is $(2, 0)$.
      The intersection of $2x + 3y = 12$ and the y-axis is $(0, 4)$.
      The intersection of $3x + y = 12$ and the x-axis is $(4, 0)$.
      To find the intersection of $2x + 3y = 12$ and $3x + y = 12$, solve the system:
$$\begin{cases} 2x + 3y = 12 \\ 3x + y = 12 \implies y = 12 - 3x \end{cases}$$

Substitute and solve:
$$2x + 3(12 - 3x) = 12 \rightarrow 2x + 36 - 9x = 12$$

$$-7x = -24 \Rightarrow x = \frac{24}{7}$$

$$y = 12 - 3\left(\frac{24}{7}\right) = 12 - \frac{72}{2} = \frac{12}{7}$$

The point of intersection is $\left(\dfrac{24}{7}, \dfrac{12}{7}\right)$.

The five corner points are $(0, 2)$, $(0, 4)$, $(2, 0)$, $(4, 0)$, and $\left(\dfrac{24}{7}, \dfrac{12}{7}\right)$.

41. Graph the system of linear inequalities:

$$\begin{cases} x \geq 0 \\ y \geq 0 \\ x + y \geq 2 \\ x + y \leq 8 \\ 2x + y \leq 10 \end{cases}$$

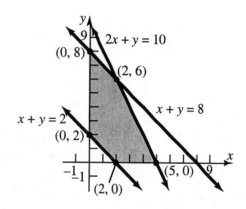

(a) Graph $x \geq 0$; $y \geq 0$. Shaded region is the first quadrant.
(b) Graph the line $x + y = 2$. Use a solid line since the inequality uses $\geq$.
     Choose a test point not on the line, such as $(0, 0)$. Since $0 + 0 \geq 2$ is false, shade the
     opposite side of the line from $(0, 0)$.
(c) Graph the line $x + y = 8$. Use a solid line since the inequality uses $\leq$.
     Choose a test point not on the line, such as $(0, 0)$. Since $0 + 0 \leq 8$ is true, shade the side
     of the line containing $(0, 0)$.
(d) Graph the line $2x + y = 10$. Use a solid line since the inequality uses $\leq$.
     Choose a test point not on the line, such as $(0, 0)$. Since $2(0) + 0 \leq 10$ is true, shade
     the side of the line containing $(0, 0)$.
(e) The overlapping region is the solution.
(f) The graph is bounded.
(g) Find the vertices:
     The intersection of $x + y = 2$ and the y-axis is $(0, 2)$.
     The intersection of $x + y = 2$ and the x-axis is $(2, 0)$.
     The intersection of $x + y = 8$ and the y-axis is $(0, 8)$.
     The intersection of $2x + y = 10$ and the x-axis is $(5, 0)$.
     To find the intersection of $x + y = 8$ and $2x + y = 10$, solve the system:
     $$\begin{cases} x + y = 8 \quad \Rightarrow \quad y = 8 - x \\ 2x + y = 10 \end{cases}$$

Substitute and solve:
$$2x + 8 - x = 10 \Rightarrow x = 2$$
$$y = 8 - 2 = 6$$
The point of intersection is (2, 6).
The five corner points are (0, 2), (0, 8), (2, 0), (5, 0), and (2, 6).

43.   Graph the system of linear inequalities:

$$\begin{cases} x \geq 0 \\ y \geq 0 \\ x + 2y \geq 1 \\ x + 2y \leq 10 \end{cases}$$

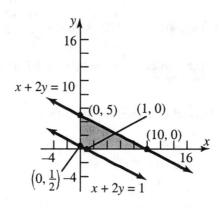

(a)   Graph $x \geq 0$; $y \geq 0$. Shaded region is the first quadrant.

(b)   Graph the line $x + 2y = 1$. Use a solid line since the inequality uses $\geq$.
Choose a test point not on the line, such as (0, 0). Since $0 + 2(0) \geq 1$ is false, shade the opposite side of the line from (0, 0).

(c)   Graph the line $x + 2y = 10$. Use a solid line since the inequality uses $\leq$.
Choose a test point not on the line, such as (0, 0). Since $0 + 2(0) \leq 10$ is true, shade the side of the line containing (0, 0).

(d)   The overlapping region is the solution.

(e)   The graph is bounded.

(f)   Find the vertices:
The intersection of $x + 2y = 1$ and the y-axis is (0, 0.5).
The intersection of $x + 2y = 1$ and the x-axis is (1, 0).
The intersection of $x + 2y = 10$ and the y-axis is (0, 5).
The intersection of $x + 2y = 10$ and the x-axis is (10, 0).
The four corner points are (0, 0.5), (0, 5), (1, 0), and (10, 0).

45.   The system of linear inequalities is:

$$\begin{cases} x \geq 0 \\ y \geq 0 \\ x \leq 4 \\ x + y \leq 6 \end{cases}$$

47.   The system of linear inequalities is:

$$\begin{cases} x \geq 0 \\ y \geq 15 \\ x \leq 20 \\ x + y \leq 50 \\ x - y \leq 0 \end{cases}$$

49. (a) Let x = the amount invested in Treasury bills.
         Let y = the amount invested in corporate bonds.
     The constraints are:

$x \geq 0, y \geq 0$	A non-negative amount must be invested.
$x + y \leq 50000$	Total investment cannot exceed \$50,000.
$y \leq 10000$	Amount invested in corporate bonds must not exceed \$10,000.
$x \geq 35000$	Amount invested in Treasury bills must be at least \$35,000.
$x > y$	Amount invested in Treasury bills must be greater than the amount invested in corporate bonds.

     (b) Graph the system.

$$\begin{cases} x \geq 0 \\ y \geq 0 \\ x + y \leq 50000 \\ y \leq 10000 \\ x \geq 35000 \\ x > y \end{cases}$$

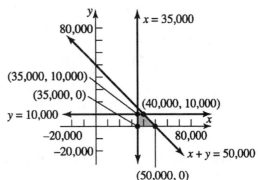

The corner points are (35000, 0), (35000, 10000), (40000, 10000), (50000, 0).

51. (a) Let x = the # of packages of the economy blend.
         Let y = the # of packages of the superior blend.
     The constraints are:

$x \geq 0, y \geq 0$	A non-negative # of packages must be produced.
$4x + 8y \leq 75 \cdot 16$	Total amount of grade A coffee cannot exceed 75 pounds. (Note: 75 pounds = (75)(16) ounces.)
$12x + 8y \leq 120 \cdot 16$	Total amount of grade B coffee cannot exceed 120 pounds. (Note: 120 pounds = (120)(16) ounces.)

     We can simplify the equations

$$4x + 8y \leq 75 \cdot 16 \qquad\qquad 12x + 8y \leq 120 \cdot 16$$
$$x + 2y \leq 75 \cdot 4 \qquad\qquad 3x + 2y \leq 120 \cdot 4$$
$$x + 2y \leq 300 \qquad\qquad 3x + 2y \leq 480$$

     (b) Graph the system.

$$\begin{cases} x \geq 0 \\ y \geq 0 \\ x + 2y \leq 300 \\ 3x + 2y \leq 480 \end{cases}$$

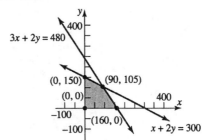

The corner points are (0, 0), (0, 150), (90, 105), (160, 0).

53.   (a)   Let x = the # of microwaves.
            Let y = the # of printers.
      The constraints are:

$x \geq 0, y \geq 0$	A non-negative # of items must be shipped.
$30x + 20y \leq 1600$	Total cargo weight cannot exceed 1600 pounds.
$2x + 3y \leq 150$	Total cargo volume cannot exceed 150 cubic feet.

      Note: $30x + 20y \leq 1600 \Rightarrow 3x + 2y \leq 160$

      (b)   Graph the system.

$$\begin{cases} x \geq 0 \\ y \geq 0 \\ 3x + 2y \leq 160 \\ 2x + 3y \leq 150 \end{cases}$$

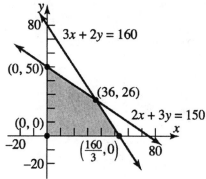

The corner points are $(0, 0)$, $(0, 50)$, $(36, 26)$, $(160/3, 0)$.

Systems of Equations and Inequalities

8.8   Linear Programming

1. $z = x + y$

Vertex	Value of $z = x + y$
(0, 3)	$z = 0 + 3 = 3$
(0, 6)	$z = 0 + 6 = 6$
(5, 6)	$z = 5 + 6 = 11$
(5, 2)	$z = 5 + 2 = 7$
(4, 0)	$z = 4 + 0 = 4$

The maximum value is 11 at (5, 6), and the minimum value is 3 at (0, 3).

3. $z = x + 10y$

Vertex	Value of $z = x + 10y$
(0, 3)	$z = 0 + 10(3) = 30$
(0, 6)	$z = 0 + 10(6) = 60$
(5, 6)	$z = 5 + 10(6) = 65$
(5, 2)	$z = 5 + 10(2) = 25$
(4, 0)	$z = 4 + 10(0) = 4$

The maximum value is 65 at (5, 6), and the minimum value is 4 at (4, 0).

5. $z = 5x + 7y$

Vertex	Value of $z = 5x + 7y$
(0, 3)	$z = 5(0) + 7(3) = 21$
(0, 6)	$z = 5(0) + 7(6) = 42$
(5, 6)	$z = 5(5) + 7(6) = 67$
(5, 2)	$z = 5(5) + 7(2) = 39$
(4, 0)	$z = 5(4) + 7(0) = 20$

The maximum value is 67 at (5, 6), and the minimum value is 20 at (4, 0).

7.   Maximize $z = 2x + y$
     Subject to $x \geq 0$, $y \geq 0$, $x + y \leq 6$, $x + y \geq 1$
     Graph the constraints.

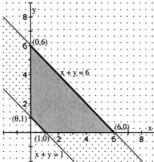

The corner points are $(0, 1)$, $(1, 0)$, $(0, 6)$, $(6, 0)$.
Evaluate the objective function:

Vertex	Value of $z = 2x + y$
$(0, 1)$	$z = 2(0) + 1 = 1$
$(0, 6)$	$z = 2(0) + 6 = 6$
$(1, 0)$	$z = 2(1) + 0 = 2$
$(6, 0)$	$z = 2(6) + 0 = 12$

The maximum value is 12 at $(6, 0)$.

9.   Minimize $z = 2x + 5y$
     Subject to $x \geq 0$, $y \geq 0$, $x + y \geq 2$, $x \leq 5$, $y \leq 3$
     Graph the constraints.

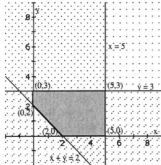

The corner points are $(0, 2)$, $(2, 0)$, $(0, 3)$, $(5, 0)$, $(5, 3)$.
Evaluate the objective function:

Vertex	Value of $z = 2x + 5y$
$(0, 2)$	$z = 2(0) + 5(2) = 10$
$(0, 3)$	$z = 2(0) + 5(3) = 15$
$(2, 0)$	$z = 2(2) + 5(0) = 4$
$(5, 0)$	$z = 2(5) + 5(0) = 10$
$(5, 3)$	$z = 2(5) + 5(3) = 25$

The minimum value is 4 at $(2, 0)$.

11. Maximize $z = 3x + 5y$

Subject to $x \geq 0$, $y \geq 0$, $x + y \geq 2$, $2x + 3y \leq 12$, $3x + 2y \leq 12$

Graph the constraints.

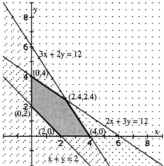

To find the intersection of $2x + 3y = 12$ and $3x + 2y = 12$, solve the system:

$$\begin{cases} 2x + 3y = 12 \\ 3x + 2y = 12 \implies y = 6 - \dfrac{3}{2}x \end{cases}$$

Substitute and solve:

$$2x + 3\left(6 - \frac{3}{2}x\right) = 12 \implies 2x + 18 - \frac{9}{2}x = 12 \implies -\frac{5}{2}x = -6$$

$$x = \frac{12}{5} \implies y = 6 - \frac{3}{2}\left(\frac{12}{5}\right) = 6 - \frac{18}{5} = \frac{12}{5}$$

The point of intersection is $(2.4, 2.4)$.

The corner points are (0, 2), (2, 0), (0, 4), (4, 0), (2.4, 2.4).

Evaluate the objective function:

Vertex	Value of $z = 3x + 5y$
(0, 2)	z = 3(0) + 5(2) = 10
(0, 4)	z = 3(0) + 5(4) = 20
(2, 0)	z = 3(2) + 5(0) = 6
(4, 0)	z = 3(4) + 5(0) = 12
(2.4, 2.4)	z = 3(2.4) + 5(2.4) = 19.2

The maximum value is 20 at (0, 4).

13. Minimize $z = 5x + 4y$

Subject to $x \geq 0$, $y \geq 0$, $x + y \geq 2$, $2x + 3y \leq 12$, $3x + y \leq 12$

Graph the constraints.

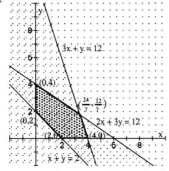

To find the intersection of $2x + 3y = 12$ and $3x + y = 12$, solve the system:

$$\begin{cases} 2x + 3y = 12 \\ 3x + y = 12 \end{cases} \Rightarrow \quad y = 12 - 3x$$

Substitute and solve:

$$2x + 3(12 - 3x) = 12 \Rightarrow 2x + 36 - 9x = 12 \Rightarrow -7x = -24 \Rightarrow x = \frac{24}{7}$$

$$y = 12 - 3\left(\frac{24}{7}\right) = 12 - \frac{72}{7} = \frac{12}{7}$$

The point of intersection is $\left(24/7, 12/7\right)$.

The corner points are $(0, 2)$, $(2, 0)$, $(0, 4)$, $(4, 0)$, $\left(24/7, 12/7\right)$.

Evaluate the objective function:

Vertex	Value of $z = 5x + 4y$
$(0, 2)$	$z = 5(0) + 4(2) = 8$
$(0, 4)$	$z = 5(0) + 4(4) = 16$
$(2, 0)$	$z = 5(2) + 4(0) = 10$
$(4, 0)$	$z = 5(4) + 4(0) = 20$
$\left(\dfrac{24}{7}, \dfrac{12}{7}\right)$	$z = 5\left(\dfrac{24}{7}\right) + 4\left(\dfrac{12}{7}\right) = \dfrac{120}{7} + \dfrac{48}{7} = \dfrac{168}{7} = 24$

The minimum value is 8 at $(0, 2)$.

15. Maximize $z = 5x + 2y$

Subject to $x \geq 0$, $y \geq 0$, $x + y \leq 10$, $2x + y \geq 10$, $x + 2y \geq 10$

Graph the constraints.

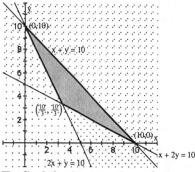

To find the intersection of $2x + y = 10$ and $x + 2y = 10$, solve the system:

$$\begin{cases} 2x + y = 10 \\ x + 2y = 10 \end{cases} \Rightarrow \quad y = 10 - 2x$$

Substitute and solve:

$$x + 2(10 - 2x) = 10 \Rightarrow x + 20 - 4x = 10 \Rightarrow -3x = -10 \Rightarrow x = \frac{10}{3}$$

$$y = 10 - 2\left(\frac{10}{3}\right) = 10 - \frac{20}{3} = \frac{10}{3}$$

The point of intersection is $\left(10/3, 10/3\right)$.

The corner points are $(0, 10)$, $(10, 0)$, $\left(10/3, 10/3\right)$.

Evaluate the objective function:

Vertex	Value of $z = 5x + 2y$
(0, 10)	$z = 5(0) + 2(10) = 20$
(10, 0)	$z = 5(10) + 2(0) = 50$
$\left(\dfrac{10}{3}, \dfrac{10}{3}\right)$	$z = 5\left(\dfrac{10}{3}\right) + 2\left(\dfrac{10}{3}\right) = \dfrac{50}{3} + \dfrac{20}{3} = \dfrac{70}{3} = 23\frac{1}{3}$

The maximum value is 50 at (10, 0).

17. Let $x =$ the number of downhill skis produced.
Let $y =$ the number of cross-country skis produced.
The total profit is: $P = 70x + 50y$. Profit is to be maximized; thus, this is the objective function.
The constraints are:

$\quad x \geq 0, \; y \geq 0$ A positive number of skis must be produced.
$\quad 2x + y \leq 40$ Only 40 hours of manufacturing time is available.
$\quad x + y \leq 32$ Only 32 hours of finishing time is available.

Graph the constraints.

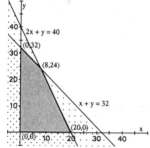

To find the intersection of $x + y = 32$ and $2x + y = 40$, solve the system:
$$\begin{cases} x + y = 32 & \Rightarrow \quad y = 32 - x \\ 2x + y = 40 \end{cases}$$

Substitute and solve:
$$2x + 32 - x = 40 \Rightarrow x = 8 \Rightarrow y = 32 - 8 = 24$$

The point of intersection is (8, 24).
The corner points are (0, 0), (0, 32), (20, 0), (8, 24).
Evaluate the objective function:

Vertex	Value of $P = 70x + 50y$
(0, 0)	$P = 70(0) + 50(0) = 0$
(0, 32)	$P = 70(0) + 50(32) = 1600$
(20, 0)	$P = 70(20) + 50(0) = 1400$
(8, 24)	$P = 70(8) + 50(24) = 1760$

The maximum profit is $1760, when 8 downhill skis and 24 cross-country skis are produced.
With the increase of the manufacturing time to 48 hours, we do the following:
The constraints are:

$\quad x \geq 0, \; y \geq 0$ A positive number of skis must be produced.
$\quad 2x + y \leq 48$ Only 48 hours of manufacturing time is available.
$\quad x + y \leq 32$ Only 32 hours of finishing time is available.

Graph the constraints.

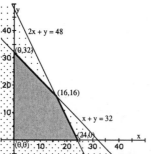

To find the intersection of $x + y = 32$ and $2x + y = 48$, solve the system:

$$\begin{cases} x + y = 32 & \Rightarrow & y = 32 - x \\ 2x + y = 48 \end{cases}$$

Substitute and solve:

$$2x + 32 - x = 48 \Rightarrow x = 16 \Rightarrow y = 32 - 16 = 16$$

The point of intersection is (16, 16).

The corner points are (0, 0), (0, 32), (24, 0), (16, 16).

Evaluate the objective function:

Vertex	Value of $P = 70x + 50y$
(0, 0)	P = 70(0) + 50(0) = 0
(0, 32)	P = 70(0) + 50(32) = 1600
(24, 0)	P = 70(24) + 50(0) = 1680
(16, 16)	P = 70(16) + 50(16) = 1920

The maximum profit is $1920, when 16 downhill skis and 16 cross-country skis are produced.

19.　Let x = the number of acres of corn planted.

Let y = the number of acres of soybeans planted.

The total profit is: $P = 250x + 200y$. Profit is to be maximized; thus, this is the objective function.

The constraints are:

$x \geq 0, \ y \geq 0$	A non-negative number of acres must be planted.
$x + y \leq 100$	Acres available to plant.
$60x + 40y \leq 1800$	Money available for cultivation costs.
$60x + 60y \leq 2400$	Money available for labor costs.

Graph the constraints.

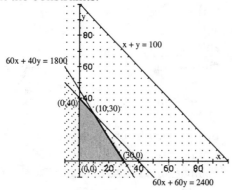

To find the intersection of $60x + 40y = 1800$ and $60x + 60y = 2400$, solve the system:

$$\begin{cases} 60x + 40y = 1800 & \Rightarrow \quad 60x = 1800 - 40y \\ 60x + 60y = 2400 \end{cases}$$

Substitute and solve:

$$1800 - 40y + 60y = 2400 \Rightarrow 20y = 600 \Rightarrow y = 30$$

$$60x = 1800 - 40(30) \Rightarrow 60x = 600 \Rightarrow x = 10$$

The point of intersection is (10, 30).

The corner points are (0, 0), (0, 40), (30, 0), (10, 30).

Evaluate the objective function:

Vertex	Value of $P = 250x + 200y$
(0, 0)	P = 250(0) + 200(0) = 0
(0, 40)	P = 250(0) + 200(40) = 8000
(30, 0)	P = 250(30) + 200(0) = 7500
(10, 30)	P = 250(10) + 200(30) = 8500

The maximum profit is $8500, when 10 acres of corn and 30 acres of soybeans are planted.

21. Let x = the number of hours that machine 1 is operated.

Let y = the number of hours that machine 2 is operated.

The total cost is: $C = 50x + 30y$. Cost is to be minimized; thus, this is the objective function.

The constraints are:

$x \geq 0, \ y \geq 0$ A positive number of hours must be used.

$x \leq 10$ 10 hours available on machine 1.

$y \leq 10$ 10 hours available on machine 2.

$60x + 40y \geq 240$ At least 240 8-inch pliers must be produced.

$70x + 20y \geq 140$ At least 140 6-inch pliers must be produced.

Graph the constraints.

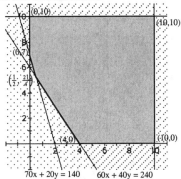

To find the intersection of $60x + 40y = 240$ and $70x + 20y = 140$, solve the system:

$$\begin{cases} 60x + 40y = 240 \\ 70x + 20y = 140 & \Rightarrow \quad 20y = 140 - 70x \end{cases}$$

Substitute and solve:
$$60x + 2(140 - 70x) = 240 \Rightarrow 60x + 280 - 140x = 240$$
$$-80x = -40 \Rightarrow x = 0.5$$
$$20y = 140 - 70(0.5) \Rightarrow 20y = 105 \Rightarrow y = 5.25$$
The point of intersection is $(0.5, 5.25)$.

The corner points are $(0, 7)$, $(0, 10)$, $(4, 0)$, $(10, 0)$, $(10, 10)$, $(0.5, 5.25)$.

Evaluate the objective function:

Vertex	Value of $C = 50x + 30y$
$(0, 7)$	$C = 50(0) + 30(7) = 210$
$(0, 10)$	$C = 50(0) + 30(10) = 300$
$(4, 0)$	$C = 50(4) + 30(0) = 200$
$(10, 0)$	$C = 50(10) + 30(0) = 500$
$(10, 10)$	$C = 50(10) + 30(10) = 800$
$(0.5, 5.25)$	$C = 50(0.5) + 30(5.25) = 182.50$

The minimum cost is $182.50, when machine 1 is used for 0.5 hours and machine 2 is used for 5.25 hours.

23.   Let x = the number of pounds of ground beef.
Let y = the number of pounds of ground pork.
The total cost is: $C = 0.75x + 0.45y$. Cost is to be minimized; thus, this is the objective function.

The constraints are:

$x \geq 0, \ y \geq 0$ A positive number of pounds must be used.

$x \leq 200$ Only 200 pounds of ground beef are available.

$y \geq 50$ At least 50 pounds of ground pork must be used.

$0.75x + 0.60y \geq 0.70(x + y) \Rightarrow 0.05x \geq 0.10y$ Leanness condition to be met.

Graph the constraints.

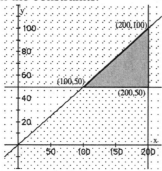

The corner points are $(100, 50)$, $(200, 50)$, $(200, 100)$.

Evaluate the objective function:

Vertex	Value of $C = 0.75x + 0.45y$
$(100, 50)$	$C = 0.75(100) + 0.45(50) = 97.50$
$(200, 50)$	$C = 0.75(200) + 0.45(50) = 172.50$
$(200, 100)$	$C = 0.75(200) + 0.45(100) = 195.00$

The minimum cost is $97.50, when 100 pounds of ground beef and 50 pounds of ground pork are used.

25. Let x = the number of racing skates manufactured.
Let y = the number of figure skates manufactured.
The total profit is: $P = 10x + 12y$. Profit is to be maximized; thus, this is the objective function.
The constraints are:

$x \geq 0, \; y \geq 0$ A positive number of skates must be manufactured.
$6x + 4y \leq 120$ Only 120 hours are available for fabrication.
$x + 2y \leq 40$ Only 40 hours are available for finishing.

Graph the constraints.

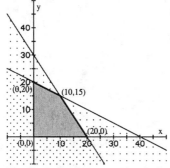

To find the intersection of $6x + 4y = 120$ and $x + 2y = 40$, solve the system:

$$\begin{cases} 6x + 4y = 120 \\ x + 2y = \; 40 \; \Rightarrow \; x = 40 - 2y \end{cases}$$

Substitute and solve:

$$6(40 - 2y) + 4y = 120 \Rightarrow 240 - 12y + 4y = 120$$
$$-8y = -120 \Rightarrow y = 15 \Rightarrow x = 40 - 2(15) = 10$$

The point of intersection is (10, 15).
The corner points are (0, 0), (0, 20), (20, 0), (10, 15).
Evaluate the objective function:

Vertex	Value of $P = 10x + 12y$
(0, 0)	P = 10(0) + 12(0) = 0
(0, 20)	P = 10(0) + 12(20) = 240
(20, 0)	P = 10(20) + 12(0) = 200
(10, 15)	P = 10(10) + 12(15) = 280

The maximum profit is $280, when 10 racing skates and 15 figure skates are produced.

27. Let x = the number of metal fasteners.
Let y = the number of plastic fasteners.
The total cost is: $C = 9x + 4y$. Cost is to be minimized; thus, this is the objective function.
The constraints are:

$x \geq 2, \; y \geq 2$ At least 2 of each fastener must be made.
$x + y \geq 6$ At least 6 fasteners are needed.
$4x + 2y \leq 24$ Only 24 hours are available.

Graph the constraints.

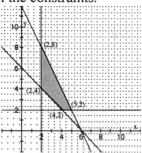

The corner points are (2, 4), (2, 8), (4, 2), (5, 2).

Evaluate the objective function:

Vertex	Value of $C = 9x + 4y$
(2, 4)	$C = 9(2) + 4(4) = 34$
(2, 8)	$C = 9(2) + 4(8) = 50$
(4, 2)	$C = 9(4) + 4(2) = 44$
(5, 2)	$C = 9(5) + 4(2) = 53$

The minimum cost is \$34, when 2 metal fasteners and 4 plastic fasteners are ordered.

29. Let x = the number of first-class seats.
     Let y = the number of coach seats.
     The constraints are:

     $8 \le x \le 16$ Restriction on first-class seats.
     $80 \le y \le 120$ Restriction on coach seats.

     (a) $\dfrac{x}{y} \le \dfrac{1}{12}$ Ratio of seats.

     If $y = 120$, then $\dfrac{x}{120} \le \dfrac{1}{12} \Rightarrow 12x \le 120 \Rightarrow x \le 10$

     The maximum revenue will be obtained with 120 coach seats and 10 first-class seats.
     (Note that the first-class seats meet their constraint.)

     (b) $\dfrac{x}{y} \le \dfrac{1}{8}$ Ratio of seats.

     If $y = 120$, then $\dfrac{x}{120} \le \dfrac{1}{8} \Rightarrow 8x \le 120 \Rightarrow x \le 15$

     The maximum revenue will be obtained with 120 coach seats and 15 first-class seats.
     (Note that the first-class seats meet their constraint.)

31. Answers will vary.

Systems of Equations and Inequalities

8.R Chapter Review

1. Solve the first equation for y, substitute into the second equation and solve:
$$\begin{cases} 2x - y = 5 & \Rightarrow \quad y = 2x - 5 \\ 5x + 2y = 8 \end{cases}$$
$$5x + 2(2x - 5) = 8 \Rightarrow 5x + 4x - 10 = 8$$
$$9x = 18 \Rightarrow x = 2 \Rightarrow y = 2(2) - 5 = 4 - 5 = -1$$
The solution is $x = 2$, $y = -1$.

3. Solve the second equation for x, substitute into the first equation and solve:
$$\begin{cases} 3x - 4y = 4 \\ x - 3y = \dfrac{1}{2} & \Rightarrow \quad x = 3y + \dfrac{1}{2} \end{cases}$$
$$3\left(3y + \frac{1}{2}\right) - 4y = 4 \Rightarrow 9y + \frac{3}{2} - 4y = 4 \Rightarrow 5y = \frac{5}{2} \Rightarrow y = \frac{1}{2} \Rightarrow x = 3\left(\frac{1}{2}\right) + \frac{1}{2} = 2$$
The solution is $x = 2$, $y = \dfrac{1}{2}$.

5. Solve the first equation for x, substitute into the second equation and solve:
$$\begin{cases} x - 2y - 4 = 0 & \Rightarrow \quad x = 2y + 4 \\ 3x + 2y - 4 = 0 \end{cases}$$
$$3(2y + 4) + 2y - 4 = 0 \Rightarrow 6y + 12 + 2y - 4 = 0$$
$$8y = -8 \Rightarrow y = -1 \Rightarrow x = 2(-1) + 4 = 2$$
The solution is $x = 2$, $y = -1$.

7. Substitute the first equation into the second equation and solve:
$$\begin{cases} y = 2x - 5 \\ x = 3y + 4 \end{cases}$$
$$x = 3(2x - 5) + 4 \Rightarrow x = 6x - 15 + 4$$
$$-5x = -11 \Rightarrow x = \frac{11}{5} \Rightarrow y = 2\left(\frac{11}{5}\right) - 5 = -\frac{3}{5}$$
The solution is $x = \dfrac{11}{5}$, $y = -\dfrac{3}{5}$.

9. Multiply each side of the first equation by 3 and each side of the second equation by -6 and add:

$$\begin{cases} x - 3y + 4 = 0 & \xrightarrow{\;3\;} & 3x - 9y + 12 = 0 \\ \dfrac{1}{2}x - \dfrac{3}{2}y + \dfrac{4}{3} = 0 & \xrightarrow{\;-6\;} & \dfrac{-3x + 9y - 8 = 0}{4 \neq 0} \end{cases}$$

There is no solution to the system. The system is inconsistent.

11. Multiply each side of the first equation by 2 and each side of the second equation by 3 and add to eliminate y:

$$\begin{cases} 2x + 3y - 13 = 0 & \xrightarrow{\;2\;} & 4x + 6y - 26 = 0 \\ 3x - 2y \quad = 0 & \xrightarrow{\;3\;} & 9x - 6y \quad = 0 \end{cases}$$
$$13x \quad - 26 = 0$$
$$13x = 26$$
$$x = 2$$

Substitute and solve for y: $\;3(2) - 2y = 0 \Rightarrow -2y = -6 \Rightarrow y = 3$

The solution of the system is $x = 2$, $y = 3$.

13. Multiply each side of the second equation by -3 and add to eliminate x:

$$\begin{cases} 3x - 2y = 8 & \longrightarrow & 3x - 2y = \quad 8 \\ x - \dfrac{2}{3}y = 12 & \xrightarrow{\;-3\;} & -3x + 2y = -36 \end{cases}$$
$$0 \neq -28$$

The system has no solution, so the system is inconsistent.

15. Multiply each side of the first equation by -2 and add to the second equation to eliminate x; and multiply each side of the first equation by -3 and add to the third equation to eliminate x:

$$\begin{cases} x + 2y - z = \quad 6 & \xrightarrow{\;-2\;} & -2x - 4y + 2z = -12 \\ 2x - y + 3z = -13 & \longrightarrow & 2x - y + 3z = -13 \\ 3x - 2y + 3z = -16 \end{cases}$$
$$-5y + 5z = -25 \xrightarrow{\;-1/5\;} y - z = 5$$
$$\xrightarrow{\;-3\;} \quad -3x - 6y + 3z = -18$$
$$\longrightarrow \quad \dfrac{3x - 2y + 3z = -16}{-8y + 6z = -34}$$

Multiply each side of the first result by 8 and add to the second result to eliminate y:

$$\begin{array}{ll} y - z = \quad 5 & \xrightarrow{\;8\;} & 8y - 8z = \quad 40 \\ -8y + 6z = -34 & \longrightarrow & -8y + 6z = -34 \end{array}$$
$$-2z = \quad 6$$
$$z = -3$$

Substituting and solving for the other variables:

$$\begin{array}{ll} y - (-3) = 5 & \qquad x + 2(2) - (-3) = 6 \\ y = 2 & \qquad x + 4 + 3 = 6 \\ & \qquad x = -1 \end{array}$$

The solution is $x = -1$, $y = 2$, $z = -3$.

17. Multiply the first equation by -1 and the second equation by 2 and then add to eliminate x; then multiply the second equation by -5 and add to the third equation to eliminate x:

$$\begin{cases} 2x - 4y + z = -15 \\ x + 2y - 4z = 27 \\ 5x - 6y - 2z = -3 \end{cases} \quad \begin{array}{l} \xrightarrow{-1} -2x + 4y - z = 15 \\ \xrightarrow{2} \underline{2x + 4y - 8z = 54} \\ \phantom{\xrightarrow{2}} \quad 8y - 9z = 69 \end{array}$$

$$\begin{array}{l} x + 2y - 4z = 27 \xrightarrow{-5} -5x - 10y + 20z = -135 \\ 5x - 6y - 2z = -3 \xrightarrow{} \underline{5x - 6y - 2z = -3} \\ \phantom{5x - 6y - 2z = -3 \xrightarrow{}} -16y + 18z = -138 \end{array}$$

Now eliminate y in the resulting system:

$$\begin{array}{l} 8y - 9z = 69 \xrightarrow{2} 16y - 18z = 138 \\ -16y + 18z = -138 \xrightarrow{} \underline{-16y + 18z = -138} \\ \phantom{-16y + 18z = -138 \xrightarrow{}} 0 = 0 \end{array}$$

$-16y + 18z = -138 \Rightarrow 18z + 138 = 16y \Rightarrow y = \dfrac{9}{8}z + \dfrac{69}{8}$, z is any real number

Substituting into the second equation and solving for the other x:

$$x + 2\left(\frac{9}{8}z + \frac{69}{8}\right) - 4z = 27$$

$x + \dfrac{9}{4}z + \dfrac{69}{4} - 4z = 27 \Rightarrow x = \dfrac{7}{4}z + \dfrac{39}{4}$, z is any real number

The solution is $x = \dfrac{7}{4}z + \dfrac{39}{4}$, $y = \dfrac{9}{8}z + \dfrac{69}{8}$, z is any real number.

19. $\begin{cases} 3x + 2y = 8 \\ x + 4y = -1 \end{cases}$

21. $A + C = \begin{bmatrix} 1 & 0 \\ 2 & 4 \\ -1 & 2 \end{bmatrix} + \begin{bmatrix} 3 & -4 \\ 1 & 5 \\ 5 & -2 \end{bmatrix} = \begin{bmatrix} 4 & -4 \\ 3 & 9 \\ 4 & 0 \end{bmatrix}$

23. $6A = 6 \cdot \begin{bmatrix} 1 & 0 \\ 2 & 4 \\ -1 & 2 \end{bmatrix} = \begin{bmatrix} 6 & 0 \\ 12 & 24 \\ -6 & 12 \end{bmatrix}$

25. $AB = \begin{bmatrix} 1 & 0 \\ 2 & 4 \\ -1 & 2 \end{bmatrix} \cdot \begin{bmatrix} 4 & -3 & 0 \\ 1 & 1 & -2 \end{bmatrix} = \begin{bmatrix} 4 & -3 & 0 \\ 12 & -2 & -8 \\ -2 & 5 & -4 \end{bmatrix}$

27. $CB = \begin{bmatrix} 3 & -4 \\ 1 & 5 \\ 5 & -2 \end{bmatrix} \cdot \begin{bmatrix} 4 & -3 & 0 \\ 1 & 1 & -2 \end{bmatrix} = \begin{bmatrix} 8 & -13 & 8 \\ 9 & 2 & -10 \\ 18 & -17 & 4 \end{bmatrix}$

29. Augment the matrix with the identity and use row operations to find the inverse:

$$A = \begin{bmatrix} 4 & 6 \\ 1 & 3 \end{bmatrix} \rightarrow \left[\begin{array}{cc|cc} 4 & 6 & 1 & 0 \\ 1 & 3 & 0 & 1 \end{array}\right]$$

$$\rightarrow \left[\begin{array}{cc|cc} 1 & 3 & 0 & 1 \\ 4 & 6 & 1 & 0 \end{array}\right] \rightarrow \left[\begin{array}{cc|cc} 1 & 3 & 0 & 1 \\ 0 & -6 & 1 & -4 \end{array}\right] \rightarrow \left[\begin{array}{cc|cc} 1 & 3 & 0 & 1 \\ 0 & 1 & -\frac{1}{6} & \frac{2}{3} \end{array}\right] \rightarrow \left[\begin{array}{cc|cc} 1 & 0 & \frac{1}{2} & -1 \\ 0 & 1 & -\frac{1}{6} & \frac{2}{3} \end{array}\right]$$

 Interchange $\quad R_2 = -4r_1 + r_2 \quad R_2 = -\frac{1}{6}r_2 \quad R_1 = -3r_2 + r_1$
$ r_1$ and r_2

$$A^{-1} = \begin{bmatrix} \frac{1}{2} & -1 \\ -\frac{1}{6} & \frac{2}{3} \end{bmatrix}$$

31. Augment the matrix with the identity and use row operations to find the inverse:

$$A = \begin{bmatrix} 1 & 3 & 3 \\ 1 & 2 & 1 \\ 1 & -1 & 2 \end{bmatrix} \rightarrow \begin{bmatrix} 1 & 3 & 3 & | & 1 & 0 & 0 \\ 1 & 2 & 1 & | & 0 & 1 & 0 \\ 1 & -1 & 2 & | & 0 & 0 & 1 \end{bmatrix}$$

$$\rightarrow \begin{bmatrix} 1 & 3 & 3 & | & 1 & 0 & 0 \\ 0 & -1 & -2 & | & -1 & 1 & 0 \\ 0 & -4 & -1 & | & -1 & 0 & 1 \end{bmatrix} \rightarrow \begin{bmatrix} 1 & 3 & 3 & | & 1 & 0 & 0 \\ 0 & 1 & 2 & | & 1 & -1 & 0 \\ 0 & -4 & -1 & | & -1 & 0 & 1 \end{bmatrix} \rightarrow \begin{bmatrix} 1 & 0 & -3 & | & -2 & 3 & 0 \\ 0 & 1 & 2 & | & 1 & -1 & 0 \\ 0 & 0 & 7 & | & 3 & -4 & 1 \end{bmatrix}$$

$R_2 = -r_1 + r_2$ $R_2 = -r_2$ $R_1 = -3r_2 + r_1$

$R_3 = -r_1 + r_3$ $R_3 = 4r_2 + r_3$

$$\rightarrow \begin{bmatrix} 1 & 0 & -3 & | & -2 & 3 & 0 \\ 0 & 1 & 2 & | & 1 & -1 & 0 \\ 0 & 0 & 1 & | & \frac{3}{7} & -\frac{4}{7} & \frac{1}{7} \end{bmatrix} \rightarrow \begin{bmatrix} 1 & 0 & 0 & | & -\frac{5}{7} & \frac{9}{7} & \frac{3}{7} \\ 0 & 1 & 0 & | & \frac{1}{7} & \frac{1}{7} & -\frac{2}{7} \\ 0 & 0 & 1 & | & \frac{3}{7} & -\frac{4}{7} & \frac{1}{7} \end{bmatrix} \longrightarrow A^{-1} = \begin{bmatrix} -\frac{5}{7} & \frac{9}{7} & \frac{3}{7} \\ \frac{1}{7} & \frac{1}{7} & -\frac{2}{7} \\ \frac{3}{7} & -\frac{4}{7} & \frac{1}{7} \end{bmatrix}$$

$R_3 = \frac{1}{7}r_3$ $R_1 = 3r_3 + r_1$

                                $R_2 = -2r_3 + r_2$

33. Augment the matrix with the identity and use row operations to find the inverse:

$$A = \begin{bmatrix} 4 & -8 \\ -1 & 2 \end{bmatrix} \rightarrow \begin{bmatrix} 4 & -8 & | & 1 & 0 \\ -1 & 2 & | & 0 & 1 \end{bmatrix}$$

$$\rightarrow \begin{bmatrix} -1 & 2 & | & 0 & 1 \\ 4 & -8 & | & 1 & 0 \end{bmatrix} \rightarrow \begin{bmatrix} -1 & 2 & | & 0 & 1 \\ 0 & 0 & | & 1 & 4 \end{bmatrix} \rightarrow \begin{bmatrix} 1 & -2 & | & 0 & -1 \\ 0 & 0 & | & 1 & 4 \end{bmatrix}$$

Interchange $R_2 = 4r_1 + r_2$ $R_1 = -r_1$

r_1 and r_2

There is no inverse because there is no way to obtain the identity on the left side. The matrix is singular.

35. $\begin{cases} 3x - 2y = 1 \\ 10x + 10y = 5 \end{cases}$ can be written as: $\begin{bmatrix} 3 & -2 & | & 1 \\ 10 & 10 & | & 5 \end{bmatrix}$

$$\rightarrow \begin{bmatrix} 3 & -2 & | & 1 \\ 1 & 16 & | & 2 \end{bmatrix} \rightarrow \begin{bmatrix} 1 & 16 & | & 2 \\ 3 & -2 & | & 1 \end{bmatrix} \rightarrow \begin{bmatrix} 1 & 16 & | & 2 \\ 0 & -50 & | & -5 \end{bmatrix} \rightarrow \begin{bmatrix} 1 & 16 & | & 2 \\ 0 & 1 & | & \frac{1}{10} \end{bmatrix} \rightarrow \begin{bmatrix} 1 & 0 & | & \frac{2}{5} \\ 0 & 1 & | & \frac{1}{10} \end{bmatrix}$$

$R_2 = -3r_1 + r_2$ Interchange $R_2 = -3r_1 + r_2$ $R_2 = -\frac{1}{50}r_2$ $R_1 = -16r_2 + r_1$

                r_1 and r_2

The solution is $x = 2/5, y = 1/10$.

37. $\begin{cases} 5x + 6y - 3z = 6 \\ 4x - 7y - 2z = -3 \\ 3x + y - 7z = 1 \end{cases}$ can be written as: $\begin{bmatrix} 5 & 6 & -3 & | & 6 \\ 4 & -7 & -2 & | & -3 \\ 3 & 1 & -7 & | & 1 \end{bmatrix}$

$$\rightarrow \begin{bmatrix} 1 & 13 & -1 & | & 9 \\ 4 & -7 & -2 & | & -3 \\ 3 & 1 & -7 & | & 1 \end{bmatrix} \rightarrow \begin{bmatrix} 1 & 13 & -1 & | & 9 \\ 0 & -59 & 2 & | & -39 \\ 0 & -38 & -4 & | & -26 \end{bmatrix} \rightarrow \begin{bmatrix} 1 & 13 & -1 & | & 9 \\ 0 & 1 & -\frac{2}{59} & | & \frac{39}{59} \\ 0 & -38 & -4 & | & -26 \end{bmatrix}$$

$R_1 = -r_2 + r_1$ $R_2 = -4r_1 + r_2$ $R_2 = -\frac{1}{59}r_2$

$$\rightarrow \begin{bmatrix} 1 & 0 & -\frac{33}{59} & \frac{24}{59} \\ 0 & 1 & -\frac{2}{59} & \frac{39}{59} \\ 0 & 0 & -\frac{312}{59} & -\frac{52}{59} \end{bmatrix} \rightarrow \begin{bmatrix} 1 & 0 & -\frac{33}{59} & \frac{24}{59} \\ 0 & 1 & -\frac{2}{59} & \frac{39}{59} \\ 0 & 0 & 1 & \frac{1}{6} \end{bmatrix} \rightarrow \begin{bmatrix} 1 & 0 & 0 & \frac{1}{2} \\ 0 & 1 & 0 & \frac{2}{3} \\ 0 & 0 & 1 & \frac{1}{6} \end{bmatrix}$$

$$R_1 = -13\,r_2 + r_1 \qquad R_3 = -\frac{59}{312}\,r_3 \qquad R_1 = \frac{33}{59}\,r_3 + r_1$$

$$R_3 = 38\,r_2 + r_3 \qquad\qquad\qquad\qquad R_2 = \frac{2}{59}\,r_3 + r_2$$

The solution is $x = 1/2,\, y = 2/3,\, z = 1/6$.

39. $\begin{cases} x & -2z = 1 \\ 2x + 3y & = -3 \\ 4x - 3y - 4z = 3 \end{cases}$ can be written as: $\begin{bmatrix} 1 & 0 & -2 & 1 \\ 2 & 3 & 0 & -3 \\ 4 & -3 & -4 & 3 \end{bmatrix}$

$$\rightarrow \begin{bmatrix} 1 & 0 & -2 & 1 \\ 0 & 3 & 4 & -5 \\ 0 & -3 & 4 & -1 \end{bmatrix} \rightarrow \begin{bmatrix} 1 & 0 & -2 & 1 \\ 0 & 1 & \frac{4}{3} & -\frac{5}{3} \\ 0 & -3 & 4 & -1 \end{bmatrix} \rightarrow \begin{bmatrix} 1 & 0 & -2 & 1 \\ 0 & 1 & \frac{4}{3} & -\frac{5}{3} \\ 0 & 0 & 8 & -6 \end{bmatrix}$$

$$R_2 = -2r_1 + r_2 \qquad R_2 = \tfrac{1}{3}r_2 \qquad\qquad R_3 = 3r_2 + r_3$$

$$R_3 = -4r_1 + r_3$$

$$\rightarrow \begin{bmatrix} 1 & 0 & -2 & 1 \\ 0 & 1 & \frac{4}{3} & -\frac{5}{3} \\ 0 & 0 & 1 & -\frac{3}{4} \end{bmatrix} \rightarrow \begin{bmatrix} 1 & 0 & 0 & -\frac{1}{2} \\ 0 & 1 & 0 & -\frac{2}{3} \\ 0 & 0 & 1 & -\frac{3}{4} \end{bmatrix}$$

$$R_3 = \tfrac{1}{8}r_3 \qquad\qquad R_1 = 2r_3 + r_1$$

$$R_2 = -\tfrac{4}{3}r_3 + r_2$$

The solution is $x = -1/2,\, y = -2/3,\, z = -3/4$.

41. $\begin{cases} x - y + z = 0 \\ x - y - 5z = 6 \\ 2x - 2y + z = 1 \end{cases}$ can be written as: $\begin{bmatrix} 1 & -1 & 1 & 0 \\ 1 & -1 & -5 & 6 \\ 2 & -2 & 1 & 1 \end{bmatrix}$

$$\rightarrow \begin{bmatrix} 1 & -1 & 1 & 0 \\ 0 & 0 & -6 & 6 \\ 0 & 0 & -1 & 1 \end{bmatrix} \rightarrow \begin{bmatrix} 1 & -1 & 1 & 0 \\ 0 & 0 & 1 & -1 \\ 0 & 0 & -1 & 1 \end{bmatrix} \rightarrow \begin{bmatrix} 1 & -1 & 0 & 1 \\ 0 & 0 & 1 & -1 \\ 0 & 0 & 0 & 0 \end{bmatrix} \rightarrow \begin{cases} x = y + 1 \\ z = -1 \end{cases}$$

$$R_2 = -r_1 + r_2 \qquad R_2 = -\tfrac{1}{6}r_2 \qquad R_1 = -r_2 + r_1$$

$$R_3 = -2r_1 + r_3 \qquad\qquad\qquad R_3 = r_2 + r_3$$

The solution is $x = y + 1,\, z = -1,\, y$ is any real number..

43. $\begin{cases} x - y - z - t = 1 \\ 2x + y - z + 2t = 3 \\ x - 2y - 2z - 3t = 0 \\ 3x - 4y + z + 5t = -3 \end{cases}$ can be written as: $\begin{bmatrix} 1 & -1 & -1 & -1 & 1 \\ 2 & 1 & -1 & 2 & 3 \\ 1 & -2 & -2 & -3 & 0 \\ 3 & -4 & 1 & 5 & -3 \end{bmatrix}$

$$\rightarrow \begin{vmatrix} 1 & -1 & -1 & -1 & | & 1 \\ 0 & 3 & 1 & 4 & | & 1 \\ 0 & -1 & -1 & -2 & | & -1 \\ 0 & -1 & 4 & 8 & | & -6 \end{vmatrix} \rightarrow \begin{vmatrix} 1 & -1 & -1 & -1 & | & 1 \\ 0 & -1 & -1 & -2 & | & -1 \\ 0 & 3 & 1 & 4 & | & 1 \\ 0 & -1 & 4 & 8 & | & -6 \end{vmatrix} \rightarrow \begin{vmatrix} 1 & -1 & -1 & -1 & | & 1 \\ 0 & 1 & 1 & 2 & | & 1 \\ 0 & 3 & 1 & 4 & | & 1 \\ 0 & -1 & 4 & 8 & | & -6 \end{vmatrix}$$

$R_2 = -2r_1 + r_2$ Interchange r_2 and r_3 $R_2 = -r_2$

$R_3 = -r_1 + r_3$

$R_4 = -3r_1 + r_4$

$$\rightarrow \begin{vmatrix} 1 & 0 & 0 & 1 & | & 2 \\ 0 & 1 & 1 & 2 & | & 1 \\ 0 & 0 & -2 & -2 & | & -2 \\ 0 & 0 & 5 & 10 & | & -5 \end{vmatrix} \rightarrow \begin{vmatrix} 1 & 0 & 0 & 1 & | & 2 \\ 0 & 1 & 1 & 2 & | & 1 \\ 0 & 0 & 1 & 1 & | & 1 \\ 0 & 0 & 1 & 2 & | & -1 \end{vmatrix} \rightarrow \begin{vmatrix} 1 & 0 & 0 & 1 & | & 2 \\ 0 & 1 & 1 & 2 & | & 1 \\ 0 & 0 & 1 & 1 & | & 1 \\ 0 & 0 & 0 & 1 & | & -2 \end{vmatrix}$$

$R_1 = r_2 + r_1$ $R_3 = -\frac{1}{2}r_3$ $R_4 = r_4 - r_3$

$R_3 = -3r_2 + r_3$ $R_4 = \frac{1}{5}r_4$

$R_4 = r_2 + r_4$

$$\rightarrow \begin{vmatrix} 1 & 0 & 0 & 0 & | & 4 \\ 0 & 1 & 0 & 0 & | & 2 \\ 0 & 0 & 1 & 0 & | & 3 \\ 0 & 0 & 0 & 1 & | & -2 \end{vmatrix}$$

$R_1 = r_1 - r_4$

$R_2 = r_2 - r_3 - r_4$

$R_3 = r_3 - r_4$

The solution is $x = 4, y = 2, z = 3, t = -2$.

45. Evaluating the determinant: $\begin{vmatrix} 3 & 4 \\ 1 & 3 \end{vmatrix} = 3(3) - 4(1) = 9 - 4 = 5$

47. Evaluating the determinant:

$$\begin{vmatrix} 1 & 4 & 0 \\ -1 & 2 & 6 \\ 4 & 1 & 3 \end{vmatrix} = 1\begin{vmatrix} 2 & 6 \\ 1 & 3 \end{vmatrix} - 4\begin{vmatrix} -1 & 6 \\ 4 & 3 \end{vmatrix} + 0\begin{vmatrix} -1 & 2 \\ 4 & 1 \end{vmatrix}$$

$$= 1[2(3) - 6(1)] - 4[-1(3) - 6(4)] + 0[-1(1) - 2(4)]$$

$$= 1(6 - 6) - 4(-3 - 24) + 0(-1 - 8)$$

$$= 1(0) - 4(-27) + 0(-9) = 0 + 108 + 0 = 108$$

49. Evaluating the determinant:

$$\begin{vmatrix} 2 & 1 & -3 \\ 5 & 0 & 1 \\ 2 & 6 & 0 \end{vmatrix} = 2\begin{vmatrix} 0 & 1 \\ 6 & 0 \end{vmatrix} - 1\begin{vmatrix} 5 & 1 \\ 2 & 0 \end{vmatrix} + (-3)\begin{vmatrix} 5 & 0 \\ 2 & 6 \end{vmatrix}$$

$$= 2(0 - 6) - 1(0 - 2) + (-3)(30 - 0) = -12 + 2 - 90 = -100$$

51. Set up and evaluate the determinants to use Cramer's Rule:
$$\begin{cases} x - 2y = 4 \\ 3x + 2y = 4 \end{cases}$$

$$D = \begin{vmatrix} 1 & -2 \\ 3 & 2 \end{vmatrix} = 1(2) - 3(-2) = 2 + 6 = 8; \quad D_x = \begin{vmatrix} 4 & -2 \\ 4 & 2 \end{vmatrix} = 4(2) - 4(-2) = 8 + 8 = 16$$

$$D_y = \begin{vmatrix} 1 & 4 \\ 3 & 4 \end{vmatrix} = 1(4) - 4(3) = 4 - 12 = -8$$

Find the solutions by Cramer's Rule: $x = \dfrac{D_x}{D} = \dfrac{16}{8} = 2 \qquad y = \dfrac{D_y}{D} = \dfrac{-8}{8} = -1$

53. Set up and evaluate the determinants to use Cramer's Rule:
$$\begin{cases} 2x + 3y = 13 \\ 3x - 2y = 0 \end{cases}$$

$$D = \begin{vmatrix} 2 & 3 \\ 3 & -2 \end{vmatrix} = -4 - 9 = -13; \quad D_x = \begin{vmatrix} 13 & 3 \\ 0 & -2 \end{vmatrix} = -26 - 0 = -26; \quad D_y = \begin{vmatrix} 2 & 13 \\ 3 & 0 \end{vmatrix} = 0 - 39 = -39$$

Find the solutions by Cramer's Rule: $x = \dfrac{D_x}{D} = \dfrac{-26}{-13} = 2 \qquad y = \dfrac{D_y}{D} = \dfrac{-39}{-13} = 3$

55. Set up and evaluate the determinants to use Cramer's Rule:
$$\begin{cases} x + 2y - z = 6 \\ 2x - y + 3z = -13 \\ 3x - 2y + 3z = -16 \end{cases}$$

$$D = \begin{vmatrix} 1 & 2 & -1 \\ 2 & -1 & 3 \\ 3 & -2 & 3 \end{vmatrix} = 1\begin{vmatrix} -1 & 3 \\ -2 & 3 \end{vmatrix} - 2\begin{vmatrix} 2 & 3 \\ 3 & 3 \end{vmatrix} + (-1)\begin{vmatrix} 2 & -1 \\ 3 & -2 \end{vmatrix}$$

$$= 1(-3 + 6) - 2(6 - 9) - 1(-4 + 3) = 3 + 6 + 1 = 10$$

$$D_x = \begin{vmatrix} 6 & 2 & -1 \\ -13 & -1 & 3 \\ -16 & -2 & 3 \end{vmatrix} = 6\begin{vmatrix} -1 & 3 \\ -2 & 3 \end{vmatrix} - 2\begin{vmatrix} -13 & 3 \\ -16 & 3 \end{vmatrix} + (-1)\begin{vmatrix} -13 & -1 \\ -16 & -2 \end{vmatrix}$$

$$= 6(-3 + 6) - 2(-39 + 48) - 1(26 - 16) = 18 - 18 - 10 = -10$$

$$D_y = \begin{vmatrix} 1 & 6 & -1 \\ 2 & -13 & 3 \\ 3 & -16 & 3 \end{vmatrix} = 1\begin{vmatrix} -13 & 3 \\ -16 & 3 \end{vmatrix} - 6\begin{vmatrix} 2 & 3 \\ 3 & 3 \end{vmatrix} + (-1)\begin{vmatrix} 2 & -13 \\ 3 & -16 \end{vmatrix}$$

$$= 1(-39 + 48) - 6(6 - 9) - 1(-32 + 39) = 9 + 18 - 7 = 20$$

$$D_z = \begin{vmatrix} 1 & 2 & 6 \\ 2 & -1 & -13 \\ 3 & -2 & -16 \end{vmatrix} = 1\begin{vmatrix} -1 & -13 \\ -2 & -16 \end{vmatrix} - 2\begin{vmatrix} 2 & -13 \\ 3 & -16 \end{vmatrix} + 6\begin{vmatrix} 2 & -1 \\ 3 & -2 \end{vmatrix}$$

$$= 1(16 - 26) - 2(-32 + 39) + 6(-4 + 3) = -10 - 14 - 6 = -30$$

Find the solutions by Cramer's Rule:

$$x = \frac{D_x}{D} = \frac{-10}{10} = -1 \qquad y = \frac{D_y}{D} = \frac{20}{10} = 2 \qquad z = \frac{D_z}{D} = \frac{-30}{10} = -3$$

57. Let $\begin{vmatrix} x & y \\ a & b \end{vmatrix} = 8$, then $\begin{vmatrix} 2x & y \\ 2a & b \end{vmatrix} = 16$ by Theorem 14.

The value of the determinant is multiplied by k when the elements of a column are multiplied by k.

59. Find the partial fraction decomposition:

$$\frac{6}{x(x-4)} = \frac{A}{x} + \frac{B}{x-4} \quad \text{(Multiply both sides by } x(x-4).)$$

$$6 = A(x-4) + Bx$$

Let $x = 4$: then $6 = A(4-4) + B(4) \Rightarrow 4B = 6 \Rightarrow B = \frac{3}{2}$

Let $x = 0$: then $6 = A(0-4) + B(0) \Rightarrow -4A = 6 \Rightarrow A = -\frac{3}{2}$

$$\frac{6}{x(x-4)} = \frac{(-3/2)}{x} + \frac{(3/2)}{x-4}$$

61. Find the partial fraction decomposition:

$$\frac{x-4}{x^2(x-1)} = \frac{A}{x} + \frac{B}{x^2} + \frac{C}{x-1} \text{(Multiply both sides by } x^2(x-1).)$$

$$x - 4 = Ax(x-1) + B(x-1) + Cx^2$$

Let $x = 1$: then $1 - 4 = A(1)(1-1) + B(1-1) + C(1)^2 \Rightarrow -3 = C \Rightarrow C = -3$

Let $x = 0$: then $0 - 4 = A(0)(0-1) + B(0-1) + C(0)^2 \Rightarrow -4 = -P \Rightarrow B = 4$

Let $x = 2$: then $2 - 4 = A(2)(2-1) + B(2-1) + C(2)^2 \Rightarrow -2 = 2A + B + 4C$

$$\Rightarrow 2A = -2 - 4 - 4(-3) \Rightarrow 2A = 6 \Rightarrow A = 3$$

$$\frac{x-4}{x^2(x-1)} = \frac{3}{x} + \frac{4}{x^2} + \frac{-3}{x-1}$$

63. Find the partial fraction decomposition:

$$\frac{x}{(x^2+9)(x+1)} = \frac{A}{x+1} + \frac{Bx+C}{x^2+9} \quad \text{(Multiply both sides by } (x+1)(x^2+9).)$$

$$x = A(x^2+9) + (Bx+C)(x+1)$$

Let $x = -1$: then $-1 = A((-1)^2 + 9) + (B(-1) + C)(-1+1)$

$$\Rightarrow -1 = A(10) + (-B+C)(0) \Rightarrow -1 = 10A \Rightarrow A = -1/10$$

Let $x = 1$: then $1 = A(1^2 + 9) + (B(1) + C)(1+1) \Rightarrow 1 = 10A + 2B + 2C$

$$\Rightarrow 1 = 10\left(-\frac{1}{10}\right) + 2B + 2C \Rightarrow 2 = 2B + 2C \Rightarrow B + C = 1$$

Let $x = 0$: then $0 = A(0^2 + 9) + (B(0) + C)(0+1) \Rightarrow 0 = 9A + C$

$$\Rightarrow 0 = 9\left(-\frac{1}{10}\right) + C \Rightarrow C = \frac{9}{10} B = 1 - C \Rightarrow B = 1 - \frac{9}{10} \Rightarrow B = \frac{1}{10}$$

$$\frac{x}{(x^2+9)(x+1)} = \frac{-(1/10)}{x+1} + \frac{((1/10)x + 9/10)}{x^2+9}$$

65. Find the partial fraction decomposition:

$$\frac{x^3}{(x^2+4)^2} = \frac{Ax+B}{x^2+4} + \frac{Cx+D}{(x^2+4)^2} \quad \text{(Multiply both sides by } (x^2+4)^2.\text{)}$$

$$x^3 = (Ax+B)(x^2+4) + Cx+D$$

$$x^3 = Ax^3 + Bx^2 + 4Ax + 4B + Cx + D \Rightarrow x^3 = Ax^3 + Bx^2 + (4A+C)x + 4B+D$$

$$A = 1; \quad B = 0$$

$$4A+C = 0 \Rightarrow 4(1)+C = 0 \Rightarrow C = -4$$

$$4B+D = 0 \Rightarrow 4(0)+D = 0 \Rightarrow D = 0$$

$$\frac{x^3}{(x^2+4)^2} = \frac{x}{x^2+4} + \frac{-4x}{(x^2+4)^2}$$

67. Find the partial fraction decomposition:

$$\frac{x^2}{(x^2+1)(x^2-1)} = \frac{x^2}{(x^2+1)(x-1)(x+1)} = \frac{A}{x-1} + \frac{B}{x+1} + \frac{Cx+D}{x^2+1}$$

$$\text{(Multiply both sides by } (x-1)(x+1)(x^2+1).\text{)}$$

$$x^2 = A(x+1)(x^2+1) + B(x-1)(x^2+1) + (Cx+D)(x-1)(x+1)$$

Let $x = 1$: then $1^2 = A(1+1)(1^2+1) + B(1-1)(1^2+1) + (C(1)+D)(1-1)(1+1)$

$$\Rightarrow 1 = 4A \Rightarrow A = \frac{1}{4}$$

Let $x = -1$: then

$$(-1)^2 = A(-1+1)((-1)^2+1) + B(-1-1)((-1)^2+1) + (C(-1)+D)(-1-1)(-1+1)$$

$$\Rightarrow 1 = -4B \Rightarrow B = -\frac{1}{4}$$

Let $x = 0$: then

$$0^2 = A(0+1)(0^2+1) + B(0-1)(0^2+1) + (C(0)+D)(0-1)(0+1)$$

$$\Rightarrow 0 = A - B - D \Rightarrow 0 = \frac{1}{4} - \left(-\frac{1}{4}\right) - D \Rightarrow D = \frac{1}{2}$$

Let $x = 2$: then

$$2^2 = A(2+1)(2^2+1) + B(2-1)(2^2+1) + (C(2)+D)(2-1)(2+1)$$

$$\Rightarrow 4 = 15A + 5B + 6C + 3D \Rightarrow 4 = 15\left(\frac{1}{4}\right) + 5\left(-\frac{1}{4}\right) + 6C + 3\left(\frac{1}{2}\right)$$

$$\Rightarrow 6C = 4 - \frac{15}{4} + \frac{5}{4} - \frac{3}{2} \Rightarrow 6C = 0 \Rightarrow C = 0$$

$$\frac{x^2}{(x^2+1)(x^2-1)} = \frac{x^2}{(x^2+1)(x-1)(x+1)} = \frac{(1/4)}{x-1} + \frac{-(1/4)}{x+1} + \frac{(1/2)}{x^2+1}$$

69. Solve the first equation for y, substitute into the second equation and solve:

$$\begin{cases} 2x + y + 3 = 0 \implies y = -2x - 3 \\ x^2 + y^2 = 5 \end{cases}$$

$$x^2 + (-2x - 3)^2 = 5 \implies x^2 + 4x^2 + 12x + 9 = 5$$

$$5x^2 + 12x + 4 = 0 \implies (5x + 2)(x + 2) = 0 \implies x = -\frac{2}{5} \quad \text{or} \quad x = -2$$

$$y = -\frac{11}{5} \qquad y = 1$$

Solutions: $\left(-2/5, -11/5\right), (-2, 1)$.

71. Multiply each side of the second equation by 2 and add the equations to eliminate xy:

$$\begin{cases} 2xy + y^2 = 10 \quad \longrightarrow \quad 2xy + y^2 = 10 \\ -xy + 3y^2 = 2 \quad \overset{2}{\longrightarrow} \quad \underline{-2xy + 6y^2 = 4} \end{cases}$$

$$7y^2 = 14 \implies y^2 = 2 \implies y = \pm\sqrt{2}$$

If $y = \sqrt{2}$: $2x\left(\sqrt{2}\right) + \left(\sqrt{2}\right)^2 = 10 \implies 2\sqrt{2}x = 8 \implies x = \frac{8}{2\sqrt{2}} = 2\sqrt{2}$

If $y = -\sqrt{2}$: $2x\left(-\sqrt{2}\right) + \left(-\sqrt{2}\right)^2 = 10 \implies -2\sqrt{2}x = 8 \implies x = \frac{8}{-2\sqrt{2}} = -2\sqrt{2}$

Solutions: $\left(2\sqrt{2}, \sqrt{2}\right), \left(-2\sqrt{2}, -\sqrt{2}\right)$

73. Substitute into the second equation into the first equation and solve:

$$\begin{cases} x^2 + y^2 = 6y \\ x^2 = 3y \end{cases}$$

$$3y + y^2 = 6y \implies y^2 - 3y = 0 \implies y(y - 3) = 0 \implies y = 0 \quad \text{or} \quad y = 3$$

If $y = 0$: $x^2 = 3(0) \implies x^2 = 0 \implies x = 0$

If $y = 3$: $x^2 = 3(3) \implies x^2 = 9 \implies x = \pm 3$

Solutions: $(0, 0), (-3, 3), (3, 3)$.

75. Factor the second equation, solve for x, substitute into the first equation and solve:

$$\begin{cases} 3x^2 + 4xy + 5y^2 = 8 \\ x^2 + 3xy + 2y^2 = 0 \implies (x + 2y)(x + y) = 0 \implies x = -2y \quad \text{or} \quad x = -y \end{cases}$$

Substitute $x = -2y$ and solve: Substitute $x = -y$ and solve:

$$3x^2 + 4xy + 5y^2 = 8$$
$$3x^2 + 4xy + 5y^2 = 8$$
$$3(-2y)^2 + 4(-2y)y + 5y^2 = 8$$
$$3(-y)^2 + 4(-y)y + 5y^2 = 8$$
$$12y^2 - 8y^2 + 5y^2 = 8$$
$$3y^2 - 4y^2 + 5y^2 = 8$$
$$9y^2 = 8$$
$$4y^2 = 8$$
$$y^2 = \frac{8}{9} \implies y = \pm\frac{2\sqrt{2}}{3}$$
$$y^2 = 2 \implies y = \pm\sqrt{2}$$

If $y = \dfrac{2\sqrt{2}}{3}$: $x = -2\left(\dfrac{2\sqrt{2}}{3}\right) = \dfrac{-4\sqrt{2}}{3}$

If $y = \dfrac{-2\sqrt{2}}{3}$: $x = -2\left(\dfrac{-2\sqrt{2}}{3}\right) = \dfrac{4\sqrt{2}}{3}$

If $y = \sqrt{2}$: $x = -\sqrt{2}$
If $y = -\sqrt{2}$: $x = \sqrt{2}$

Solutions: $\left(-\dfrac{4\sqrt{2}}{3}, \dfrac{2\sqrt{2}}{3}\right), \left(\dfrac{4\sqrt{2}}{3}, -\dfrac{2\sqrt{2}}{3}\right), \left(-\sqrt{2}, \sqrt{2}\right), \left(\sqrt{2}, -\sqrt{2}\right)$

77. Multiply each side of the second equation by $-y$ and add the equations to eliminate y:

$\begin{cases} x^2 - 3x + y^2 + y = -2 \quad \longrightarrow \quad x^2 - 3x + y^2 + y = -2 \\ \dfrac{x^2 - x}{y} + y + 1 = 0 \quad \xrightarrow{-y} \quad -x^2 + x - y^2 - y = 0 \end{cases}$

$-2x = -2 \Rightarrow x = 1$

If $x = 1$: $1^2 - 3(1) + y^2 + y = -2 \Rightarrow y^2 + y = 0 \Rightarrow y(y+1) = 0$
$\Rightarrow y = 0$ or $y = -1$

Note that $y \neq 0$ because that would cause division by zero in the original system.
Solution: $(1, -1)$

79. $3x + 4y \le 12$

(a) Graph the line $3x + 4y = 12$. Use a solid line since the inequality uses $\le$.
Choose a test point not on the line, such as $(0, 0)$.
Since $3(0) + 4(0) \le 12$ is true, shade the side of the line containing $(0, 0)$.

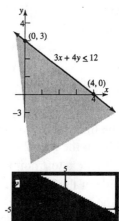

(b) Use the SHADE function in the calculator's DRAW menu: $\text{Shade}\left(-5, -(3/4)x + 3\right)$.

81. Graph the system of linear inequalities:
$\begin{cases} -2x + y \le 2 \\ x + y \ge 2 \end{cases}$

(a) Graph the line $-2x + y = 2$. Use a solid line since the inequality uses $\le$.
Choose a test point not on the line, such as $(0, 0)$.
Since $-2(0) + 0 \le 2$ is true, shade the side of the line containing $(0, 0)$.

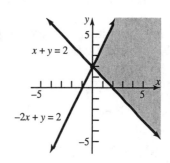

(b)   Graph the line $x + y = 2$. Use a solid line since the inequality uses $\geq$.
Choose a test point not on the line, such as $(0, 0)$. Since $0 + 0 \geq 2$ is false, shade the opposite side of the line from $(0, 0)$.

(c)   The overlapping region is the solution.

(d)   The graph is unbounded.

(e)   Find the vertices:
To find the intersection of $x + y = 2$ and $-2x + y = 2$, solve the system:
$$\begin{cases} x + y = 2 & \Rightarrow \quad x = 2 - y \\ -2x + y = 2 \end{cases}$$
Substitute and solve:
$$-2(2 - y) + y = 2 \Rightarrow -4 + 2y + y = 2 \Rightarrow 3y = 6 \Rightarrow y = 2$$
$$x = 2 - 2 = 0$$
The point of intersection is $(0, 2)$. The corner point is $(0, 2)$.

83.   Graph the system of linear inequalities:
$$\begin{cases} x \geq 0 \\ y \geq 0 \\ x + y \leq 4 \\ 2x + 3y \leq 6 \end{cases}$$

(a)   Graph $x \geq 0; y \geq 0$. Shaded region is the first quadrant.

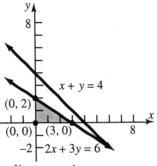

(b)   Graph the line $x + y = 4$. Use a solid line since the inequality uses $\leq$.
Choose a test point not on the line, such as $(0, 0)$. Since $0 + 0 \leq 4$ is true, shade the side of the line containing $(0, 0)$.

(c)   Graph the line $2x + 3y = 6$. Use a solid line since the inequality uses $\leq$.
Choose a test point not on the line, such as $(0, 0)$. Since $2(0) + 3(0) \leq 6$ is true, shade the side of the line containing $(0, 0)$.

(d)   The overlapping region is the solution.

(e)   The graph is bounded.

(f)   Find the vertices:
The x-axis and y-axis intersect at $(0, 0)$.
The intersection of $2x + 3y = 6$ and the y-axis is $(0, 2)$.
The intersection of $2x + 3y = 6$ and the x-axis is $(3, 0)$.
The three corner points are $(0, 0)$, $(0, 2)$, and $(3, 0)$.

85.   Graph the system of linear inequalities:
$$\begin{cases} x \geq 0 \\ y \geq 0 \\ 2x + y \leq 8 \\ x + 2y \geq 2 \end{cases}$$

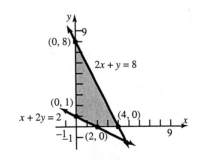

(a)   Graph $x \geq 0; y \geq 0$. Shaded region is in the first quadrant.
(b)   Graph the line $2x + y = 8$. Use a solid line since the inequality uses $\leq$.
      Choose a test point not on the line, such as $(0, 0)$. Since $2(0) + 0 \leq 8$ is true,
      shade the side of the line containing $(0, 0)$.
(c)   Graph the line $x + 2y = 2$. Use a solid line since the inequality uses $\geq$.
      Choose a test point not on the line, such as $(0, 0)$. Since $0 + 2(0) \geq 2$ is false, shade the
      opposite side of the line from $(0, 0)$.
(d)   The overlapping region is the solution.
(e)   The graph is bounded
(f)   Find the vertices:
      The intersection of $x + 2y = 2$ and the y-axis is $(0, 1)$.
      The intersection of $x + 2y = 2$ and the x-axis is $(2, 0)$.
      The intersection of $2x + y = 8$ and the y-axis is $(0, 8)$.
      The intersection of $2x + y = 8$ and the x-axis is $(4, 0)$.
      The four corner points are $(0, 1)$, $(0, 8)$, $(2, 0)$, and $(4, 0)$.

87.   Graph the system of inequalities:
$$\begin{cases} x^2 + y^2 \leq 16 \\ x + y \geq 2 \end{cases}$$

(a)   Graph the circle $x^2 + y^2 = 16$. Use a solid line since the
      inequality uses $\leq$. Choose a test point not on the circle, such
      as $(0, 0)$. Since $0^2 + 0^2 \leq 16$ is true, shade the side of the
      circle containing $(0, 0)$.
(b)   Graph the line $x + y = 2$. Use a solid line since the
      inequality uses $\geq$. Choose a test point not on the line, such
      as $(0, 0)$. Since $0 + 0 \geq 2$ is false, shade the opposite side of
      the line from $(0, 0)$.

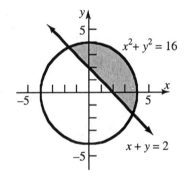

(c)   The overlapping region is the solution.

89.   Graph the system of inequalities:
$$\begin{cases} y \leq x^2 \\ xy \leq 4 \end{cases}$$

(a)   Graph the parabola $y = x^2$. Use a solid line since the
      inequality uses $\leq$. Choose a test point not on the parabola,
      such as $(1, 2)$. Since $2 \leq 1^2$ is false, shade the opposite side
      of the parabola from $(1, 2)$.
(b)   Graph the hyperbola $xy = 4$. Use a solid line since the
      inequality uses $\leq$. Choose a test point not on the hyperbola,
      such as $(1, 2)$. Since $1 \cdot 2 \leq 4$ is true, shade the same side
      of the hyperbola as $(1, 2)$.

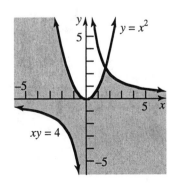

(c)   The overlapping region is the solution.

91. Maximize $z = 3x + 4y$ Subject to $x \geq 0$, $y \geq 0$, $3x + 2y \geq 6$, $x + y \leq 8$
Graph the constraints.

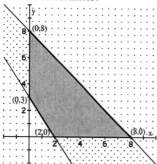

The corner points are (0, 3), (2, 0), (0, 8), (8, 0).

Evaluate the objective function:

Vertex	Value of $z = 3x + 4y$
(0, 3)	$z = 3(0) + 4(3) = 12$
(0, 8)	$z = 3(0) + 4(8) = 32$
(2, 0)	$z = 3(2) + 4(0) = 6$
(8, 0)	$z = 3(8) + 4(0) = 24$

The maximum value is 32 at (0, 8).

93. Minimize $z = 3x + 5y$

Subject to $x \geq 0$, $y \geq 0$, $x + y \geq 1$, $3x + 2y \leq 12$, $x + 3y \leq 12$
Graph the constraints.

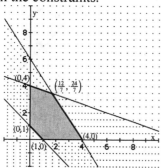

To find the intersection of $3x + 2y = 12$ and $x + 3y = 12$, solve the system:

$$\begin{cases} 3x + 2y = 12 \\ x + 3y = 12 \end{cases} \Rightarrow x = 12 - 3y$$

Substitute and solve:

$$3(12 - 3y) + 2y = 12 \Rightarrow 36 - 9y + 2y = 12 \Rightarrow -7y = -24 \Rightarrow y = 24 / 7$$

$$x = 12 - 3(24 / 7) = 12 - 72 / 7 = 12 / 7$$

The point of intersection is $\left(12 / 7, 24 / 7 \right)$.

The corner points are (0, 1), (1, 0), (0, 4), (4, 0), $\left(12 / 7, 24 / 7 \right)$.

Evaluate the objective function:

Vertex	Value of $z = 3x + 5y$
(0, 1)	$z = 3(0) + 5(1) = 5$
(0, 4)	$z = 3(0) + 5(4) = 20$
(1, 0)	$z = 3(1) + 5(0) = 3$
(4, 0)	$z = 3(4) + 5(0) = 12$
$(12/7, 24/7)$	$z = 3(12/7) + 5(24/7) = 36/7 + 120/7 = 156/7 \approx 22.3$

The minimum value is 3 at (1, 0).

95. Multiply each side of the first equation by –2 and eliminate x:

$$\begin{cases} 2x + 5y = 5 \\ 4x + 10y = A \end{cases} \xrightarrow{\ -2\ } \begin{aligned} -4x - 10y &= -10 \\ 4x + 10y &= A \\ \hline 0 &= A - 10 \end{aligned}$$

If there are to be infinitely many solutions, the sum in elimination should be $0 = 0$.
Therefore, $A - 10 = 0$ or $A = 10$.

97. $y = ax^2 + bx + c$

At (0, 1) the equation becomes:

$$1 = a(0)^2 + b(0) + c$$
$$c = 1$$

At (1, 0) the equation becomes:

$$0 = a(1)^2 + b(1) + c$$
$$0 = a + b + c$$
$$a + b + c = 0$$

At (–2, 1) the equation becomes:

$$1 = a(-2)^2 + b(-2) + c = 4a - 2b + c \Rightarrow 4a - 2b + c = 1$$

The system of equations is:

$$\begin{cases} a + b + c = 0 \\ 4a - 2b + c = 1 \\ c = 1 \end{cases}$$

Substitute $c = 1$ into the first and second equations and simplify:

$$\begin{cases} a + b + 1 = 0 \ \Rightarrow\ a + b = -1 \ \Rightarrow\ a = -b - 1 \\ 4a - 2b + 1 = 1 \ \Rightarrow\ 4a - 2b = 0 \end{cases}$$

Solve the first equation for a, substitute into the second equation and solve:

$$4(-b - 1) - 2b = 0 \Rightarrow -4b - 4 - 2b = 0$$

$$-6b = 4 \Rightarrow b = -\frac{2}{3} \Rightarrow a = \frac{2}{3} - 1 = -\frac{1}{3}$$

The quadratic function is $y = -\dfrac{1}{3}x^2 - \dfrac{2}{3}x + 1$.

99. Let x = the number of pounds of coffee that costs \$3.00 per pound.
Let y = the number of pounds of coffee that costs \$6.00 per pound.
Then $x + y = 100$ represents the total amount of coffee in the blend.
The value of the blend will be represented by the equation: $3x + 6y = 3.90(100)$.
Solve the system of equations:

$$\begin{cases} x + y = 100 \ \Rightarrow\ y = 100 - x \\ 3x + 6y = 390 \end{cases}$$

Solve by substitution:
$$3x + 6(100 - x) = 390 \Rightarrow 3x + 600 - 6x = 390$$
$$-3x = -210 \Rightarrow x = 70$$
$$y = 100 - 70 = 30$$

The blend is made up of 70 pounds of the $3 per pound coffee and 30 pounds of the $6 per pound coffee.

101. Let x = the number of small boxes.
Let y = the number of medium boxes.
Let z = the number of large boxes.

Oatmeal raisin equation: $x + 2y + 2z = 15$
Chocolate chip equation: $x + y + 2z = 10$
Shortbread equation: $y + 3z = 11$

Multiply each side of the second equation by –1 and add to the first equation to eliminate x:

$$\begin{cases} x + 2y + 2z = 15 \\ x + y + 2z = 10 \\ \phantom{x + {}} y + 3z = 11 \end{cases} \begin{array}{l} \longrightarrow \\ \xrightarrow{-1} \end{array} \begin{array}{rcl} x + 2y + 2z &=& 15 \\ -x - y - 2z &=& -10 \\ \hline y &=& 5 \end{array}$$

Substituting and solving for the other variables:
$$\begin{array}{ll} 5 + 3z = 11 & x + 5 + 2(2) = 10 \\ 3z = 6 & x + 9 = 10 \\ z = 2 & x = 1 \end{array}$$

1 small box, 5 medium boxes, and 2 large boxes of cookies should be purchased.

103. Let x = the speed of the boat in still water.
Let y = the speed of the river current.
Let d = the distance from Chiritza to the Flotel Orellana (100 kilometers)

	Rate	Time	Distance
trip downstream	$x + y$	5 / 2	100
trip downstream	$x - y$	3	100

The system of equations is:
$$\begin{cases} (x + y)(5/2) = 100 & \Rightarrow & 5x + 5y = 200 \\ (x - y)(3) = d & \Rightarrow & 3x - 3y = 100 \end{cases}$$

$$\begin{array}{l} 5x + 5y = 200 \xrightarrow{3} & 15x + 15y = 600 \\ 3x - 3y = 100 \xrightarrow{5} & \underline{+\ 15x - 15y = 500} \\ & 30x = 1100 \end{array} \qquad \therefore x = \frac{1100}{30} = \frac{110}{3}$$

$$\Rightarrow 3(110/3) - 3y = 100 \Rightarrow 110 - 3y = 100 \Rightarrow 10 = 3y \Rightarrow y = \frac{10}{3}$$

The speed of the boat = $110/3 \approx 36.67$ km / hr; the speed of the current = $10/3 \approx 3.33$ km / hr.

105. Let x = the number of hours for Bruce to do the job alone.
Let y = the number of hours for Bryce to do the job alone.
Let z = the number of hours for Marty to do the job alone.
Then $1/x$ represents the fraction of the job that Bruce does in one hour.
$1/y$ represents the fraction of the job that Bryce does in one hour.
$1/z$ represents the fraction of the job that Marty does in one hour.
The equation representing Bruce and Bryce working together is:
$$\frac{1}{x} + \frac{1}{y} = \frac{1}{(4/3)} = \frac{3}{4} = 0.75$$
The equation representing Bryce and Marty working together is:
$$\frac{1}{y} + \frac{1}{z} = \frac{1}{(8/5)} = \frac{5}{8} = 0.675$$
The equation representing Bruce and Marty working together is:
$$\frac{1}{x} + \frac{1}{z} = \frac{1}{(8/3)} = \frac{3}{8} = 0.375$$

Solve the system of equations:
$$\begin{cases} x^{-1} + y^{-1} = 0.75 \\ y^{-1} + z^{-1} = 0.675 \\ x^{-1} + z^{-1} = 0.375 \end{cases}$$

Let $u = x^{-1},\ v = y^{-1},\ w = z^{-1}$
$$\begin{cases} u + v = 0.75 \quad \rightarrow \quad u = 0.75 - v \\ v + w = 0.675 \quad \rightarrow \quad w = 0.675 - v \\ u + w = 0.375 \end{cases}$$

Substitute into the third equation and solve:
$$0.75 - v + 0.675 - v = 0.375 \Rightarrow -2v = -1 \Rightarrow v = 0.5$$
$$u = 0.75 - 0.5 = 0.25$$
$$w = 0.675 - 0.5 = 0.125$$
Solve for x, y, and z: $x = 4,\ y = 2,\ z = 8$ (reciprocals)
Bruce can do the job in 4 hours, Bryce in 2 hours, and Marty in 8 hours.

107. Let x = the number of gasoline engines produced each week.
Let y = the number of diesel engines produced each week.
The total cost is: $C = 450x + 550y$. Cost is to be minimized; thus, this is the objective function.
The constraints are:
$$20 \le x \le 60 \qquad \text{number of gasoline engines needed and capacity each week.}$$
$$15 \le y \le 40 \qquad \text{number of diesel engines needed and capacity each week.}$$
$$x + y \ge 50 \qquad \text{number of engines produced to prevent layoffs.}$$
Graph the constraints.

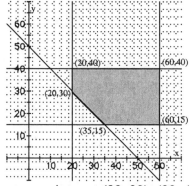

The corner points are $(20, 30)$, $(20, 40)$, $(35, 15)$, $(60, 15)$, $(60, 40)$.

Evaluate the objective function:

Vertex	Value of $C = 450x + 550y$
(20, 30)	$C = 450(20) + 550(30) = 25{,}500$
(20, 40)	$C = 450(20) + 550(40) = 31{,}000$
(35, 15)	$C = 450(35) + 550(15) = 24{,}000$
(60, 15)	$C = 450(60) + 550(15) = 35{,}250$
(60, 40)	$C = 450(60) + 550(40) = 49{,}000$

The minimum cost is \$24,000, when 35 gasoline engines and 15 diesel engines are produced.
The excess capacity is 15 gasoline engines, since only 20 gasoline engines had to be delivered.

Systems of Equations and Inequalities

8.CR Cumulative Review

1. $2x^2 - x = -3$
    $2x^2 - x + 3 = 0$

    $$x = \frac{-(-1) \pm \sqrt{(-1)^2 - 4 \cdot 2 \cdot 3}}{2 \cdot 2} = \frac{1 \pm \sqrt{1 - 24}}{4}$$

    $$= \frac{1 \pm \sqrt{-23}}{4} \Rightarrow \text{no real solution}$$

    The solution set is $\varnothing$.

3. $2x^3 - 3x^2 - 8x - 3 = 0$
    The graph of $y_1 = 2x^3 - 3x^2 - 8x - 3$
    appears to have an x-intercept at $x = 3$.

    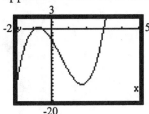

    Using synthetic division:

    $$3 \overline{) \begin{array}{cccc} 2 & -3 & -8 & -3 \\ & 6 & 9 & 3 \\ \hline 2 & 3 & 1 & 0 \end{array}}$$

    Therefore,
    $2x^3 - 3x^2 - 8x - 3 = 0$

    $(x - 3)(2x^2 + 3x + 1) = 0$

    $(x - 3)(2x + 1)(x + 1) = 0$

    $x = 3$ or $x = -\dfrac{1}{2}$ or $x = -1$

    The solution set is $\left\{ -1, -\dfrac{1}{2}, 3 \right\}$.

5. $\log_3(x - 1) + \log_3(2x + 1) = 2$

    $\log_3\big((x - 1)(2x + 1)\big) = 2$

    $(x - 1)(2x + 1) = 3^2$

    $2x^2 - x - 1 = 9$

    $2x^2 - x - 10 = 0$

    $(2x - 5)(x + 2) = 0$

    $x = \dfrac{5}{2}$ or $x = -2$

    Since $x = -2$ makes the original logarithms
    undefined, the solution set is $\left\{ \dfrac{5}{2} \right\}$.

7. $f(x) = \dfrac{2x^3}{x^4 + 1}$

    $$f(-x) = \frac{2(-x)^3}{(-x)^4 + 1} = \frac{-2x^3}{x^4 + 1} = -f(x),$$

    therefore f is an odd function and its graph
    is symmetric with respect to the origin.

9. $f(x) = 3^{x-2} + 1$

Using the graph of $y = 3^x$, shift the graph
horizontally 2 units to the right, then shift
the graph vertically 1 unit upward.
Domain: $(-\infty, \infty)$
Range: $(1, \infty)$
Horizontal Asymptote: $y = 1$

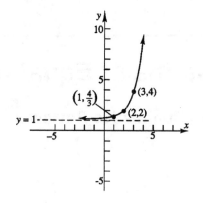

11. (a) This relation is not a function since the points $(2, 15900)$ and $(2, 16980)$ cause the
graph to fail the Vertical Line Test.

(b)

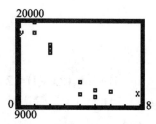

(c) Using EXPREGression yields $P = 21952.6(0.8671)^n$

(d) $P(a) = 21952.6(0.8671)^n$

(e) $P(7) = 21952.6(0.8671)^7 \approx \$8090$

Chapter 9

Sequences; Induction; The Binomial Theorem

9.1 Sequences

1. $a_1 = 1,\ a_2 = 2,\ a_3 = 3,\ a_4 = 4,\ a_5 = 5$

3. $a_1 = \dfrac{1}{1+2} = \dfrac{1}{3},\ a_2 = \dfrac{2}{2+2} = \dfrac{2}{4} = \dfrac{1}{2},\ a_3 = \dfrac{3}{3+2} = \dfrac{3}{5},\ a_4 = \dfrac{4}{4+2} = \dfrac{4}{6} = \dfrac{2}{3},$
   $a_5 = \dfrac{5}{5+2} = \dfrac{5}{7}$

5. $a_1 = (-1)^{1+1}(1^2) = 1,\ a_2 = (-1)^{2+1}(2^2) = -4,\ a_3 = (-1)^{3+1}(3^2) = 9,$
   $a_4 = (-1)^{4+1}(4^2) = -16,\ a_5 = (-1)^{5+1}(5^2) = 25$

7. $a_1 = \dfrac{2^1}{3^1+1} = \dfrac{2}{4} = \dfrac{1}{2},\ a_2 = \dfrac{2^2}{3^2+1} = \dfrac{4}{10} = \dfrac{2}{5},\ a_3 = \dfrac{2^3}{3^3+1} = \dfrac{8}{28} = \dfrac{2}{7},$
   $a_4 = \dfrac{2^4}{3^4+1} = \dfrac{16}{82} = \dfrac{8}{41},\ a_5 = \dfrac{2^5}{3^5+1} = \dfrac{32}{244} = \dfrac{8}{61}$

9. $a_1 = \dfrac{(-1)^1}{(1+1)(1+2)} = \dfrac{-1}{2\cdot 3} = -\dfrac{1}{6},\ a_2 = \dfrac{(-1)^2}{(2+1)(2+2)} = \dfrac{1}{3\cdot 4} = \dfrac{1}{12},$
   $a_3 = \dfrac{(-1)^3}{(3+1)(3+2)} = \dfrac{-1}{4\cdot 5} = -\dfrac{1}{20},\ a_4 = \dfrac{(-1)^4}{(4+1)(4+2)} = \dfrac{1}{5\cdot 6} = \dfrac{1}{30},$
   $a_5 = \dfrac{(-1)^5}{(5+1)(5+2)} = \dfrac{-1}{6\cdot 7} = -\dfrac{1}{42}$

11. $a_1 = \dfrac{1}{e^1} = \dfrac{1}{e},\ a_2 = \dfrac{2}{e^2},\ a_3 = \dfrac{3}{e^3},\ a_4 = \dfrac{4}{e^4},\ a_5 = \dfrac{5}{e^5}$

13. $\dfrac{n}{n+1}$

15. $\dfrac{1}{2^{n-1}}$

17. $(-1)^{n+1}$

19. $(-1)^{n+1}n$

21. $a_1 = 2,\ a_2 = 3+2 = 5,\ a_3 = 3+5 = 8,\ a_4 = 3+8 = 11,\ a_5 = 3+11 = 14$

23. $a_1 = -2,\ a_2 = 2+(-2) = 0,\ a_3 = 3+0 = 3,\ a_4 = 4+3 = 7,\ a_5 = 5+7 = 12$

25. $a_1 = 5,\ a_2 = 2 \cdot 5 = 10,\ a_3 = 2 \cdot 10 = 20,\ a_4 = 2 \cdot 20 = 40,\ a_5 = 2 \cdot 40 = 80$

27. $a_1 = 3,\ a_2 = \dfrac{3}{2},\ a_3 = \dfrac{(3/2)}{3} = \dfrac{1}{2},\ a_4 = \dfrac{(1/2)}{4} = \dfrac{1}{8},\ a_5 = \dfrac{(1/8)}{5} = \dfrac{1}{40}$

29. $a_1 = 1,\ a_2 = 2,\ a_3 = 2 \cdot 1 = 2,\ a_4 = 2 \cdot 2 = 4,\ a_5 = 4 \cdot 2 = 8$

31. $a_1 = A,\ a_2 = A + d,\ a_3 = (A + d) + d = A + 2d,\ a_4 = (A + 2d) + d = A + 3d,$
$a_5 = (A + 3d) + d = A + 4d$

33. $a_1 = \sqrt{2},\ a_2 = \sqrt{2 + \sqrt{2}},\ a_3 = \sqrt{2 + \sqrt{2 + \sqrt{2}}},\ a_4 = \sqrt{2 + \sqrt{2 + \sqrt{2 + \sqrt{2}}}},$
$a_5 = \sqrt{2 + \sqrt{2 + \sqrt{2 + \sqrt{2 + \sqrt{2}}}}}$

35. $\displaystyle\sum_{k=1}^{5} (k + 2) = 3 + 4 + 5 + 6 + 7$

37. $\displaystyle\sum_{k=1}^{8} \dfrac{k^2}{2} = \dfrac{1}{2} + 2 + \dfrac{9}{2} + 8 + \dfrac{25}{2} + 18 + \dfrac{49}{2} + 32$

39. $\displaystyle\sum_{k=0}^{n} \dfrac{1}{3^k} = 1 + \dfrac{1}{3} + \dfrac{1}{9} + \dfrac{1}{27} + \cdots + \dfrac{1}{3^n}$

41. $\displaystyle\sum_{k=0}^{n-1} \dfrac{1}{3^{k+1}} = \dfrac{1}{3} + \dfrac{1}{9} + \dfrac{1}{27} + \cdots + \dfrac{1}{3^n}$

43. $\displaystyle\sum_{k=2}^{n} (-1)^k \ln k = \ln 2 - \ln 3 + \ln 4 - \ln 5 + \cdots + (-1)^n \ln n$

45. $1 + 2 + 3 + \cdots + 20 = \displaystyle\sum_{k=1}^{20} k$ 47. $\dfrac{1}{2} + \dfrac{2}{3} + \dfrac{3}{4} + \cdots + \dfrac{13}{13+1} = \displaystyle\sum_{k=1}^{13} \dfrac{k}{k+1}$

49. $1 - \dfrac{1}{3} + \dfrac{1}{9} - \dfrac{1}{27} + \cdots + (-1)^6 \left(\dfrac{1}{3^6} \right) = \displaystyle\sum_{k=0}^{6} (-1)^k \left(\dfrac{1}{3^k} \right)$ or $\displaystyle\sum_{k=1}^{7} (-1)^{k-1} \left(\dfrac{1}{3^{k-1}} \right)$

51. $3 + \dfrac{3^2}{2} + \dfrac{3^3}{3} + \cdots + \dfrac{3^n}{n} = \displaystyle\sum_{k=1}^{n} \dfrac{3^k}{k}$

53. $a + (a + d) + (a + 2d) + \cdots + (a + nd) = \displaystyle\sum_{k=0}^{n} (a + kd)$

55. (a) $\displaystyle\sum_{k=1}^{10} 5 = \underbrace{5+5+5+...+5}_{10 \text{ times}} = 50$

(b) use the sum(seq) feature:

```
seq(5,A,1,10,1)→
L₁
{5 5 5 5 5 5 5 ...
sum(L₁)
                50
```

57. (a) $\displaystyle\sum_{k=1}^{6} k = 1+2+3+4+5+6 = 21$

(b) use the sum(seq) feature

```
seq(A,A,1,6,1)→L
₁
       {1 2 3 4 5 6}
sum(L₁)
                21
```

59. (a) $\displaystyle\sum_{k=1}^{5} (5k+3) = 8+13+18+23+28 = 90$

(b) use the sum(seq) feature

```
seq(5*A+3,A,1,5,
1)→L₁
   {8 13 18 23 28}
sum(L₁)
                90
```

61. (a) $\displaystyle\sum_{k=1}^{3} (k^2+4) = 5+8+13 = 26$

(b) use the sum(seq) feature

```
seq(A^2+4,A,1,3,
1)→L₁
          {5 8 13}
sum(L₁)
                26
```

63. (a) $\displaystyle\sum_{k=1}^{6} (-1)^k 2^k = (-1)^1 \cdot 2^1 + (-1)^2 \cdot 2^2 + (-1)^3 \cdot 2^3 + (-1)^4 \cdot 2^4 + (-1)^5 \cdot 2^5 + (-1)^6 \cdot 2^6$

$$= -2+4-8+16-32+64 = 42$$

(b) use the sum(seq) feature

```
seq((-1)^A*(2^A)
,A,1,6,1)→L₁
{-2 4 -8 16 -32...
sum(L₁)
                42
```

65. (a) $\displaystyle\sum_{k=1}^{4} (k^3-1) = 0+7+26+63 = 96$

(b) use the sum(seq) feature

```
seq(A^3-1,A,1,4,
1)→L₁
       {0 7 26 63}
sum(L₁)
                96
```

67. (a) $B_1 = 1.01(3000) - 100 = \$2930$

     (b)   Put the graphing utility in SEQuence mode. Enter Y= as follows, then examine the TABLE:

 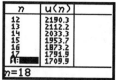

           From the table we see that the balance is below \$2000 after 14 payments have been made. The balance then is \$1953.70.

     (c)   Scrolling down the table, we find that balance is paid off in the 36th month. The last payment is \$83.78. There are 35 payments of \$100 and the last payment of \$83.78. The total amount paid is: $35(100) + 83.78(1.01) = \$3584.62$. (we have to add the interest for the last month).

     (d)   The interest expense is: $3584.62 - 3000.00 = \$584.62$

69. (a) $p_1 = 1.03(2000) + 20 = 2080;$ $p_2 = 1.03(2080) + 20 = 2162$

     (b)   Scrolling down the table, we find the trout population exceeds 5000 at the beginning of the 26th month when the population is 5084.

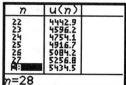

71. (a)   Since the fund returns 8% compound annually, this is equivalent to a return of 2% each quarter. Defining a recursive sequence, we have:
           $$A_0 = 0, \quad A_n = 1.02A_{n-1} + 500$$

     (b)   Insert the formulas in your graphing utility and use the table feature to find when the value of the account will exceed \$100,000:

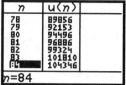

           In the 83rd quarter (during the 21st year) the value of the account will exceed \$100,000 with a value of \$101,810.

     (c)   Find the value of the account in 25 years or 100 quarters:

n	$u(n)$
96	139042
97	142323
98	145670
99	149083
100	152565
101	156116
102	159738

           $n=102$

           The value of the account will be \$156,116.15.

73. (a) Since the interest rate is 6% per annum compounded monthly, this is equivalent to a rate of 0.5% each month. Defining a recursive sequence, we have:
$$A_0 = 150,000, \quad A_n = 1.005A_{n-1} - 899.33$$

(b) $1.005(150,000) - 899.33 = \$149,850.67$

(c) Enter the recursive formula in Y= and create the table:

```
Plot1 Plot2 Plot3
nMin=1
\.u(n)⊟(u(n-1))*1
.005-899.33
 u(nMin)⊟(15000...
\.v(n)=
 v(nMin)=
\.w(n)=
```

n	u(n)
1	150000
2	149851
3	149701
4	149550
5	149398
6	149246
7	149093

n=7

(d) Scroll through the table:

n	u(n)
54	140963
55	140769
56	140573
57	140377
58	140180
59	139981
60	139782

n=60

At the beginning of the 59th month, or after 58 payments have been made, the balance is below \$140,000. The balance is \$139,981.

(e) Scroll through the table:

n	u(n)
355	5298.7
356	4425.9
357	3548.7
358	2667.1
359	1781.1
360	890.65
361	-4.231

n=355

The loan will be paid off at the end of 360 months or 30 years.
Total amount paid = (359)(\$899.33) + \$890.65(1.005) = \$323,754.57.
That is, after 359 payments of \$899.33 plus a final payment of \$895.10.

(f) The total interest expense is the difference of the total of the payments and the original loan: $323,754.57 - 150,000 = \$173,754.57$

(g) (a) Since the interest rate is 6% per annum compounded monthly, this is equivalent to a rate of 0.5% each month. Defining a recursive sequence, we have:
$$A_0 = 150,000, \quad A_n = 1.005A_{n-1} - 999.33$$

(b) $1.005(150,000) - 999.33 = \$149,750.67$

(c) Enter the recursive formula in Y= and create the table:

```
Plot1 Plot2 Plot3
nMin=1
\.u(n)⊟(u(n-1))*1
.005-999.33
 u(nMin)⊟(15000...
\.v(n)=
 v(nMin)=
\.w(n)=
```

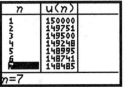

n	u(n)
1	150000
2	149751
3	149500
4	149248
5	148995
6	148741
7	148485

n=7

(d) Scroll through the table:

n	u(n)
34	141079
35	140785
36	140489
37	140192
38	139894
39	139594
40	139293

n=40

At the beginning of the 38th month, or after 37 payments have been made, the balance is below \$140,000. The balance is \$139,894.

535

(e) Scroll through the table:

n	$u(n)$
275	4294.6
276	3316.7
277	2333.9
278	1346.3
279	353.69
280	-643.9
	-1646

$n=281$

The loan will be paid off at the end of 279 months or 23 years and 3 months.
Total amount paid $= (278)(\$999.33) + 353.69(1.005) = \$278{,}169.20$
That is, after 278 payments of \$999.33 plus a final payment of \$355.46.

(f) The total interest expense is the difference of the total of the payments and the original loan: $279{,}169.20 - 150{,}000 = \$129{,}169.20$

75. $a_1 = 1, \ a_2 = 1, \ a_3 = 2, \ a_4 = 3, \ a_5 = 5, \ a_6 = 8, \ a_7 = 13, \ a_8 = 21, \ a_n = a_{n-1} + a_{n-2}$
$a_8 = a_7 + a_6 = 13 + 8 = 21$
After 7 months there are 21 mature pairs of rabbits.

77. 1, 1, 2, 3, 5, 8, 13   This is the Fibonacci sequence.

79.   To show that $1 + 2 + 3 + ... + (n-1) + n = \dfrac{n(n+1)}{2}$

Let

$S = 1 + 2 + 3 + ... + (n-1) + n,$ we can reverse the order to get

$+S = n + (n-1) + (n-2) + ... + 2 + 1,$ now add these two lines to get

$2S = [1+n] + [2 + (n-1)] + [3 + (n-2)] + ... + [(n-1) + 2] + [n+1]$

$\underbrace{\qquad\qquad\qquad\qquad\qquad\qquad}_{n \text{ terms}}$

So we have

$2S = [1+n] + [1+n] + [1+n] + ... + [n+1] + [n+1] = n \cdot [n+1]$

$\underbrace{\qquad\qquad\qquad\qquad\qquad}_{n \text{ terms}}$

$\therefore \ S = \dfrac{n \cdot (n+1)}{2}$

536

Chapter 9

Sequences; Induction; The Binomial Theorem

9.2 Arithmetic Sequences

1. $d = a_{n+1} - a_n = (n+1+4) - (n+4) = n+5-n-4 = 1$
   $a_1 = 1+4 = 5, \quad a_2 = 2+4 = 6, \quad a_3 = 3+4 = 7, \quad a_4 = 4+4 = 8$

3. $d = a_{n+1} - a_n = (2(n+1)-5) - (2n-5) = 2n+2-5-2n+5 = 2$
   $a_1 = 2 \cdot 1 - 5 = -3, \quad a_2 = 2 \cdot 2 - 5 = -1, \quad a_3 = 2 \cdot 3 - 5 = 1, \quad a_4 = 2 \cdot 4 - 5 = 3$

5. $d = a_{n+1} - a_n = (6 - 2(n+1)) - (6-2n) = 6-2n-2-6+2n = -2$
   $a_1 = 6 - 2 \cdot 1 = 4, \quad a_2 = 6 - 2 \cdot 2 = 2, \quad a_3 = 6 - 2 \cdot 3 = 0, \quad a_4 = 6 - 2 \cdot 4 = -2$

7. $d = a_{n+1} - a_n = \left(\dfrac{1}{2} - \dfrac{1}{3}(n+1)\right) - \left(\dfrac{1}{2} - \dfrac{1}{3}n\right) = \dfrac{1}{2} - \dfrac{1}{3}n - \dfrac{1}{3} - \dfrac{1}{2} + \dfrac{1}{3}n = -\dfrac{1}{3}$

   $a_1 = \dfrac{1}{2} - \dfrac{1}{3} \cdot 1 = \dfrac{1}{6}, \quad a_2 = \dfrac{1}{2} - \dfrac{1}{3} \cdot 2 = -\dfrac{1}{6}, \quad a_3 = \dfrac{1}{2} - \dfrac{1}{3} \cdot 3 = -\dfrac{1}{2}, \quad a_4 = \dfrac{1}{2} - \dfrac{1}{3} \cdot 4 = -\dfrac{5}{6}$

9. $d = a_{n+1} - a_n = \ln\left(3^{n+1}\right) - \ln\left(3^n\right) = (n+1)\ln(3) - n\ln(3) = \ln 3(n+1-n) = \ln(3)$
   $a_1 = \ln\left(3^1\right) = \ln(3), \quad a_2 = \ln\left(3^2\right) = 2\ln(3), \quad a_3 = \ln\left(3^3\right) = 3\ln(3), \quad a_4 = \ln\left(3^4\right) = 4\ln(3)$

11. $a_n = a + (n-1)d = 2 + (n-1)3 = 2 + 3n - 3 = 3n - 1$
    $a_5 = 3 \cdot 5 - 1 = 14$

13. $a_n = a + (n-1)d = 5 + (n-1)(-3) = 5 - 3n + 3 = 8 - 3n$
    $a_5 = 8 - 3 \cdot 5 = -7$

15. $a_n = a + (n-1)d = 0 + (n-1)\dfrac{1}{2} = \dfrac{1}{2}n - \dfrac{1}{2} = \dfrac{1}{2}(n-1)$

    $a_5 = \dfrac{1}{2} \cdot 5 - \dfrac{1}{2} = 2$

17. $a_n = a + (n-1)d = \sqrt{2} + (n-1)\sqrt{2} = \sqrt{2} + \sqrt{2}n - \sqrt{2} = \sqrt{2}n$
    $a_5 = 5\sqrt{2}$

19. $a_1 = 2, \quad d = 2, \quad a_n = a + (n-1)d$
    $a_{12} = 2 + (12-1)2 = 2 + 11(2) = 2 + 22 = 24$

21. $a_1 = 1, \ d = -2 - 1 = -3, \quad a_n = a + (n-1)d$
$a_{10} = 1 + (10 - 1)(-3) = 1 + 9(-3) = 1 - 27 = -26$

23. $a_1 = a, \ d = (a+b) - a = b, \quad a_n = a + (n-1)d$
$a_8 = a + (8-1)b = a + 7b$

25. $a_8 = a + 7d = 8 \qquad a_{20} = a + 19d = 44$
Solve the system of equations:
$$8 - 7d + 19d = 44$$
$$12d = 36 \Rightarrow d = 3 \Rightarrow a = 8 - 7(3) = 8 - 21 = -13$$
Recursive formula: $a_1 = -13 \qquad a_n = a_{n-1} + 3; \ a_n = a + (n-1)d = -13 + (n-1)3 = 3n - 16$

27. $a_9 = a + 8d = -5 \qquad a_{15} = a + 14d = 31$
Solve the system of equations:
$$-5 - 8d + 14d = 31 \Rightarrow 6d = 36 \Rightarrow d = 6$$
$$a = -5 - 8(6) = -5 - 48 = -53$$
Recursive formula: $a_1 = -53 \qquad a_n = a_{n-1} + 6; \ a_n = a + (n-1)d = -53 + (n-1)6 = 6n - 59$

29. $a_{15} = a + 14d = 0 \qquad a_{40} = a + 39d = -50$
Solve the system of equations:
$$-14d + 39d = -50 \Rightarrow 25d = -50 \Rightarrow d = -2$$
$$a = -14(-2) = 28$$
Recursive formula: $a_1 = 28 \qquad a_n = a_{n-1} - 2; \ a_n = a + (n-1)d = 28 + (n-1)(-2) = 30 - 2n$

31. $a_{14} = a + 13d = -1 \qquad a_{18} = a + 17d = -9$
Solve the system of equations:
$$-1 - 13d + 17d = -9$$
$$4d = -8 \Rightarrow d = -2 \Rightarrow a = -1 - 13(-2) = -1 + 26 = 25$$
Recursive formula: $a_1 = 25 \qquad a_n = a_{n-1} - 2; \ a_n = a + (n-1)d = 25 + (n-1)(-2) = 27 - 2n$

33. $S_n = \dfrac{n}{2}(a + a_n) = \dfrac{n}{2}(1 + (2n - 1)) = \dfrac{n}{2}(2n) = n^2$

35. $S_n = \dfrac{n}{2}(a + a_n) = \dfrac{n}{2}(7 + (2 + 5n)) = \dfrac{n}{2}(9 + 5n)$

37. $a_1 = 2, \ d = 4 - 2 = 2, \quad a_n = a + (n-1)d$
$$70 = 2 + (n-1)2 \Rightarrow 70 = 2 + 2n - 2 \Rightarrow 70 = 2n \Rightarrow n = 35$$
$$S_n = \dfrac{n}{2}(a + a_n) = \dfrac{35}{2}(2 + 70) = \dfrac{35}{2}(72) = 35(36) = 1260$$

39. $a_1 = 5, \ d = 9 - 5 = 4, \quad a_n = a + (n-1)d$
$$49 = 5 + (n-1)4 \Rightarrow 49 = 5 + 4n - 4 \Rightarrow 48 = 4n \Rightarrow n = 12$$
$$S_n = \dfrac{n}{2}(a + a_n) = \dfrac{12}{2}(5 + 49) = 6(54) = 324$$

41. Using the sum of the sequence feature:

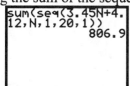

43. $d = 5.2 - 2.8 = 2.4$
     $a = 2.8$
     $36.4 = 2.8 + (n-1)2.4$
     $36.4 = 2.8 + 2.4n - 2.4$
     $36 = 2.4n$
     $n = 15$
     $a_n = 2.8 + (n-1)2.4 = 2.8 + 2.4n - 2.4 = 2.4n + 0.4$

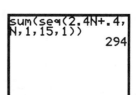

45. $d = 7.48 - 4.9 = 2.58$
     $a = 4.9$
     $66.82 = 4.9 + (n-1)2.58$
     $66.82 = 4.9 + 2.58n - 2.58$
     $64.5 = 2.58n$
     $n = 25$
     $a_n = 4.9 + (n-1)2.58 = 4.9 + 2.58n - 2.58$
     $a_n = 2.58n + 2.32$

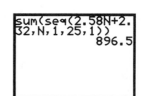

47. Find the common difference of the terms and solve the system of equations:
     $$(2x+1) - (x+3) = d \implies x - 2 = d$$
     $$(5x+2) - (2x+1) = d \implies 3x + 1 = d$$
     $$3x + 1 = x - 2 \implies 2x = -3 \implies x = -\frac{3}{2}$$

49. The total number of seats is: $S = 25 + 26 + 27 + \cdots$
     This is the sum of an arithmetic sequence with $d = 1$, $a = 25$, and $n = 30$.
     Find the sum of the sequence: $S_{30} = \frac{30}{2}[2(25) + (30-1)(1)] = 15(50 + 29) = 15(79) = 1185$
     There are 1185 seats in the theater.

51. The lighter colored tiles have 20 tiles in the bottom row and 1 tile in the top row. The number
     decreases by 1 as we move up the triangle. This is an arithmetic sequence with
     $a_1 = 20$, $d = -1$, and $n = 20$. Find the sum:
     $$S = \frac{20}{2}[2(20) + (20-1)(-1)] = 10(40 - 19) = 10(21) = 210 \text{ lighter tiles.}$$
     The darker colored tiles have 19 tiles in the bottom row and 1 tile in the top row. The number
     decreases by 1 as we move up the triangle. This is an arithmetic sequence with
     $a_1 = 19$, $d = -1$, and $n = 19$. Find the sum:
     $$S = \frac{19}{2}[2(19) + (19-1)(-1)] = \frac{19}{2}(38 - 18) = \frac{19}{2}(20) = 190 \text{ darker tiles.}$$

53.   Find n in an arithmetic sequence with $a_1 = 10$, $d = 4$, $s_n = 2040$.

$$s_n = \frac{n}{2}\left[2a_1 + (n-1)d\right] \Rightarrow 2040 = \frac{n}{2}\left[2(10) + (n-1)4\right]$$

$$4080 = n\left[20 + 4n - 4\right] \Rightarrow 4080 = n(4n + 16)$$

$$4080 = 4n^2 + 16n \Rightarrow 1020 = n^2 + 4n$$

$$n^2 + 4n - 1020 = 0 \Rightarrow (n + 34)(n - 30) = 0 \Rightarrow n = -34 \text{ or } n = 30$$

There are 30 rows in the corner section of the stadium.

55.   Answers will vary.

Sequences; Induction; The Binomial Theorem

9.3 Geometric Sequences; Geometric Series

1. $r = \dfrac{3^{n+1}}{3^n} = 3^{n+1-n} = 3$

   $a_1 = 3^1 = 3, \ a_2 = 3^2 = 9, \ a_3 = 3^3 = 27, \ a_4 = 3^4 = 81$

3. $r = \dfrac{-3(1/2)^{n+1}}{-3(1/2)^n} = \left(\dfrac{1}{2}\right)^{n+1-n} = \dfrac{1}{2}$

   $a_1 = -3\left(\dfrac{1}{2}\right)^1 = -\dfrac{3}{2}, \ a_2 = -3\left(\dfrac{1}{2}\right)^2 = -\dfrac{3}{4}, \ a_3 = -3\left(\dfrac{1}{2}\right)^3 = -\dfrac{3}{8}, \ a_4 = -3\left(\dfrac{1}{2}\right)^4 = -\dfrac{3}{16}$

5. $r = \dfrac{\left(\dfrac{2^{n+1-1}}{4}\right)}{\left(\dfrac{2^{n-1}}{4}\right)} = \dfrac{2^n}{2^{n-1}} = 2^{n-(n-1)} = 2$

   $a_1 = \dfrac{2^{1-1}}{4} = \dfrac{2^0}{2^2} = 2^{-2} = \dfrac{1}{4}, \ a_2 = \dfrac{2^{2-1}}{4} = \dfrac{2^1}{2^2} = 2^{-1} = \dfrac{1}{2}, \ a_3 = \dfrac{2^{3-1}}{4} = \dfrac{2^2}{2^2} = 1,$

   $a_4 = \dfrac{2^{4-1}}{4} = \dfrac{2^3}{2^2} = 2$

7. $r = \dfrac{2^{\left(\frac{n+1}{3}\right)}}{2^{\left(\frac{n}{3}\right)}} = 2^{\left(\frac{n+1}{3} - \frac{n}{3}\right)} = 2^{1/3}$

   $a_1 = 2^{1/3}, \ a_2 = 2^{2/3}, \ a_3 = 2^{3/3} = 2, \ a_4 = 2^{4/3}$

9. $r = \dfrac{\left(\dfrac{3^{n+1-1}}{2^{n+1}}\right)}{\left(\dfrac{3^{n-1}}{2^n}\right)} = \dfrac{3^n}{3^{n-1}} \cdot \dfrac{2^n}{2^{n+1}} = 3^{n-(n-1)} \cdot 2^{n-(n+1)} = 3 \cdot 2^{-1} = \dfrac{3}{2}$

   $a_1 = \dfrac{3^{1-1}}{2^1} = \dfrac{3^0}{2} = \dfrac{1}{2}, \ a_2 = \dfrac{3^{2-1}}{2^2} = \dfrac{3^1}{2^2} = \dfrac{3}{4}, \ a_3 = \dfrac{3^{3-1}}{2^3} = \dfrac{3^2}{2^3} = \dfrac{9}{8},$

   $a_4 = \dfrac{3^{4-1}}{2^4} = \dfrac{3^3}{2^4} = \dfrac{27}{16}$

11. $\{n+2\}$ Arithmetic

$d = (n+1+2) - (n+2) = n+3-n-2 = 1$

13. $\{4n^2\}$ Examine the terms of the sequence: 4, 16, 36, 64, 100, ...

There is no common difference; there is no common ratio; neither.

15. $\left\{3 - \dfrac{2}{3}n\right\}$ Arithmetic

$d = \left(3 - \dfrac{2}{3}(n+1)\right) - \left(3 - \dfrac{2}{3}n\right) = 3 - \dfrac{2}{3}n - \dfrac{2}{3} - 3 + \dfrac{2}{3}n = -\dfrac{2}{3}$

17. 1, 3, 6, 10, ...   Neither

There is no common difference or common ratio.

19. $\left\{\left(\dfrac{2}{3}\right)^n\right\}$ Geometric $r = \dfrac{\left(\dfrac{2}{3}\right)^{n+1}}{\left(\dfrac{2}{3}\right)^n} = \left(\dfrac{2}{3}\right)^{n+1-n} = \dfrac{2}{3}$

21. $-1, -2, -4, -8, ...$ Geometric $r = \dfrac{-2}{-1} = \dfrac{-4}{-2} = \dfrac{-8}{-4} = 2$

23. $\left\{3^{n/2}\right\}$ Geometric $r = \dfrac{3^{\left(\frac{n+1}{2}\right)}}{3^{\left(\frac{n}{2}\right)}} = 3^{\left(\frac{n+1}{2} - \frac{n}{2}\right)} = 3^{1/2}$

25. $a_5 = 2 \cdot 3^{5-1} = 2 \cdot 3^4 = 2 \cdot 81 = 162$ $a_n = 2 \cdot 3^{n-1}$

27. $a_5 = 5(-1)^{5-1} = 5(-1)^4 = 5 \cdot 1 = 5$ $a_n = 5 \cdot (-1)^{n-1}$

29. $a_5 = 0 \cdot \left(\dfrac{1}{2}\right)^{5-1} = 0 \cdot \left(\dfrac{1}{2}\right)^4 = 0$ $a_n = 0 \cdot \left(\dfrac{1}{2}\right)^{n-1} = 0$

31. $a_5 = \sqrt{2} \cdot \left(\sqrt{2}\right)^{5-1} = \sqrt{2} \cdot \left(\sqrt{2}\right)^4 = \sqrt{2} \cdot 4 = 4\sqrt{2}$ $a_n = \sqrt{2} \cdot \left(\sqrt{2}\right)^{n-1} = \left(\sqrt{2}\right)^n$

33. $a = 1, \ r = \dfrac{1}{2}, \ n = 7$ $a_7 = 1 \cdot \left(\dfrac{1}{2}\right)^{7-1} = \left(\dfrac{1}{2}\right)^6 = \dfrac{1}{64}$

35. $a = 1, \ r = -1, \ n = 9$ $a_9 = 1 \cdot (-1)^{9-1} = (-1)^8 = 1$

37. $a = 0.4, \ r = 0.1, \ n = 8$ $a_8 = 0.4 \cdot (0.1)^{8-1} = 0.4(0.1)^7 = 0.00000004$

39. $a = \dfrac{1}{4}, \ r = 2 \qquad S_n = a\left(\dfrac{1 - r^n}{1 - r}\right) = \dfrac{1}{4}\left(\dfrac{1 - 2^n}{1 - 2}\right) = \dfrac{1}{4}\left(2^n - 1\right)$

41. $a = \dfrac{2}{3}, \ r = \dfrac{2}{3} \qquad S_n = a\left(\dfrac{1 - r^n}{1 - r}\right) = \dfrac{2}{3}\left(\dfrac{1 - \left(\dfrac{2}{3}\right)^n}{1 - \dfrac{2}{3}}\right) = \dfrac{2}{3}\left(\dfrac{1 - \left(\dfrac{2}{3}\right)^n}{\dfrac{1}{3}}\right) = 2\left(1 - \left(\dfrac{2}{3}\right)^n\right)$

43. $a = -1, \ r = 2 \qquad S_n = a\left(\dfrac{1 - r^n}{1 - r}\right) = -1\left(\dfrac{1 - 2^n}{1 - 2}\right) = 1 - 2^n$

45. Using the sum of the sequence feature: 47. Using the sum of the sequence feature:

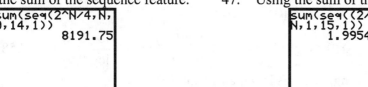

```
sum(seq(2^N/4,N,
0,14,1))
         8191.75
```

```
sum(seq((2/3)^N,
N,1,15,1))
      1.995432683
```

49. Using the sum of the sequence feature:

```
sum(seq(-1*2^N,N
,0,14,1))
          -32767
```

51. $a = 1, \ r = \dfrac{1}{3} \qquad$ Since $|r| < 1, \ S_n = \dfrac{a}{1 - r} = \dfrac{1}{\left(1 - \dfrac{1}{3}\right)} = \dfrac{1}{\left(\dfrac{2}{3}\right)} = \dfrac{3}{2}$

53. $a = 8, \ r = \dfrac{1}{2} \qquad$ Since $|r| < 1, \ S_n = \dfrac{a}{1 - r} = \dfrac{8}{\left(1 - \dfrac{1}{2}\right)} = \dfrac{8}{\left(\dfrac{1}{2}\right)} = 16$

55. $a = 2, \ r = -\dfrac{1}{4} \qquad$ Since $|r| < 1, \ S_n = \dfrac{a}{1 - r} = \dfrac{2}{\left(1 - \left(-\dfrac{1}{4}\right)\right)} = \dfrac{2}{\left(\dfrac{5}{4}\right)} = \dfrac{8}{5}$

57. $a = 5, \ r = \dfrac{1}{4} \qquad$ Since $|r| < 1, \ S_n = \dfrac{a}{1 - r} = \dfrac{5}{\left(1 - \dfrac{1}{4}\right)} = \dfrac{5}{\left(\dfrac{3}{4}\right)} = \dfrac{20}{3}$

59. $a = 6, \ r = -\dfrac{2}{3} \qquad$ Since $|r| < 1, \ S_n = \dfrac{a}{1 - r} = \dfrac{6}{\left(1 - \left(-\dfrac{2}{3}\right)\right)} = \dfrac{6}{\left(\dfrac{5}{3}\right)} = \dfrac{18}{5}$

61. Find the common ratio of the terms and solve the system of equations:

$$\frac{x+2}{x} = r; \quad \frac{x+3}{x+2} = r$$

$$\frac{x+2}{x} = \frac{x+3}{x+2} \Rightarrow x^2 + 4x + 4 = x^2 + 3x \Rightarrow x = -4$$

63. This is a geometric series with $a = \$18,000, \quad r = 1.05, \quad n = 5$. Find the 5th term:

$$a_5 = 18000(1.05)^{5-1} = 18000(1.05)^4 = \$21,879.11$$

65. (a) Find the 10th term of the geometric sequence:

$a = 2, \ r = 0.9, \ n = 10 \qquad a_{10} = 2(0.9)^{10-1} = 2(0.9)^9 \approx 0.77$ feet

(b) Find n when $a_n < 1$:

$$2(0.9)^{n-1} < 1 \Rightarrow (0.9)^{n-1} < 0.5$$

$$(n-1)\log(0.9) < \log(0.5) \Rightarrow n-1 > \frac{\log(0.5)}{\log(0.9)} \Rightarrow n > \frac{\log(0.5)}{\log(0.9)} + 1 \approx 7.58$$

On the 8th swing the arc is less than 1 foot.

(c) Find the sum of the first 15 swings:

$$S_{15} = 2\left(\frac{1-(0.9)^{15}}{1-0.9}\right) = 2\left(\frac{1-(0.9)^{15}}{0.1}\right) = 20\left(1-(0.9)^{15}\right) = 15.88 \text{ feet}$$

(d) Find the infinite sum of the geometric series:

$$S = \frac{2}{1-0.9} = \frac{2}{0.1} = 20 \text{ feet}$$

67. Both options are geometric sequences:

Option A: $a = \$20,000; \quad r = 1.06; \quad n = 5$

$$a_5 = 20,000(1.06)^{5-1} = 20,000(1.06)^4 = \$25,250$$

$$S_5 = 20000\left(\frac{1-(1.06)^5}{1-1.06}\right) = \$112,742$$

Option B: $a = \$22,000; \quad r = 1.03; \quad n = 5$

$$a_5 = 22,000(1.03)^{5-1} = 22,000(1.03)^4 = \$24,761$$

$$S_5 = 22000\left(\frac{1-(1.03)^5}{1-1.03}\right) = \$116,801$$

Option A provides more money in the 5th year, while Option B provides the greatest total amount of money over the 5 year period.

69. Option 1: Total Salary $= \$2,000,000(7) + \$100,000(7) = \$14,700,000$

Option 2: Geometric series with: $a = \$2,000,000, \quad r = 1.045, \quad n = 7$

Find the sum of the geometric series:

$$S = 2,000,000\left(\frac{1-(1.045)^7}{1-1.045}\right) \approx \$16,038,304$$

Option 3:   Arithmetic series with: $a = \$2,000,000,$ $d = \$95,000,$ $n = 7$
Find the sum of the arithmetic series:
$$S_7 = \frac{7}{2}(2(2,000,000) + (7-1)(95,000)) = \$15,995,000$$
Option 2 provides the most money; Option 1 provides the least money.

71.   This is a geometric sequence with $a = 1,$ $r = 2,$ $n = 64.$
Find the sum of the geometric series:
$$S_{64} = 1\left(\frac{1-2^{64}}{1-2}\right) = \frac{1-2^{64}}{-1} = 2^{64} - 1 = 1.845 \times 10^{19} \text{ grains}$$

73.   The common ratio, $r = 0.90 < 1.$ The sum is: $S = \dfrac{1}{1-0.9} = \dfrac{1}{0.10} = 10.$
The multiplier is 10.

75.   This is an infinite geometric series with $a = 4,$ and $r = \dfrac{1.03}{1.09}.$

Find the sum: Price $= \dfrac{4}{\left(1 - \dfrac{1.03}{1.09}\right)} \approx \$72.67.$

77.   Yes, a sequence can be both arithmetic and geometric. For example, the constant sequence
$3,3,3,3,.....$ can be viewed as an arithmetic sequence with $a = 3$ and $d = 0.$ Alternatively,
the same sequence can be viewed as a geometric sequence with $a = 3$ and $r = 1.$

79.   Answers will vary.

Sequences; Induction; The Binomial Theorem

9.4 Mathematical Induction

1. I: $n = 1$: $2 \cdot 1 = 2$ and $1(1+1) = 2$

    II: If $2 + 4 + 6 + \cdots + 2k = k(k+1)$

    then $2 + 4 + 6 + \cdots + 2k + 2(k+1)$

    $$= [2 + 4 + 6 + \cdots + 2k] + 2(k+1) = k(k+1) + 2(k+1)$$

    $$= (k+1)(k+2) = (k+1)\big((k+1)+1\big)$$

    Conditions I and II are satisfied; the statement is true.

3. I: $n = 1$: $1 + 2 = 3$ and $\dfrac{1}{2} \cdot 1(1+5) = 3$

    II: If $3 + 4 + 5 + \cdots + (k+2) = \dfrac{1}{2} \cdot k(k+5)$

    then $3 + 4 + 5 + \cdots + (k+2) + [(k+1)+2]$

    $$= [3 + 4 + 5 + \cdots + (k+2)] + (k+3) = \frac{1}{2} \cdot k(k+5) + (k+3)$$

    $$= \frac{1}{2}k^2 + \frac{5}{2}k + k + 3 = \frac{1}{2}k^2 + \frac{7}{2}k + 3 = \frac{1}{2} \cdot \left(k^2 + 7k + 6\right)$$

    $$= \frac{1}{2} \cdot (k+1)(k+6) = \frac{1}{2} \cdot (k+1)\big((k+1)+5\big)$$

    Conditions I and II are satisfied; the statement is true.

5. I: $n = 1$: $3 \cdot 1 - 1 = 2$ and $\dfrac{1}{2} \cdot 1(3 \cdot 1 + 1) = 2$

    II: If $2 + 5 + 8 + \cdots + (3k - 1) = \dfrac{1}{2} \cdot k(3k+1)$

    then $2 + 5 + 8 + \cdots + (3k-1) + [3(k+1)-1]$

    $$= [2 + 5 + 8 + \cdots + (3k-1)] + (3k+2) = \frac{1}{2} \cdot k(3k+1) + (3k+2)$$

    $$= \frac{3}{2}k^2 + \frac{1}{2}k + 3k + 2 = \frac{3}{2}k^2 + \frac{7}{2}k + 2 = \frac{1}{2} \cdot \left(3k^2 + 7k + 4\right)$$

    $$= \frac{1}{2} \cdot (k+1)(3k+4) = \frac{1}{2} \cdot (k+1)(3(k+1)+1)$$

    Conditions I and II are satisfied; the statement is true.

7.   I: $n = 1$: $2^{1-1} = 1$ and $2^1 - 1 = 1$

    II: If $1 + 2 + 2^2 + \cdots + 2^{k-1} = 2^k - 1$

        then $1 + 2 + 2^2 + \cdots + 2^{k-1} + 2^{k+1-1} = \left[1 + 2 + 2^2 + \cdots + 2^{k-1}\right] + 2^k = 2^k - 1 + 2^k$

$$= 2 \cdot 2^k - 1 = 2^{k+1} - 1$$

Conditions I and II are satisfied; the statement is true.

9.   I: $n = 1$: $4^{1-1} = 1$ and $\dfrac{1}{3} \cdot \left(4^1 - 1\right) = 1$

    II: If $1 + 4 + 4^2 + \cdots + 4^{k-1} = \dfrac{1}{3} \cdot \left(4^k - 1\right)$

        then $1 + 4 + 4^2 + \cdots + 4^{k-1} + 4^{k+1-1}$

$$= \left[1 + 4 + 4^2 + \cdots + 4^{k-1}\right] + 4^k = \dfrac{1}{3} \cdot \left(4^k - 1\right) + 4^k$$

$$= \dfrac{1}{3} \cdot 4^k - \dfrac{1}{3} + 4^k = \dfrac{4}{3} \cdot 4^k - \dfrac{1}{3} = \dfrac{1}{3}\left(4 \cdot 4^k - 1\right) = \dfrac{1}{3} \cdot \left(4^{k+1} - 1\right)$$

Conditions I and II are satisfied; the statement is true.

11.   I: $n = 1$: $\dfrac{1}{1(1+1)} = \dfrac{1}{2}$ and $\dfrac{1}{1+1} = \dfrac{1}{2}$

    II: If $\dfrac{1}{1 \cdot 2} + \dfrac{1}{2 \cdot 3} + \dfrac{1}{3 \cdot 4} + \cdots + \dfrac{1}{k(k+1)} = \dfrac{k}{k+1}$

        then $\dfrac{1}{1 \cdot 2} + \dfrac{1}{2 \cdot 3} + \dfrac{1}{3 \cdot 4} + \cdots + \dfrac{1}{k(k+1)} + \dfrac{1}{(k+1)(k+1+1)}$

$$= \left[\dfrac{1}{1 \cdot 2} + \dfrac{1}{2 \cdot 3} + \dfrac{1}{3 \cdot 4} + \cdots + \dfrac{1}{k(k+1)}\right] + \dfrac{1}{(k+1)(k+2)}$$

$$= \dfrac{k}{k+1} + \dfrac{1}{(k+1)(k+2)} = \dfrac{k}{k+1} \cdot \dfrac{k+2}{k+2} + \dfrac{1}{(k+1)(k+2)}$$

$$= \dfrac{k^2 + 2k + 1}{(k+1)(k+2)} = \dfrac{(k+1)(k+1)}{(k+1)(k+2)} = \dfrac{k+1}{k+2} = \dfrac{k+1}{(k+1)+1}$$

Conditions I and II are satisfied; the statement is true.

13.   I: $n = 1$: $1^2 = 1$ and $\dfrac{1}{6} \cdot 1(1+1)(2 \cdot 1 + 1) = 1$

    II: If $1^2 + 2^2 + 3^2 + \cdots + k^2 = \dfrac{1}{6} \cdot k(k+1)(2k+1)$

        then $1^2 + 2^2 + 3^2 + \cdots + k^2 + (k+1)^2$

$$= \left[1^2 + 2^2 + 3^2 + \cdots + k^2\right] + (k+1)^2 = \dfrac{1}{6}k(k+1)(2k+1) + (k+1)^2$$

$$= (k+1)\left[\dfrac{1}{6}k(2k+1) + k + 1\right] = (k+1)\left[\dfrac{1}{3}k^2 + \dfrac{1}{6}k + k + 1\right]$$

$$= (k+1)\left[\dfrac{1}{3}k^2 + \dfrac{7}{6}k + 1\right] = \dfrac{1}{6}(k+1)\left[2k^2 + 7k + 6\right]$$

$$= \frac{1}{6} \cdot (k+1)(k+2)(2k+3) = \frac{1}{6} \cdot (k+1)\big((k+1)+1\big)\big(2(k+1)+1\big)$$

Conditions I and II are satisfied; the statement is true.

15. I: $n = 1$: $5 - 1 = 4$ and $\frac{1}{2} \cdot 1(9-1) = 4$

    II: If $4 + 3 + 2 + \cdots + (5-k) = \frac{1}{2} \cdot k(9-k)$

           then $4 + 3 + 2 + \cdots + (5-k) + (5-(k+1))$

$$= \big[4 + 3 + 2 + \cdots + (5-k)\big] + (4-k) = \frac{1}{2}k(9-k) + (4-k)$$

$$= \frac{9}{2}k - \frac{1}{2}k^2 + 4 - k = -\frac{1}{2}k^2 + \frac{7}{2}k + 4 = -\frac{1}{2} \cdot \big[k^2 - 7k - 8\big]$$

$$= -\frac{1}{2} \cdot (k+1)(k-8) = \frac{1}{2} \cdot (k+1)(8-k) = \frac{1}{2} \cdot (k+1)[9 - (k+1)]$$

Conditions I and II are satisfied; the statement is true.

17. I: $n = 1$: $1(1+1) = 2$ and $\frac{1}{3} \cdot 1(1+1)(1+2) = 2$

    II: If $1 \cdot 2 + 2 \cdot 3 + 3 \cdot 4 + \cdots + k(k+1) = \frac{1}{3} \cdot k(k+1)(k+2)$

           then $1 \cdot 2 + 2 \cdot 3 + 3 \cdot 4 + \cdots + k(k+1) + (k+1)(k+1+1)$

$$= \big[1 \cdot 2 + 2 \cdot 3 + 3 \cdot 4 + \cdots + k(k+1)\big] + (k+1)(k+2)$$

$$= \frac{1}{3} \cdot k(k+1)(k+2) + (k+1)(k+2) = (k+1)(k+2)\left[\frac{1}{3}k + 1\right]$$

$$= \frac{1}{3} \cdot (k+1)(k+2)(k+3) = \frac{1}{3} \cdot (k+1)\big((k+1)+1\big)\big((k+1)+2\big)$$

Conditions I and II are satisfied; the statement is true.

19. I: $n = 1$: $1^2 + 1 = 2$ is divisible by 2
    II: If $k^2 + k$ is divisible by 2
           then $(k+1)^2 + (k+1) = k^2 + 2k + 1 + k + 1 = (k^2 + k) + (2k+2)$
           Since $k^2 + k$ is divisible by 2 and $2k + 2$ is divisible by 2, then $(k+1)^2 + (k+1)$
           is divisible by 2. Conditions I and II are satisfied; the statement is true.

21. I: $n = 1$: $1^2 - 1 + 2 = 2$ is divisible by 2
    II: If $k^2 - k + 2$ is divisible by 2
           then $(k+1)^2 - (k+1) + 2 = k^2 + 2k + 1 - k - 1 + 2 = (k^2 - k + 2) + (2k)$
           Since $k^2 - k + 2$ is divisible by 2 and $2k$ is divisible by 2, then
           $(k+1)^2 - (k+1) + 2$ is divisible by 2. Conditions I and II are satisfied; the statement is true.

23. I: $n = 1$: If $x > 1$ then $x^1 = x > 1$.
    II: Assume, for some natural number k, that if $x > 1$, then $x^k > 1$.

Show that if $x^k > 1$, then $x^{k+1} > 1$:

$$x^{k+1} = x^k \cdot x > 1 \cdot x = x > 1$$

$\uparrow$

$(x^k > 1)$ Conditions I and II are satisfied; the statement is true.

25. I: $n = 1$: $a - b$ is a factor of $a^1 - b^1 = a - b$.

II: If $a - b$ is a factor of $a^k - b^k$

Show that $a - b$ is a factor of $a^{k+1} - b^{k+1} = a \cdot a^k - b \cdot b^k$

$$= a \cdot a^k - a \cdot b^k + a \cdot b^k - b \cdot b^k = a\left(a^k - b^k\right) + b^k(a - b)$$

Since $a - b$ is a factor of $a^k - b^k$ and $a - b$ is a factor of $a - b$, then

$a - b$ is a factor of $a^{k+1} - b^{k+1}$. Conditions I and II are satisfied; the statement is true.

27. $n = 1$: $1^2 - 1 + 41 = 41$ is a prime number.
$n = 41$: $41^2 - 41 + 41 = 41^2$ is not a prime number.

29. I: $n = 1$: $ar^{1-1} = a$ and $a\left(\dfrac{1 - r^1}{1 - r}\right) = a,$ because $a \neq 1$.

II: If $a + ar + ar^2 + \cdots + ar^{k-1} = a\left(\dfrac{1 - r^k}{1 - r}\right)$

then $a + ar + ar^2 + \cdots + ar^{k-1} + ar^{k+1-1} = \left[a + ar + ar^2 + \cdots + ar^{k-1}\right] + ar^k = a\left(\dfrac{1 - r^k}{1 - r}\right) + ar^k$

$$= \frac{a(1 - r^k) + ar^k(1 - r)}{1 - r} = \frac{a - ar^k + ar^k - ar^{k+1}}{1 - r} = a\left(\frac{1 - r^{k+1}}{1 - r}\right)$$

Conditions I and II are satisfied; the statement is true.

31. I: $n = 3$:   The number of diagonals of a triangle is $\dfrac{1}{2} \cdot 3(3 - 3) = 0,$ which is true.

II: Assume that for any integer $k \geq 3$, the number of diagonals of a convex polygon

with k sides (k vertices) is $\dfrac{1}{2} \cdot k(k - 3)$. A convex polygon with $k + 1$ sides

($k + 1$ vertices) consists of a convex polygon with k sides (k vertices) plus

a triangle for a total of $k + 1$ vertices. The number of diagonals of this

convex polygon consists of the original ones plus $k - 1$ additional ones,

namely, $\dfrac{1}{2} \cdot k(k - 3) + (k - 1) = \dfrac{1}{2}k^2 - \dfrac{3}{2}k + k - 1 = \dfrac{1}{2}k^2 - \dfrac{1}{2}k - 1$

$$= \frac{1}{2} \cdot \left(k^2 - k - 2\right) = \frac{1}{2} \cdot (k + 1)(k - 2) = \frac{1}{2} \cdot (k + 1)\left((k + 1) - 3\right)$$

Conditions I and II are satisfied; the statement is true.

33. Answers will vary.

Chapter 9

Sequences; Induction; The Binomial Theorem

9.5 The Binomial Theorem

1. $\binom{5}{3} = \dfrac{5!}{3!\,2!} = \dfrac{5\cdot4\cdot3\cdot2\cdot1}{3\cdot2\cdot1\cdot2\cdot1} = \dfrac{5\cdot4}{2\cdot1} = 10$

3. $\binom{7}{5} = \dfrac{7!}{5!\,2!} = \dfrac{7\cdot6\cdot5\cdot4\cdot3\cdot2\cdot1}{5\cdot4\cdot3\cdot2\cdot1\cdot2\cdot1} = \dfrac{7\cdot6}{2\cdot1} = 21$

5. $\binom{50}{49} = \dfrac{50!}{49!\,1!} = \dfrac{50\cdot49!}{49!\cdot1} = \dfrac{50}{1} = 50$

7. $\binom{1000}{1000} = \dfrac{1000!}{1000!\,0!} = \dfrac{1}{1} = 1$

9. $\binom{55}{23} = \dfrac{55!}{23!\,32!} = 1.8664\times10^{15}$

11. $\binom{47}{25} = \dfrac{47!}{25!\,22!} = 1.4834\times10^{13}$

13. $(x+1)^5 = \binom{5}{0}x^5 + \binom{5}{1}x^4 + \binom{5}{2}x^3 + \binom{5}{3}x^2 + \binom{5}{4}x^1 + \binom{5}{5}x^0$

$= x^5 + 5x^4 + 10x^3 + 10x^2 + 5x + 1$

15. $(x-2)^6 = \binom{6}{0}x^6 + \binom{6}{1}x^5(-2) + \binom{6}{2}x^4(-2)^2 + \binom{6}{3}x^3(-2)^3 + \binom{6}{4}x^2(-2)^4$

$+ \binom{6}{5}x(-2)^5 + \binom{6}{6}x^0(-2)^6$

$= x^6 + 6x^5(-2) + 15x^4\cdot4 + 20x^3(-8) + 15x^2\cdot16 + 6x\cdot(-32) + 64$

$= x^6 - 12x^5 + 60x^4 - 160x^3 + 240x^2 - 192x + 64$

17. $(3x+1)^4 = \binom{4}{0}(3x)^4 + \binom{4}{1}(3x)^3 + \binom{4}{2}(3x)^2 + \binom{4}{3}(3x) + \binom{4}{4}$

$= 81x^4 + 4\cdot27x^3 + 6\cdot9x^2 + 4\cdot3x + 1 = 81x^4 + 108x^3 + 54x^2 + 12x + 1$

19. $(x^2+y^2)^5 = \binom{5}{0}(x^2)^5(y^2)^0 + \binom{5}{1}(x^2)^4(y^2) + \binom{5}{2}(x^2)^3(y^2)^2 + \binom{5}{3}(x^2)^2(y^2)^3$

$+ \binom{5}{4}x^2(y^2)^4 + \binom{5}{5}(y^2)^5$

$= x^{10} + 5x^8y^2 + 10x^6y^4 + 10x^4y^6 + 5x^2y^8 + y^{10}$

21. $\left(\sqrt{x}+\sqrt{2}\right)^6 = \binom{6}{0}\left(\sqrt{x}\right)^6\left(\sqrt{2}\right)^0 + \binom{6}{1}\left(\sqrt{x}\right)^5\left(\sqrt{2}\right)^1 + \binom{6}{2}\left(\sqrt{x}\right)^4\left(\sqrt{2}\right)^2 + \binom{6}{3}\left(\sqrt{x}\right)^3\left(\sqrt{2}\right)^3$

$\qquad\qquad \binom{6}{4}\left(\sqrt{x}\right)^2\left(\sqrt{2}\right)^4 + \binom{6}{5}\left(\sqrt{x}\right)\left(\sqrt{2}\right)^5 + \binom{6}{6}\left(\sqrt{x}\right)^0\left(\sqrt{2}\right)^6$

$\qquad = x^3 + 6\sqrt{2}x^{5/2} + 15\cdot 2x^2 + 20\cdot 2\sqrt{2}x^{3/2} + 15\cdot 4x + 6\cdot 4\sqrt{2}x^{1/2} + 8$

$\qquad = x^3 + 6\sqrt{2}x^{5/2} + 30x^2 + 40\sqrt{2}x^{3/2} + 60x + 24\sqrt{2}x^{1/2} + 8$

23. $(ax+by)^5 = \binom{5}{0}(ax)^5 + \binom{5}{1}(ax)^4\cdot by + \binom{5}{2}(ax)^3(by)^2 + \binom{5}{3}(ax)^2(by)^3$

$\qquad\qquad + \binom{5}{4}ax(by)^4 + \binom{5}{5}(by)^5$

$\qquad = a^5x^5 + 5a^4x^4by + 10a^3x^3b^2y^2 + 10a^2x^2b^3y^3 + 5axb^4y^4 + b^5y^5$

25. $n = 10,\ j = 4,\ x = x,\ a = 3$

$\qquad \binom{10}{4}x^6\cdot 3^4 = \dfrac{10!}{4!\,6!}\cdot 81x^6 = \dfrac{10\cdot 9\cdot 8\cdot 7}{4\cdot 3\cdot 2\cdot 1}\cdot 81x^6 = 17{,}010x^6$

The coefficient of x^6 is 17,010.

27. $n = 12,\ j = 5,\ x = 2x,\ a = -1$

$\qquad \binom{12}{5}(2x)^7\cdot(-1)^5 = \dfrac{12!}{5!\,7!}\cdot 128x^7(-1) = \dfrac{12\cdot 11\cdot 10\cdot 9\cdot 8}{5\cdot 4\cdot 3\cdot 2\cdot 1}\cdot(-128)x^7 = -101{,}376x^7$

The coefficient of x^7 is $-101{,}376$.

29. $n = 9,\ j = 2,\ x = 2x,\ a = 3$

$\qquad \binom{9}{2}(2x)^7\cdot 3^2 = \dfrac{9!}{2!\,7!}\cdot 128x^7(9) = \dfrac{9\cdot 8}{2\cdot 1}\cdot 128x^7\cdot 9 = 41{,}472x^7$

The coefficient of x^7 is 41,472.

31. $n = 7,\ j = 4,\ x = x,\ a = 3$

$\qquad \binom{7}{4}x^3\cdot 3^4 = \dfrac{7!}{4!\,3!}\cdot 81x^3 = \dfrac{7\cdot 6\cdot 5}{3\cdot 2\cdot 1}\cdot 81x^3 = 2835x^3$

33. $n = 9,\ j = 2,\ x = 3x,\ a = -2$

$\qquad \binom{9}{2}(3x)^7\cdot(-2)^2 = \dfrac{9!}{2!\,7!}\cdot 2187x^7\cdot 4 = \dfrac{9\cdot 8}{2\cdot 1}\cdot 8748x^7 = 314{,}928x^7$

35. The constant term in $\binom{12}{j}\left(x^2\right)^{12-j}\left(\dfrac{1}{x}\right)^j$ occurs when:

$\qquad 2(12-j) = j \implies 24 - 2j = j \implies 3j = 24 \implies j = 8.$

Evaluate the 9th term:

$\qquad \binom{12}{8}\left(x^2\right)^4\cdot\left(\dfrac{1}{x}\right)^8 = \dfrac{12!}{8!\,4!}x^8\cdot\dfrac{1}{x^8} = \dfrac{12\cdot 11\cdot 10\cdot 9}{4\cdot 3\cdot 2\cdot 1}x^0 = 495$

37. The x^4 term in $\binom{10}{j}(x)^{10-j}\left(\dfrac{-2}{\sqrt{x}}\right)^j$ occurs when:

$$10 - j - \frac{1}{2}j = 4 \implies -\frac{3}{2}j = -6 \implies j = 4.$$

Evaluate the 5th term:

$$\binom{10}{4}(x)^6 \cdot \left(\frac{-2}{\sqrt{x}}\right)^4 = \frac{10!}{6!\,4!}x^6 \cdot \frac{16}{x^2} = \frac{10\cdot 9\cdot 8\cdot 7}{4\cdot 3\cdot 2\cdot 1}\cdot 16x^4 = 3360x^4$$

The coefficient is 3360.

39. $(1.001)^5 = \left(1 + 10^{-3}\right)^5 = \binom{5}{0}\cdot 1^5 + \binom{5}{1}\cdot 1^4\cdot 10^{-3} + \binom{5}{2}\cdot 1^3\cdot \left(10^{-3}\right)^2 + \binom{5}{3}\cdot 1^2\cdot \left(10^{-3}\right)^3 + \dots$

$$= 1 + 5(0.001) + 10(0.000001) + 10(0.000000001) + \dots$$
$$= 1 + 0.005 + 0.000010 + 0.000000010 + \dots$$
$$= 1.00501 \quad \text{(correct to 5 decimal places)}$$

41. $\dbinom{n}{n-1} = \dfrac{n!}{(n-1)!(n-(n-1))!} = \dfrac{n!}{(n-1)!(1)!} = n$

$$\binom{n}{n} = \frac{n!}{n!(n-n)!} = \frac{n!}{n!\,0!} = \frac{n!}{n!\cdot 1} = \frac{n!}{n!} = 1$$

43. Show that $\dbinom{n}{0} + \dbinom{n}{1} + \dots + \dbinom{n}{n} = 2^n$

$$2^n = (1+1)^n$$

$$= \binom{n}{0}\cdot 1^n + \binom{n}{1}\cdot 1^{n-1}\cdot 1 + \binom{n}{2}\cdot 1^{n-2}\cdot 1^2 + \dots + \binom{n}{n}\cdot 1^{n-n}\cdot 1^n$$

$$= \binom{n}{0} + \binom{n}{1} + \dots + \binom{n}{n}$$

45. $\dbinom{5}{0}\left(\dfrac{1}{4}\right)^5 + \dbinom{5}{1}\left(\dfrac{1}{4}\right)^4\left(\dfrac{3}{4}\right) + \dbinom{5}{2}\left(\dfrac{1}{4}\right)^3\left(\dfrac{3}{4}\right)^2 + \dbinom{5}{3}\left(\dfrac{1}{4}\right)^2\left(\dfrac{3}{4}\right)^3$

$$+ \binom{5}{4}\left(\frac{1}{4}\right)\left(\frac{3}{4}\right)^4 + \binom{5}{5}\left(\frac{3}{4}\right)^5 = \left(\frac{1}{4} + \frac{3}{4}\right)^5 = (1)^5 = 1$$

47. We can use Mathematical Induction to prove the Binomial Theorem.

I: $n = 1$: $(x+a)^1 = x + a = \dbinom{1}{0}x^1 + \dbinom{1}{1}a^1$. Therefore, the Theorem holds for $n = 1$.

II: Now assume the Theorem holds for some natural number k.
     That is, assume

$$(x+a)^k = \binom{k}{0}x^k + \binom{k}{1}ax^{k-1} + \dots + \binom{k}{j-1}a^{j-1}x^{k-j+1} + \binom{k}{j}a^j x^{k-j} + \dots + \binom{k}{k}a^k$$

We now calculate $(x+a)^{k+1}$:

$$(x+a)^{k+1} = (x+a)(x+a)^k$$

$$= (x+a)\left(\binom{k}{0}x^k + \binom{k}{1}ax^{k-1} + \dots + \binom{k}{j-1}a^{j-1}x^{k-j+1} + \binom{k}{j}a^jx^{k-j} + \dots + \binom{k}{k}a^k\right)$$

$$= x\left(\binom{k}{0}x^k + \binom{k}{1}ax^{k-1} + \dots + \binom{k}{j-1}a^{j-1}x^{k-j+1} + \binom{k}{j}a^jx^{k-j} + \dots + \binom{k}{k}a^k\right)$$

$$+ a\left(\binom{k}{0}x^k + \binom{k}{1}ax^{k-1} + \dots + \binom{k}{j-1}a^{j-1}x^{k-j+1} + \binom{k}{j}a^jx^{k-j} + \dots + \binom{k}{k}a^k\right)$$

$$= \left(\binom{k}{0}x^{k+1} + \binom{k}{1}ax^k + \dots + \binom{k}{j-1}a^{j-1}x^{k-j+2} + \binom{k}{j}a^jx^{k-j+1} + \dots + \binom{k}{k}a^kx\right)$$

$$+ \left(\binom{k}{0}ax^k + \binom{k}{1}a^2x^{k-1} + \dots + \binom{k}{j-1}a^jx^{k-j+1} + \binom{k}{j}a^{j+1}x^{k-j} + \dots + \binom{k}{k}a^{k+1}\right)$$

$$= \binom{k}{0}x^{k+1} + \left(\binom{k}{1}+\binom{k}{0}\right)ax^k + \dots + \left(\binom{k}{j}+\binom{k}{j-1}\right)a^jx^{k-j+1} + \dots + \left(\binom{k}{k}+\binom{k}{k-1}\right)a^kx + \binom{k}{k}a^{k+1}$$

Note that

$$\binom{k}{1}=1=\binom{k+1}{0}; \quad \binom{k}{1}+\binom{k}{0}=\binom{k+1}{1}; \quad \binom{k}{2}+\binom{k}{1}=\binom{k+1}{2};\dots; \binom{k}{j}+\binom{k}{j-1}=\binom{k+1}{j}$$

and $\binom{k}{k}=1=\binom{k+1}{k+1}$.

So we have $(x+a)^{k+1} = \binom{k+1}{0}x^{k+1} + \binom{k+1}{1}ax^k + \dots + \binom{k+1}{j}a^jx^{k-j+1} + \dots + \binom{k+1}{k+1}a^{k+1}$

Conditions I and II are satisfied; the Theorem is true.

Sequences; Induction; The Binomial Theorem

9.R   Chapter Review

1. $a_1 = (-1)^1 \dfrac{1+3}{1+2} = -\dfrac{4}{3}, \ a_2 = (-1)^2 \dfrac{2+3}{2+2} = \dfrac{5}{4}, \ a_3 = (-1)^3 \dfrac{3+3}{3+2} = -\dfrac{6}{5},$

$a_4 = (-1)^4 \dfrac{4+3}{4+2} = \dfrac{7}{6}, \ a_5 = (-1)^5 \dfrac{5+3}{5+2} = -\dfrac{8}{7}$

3. $a_1 = \dfrac{2^1}{1^2} = \dfrac{2}{1} = 2, \ a_2 = \dfrac{2^2}{2^2} = \dfrac{4}{4} = 1, \ a_3 = \dfrac{2^3}{3^2} = \dfrac{8}{9}, \ a_4 = \dfrac{2^4}{4^2} = \dfrac{16}{16} = 1, \ a_5 = \dfrac{2^5}{5^2} = \dfrac{32}{25}$

5. $a_1 = 3, \ a_2 = \dfrac{2}{3} \cdot 3 = 2, \ a_3 = \dfrac{2}{3} \cdot 2 = \dfrac{4}{3}, \ a_4 = \dfrac{2}{3} \cdot \dfrac{4}{3} = \dfrac{8}{9}, \ a_5 = \dfrac{2}{3} \cdot \dfrac{8}{9} = \dfrac{16}{27}$

7. $a_1 = 2, \ a_2 = 2 - 2 = 0, \ a_3 = 2 - 0 = 2, \ a_4 = 2 - 2 = 0, \ a_5 = 2 - 0 = 2$

9. $\displaystyle\sum_{k=1}^{4}(4k+2) = (4 \cdot 1 + 2) + (4 \cdot 2 + 2) + (4 \cdot 3 + 2) + (4 \cdot 4 + 2) = (6) + (10) + (14) + (18) = 48$

11. $1 - \dfrac{1}{2} + \dfrac{1}{3} - \dfrac{1}{4} + \cdots + \dfrac{1}{13} = \displaystyle\sum_{k=1}^{13}(-1)^{k+1}\left(\dfrac{1}{k}\right)$

13. $\{n+5\}$ Arithmetic

$d = (n+1+5) - (n+5) = n+6-n-5 = 1$

$S_n = \dfrac{n}{2}[6 + n + 5] = \dfrac{n}{2}(n+11)$

15. $\{2n^3\}$ Examine the terms of the sequence: 2, 16, 54, 128, 250, ...

There is no common difference; there is no common ratio; neither.

17. $\{2^{3n}\}$ Geometric $r = \dfrac{2^{3(n+1)}}{2^{3n}} = \dfrac{2^{3n+3}}{2^{3n}} = 2^{3n+3-3n} = 2^3 = 8$

$S_n = 8\left(\dfrac{1-8^n}{1-8}\right) = 8\left(\dfrac{1-8^n}{-7}\right) = \dfrac{8}{7}\left(8^n - 1\right)$

19.   0, 4, 8, 12, ...   Arithmetic $d = 4 - 0 = 4$

$S_n = \dfrac{n}{2}(2(0) + (n-1)4) = \dfrac{n}{2}(4(n-1)) = 2n(n-1)$

21. $3, \dfrac{3}{2}, \dfrac{3}{4}, \dfrac{3}{5}, \dfrac{3}{16}, \dots$ Geometric $r = \dfrac{(3/2)}{3} = \dfrac{3}{2} \cdot \dfrac{1}{3} = \dfrac{1}{2}$

$$S_n = 3\left(\dfrac{1 - \left(\dfrac{1}{2}\right)^n}{1 - \dfrac{1}{2}}\right) = 3\left(\dfrac{1 - \left(\dfrac{1}{2}\right)^n}{\left(\dfrac{1}{2}\right)}\right) = 6\left(1 - \left(\dfrac{1}{2}\right)^n\right)$$

23. Neither.   There is no common difference or common ratio.

25. (a) $\displaystyle\sum_{k=1}^{5}(k^2 + 12) = 13 + 16 + 21 + 28 + 37 = 115$

(b) use the sum(seq) feature:

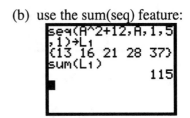

27. (a) $\displaystyle\sum_{k=1}^{10}(3k - 9) = \sum_{k=1}^{10}3k - \sum_{k=1}^{10}9 = 3\sum_{k=1}^{10}k - \sum_{k=1}^{10}9 = 3\left(\dfrac{10(10+1)}{2}\right) - 10(9) = 165 - 90 = 75$

(b) use the sum(seq) feature:

```
seq(3*A-9,A,1,10
,1)→L₁
{-6 -3 0 3 6 9 …
sum(L₁)
                75
```

29. (a) $\displaystyle\sum_{k=1}^{7}\left(\dfrac{1}{3}\right)^k = \dfrac{1}{3}\left(\dfrac{1 - \left(\dfrac{1}{3}\right)^7}{1 - \dfrac{1}{3}}\right) = \dfrac{1}{3}\left(\dfrac{1 - \left(\dfrac{1}{3}\right)^7}{\left(\dfrac{2}{3}\right)}\right) = \dfrac{1}{2}\left(1 - \dfrac{1}{2187}\right) = \dfrac{1}{2} \cdot \dfrac{2186}{2187} = \dfrac{1093}{2187} \approx 0.49977$

(b) use the sum(seq) feature:

```
seq((1/3)^A,A,1,
7,1)→L₁
{.3333333333 .1…
sum(L₁)
        .4997713763
```

31. (a) Arithmetic $a = 3$, $d = 4$, $a_n = a + (n-1)d$
$$a_9 = 3 + (9-1)4 = 3 + 8(4) = 3 + 32 = 35$$

(b) scroll to the end of the list:

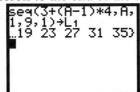

33.   (a) Geometric $a=1,\ r=\dfrac{1}{10},\ n=11;\ a_n=ar^{n-1}$

$$a_{11}=1\cdot\left(\frac{1}{10}\right)^{11-1}=\left(\frac{1}{10}\right)^{10}=\frac{1}{10^{10}}=\frac{1}{10{,}000{,}000{,}000}$$

(b) scroll to the end of the list:

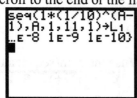

35.   (a) Arithmetic $a=\sqrt{2},\ d=\sqrt{2},\ n=9,\ a_n=a+(n-1)d$

$$a_9=\sqrt{2}+(9-1)\sqrt{2}=\sqrt{2}+8\sqrt{2}=9\sqrt{2}\approx12.7279$$

(b) scroll to the end of the list:

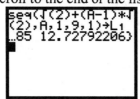

37. $a_7=a+6d=31 \qquad a_{20}=a+19d=96;$ $\qquad\qquad a_n=a+(n-1)d$

Solve the system of equations:

$$31-6d+19d=96$$
$$13d=65$$
$$d=5$$
$$a=31-6(5)=31-30=1$$

General formula: $a_n=5n-4$

39. $a_{10}=a+9d=0 \qquad a_{18}=a+17d=8;$ $\qquad a_n=a+(n-1)d$

Solve the system of equations:

$$-9d+17d=8$$
$$8d=8$$
$$d=1$$
$$a=-9(1)=-9$$

General formula: $a_n=n-10$

41. $a=3,\ r=\dfrac{1}{3}$ Since $|r|<1,\ S_n=\dfrac{a}{1-r}=\dfrac{3}{\left(1-\dfrac{1}{3}\right)}=\dfrac{3}{\left(\dfrac{2}{3}\right)}=\dfrac{9}{2}$

43. $a=2,\ r=-\dfrac{1}{2}$ Since $|r|<1,\ S_n=\dfrac{a}{1-r}=\dfrac{2}{\left(1-\left(-\dfrac{1}{2}\right)\right)}=\dfrac{2}{\left(\dfrac{3}{2}\right)}=\dfrac{4}{3}$

45. $a = 4$, $r = \dfrac{1}{2}$ Since $|r| < 1$, $S_n = \dfrac{a}{1-r} = \dfrac{4}{\left(1 - \dfrac{1}{2}\right)} = \dfrac{4}{\left(\dfrac{1}{2}\right)} = 8$

47. I: $n = 1$: $3 \cdot 1 = 3$ and $\dfrac{3 \cdot 1}{2}(1 + 1) = 3$

    II: If $3 + 6 + 9 + \cdots + 3k = \dfrac{3k}{2}(k + 1)$

        then $3 + 6 + 9 + \cdots + 3k + 3(k + 1)$

$$= \left[3 + 6 + 9 + \cdots + 3k\right] + 3(k + 1) = \dfrac{3k}{2}(k + 1) + 3(k + 1)$$

$$= (k + 1)\left(\dfrac{3k}{2} + 3\right) = \dfrac{3}{2}(k + 1)(k + 2) = \dfrac{3(k + 1)}{2}\big((k + 1) + 1\big)$$

Conditions I and II are satisfied; the statement is true.

49. I: $n = 1$: $2 \cdot 3^{1-1} = 2$ and $3^1 - 1 = 2$
    II: If $2 + 6 + 18 + \cdots + 2 \cdot 3^{k-1} = 3^k - 1$

        then $2 + 6 + 18 + \cdots + 2 \cdot 3^{k-1} + 2 \cdot 3^{k+1-1}$

$$= \left[2 + 6 + 18 + \cdots + 2 \cdot 3^{k-1}\right] + 2 \cdot 3^k = 3^k - 1 + 2 \cdot 3^k = 3 \cdot 3^k - 1 = 3^{k+1} - 1$$

Conditions I and II are satisfied; the statement is true.

51. I: $n = 1$: $(3 \cdot 1 - 2)^2 = 1$ and $\dfrac{1}{2} \cdot 1(6 \cdot 1^2 - 3 \cdot 1 - 1) = 1$

    II: If $1^2 + 4^2 + 7^2 + \cdots + (3k - 2)^2 = \dfrac{1}{2} \cdot k\left(6k^2 - 3k - 1\right)$

        then $1^2 + 4^2 + 7^2 + \cdots + (3k - 2)^2 + \big(3(k + 1) - 2\big)^2$

$$= \left[1^2 + 4^2 + 7^2 + \cdots + (3k - 2)^2\right] + (3k + 1)^2$$

$$= \dfrac{1}{2} \cdot k\left(6k^2 - 3k - 1\right) + (3k + 1)^2$$

$$= \dfrac{1}{2} \cdot \left[6k^3 - 3k^2 - k + 18k^2 + 12k + 2\right] = \dfrac{1}{2} \cdot \left[6k^3 + 15k^2 + 11k + 2\right]$$

$$= \dfrac{1}{2} \cdot (k + 1)\left[6k^2 + 9k + 2\right] = \dfrac{1}{2} \cdot (k + 1)\left[6k^2 + 12k + 6 - 3k - 3 - 1\right]$$

$$= \dfrac{1}{2} \cdot (k + 1)\left[6(k^2 + 2k + 1) - 3(k + 1) - 1\right]$$

$$= \dfrac{1}{2} \cdot (k + 1)\left[6(k + 1)^2 - 3(k + 1) - 1\right]$$

Conditions I and II are satisfied; the statement is true.

53. $\dbinom{5}{2} = \dfrac{5!}{2! \, 3!} = \dfrac{5 \cdot 4 \cdot 3 \cdot 2 \cdot 1}{2 \cdot 1 \cdot 3 \cdot 2 \cdot 1} = \dfrac{5 \cdot 4}{2 \cdot 1} = 10$

55. $(x+2)^5 = \binom{5}{0}x^5 + \binom{5}{1}x^4 \cdot 2 + \binom{5}{2}x^3 \cdot 2^2 + \binom{5}{3}x^2 \cdot 2^3 + \binom{5}{4}x^1 \cdot 2^4 + \binom{5}{5} \cdot 2^5$

$\qquad = x^5 + 5 \cdot 2x^4 + 10 \cdot 4x^3 + 10 \cdot 8x^2 + 5 \cdot 16x + 1 \cdot 32$

$\qquad = x^5 + 10x^4 + 40x^3 + 80x^2 + 80x + 32$

57. $(2x+3)^5 = \binom{5}{0}(2x)^5 + \binom{5}{1}(2x)^4 \cdot 3 + \binom{5}{2}(2x)^3 \cdot 3^2 + \binom{5}{3}(2x)^2 \cdot 3^3$

$\qquad\qquad\qquad\qquad + \binom{5}{4}(2x)^1 \cdot 3^4 + \binom{5}{5} \cdot 3^5$

$\qquad = 32x^5 + 5 \cdot 16x^4 \cdot 3 + 10 \cdot 8x^3 \cdot 9 + 10 \cdot 4x^2 \cdot 27 + 5 \cdot 2x \cdot 81 + 1 \cdot 243$

$\qquad = 32x^5 + 240x^4 + 720x^3 + 1080x^2 + 810x + 243$

59. $n = 9, \ j = 2, \ x = x, \ a = 2$

$\qquad \binom{9}{2}x^7 \cdot 2^2 = \dfrac{9!}{2! \, 7!} \cdot 4x^7 = \dfrac{9 \cdot 8}{2 \cdot 1} \cdot 4x^7 = 144x^7$

The coefficient of x^7 is 144.

61. $n = 7, \ j = 5, \ x = 2x, \ a = 1$

$\qquad \binom{7}{5}(2x)^2 \cdot 1^5 = \dfrac{7!}{5! \, 2!} \cdot 4x^2(1) = \dfrac{7 \cdot 6}{2 \cdot 1} \cdot 4x^2 = 84x^2$

The coefficient of x^2 is 84.

63.   This is an arithmetic sequence with $a = 80, \ d = -3, \ n = 25$

(a) $a_{25} = 80 + (25 - 1)(-3) = 80 - 72 = 8$ bricks

(b) $S_{25} = \dfrac{25}{2}(80 + 8) = 25(44) = 1100$ bricks

$\qquad$ 1100 bricks are needed to build the steps.

65.   This is a geometric sequence with $a = 20, \ r = \dfrac{3}{4}$.

(a)   After striking the ground the third time, the height is $20\left(\dfrac{3}{4}\right)^3 = \dfrac{135}{16} \approx 8.44$ feet.

(b)   After striking the ground the nth time, the height is $20\left(\dfrac{3}{4}\right)^n$ feet.

(c)   If the height is less than 6 inches or 0.5 feet, then:

$$0.5 = 20\left(\dfrac{3}{4}\right)^n \Rightarrow 0.025 = \left(\dfrac{3}{4}\right)^n \Rightarrow \log(0.025) = n\log(3/4) \Rightarrow n = \dfrac{\log(0.025)}{\log(3/4)} \approx 12.82$$

$\qquad$ The height is less than 6 inches after the 13th strike.

(d)   Since this is a geometric sequence with $|r| < 1$, the distance is the sum of the two infinite geometric series - the distances going down plus the distances going up.

$$\text{Distance going down: } S_{down} = \dfrac{20}{\left(1 - \dfrac{3}{4}\right)} = \dfrac{20}{\left(\dfrac{1}{4}\right)} = 80 \text{ feet.}$$

Distance going up: $S_{up} = \dfrac{15}{\left(1 - \dfrac{3}{4}\right)} = \dfrac{15}{\left(\dfrac{1}{4}\right)} = 60$ feet.

The total distance traveled is 140 feet.

67. (a) $b_1 = 5{,}000, \quad b_n = 1.015b_{n-1} - 100$

$b_2 = 1.015b_{(2-1)} - 100 = 1.015b_1 - 100 = 1.015(5000) - 100 = \$4975$

(b) Enter the recursive formula in Y= and draw the graph:

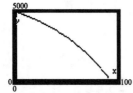

(c) Scroll through the table:

n	$u(n)$
30	4100
31	4061.5
32	4022.5
33	3982.8
34	3942.5
35	3901.7
36	3860.2

$n=33$

At the beginning of the 33rd month, or after 32 payments have been made, the balance is below \$4,000. The balance is \$3982.8.

(d) Scroll through the table:

n	$u(n)$
90	395.82
91	301.75
92	206.28
93	109.37
94	11.014
95	-88.82
96	-190.2

$n=94$

The balance will be paid off at the end of 94 months or 7 years and 10 months.
Total payments $= 100(93) + 11.01 = \$9{,}311.01$

(e) The total interest expense is the difference of the total of the payments and the original balance: $100(93) + 11.01 - 5{,}000 = \$4{,}311.01$

Chapter 9

Sequences; Induction; The Binomial Theorem

9.CR   Cumulative Review

1. $\left|x^2\right| = 9$

    $x^2 = 9 \quad$ or $\quad x^2 = -9$

    $x = \pm 3 \quad$ or $\quad x = \pm 3i$

3. $2e^x = 5$

    $e^x = \dfrac{5}{2} = 2.5$

    $\ln\left(e^x\right) = \ln(2.5)$

    $x = \ln(2.5) \approx 0.916$

5. $f(x) = \dfrac{1}{x+3} - 2$

    (a) Using the graph of $y = \dfrac{1}{x}$, horizontally shift the graph to the left 3 units, and vertically shift the graph down 2 units

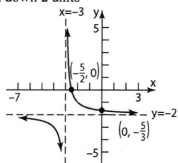

    (b)   From the graph, we can see that the domain of f is $\{x \mid x \neq -3\}$ or $(-\infty, -3) \cup (-3, \infty)$.
    (c)   From the graph, we can see that the range of f is $\{y \mid y \neq -2\}$ or $(-\infty, -2) \cup (-2, \infty)$.
    (d)   From the graph, we can see that $x = -3$ is a vertical asymptote for f and $y = -2$ is a horizontal asymptote for f.

7.   Center: $(0, 0)$; Focus: $(0, 3)$; Vertex: $(0, 4)$; Major axis is the y-axis; $a = 4$; $c = 3$.
     Find b: $b^2 = a^2 - c^2 = 16 - 9 = 7 \Rightarrow b = \sqrt{7}$

     Write the equation using rectangular coordinates: $\dfrac{x^2}{7} + \dfrac{y^2}{16} = 1$

9. $f(x) = 4x^5 + 23x^4 + 42x^3 + 60x^2 + 90x - 27$

Step 1: $f(x)$ has at most 5 real zeros.

Step 2:   Possible rational zeros:

$p = \pm 1, \pm 2, \pm 3, \pm 9, \pm 27; \quad q = \pm 1, \pm 2, \pm 4;$

$\dfrac{p}{q} = \pm 1, \pm \dfrac{1}{2}, \pm \dfrac{1}{4}, \pm 2, \pm 3, \pm \dfrac{3}{2}, \pm \dfrac{3}{4}, \pm 9, \pm \dfrac{9}{2}, \pm \dfrac{9}{4}, \pm 27, \pm \dfrac{27}{2}, \pm \dfrac{27}{4}$

Step 3:   Using the Bounds on Zeros Theorem:

$f(x) = 4\left(x^5 + 5.75x^4 + 10.5x^3 + 15x^2 + 22.5x - 6.75\right)$

$a_4 = 5.75, \quad a_3 = 10.5, \quad a_2 = 15, \quad a_1 = 22.5, \quad a_0 = -6.75$

$\text{Max}\left\{1, |-6.75| + |22.5| + |15| + |10.5| + |5.75|\right\} = \text{Max}\left\{1, 60.5\right\} = 60.5$

$1 + \text{Max}\left\{|-6.75|, |22.5|, |15|, |10.5|, |5.75|\right\} = 1 + 22.5 = 23.5$

The smaller of the two numbers is 23.5. Thus, every zero of f lies between -23.5 and 23.5.

Graphing using the bounds and ZOOM-FIT: (Second graph has a better window.)

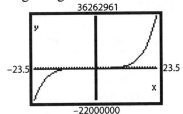
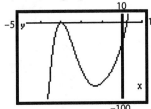

Step 4:   From the graph it appears that there are x-intercepts at -3 and $1/4$.

Using synthetic division with -3:

$$
\begin{array}{r|rrrrrr}
-3 & 4 & 23 & 42 & 60 & 90 & -27 \\
   &   & -12 & -33 & -27 & -99 & 27 \\
\hline
   & 4 & 11 & 9 & 33 & -9 & 0
\end{array}
$$

Since the remainder is 0, $x + 3$ is a factor. The other factor is the quotient: $4x^4 + 11x^3 + 9x^2 + 33x - 9$.

Using synthetic division with $1/4$ on the quotient:

$$
\begin{array}{r|rrrrr}
\frac{1}{4} & 4 & 11 & 9 & 33 & -9 \\
            &   & 1 & 3 & 3 & 9 \\
\hline
            & 4 & 12 & 12 & 36 & 0
\end{array}
$$

Since the remainder is 0, $x - \dfrac{1}{4}$ is a factor. The other factor is the quotient:

$4x^3 + 12x^2 + 12x + 36 = 4\left(x^3 + 3x^2 + 3x + 9\right)$.

Note that $x^3 + 3x^2 + 3x + 9 = x^2(x + 3) + 3(x + 3) = (x + 3)\left(x^2 + 3\right)$

Factoring,

$$f(x) = 4\left(x - \frac{1}{4}\right)(x + 3)^2\left(x^2 + 3\right) = (4x - 1)(x + 3)^2\left(x^2 + 3\right)$$

The real zeros are -3 (multiplicity 2) and $1/4$ (multiplicity 1).

Therefore the x-intercepts are -3 and $1/4$.

The y-intercept is $f(0) = -27$.

Using MAXIMUM and MINIMUM we find the turning points.

    f has a relative maximum at $(-3,0)$

    f has a relative minimum at $(-1.32,-84.06)$

    f is increasing on $(-\infty,-3)\cup(-1.32,\infty)$

    f is decreasing on $(-3,-1.32)$

Graphing:

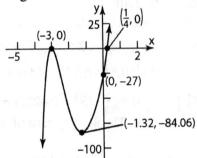

Chapter 10

Counting and Probability

10.1 Sets and Counting

1. $A \cup B = \{1, 3, 5, 7, 9\} \cup \{1, 5, 6, 7\} = \{1, 3, 5, 6, 7, 9\}$

3. $A \cap B = \{1, 3, 5, 7, 9\} \cap \{1, 5, 6, 7\} = \{1, 5, 7\}$

5. $(A \cup B) \cap C = (\{1, 3, 5, 7, 9\} \cup \{1, 5, 6, 7\}) \cap \{1, 2, 4, 6, 8, 9\}$
   $= \{1, 3, 5, 6, 7, 9\} \cap \{1, 2, 4, 6, 8, 9\}$
   $= \{1, 6, 9\}$

7. $(A \cap B) \cup C = (\{1, 3, 5, 7, 9\} \cap \{1, 5, 6, 7\}) \cup \{1, 2, 4, 6, 8, 9\}$
   $= \{1, 5, 7\} \cup \{1, 2, 4, 6, 8, 9\}$
   $= \{1, 2, 4, 5, 6, 7, 8, 9\}$

9. $(A \cup C) \cap (B \cup C)$
   $= (\{1, 3, 5, 7, 9\} \cup \{1, 2, 4, 6, 8, 9\}) \cap (\{1, 5, 6, 7\} \cup \{1, 2, 4, 6, 8, 9\})$
   $= \{1, 2, 3, 4, 5, 6, 7, 8, 9\} \cap \{1, 2, 4, 5, 6, 7, 8, 9\}$
   $= \{1, 2, 4, 5, 6, 7, 8, 9\}$

11. $\overline{A} = \{0, 2, 6, 7, 8\}$

13. $\overline{A \cap B} = \overline{\{1, 3, 4, 5, 9\} \cap \{2, 4, 6, 7, 8\}} = \overline{\{4\}} = \{0, 1, 2, 3, 5, 6, 7, 8, 9\}$

15. $\overline{A} \cup \overline{B} = \{0, 2, 6, 7, 8\} \cup \{0, 1, 3, 5, 9\} = \{0, 1, 2, 3, 5, 6, 7, 8, 9\}$

17. $\overline{A \cap \overline{C}} = \overline{\{1, 3, 4, 5, 9\} \cap \{0, 2, 5, 7, 8, 9\}} = \overline{\{5, 9\}} = \{0, 1, 2, 3, 4, 6, 7, 8\}$

19. $\overline{A \cup B \cup C} = \overline{\{1, 3, 4, 5, 9\} \cup \{2, 4, 6, 7, 8\} \cup \{1, 3, 4, 6\}}$
    $= \overline{\{1, 2, 3, 4, 5, 6, 7, 8, 9\}} = \{0\}$

21. $\{a\}, \{b\}, \{c\}, \{d\}, \{a, b\}, \{a, c\}, \{a, d\}, \{b, c\}, \{b, d\}, \{c, d\}, \{a, b, c\}, \{a, b, d\},$
    $\{a, c, d\}, \{b, c, d\}, \{a, b, c, d\}, \varnothing$

23. $n(A) = 15, n(B) = 20, n(A \cap B) = 10$
   $n(A \cup B) = n(A) + n(B) - n(A \cap B) = 15 + 20 - 10 = 25$

25. $n(A \cup B) = 50, n(A \cap B) = 10, n(B) = 20$
   $n(A \cup B) = n(A) + n(B) - n(A \cap B)$
   $50 = n(A) + 20 - 10$
   $40 = n(A)$

27.   From the figure:
   $n(A) = 15 + 3 + 5 + 2 = 25$

29.   From the figure:
   $n(A \text{ or } B) = n(A \cup B) = n(A) + n(B) - n(A \cap B) = 25 + 20 - 8 = 37$

31.   From the figure:
   $n(A \text{ but not } C) = n(A) - n(A \cap C) = 25 - 7 = 18$

33.   From the figure:
   $n(A \text{ and } B \text{ and } C) = n(A \cap B \cap C) = 5$

35.   Let $A = \{\text{those who will purchase a major appliance}\}$
   $B = \{\text{those who will buy a car}\}$
   $n(U) = 500, \ n(A) = 200, \ n(B) = 150, \ n(A \cap B) = 25$
   $n(A \cup B) = n(A) + n(B) - n(A \cap B) = 200 + 150 - 25 = 325$
   $n(\text{purchase neither}) = 500 - 325 = 175$
   $n(\text{purchase only a car}) = 150 - 25 = 125$

37.   Construct a Venn diagram:

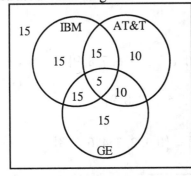

   (a)   15
   (b)   15
   (c)   15
   (d)   25
   (e)   40

39.   (a) $n(\text{married or widowed}) = n(\text{married}) + n(\text{widowed})$
      $= 58,986 + 2,542 = 61,528 \text{ thousand}$
   (b) $n(\text{widowed or divorced}) = n(\text{widowed}) + n(\text{divorced})$
      $= 2,542 + 8,543 = 11,085 \text{ thousand}$
   (c) $n(\text{married, widowed or divorced})$
      $= n(\text{married}) + n(\text{widowed}) + n(\text{divorced})$
      $= 58,986 + 2,542 + 8,543 = 70,071 \text{ thousand}$

41.   Answers will vary.

43.   Set A is a proper subset of set B provided every element of A is also an element of B, and $A \neq B$.

Counting and Probability

10.2 Permutations and Combinations

1. $P(6, 2) = \dfrac{6!}{(6-2)!} = \dfrac{6!}{4!} = \dfrac{6 \cdot 5 \cdot 4!}{4!} = 30$

3. $P(4, 4) = \dfrac{4!}{(4-4)!} = \dfrac{4!}{0!} = \dfrac{4 \cdot 3 \cdot 2 \cdot 1}{1} = 24$

5. $P(7, 0) = \dfrac{7!}{(7-0)!} = \dfrac{7!}{7!} = 1$

7. $P(8, 4) = \dfrac{8!}{(8-4)!} = \dfrac{8!}{4!} = \dfrac{8 \cdot 7 \cdot 6 \cdot 5 \cdot 4!}{4!} = 1680$

9. $C(8, 2) = \dfrac{8!}{(8-2)!\,2!} = \dfrac{8!}{6!\,2!} = \dfrac{8 \cdot 7 \cdot 6!}{6! \cdot 2 \cdot 1} = 28$

11. $C(7, 4) = \dfrac{7!}{(7-4)!\,4!} = \dfrac{7!}{3!\,4!} = \dfrac{7 \cdot 6 \cdot 5 \cdot 4!}{4! \cdot 3 \cdot 2 \cdot 1} = 35$

13. $C(15, 15) = \dfrac{15!}{(15-15)!\,15!} = \dfrac{15!}{0!\,15!} = \dfrac{15!}{15! \cdot 1} = 1$

15. $C(26, 13) = \dfrac{26!}{(26-13)!\,13!} = \dfrac{26!}{13!\,13!} = 10,400,600$

17. {*abc, abd, abe, acb, acd, ace, adb, adc, ade, aeb, aec, aed, bac, bad, bae, bca, bcd, bce, bda, bdc, bde, bea, bec, bed, cab, cad, cae, cba, cbd, cbe, cda, cdb, cde, cea, ceb, ced, dab, dac, dae, dba, dbc, dbe, dca, dcb, dce, dea, deb, dec, eab, eac, ead, eba, ebc, ebd, eca, ecb, ecd, eda, edb, edc*}
$$P(5,3) = \dfrac{5!}{(5-3)!} = \dfrac{5!}{2!} = \dfrac{5 \cdot 4 \cdot 3 \cdot 2!}{2!} = 60$$

19. {123, 124, 132, 134, 142, 143, 213, 214, 231, 234, 241, 243, 312, 314, 321, 324, 341, 342, 412, 413, 421, 423, 431, 432}
$$P(4,3) = \dfrac{4!}{(4-3)!} = \dfrac{4!}{1!} = \dfrac{4 \cdot 3 \cdot 2 \cdot 1}{1} = 24$$

21. {*abc, abd, abe, acd, ace, ade, bcd, bce, bde, cde*}
$$C(5,3) = \dfrac{5!}{(5-3)!\,3!} = \dfrac{5 \cdot 4 \cdot 3!}{2 \cdot 1 \cdot 3!} = 10$$

23. $\{123, 124, 134, 234\}$ $\qquad C(4,3) = \dfrac{4!}{(4-3)!\,3!} = \dfrac{4\cdot 3!}{1!\,3!} = 4$

25. There are 5 choices of shirts and 3 choices of ties; there are $(5)(3) = 15$ combinations.

27. There are 4 choices for the first letter in the code and 4 choices for the second letter in the code; there are $(4)(4) = 16$ possible two-letter codes.

29. There are two choices for each of three positions; there are $(2)(2)(2) = 8$ possible three-digit numbers.

31. To line up the four people, there are 4 choices for the first position, 3 choices for the second position, 2 choices for the third position, and 1 choice for the fourth position. Thus there are $(4)(3)(2)(1) = 24$ possible ways four people can be lined up.

33. Since no letter can be repeated, there are 5 choices for the first letter, 4 choices for the second letter, and 3 choices for the third letter. Thus, there are $(5)(4)(3) = 60$ possible three-letter codes.

35. There are 26 possible one-letter names. There are $(26)(26) = 676$ possible two-letter names. There are $(26)(26)(26) = 17576$ possible three-letter names. Thus, there are $26 + 676 + 17576 = 18{,}278$ possible companies that can be listed on the New York Stock Exchange.

37. A committee of 4 from a total of 7 students is given by:
$$C(7,4) = \frac{7!}{(7-4)!\,4!} = \frac{7!}{3!\,4!} = \frac{7\cdot 6\cdot 5\cdot 4!}{3\cdot 2\cdot 1\cdot 4!} = 35$$
35 committees are possible.

39. There are 2 possible answers for each question. Therefore, there are $2^{10} = 1024$ different possible arrangements of the answers.

41. There are 9 choices for the first digit, and 10 choices for each of the other three digits. Thus, there are $(9)(10)(10)(10) = 9000$ possible four-digit numbers.

43. There are 5 choices for the first position, 4 choices for the second position, 3 choices for the third position, 2 choices for the fourth position, and 1 choice for the fifth position. Thus, there are $(5)(4)(3)(2)(1) = 120$ possible arrangements of the books.

45. There are 8 choices for the DOW stocks, 15 choices for the NASDAQ stocks, and 4 choices for the global stocks. Thus, there are $(8)(15)(4) = 480$ different portfolios.

47. The first person can have any of 365 days, the second person can have any of the remaining 364 days. Thus, there are $(365)(364) = 132{,}860$ possible ways two people can have different birthdays.

49. Choosing 2 boys from the 4 boys can be done C(4,2) ways, and choosing 3 girls from the 8 girls can be done in C(8,3) ways. Thus, there are a total of:

$$C(4,2) \cdot C(8,3) = \frac{4!}{(4-2)!\,2!} \cdot \frac{8!}{(8-3)!\,3!} = \frac{4!}{2!\,2!} \cdot \frac{8!}{5!\,3!}$$

$$= \frac{4 \cdot 3!}{2 \cdot 1 \cdot 2 \cdot 1} \cdot \frac{8 \cdot 7 \cdot 6 \cdot 5!}{5!\,3!} = 336$$

51. This is a permutation with repetition. There are $\dfrac{9!}{2!\,2!} = 90,720$ different words.

53. (a) $C(7,2) \cdot C(3,1) = 21 \cdot 3 = 63$
     (b) $C(7,3) = 35$
     (c) $C(3,3) = 1$

55. There are C(100, 22) ways to form the first committee. There are 78 senators left, so there are C(78, 13) ways to form the second committee. There are C(65, 10) ways to form the third committee. There are C(55, 5) ways to form the fourth committee. There are C(50, 16) ways to form the fifth committee. There are C(34, 17) ways to form the sixth committee. There are C(17, 17) ways to form the seventh committee.
The total number of committees =

$$= C(100,22) \cdot C(78,13) \cdot C(65,10) \cdot C(55,5) \cdot C(50,16) \cdot C(34,17) \cdot C(17,17)$$

$$\approx 1.157 \times 10^{76}$$

57. There are 9 choices for the first position, 8 choices for the second position, 7 for the third position, etc. There are $9 \cdot 8 \cdot 7 \cdot 6 \cdot 5 \cdot 4 \cdot 3 \cdot 2 \cdot 1 = 9! = 362,880$ possible batting orders.

59. The team must have 1 pitcher and 8 position players (non-pitchers). For pitcher, choose 1 player from a group of 4 players, i.e. C(4, 1). For position players, choose 8 players from a group of 11 players, i.e. C(11, 8). Therefore, the number different teams possible is

$$C(4,1) \cdot C(11,8) = \frac{4!}{(4-1)!\cdot 1!} \cdot \frac{11!}{(11-8)!\cdot 8!} = \frac{4!}{3!} \cdot \frac{11!}{3!\cdot 8!} = \frac{4 \cdot 3!}{3!} \cdot \frac{11 \cdot 10 \cdot 9 \cdot 8!}{3!\cdot 8!}$$

$$= 4 \cdot \left(\frac{11 \cdot 10 \cdot 9}{3!} \right) = 4 \cdot \left(\frac{990}{6} \right) = 4 \cdot 165 = 660$$

61. Choose 2 players from a group of 6 players. Therefore, there are $C(6,2) = 15$ different teams possible.

63 – 65.   Answers will vary.

Chapter 10

Counting and Probability

10.3 Probability of Equally Likely Outcomes

1. Probabilities must be between 0 and 1, inclusive. Thus, $0, 0.01, 0.35$, and 1 are probabilities.

3. All the probabilities are between 0 and 1.
   The sum of the probabilities is $0.2 + 0.3 + 0.1 + 0.4 = 1$.
   This is a probability model.

5. All the probabilities are between 0 and 1.
   The sum of the probabilities is $0.3 + 0.2 + 0.1 + 0.3 = 0.9$.
   This is not a probability model.

7. The sample space is: $S = \{HH, HT, TH, TT\}$.
   Each outcome is equally likely to occur; so $P(E) = \dfrac{n(E)}{n(S)}$.
   The probabilities are: $P(HH) = \dfrac{1}{4}$, $P(HT) = \dfrac{1}{4}$, $P(TH) = \dfrac{1}{4}$, $P(TT) = \dfrac{1}{4}$.

9. The sample space of tossing two fair coins and a fair die is:
   $$S = \{HH1, HH2, HH3, HH4, HH5, HH6, HT1, HT2, HT3, HT4, HT5,$$
   $$HT6, TH1, TH2, TH3, TH4, TH5, TH6, TT1, TT2, TT3, TT4, TT5, TT6\}$$
   There are 24 equally likely outcomes and the probability of each is $\dfrac{1}{24}$.

11. The sample space for tossing three fair coins is:
    $$S = \{HHH, HHT, HTH, THH, HTT, THT, TTH, TTT\}$$
    There are 8 equally likely outcomes and the probability of each is $\dfrac{1}{8}$.

13. The sample space is:
    $$S = \{1 \text{ Yellow}, 1 \text{ Red}, 1 \text{ Green}, 2 \text{ Yellow}, 2 \text{ Red}, 2 \text{ Green}, 3 \text{ Yellow}, 3 \text{ Red},$$
    $$3 \text{ Green}, 4 \text{ Yellow}, 4 \text{ Red}, 4 \text{ Green}\}$$
    There are 12 equally likely events and the probability of each is $\dfrac{1}{12}$. The probability of getting a 2 or 4 followed by a Red is $P(2 \text{ Red}) + P(4 \text{ Red}) = \dfrac{1}{12} + \dfrac{1}{12} = \dfrac{1}{6}$.

15. The sample space is:

S = {1 Yellow Forward, 1 Yellow Backward, 1 Red Forward, 1 Red Backward, 1 Green Forward, 1 Green Backward, 2 Yellow Forward, 2 Yellow Backward, 2 Red Forward, 2 Red Backward, 2 Green Forward, 2 Green Backward, 3 Yellow Forward, 3 Yellow Backward, 3 Red Forward, 3 Red Backward, 3 Green Forward, 3 Green Backward, 4 Yellow Forward, 4 Yellow Backward, 4 Red Forward, 4 Red Backward, 4 Green Forward, 4 Green Backward}

There are 24 equally likely events and the probability of each is $\frac{1}{24}$.

The probability of getting a 1, followed by a Red or Green, followed by a Backward is

$$P(1 \text{ Red Backward}) + P(1 \text{ Green Backward}) = \frac{1}{24} + \frac{1}{24} = \frac{1}{12}.$$

17. The sample space is:

S = {1 1 Yellow, 1 1 Red, 1 1 Green, 1 2 Yellow, 1 2 Red, 1 2 Green, 1 3 Yellow, 1 3 Red, 1 3 Green, 1 4 Yellow, 1 4 Red, 1 4 Green, 2 1 Yellow, 2 1 Red, 2 1 Green, 2 2 Yellow, 2 2 Red, 2 2 Green, 2 3 Yellow, 2 3 Red, 2 3 Green, 2 4 Yellow, 2 4 Red, 2 4 Green, 3 1 Yellow, 3 1 Red, 3 1 Green, 3 2 Yellow, 3 2 Red, 3 2 Green, 3 3 Yellow, 3 3 Red, 3 3 Green, 3 4 Yellow, 3 4 Red, 3 4 Green, 4 1 Yellow, 4 1 Red, 4 1 Green, 4 2 Yellow, 4 2 Red, 4 2 Green, 4 3 Yellow, 4 3 Red, 4 3 Green, 4 4 Yellow, 4 4 Red, 4 4 Green}

There are 48 equally likely events and the probability of each is $\frac{1}{48}$.

The probability of getting a 2, followed by a 2 or 4, followed by a Red or Green is

$$P(2\ 2 \text{ Red}) + P(2\ 4 \text{ Red}) + P(2\ 2 \text{ Green}) + P(2\ 4 \text{ Green}) = \frac{1}{48} + \frac{1}{48} + \frac{1}{48} + \frac{1}{48} = \frac{1}{12}$$

19. A, B, C, F

21. B

23. Let $P(\text{tails}) = x$, then $P(\text{heads}) = 4x$

$$x + 4x = 1 \Rightarrow 5x = 1 \Rightarrow x = \frac{1}{5} \qquad P(\text{tails}) = \frac{1}{5}, \quad P(\text{heads}) = \frac{4}{5}$$

25. $P(2) = P(4) = P(6) = x \qquad P(1) = P(3) = P(5) = 2x$

$P(1) + P(2) + P(3) + P(4) + P(5) + P(6) = 1$

$$2x + x + 2x + x + 2x + x = 1 \Rightarrow 9x = 1 \Rightarrow x = \frac{1}{9}$$

$$P(2) = P(4) = P(6) = \frac{1}{9} \qquad P(1) = P(3) = P(5) = \frac{2}{9}$$

27. $P(E) = \dfrac{n(E)}{n(S)} = \dfrac{n\{1,2,3\}}{10} = \dfrac{3}{10}$

29. $P(E) = \dfrac{n(E)}{n(S)} = \dfrac{n\{2,4,6,8,10\}}{10} = \dfrac{5}{10} = \dfrac{1}{2}$

31. $P(\text{white}) = \dfrac{n(\text{white})}{n(S)} = \dfrac{5}{5+10+8+7} = \dfrac{5}{30} = \dfrac{1}{6}$

33. The sample space is: S = {BBB, BBG, BGB, GBB, BGG, GBG, GGB, GGG}

$$P(3 \text{ boys}) = \frac{n(3 \text{ boys})}{n(S)} = \frac{1}{8}$$

35. The sample space is:

S = {BBBB, BBBG, BBGB, BGBB, GBBB, BBGG, BGBG, GBBG, BGGB, GBGB, GGBB, BGGG, GBGG, GGBG, GGGB, GGGG}

$$P(1 \text{ girl, } 3 \text{ boys}) = \frac{n(1 \text{ girl, } 3 \text{ boys})}{n(S)} = \frac{4}{16} = \frac{1}{4}$$

37. $P(\text{sum of two die is } 7) = \dfrac{n(\text{sum of two die is } 7)}{n(S)}$

$$= \frac{n\{1,6 \text{ or } 2,5 \text{ or } 3,4 \text{ or } 4,3 \text{ or } 5,2 \text{ or } 6,1\}}{n(S)} = \frac{6}{36} = \frac{1}{6}$$

39. $P(\text{sum of two die is } 3) = \dfrac{n(\text{sum of two die is } 3)}{n(S)} = \dfrac{n\{1,2 \text{ or } 2,1\}}{n(S)} = \dfrac{2}{36} = \dfrac{1}{18}$

41. $P(A \cup B) = P(A) + P(B) - P(A \cap B) = 0.25 + 0.45 - 0.15 = 0.55$

43. $P(A \cup B) = P(A) + P(B) = 0.25 + 0.45 = 0.70$

45. $P(A \cup B) = P(A) + P(B) - P(A \cap B)$
    $0.85 = 0.60 + P(B) - 0.05$
    $P(B) = 0.85 - 0.60 + 0.05 = 0.30$

47. $P(\text{not victim}) = 1 - P(\text{victim}) = 1 - 0.253 = 0.747$

49. $P(\text{not in } 70's) = 1 - P(\text{in } 70's) = 1 - 0.3 = 0.7$

51. $P(\text{white or green}) = P(\text{white}) + P(\text{green}) = \dfrac{n(\text{white}) + n(\text{green})}{n(S)} = \dfrac{9+8}{9+8+3} = \dfrac{17}{20}$

53. $P(\text{not white}) = 1 - P(\text{white}) = 1 - \dfrac{n(\text{white})}{n(S)} = 1 - \dfrac{9}{20} = \dfrac{11}{20}$

55. $P(\text{strike or one}) = P(\text{strike}) + P(\text{one}) = \dfrac{n(\text{strike}) + n(\text{one})}{n(S)} = \dfrac{3+1}{8} = \dfrac{4}{8} = \dfrac{1}{2}$

57. There are 30 households out of 100 with an income of $30,000 or more.

$$P(E) = \frac{n(E)}{n(S)} = \frac{n(30,000 \text{ or more})}{n(\text{total households})} = \frac{30}{100} = \frac{3}{10}$$

59. There are 40 households out of 100 with an income of less than $20,000.

$$P(E) = \frac{n(E)}{n(S)} = \frac{n(\text{less than } \$20,000)}{n(\text{total households})} = \frac{40}{100} = \frac{2}{5}$$

61. (a) $P(1 \text{ or } 2) = P(1) + P(2) = 0.24 + 0.33 = 0.57$

(b) $P(1 \text{ or more}) = P(1) + P(2) + P(3) + P(4 \text{ or more})$
$$= 0.24 + 0.33 + 0.21 + 0.17 = 0.95$$

(c) $P(3 \text{ or fewer}) = P(0) + P(1) + P(2) + P(3) = 0.05 + 0.24 + 0.33 + 0.21 = 0.83$

(d) $P(3 \text{ or more}) = P(3) + P(4 \text{ or more}) = 0.21 + 0.17 = 0.38$

(e) $P(\text{less than } 2) = P(0) + P(1) = 0.05 + 0.24 = 0.29$

(f) $P(\text{less than } 1) = P(0) = 0.05$

(g) $P(1, 2, \text{ or } 3) = P(1) + P(2) + P(3) = 0.24 + 0.33 + 0.21 = 0.78$

(h) $P(2 \text{ or more}) = P(2) + P(3) + P(4 \text{ or more}) = 0.33 + 0.21 + 0.17 = 0.71$

63. (a) $P(\text{freshman or female}) = P(\text{freshman}) + P(\text{female}) - P(\text{freshman and female})$
$$= \frac{n(\text{freshman}) + n(\text{female}) - n(\text{freshman and female})}{n(S)}$$
$$= \frac{18 + 15 - 8}{33} = \frac{25}{33}$$

(b) $P(\text{sophomore or male}) = P(\text{sophomore}) + P(\text{male}) - P(\text{sophomore and male})$
$$= \frac{n(\text{sophomore}) + n(\text{male}) - n(\text{sophomore and male})}{n(S)}$$
$$= \frac{15 + 18 - 8}{33} = \frac{25}{33}$$

65. $P(\text{at least 2 with same birthday}) = 1 - P(\text{none with same birthday})$
$$= 1 - \frac{n(\text{different birthdays})}{n(S)}$$
$$= 1 - \frac{365 \cdot 364 \cdot 363 \cdot 362 \cdot 361 \cdot 360 \cdot \ldots \cdot 354}{365^{12}}$$
$$= 1 - 0.833 = 0.167$$

67. The sample space for picking 5 out of 10 numbers in a particular order contains
$$P(10,5) = \frac{10!}{(10-5)!} = \frac{10!}{5!} = 30,240 \quad \text{possible outcomes.}$$
One of these is the desired outcome. Thus, the probability of winning is:
$$P(E) = \frac{n(E)}{n(S)} = \frac{n(\text{winning})}{n(\text{total possible outcomes})} = \frac{1}{30240} \approx 0.0000331$$

69. (a) $P(3 \text{ heads}) = \dfrac{C(5,3)}{2^5} = \dfrac{10}{32} = \dfrac{5}{16}$ (b) $P(0 \text{ heads}) = \dfrac{C(5,0)}{2^5} = \dfrac{1}{32}$

71. (a) $P(\text{sum} = 7 \text{ three times}) = P(\text{sum} = 7) \cdot P(\text{sum} = 7) \cdot P(\text{sum} = 7)$
$$= \frac{1}{6} \cdot \frac{1}{6} \cdot \frac{1}{6} = \frac{1}{216} \approx 0.00463$$

(b) $P(\text{sum} = 7 \text{ or } 11 \text{ at least twice})$
$$= P(\text{sum} = 7 \text{ or } 11) \cdot P(\text{sum} = 7 \text{ or } 11) \cdot P(\text{sum} \neq 7 \text{ or } 11) +$$
$$P(\text{sum} = 7 \text{ or } 11) \cdot P(\text{sum} = 7 \text{ or } 11) \cdot P(\text{sum} = 7 \text{ or } 11)$$
$$= 3\left(\frac{8}{36} \cdot \frac{8}{36} \cdot \frac{28}{36}\right) + \frac{8}{36} \cdot \frac{8}{36} \cdot \frac{8}{36} \approx 0.126$$

73. $P(\text{all 5 defective}) = \dfrac{n(\text{5 defective})}{n(S)} = \dfrac{1}{C(30,5)} = 7.02 \times 10^{-6}$

$P(\text{at least 2 defective}) = 1 - (P(\text{none defective}) + P(\text{one defective}))$

$$= 1 - \left(\frac{C(5,0) \cdot C(25,5)}{C(30,5)} + \frac{C(5,1) \cdot C(25,4)}{C(30,5)} \right) = 1 - 0.817 = 0.183$$

75. $P(\text{one of 5 coins is valued at more than } \$10,000) = \dfrac{C(49,4) \cdot C(1,1)}{C(50,5)} = 0.1$

Chapter 10

Counting and Probability

10.4 Obtaining Probabilities From Data

1. (a)

Cause of Death	Probability
Accidents and adverse effects	0.436
Homicide and legal intervention	0.180
Suicide	0.135
Malignant neoplasms	0.055
Diseases of heart	0.035
Human immunodeficiency virus infection	0.006
Congenital anomalies	0.015
Chronic obstructive pulmonary diseases	0.008
Pneumonia and influenza	0.007
Cerebrovascular diseases	0.006
All other causes	0.118

(b) $P(\text{suicide}) = 0.1350 = 13.50\%$

(c) $P(\text{suicide or malignant neoplasms}) = P(\text{suicide}) + P(\text{malignant neoplasms})$
$$= 0.1350 + 0.0555 = 0.1905 = 19.05\%$$

(d) $P(\text{not suicide nor malignant neoplasms}) = 1 - P(\text{suicide or malignant neoplasms})$
$$= 1 - 0.1905 = 0.8095 = 80.95\%$$

3. (a)

Seatbelt Worn	Probability
Never	0.0262
Rarely	0.0678
Sometimes	0.1156
Most of the Time	0.2632
Always	0.5272

(b) $P(\text{Never}) = 0.0262 = 2.62\%$

(c) $P(\text{Never or Rarely}) = P(\text{Never}) + P(\text{Rarely})$
$$= 0.0262 + 0.0678 = 0.0940 = 9.40\%$$

5.   (a)

Weight (in grams)	Probability
Less than 500	0.0015
500 – 999	0.0057
1000 – 1499	0.0073
1500 – 1999	0.0150
2000 – 2499	0.0463
2500 – 2999	0.1650
3000 – 3499	0.3702
3500 – 3999	0.2884
4000 – 4499	0.0851
4500 – 4999	0.0139
5000 or more	0.0016

(b) $P(3500 - 3999) = 0.2884 = 28.84\%$

(c) $P(3500 - 4499) = P(3500 - 3999 \text{ or } 4000 - 4499) = P(3500 - 3999) + P(4000 - 4499)$
$$= 0.2884 + 0.0851 = 0.3735 = 37.35\%$$

(d) $P(\text{not } 5000 \text{ or more}) = 1 - P(5000 \text{ or more}) = 1 - 0.0016 = 0.9984 = 99.84\%$

7. $P(\text{Titleist}) = \dfrac{n(\text{Titleist})}{n(S)} = \dfrac{4}{10} = \dfrac{2}{5} = 0.40$

9. $P(2\text{boys, 1 girl}) = \dfrac{n(2\text{boys, 1 girl})}{n(S)} = \dfrac{20}{50} = \dfrac{2}{5} = 0.40$

11. $P(\text{tornado, 5 - 6PM}) = \dfrac{n(\text{tornado, 5 - 6PM})}{n(S)} = \dfrac{3262}{28538} = 0.1143 = 11.43\%$

$P(\text{tornado, not 5 - 6PM}) = 1 - P(\text{tornado, 5 - 6PM})$
$$= 1 - \dfrac{3262}{28538} = 1 - 0.1143 = 0.8857 = 88.57\%$$

13. $P(\text{cloudy}) = \dfrac{n(\text{cloudy})}{n(S)} = \dfrac{11.2}{30} = 0.3733 = 37.33\%$

$P(\text{clear}) = \dfrac{n(\text{clear})}{n(S)} = \dfrac{7.3}{30} = 0.2433 = 24.33\%$

$P(\text{not clear}) = 1 - P(\text{clear}) = 1 - 0.2433 = 0.7567 = 75.67\%$

15. $P(\text{thunderstorm day}) = \dfrac{n(\text{thunderstorm day})}{n(S)} = \dfrac{6.4}{30} = 0.2133 = 21.33\%$

$P(\text{not thunderstorm day}) = 1 - P(\text{thunderstorm day})$
$$= 1 - 0.2133 = 0.7867 = 78.67\%$$

17.   (a)

Field of Home Run	Probability
Left	0.4194
Left center	0.3387
Center	0.1935
Right center	0.0484
Right	0

    (b) P(left field) $= 0.4194 = 41.94\%$

    (c) P(center field) $= 0.1935 = 19.35\%$

    (d) P(right field) $= 0 = 0\%$

    (e)   Answers will vary.

19.   Use the randInt function on the calculator as follows (answers will vary):

    (a)   randInt(1,6,100)

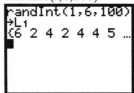 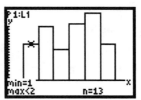

The plot shows the probability of rolling a "1" to be $\dfrac{13}{100} = 0.13$.

    (b)   randInt(1,6,100)

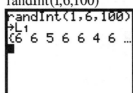 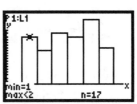

The plot shows the probability of rolling a "1" to be $\dfrac{17}{100} = 0.17$.

    (c)   randInt(1,6,500)

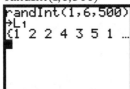 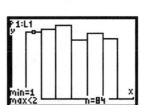

The plot shows the probability of rolling a "1" to be $\dfrac{84}{500} = 0.168$.

    (d)   The simulation in part (c) yields the closest estimate to the probability obtained using equally likely outcomes, $\dfrac{1}{6} \approx 0.16\overline{6}$.

Counting and Probability

10.R Chapter Review

1. $\{\text{Melody}\}, \{\text{Dave}\}, \{\text{Joanne}\}, \{\text{Erica}\},$
    $\{\text{Melody}, \text{Dave}\}, \{\text{Melody}, \text{Joanne}\}, \{\text{Melody}, \text{Erica}\},$
    $\{\text{Dave}, \text{Joanne}\}, \{\text{Dave}, \text{Erica}\}, \{\text{Joanne}, \text{Erica}\},$
    $\{\text{Melody}, \text{Dave}, \text{Joanne}\}, \{\text{Melody}, \text{Dave}, \text{Erica}\}, \{\text{Melody}, \text{Joanne}, \text{Erica}\}, \{\text{Dave}, \text{Joanne}, \text{Erica}\}$
    $\{\text{Melody}, \text{Dave}, \text{Joanne}, \text{Erica}\}, \varnothing$

3. $A \cup B = \{1, 3, 5, 7\} \cup \{3, 5, 6, 7, 8\} = \{1, 3, 5, 6, 7, 8\}$

5. $A \cap C = \{1, 3, 5, 7\} \cap \{2, 3, 7, 8, 9\} = \{3, 7\}$

7. $\overline{A} \cup \overline{B} = \overline{\{1, 3, 5, 7\}} \cup \overline{\{3, 5, 6, 7, 8\}} = \{2, 4, 6, 8, 9\} \cup \{1, 2, 4, 9\} = \{1, 2, 4, 6, 8, 9\}$

9. $\overline{B \cap C} = \overline{\{3, 5, 6, 7, 8\} \cap \{2, 3, 7, 8, 9\}} = \overline{\{3, 7, 8\}} = \{1, 2, 4, 5, 6, 9\}$

11. $n(A) = 8,\ n(B) = 12,\ n(A \cap B) = 3$
    $n(A \cup B) = n(A) + n(B) - n(A \cap B) = 8 + 12 - 3 = 17$

13. From the figure:
    $n(A) = 20 + 2 + 6 + 1 = 29$

15. From the figure:
    $n(A \text{ and } C) = n(A \cap C) = 1 + 6 = 7$

17. From the figure:
    $n(\text{neither in } A \text{ nor in } C) = n(\overline{A \cup C}) = 20 + 5 = 25$

19. $P(8,3) = \dfrac{8!}{(8-3)!} = \dfrac{8!}{5!} = \dfrac{8 \cdot 7 \cdot 6 \cdot 5!}{5!} = 336$

21. $C(8,3) = \dfrac{8!}{(8-3)!\,3!} = \dfrac{8!}{5!\,3!} = \dfrac{8 \cdot 7 \cdot 6 \cdot 5!}{5! \cdot 3 \cdot 2 \cdot 1} = 56$

23. There are 2 choices of material, 3 choices of color, and 10 choices of size. The complete assortment would have: $2 \cdot 3 \cdot 10 = 60$ suits.

25. There are two possible outcomes for each game or
    $2 \cdot 2 \cdot 2 \cdot 2 \cdot 2 \cdot 2 \cdot 2 = 2^7 = 128$ outcomes for 7 games.

27. Since order is significant, this is a permutation.
    $$P(9,4) = \frac{9!}{(9-4)!} = \frac{9!}{5!} = \frac{9 \cdot 8 \cdot 7 \cdot 6 \cdot 5!}{5!} = 3024 \text{ ways to seat 4 people in 9 seats.}$$

29. Choose 4 runners - order is not significant:
    $$C(8,4) = \frac{8!}{(8-4)!\,4!} = \frac{8!}{4!\,4!} = \frac{8 \cdot 7 \cdot 6 \cdot 5 \cdot 4!}{4 \cdot 3 \cdot 2 \cdot 1 \cdot 4!} = 70 \text{ ways a squad can be chosen.}$$

31. Choose 14 teams 2 at a time:
    $$C(14,2) = \frac{14!}{(14-2)!\,2!} = \frac{14!}{12!\,2!} = \frac{14 \cdot 13 \cdot 12!}{12! \cdot 2 \cdot 1} = 91 \text{ ways to pair 14 teams.}$$

33. There are $8 \cdot 10 \cdot 10 \cdot 10 \cdot 10 \cdot 2 = 1,600,000$ possible phone numbers.

35. There are $24 \cdot 9 \cdot 10 \cdot 10 \cdot 10 = 216,000$ possible license plates.

37. Since there are repeated letters:
    $$\frac{7!}{2! \cdot 2!} = \frac{7 \cdot 6 \cdot 5 \cdot 4 \cdot 3 \cdot 2 \cdot 1}{2 \cdot 1 \cdot 2 \cdot 1} = 1260 \text{ different words can be formed.}$$

39. (a) $C(9,4) \cdot C(9,3) \cdot C(9,2) = \dfrac{9!}{5! \cdot 4!} \cdot \dfrac{9!}{6! \cdot 3!} \cdot \dfrac{9!}{7! \cdot 2!}$

    $$= \frac{9 \cdot 8 \cdot 7 \cdot 6 \cdot 5 \cdot 4 \cdot 3 \cdot 2 \cdot 1}{5 \cdot 4 \cdot 3 \cdot 2 \cdot 1 \cdot 4 \cdot 3 \cdot 2 \cdot 1} \cdot \frac{9 \cdot 8 \cdot 7 \cdot 6 \cdot 5 \cdot 4 \cdot 3 \cdot 2 \cdot 1}{6 \cdot 5 \cdot 4 \cdot 3 \cdot 2 \cdot 1 \cdot 3 \cdot 2 \cdot 1} \cdot \frac{9 \cdot 8 \cdot 7 \cdot 6 \cdot 5 \cdot 4 \cdot 3 \cdot 2 \cdot 1}{7 \cdot 6 \cdot 5 \cdot 4 \cdot 3 \cdot 2 \cdot 1 \cdot 2 \cdot 1}$$

    $$= \frac{9 \cdot 8 \cdot 7 \cdot 6}{4 \cdot 3 \cdot 2 \cdot 1} \cdot \frac{9 \cdot 8 \cdot 7}{3 \cdot 2 \cdot 1} \cdot \frac{9 \cdot 8}{2 \cdot 1} = \frac{109734912}{288} = 381,024$$

    (b) $C(9,4) \cdot C(5,3) \cdot C(2,2) = \dfrac{9!}{5! \cdot 4!} \cdot \dfrac{5!}{2! \cdot 3!} \cdot \dfrac{2!}{0! \cdot 2!}$

    $$= \frac{9 \cdot 8 \cdot 7 \cdot 6 \cdot 5 \cdot 4 \cdot 3 \cdot 2 \cdot 1}{5 \cdot 4 \cdot 3 \cdot 2 \cdot 1 \cdot 4 \cdot 3 \cdot 2 \cdot 1} \cdot \frac{5 \cdot 4 \cdot 3 \cdot 2 \cdot 1}{2 \cdot 1 \cdot 3 \cdot 2 \cdot 1} \cdot \frac{2 \cdot 1}{1 \cdot 2 \cdot 1} = \frac{9 \cdot 8 \cdot 7 \cdot 6}{4 \cdot 3 \cdot 2 \cdot 1} \cdot \frac{5 \cdot 4}{2 \cdot 1} \cdot \frac{1}{1} = \frac{60480}{48} = 1260$$

41. (a)

Age	Probability
20 – 24	0.1709
25 – 29	0.1410
30 – 34	0.1344
35 – 39	0.1227
40 – 44	0.0991
45 – 49	0.0816
50 – 54	0.0602
55 – 59	0.0460
60 – 64	0.0389
65 – 69	0.0321
70 – 74	0.0293
75 – 79	0.0249
80 – 84	0.0190

(b) $P(25-29) = 0.1410 = 14.10\%$

(c) $P(20-29) = P(20-24 \text{ or } 25-29) = P(20-24) + P(25-29)$
$$= 0.1709 + 0.1410 = 0.3119 = 31.19\%$$

(d) $P(\text{not } 20-24) = 1 - P(20-24) = 1 - 0.1709 = 0.8291 = 82.91\%$

43. (a) $365 \cdot 364 \cdot 363 \cdot 362 \cdot \ldots \cdot 348 = 8.634628387 \times 10^{45}$

(b) $P(\text{no one has same birthday}) = \dfrac{365 \cdot 364 \cdot 363 \cdot 362 \cdot \ldots \cdot 348}{365^{18}} = 0.6531 = 65.31\%$

(c) $P(\text{at least 2 have same birthday}) = 1 - P(\text{no one has same birthday})$
$$= 1 - 0.6531 = 0.3469 = 34.69\%$$

45. (a) $P(\text{unemployed}) = 0.054 = 5.4\%$

(b) $P(\text{not unemployed}) = 1 - P(\text{unemployed}) = 1 - 0.054 = 0.946 = 94.6\%$

47. $P(\$1 \text{ bill}) = \dfrac{n(\$1 \text{ bill})}{n(S)} = \dfrac{4}{9}$

49. Let S be all possible selections, let D be a card that is divisible by 5, and let PN be a 1 or a prime number.

$n(S) = 100$

$n(D) = 20$ (There are 20 numbers divisible by 5 between 1 and 100.)

$n(PN) = 26$ (There are 25 prime numbers less than or equal to 100.)

$P(D) = \dfrac{n(D)}{n(S)} = \dfrac{20}{100} = \dfrac{1}{5} = 0.2$

$P(PN) = \dfrac{n(PN)}{n(S)} = \dfrac{26}{100} = \dfrac{13}{50} = 0.26$

51.   (a) $P(5 \text{ heads}) = \dfrac{n(5 \text{ heads})}{n(S)} = \dfrac{C(10,5)}{2^{10}} = \dfrac{\left(\dfrac{10!}{5!\,5!}\right)}{1024} = \dfrac{252}{1024} \approx 0.2461$

     (b) $P(\text{all heads}) = \dfrac{n(\text{all heads})}{n(S)} = \dfrac{1}{2^{10}} = \dfrac{1}{1024} = 0.00098$

53.   (a) $P(\text{all students}) = \dfrac{C(8,5)}{C(18,5)} = \dfrac{56}{8568} \approx 0.0065$

     (b) $P(\text{all faculty}) = \dfrac{C(10,5)}{C(18,5)} = \dfrac{252}{8568} \approx 0.0294$

     (c) $P(2 \text{ students and } 3 \text{ faculty}) = \dfrac{C(8,2) \cdot C(10,3)}{C(18,5)} = \dfrac{28 \cdot 120}{8568} \approx 0.3922$

55.   Use the randInt function on the calculator as follows (answers will vary):

     (a)   randInt(1,6,100)

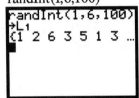 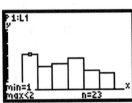

The plot shows the probability of rolling a "1" to be $\dfrac{23}{100} = 0.23$.

     (b)   randInt(1,6,100)

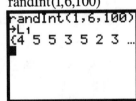 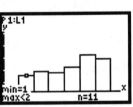

The plot shows the probability of rolling a "1" to be $\dfrac{11}{100} = 0.11$.

     (c)   randInt(1,6,500)

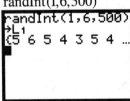 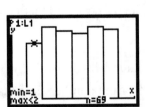

The plot shows the probability of rolling a "1" to be $\dfrac{69}{500} = 0.138$.

     (d)   The simulation in part (c) yields the closest estimate to the probability obtained using equally likely outcomes, $\dfrac{1}{6} = 0.16\overline{6}$.

Counting and Probability

10.CR   Cumulative Review

1. $3x^2 - 2x = -1 \Rightarrow 3x^2 - 2x + 1 = 0$

$$x = \frac{-b \pm \sqrt{b^2 - 4ac}}{2a} = \frac{-(-2) \pm \sqrt{(-2)^2 - 4(3)(1)}}{2(3)}$$

$$= \frac{2 \pm \sqrt{4 - 12}}{6} = \frac{2 \pm \sqrt{-8}}{6} = \frac{2 \pm 2\sqrt{2}i}{6} = \frac{1 \pm \sqrt{2}i}{3}$$

The solution set is $\left\{\dfrac{1}{3} - \dfrac{\sqrt{2}}{3}i, \dfrac{1}{3} + \dfrac{\sqrt{2}}{3}i\right\}$.

3. $y = 2(x+1)^2 - 4$

Using the graph of $y = x^2$, horizontally shift to the left 1 unit, vertically stretch by a factor of 2, and vertically shift down 4 units.

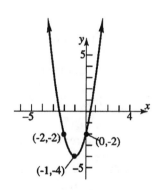

5. $f(x) = 5x^4 - 9x^3 - 7x^2 - 31x - 6$

Step 1: $f(x)$ has at most 4 real zeros.

Step 2: Possible rational zeros:
$p = \pm 1, \pm 2, \pm 3, \pm 6; \quad q = \pm 1, \pm 5;$

$$\frac{p}{q} = \pm 1, \pm \frac{1}{5}, \pm 2, \pm \frac{2}{5}, \pm 3, \pm \frac{4}{5}, \pm 6, \pm \frac{6}{5}$$

Step 3: Using the Bounds on Zeros Theorem:
$f(x) = 5\left(x^4 - 1.8x^3 - 1.4x^2 - 6.2x - 1.2\right)$

$a_3 = -1.8, \quad a_2 = -1.4, \quad a_1 = -6.2, \quad a_0 = -1.2$

$\text{Max}\left\{1, |-1.2| + |-6.2| + |\ -1.4\ | + |-1.8|\right\} = \text{Max}\left\{1, 6.2\right\} = 6.2$

$1 + \text{Max}\left\{|-1.2|, |\ -6.2|, |-1.4|, |-1.8|\right\} = 1 + 6.2 = 7.2$

The smaller of the two numbers is 6.2. Thus, every zero of f lies between –6.2 and 6.2.

Graphing using the bounds and ZOOM-FIT: (Second graph has a better window.)

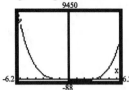 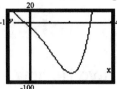

Step 4: From the graph it appears that there are x-intercepts at –1/5 and 3.
Using synthetic division with 3:

$$
\begin{array}{r|rrrrr}
3 & 5 & -9 & -7 & -31 & -6 \\
  &   & 15 & 18 & 33 & 6 \\
\hline
  & 5 & 6 & 11 & 2 & 0
\end{array}
$$

Since the remainder is 0, $x-3$ is a factor. The other factor is the quotient: $5x^3+6x^2+11x+2$.

Using synthetic division with 2 on the quotient:

$$
\begin{array}{r|rrrr}
-\dfrac{1}{5} & 5 & 6 & 11 & 2 \\
  &   & -1 & -1 & -2 \\
\hline
  & 5 & 5 & 10 & 0
\end{array}
$$

Since the remainder is 0, $x-\left(-\dfrac{1}{5}\right)=x+\dfrac{1}{5}$ is a factor. The other factor is the quotient: $5x^2+5x+10=5\left(x^2+x+2\right)$.

Factoring, $f(x)=5(x^2+x+2)(x-3)\left(x+\dfrac{1}{5}\right)$

The real zeros are 3 and $-\dfrac{1}{5}$.

The complex zeros come from solving $x^2+x+2=0$.

$$x=\dfrac{-b\pm\sqrt{b^2-4ac}}{2a}=\dfrac{-1\pm\sqrt{1^2-4(1)(2)}}{2(1)}=\dfrac{-1\pm\sqrt{1-8}}{2}=\dfrac{-1\pm\sqrt{-7}}{2}=\dfrac{-1\pm\sqrt{7}i}{2}$$

Therefore, the over the set of complex numbers, $f(x)=5x^4-9x^3-7x^2-31x-6$ has

zeros $-\dfrac{1}{5}, 3, -\dfrac{1}{2}-\dfrac{\sqrt{7}}{2}i, -\dfrac{1}{2}+\dfrac{\sqrt{7}}{2}i$.

7. $\log_3(9)=\log_3\left(\left(3^2\right)\right)=2$

9. $f(x)=\log\left(x^2-4\right)$
f will be defined provided $x^2-4>0$.
Solving the inequality:
$$p(x)=x^2-4>0$$
$$(x+2)(x-2)>0$$

The zeros are $x = -2$, $x = 2$.

Interval	Test Number	$p(x)$	Positive/Negative
$-\infty < x < -2$	-3	5	Positive
$-2 < x < 2$	0	-4	Negative
$2 < x < \infty$	3	5	Positive

The solution set is $\{x \mid x < -2 \text{ or } x > 2\}$; $(-\infty, -2) \cup (2, \infty)$.

Therefore, the domain of f is $\{x \mid x < -2 \text{ or } x > 2\}$; $(-\infty, -2) \cup (2, \infty)$.

11. Multiply each side of the first equation by -3 and add to the second equation to eliminate x; and multiply each side of the first equation by 2 and add to the third equation to eliminate x:

$$\begin{cases} x - 2y + z = 15 & \xrightarrow{\;-3\;} & -3x + 6y - 3z = -45 \\ 3x + y - 3z = -8 & \longrightarrow & \underline{3x + y - 3z = -8} \\ -2x + 4y - z = -27 & & 7y - 6z = -53 \end{cases}$$

$$\begin{aligned} x - 2y + z = 15 & \xrightarrow{\;2\;} & 2x - 4y + 2z = 30 \\ -2x + 4y - z = -27 & \longrightarrow & \underline{-2x + 4y - z = -27} \\ & & z = 3 \end{aligned}$$

Substituting and solving for the other variables:

$z = 3 \Rightarrow 7y - 6(3) = -53$

$7y = -35$

$y = -5$

$z = 3, y = -5 \Rightarrow x - 2(-5) + 3 = 15$

$x + 10 + 3 = 15 \Rightarrow x = 2$

The solution is $x = 2$, $y = -5$, $z = 3$.